Lecture Notes in Computer Science 14682

Founding Editors

Gerhard Goos
Juris Hartmanis

The series Lecture Notes in Computer Science (LNCS), including its subseries Lecture Notes in Artificial Intelligence (LNAI) and Lecture Notes in Bioinformatics (LNBI), has established itself as a medium for the publication of new developments in computer science and information technology research, teaching, and education.

LNCS enjoys close cooperation with the computer science R & D community, the series counts many renowned academics among its volume editors and paper authors, and collaborates with prestigious societies. Its mission is to serve this international community by providing an invaluable service, mainly focused on the publication of conference and workshop proceedings and postproceedings. LNCS commenced publication in 1973.

Arie Gurfinkel · Vijay Ganesh
Editors

Computer Aided Verification

36th International Conference, CAV 2024
Montreal, QC, Canada, July 24–27, 2024
Proceedings, Part II

 Springer

Editors
Arie Gurfinkel
University of Waterloo
Waterloo, ON, Canada

Vijay Ganesh
Georgia Institute of Technology
Atlanta, GA, USA

ISSN 0302-9743   ISSN 1611-3349 (electronic)
Lecture Notes in Computer Science
ISBN 978-3-031-65629-3   ISBN 978-3-031-65630-9 (eBook)
https://doi.org/10.1007/978-3-031-65630-9

This Springer imprint is published by the registered company Springer Nature Switzerland AG
The registered company address is: Gewerbestrasse 11, 6330 Cham, Switzerland

If disposing of this product, please recycle the paper.

Preface

It was our privilege to serve as the program chairs for CAV 2024, the 36th International Conference on Computer-Aided Verification. CAV 2024 was held in Montreal, Canada, on July 24–27, 2024, and the pre-conference workshops were held on July 22–23, 2024.

CAV is an annual conference dedicated to the advancement of the theory and practice of computer-aided formal analysis methods for hardware and software systems. The primary focus of CAV is to extend the frontiers of verification techniques by expanding to new domains such as security, quantum computing, and machine learning. This puts CAV at the cutting edge of formal methods research. This year's program is a reflection of this commitment.

CAV 2024 received 317 submissions. We accepted 16 tool papers, 2 case-study papers, and 51 regular papers, which amounts to an acceptance rate of roughly 26% in each category. The accepted papers cover a wide spectrum of topics, from theoretical results to applications of formal methods. These papers apply or extend formal methods to a wide range of domains such as concurrency, machine learning and neural networks, quantum systems, as well as hybrid and stochastic systems. The program featured keynote talks by Noriko Arai (National Institute of Informatics, Japan), Leonardo de Moura (Amazon Web Services, USA), and Erika Abraham (RWTH Aachen University, Germany). In addition to the contributed talks, CAV 2024 also hosted the CAV Award ceremony, and a report from the Synthesis Competition (SYNTCOMP) chairs. Furthermore, we continued the tradition of Logic Lounge, a series of discussions on computer science topics targeting a general audience. This year's Logic Lounge speaker was Scott J. Shapiro (Yale Law School) who spoke about topics at the intersection of formal methods and the law.

In addition to the main conference, CAV 2024 hosted the following workshops: Verification Mentoring Workshop (VMW), Correct Data Compression (CoDaC), Workshop on Synthesis (SYNT), Workshop on Verification of Probabilistic Programs (VeriProP), Developing an Open-Source, State-of-the-Art Symbolic Model-Checking Framework for the Model-Checking Research Community (OSSyM), Formal Reasoning in Distributed Algorithms (FRIDA), Workshop on Hyperproperties: Advances in Theory and Practice (HYPER), Symposium on AI Verification (SAIV), Deep Learning-aided Verification (DAV), and International Workshop on Satisfiability Modulo Theories (SMT).

Organizing a flagship conference like CAV requires a great deal of effort from the community. The Program Committee for CAV 2024 consisted of 90 members—a committee of this size ensures that each member has to review only a reasonable number of papers in the allotted time. In all, the committee members wrote over 900 reviews while investing significant effort to maintain and ensure the high quality of the conference program. We are grateful to the CAV 2024 Program Committee for their outstanding efforts in evaluating the submissions and making sure that each paper got a fair chance.

Like recent years in CAV, we made artifact evaluation mandatory for tool paper submissions, but optional for the rest of the accepted papers. This year we received 54 artifact submissions, all of which received at least one badge. The Artifact Evaluation Committee consisted of 92 members who put in significant effort to evaluate each artifact. The goal of this process was to provide constructive feedback to tool developers and help make the research published in CAV more reproducible. We are also very grateful to the Artifact Evaluation Committee for their hard work and dedication in evaluating the submitted artifacts.

CAV 2024 would not have been possible without the tremendous help we received from several individuals, and we would like to thank everyone who helped make CAV 2024 a success. We would like to thank Mirco Giacobbe and Milan Ceska for chairing the Artifact Evaluation Committee. We also thank Temegshen Kahsai for chairing the workshop organization. Norine Coenen and Hadar Frenkel for leading publicity efforts, Eric Koskinen and Grigory Fedyukovich as the fellowship chairs, Grigory Fedyukovich as sponsorship chair, and John (Zhengyang) Lu as the website chair. Hari Govind V. K. helped prepare the proceedings. We also thank Grigory Fedyukovich, Eric Koskinen, Umang Mathur, Yoni Zohar, and Jingbo Wang for organizing the Verification Mentoring Workshop. Last but not least, we would like to thank the members of the CAV Steering Committee (Kenneth McMillan, Aarti Gupta, Orna Grumberg, and Daniel Kroening) for helping us with several important aspects of organizing CAV 2024.

We hope that you will find the proceedings of CAV 2024 scientifically interesting and thought-provoking!

June 2024

Arie Gurfinkel
Vijay Ganesh

Organization

Steering Committee

Aarti Gupta   Princeton University
Daniel Kroening   University of Oxford
Kenneth McMillan   University of Texas at Austin
Ornal Grumberg   Technion

Conference Co-chairs

Arie Gurfinkel   University of Waterloo
Vijay Ganesh   Georgia Institute of Technology

Artifact Evaluation Co-chairs

Mirco Giacobbe   University of Birmingham
Milan Ceska   Brno University of Technology

Local Chair

Xujie Si   University of Toronto

Area Chairs

Alexandra Silva   Cornell University
Anthony Widjaja Lin   Technical University of Kaiserslautern
Borzoo Bonakdarpour   Michigan State University
Corina Pasareanu   NASA
Kristin Yvonne Rozier   Iowa State University
Laura Kovacs   TU Wien

Workshop Chair

Temesghen Kahsai   Amazon

Fellowship Chairs

Grigory Fedyukovich   Florida State University
Eric Koskinen   Stevens Institute of Technology

Publicity Chairs

Norine Coenen   CISPA Helmholtz Center for Information Security
Hadar Frenkel   CISPA Helmholtz Center for Information Security

Publication Chair

Hari Govind V. K.   University of Waterloo

Website Chair

John (Zhengyang) Lu   University of Waterloo

Program Committee

Aditya Thakur   University of California, Davis
Ahmed Bouajjani   IRIF
Aina Niemetz   Stanford University
Akash Lal   Microsoft Research
Alan Hu   University of British Columbia
Alessandro Cimatti   Fondazione Bruno Kessler
Alexander Nadel   Technion & Intel
Alexandra Silva   Cornell University
Amir Goharshady   Hong Kong University of Science and Technology
Anastasia Mavridou   KBR Inc.
Andrew Reynolds   University of Iowa
Anna Slobodova   Intel

Anthony Widjaja Lin   Technical University of Kaiserslautern
Azadeh Farzan   University of Toronto
B. Srivathsan   Chennai Mathematical Institute
Benjamin Kaminski   Saarland University
Bernd Finkbeiner   CISPA Helmholtz Center for Information Security
Bettina Könighofer   Graz University of Technology
Bor-Yuh Evan Chang   University of Colorado
Borzoo Bonakdarpour   Michigan State University
Caterina Urban   Inria
Cezara Dragoi   Inria
Christopher Hahn   Google
Constantin Enea   Ecole Polytechnique
Corina Pasareanu   NASA
Deepak D'Souza   Indian Institute of Science
Dejan Jovanović   Amazon
Elizabeth Polgreen   University of Edinburgh
Elvira Albert   Universidad Complutense de Madrid
Erika Abraham   RWTH Aachen University
Eunsuk Kang   Carnegie Mellon University
Florin Manea   University of Göttingen
Gagandeep Singh   University of Illinois Urbana-Champaign
Grigory Fedyukovich   Florida State University
Guy Amir   Hebrew University of Jerusalem
Hadar Frenkel   CISPA Helmholtz Center for Information Security
Hongce Zhang   Hong Kong University of Science and
                                 Technology, China

Ichiro Hasuo   National Institute of Informatics
Isil Dillig   University of Texas at Austin
Jana Hofmann   Azure Research, Microsoft
Jianwen Li   East China Normal University
Jingbo Wang   University of Southern California
Jorge A. Navas   Certora
Ken McMillan   University of Texas at Austin
Kristin Yvonne Rozier   Iowa State University
Kshitij Bansal   Google
Kuldeep Meel   University of Toronto
Kumar Madhukar   Indian Institute of Technology Delhi
Laura Kovacs   TU Wien
Liana Hadarean   Amazon
Loris D'Antoni   University of Wisconsin-Madison
Mathias Preiner   Stanford University
Matthias Heizmann   University of Freiburg

Mihaela Sighireanu	Université Paris-Saclay
Mirco Giacobbe	University of Birmingham
Naijun Zhan	Chinese Academy of Sciences
Natasha Sharygina	University of Lugano
Nathalie Sznajder	Sorbonne Université
Nikolaj Bjørner	Microsoft Research
Ning Luo	Northwestern University
Oded Padon	VMware Research
Orna Grumberg	Technion
Pascal Fontaine	Université de Liège
Peter Schrammel	University of Sussex
Qirun Zhang	Georgia Institute of Technology
Ranjit Jhala	University of California, San Diego
Ravi Mangal	Carnegie Mellon University
Rayna Dimitrova	CISPA Helmholtz Center for Information Security
Rohit Dureja	Advanced Micro Devices, Inc.
Roland Yap	National University of Singapore
Rose Bohrer	Worcester Polytechnic Institute
Ruzica Piskac	Yale University
S. Akshay	Indian Institute of Technology Bombay
Sebastian Junges	Radboud University
Serdar Tasiran	Amazon
Sharon Shoham	Tel Aviv University
Shuvendu Lahiri	Microsoft Research
Sorav Bansal	Indian Institute of Technology Delhi
Sriram Sankaranarayanan	University of Colorado Boulder
Subhajit Roy	Indian Institute of Technology Kanpur
Subodh Sharma	Indian Institute of Technology Delhi
Suguman Bansal	Georgia Institute of Technology
Supratik Chakraborty	Indian Institute of Technology Bombay
Temesghen Kahsai	Amazon
Umang Mathur	National University of Singapore
Xujie Si	University of Toronto
Yakir Vizel	Technion
Yann Thierry-Mieg	LIP6
Yu-Fang Chen	Academia Sinica
Zvonimir Rakamaric	Amazon

Artifact Evaluation Committee

Abhinandan Pal	University of Birmingham
Adwait Godbole	UC Berkeley
Akshatha Shenoy	Tata Consultancy Services Ltd.
Alejandro Hernández-Cerezo	Complutense University of Madrid
Alvin George	IISc Bangalore
Ameer Hamza	Florida State University
Andreas Katis	KBR Inc. at NASA Ames Research Center
Anna Becchi	Fondazione Bruno Kessler
Benjamin Mikek	Georgia Institute of Technology
Bohua Zhan	Institute of Software, Chinese Academy of Sciences
Chenyu Zhou	University of Southern California
Daniel Dietsch	University Freiburg
Daniel Riley	Florida State University
Diptarko Roy	University of Oxford
Edoardo Manino	University of Manchester
Ennio Visconti	TU Wien
Enrico Magnago	Amazon Web Services
Filip Cano	Graz University of Technology
Filip Macák	Brno University of Technology
Florian Renkin	IRIF
Francesco Parolini	Sorbonne Université
Francesco Pontiggia	TU Wien
Gianluca Redondi	Fondazione Bruno Kessler
Giulio Garbi	University of Molise
Haoze Wu	Stanford University
Jacqueline Mitchell	University of Southern California
Jialuo Chen	Zhejiang University
Jie An	National Institute of Informatics
Jiong Yang	National University of Singapore
Julia Klein	University of Konstanz
Kartik Nagar	IIT Madras
Kaushik Mallik	Institute of Science and Technology Austria
Kazuki Watanabe	National Institute of Informatics, Tokyo
Kevin Cheang	Amazon Web Services
Konstantin Kueffner	Institute of Science and Technology Austria
Lelio Brun	National Institute of Informatics
Lorenz Leutgeb	Max Planck Institute for Informatics
Luca Arnaboldi	University of Birmingham
Lucas Zavalia	Florida State University

Malinda Dilhara	University of Colorado Boulder
Marcel Moosbrugger	TU Wien
Marck van der Vegt	Radboud University
Marco Casadio	Heriot-Watt University
Marco Lewis	Newcastle University
Marek Chalupa	Institute of Science and Technology Austria
Mário Pereira	NOVA University Lisbon
Marius Mikučionis	Aalborg University
Mathias Fleury	University of Freiburg
Matteo Marescotti	Meta Platforms
Matthias Schlaipfer	Amazon Web Services
Maximilian Weininger	Institute of Science and Technology Austria
Mertcan Temel	Intel Corporation
Mihir Mehta	University of Texas at Austin
N. Ege Saraç	Institute of Science and Technology Austria
Natasha Jeppu	Amazon Web Services
Neea Rusch	Augusta University
Neta Elad	Tel Aviv University
Nham Le	University of Waterloo
Oliver Markgraf	Max Planck Institute Kaiserslautern
Omar Inverso	Gran Sasso Science Institute
Omri Isac	Hebrew University of Jerusalem
Oyendrila Dobe	Michigan State University
P. Habeeb	Indian Institute of Science
Patrick Trentin	Amazon Web Services
Philippe Heim	CISPA Helmholtz Center for Information Security
Po-Chun Chien	LMU Munich
Ranadeep Biswas	Informal Systems
Remi Desmartin	Heriot-Watt University
Roman Andriushchenko	Brno University of Technology
Samuel Pastva	Institute of Science and Technology Austria
Sayan Mukherjee	Université libre de Bruxelles
Shengping Xiao	East China Normal University
Shubham Ugare	University of Illinois Urbana-Champaign
Shufang Zhu	University of Oxford
Shuo Ding	Georgia Institute of Technology
Siddharth Priya	University of Waterloo
Sidi Mohamed Beillahi	University of Toronto
Stefan Pranger	Graz University of Technology
Tobias Meggendorfer	Lancaster University Leipzig
Tobias Winkler	RWTH Aachen University
Tzu-Han Hsu	Michigan State University

Wael-Amine Boutglay	Université Paris Cité and Mohammed VI Polytechnic University
Xidan Song	University of Manchester
Xindi Zhang	Institute of Software, Chinese Academy of Sciences
Xiyue Zhang	University of Oxford
Yannan Li	Oracle
Yannik Schnitzer	University of Oxford
Yizhak Elboher	Hebrew University of Jerusalem
Yuzhou Fang	University of Southern California
Zhe Tao	University of California, Davis
Zhendong Ang	National University of Singapore
Zhiwei Zhang	Rice University

Additional Reviewers

Albarghouthi, Aws
Amarilli, Antoine
Ang, Zhendong
Antal, László
Banerjee, Subarno
Batz, Kevin
Becchi, Anna
Ben Shimon, Yoav
Biagiola, Matteo
Blicha, Martin
Bossut, Camille
Britikov, Konstantin
Campion, Marco
De Palma, Alessandro
Ding, Shuo
Dobe, Oyendrila
Eeralla, Ajay
Elad, Neta
Elboher, Yizhak
Emmi, Michael
Frenkel, Eden
Georgiou, Pamina
Gerlach, Carolina
Gürtler, Tobias
Hartmanns, Arnd
Hoad, Stuart
Hong, Chih-Duo

Hsu, Tzu-Han
Hunt, Warren
Hyvärinen, Antti
Ivrii, Alexander
Karmarkar, Hrishikesh
Koll, Charles
Labbaf, Faezeh
Lester, Martin Mariusz
Lotan, Raz
Luo, Ziyan
Magnago, Enrico
Metta, Ravindra
Metzger, Niklas
Mikek, Benjamin
Moosbrugger, Marcel
Morris, Jason
Mover, Sergio
Mukhopadhyay, Diganta
Nalbach, Jasper
Otoni, Rodrigo
Pailoor, Shankara
Patterson, Zachary
Piskachev, Goran
Promies, Valentin
Quatmann, Tim
Rappoport, Omer
Ravitch, Tristan

Rawson, Michael
Ritzert, Martin
Saatcioglu, Goktug
Shenoy, Akshatha
Shetty, Abhishek
Shi, Zheng
Tarrach, Thorsten
Trivedi, Ashutosh
Tunç, Hünkar Can
Verscht, Lena

Visconti, Ennio
Winkler, Tobias
Zhang, Minjian
Kaivola, Roope
Kaufmann, Daniela
Kolárik, Tomáš
Le, Nham
Li, Yong
Lu, Zhengyang
Löding, Christof

Invited Talks

How to Solve Math Problems Without Talent

Noriko Arai

National Institute of Informatics, Japan

The desire to solve mathematical problems without inherent talent has been a long-standing aspiration of humanity since ancient times. In this lecture, we delve into the complexity theory of proofs, examining the relationship between talent and the cost of proof. Additionally, we discuss the possibilities and limitations of using a fusion of computational methods, including computer algebra and natural language processing, to solve mathematical problems with machines. Join us as we explore the frontier of machine-enabled mathematical problem-solving, reflecting on its potential and boundaries in fulfilling this age-old human ambition.

Bridging Formal Mathematics and Software Verification

Leonardo de Moura

Amazon Web Services, USA

This talk will explore the dual applications of Lean 4, the latest iteration of the Lean proof assistant and programming language, in advancing formal mathematics and software verification. We begin with an overview of its design and implementation. We will detail how Lean 4 enables the formalization of complex mathematical theories and proofs, thereby enhancing collaboration and reliability in mathematical research. This endeavor is supported by a philosophy that promotes decentralized innovation, empowering a diverse community of researchers, developers, and enthusiasts to collaboratively push the boundaries of mathematical practice. Simultaneously, we will discuss software verification applications using Lean 4 at AWS. By leveraging Lean's dual capabilities as both a proof assistant and a functional programming language, we achieve a cohesive approach to software development and verification. Additionally, the talk will outline future directions for Lean 4, including efforts to expand its user community, enhance user experience, and further integrate formal methods into both academic research and industrial applications.

The Art of SMT Solving

Erika Ábrahám

RWTH Aachen University, Germany

Satisfiability Modulo Theories (SMT) solving [3, 4, 9] is a technology for the fully automated solution of logical formulas. SMT solvers can be used as general-purpose off-the-shelf tools. Due to their impressive efficiency, they are nowadays frequently used in a wide variety of applications [2]. A typical application encodes real-world problems as logical formulas, whose solutions can be decoded to solutions of the original real-world problem.

Besides its unquestionable practical impact, SMT solving has another great merit: it inspired truly elegant ideas, which do not only enable the construction of efficient software tools, but provide also interesting theoretical insights.

For *propositional logic* where each formula has a finite number of Boolean variables, we could enumerate and check all possible variable assignments, but due to its bad average complexity, this exploration approach is not applicable in practice. Alternatively, the proof system of Boolean resolution can be applied, but the applicability of this method is also restricted to rather small problems. However, in the 90s, *SAT solvers* succeeded to become impressively powerful due to an elegant combination of these two methods, where the proof construction is guided by an exploration of the assignment space equipped with a smart look-ahead mechanism [5, 6, 10].

The effectivity of SAT solvers gave motivation to extend the scope of solver technologies to formulas of *quantifier-free first-order logic over different theories*. On the one hand, *eager SMT solving* approaches have been proposed for certain theories to transform their formulas to propositional logic and use SAT solving to check the result for satisfiability. On the other hand, *(full/less) lazy SMT solving* uses SAT solving to explore the Boolean structure of the formula, and employs theory solvers to check the consistency of Boolean assignments in the theory domains.

Recently, the idea of symbiotic combination of exploration and proof construction has been also generalized to theories, most notably quantifier-free real algebra [7], in the framework of the *model constructing satisfiability calculus (MCSAT)* [11]. In this approach, exploration-guided proof construction is designed to run *both* in the Boolean space and in the theory domain, simultaneously in a consistent manner.

Both the SAT and the MCSAT approaches are based on the generalization of "wrong guesses", made during exploration, into pieces of a proof, which are collected and used to synthesize a global proof during the solving process. While being one of the currently best approaches, for large or complex formulas, a large number of "proof pieces" cause high effort for their processing and restrict scalability.

Thus the question comes up whether there are also other ways to store such information in a more structured way, allowing a less costly processing. This idea is taken up by the *cylindrical algebraic covering* method [1, 8], developed for the satisfiability check of conjunctions of polynomial constraints.

In this talk we give an introduction to the mechanisms of SAT and SMT solving, discuss the above ideas, and illustrate the usage of SMT solvers on a few application examples.

References

1. Ábrahám, E., Davenport, J.H., England, M., Kremer, G.: Deciding the consistency of non-linear real arithmetic constraints with a conflict driven search using cylindrical algebraic coverings. J. Log. Algebraic Methods Program. **119**, 100633 (2021). https://doi.org/10.1016/j.jlamp.2020.100633
2. Ábrahám, E., Kovács, J., Remke, A.: SMT: something you must try. In: Herber, P., Wijs, A. (eds) iFM 2023. LNCS, vol. 14300, pp. 3–18. Springer, Cham (2024). https://doi.org/10.1007/978-3-031-47705-8_1
3. Ábrahám, E., Kremer, G.: SMT solving for arithmetic theories: theory and tool support. In: Proceedings SYNASC 2017, pp. 1–8. IEEE (2017). https://doi.org/10.1109/SYNASC.2017.00009
4. Barrett, C., Sebastiani, R., Seshia, S.A., Tinelli, C.: Satisfiability modulo theories. In: Handbook of Satisfiability, Frontiers in Artificial Intelligence and Applications, vol. 185, chap. 26, pp. 825–885. IOS Press (2009)
5. Davis, M., Putnam, H.: A computing procedure for quantification theory. J. ACM **7**(3), 201–215 (1960)
6. Davis, M., Logemann, G., Loveland, D.W.: A machine program for theorem-proving. Commun. ACM **5**(7), 394–397 (1962). https://doi.org/10.1145/368273.368557
7. Jovanović, D., de Moura, L.: Solving non-linear arithmetic. In: Gramlich, B., Miller, D., Sattler, U. (eds.) IJCAR 2012. LNCS, vol. 7364, pp. 339–354. Springer, Heidelberg (2012). https://doi.org/10.1007/978-3-642-31365-3_27
8. Kremer, G., Ábrahám, E., England, M., Davenport, J.H.: On the implementation of cylindrical algebraic coverings for satisfiability modulo theories solving. In: Proceedings SYNASC 2021, pp. 37–39. IEEE (2021). https://doi.org/10.1109/SYNASC54541.2021.00018
9. Kroening, D., Strichman, O.: Decision Procedures: An Algorithmic Point of View. Springer, Heidelberg (2008). https://doi.org/10.1007/978-3-662-50497-0
10. Moskewicz, M., Madigan, C.F., Zhao, Y., Zhang, L., Malik, S.: Chaff: engineering an efficient SAT solver. In: Proceedings 38th Design Automation Conference (2001)
11. de Moura, L., Jovanović, D.: A model-constructing satisfiability calculus. In: Giacobazzi, R., Berdine, J., Mastroeni, I. (eds.) VMCAI 2013. LNCS, vol. 7737, pp. 1–12. Springer, Heidelberg (2013). https://doi.org/10.1007/978-3-642-35873-9_1

Contents – Part II

Concurrency

The VerCors Verifier: A Progress Report 3
Lukas Armborst, Pieter Bos, Lars B. van den Haak, Marieke Huisman,
Robert Rubbens, Ömer Şakar, and Philip Tasche

Parsimonious Optimal Dynamic Partial Order Reduction 19
Parosh Aziz Abdulla, Mohamed Faouzi Atig, Sarbojit Das,
Bengt Jonsson, and Konstantinos Sagonas

Collective Contracts for Message-Passing Parallel Programs 44
Ziqing Luo and Stephen F. Siegel

Distributed Systems

mypyvy: A Research Platform for Verification of Transition Systems
in First-Order Logic 71
James R. Wilcox, Yotam M. Y. Feldman, Oded Padon, and Sharon Shoham

Efficient Implementation of an Abstract Domain of Quantified First-Order
Formulas 86
Eden Frenkel, Tej Chajed, Oded Padon, and Sharon Shoham

Verifying Cake-Cutting, Faster 109
Noah Bertram, Tean Lai, and Justin Hsu

Runtime Verification and Monitoring

General Anticipatory Runtime Verification 133
Raik Hipler, Hannes Kallwies, Martin Leucker, and César Sánchez

Proactive Real-Time First-Order Enforcement 156
François Hublet, Leonardo Lima, David Basin, Srđan Krstić,
and Dmitriy Traytel

Predictive Monitoring with Strong Trace Prefixes 182
Zhendong Ang and Umang Mathur

Case Studies and Tools

Monitoring Unmanned Aircraft: Specification, Integration,
and Lessons-Learned 207
    Jan Baumeister, Bernd Finkbeiner, Florian Kohn, Florian Löhr,
    Guido Manfredi, Sebastian Schirmer, and Christoph Torens

Testing the Migration from Analog to Software-Based Railway
Interlocking Systems 219
    Anna Becchi, Alessandro Cimatti, and Giuseppe Scaglione

soid: A Tool for Legal Accountability for Automated Decision Making 233
    Samuel Judson, Matthew Elacqua, Filip Cano, Timos Antonopoulos,
    Bettina Könighofer, Scott J. Shapiro, and Ruzica Piskac

Machine Learning and Neural Networks

Marabou 2.0: A Versatile Formal Analyzer of Neural Networks 249
    Haoze Wu, Omri Isac, Aleksandar Zeljić, Teruhiro Tagomori,
    Matthew Daggitt, Wen Kokke, Idan Refaeli, Guy Amir, Kyle Julian,
    Shahaf Bassan, Pei Huang, Ori Lahav, Min Wu, Min Zhang,
    Ekaterina Komendantskaya, Guy Katz, and Clark Barrett

Monitizer: Automating Design and Evaluation of Neural Network Monitors ... 265
    Muqsit Azeem, Marta Grobelna, Sudeep Kanav, Jan Křetínský,
    Stefanie Mohr, and Sabine Rieder

Guiding Enumerative Program Synthesis with Large Language Models 280
    Yixuan Li, Julian Parsert, and Elizabeth Polgreen

Enchanting Program Specification Synthesis by Large Language Models
Using Static Analysis and Program Verification 302
    Cheng Wen, Jialun Cao, Jie Su, Zhiwu Xu, Shengchao Qin, Mengda He,
    Haokun Li, Shing-Chi Cheung, and Cong Tian

Verifying Global Two-Safety Properties in Neural Networks
with Confidence 329
    Anagha Athavale, Ezio Bartocci, Maria Christakis, Matteo Maffei,
    Dejan Nickovic, and Georg Weissenbacher

Certified Robust Accuracy of Neural Networks Are Bounded Due to Bayes
Errors 352
    Ruihan Zhang and Jun Sun

Boosting Few-Pixel Robustness Verification via Covering Verification
Designs 377
  Yuval Shapira, Naor Wiesel, Shahar Shabelman,
  and Dana Drachsler-Cohen

Unifying Qualitative and Quantitative Safety Verification
of DNN-Controlled Systems 401
  Dapeng Zhi, Peixin Wang, Si Liu, C.-H. Luke Ong, and Min Zhang

Author Index 427

Concurrency

The VerCors Verifier: A Progress Report

Lukas Armborst[1], Pieter Bos[1], Lars B. van den Haak[2],
Marieke Huisman[1], Robert Rubbens[1(✉)], Ömer Şakar[1],
and Philip Tasche[1]

[1] Formal Methods and Tools, University of Twente, Enschede,
The Netherlands
{l.armborst,p.h.bos,m.huisman,r.b.rubbens,o.f.o.sakar,
p.b.h.tasche}@utwente.nl
[2] Software Engineering Technology,
Technical University of Eindhoven, Eindhoven, The Netherlands
l.b.v.d.haak@tue.nl

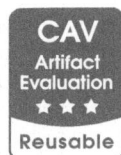

Abstract. This paper gives an overview of the most recent developments on the VerCors verifier. VerCors is a deductive verifier for concurrent software, written in multiple programming languages, where the specifications are written in terms of pre-/postcondition contracts using permission-based separation logic. In essence, VerCors is a program transformation tool: it translates an annotated program into input for the Viper framework, which is then used as verification back-end. The paper discusses the different programming languages and features for which VerCors provides verification support. It also discusses how the tool internally has been reorganised to become easily extendible, and to improve the connection and interaction with Viper. In addition, we also introduce two tools built on top of VerCors, which support correctness-preserving transformations of verified programs. Finally, we discuss how the VerCors verifier has been used on a range of realistic case studies.

1 Introduction

With the ever-growing digitalisation of our society, we depend more and more on the reliability of the underlying software. To provide guarantees about this reliability, we need tools that can do a formal analysis directly at the implementation level of the software. The VerCors verifier [12] contributes to this goal: it enables the verification of pre-/postcondition contract specifications for (concurrent) programs, written in a range of different programming languages.

Work on the VerCors verifier started in 2011 [2], focussing initially on the verification of concurrent Java programs, using permission-based separation logic. Over time, VerCors has expanded into a verification environment that supports reasoning about programs in a wide range of different programming languages. An important design goal of the VerCors verifier was to make a tool that

Work on this project is support by the NWO VICI 639.023.710 Mercedes project and the NWO TTW 17249 ChEOPS project.

A. Gurfinkel and V. Ganesh (Eds.): CAV 2024, LNCS 14682, pp. 3–18, 2024.
https://doi.org/10.1007/978-3-031-65630-9_1

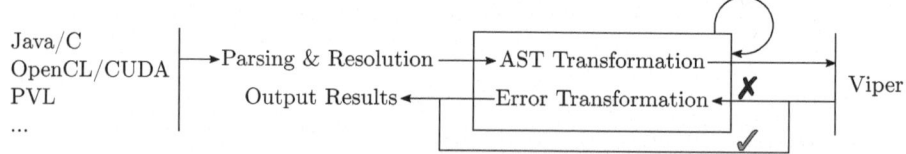

Fig. 1. Overview of the tool architecture. Tool interface boundaries are indicated with vertical lines. The circular arrow indicates that AST and error transformation steps might by applied multiple times. The red X (Color figure online) indicates a verification error, the green checkmark indicates succesful verification.

(1) would verify a program *as is*, i.e., without the need to manually simplify the implementation and only requiring additional verification annotations in comments, and (2) would have a high degree of automation, to make it accessible to a large group of potential users. Ultimately, VerCors should make verification available as a part of the build process, similar to type checking. VerCors is developed as a program transformation tool: it takes as input an annotated program, and it transforms this in multiple steps into input for the Viper framework [38], which is an intermediate representation framework for separation-logic-style specifications. An overview of the architecture is provided in Fig. 1. The transformation is set up in such a way that it is sound but incomplete: if Viper verifies the program, it is guaranteed that the original program satisfies its specification. However, if verification fails the program might or might not respect its verification annotations.

This paper reports on the recent steps that have been taken to further develop the VerCors verifier towards its ultimate goals. It describes in particular new developments on the VerCors verifier since 2017, when the last tool paper on VerCors was published [12]. Notable developments since then are:

- improved front-end support for programming languages such as Java, C and OpenCL, described in Sect. 2.1;
- added front-end support for other programming languages, such as Halide [44], SystemC [27], LLVM IR [31] and SYCL [58], described in Sects. 2.2 and 2.3;
- updated the internals of the tool to improve support for typing and transformation, as well as in the interaction with Viper, described in Sect. 3;
- a collection of transformation tools built on top of VerCors to step-wise derive verified, complex implementations, described in Sect. 4; and
- a wide range of practical case studies to understand how verification can be used in practice, described in Sect. 5.

2   New and Improved Language Support

This section describes the progress on programming languages supported by VerCors. First we describe new features that are provided for languages that were already supported by VerCors, namely Java and C/C++, as well as the improved support to reason about GPU kernels. Next, we describe new languages for which direct support has been added to VerCors (JavaBIP and SYCL). The last subsection covers programming languages that are not directly supported by VerCors, but can be encoded – by VerCors itself, or by an external tool – into an existing VerCors language: SystemC, LLVM IR and Halide. For these encodings, we typically transform a program to PVL, which is VerCors' internal language. It is similar to Java, supporting classes and methods for example, but also has additional constructs such as parallel blocks, which we use to prototype new verification features.

2.1 Improved Existing Language Support

Java: Exceptions. As mentioned above, Java was the first programming language supported by VerCors. It has support for several non-trivial features of the language, such as the `import` statement, locks (specified using lock invariants), arrays, instance and `static` fields.

A missing feature that hindered practical applicability was the support to reason about exceptions. To improve this, we first added support for exceptional contracts using `signals` clauses. Similar to `ensures`, a `signals` clause specifies the postcondition that must hold when an exception of the indicated type is thrown. In addition, it can also specify properties over the object that is thrown.

Support for exception-related statements and modifiers such as `try_catch`, `throw` and `throws` is encoded by transforming them in several steps, to keep the implementation modular. For example, `throws` modifiers are encoded into `signals` clauses, and `try_catch` and throwing method calls are encoded into `goto`'s. After the transformations, the only primitives that remain are `goto`, `return`, `requires` and `ensures`. In addition, abrupt termination primitives such as `break` and `continue` are transformed into exceptional statements, such that they can be handled using the same code that encodes exceptional behaviour. For more details about the support for exceptions, see [47,48].

C/C++. Support for basic features of the C and C++ languages works similar to the verification of those features in Java. In particular, a C/C++ program can only be verified if it does not have undefined behaviour. However, also C-specific features had to be covered, such as *allocating* and *freeing* memory (`malloc` and `free`), *array initialisers*, *structures*, *casts* between primitive types and implicit type conversion rules. Furthermore, VerCors now uses the truncated [33] definition for division and modulo in the C, Java and C++ languages.

GPU Kernels: OpenCL/CUDA. VerCors initially supported verifying data race freedom and functional correctness of GPU kernels using barriers and atomic operations by manually encoding kernels into PVL (using parallel blocks) [13]. Support for verification directly at the level of the OpenCL [59] or CUDA [35] program has now been added, by implementing a translation from kernels into parallel blocks. In addition, support for both dynamic and static *local memory* (called *shared memory* in CUDA) is added, allowing verification of kernels that use faster data sharing for threads within the same workgroup. Support for local and global memory fences for barriers is present for OpenCL, only allowing redistribution of memory permissions when the appropriate fence is used.

2.2 Newly Supported Frameworks

JavaBIP. VerCors has direct support for JavaBIP [11]. BIP [6] ("Behavior, Interaction, Priority") is a framework for rigorous system design. JavaBIP provides support for BIP as a Java library. Each JavaBIP class is modelled by a separate BIP state machine. This connection is made through annotations. The @State class annotation indicates the possible states, and the @Transition annotation indicates that a method makes a transition. Whenever a transition must be taken, the JavaBIP runtime engine looks up and executes the corresponding method. Essentially, the user declaratively specifies the state machine and implements the transition methods, and JavaBIP provides state machine behaviour.

The BIP methodology assumes that conditions on the behaviours of the system are encoded by the user in the BIP state machine, e.g. by adding guards to transitions, and by assuming implicit invariants in the state machine, such as "in state S, field f is positive". However, the JavaBIP platform does not provide tool support to check if an implementation actually guarantees these invariants. To address this shortcoming, we prototyped verification support for JavaBIP using VerCors [10]. In the JavaBIP state machine, the user makes implicit invariants explicit by adding contract annotations on the states and transitions. Guards and contracts are then verified deductively using VerCors, thus ensuring that the implementation corresponds to the assumptions for the BIP state machine.

SYCL. SYCL is a high-level programming language that enables the use of different heterogeneous devices in a single application [58]. It is built in C++ and targets different devices such as CPUs, GPUs and FPGAs. It abstracts away from the device-specific details (in contrast to e.g. OpenCL for GPUs), by building on top of existing (lower-level) APIs such as OpenCL, CUDA and HIP.

VerCors provides prototype verification support for a subset of SYCL, focussing on its basic and nd-range kernels, buffers and data accessors [60]. A contract is specified for the host function and SYCL kernel. VerCors automatically adds predefined specifications for the various SYCL data types and functions, and uses the kernel contract to automatically handle the permissions related to the data transfer and access through SYCL's buffer and accessor constructs.

2.3 Programming Languages Encoded into VerCors

SystemC. VerCors is able to verify embedded systems at the design stage, as it supports the hardware/software co-design language SystemC [27]. The VeSUV tool [57] takes designs written in a widely-used subset of SystemC and encodes their semantics, as well as the scheduling semantics of SystemC, into PVL. The user can then add properties to the encoded PVL program and verify them normally with VerCors. This approach allows VerCors to verify both local and global safety properties and to reason about the timing behaviour of the system, which is typically difficult for deductive verifiers.

LLVM IR. VCLLVM is a prototype tool that adds support for LLVM IR [31] to VerCors [40,41]. Building verification support for LLVM IR is part of a larger project that aims to develop verification support for any programming language that compiles into LLVM IR. VCLLVM takes as input an annotated LLVM IR file. It uses the existing LLVM infrastructure to parse and analyse the program. The program and the annotations are then encoded by VCLLVM into input for VerCors, and VerCors is used for the verification.

Halide. HaliVer [24] is a tool that adds verification support for Halide [44] and uses VerCors as its verifier. Halide is a Domain Specific Language designed to write high-performance image and tensor processing code. Halide decouples the *algorithmic* part, which defines *what* should be computed, from the schedule, which defines how a computation should be optimised. HaliVer makes it possible to add and verify annotations that describe the behaviour of Halide programs. Verification can be done at two levels: (1) *front-end verification* encodes the algorithmic part of the Halide program directly into PVL, together with its annotations, to verify its functional correctness, while (2) *back-end verification* transforms the annotations to match the Halide-generated and optimised C code, which VerCors can then verify. This allows to verify complex optimised code, without formal verification of the whole Halide compiler. The HaliVer tool is integrated into the Halide compiler and transforms the annotations similar to how the compiler transforms the code.

3 VerCors Implementation Changes

In order to improve the user experience for VerCors users, as well as the extendability of the tool, some major updates to its implementation have been made. We describe the important changes.

Internal Transformation Steps. The effect of VerCors as a program transformer is achieved by a sequence of approximately eighty rewrite steps. Each step descends into the program tree recursively and rewrites nodes where appropriate. In earlier versions of VerCors there were several transformations containing over 1000 lines of code each, which made it hard to guarantee that they were correct rewrites. We reorganised the internal structure of VerCors and split those large transformations into multiple small rewrites. The smaller steps also help facilitate abstractions that newly supported languages like SYCL can build on.

Name Resolution. Earlier versions of VerCors used text names, which ended up with a large number of prefixes. If one was missing, it was hard to see which rewrite caused that. Schemes with de Bruijn-indexed names [17] are thwarted by declarations shifting around, and forgetting to account for it. Therefore, we made the rewriters blind to the declaration names. Instead, direct references to the referred declaration are stored in the tree. This means that names are resolved once at the start, and from then on there is nothing to resolve anymore: the name is a pointer to the declaration itself. When rewriting such a reference we look up the successor of the referent in a map. The circularity of this approach is resolved by storing the reference as a lazily evaluated value.

Typing Coercions. To ensure that all (intermediate) program trees during parsing and rewriting are correct, it is imperative that the program is well-typed. This is arranged by having each node in the tree assert typing constraints on its sub-nodes using the internal typing rules of VerCors. Moreover, certain rewriters need to know what typing rules were applied to the current node for it to be allowed in its current position, for example, if we want to store the sequence {null, null, null} in a variable of type seq<int[]>. This is achieved by temporarily storing the typing rule(s) that are applied to a node in the program tree, as a *coercion*. In this case, the sequence stores a coercion capturing that "seq<null_type> can be mapped to seq<int[]>, because null_type can be coerced to int[]". As a result, the rewriter for arrays only needs to consider places with the appropriate coercions.

Triggers. A known challenge in verification are quantifiers, which need instantiation in the proof. In the SMT community, triggers are used to manually provide hints about potential instantiations [21]. Initially, VerCors automatically generated triggers for quantifiers. However, for complicated examples it is important to have explicit control over triggers, to avoid matching loops [8]. Therefore, while VerCors still generates triggers, VerCors now also allows the user to specify triggers explicitly.

To enable the use of triggers for parallel block specifications, additional rewrites may be necessary. For a parallel block, the annotations are given per thread, and during the verification process these annotations are quantified over the range of all threads. However, in some cases this results in quantified formulas containing arithmetic expressions, which are not allowed in triggers. For example in the case of a flattened multi-dimensional array, we obtain specifications like: $\forall$ int i, int j; $0 \leq i < 8 \wedge 0 \leq j < 10 \wedge j\%2 = 0 \Rightarrow A[(j*8)+i] > 0$. We would like to use the following trigger: $A[(j*8)+i]$. However, as arithmetic operators are not allowed in triggers, this trigger cannot be used. To fix this, VerCors can now automatically rewrite this expression to $\forall$ int k; $0 \leq k < 8*10 \wedge (k/8)\%2 = 0 \Rightarrow A[k] > 0$. This quantifier now has the following valid trigger: $A[k]$. This rewrite is general, and applies for most surjective mappings from variables to values.

Error Reporting. Errors that are reported about input programs are now modelled close to the input language. Earlier the tool reported simply that a formula

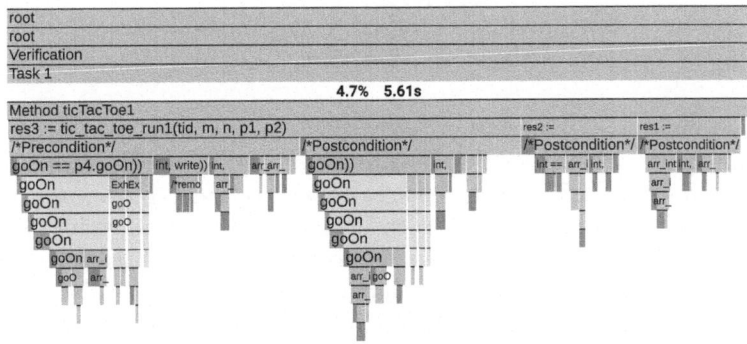

Fig. 2. Flame graph render of a verification profile

is false, or another technical error from the back-end. We extended the rewriters to indicate how errors reported in Viper [38] should be translated backwards in correspondence to the changes that occur in that rewriter. In certain cases such translations can consist of several steps, which have to be merged/combined, as rewriters build on abstractions within the internal VerCors language. Essentially, whenever a transformation creates an AST node that might cause a failure in the output AST, the transformation also has to define how to map the error back onto the input AST. The end result is that errors at the SMT level can be translated back to the input source level at the correct location.

Progress and Profiling. While VerCors is verifying a file, it now occasionally updates the user interface to show the proof goal it is working on. Since verification often gets stuck on a specific proof goal, this is helpful in diagnosing where the program needs further specifications or fixes. Currently this is reported in a rather technical manner, but we plan to soon adopt a better model, reporting in terms of the input program. This is inspired by the approach in the WP interface of Frama-C [7], where proof goals and their status are reported in line with the input file before the file is verified.

To keep the verify-edit-verify loop manageable, it also helps to be able to diagnose the verification time as a whole. For this purpose VerCors can now output a fine-grained profile, which contains timing information that can later be rendered to e.g. a flame graph as in Fig. 2. The tasks in the profile can be viewed as a tree structure, where a task is nested under its parent task. Tasks are divided up from global phases, down to the branch conditions under which a proof goal is verified. The detailed information about proof goals is supported through the symbolic execution back-end of Viper.

4   Deriving Verified, Optimised Programs

Program verification is a hard and challenging problem, and verifying a program that has been optimised for performance can be even harder. To alleviate this problem, we have developed two program correctness-preserving optimisation tools on top of VerCors: Alpinist and VeyMont.

Alpinist. Alpinist is an annotation-aware GPU program optimiser [52]. Part of the GPU program development cycle is to incrementally optimise the GPU program for performance. These incremental optimisations are performed on the source level, prior to compilation. Such optimisations can introduce errors. To address this problem, Alpinist automatically applies frequently-used GPU program optimisations, notably loop unrolling, tiling, kernel fusion, iteration merging, matrix linearisation and data prefetching, in an *annotation-aware* manner, which means that besides transforming the GPU program itself, it also transforms the annotations. The provability of the resulting annotated optimised GPU program is preserved by this transformation. Alpinist works in four different phases: *parsing, applicability checking, transformation* and *output*. The strength of Alpinist's approach lies in particular in the *applicability checking*, where different analysis techniques, including deductive verification can be used to check whether the optimisation is indeed applicable, before applying it. An example of an applicability check is whether a loop can be safely unrolled a certain number of times (as specified by the user): Alpinist unrolls a loop n times only if it can prove that the loop is executed at least n times.

VeyMont. VeyMont supports the derivation of correct parallel programs from sequential programs [16]. First, a sequential global program is verified. The sequential program has a restricted form, similar to choreographic programs and session types [26,36]. A sequential VeyMont program contains endpoints, communication statements between these endpoints, conditional statements, and loops, where for conditional statements all endpoints must agree on which branch is taken ("branch unanimity"). There are no local variables, instead all state is encapsulated by the endpoints. VeyMont can also generate permissions, however, this assumes a simple ownership structure without sharing.

After the global program is verified, VeyMont transforms it into a concurrent program, where an implementation is derived for each endpoint by projection [16]. For example, if an endpoint is in a receiving position in a communication statement, the projection will produce code that reads from the receiving end of the channel. If an endpoint is not involved in a communication, the projection will produce a no-op. The meta-theory behind VeyMont shows that this transformed program behaves in the same way as the sequential program [29]. In future work, we want to make VeyMont usable for a larger class of programs, in particular by providing support for the user to specify permissions, and by allowing parametrisation of global programs over the number of endpoints.

5   Case Studies

In order to evaluate and improve the usability and applicability of VerCors, we have developed a number of case studies using VerCors over the last years.

5.1   Tunnel Control Software Components

In collaboration with the company Technolution[1], several Java components of a tunnel control system were analysed with VerCors. The architecture of the software is governed by the Dutch tunnel standard specification (called BSTTI) [45]. First, we investigated the connection between the BSTTI and the implementation [42]. Next, we looked into a benign but unexplained runtime behaviour of the control software implementation [37]. Technolution suspected there was a concurrency bug in the code, but had not yet found a likely explanation.

After analysis and annotating the Java code, two possible explanations were found, and later confirmed by Technolution. First, there was a mutable internal data structure, which was accidentally aliased into a reference which was assumed to be immutable. Second, several methods allowed inspection and hence the leaking of an internal data structure, which was not designed to be thread safe. The collaboration with Technolution strengthened our ideas about what is needed for further adoption of verification in industry, as we not only encountered the problems ourselves, but also were able to confirm these findings with Technolution. These ideas are: language support has to be improved, code written without verification in mind is difficult to verify, and ultimately verification should be part of the development chain.

5.2   Verification of Red-Black Trees and their Parallel Merge

Another case study inspired by industrial code, this time from NLnet Labs[2], involved the verification of red-black (RB) trees. In the industrial C code, data was parsed by several threads concurrently, each constructing its own red-black tree. Afterwards, all those trees are merged in parallel into one. As a first step, Nguyen in his master thesis [39] implemented an RB tree in Java and verified parts of its functionality. This was later extended by verifying the delete functionality, as well as a version of the parallel merging process [4]. It uses a linked-list data structure to store batches of RB tree nodes, prepared by a producer thread and queueing for a consumer thread. This case study particularly highlights the use of two concepts supported by VerCors: (1) The producer-consumer pattern was proved using *ghost variables*, i.e. variables that only exist for specification and verification, and are not part of the executable code. While ghost variables are not unique to VerCors, the case study provides a useful example how they can assist in verifying concurrent programs in VerCors. (2) The delete operator was verified using the *separating implication* operator ("magic wand"), which is the separation logic counterpart to the logical implication "⇒" [14,53]. Many tools based on separation logic do not support the magic wand, but this case study shows its usefulness.

---

[1] https://www.technolution.com/.
[2] https://nlnetlabs.nl/.

5.3 GPU Case Studies

We developed several verification case studies for GPU code. Notably, we studied the verification of various prefix sum implementations, which is a frequently used library function for GPU kernels [51]. After that, we verified two other GPU algorithms (Parallel Stream Compaction and Summed-Area Table) that use prefix sum, to show how to verify code reusing existing verification results [50]. Initially, we verified encodings of the algorithms in PVL, but to show practical applicability of our approach, we also verified CUDA versions for most of them [49]. These case studies helped us to improve our GPU support and understand how these proofs work.

5.4 Student Projects

Several students have done case studies with VerCors. We find these student projects important, as they show the usability of VerCors for users who are not involved in the development of VerCors.

Sequential SCC Algorithm. The strongly connected components (SCC) algorithm finds the maximal subsets of nodes in a directed graph, such that every node in the component can reach any other node in the component, without leaving the component. It is an important ingredient for many model checking algorithms, and thus its correctness is essential. We had two student projects on the verification of a variation of Tarjan's SCC algorithm [56] in PVL. Hollander [25] provided an overall outline of the correctness proof, which was proven correct with VerCors, however using some unproven lemmas. Boerman [15] then followed up on this, and proved two of these remaining lemmas, to complete the soundness proof of the algorithm. In addition, Boerman identified several bottlenecks that slowed down the proof, and documented how they were resolved.

Distributed Locks. An implementation of a distributed re-entrant lock was verified to be memory safe and functionally correct by Ledelay [32]. The case study was provided by the company BetterBe[3]. To make verification tractable, Ledelay split up the implementation into four intermediate versions of increasing complexity, adding more aspects of the original code of BetterBe in each layer. The first layer was based on an earlier verified re-entrant lock [3]. The second layer added read/write functionality to the lock, and the third layer added an abstraction for a database. Finally, the fourth phase added a "fail-fast" optimisation, where a lock can safely skip a database query in certain cases. Layers one and two were fully verified. Verification of the later layers was not completed due

---

[3] https://www.betterbe.com/.

to time constraints. During verification, the multiple layers of abstraction sometimes made verification slower, or required additional verification annotations in other places. This was important input to improve the performance of VerCors.

Other Student Projects. Sessink verified (parts of) the implementation of the ArrayList class of Java's standard library [54]. This is relevant for verifying real-life code bases, which often make use of library features. Budde verified Kahn's topological sorting algorithm [18]. Like the SCC algorithm above, this is a base component in more complex procedures, such as task scheduling.

6 Conclusions, Related Work and Future Work

This paper gave an overview of recent work around the VerCors verifier. We described how we improved the support for programming languages that can be reasoned about, as well as the internals and verification support of the tool. We also discussed various case studies, which demonstrate the usability of the tool.

Related Work. There are several other deductive program verifiers for high-level programs, such as KeY [1], Dafny [34], OpenJML [20] Why3 [23], VeriFast [28], Frama-C [7], Whiley [43] RESOLVE [55] and the verifiers that are built on top of Viper, such as Nagini [22], Prusti [5] and Gobra [61]. The main characteristics that distinguish VerCors from these other tools are its focus on concurrency (only a few other verifiers, such as VeriFast and the Viper-based Gobra and Nagini, also support this), and its focus on extendability and support for many different programming languages and concurrency paradigms. However, we are often inspired by verification features and how they are built into other tools. There are also some tools that focus specifically on the analysis of GPU programs, such as GPUVerify [9] and Faisal [19]. They tailor their verification support specifically to GPU programs, whereas VerCors is fully general.

There also is related work on developing verification theories for concurrent software, such as Iris [30] and TaDa [46]. These form an inspiration for the verification logic supported by VerCors. However, our approach ultimately focuses on the applicability of our techniques, rather than covering all edge cases by developing a fully generic verification technique.

Future Work. Annotation generation is an important aspect of future work. HaliVer, Alpinist and VeyMont already address this for specific cases, but we also plan to develop techniques to generate annotations from scratch. Further, we would like to exploit the generality of VerCors further, to make it easier to support new programming languages. One future project is to investigate if we can use support for LLVM IR to develop verifiers for any language that compiles into LLVM IR. Finally, we continuously work on improving VerCors' usability.

References

1. Ahrendt, W., Beckert, B., Bubel, R., Hähnle, R., Schmitt, P.H., Ulbrich, M.: In: Deductive Software Verification – The KeY Book. LNCS, vol. 10001. Springer, Heidelberg (2016). https://doi.org/10.1007/978-3-319-49812-6. ISBN: 9783319498126
2. Amighi, A., Blom, S., Huisman, M., Zaharieva-Stojanovski, M.: The VerCors project: setting up basecamp. In: Programming Languages meets Program Verification (PLPV 2012), pp. 71–82. ACM (2012). https://doi.org/10.1145/2103776. 2103785
3. Amighi, A.: Specification and verification of synchronisation classes in Java: a practical approach. Ph.D. thesis. University of Twente (2018). https://doi.org/10. 3990/1.9789036544399
4. Armborst, L., Huisman, M.: Permission-based verification of red-black trees and their merging. In: 2021 IEEE/ACM 9th International Conference on Formal Methods in Software Engineering (FormaliSE), pp. 111–123 (2021). https://doi.org/10. 1109/FormaliSE52586.2021.00017
5. Astrauskas, V., et al.: The Prusti project: formal verification for Rust. In: Deshmukh, J.V., Havelund, K., Perez, I. (eds.). NASA Formal Methods, pp. 88–108. Springer, Heidelberg (2022). https://doi.org/10.1007/978-3-031-06773-0_5. ISBN: 978-3-031-06773-0
6. Basu, A., Bozga, M., Sifakis, J.: Modeling heterogeneous real-time components in BIP. In: Fourth IEEE International Conference on Software Engineering and Formal Methods (SEFM 2006), pp. 3–12 (2006). https://doi.org/10.1109/SEFM. 2006.27
7. Baudin, P., et al.: The dogged pursuit of bug-free C programs: the Frama-C software analysis platform. Commun. ACM **64**(8), 56–68 (2021). https://doi.org/10. 1145/3470569
8. Becker, Nils, Müller, Peter, Summers, Alexander J..: The axiom profiler: understanding and debugging SMT quantifier instantiations. In: Vojnar, Tomáš, Zhang, Lijun (eds.) TACAS 2019. LNCS, vol. 11427, pp. 99–116. Springer, Cham (2019). https://doi.org/10.1007/978-3-030-17462-0_6
9. Betts, A., Chong, N., Donaldson, A., Qadeer, S., Thomson, P.: GPUVerify: a verifier for GPU kernels. In: Proceedings of the ACM International Conference on Object Oriented Programming Systems Languages and Applications (OOPSLA 2012), pp. 113–132. ACM (2012). https://doi.org/10.1145/2384616.2384625
10. Bliudze, S., van den Bos, P., Huisman, M., Rubbens, R., Safina, L.: Java-BIP meets VerCors: towards the safety of concurrent software systems in Java. In: Lambers, L., Uchitel, S. (eds.). Fundamental Approaches to Software Engineering, pp. 143–150. Springer, Cham (2023). https://doi.org/10.1007/978-3-031-30826-0_8. ISBN: 978-3-031-30826-0
11. Bliudze, S., Mavridou, A., Szymanek, R., Zolotukhina, A.: Exogenous coordination of concurrent software components with JavaBIP. In: Software: Practice and Experience, vol. 47, no. 11, pp. 1801–1836 (2017). https://doi.org/10.1002/spe. 2495. eprint: https://onlinelibrary.wiley.com/doi/pdf/10.1002/spe.2495
12. Blom, S., Darabi, S., Huisman, M., Oortwijn, W.: The VerCors tool set: verification of parallel and concurrent software. In: Polikarpova, N., Schneider, S. (eds.) Integrated Formal Methods 2017. LNCS, vol. 10510, pp. 102 –110. Springer, Cham (2017). https://doi.org/10.1007/978-3-319-66845-1_7
13. Blom, S., Huisman, M., Mihelčić, M.: Specification and verification of GPGPU programs. Sci. Comput. Program. **95**, 376–388 (2014). https://doi.org/10.1016/j. scico.2014.03.013. ISSN: 0167-6423

14. Blom, S., Huisman, M.: Witnessing the elimination of magic wands. Int. J. Softw. Tools Technol. Transfer **17**(6), 757–781 (2015). https://doi.org/10.1007/s10009-015-0372-3. ISSN: 1433-2787
15. Boerman, J.: Formal verification of a sequential SCC algorithm. MA thesis. University of Twente (2023). http://essay.utwente.nl/94474/
16. van den Bos, P., Jongmans, S.: VeyMont: parallelising verified programs instead of verifying parallel programs. In: Chechik, M., Katoen, J., Leucker, M. (eds.) Formal Methods, pp. 321–339. Springer, Heidelberg (2023). https://doi.org/10.1007/978-3-031-27481-7_19. ISBN: 978-3-031-27481-7
17. de Bruijn, N.G.: Lambda calculus notation with nameless dummies, a tool for automatic formula manipulation, with application to the Church-Rosser theorem. In: Indagationes Mathematicae (Proceedings), vol. 75, no. 5, pp. 381–392. Elsevier (1972). https://doi.org/10.1016/1385-7258(72)90034-0
18. Budde, N.: Verified version of Kahn's topological sorting algorithm (2023). https://github.com/utwente-fmt/vercors/tree/5e3eb17/examples/concepts/algo/KahnsTopologicalSort.pvl. Accessed 17 Jan 2024
19. Cogumbreiro, T., Lange, J., Rong, D.L.Z., Zicarelli, H.: Checking data-race freedom of GPU kernels, compositionally. In: Silva, A., Leino, K.R.M. (eds.) CAV 2021. LNCS, vol. 12759, pp. 403– 426. Springer, Heidelberg (2021). https://doi.org/10.1007/978-3-030-81685-8_19
20. Cok, D.: OpenJML: software verification for Java 7 using JML, Open-JDK, and Eclipse. In: Dubois, C., Giannakopoulou, D., Mery, D. (eds.) 1st Workshop on Formal Integrated Development Environment, (F-IDE). EPTCS. 2014, vol. 149, pp. 79–92 (2014). https://doi.org/10.4204/EPTCS.149.8
21. Dross, C., Conchon, S., Paskevich, A.: Reasoning with triggers. Research Report RR-7986. INRIA, p. 29 (2012). https://inria.hal.science/hal-00703207
22. Eilers, M., Müller, P.: Nagini: a static verifier for Python. In: Chockler, H., Weissenbacher, G. (eds.) CAV 2018. LNCS, vol. 10981, pp. 596–603. Springer, Cham (2018). https://doi.org/10.1007/978-3-319-96145-3_33
23. Filliâtre, J.-C., Paskevich, A.: Why3—where programs met provers. In: Felleisen, M., Gardner, P. (eds.) ESOP. LNCS, vol. 7792, pp. 125–128. Springer, Cham (2013). https://doi.org/10.1007/978-3-642-37036-6_8
24. van den Haak, L., Wijs, A., Huisman, M., van den Brand, M.: HaliVer: deductive verification and scheduling languages join forces. In: TACAS 2024. LNCS. Springer, Cham (2024)
25. Hollander, J.: Verification of a model checking algorithm in VerCors. MA thesis. University of Twente (2021). http://essay.utwente.nl/88268/
26. Honda, K., Vasconcelos, V.T., Kubo, M.: Language primitives and type discipline for structured communication-based programming. In: Hankin, C. (ed.) Programming Languages and Systems - ESOP 1998. LNCS, vol. 1381, pp. 122–138. Springer, Heidelberg (1998). https://doi.org/10.1007/BFB0053567
27. IEEE Standards Association. IEEE Std. 1666–2011, Open SystemC Language Reference Manual. IEEE Press (2011). https://doi.org/10.1109/IEEESTD.2012.6134619
28. Jacobs, B., Smans, J., Philippaerts, P., Vogels, F., Penninckx, W., Piessens, F.: VeriFast: a powerful, sound, predictable, fast verifier for C and Java. In: Bobaru, M., Havelund, K., Holzmann, G.J., Joshi, R.: NASA Formal Methods Symposium, pp. 41–55. Springer, Cham (2011). https://doi.org/10.1007/978-3-642-20398-5_4
29. Jongmans, S., van den Bos, P.: A predicate transformer for choreographies - computing preconditions in choreographic programming. In: Sergey, I. (ed.) Programming Languages and Systems - 31st European Symposium on Programming,

ESOP 2022, Held as Part of the European Joint Conferences on Theory and Practice of Software, ETAPS 2022, Munich, 2–7 April 2022, Proceedings. LNCS, vol. 13240, pp. 520–547. Springer, Heidelberg (2022). https://doi.org/10.1007/978-3-030-99336-8_19

30. Jung, R., Krebbers, R., Jourdan, J., Bizjak, A., Birkedal, L., Dreyer, D.: Iris from the ground up: a modular foundation for higher-order concurrent separation logic. J. Funct. Program. **28** (2018). https://doi.org/10.1017/S0956796818000151

31. Lattner, C., Adve, V.: LLVM: a compilation framework for lifelong program analysis & transformation. In: International Symposium on Code Generation and Optimization, 2004. CGO 2004, pp. 75–86. IEEE (2004). https://doi.org/10.5555/977395.977673

32. Ledelay, J.: Verification of Distributed Locks: A Case Study. MA thesis. University of Twente (2023). http://essay.utwente.nl/95192/

33. Leijen, D.: Division and Modulus for Computer Scientists (2003). https://www.microsoft.com/en-us/research/publication/divisionand-modulus-for-computer-scientists/

34. Leino, K.: Accessible software verification with Dafny. IEEE Softw. **34**(6), 94–97 (2017). https://doi.org/10.1109/MS.2017.4121212

35. Lindholm, L., Nickolls, J., Oberman, S., Montrym, J.: NVIDIA Tesla: a unified graphics and computing architecture. IEEE Micro **28**(2), 39–55 (2008). https://doi.org/10.1109/MM.2008.31

36. Montesi, F.: Introduction to Choreographies. Cambridge University Press (2023). https://doi.org/10.1017/9781108981491

37. Monti, R.E., Rubbens, R., Huisman, M.: On deductive verification of an industrial concurrent software component with VerCors. In: Margaria, T., Steffen, B. (eds.) Leveraging Applications of Formal Methods, Verification and Validation. Verification Principles. ISoLA 2022. LNCS, vol. 13701, pp. 517–534. Springer, Heidelberg (2022). https://doi.org/10.1007/978-3-031-19849-6_29. ISBN: 978-3-031-19849-6

38. Müller, P., Schwerhoff, M., Summers, A.: Viper - a verification infrastructure for permission-based reasoning. In: Jobstmann, B., Leino, K.R.M. (eds.) Verification, Model Checking, and Abstract Interpretation. VMCAI. Springer, Heidelberg (2016). https://doi.org/10.1007/978-3-662-49122-5_2

39. Nguyen, H.: Formal verification of a red-black tree data structure. MA thesis. University of Twente (2019). http://essay.utwente.nl/77569/

40. van Oorschot, D.: VCLLVM: A Transformation Tool for LLVM IR programs to aid Deductive Verification". MA thesis. University of Twente (2023). http://essay.utwente.nl/96536/

41. van Oorschot, D., Huisman, M., Şakar, Ö.: First steps towards deductive verification of LLVM IR. In: FASE 2024, LNCS. Springer, Cham (2024)

42. Oortwijn, W., Huisman, M.: Formal verification of an industrial safety-critical traffic tunnel control system. In: Ahrendt, W., Tarifa, S.L.T. (eds.) Integreated Formal Methods (iFM) 2019. LNCS, vol. 11918. Springer, Heidelberg (2019). https://doi.org/10.1007/978-3-030-34968-4_23

43. Pearce, D.J., Utting, M., Groves, L.: An introduction to software verification with Whiley. In: Bowen, J.P., Liu, Z., Zhang, Z. (eds.) Engineering Trustworthy Software Systems - 4th International School, SETSS 2018, Chongqing, 7–12 April 2018, Tutorial Lectures. LNCS, vol. 11430, pp. 1–37. Springer, Heidelberg (2018). https://doi.org/10.1007/978-3-030-17601-3_1

44. Ragan-Kelley, J., Barnes, C., Adams, A., Paris, S., Durand, F., Amarasinghe, S.: Halide: a language and compiler for optimizing parallelism, locality, and recompu-

tation in image processing pipelines. In: ACM Sigplan Notices. PLDI 2013, vol. 48, no. 6, pp. 519–530 (2013). https://doi.org/10.1145/2491956.2462176

45. Rijkswaterstaat. Landelijke Tunnelstandaard (National Tunnel Standard). https://standaarden.rws.nl/link/standaard/6080. Accessed 17 Jan 2024

46. da Rocha Pinto, P., Dinsdale-Young, T., Gardner, P.: TaDA: a logic for time and data abstraction. In: European Conference on Object-Oriented Programming (ECOOP). LNCS, vol. 8586. Springer, Heidelberg (2014). https://doi.org/10.1007/978-3-662-44202-9_9

47. Rubbens, R.: Improving Support for Java Exceptions and Inheritance in VerCors. MA thesis. University of Twente (2020). http://essay.utwente.nl/81338/

48. Rubbens, R., Lathouwers, S., Huisman, M.: Modular transformation of Java exceptions modulo errors. In: Lluch-Lafuente, A., Mavridou, A. (eds.) Formal Methods for Industrial Critical Systems - 26th International Conference, FMICS 2021, Paris, 24–26 August 2021, Proceedings. LNCS, Vol. 12863, pp. 67–84. Springer, Heidelberg (2021). https://doi.org/10.1007/978-3-030-85248-1_5

49. Safari, M., Huisman, M.: Formal verification of parallel prefix sum and stream compaction algorithms in CUDA. Theor. Comput. Sci. **912**, 81–98 (2022). https://doi.org/10.1016/J.TCS.2022.02.027

50. Safari, M., Huisman, M.: Formal verification of parallel stream compaction and summed-area table algorithms. In: Pun, V.K.I., Stolz, V., Simao, A. (eds.) Theoretical Aspects of Computing – ICTAC 2020, pp. 181–199. Springer, Heidelberg (2020). https://doi.org/10.1007/978-3-030-64276-1_10

51. Safari, M., Oortwijn, W., Joosten, S., Huisman, M.: Formal verification of parallel prefix sum. In: Lee, R., Jha, S., Mavridou, A., Giannakopoulou, D. (eds.) NASA Formal Methods Symposium, pp. 170–186. Springer, Heidelberg (2020). https://doi.org/10.1007/978-3-030-55754-6_10

52. Şakar, Ö., Safari, M., Huisman, M., Wijs, A.: Alpinist: an annotation-aware GPU program optimizer. In: Fisman, D., Rosu, G. (eds.) Tools and Algorithms for the Construction and Analysis of Systems, TACAS 2022. LNCS, Vol. 13244, pp. 332–352. Springer, Heidelberg (2022). https://doi.org/10.1007/978-3-030-99527-0_18

53. Schwerhoff, M., Summers, A.J.: Lightweight support for magic wands in an automatic verifier. In: Boyland, J.T. (ed.) 29th European Conference on Object-Oriented Programming, ECOOP 2015, 5–10 July 2015, Prague. LIPIcs, vol. 37, pp. 614–638. Schloss Dagstuhl - Leibniz-Zentrum fur Informatik (2015). https://doi.org/10.4230/LIPICS.ECOOP.2015.614

54. Sessink, J.: Verified version of Java's ArrayList (2022). https://github.com/utwente-fmt/vercors/tree/5e3eb17/examples/concepts/arrays/ArrayList.java. Accessed 17 Jan 2024

55. Sitaraman, M., Weide, B.W.: A synopsis of twenty five years of RESOLVE PhD research efforts: software development effort estimation using ensemble techniques. ACM SIGSOFT Softw. Eng. Notes **43**(3), 17 (2018). https://doi.org/10.1145/3229783.3229794

56. Tarjan, R.E.: Depth-first search and linear graph algorithms. SIAM J. Comput. **1**(2), 146–160 (1972). https://doi.org/10.1137/0201010

57. Tasche, P., Monti, R.E., Drerup, S.E., Blohm, P., Herber, P., Huisman, M.: Deductive verification of parameterized embedded systems modeled in SystemC. In: Dimitrova, R., Lahav, O., Wolff, S. (eds.)25th International Conference on Verification, Model Checking, and Abstract Interpretation (VMCAI 2024). LNCS, vol. 14500. Springer, Heidelberg (2024). https://doi.org/10.1007/978-3-031-50521-8_9

58. The Khronos SYCLWorking Group. SYCLTM 2020 Specification (revision 8). Specification. The Khronos Group (2023). https://registry.khronos.org/SYCL/specs/sycl-2020/pdf/sycl-2020.pdf
59. The OpenCL 1.2 Specification. Khronos Group (2011)
60. Wittingen, E.: Deductive verification for SYCL. MA thesis. University of Twente (2023). https://purl.utwente.nl/essays/97976
61. Wolf, F.A., Arquint, L., Clochard, M., Oortwijn, W., Pereira, J.C., Muller, P.: Gobra: modular specification and verification of Go programs. In: Silva, A., Leino, K.R.M. (eds.) Computer Aided Verification. LNCS, vol. 12759, pp. 367–379. Springer, Heidelberg (2021). https://doi.org/10.1007/978-3-030-81685-8_17. ISBN: 978-3-030-81685-8

Parsimonious Optimal Dynamic Partial Order Reduction

Parosh Aziz Abdulla[1], Mohamed Faouzi Atig[1], Sarbojit Das[1(✉)],
Bengt Jonsson[1], and Konstantinos Sagonas[1,2]

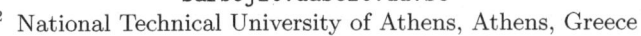

[1] Uppsala University, Uppsala, Sweden
sarbojit.das@it.uu.se
[2] National Technical University of Athens, Athens, Greece

Abstract. Stateless model checking is a fully automatic verification technique for concurrent programs that checks for safety violations by exploring all possible thread schedulings. It becomes effective when coupled with Dynamic Partial Order Reduction (DPOR), which introduces an equivalence on schedulings and reduces the amount of needed exploration. DPOR algorithms that are *optimal* are particularly effective in that they guarantee to explore *exactly* one execution from each equivalence class. Unfortunately, existing sequence-based optimal algorithms may in the worst case consume memory that is exponential in the size of the analyzed program. In this paper, we present Parsimonious-OPtimal DPOR (POP), an optimal DPOR algorithm for analyzing multi-threaded programs under sequential consistency, whose space consumption is polynomial in the worst case. POP combines several novel algorithmic techniques, including (i) a parsimonious race reversal strategy, which avoids multiple reversals of the same race, (ii) an eager race reversal strategy to avoid storing initial fragments of to-be-explored executions, and (iii) a space-efficient scheme for preventing redundant exploration, which replaces the use of sleep sets. Our implementation in NIDHUGG shows that these techniques can significantly speed up the analysis of concurrent programs, and do so with low memory consumption. Comparison to TruSt, a related optimal DPOR algorithm that represents executions as graphs, shows that POP's implementation achieves similar performance for smaller benchmarks, and scales much better than TruSt's on programs with long executions.

1 Introduction

Testing and verification of multi-threaded programs is challenging, since it requires reasoning about all the ways in which operations executed by different threads can interfere. A successful technique for finding concurrency bugs in multithreaded programs and for verifying their absence is *stateless model checking* (SMC) [20]. Given a terminating program and fixed input data, SMC systematically explores the set of all thread schedulings that are possible during program runs. A dedicated runtime scheduler drives the SMC exploration by making decisions on scheduling whenever such choices may affect the interaction between threads. Given enough time, the exploration covers all possible executions and

© The Author(s) 2024
A. Gurfinkel and V. Ganesh (Eds.): CAV 2024, LNCS 14682, pp. 19–43, 2024.
https://doi.org/10.1007/978-3-031-65630-9_2

detects any unexpected program results, program crashes, or assertion violations. The technique is entirely automatic, has no false positives, does not consume excessive memory, and can reproduce the concurrency bugs it detects. SMC has been implemented in many tools (e.g., VeriSoft [21], CHESS [39], Concuerror [15], NIDHUGG [2], rInspect [48], CDSCHECKER [41], RCMC [28], and GENMC [34]), and successfully applied to realistic programs (e.g., [22] and [32]).

To reduce the number of explored executions, SMC tools typically employ *dynamic partial order reduction* (DPOR) [1, 18, 28]. DPOR defines an equivalence relation on executions, typically Mazurkiewicz trace equivalence [36], which preserves many important correctness properties, such as reachability of local states and assertion violations, and explores at least one execution in each equivalence class. Thus, to analyze a program, it suffices to explore one execution from each equivalence class. DPOR was originally developed [18] for models of concurrency where executions are expressed as sequences of interactions between threads/processes and shared objects. Subsequently, sequence-based DPOR has been adapted and refined to a number of programming models, including actor programs [46], abstract computational models [27], event driven programs [4, 24, 35], and MPI programs [42]; it has been extended with features for efficiently handling spinloops and blocking constructs [25], and been adapted for weak concurrency memory models, such as TSO and PSO [2, 48]. DPOR has also been adapted for weak memory models by representing executions as graphs, where nodes represent read and write operations, and edges represent reads-from and coherence relations; this allows the algorithm to be parametric on a specific memory model, at the cost of calling a memory-model oracle [28, 30]

An important improvement has been the introduction of *optimal* DPOR algorithms, which are efficient in that they guarantee to explore *exactly* one execution from each equivalence class. The first optimal DPOR algorithm was designed for the sequence-based representation [1]. Subsequently, optimal DPOR algorithms for even weaker equivalences than Mazurkiewicz trace equivalence have been developed [6, 9, 11]. In some DPOR algorithms [1, 9, 11], optimality comes at the price of added memory consumption which in the worst case can be exponential in the size of the program [3]. Even though most benchmarks in the literature show a modest memory overhead as the price for optimality, it would be desirable to have an optimal DPOR algorithm whose memory consumption is guaranteed to be polynomial in the size of the program. Such an algorithm, called TruSt [29], was recently presented, but for a graph-based setting [30]. It would be desirable to develop a polynomial-space optimal DPOR algorithm also for sequence-based settings. One reason is that a majority of past work on DPOR is sequence-based; hence such an algorithm could be adapted to various programming models and features, some of which were recalled above. Another reason is that sequence-based models represent computations adhering to sequential consistency (SC) and TSO more naturally than graph-based models. For SC, representing executions as sequences of events makes executions consistent by construction and alleviates the need to resort to a potentially expensive memory-model oracle for SC.

In this paper, we present the Parsimonious-OPtimal DPOR (POP) algorithm for analyzing multi-threaded programs under SC (Sect. 4). POP is designed for programs in which threads interact by atomic reads, writes, and RMWs to shared variables, and combines several novel algorithmic techniques.

- A *parsimonious race reversal* technique (Sect. 4.1), which considers a race if and only if its reversal will generate a previously unexplored execution; in contrast, most existing DPOR algorithms reverse races indiscriminately, only to thereafter discard redundant reversals (e.g., by sleep sets or similar mechanisms).
- An *eager race reversal* strategy (Sect. 4.2), which immediately starts exploration of the new execution resulting from a race reversal; this prevents accumulation of a potentially exponential number of execution fragments generated by race reversals.
- In order to avoid exploring several executions in the same equivalence class, a naïve realization of POP would employ an adaptation of sleep sets [19]. However, these can in the worst case become exponentially large. Therefore, POP employs a *parsimonious characterization* of sleep sets (Sect. 4.3): instead of representing the elements of the sleep set explicitly, POP uses a characterization of them, which allows to detect and prevent redundant exploration, and uses at most polynomial space. This sleep set characterization is computed only from its generating race, implying that explorations of different executions share no state, making POP suitable for parallelization.

We prove (in the appendices of the longer version of this paper [5]) that the POP algorithm is *correct* (explores at least one execution in each equivalence class), *optimal* (explores exactly one execution in each equivalence class), does not suffer from blocked explorations, and requires only polynomial size memory.

We have implemented POP DPOR in an extension of the NIDHUGG tool [2]. Using a wide variety of benchmarks (Sect. 6), which are available in the paper's artifact, we show that POP's implementation indeed has its claimed properties, it always outperforms Optimal DPOR's implementation, and offers performance which is on par with TruSt's, the state-of-the-art graph-based DPOR algorithm. Moreover, by being sequence-based, it scales much better than TruSt's implementation on programs with long executions.

2   Main Concepts

In this section, we informally present the core principles of our approach, in particular the three novel algorithmic techniques of parsimonious race reversal, eager race reversal, and parsimonious characterization of sleep sets, along with how they relate to previous sequence-based DPOR algorithms, on a simple example, shown in Fig. 1. In this code, four threads (p, q, r, s) access three shared variables (g, x, y, z), using five thread-local

Initially: $x = y = z = 0$

p	q	r	s
$x = 1$	$y = 1$	$g = 1$	$c = y$
	$z = 1$	$a = y$	$d = z$
		$b = x$	$e = x$

Fig. 1. Program code.

registers (a, b, c, d, e).[1] DPOR algorithms typically first explore an arbitrary execution, which is then inspected to detect races. Assume that this execution is E_1 (the leftmost execution in Fig. 2). To detect races in an execution E, one first computes its happens-before order, denoted $\xrightarrow{hb}_E$, which is the smallest transitive relation that orders two events that (i) are in the same thread, or (ii) access a common shared variable and at least one of them is a write. A *race* consists of two events in different threads that are adjacent in the $\xrightarrow{hb}_E$ order. In execution E_1 there are two races on x, two races on y, and one race on z. The two races on y are marked with yellow arrows, as we are going to discuss them now. POP first reverses the race between events y = 1 and a = y. For each race, a DPOR algorithm constructs an initial fragment of an alternative execution, called a *schedule*, which reverses the race and branches off from the explored execution just before the race. POP constructs a minimal schedule consisting of the events that happen before (in the $\xrightarrow{hb}_{E_1}$ order) the second event followed by the second event of the race, while omitting the first event of the race, resulting in the event sequence $\langle g = 1 \cdot a = y \rangle$, which is inserted as an alternative continuation after x = 1 (the branch to the right of x = 1).

In comparison, early DPOR algorithms, including the "classic" DPOR algorithm by Flanagan and Godefroid [18] and the Source DPOR algorithm of Abdulla *et al.* [1] construct a schedule consisting of just one event that can initiate an execution which reverses the race ($\langle g = 1 \rangle$ in this case). Storing just one event saves space, but the execution afterwards is uncontrolled and may deviate from the path towards the second racing event a = y, potentially leading to redundant exploration. To avoid redundancy, we need schedules which consist of paths to the second racing event.

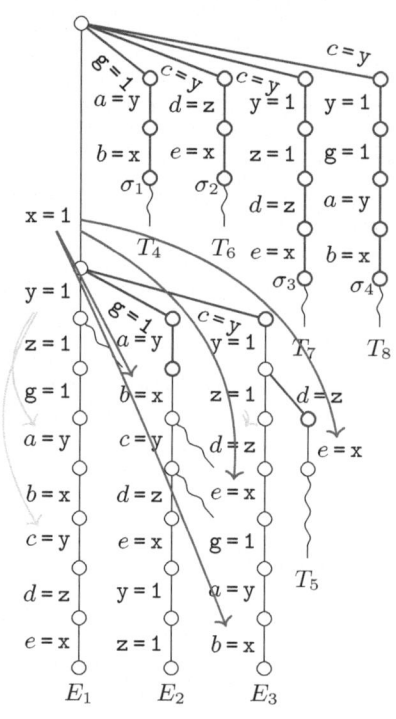

Eager Race Reversal: Following an eager race reversal strategy, POP continues the exploration with this branch and explores E_2. POP can in principle be implemented so that the schedules constructed as alternative continuations of an event are all collected before they are explored. However, such a strategy can in the worst case consume memory that is exponential in the program size. The reason is that, for some programs, the number of schedules that

Fig. 2. Part of the exploration tree for the program in Fig. 1. Completed executions are denoted E_i; truncated subtrees are denoted T_i.

---

[1] Throughout this paper, we assume that threads are spawned by a main thread, and that all shared variables get initialized to 0, also by the main thread.

branch off at a particular point in an execution may become exponential in the size of the program; this was first observed by Abdulla *et al.* [3, Sect. 9]; an illustrating shared-variable program is given by Kokologiannakis *et al.* [29, Sect. 2.3]. POP avoids this problem by *exploring schedules eagerly*: immediately after the creation of a schedule, exploration switches to continuations of that schedule. This strategy can be realized by an algorithm that calls a recursive function to initiate exploration of a new schedule. We establish, in Lemma 1, that the recursion depth of such an algorithm is at most $n(n-1)/2$, where n is the length of the longest execution of the program.

Continuing exploration, POP encounters the race on x in E_2 involving events x = 1 and b = x. (In Fig. 2, we show races by red arrows.) POP constructs the schedule $\sigma_1 := \langle g = 1 \cdot a = y \cdot b = x \rangle$ (second branch from the root) and explores the subsequent part of T_4 (tree T_4 represents all the extensions after σ_1). After exploring T_4 (second branch from the root), POP comes back to E_2.

Parsimonious Race Reversal: To illustrate POP's mechanism for reversing each race only once, let us next consider races in execution E_2. There is one race on y, between a = yand y = 1in E_2, for which POP would construct the schedule $\sigma := \langle c = y \cdot y = 1 \rangle$ However, a prefix of σ, namely $\langle c = y \rangle$ will be constructed from a race in E_1 between y = 1and c = y and inserted as an alternative continuation after x = 1 (the rightmost child of x = 1 in Fig. 2). Thus, any continuation of σ after x = 1 can also be explored as a continuation after the rightmost child of x = 1, implying that inserting σ as an alternative continuation after x = 1 would lead to redundant exploration. POP avoids such redundant exploration by forbidding to consider races whose first event (in this case a = y) is in some schedule: reversing a race whose first event is in a schedule yields a fragment that is explored in some other execution. The execution E_2 also exhibits two races on x, both including x = 1, with the events b = x and e = x These races have already occurred in E_1, and should therefore not be considered, since the schedules they would generate will be generated from the corresponding races in E_1. POP achieves this by forbidding to consider races whose second event is not fresh. A second event of a race is *fresh* if it happens-after (in the $\xrightarrow{\text{hb}}$ order) the last event of each schedule that appears between the two racing events. Returning to the two races on x in E_2, their second events are not fresh, and hence they are not reversed.

Let us continue the exploration of E_2 in Fig. 2 to illustrate how the eager race reversal strategy affects the order in which branches are explored. In E_2, there are two more races, on y and z, whose reversals produce two branches after b = x and c = y, denoted by wavy edges. After their exploration, since there are no more races in E_2, POP returns to E_1, where the race between events y = 1 and c = y induces the schedule $\langle c = y \rangle$, initiating exploration of E_3. While exploring E_3, the race inolving events z = 1 and d = z in E_3 induces the schedule $\langle d = z \rangle$, initiating exploration of the subtree T_5, during which the race on x involving x = 1 and e = x induces the schedule $\sigma_2 := \langle c = y \cdot d = z \cdot e = x \rangle$, and explores the subsequent part of the tree T_6. After finishing exploration of T_6 and T_5, POP comes back to E_3, where the race involving events x = 1 and e = x induces the schedule $\sigma_3 :=$

$\langle c = y \cdot y = 1 \cdot z = 1 \cdot d = z \cdot e = x \rangle$ initiating exploration of T_7, whereafter exploration of E_3 resumes.

Parsimonious Characterization of Sleep Sets: Even though the parsimonious race reversal strategy guarantees that the initial fragments of alternative executions are inequivalent, one must prevent that their continuations become equivalent. This happens when POP continues after a *read schedule*, generated from a race whose second event is a read event. To illustrate this problem, let us consider the race involving events $x = 1$ and $b = x$ in E_3, which produces the read schedule $\sigma_4 := \langle c = y \cdot y = 1 \cdot g = 1 \cdot a = y \cdot b = x \rangle$, initiating exploration of T_8. Note that the schedule σ_4 is not conflicting with the read schedules σ_2 and σ_3. At this point, we need to be careful: there is a danger that σ_4 will be continued using the other two schedules (σ_2 and σ_3), whereas the explorations starting with schedules σ_2 and σ_3 can be continued using σ_4; we would then explore equivalent executions, consisting of these three schedules in either order. The same problem occurs with σ_1 and σ_3, as they do not conflict. The DPOR technique for avoiding such redundant exploration is *sleep sets* [19]. In its standard form, a sleep set is a set of events that should not be performed before some conflicting event. Since POP uses schedules as beginnings of alternative explorations, the appropriate adaptation would be to let a sleep set be a set of read schedules that should not be performed unless some conflicting event is performed before that. In Fig. 2, this would mean that after exploring the continuations of σ_2 and σ_3, these schedules are added to the sleep set when starting to explore the continuations of σ_4, and σ_1 is added to the sleep set when starting to explore the continuations of σ_3. This mechanism is simple to combine with parsimonious race reversal and eager exploration of schedules. Unfortunately, there are programs where the number of read schedules that would be added to such a sleep set is exponential in the size of the program, whence the worst-case memory consumption may be exponential in the size of the program. POP avoids this problem by a *parsimonious characterization of sleep sets*, which consumes memory that is polynomial in the size of the program. The idea is to totally order the read schedules. When continuing exploration after a read schedule σ, the read schedules that precede σ in this order are represented by POP's parsimonious characterization in polynomial space, even though the number of represented schedules may be exponential. In principle, there are several ways to order the read schedules. POP uses one such ordering, namely σ_1, σ_2, σ_3 and σ_4. We provide the details about this representation in Sect. 4.3.

3 Programs, Executions, and Equivalence

We consider programs consisting of a finite set of *threads* that share a finite set of *(shared) variables*. Each thread has a finite set of local registers and runs a deterministic code, built in a standard way from expressions (over local registers) and atomic commands, using standard control flow constructs (sequential composition, selection, and bounded loop constructs). Atomic commands either write the value of an expression to a shared variable, or assign the value of a shared variable to a register, or can atomically both read and modify a shared variable. Conditional control flow constructs can branch on the value of an expression. From here on, we use t to range over threads, and x, y, z to range over shared variables. The local state of a thread is defined as usual by its program counter and the contents of its registers. The global state of a program consists of the local state of each thread together with the valuation of the shared variables. The program has a unique initial state, in which shared variables have predefined initial values. We assume that memory is sequentially consistent.

The execution of a program statement is an *event*, which affects or is affected by the global state of the program. An event is represented by a tuple $\langle t, i, \text{T}, x \rangle$, where t is the thread performing the event, i is a positive integer, denoting that the event results from the i-th execution step in thread t. T is the type of the event (either R for read or W for write and read-modify-write), and x is the accessed variable. If e is the event $\langle t, i, \text{T}, x \rangle$, we write $e.th$ for t, $e.\text{T}$ for T, and $e.var$ for x. An *access* is a pair $\langle \text{T}, x \rangle$ consisting of a type and a variable. We write $e.acc$ for $\langle e.\text{T}, e.var \rangle$. We say that two accesses $\langle \text{T}, x \rangle$ and $\langle \text{T}', x' \rangle$ are *dependent*, denoted $\langle \text{T}, x \rangle \bowtie \langle \text{T}', x' \rangle$, if $x = x'$ and at least one of T and T' is W. We say that two events e and e' are *dependent*, denoted $e \bowtie e$, if $e.th = e'.th$ or $e.acc \bowtie e'.acc$. As is customary in DPOR algorithms, we can let an event represent the combined effect of a sequence of statements, if at most one of them accesses a shared variable.

An *execution sequence* (or just *execution*) E is a finite sequence of events, starting from the initial state of the program. We let $\texttt{enabled}(E)$ denote the set of events that can be performed in the state to which E leads. An execution E is *maximal* if $\texttt{enabled}(E) = \emptyset$. We let $\texttt{dom}(E)$ denote the set of events in E; we also write $e \in E$ to denote $e \in \texttt{dom}(E)$. We use u and w, possibly with superscripts, to range over sequences of events (not necessarily starting from the initial state), $\langle \rangle$ to denote the empty sequence, and $\langle e \rangle$ to denote the sequence with only the event e. We let $w \cdot w'$ denote the concatenation of sequences w and w', and let $w \backslash e$ denote the sequence w with the first occurrence of e (if any) removed. For a sequence $u = e_1 \cdot e_2 \cdot \ldots \cdot e_m$, we let $w \backslash u$ denote $(\cdots ((w \backslash e_1) \backslash e_2) \backslash \cdots) \backslash e_m$.

The basis for a DPOR algorithm is an equivalence relation on the set of execution sequences. The definition of this equivalence is based on a happens-before relation on the events of each execution sequence, which captures the data and control dependencies that must be respected by any equivalent execution.

Definition 1 (Happens-before). *Given an execution sequence E, we define the* happens-before *relation on E, denoted $\xrightarrow{\text{hb}}_E$, as the smallest irreflexive partial order on $\texttt{dom}(E)$ such that $e \xrightarrow{\text{hb}}_E e'$ if e occurs before e' in E, and $e \bowtie e'$.*

The hb-*trace* (or *trace* for short) of E is the directed graph $(\texttt{dom}(E), \xrightarrow{\text{hb}}_E)$.

Definition 2 (Equivalence). *Two execution sequences E and E' are equivalent, denoted $E \simeq E'$, if they have the same* hb-*trace. We let $[E]_\simeq$ denote the equivalence class of E.*

The equivalence relation $\simeq$ partitions the set of execution sequences into equivalence classes, paving the way for an optimal DPOR algorithm which explores precisely one execution in each equivalence class.

4   Design of the POP Algorithm

In this section, we explain the design of POP, which is optimal in the sense that it explores precisely one execution in each equivalence class defined by Definition 2. We first need some auxiliary definitions

Definition 3 (Compatible sequences and happens-before prefix). *For two execution sequences $E \cdot w$ and $E \cdot w'$,*

- *the sequences w and w' are* compatible, *denoted $w \sim w'$, iff there are sequences w'' and w''' s.t. $E \cdot w \cdot w'' \simeq E \cdot w' \cdot w'''$,*
- *the sequence w is a* happens-before prefix *of w', denoted $w \sqsubseteq w'$, iff there is a sequence w'' s.t. $E \cdot w \cdot w'' \simeq E \cdot w'$.*

We illustrate the definition on the example in Fig. 2. Assuming $E_3 = \langle \mathtt{x = 1} \rangle \cdot w'$, it is true that $\sigma_4 \sqsubseteq w'$, since $\langle \mathtt{x = 1} \rangle \cdot \sigma_4 \cdot w'' \simeq \langle \mathtt{x = 1} \rangle \cdot w'$, where w'' is the sequence $\langle \mathtt{z = 1} \cdot d = \mathtt{z} \cdot e = \mathtt{x} \rangle$. However, $\sigma_1 \not\sim \sigma_4$, since σ_1's access to y and σ_4's second access to y are in conflict.

Definition 4 (Schedule). *A sequence of events σ is called a* schedule *if all its events happen-before its last one, i.e., $e' \xrightarrow{\text{hb}} e$ where e is its last event, and e' is any other event in σ. The last event e of a schedule σ is called the* head *of σ, sometimes denoted $hd(\sigma)$. For an execution sequence $E \cdot w$ and event $e \in w$, define the schedule $e \downarrow^w$ to be the subsequence w' of w such that (i) $e \in w'$, and (ii) for each $e' \in w$ it holds that $e' \in w'$ iff $e' \xrightarrow{\text{hb}}_{E \cdot w} e$.*

4.1   Parsimonious Race Reversals

A central mechanism of many DPOR algorithms is to detect and reverse races. Intuitively, a race is a conflict between two consecutive accesses to a shared variable, where at least one access writes to the variable (i.e., it is a write or a read-modify-write).

Definition 5 (Race). *Let E be an execution sequence. Two events e and e' in E are* racing *in E if (i) e and e' are performed by different threads, (ii) $e \xrightarrow{\text{hb}}_E e'$. (iii) there is no other event e'' with $e \xrightarrow{\text{hb}}_E e'' \xrightarrow{\text{hb}}_E e'$.*

Intuitively, a race arises when two different threads perform dependent accesses to a shared variable, which are adjacent in the $\xrightarrow{\text{hb}}_E$ order. If e and e' are racing in E, then to reverse the race, E is decomposed as $E = E_1 \cdot e \cdot E_2$ with e' in E_2, thereafter the schedule $\sigma = e' \downarrow^{E_2}$ is formed as the initial fragment of an alternative execution, which extends E_1.

The key idea of parsimonious race reversal is to reverse a race *only if* such a reversal generates an execution that has not been explored before. To be able to do so, POP remembers whenever an event in a new execution is in a schedule, and whether it is a schedule head. This can be done, e.g., by marking events in schedules, and specifically marking the schedule head. From now on, we consider such markings to be included in the events of executions. They play an important role in selecting races.

Definition 6 (Fresh event). *For an execution* $E \cdot w \cdot e' \cdot w'$, *the event* e' *is called* fresh *in* $w \cdot e' \cdot w'$ *after* E *if (i) if* e' *is in a schedule, then it is the head of that schedule, and (ii) for each head* e_h *of a schedule in* w *it is the case that* $e_h \xrightarrow{\text{hb}}_{E \cdot w \cdot e} e'$.

Definition 7 (Parsimonious race). *Let* E *be an execution sequence. Two events* e *and* e' *in* E *are in a* parsimonious race, *denoted* $e \lesssim_E e'$ *if (i)* e *and* e' *are racing in* E, *(ii)* e *is not in a schedule in* E, *and (iii)* e' *is fresh in* $w \cdot e'$ *after* E_1, *where* $E = E_1 \cdot e \cdot w \cdot e' \cdot w'$

Conditions (ii) and (iii) are the additional conditions for a race to be parsimonious. They filter out races, whose reversals would lead to previously explored executions. Let us provide the intuition behind these conditions. (ii) If e is in a schedule, then that schedule, call it σ, was generated by a race in an earlier explored execution E'. Hence σ was contained in E'. Moreover e' would race with the head of σ also in E'; if e' appeared after σ the resulting new schedule had been generated already in E'; if e' appeared before σ, then we would only undo a previous race reversal. This is illustrated in Fig. 2 by the race on y, between $a = y$ and $y = 1$ in E_2. (iii) If e' is not fresh, then e' appeared with the same happens-before predecessors in an earlier explored execution E', where it was in a race that would generate the same schedule as in E. This is illustrated in Fig. 2 by the race on x, between $b = x$ and $e = x$. in E_2, which was considered already in E_1.

4.2   The Parsimonious-OPtimal DPOR (POP) Algorithm

We will now describe the mechanism of the POP algorithm, without going into details regarding its handling of sleep sets (this will be done in Sect. 4.3). In particular, we will show how the *eager race reversal strategy* is represented in pseudo-code. Recall from Sect. 2 that a DPOR algorithm with parsimonious race reversal could be implemented so that the schedules that constructed from races with a particular event e are all collected before they are explored. However, for some programs, the number of schedules created from races with an event e can be exponential in the length of the longest program execution. In order not to consume exponential memory, POP explores schedules *eagerly*: immediately after the creation of a schedule, exploration switches to continuations of that schedule.

The POP algorithm is shown as Algorithm 1, where lines without background shading are concerned with the exploration and race handling, and the other

---

Algorithm 1: POP (Recursive)

---

1   Pick $e \in$ enabled $(\langle \rangle)$

2

3   Explore $(\langle e \rangle)$

4   Explore (E)

5   **foreach** e s.t. $e \lesssim_E e'$, where $e' = $ last (E) **do**

6   **let** $E = E_1 \cdot e \cdot E_2$

7   **let** $\sigma = e' \downarrow^{E_2}$

8   **if**   **then**

9

10

11

12

13   Explore $(E_1 \cdot \sigma)$

14   **if** $\exists e \in$ enabled (E) s.t.   **then**

15

16   Explore $(E \cdot e)$

---

lines, which are marked with green background, are concerned with sleep sets. POP takes an input program, and explores its executions by repeated calls to the procedure Explore. For each prefix E' of an execution that is under exploration, the algorithm maintains a characterization $SSChar[E']$ of the sleep set at E', to be described in Sect. 4.3, in order to prevent redundant exploration of read schedules. This characterization is manipulated by POP through two functions:

MkSchedChar (σ, E_1, e, E_2) constructs a characterization of the sleep set for a newly constructed σ, constructed from a race $e \lesssim_{E_1 \cdot e \cdot E_2}$ last (E_2),

UpdSeq $(w, SSChar)$ updates the sleep set characterization $SSChar$ wrt. processing of the sequence w. However, if a characterized read schedule (i.e., a schedule in the sleep set) would be performed while exploring w, the function returns *block* instead of the updated characterization.

The algorithm first picks an enabled event e (line 1), initializes the characterizations of sleep sets of $\langle \rangle$ and $\langle e \rangle$ (line 2), whereafter it calls Explore $(\langle e \rangle)$ (line 3). Each call to Explore (E) consists of a race reversal phase (lines 5 to 13) and an exploration phase (lines 14 to 16). In the race reversal phase, POP considers all parsimonious races between an event e in E and the last event e' of E (line 5). For each such race, of form $e \lesssim_E e'$, POP decomposes E as $E_1 \cdot e \cdot E_2$ (line 6), and forms the schedule σ that reverses the race as $e' \downarrow^{E_2}$ (line 7). It then intends to call Explore $(E_1 \cdot \sigma)$ in order to recursively switch the exploration to the newly reversed race, according to the eager race reversal strategy. Before that it checks whether exploring $E_1 \cdot \sigma$ will complete a schedule in the sleep set by calling UpdSeq $(\sigma, SSChar[E_1])$ (line 8). If not, $SSChar[E_1 \cdot \sigma]$ is computed (line 9), and if e' is a read event also extended with the new sleep set for σ (lines 11 to 12). After these preparations, Explore $(E_1 \cdot \sigma)$ is called recursively (line

13). After the return of all recursive calls initiated in the race reversal phase, `Explore` enters the exploration phase. There it picks an event e that is enabled for execution, and check that e is not the head of a schedule in the sleep set by calling `UpdSeq`($\langle e \rangle$, $SSChar[E]$) (line 14) If the check succeeds, exploration of e is prepared by updating $SSChar[E_1 \cdot e]$ (line 15) and then performed by calling `Explore`($E \cdot e$)(line 16).

We establish (in Lemma 1) that the recursion depth of Algorithm 1 is at most $n(n-1)/2$, where n is the length of the longest execution of the analyzed program.

4.3 Parsimonious Sleep Set Characterization

As described in Sect. 2, POP needs a sleep set mechanism to avoid redundant exploration of read schedules. Such a mechanism is needed whenever POP explores reversals of races with a write event e_W that appears after an execution E_1. Then each parsimonious race $e_W \lesssim_{E'} e_R$ between e_W and a read event e_R results in a schedule σ, which will be explored as a continuation of E_1. For any two such schedules, σ and σ', POP must ensure that *either* the exploration starting with σ does not continue in a way that includes σ', *or* (vice versa) that the exploration starting with σ' does not continue in a way that includes σ. In Sect. 2, it was further described that to achieve this, POP must for each such explored write event e_W establish a total order between the read schedules resulting from races with e_W, and ensure that an exploration starting with σ does not continue in a way that includes another schedule σ' which precedes σ in this order. It was also observed that, since there can be an exponential number of such schedules, the naïve approach of enumerating the schedules that precede σ can in the worst case consume space exponentical in the length of the longest execution.

In this section, we will describe one way to realize such a sleep set mechanism. We first define, for each explored write event e_W, a total order between the read-schedules resulting from races with e_W. Thereafter we define a succinct (polynomial-space) characterization of all schedules that precede any given such schedule σ. Finally, we define a polynomial-space mechanism for POP to monitor exploration so that exploration after the schedule σ does not explore another read schedule which precedes σ in the order.

First, for a variable x, we define a *read-x-schedule* to be a schedule whose head is a read on x, and which does not contain any other read or write on x. A *read-schedule* is a *read-x-schedule* for some variable x. Then a read-x-schedule is a schedule that may be formed when reversing a parsimonious race between a write on x and a read on x. Such a schedule σ cannot include a write on x, since then it could not have been formed from a race. Also, it cannot include a read on x, since that extra read will both happen-before $hd(\sigma)$, and happen-after the write on x, contradicting that there was a race between the write and $hd(\sigma)$.

Let us now define the order $\propto$, which for each write event e_W totally orders the schedules that result from parsimonious races between e_W and a subsequent read. Let σ be formed from a race $e_W \lesssim_E e_R$ between e_W and another read event

e_R in E and σ' be formed from a race $e_W \precsim_{E'} e'_R$ between e_W and another read event e'_R. Then $\sigma' \propto \sigma$ if either

(A) E' is a prefix of E, i.e., e'_R occurs before e_R in E, or
(B) for the longest common prefix $\hat{E}$ of E and E', E has a prefix of form $\hat{E} \cdot \hat{e}$ for some non-schedule event $\hat{e}$, whereas E' has a prefix of form $\hat{E} \cdot \hat{\sigma}$ for some schedule $\hat{\sigma}$ (which is induced by a race whose first event is $\hat{e}$), or
(C) for the longest common prefix $\hat{E}$ of E and E', E has a prefix of form $\hat{E} \cdot \sigma_i$ for some schedule σ_i, whereas E' has a prefix of form $\hat{E} \cdot \sigma'_i$ for some schedule σ'_i, and $\sigma'_i \propto \sigma_i$.

Schedules of form (A) are called *contained schedules* (wrt. σ). An example can be found in Fig. 2. Consider the schedules $\sigma_3 := \langle c = y \cdot y = 1 \cdot z = 1 \cdot d = z \cdot e = x \rangle$ from the race $x = 1 \precsim_{E_3} e = x$ in E_3, and $\sigma_4 := \langle c = y \cdot y = 1 \cdot g = 1 \cdot a = y \cdot b = x \rangle$ from the race $x = 1 \precsim_{E_3} b = x$ in E_3. As $e = x$ occurs before $b = x$ in E_3, (A) implies that $\sigma_3 \propto \sigma_4$. Schedules of form (B) are called *conflicting schedules*, because e' occurs in an execution which branches off from (thus conflicts with) E because of a race involving an event $\hat{e}$ in E. For example, consider the schedules $\sigma_2 := \langle c = y \cdot d = z \cdot e = x \rangle$, which is constructed from the race between $x = 1$ and $e = x$ in T_5, and σ_4 constructed from the race $x = 1 \precsim_{E_3} b = x$ in E_3. Since T_5 branches off from (and thus conflicts with) E_3 after the prefix $\hat{E} := \langle x = 1 \cdot c = y \cdot y = 1 \rangle$ with the schedule $\hat{\sigma} := \langle d = z \rangle$, we have $\sigma_2 \propto \sigma_4$ according to case (B). Schedules of form (C) are called *inherited schedules*, because the order $\sigma' \propto \sigma$ is inherited from the order $\sigma'_i \propto \sigma_i$. For example, consider the schedules $\langle g = 1 \cdot a = y \rangle$ (second branch after $x = 1$), and $\langle c = y \rangle$ (third branch after $x = 1$), for which $\langle g = 1 \cdot a = y \rangle \propto \langle c = y \rangle$ because of (A). Now consider the schedules $\sigma_1 := \langle g = 1 \cdot a = y \cdot b = x \rangle$ from the race $x = 1 \precsim_{E_2} b = x$ in E_2, and σ_2 from the race between the events $x = 1$ and $e = x$ from an execution in T_5. As $\langle g = 1 \cdot a = y \rangle$ is a prefix of σ_1 and $\langle c = y \rangle$ is a prefix of σ_2, according to (C), the order $\langle g = 1 \cdot a = y \rangle \propto \langle c = y \rangle$ is inherited as $\sigma_1 \propto \sigma_2$.

It is clear that these rules define a total order on the read schedules that branch off after E_1. We next define a succinct way to characterize, for a given schedule σ, the set of schedules σ' such that $\sigma' \propto \sigma$. Given $E = E_1 \cdot e_W \cdot w \cdot e_R$ and σ formed from the race $e_W \precsim_E e_R$, let $w = w_0 \cdot \sigma_1 \cdot w_1 \cdot \sigma_2 \cdots \sigma_m \cdot w_m$, where $\sigma_1, \ldots, \sigma_m$ are the schedules in w. We note that σ, since $e_W \precsim_E e_R$ is parsimonious, includes all σ_i (including their heads) for $1 \leq i \leq m$, and may also include events in the sequences $w_0, \ldots, w_m$. This means that $w \backslash \sigma$ is of form $w'_0 \cdot \ldots \cdot w'_m$, where w'_i is the sequence remaining in w_i after removing σ; in particular $w \backslash \sigma$ does not contain any events in any schedule σ_i. The following proposition characterizes how to detect a schedule σ' with $\sigma' \propto \sigma$ in an exploration that is initiated as a continuation of $E_1 \cdot \sigma$.

Proposition 1. *Let $E = E_1 \cdot e_W \cdot w \cdot e_R$, let $w = w_0 \cdot \sigma_1 \cdot w_1 \cdots \cdots w_m$, and let σ be formed from $e_W \precsim_E e_R$. Let $w'_j = w_j \backslash \sigma$ for $j = 0, \ldots, m$, and $e_j = hd(\sigma_j)$ for $j = 1, \ldots, m$. Let $E_1 \cdot \sigma \cdot u \cdot e'_R$ be an execution where e'_R is a read event on x, and let $\sigma' = e'_R \downarrow^{\sigma \cdot u \cdot e'_R}$. Then $\sigma' \propto \sigma$ iff σ' is a read-x-schedule such that either*

(A) (i) $(e'_R \downarrow^{u \cdot e'_R}) \sqsubseteq w \backslash \sigma$, and (ii) if e'_R is in w'_j then $e_k \xrightarrow{hb} e'_R$ for $1 \leq k \leq j$,

(B) for some j with $0 \leq j \leq m$ we have (i) $(e'_R \downarrow^{u \cdot e'_R}) \not\prec w'_0 \cdot \ldots \cdot w'_j$, and

 (ii) if j is the smallest index s.t. (i) holds, then $e_k \xrightarrow{\text{hb}} e'_R$ for $1 \leq k \leq j$, or

(C) for some i with $1 \leq i \leq m$ s.t. σ_i is a read-schedule, and σ'_i with $\sigma'_i \propto \sigma_i$

 1) if $hd(\sigma_i).var \neq x$ then (i) $(hd(\sigma'_i) \downarrow^{w'_0 \cdot \ldots \cdot w'_i \cdot \sigma'_i}) \sqsubseteq u$,

  (ii) $hd(\sigma'_i) \xrightarrow{\text{hb}} e'_R$, and (iii) $e_k \xrightarrow{\text{hb}} e'_R$ for $1 \leq k \leq i$.

 2) if $hd(\sigma_i).var = x$ then (i) $(hd(\sigma'_i) \downarrow^{w'_0 \cdot \ldots \cdot w'_i \cdot \sigma'_i}) \sqsubseteq u \cdot e'_R$,

  (ii) $hd(\sigma'_i) = e'_R$, and (iii) $e_k \xrightarrow{\text{hb}} e'_R$ for $1 \leq k \leq i$. $\square$

Let us motivate this proposition.

(A) Since $\sigma \sqsubseteq w \cdot e_R$, condition (i) implies that $\sigma' = e'_R \downarrow^{\sigma \cdot u \cdot e'_R} \sqsubseteq w$, implying that σ' is a contained schedule (wrt. σ).

(B) Since $\sigma \sqsubseteq w \cdot e_R$, condition (i) implies that $\sigma' = e'_R \downarrow^{\sigma \cdot u \cdot e'_R} \not\prec w_0 \cdot \sigma_1 \cdot \ldots \cdot \sigma_j \cdot w_j$, implying that σ' is a conflicting schedule.

(C) Let us first consider case 1). Since $\sigma \sqsubseteq w \cdot e_R$, condition (i) implies that $(hd(\sigma'_i) \downarrow^{w_0 \cdot \sigma_1 \cdot \ldots \cdot \sigma_j \cdot w_j \cdot \sigma'_i}) \sqsubseteq \sigma \cdot u$, implying that σ' is an inherited schedule. Condition (ii) ensures that e'_R appears in the exploration that follows $hd(\sigma'_i)$, in which case $hd(\sigma'_i) \xrightarrow{\text{hb}} e'_R$ is necessary for e'_R to be fresh. Case 2) is a slight modification for these case that the head of σ'_i and e'_R read from the same variable, in which case e'_R must be $hd(\sigma'_i)$ (since a read-x-schedule cannot contain another read on x).

In each case, the last condition ensures that e'_R is fresh, and thus part of a parsimonious race.

 Let us illustrate, using Fig. 2, how some continuations of read schedules can be characterized according to Proposition 1. First, consider σ_4 (top right in Fig. 2), derived from the race $\mathbf{x} = 1 \precsim_{E_3} \mathbf{b} = \mathbf{x}$ in E_3. Decomposing E_3 as $\mathbf{x} = 1 \cdot w \cdot \mathbf{b} = \mathbf{x}$, where $w := \langle \mathbf{c} = \mathbf{y} \cdot \mathbf{y} = 1 \cdot \mathbf{z} = 1 \cdot \mathbf{d} = \mathbf{z} \cdot \mathbf{e} = \mathbf{x} \cdot \mathbf{g} = 1 \cdot \mathbf{a} = \mathbf{y} \rangle$, we obtain $w \setminus \sigma_4 = \langle \mathbf{z} = 1 \cdot \mathbf{d} = \mathbf{z} \cdot \mathbf{e} = \mathbf{x} \rangle$.

(A) Assume that the exploration continues after σ_4 as $\langle \mathbf{z} = 1 \cdot \mathbf{d} = \mathbf{z} \cdot \mathbf{e} = \mathbf{x} \rangle$. Letting u be $\langle \mathbf{z} = 1 \cdot \mathbf{d} = \mathbf{z} \rangle$ and e'_R be $\mathbf{e} = \mathbf{x}$, we see that $\sigma' = u \cdot e'_R$ matches the conditions in case (A), since (i) $\sigma' \sqsubseteq w \setminus \sigma_4$ and (ii) e'_R happens-after the head of the only schedule $\langle \mathbf{c} = \mathbf{y} \rangle$ in E_3.

(B) Assume next that the exploration continues after σ_4 as $\langle \mathbf{d} = \mathbf{z} \cdot \mathbf{e} = \mathbf{x} \rangle$. Letting u be $\langle \mathbf{d} = \mathbf{z} \rangle$ and e'_R be $\mathbf{e} = \mathbf{x}$, we see that $\sigma' = u \cdot e'_R$ matches the conditions in case (B), since (i) $\mathbf{e} = \mathbf{x} \downarrow^{\langle \mathbf{d} = \mathbf{z} \cdot \mathbf{e} = \mathbf{x} \rangle} = \langle \mathbf{d} = \mathbf{z} \cdot \mathbf{e} = \mathbf{x} \rangle$ and $\langle \mathbf{d} = \mathbf{z} \cdot \mathbf{e} = \mathbf{x} \rangle \not\prec (w \setminus \sigma_4)$, and (ii) $\mathbf{e} = \mathbf{x}$ happens-after the head of the only schedule $\mathbf{c} = \mathbf{y}$ in E_3.

(C) Let us next consider σ_2 (top middle in Fig. 2), derived from the race $\mathbf{x} = 1 \precsim_{E'} \mathbf{e} = \mathbf{x}$ in the first explored execution E' from T_5. Decomposing E' as $\mathbf{x} = 1 \cdot w \cdot \mathbf{e} = \mathbf{x}$, where $w := \langle \mathbf{c} = \mathbf{y} \cdot \mathbf{y} = 1 \cdot \mathbf{d} = \mathbf{z} \rangle$ we obtain $w \setminus \sigma_2 = \langle \mathbf{y} = 1 \rangle$. Assume next that the exploration continues after σ_2 as $\langle \mathbf{g} = 1 \cdot \mathbf{a} = \mathbf{y} \cdot \mathbf{b} = \mathbf{x} \rangle$. Letting u be $\langle \mathbf{g} = 1 \cdot \mathbf{a} = \mathbf{y} \rangle$ and e'_R be $\mathbf{b} = \mathbf{x}$, we see that $\sigma' = u \cdot e'_R$ matches the conditions in case (C)1), since there is the schedule $\sigma_i = \langle \mathbf{c} = \mathbf{y} \rangle$ for which there is another schedule $\sigma'_i = \langle \mathbf{g} = 1 \cdot \mathbf{a} = \mathbf{y} \rangle$ with $\sigma'_i \propto \sigma_i$. The conditions in case (C)1) are satisfied, since (i) $\mathbf{a} = \mathbf{y} \downarrow^{\langle \mathbf{y} = 1 \cdot \mathbf{g} = 1 \cdot \mathbf{a} = \mathbf{y} \rangle} \sqsubseteq u$, (ii) $\mathbf{a} = \mathbf{y} \xrightarrow{\text{hb}} e'_R$, and (iii) there is no schedule before the event $\mathbf{c} = \mathbf{y}$ in E'.

Based on Proposition 1, we now describe a technique to monitor the exploration of executions in order to detect when it is about to explore a schedule in a sleep set. It is based on annotating each newly constructed read schedule σ with a characterization of the schedules σ' with $\sigma' \propto \sigma$ that must be avoided in the exploration that continues after σ. We use the same notation and set-up as for Proposition 1. For $i = 0, \ldots, m$, let P_i denote $P_i = w_0'\{e_1\}w_1' \cdots \{e_i\}w_i'$, where w_j' is $w_j\backslash\sigma$ for $j = 0, \ldots, i$, and e_j is $hd\,(\sigma_j)$ for $j = 1, \ldots, i$. From Proposition 1 we see that (i) P_m and x contains sufficient information to characterize the contained and conflicting schedules that must be avoided, and (ii) for each $i = 1, \ldots, m$, such that σ_i is a read-schedule, P_{i-1} together with a characterization of the schedules σ_i' with $\sigma_i' \propto \sigma_i$ contain sufficient information to characterize the schedules inherited from schedules σ_i' with $\sigma_i' \propto \sigma_i$ that must be avoided. Let us therefore define a *schedule expression* as an expression of form (i) $P_m \triangleright x$, characterizing the set of contained and conflicting read-x-schedules, according to cases (A) and (B) in Proposition 1, or of form (ii) $P_{i-1}[\varphi_i] \triangleright x$ for some $i = 1, \ldots, m$, such that σ_i is a read-schedule, and φ_i is a schedule expression characterizing schedules σ_i' with $\sigma_i' \propto \sigma_i$. Let us go through one example of each form of schedule expressions using Fig. 2. While exploring continuations of σ_4, POP creates two schedule expressions; (i) $P_1 \triangleright x = \{c\!=\!y\}\langle z\!=\!1 \cdot d\!=\!z \cdot e\!=\!x\rangle \triangleright x$ representing the schedules σ_2 and σ_3, and (ii) $P_0[\varphi_1] \triangleright x = \langle\rangle[\langle z\!=\!1 \cdot g\!=\!1 \cdot a\!=\!y \cdot b\!=\!x\rangle \triangleright y] \triangleright x$, representing only σ_1. Notice that, expression (ii) is useless in this case as σ_1 is conflicting with σ_4, i.e., σ_1 is not a feasible continuation after σ_4. However, the same expression is useful to prevent doing σ_1, when exploring a continuation of σ_2.

In order to detect when exploration is about to explore a schedule that must be avoided, the "state" of each schedule expression will during exploration be maintained by POP in a *sleep set expression*, which is obtained from a schedule expression φ by (i) augmenting each event e which occurs in some sequence w_i in φ (i.e., not inside brackets $\{\cdot\}$) with a *conflict set* (denoted C) of encountered events that conflict with e or happen-after an event that conflicts with e; we use the notation e^C to denote such an augmented event, (ii) augmenting each enclosed subexpression of form $P \triangleright x$ or $P[\varphi] \triangleright x$ with the set (denoted D) of encountered read-x-events that are heads of read-schedules that are characterized by $P \triangleright x$; we use the notation $[P \triangleright x]^D$ (or $[P[\varphi] \triangleright x]^D$), and (iii) augmenting each occuring variable x that occurs after $\triangleright$ in a subexpression of form $P \triangleright x$ or $P[\varphi] \triangleright x$ with the set of previously encountered read events on x; we use the notation $\triangleright x^R$, where R is this set of read events. If a read on x happens-after a read in R, it cannot be the head of a read-x-schedule, and should thus not be blocked (recall from the definition of read-x-schedules that its head cannot happen-after another read on the same variable). When a sleep set expression is created and initialized, its augmenting sets are empty. We identify a schedule expression with its initialized sleep set expression. We use ψ, possibly with sub- or superscripts, to range over sleep set expressions.

Algorithm 2 shows POP's implementation of the sleep set expression manipulation functions $\texttt{MkSchedChar}(\sigma, E_1, e, E_2)$ and $\texttt{UpdSeq}(w, SSChar)$, which are

---

Algorithm 2: Functions for Parsimonious Sleep Set Characterization

---

1 MkSchedChar(σ, E_1, e, E_2)

2   **let** $x = hd(\sigma).var$

3   **let** $E_2 = w_0 \cdot \sigma_1 \cdot w_1 \cdots \sigma_m \cdot w_m \cdot e'$

4   **for** $i = 0, \ldots, m$ **let** $P_i = (w_0 \backslash \sigma)\{hd(\sigma_1)\}(w_1 \backslash \sigma) \cdots \{hd(\sigma_i)\}(w_i \backslash \sigma)$

5   **for** $i = 0, \ldots, m$ **let** $u_i = e \cdot w_0 \cdot \sigma_1 \cdot \ldots \cdot \sigma_i \cdot w_i$

6   **return** $\left(\{P_m \rhd x\} \cup \bigcup_{i=1}^{m} \{P_{i-1}[\varphi_i] \rhd x \mid \varphi_i \in SchedChar[E_1 \cdot u_{i-1}](\sigma_i)\} \right)$

7 UpdSeq$(w, SSChar)$

8   **if** $w = \langle \rangle$ **then return** $(SSChar)$

9   **else if** $\exists \psi \in SSChar : \text{UpdSE}(fst(w), \psi) = block$ **then return** $block$

10   **else return** (UpdSeq$(rest(w), \{\text{UpdSE}(fst(w), \psi) \mid \psi \in SSChar \wedge$

11   **if** $e.\text{T} = \text{W}$ **then** ψ does not contain $\rhd(e.var))\})$

12 UpdSE$(e, P \rhd x^R)$

13   **if** UpdP$(e, P, x, R) = block$ **then return** $block$

14   **else return** (UpdP$(e, P, x, R) \rhd x$)

15 UpdSE$(e, P[\psi']^D \rhd x^R)$

16   **if** UpdP$(e, P, x, R) = block$ **then return** $block$

17   **if** UpdP$(e, P, x, R) = indep$ **then**

18   **if** $(e.\text{T} = \text{R} \wedge e.var = x \wedge (e \in D \vee \exists e' \in D : [e'.var \neq x \wedge e' \xrightarrow{\text{hb}} e])$ **then**

19   **if** $\not\exists e'_R \in R : e'_R \xrightarrow{\text{hb}} e$ **then return** $block$ **else** add e to R

20   **else**

21   **if** UpdSE$(e, \psi') = block$ **then return** $(P[\psi']^{D \cup \{e\}} \rhd x)$

22   **else return** $(P[\text{UpdSE}(e, \psi')] \rhd x)$

23   **else return** (UpdP$(e, P, x)[\psi']^D \rhd x$)

24 UpdP(e, P, x, R)

25   **let** $P = w'_0\{e'_1\}w'_1 \cdots \{e'_i\}w'_i$

26   **for** $j = 0, \ldots, i$ **do**

27   **let** $w'_j = e_1^{C_1} \cdot \ldots \cdot e_k^{C_k}$

28   **for** $l = 1, \ldots, k$ **do**

29   **if** $e \bowtie C_l \vee e \leftrightarrow e_l$ **then** add e to C_l ; **go to** line 32

30   **if** $e = e_l$ **then** remove e from w'_j ; **go to** line 32

31   **return** $indep$

32   **if** $(e.\text{T} = \text{R} \wedge e.var = x \wedge \forall n : 1 \leq n \leq j : e'_n \xrightarrow{\text{hb}} e)$ **then**

33   **if** $\not\exists e'_R \in R : e'_R \xrightarrow{\text{hb}} e$ **then return** $block$ **else** add e to R

34   **else return** *the updated version of* P

---

called by Algorithm 1. A set of sleep set expressions is called a *sleep set characterization*. The function MkSchedChar(σ, E_1, e, E_2) (line 1), constructs the set of schedule expressions (which can be seen as initialized sleep set expressions) for σ according to the description given earlier in this section. The function UpdSeq$(w, SSChar)$ updates the sleep set characterization *SSChar* wrt. processing of the sequence w. At its top level, UpdSeq$(w, SSChar)$ updates each sleep set expression ψ in *SSChar* with the sequence of events in w, one by one, each time calling $\mathtt{UpdSE}(e, \psi)$. If e is a write on a variable y, then in this process, all sleep set expressions containing $\rhd y$ are discarded, since it is from now impossible to complete a read-y-schedule. The function $\mathtt{UpdSE}(e, \psi)$ comes in two versions (at line 12 and line 15). Both versions first call $\mathtt{UpdP}(e, P, x, R)$, which updates the sleep set expressions with respect to contained and conflicting read-x-schedules characterized by $P \rhd x^R$. If e is the head of such a schedule, then $\mathtt{UpdP}(e, P, x, R)$ returns *block*; if e is independent with all of P, then $\mathtt{UpdP}(e, P, x, R)$ returns *indep*; otherwise it returns the updated version of P. In the code for $\mathtt{UpdP}$, we let let $e \leftrightarrow e'$ denote that e and e' are performed by *different* threads and access the same variable and at least one of e and e' writes. For an event e and a set C of events, let $e \bowtie C$ denote that there is some $e' \in C$ with $e \bowtie e'$. When called, $\mathtt{UpdP}(e, P, x, R)$ traverses the sequences $w'_0, \ldots, w'_i$, one event at a time, and stops at the first event $e_l^{C_l}$ such that either (i) e conflicts with e_l or depends with an event in C_l, in which case e is added to C_l (line 29), or (ii) $e = e_l$, in which case e is removed from the sequence (of form w'_j) (line 30). If in addition e is a read on x and happens after the relevant schedule heads among $e'_1, \ldots, e'_i$ for being fresh, then if e does not happen after a read in R, $\mathtt{UpdP}(e, P, x, R)$ returns *blocked* (since in case (i) it is the head of a conflicting schedule and in case (ii) of a contained schedule), else e is added to R (line 33). If on the other hand, e is not a read on x or does not happen after the relevant schedule heads among $e'_1, \ldots, e'_i$, then $\mathtt{UpdP}(e, P, x, R)$ returns the updated version of P. Finally, if there is no event $e_l^{C_l}$ in $w'_0, \ldots, w'_i$ satisfying conditions (i) or (ii), then $\mathtt{UpdP}$ returns *indep* (line 31).

Let us now consider $\mathtt{UpdSE}(e, \psi)$, which comes in two versions, depending on the form of ψ. If ψ is of form $P \rhd x^R$ (line 12), it calls $\mathtt{UpdP}(e, P, x, R)$ and forwards its return value. If ψ is of form $P[\psi']^D \rhd x^R)$ (line 15), it also calls $\mathtt{UpdP}(e, P, x, R)$. Also this version forwards the return value *block*. In addition, if $\mathtt{UpdP}(e, P, x, R)$ returns *indep*, meaning that e is independent of P, then (i) if some event already in D (being the head of a schedule characterized by ψ') happens-before e (or is the same as e if it reads from x), and e is a read on x, then if e does not happen after a read in R, the function returns *blocked* (since e is the head of an inherited schedule), else e is added to R (line 19), (ii) otherwise, processing is continued recursively on ψ' by calling $\mathtt{UpdSE}(e, \psi')$. If this call returns *blocked*, then e is added to D (line 21), otherwise the inner sleep set expression ψ' is updated. Finally, if $\mathtt{UpdP}(e, P, x, R)$ returns neither *blocked* nor *indep*, the updated sleep set expression is returned (line 23).

5   Correctness and Space Complexity

In this section, we state theorems of correctness, optimality, and space complexity of POP. We first consider correctness and optimality.

Theorem 1. *For a terminating program P, the POP algorithm has the properties that (i) for each maximal execution E of P, it explores some execution E'*

with $E' \simeq E$, and (ii) it never explores two different but equivalent maximal executions, and (iii) it is never blocked (at line 14) unless it has explored a maximal execution.

We thereafter consider space complexity.

Lemma 1. *The number of nested recursive calls to* Explore *at line 13 is at most $n(n-1)/2$, where n is the length of the longest execution of the program.*

Note that in this lemma, we do not count the calls at line 16, since they are considered as normal exploration of some execution. Only the calls at line 13 start the exploration of a new execution.

Theorem 2. *Algorithm 1 needs space which is polynomial in n, where n is the length of the longest execution of the analyzed program.*

6   Implementation and Evaluation

Our implementation, which is available in the artifact of this paper, was done in a fork of NIDHUGG. NIDHUGG is a state-of-the-art stateless model checker for C/C++ programs with Pthreads, which works at the level of LLVM Intermediate Representation, typically produced by the Clang compiler. NIDHUGG comes with a selection of DPOR algorithms, one of which is Optimal DPOR [1] nowadays also enhanced with Partial Loop Purity elimination and support for await statements [25]. In our NIDHUGG fork, we have added the POP algorithm as another selection. Its implementation involved: (i) designing an efficient data structure to simulate recursive calls to Explore, i.e., follow the next schedule to explore and backtrack to the previous execution when no further races to reverse, (ii) developing a procedure to filter out races that are not parsimonious, and (iii) implementing a more optimized data structure than Algorithm 2 that stores sleep set characterizations as trees.

In this section, we evaluate the performance of POP's implementation and compare it, in terms of time and memory, against the implementations of Optimal DPOR in NIDHUGG commit 5805d77 and the graph-based Truly Stateless (TruSt) Optimal DPOR algorithm [29] as implemented in GENMC v0.10.0 using options -sc --disable-instruction-caching. All tools employed LLVM 14.0.6, and the numbers we present are measured on a desktop with a Ryzen 7950X CPU running Debian 12.4.

Table 1 contains the results of our evaluation. Its first nine benchmarks are from the DPOR literature, and are all parametric on the number of threads (shown in parentheses). The last benchmark, length-param, is synthetic and is additionally parametric on the length of its executions. Since these DPOR algorithms are optimal, they explore the same number of executions (2nd column) in all ten benchmarks. We will analyze the results in five groups (cf. Table 1).

The first group consists of three programs (circular-buffer from SCT-Bench [47], fib-bench from SV-Comp [45], and the linuxrwlocks from SATCheck [16]). Here, all algorithms consume memory that stays constant as the size of

Table 1. Time and memory performance of three optimal DPOR algorithms on ten benchmark programs which are parametric in the number of threads used.

Benchmark	Executions	Time (secs)			Memory (MB)		
		TruSt	Optimal	POP	TruSt	Optimal	POP
circular-buffer(7)	3432	0.62	0.45	0.43	85	84	84
circular-buffer(8)	12870	2.63	1.79	1.66	85	84	84
circular-buffer(9)	48620	11.04	7.21	6.67	85	84	84
fib-bench(4)	19605	1.08	1.93	1.82	85	84	84
fib-bench(5)	218243	14.59	24.66	24.10	85	84	84
fib-bench(6)	2364418	186.25	301.30	297.40	85	84	84
linuxrwlocks(6)	99442	3.61	13.71	12.88	90	91	91
linuxrwlocks(7)	829168	32.75	127.66	121.17	90	91	91
linuxrwlocks(8)	6984234	311.93	1176.13	1119.23	90	91	91
filesystem(22)	512	0.72	0.62	0.34	86	84	84
filesystem(24)	2048	2.84	2.97	1.32	86	187	84
filesystem(26)	8192	11.88	15.71	5.66	85	622	84
indexer(15)	4096	11.07	8.58	5.65	89	116	90
indexer(16)	32768	90.14	80.37	46.46	89	464	90
indexer(17)	262144	736.78	827.02	399.87	89	3030	90
lastzero(10)	3328	0.07	0.34	0.27	85	84	84
lastzero(15)	147456	3.19	24.46	15.09	85	276	84
lastzero(20)	6029312	152.13	1828.92	786.19	85	8883	84
exp-mem3(7)	10080	0.22	0.67	0.54	86	104	85
exp-mem3(8)	80640	1.96	6.15	4.61	86	506	85
exp-mem3(9)	725760	19.11	73.68	44.83	86	4489	85
dispatcher(4)	6854	1.15	1.75	1.47	90	90	90
dispatcher(5)	151032	34.66	55.07	42.76	89	407	90
dispatcher(6)	4057388	1245.13	2333.51	1424.57	89	9097	90
poke(10)	135944	88.54	96.30	63.45	90	791	90
poke(15)	728559	874.76	891.26	479.03	89	5527	90
poke(20)	2366924	4502.45	4356.59	2008.92	90	22383	90
length-param(2,1024)	4	0.14	0.05	0.06	85	84	84
length-param(2,8196)	4	7.95	0.16	0.14	95	101	89
length-param(2,65536)	4	1413.00	1.13	0.90	389	441	343

the program and the number of executions explored increase. We can therefore compare the raw performance of the implementation of these three DPOR algorithms. POP's implementation is fastest on circular-buffer, while TruSt's is fastest on the two other programs. However, notice that all three implementations scale similarly.

The second group consists of the two benchmarks (filesystem and indexer) from the "classic" DPOR paper of Flanagan and Godefroid [18]. Here,

Optimal DPOR shows an increase in memory consumption (measured in MB), while the other two algorithms use constant memory. POP is fastest here by approximately $2\times$.

The third group, consisting of lastzero [1] and exp-mem3,[2] two synthetic benchmarks also used in the TruSt paper [29, Table 1], shows a similar picture in terms of memory consumption: Optimal DPOR's increases more noticeably here, while the two other algorithms use memory that stays constant. Time-wise, TruSt is 2–$5\times$ faster than POP, which in turn is $2\times$ faster than Optimal.

The fourth group, consisting of two concurrent data structure programs (dispatcher and poke) from the Quasi-Optimal POR paper [40], shows Optimal's memory explosion more profoundly, and provides further evidence of the good memory performance of the TruSt and POP algorithms. Time-wise, there is no clear winner here, with TruSt's implementation being a bit faster on dispatcher, and with POP's being faster and scaling slightly better than TruSt's on poke.

Finally, let us examine the algorithms' performance on length-param(T,N), a synthetic but simple program in which a number of threads (just two here) issue N stores and loads to thread-specific global variables, followed by a store and a load to a variable shared between threads. The total number of executions is just four here, but the executions grow in length. One can clearly see the superior time performance of sequence-based DPOR algorithms, such as Optimal and POP, compared to TruSt's graph-based algorithm that needs to perform consistency checks for the executions it constructs. As can be seen, these checks can become quite expensive (esp. if their implementation has sub-optimal complexity, as it is probably the case here). In contrast, sequence-based DPOR algorithms naturally generate consistent executions (for memory models such as SC). We can also notice that POP performs slightly better than Optimal in terms of memory.

Wrapping up our evaluation, we can make the following two general claims:

1. Both POP and TruSt live up to their promise about performing SMC exploration which is optimal (w.r.t. the Mazurkiewicz equivalence) but also with polynomial (in fact, in practice, constant) space consumption.
2. The implementation of the POP algorithm consistently outperforms that of Optimal DPOR in NIDHUGG. This is mostly due to increased simplicity.

7   Related Work

Since its introduction in the tools Verisoft [20,21] and CHESS [39], stateless model checking has been an important technique for analyzing correctness of concurrent programs. Dynamic partial order reduction [18,44] has enabled a significantly increased efficiency for covering all interleavings, which has been

---

[2] exp-mem3 is slight variant of the exp-mem program used in the TruSt paper. It uses atomic stores and loads instead of fetch-and-adds (FAAs), because the current implementation of Optimal DPOR (and POP) in NIDHUGG employs an optimization which treats independent FAAs as non-conflicting [25] and explores only one trace on the exp-mem program independently of the benchmark's parameter.

adapted to many different settings and computational models, including actor programs [46], abstract computational models [27], event driven programs [4,24, 35], and MPI programs [42]. DPOR has been adapted for weak memory models including TSO [2,16,48], Release-Acquire [8], POWER [7], and C11 [28], and also been applied to real life programs [32]. DPOR has been extended with features for efficiently handling spinloops and blocking constructs [25,31],

An important advancement has been the introduction of *optimal* DPOR algorithms, which guarantee to explore *exactly* one execution from each equivalence class [1], and therefore achieve exponential-time reduction over non-optimal algorithms. This saving came at the cost of worst-case exponential (in the size of the program) memory consumption [3]. The strive for covering the space of all interleavings with fewer representative executions inspired DPOR algorithms for even weaker equivalences than Mazurkiewicz trace equivalence, such as equivalence based on observers [11], reads-from equivalence [6,13,14], conditional independence [10], context-sensitive independence and observers [9], or on the maximal causal model [23]. These approaches explore fewer traces than approaches based on Mazurkiewicz trace equivalence at the cost of potentially expensive (often NP-hard) consistency checks. Another line of work uses unfoldings [37] to further reduce the number of interleavings that must be considered [26,40,43]; these techniques incur significantly larger cost per test execution than the previously mentioned ones.

DPOR has also been adapted for weak memory models using an approach in which executions are represented as graphs, where nodes represent read and write operations, and edges represent reads-from and coherence relations; this allows the algorithm to be parametric on a specific memory model, at the cost of calling a memory-model oracle [28,30,33]. For this graph-based setting, an optimal DPOR algorithm with worst-case polynomial space consumption, called TruSt, was recently presented [29]. POP is also optimal with worst-case polynomial space consumption. Since it is designed for a sequence-based representation of executions, POP must be designed differently. In analogy with the parsimonious race reversal technique, TruSt has a technique for reversing each race only once, which is based on a *maximal extension* criterion. POP adapts TruSt's strategy of eager race reversal to avoid potentially space-consuming accumulation of schedules. Finally, since TruSt operates in a graph-based setting, it reverses write-read races by changing the source of a read-from relation in the graph, instead of constructing a new schedule. Therefore redundant exploration of read-schedules is prevented by careful book-keeping instead of using sleep sets, which POP represents in a compact parsimonious way. The experimental results show that TruSt and POP have comparable performance for small and modest-size programs, but that POP is superior for programs with long executions, since the graph-based approach has difficulties to scale for long executions.

An alternative to DPOR for limiting the number of explored executions is to cover only a subset of all executions. Various heuristics for choosing this subset have been developed, including delay bounding [17], preemption bounding [38], and probabilistic strategies [12]. Such techniques can be effective in finding bugs in concurrent programs, but not prove their absence.

8 Conclusion

In this paper, we have presented POP, a new optimal DPOR algorithm for analyzing multi-threaded programs under SC. POP combines several novel algorithmic techniques, which allow efficiency improvements over previous such DPOR algorithms, both in time and space. In particular, its space consumption is polynomial in the size of the analyzed program. Our experiments on a wide variety of benchmarks show that POP always outperforms Optimal DPOR, the state-of-the-art sequence-based optimal DPOR algorithm, and offers performance comparable with TruSt, the state-of-the-art graph-based DPOR algorithm. Moreover, by being sequence-based, its implementation scales much better than TruSt's on programs with long executions.

As future work, it would be interesting to investigate the effect of applying POP's novel algorithmic techniques on DPOR algorithms tailored for different computational models, and for analyzing programs under weak concurrency memory models such as TSO and PSO.

Acknowledgements. This research was partially funded by research grants from the Swedish Research Council (Vetenskapsrådet) and from the Swedish Foundation for Strategic Research through project aSSIsT. We thank these funding agencies and the anonymous CAV 2024 reviewers for their comments.

References

1. Abdulla, P., Aronis, S., Jonsson, B., Sagonas, K.: Optimal dynamic partial order reduction. In: Symposium on Principles of Programming Languages, pp. 373–384. POPL 2014, ACM, New York, NY, USA (2014). https://doi.org/10.1145/2535838. 2535845
2. Abdulla, P.A., Aronis, S., Atig, M.F., Jonsson, B., Leonardsson, C., Sagonas, K.: Stateless model checking for TSO and PSO. In: Baier, C., Tinelli, C. (eds.) TACAS 2015. LNCS, vol. 9035, pp. 353–367. Springer, Heidelberg (2015). https://doi.org/10.1007/978-3-662-46681-0_28
3. Abdulla, P.A., Aronis, S., Jonsson, B., Sagonas, K.: Source sets: a foundation for optimal dynamic partial order reduction. J. ACM **64**(4), 25:1–25:49 (2017). https://doi.org/10.1145/3073408
4. Abdulla, P.A., Atig, M.F., Bønneland, F.M., Das, S., Jonsson, B., Lång, M., Sagonas, K.: Tailoring stateless model checking for event-driven multi-threaded programs. In: André, É., Sun, J. (eds.) Automated Technology for Verification and Analysis - 21st International Symposium, ATVA 2023, Proceedings, Part II. LNCS, vol. 14216, pp. 176–198. Springer (2023). https://doi.org/10.1007/978-3-031-45332-8_9
5. Abdulla, P.A., Atig, M.F., Das, S., Jonsson, B., Sagonas, K.: Parsimonious optimal dynamic partial order reduction (2024). https://doi.org/10.48550/arXiv.2405. 11128, https://doi.org/10.48550/arXiv.2405.11128, Extended Version with Proofs

6. Abdulla, P.A., Atig, M.F., Jonsson, B., Lång, M., Ngo, T.P., Sagonas, K.: Optimal stateless model checking for reads-from equivalence under sequential consistency. Proc. ACM Program. Lang. **3**(OOPSLA), 150:1–150:29 (2019). https://doi.org/10.1145/3360576

7. Abdulla, P.A., Atig, M.F., Jonsson, B., Leonardsson, C.: Stateless model checking for POWER. In: Chaudhuri, S., Farzan, A. (eds.) CAV 2016. LNCS, vol. 9780, pp. 134–156. Springer, Cham (2016). https://doi.org/10.1007/978-3-319-41540-6_8

8. Abdulla, P.A., Atig, M.F., Jonsson, B., Ngo, T.P.: Optimal stateless model checking under the release-acquire semantics. Proc. ACM on Program. Lang. **2**(OOPSLA), 135:1–135:29 (2018). https://doi.org/10.1145/3276505

9. Albert, E., de la Banda, M.G., Gómez-Zamalloa, M., Isabel, M., Stuckey, P.J.: Optimal dynamic partial order reduction with context-sensitive independence and observers. J. Syst. Softw. **202**, 111730 (2023). https://doi.org/10.1016/J.JSS.2023.111730

10. Albert, E., Gómez-Zamalloa, M., Isabel, M., Rubio, A.: Constrained dynamic partial order reduction. In: Chockler, H., Weissenbacher, G. (eds.) CAV 2018. LNCS, vol. 10982, pp. 392–410. Springer, Cham (2018). https://doi.org/10.1007/978-3-319-96142-2_24

11. Aronis, S., Jonsson, B., Lång, M., Sagonas, K.: Optimal dynamic partial order reduction with observers. In: Beyer, D., Huisman, M. (eds.) TACAS 2018. LNCS, vol. 10806, pp. 229–248. Springer, Cham (2018). https://doi.org/10.1007/978-3-319-89963-3_14

12. Burckhardt, S., Kothari, P., Musuvathi, M., Nagarakatte, S.: A randomized scheduler with probabilistic guarantees of finding bugs. In: Proceedings of the Fifteenth Edition of ASPLOS on Architectural Support for Programming Languages and Operating Systems, pp. 167–178. ASPLOS XV, ACM, New York, NY, USA (2010). https://doi.org/10.1145/1736020.1736040

13. Chalupa, M., Chatterjee, K., Pavlogiannis, A., Sinha, N., Vaidya, K.: Data-centric dynamic partial order reduction. Proc. ACM on Program. Lang. **2**(POPL), 31:1–31:30 (2018). https://doi.org/10.1145/3158119

14. Chatterjee, K., Pavlogiannis, A., Toman, V.: Value-centric dynamic partial order reduction. Proc. ACM Program. Lang. **3**(OOPSLA), 124:1–124:29 (2019). https://doi.org/10.1145/3360550

15. Christakis, M., Gotovos, A., Sagonas, K.: Systematic testing for detecting concurrency errors in Erlang programs. In: Sixth IEEE International Conference on Software Testing, Verification and Validation, pp. 154–163. ICST 2013, IEEE, Los Alamitos, CA, USA (2013). https://doi.org/10.1109/ICST.2013.50

16. Demsky, B., Lam, P.: SATCheck: SAT-directed stateless model checking for SC and TSO. In: Proceedings of the 2015 ACM SIGPLAN International Conference on Object-Oriented Programming, Systems, Languages, and Applications, pp. 20–36. OOPSLA 2015, ACM, New York, NY, USA (2015). https://doi.org/10.1145/2814270.2814297

17. Emmi, M., Qadeer, S., Rakamaric, Z.: Delay-bounded scheduling. In: Proceedings of the 38th ACM SIGPLAN-SIGACT Symposium on Principles of Programming Languages, pp. 411–422. POPL 2011, ACM (2011). https://doi.org/10.1145/1926385.1926432

18. Flanagan, C., Godefroid, P.: Dynamic partial-order reduction for model checking software. In: Principles of Programming Languages, (POPL), pp. 110–121. ACM, New York, NY, USA (2005). https://doi.org/10.1145/1040305.1040315

19. Godefroid, P. (ed.): Partial-Order Methods for the Verification of Concurrent Systems. LNCS, vol. 1032. Springer, Heidelberg (1996). https://doi.org/10.1007/3-540-60761-7

20. Godefroid, P.: Model checking for programming languages using VeriSoft. In: Principles of Programming Languages, (POPL), pp. 174–186. ACM Press, New York, NY, USA (1997). https://doi.org/10.1145/263699.263717

21. Godefroid, P.: Software model checking: the VeriSoft approach. Formal Methods Syst. Des. **26**(2), 77–101 (2005). https://doi.org/10.1007/s10703-005-1489-x

22. Godefroid, P., Hanmer, R.S., Jagadeesan, L.: Model checking without a model: an analysis of the heart-beat monitor of a telephone switch using VeriSoft. In: Proceedings of the ACM SIGSOFT International Symposium on Software Testing and Analysis, pp. 124–133. ISSTA, ACM, New York, NY, USA (1998). https://doi.org/10.1145/271771.271800

23. Huang, J.: Stateless model checking concurrent programs with maximal causality reduction. In: Proceedings of the 36th ACM SIGPLAN Conference on Programming Language Design and Implementation, pp. 165–174. PLDI 2015, ACM, New York, NY, USA (2015). https://doi.org/10.1145/2737924.2737975

24. Jensen, C.S., Møller, A., Raychev, V., Dimitrov, D., Vechev, M.T.: Stateless model checking of event-driven applications. In: Proceedings of the 2015 ACM SIGPLAN International Conference on Object-Oriented Programming, Systems, Languages, and Applications, pp. 57–73. OOPSLA 2015, ACM, New York, NY, USA (2015). https://doi.org/10.1145/2814270.2814282

25. Jonsson, B., Lång, M., Sagonas, K.: Awaiting for godot: stateless model checking that avoids executions where nothing happens. In: Griggio, A., Rungta, N. (eds.) 22nd Formal Methods in Computer-Aided Design, pp. 284–293. FMCAD 2022, IEEE (2022). https://doi.org/10.34727/2022/ISBN.978-3-85448-053-2_35

26. Kähkönen, K., Saarikivi, O., Heljanko, K.: Using unfoldings in automated testing of multithreaded programs. In: IEEE/ACM International Conference on Automated Software Engineering, pp. 150–159. ASE'12, ACM, New York, NY, USA (2012). https://doi.org/10.1145/2351676.2351698, http://dl.acm.org/citation.cfm?id=2351676

27. Kastenberg, H., Rensink, A.: Dynamic partial order reduction using probe sets. In: van Breugel, F., Chechik, M. (eds.) CONCUR 2008. LNCS, vol. 5201, pp. 233–247. Springer, Heidelberg (2008). https://doi.org/10.1007/978-3-540-85361-9_21

28. Kokologiannakis, M., Lahav, O., Sagonas, K., Vafeiadis, V.: Effective stateless model checking for C/C++ concurrency. Proc. ACM on Program. Lang. **2**(POPL), 17:1–17:32 (2018). https://doi.org/10.1145/3158105

29. Kokologiannakis, M., Marmanis, I., Gladstein, V., Vafeiadis, V.: Truly stateless, optimal dynamic partial order reduction. Proc. ACM Program. Lang. **6**(POPL), 1–28 (2022). https://doi.org/10.1145/3498711

30. Kokologiannakis, M., Raad, A., Vafeiadis, V.: Model checking for weakly consistent libraries. In: Proceedings of the 40th ACM SIGPLAN Conference on Programming Language Design and Implementation, pp. 96–110. PLDI 2019, ACM, New York, NY, USA (2019). https://doi.org/10.1145/3314221.3314609

31. Kokologiannakis, M., Ren, X., Vafeiadis, V.: Dynamic partial order reductions for Spinloops. In: Formal Methods in Computer Aided Design, pp. 163–172. FMCAD 2021, IEEE (2021). https://doi.org/10.34727/2021/isbn.978-3-85448-046-4_25

32. Kokologiannakis, M., Sagonas, K.: Stateless model checking of the Linux kernel's read-copy update (RCU). Softw. Tools Technol. Transf. **21**(3), 287–306 (2019). https://doi.org/10.1007/s10009-019-00514-6

33. Kokologiannakis, M., Vafeiadis, V.: HMC: model checking for hardware memory models. In: Larus, J.R., Ceze, L., Strauss, K. (eds.) Architectural Support for Programming Languages and Operating Systems, pp. 1157–1171. ASPLOS '20, ACM (2020). https://doi.org/10.1145/3373376.3378480

34. Kokologiannakis, M., Vafeiadis, V.: GENMC: a model checker for weak memory models. In: Silva, A., Leino, K.R.M. (eds.) CAV 2021. LNCS, vol. 12759, pp. 427–440. Springer, Cham (2021). https://doi.org/10.1007/978-3-030-81685-8_20

35. Maiya, P., Gupta, R., Kanade, A., Majumdar, R.: Partial order reduction for event-driven multi-threaded programs. In: Chechik, M., Raskin, J.-F. (eds.) TACAS 2016. LNCS, vol. 9636, pp. 680–697. Springer, Heidelberg (2016). https://doi.org/10.1007/978-3-662-49674-9_44

36. Mazurkiewicz, A.: Trace theory. In: Brauer, W., Reisig, W., Rozenberg, G. (eds.) ACPN 1986. LNCS, vol. 255, pp. 278–324. Springer, Heidelberg (1987). https://doi.org/10.1007/3-540-17906-2_30

37. McMillan, K.L.: A technique of a state space search based on unfolding. Formal Methods Syst. Des. **6**(1), 45–65 (1995). https://doi.org/10.1007/BF01384314

38. Musuvathi, M., Qadeer, S.: Iterative context bounding for systematic testing of multithreaded programs. In: Proceedings of the ACM SIGPLAN 2007 Conference on Programming Language Design and Implementation, pp. 446–455. PLDI 2007, ACM (2007). https://doi.org/10.1145/1250734.1250785

39. Musuvathi, M., Qadeer, S., Ball, T., Basler, G., Nainar, P.A., Neamtiu, I.: Finding and reproducing heisenbugs in concurrent programs. In: Proceedings of the 8th USENIX Symposium on Operating Systems Design and Implementation, pp. 267–280. OSDI '08, USENIX Association, Berkeley, CA, USA (2008). http://dl.acm.org/citation.cfm?id=1855741.1855760

40. Nguyen, H.T.T., Rodríguez, C., Sousa, M., Coti, C., Petrucci, L.: Quasi-optimal partial order reduction. In: Chockler, H., Weissenbacher, G. (eds.) CAV 2018. LNCS, vol. 10982, pp. 354–371. Springer, Cham (2018). https://doi.org/10.1007/978-3-319-96142-2_22

41. Norris, B., Demsky, B.: A practical approach for model checking C/C++11 code. ACM Trans. Program. Lang. Syst. **38**(3), 10:1–10:51 (2016). https://doi.org/10.1145/2806886

42. Palmer, R., Gopalakrishnan, G., Kirby, R.M.: Semantics driven dynamic partial-order reduction of MPI-based parallel programs. In: Ur, S., Farchi, E. (eds.) Proceedings of the 5th Workshop on Parallel and Distributed Systems: Testing, Analysis, and Debugging, pp. 43–53. PADTAD 2007, ACM (2007). https://doi.org/10.1145/1273647.1273657

43. Rodríguez, C., Sousa, M., Sharma, S., Kroening, D.: Unfolding-based partial order reduction. In: 26th International Conference on Concurrency Theory (CONCUR 2015). LIPIcs, vol. 42, pp. 456–469. Schloss Dagstuhl–Leibniz-Zentrum fuer Informatik (2015). https://doi.org/10.4230/LIPIcs.CONCUR.2015.456

44. Sen, K., Agha, G.: A race-detection and flipping algorithm for automated testing of multi-threaded programs. In: Bin, E., Ziv, A., Ur, S. (eds.) HVC 2006. LNCS, vol. 4383, pp. 166–182. Springer, Heidelberg (2007). https://doi.org/10.1007/978-3-540-70889-6_13

45. SV-COMP: Competition on Software Verification (2019). https://sv-comp.sosy-lab.org/2019. Accessed 24 Mar 2019

46. Tasharofi, S., Karmani, R.K., Lauterburg, S., Legay, A., Marinov, D., Agha, G.: TransDPOR: a novel dynamic partial-order reduction technique for testing actor programs. In: Giese, H., Rosu, G. (eds.) FMOODS/FORTE -2012. LNCS, vol. 7273, pp. 219–234. Springer, Heidelberg (2012). https://doi.org/10.1007/978-3-642-30793-5_14
47. Thomson, P., Donaldson, A.F., Betts, A.: Concurrency testing using controlled schedulers: An empirical study. ACM Trans. Parallel Comput. **2**(4), 23:1–23:37 (2016). https://doi.org/10.1145/2858651
48. Zhang, N., Kusano, M., Wang, C.: Dynamic partial order reduction for relaxed memory models. In: Programming Language Design and Implementation (PLDI), pp. 250–259. ACM, New York, NY, USA (2015). https://doi.org/10.1145/2737924.2737956

Collective Contracts for Message-Passing Parallel Programs

Ziqing Luo$^{(\boxtimes)}$ 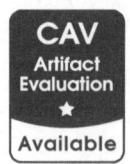 and Stephen F. Siegel

University of Delaware, Newark, DE 19716, USA
{ziqing,siegel}@udel.edu

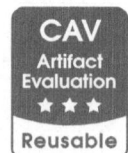

Abstract. Procedure contracts are a well-known approach for specifying programs in a modular way. We investigate a new contract theory for collective procedures in parallel message-passing programs. As in the sequential setting, one can verify that a procedure f conforms to its contract using only the contracts, and not the implementations, of the collective procedures called by f. We apply this approach to C programs that use the Message Passing Interface (MPI), introducing a new contract language that extends the ANSI/ISO C Specification Language. We present contracts for the standard MPI collective functions, as well as many user-defined collective functions. A prototype verification system has been implemented using the CIVL model checker for checking contract satisfaction within small bounds on the number of processes.

Keywords: contract · message-passing · MPI · verification · collective

1 Introduction

Procedure contracts [27,46,47] are a well-known way to decompose program verification. In this approach, each procedure f is specified independently with pre- and postconditions or other invariants. To verify f, one needs only the contracts, not the implementations, of the procedures called by f.

Contract languages have been developed for many programming languages. These include the *Java Modeling Language* (JML) [38] for Java and the *ANSI C Specification Language* (ACSL) [10] for C. A number of tools have been developed which (partially) automate the process of verifying that a procedure satisfies its contract; an example for C is Frama-C [18] with the WP plugin [9].

In this paper, we explore a procedure contract system for message-passing parallel programs, specifically for programs that use the Message-Passing Interface (MPI) [45], the de facto standard for high performance computing.

Our contracts apply to *collective-style* procedures in these programs. These are procedures f called by all processes and that are *communication-closed*: any message issued by a send statement in f is received by a receive statement in f, and vice-versa. The processes executing f coordinate in order to accomplish a coherent change in the global state. Examples include all of the standard blocking MPI collective functions [45, Chapter 5], but also many user-defined procedures,

© The Author(s) 2024
A. Gurfinkel and V. Ganesh (Eds.): CAV 2024, LNCS 14682, pp. 44–68, 2024.
https://doi.org/10.1007/978-3-031-65630-9_3

such as a procedure to exchange ghost cells in a stencil computation. (We will use the term *collective* as shorthand for *collective-style* when there is no chance of ambiguity.) These procedures are typically specified informally by describing the effect they produce when called by all processes, rather than the effect of an individual process. They should be formally specified and verified in the same way.

Developers often construct applications by composing collective procedures. As examples, consider the Monte Carlo particle transport code OpenMC [53] (over 24K lines of C++/MPI code) and module `parcsr_ls` in the algebraic multigrid solver AMG [62] (over 35K lines of C/MPI code). Through manual inspection, we confirmed that every function in these codes that involves MPI communication is collective-style.

We begin in Sect. 2 with a toy message-passing language, so the syntax, semantics, and theoretical results can be stated and proved precisely. The main result is a theorem that justifies a method for verifying a collective procedure using only the contracts of the collective procedures called, as in the sequential case.

Section 3 describes changes needed to apply this system to C/MPI programs. We handle a significant subset of MPI that does not include `MPI_ANY_SOURCE` ("wildcard") receives. This means program behavior is largely independent of interleaving [55]. There are enough issues to deal with, such as MPI datatypes, input nondeterminism, and nontermination, that we feel it best to leave wildcards for a sequel. A prototype verification system for such programs, using the CIVL model checker, is described and evaluated in Sect. 4. Related work is discussed in Sect. 5. In Sect. 6, we wrap up with a discussion of the advantages and limitations of our system, and work that remains.

In summary, this paper makes the following contributions: (1) a contract theory for collective message-passing procedures, with mathematically precise syntax and semantics, (2) a theorem justifying a method for verifying that a collective procedure conforms to its contract, (3) a contract language for a large subset of MPI, based on the theory but also dealing with additional intricacies of MPI, and (4) a prototype verification tool for checking that collective-style MPI procedures conform to their contracts.

2 A Theory of Collective Contracts

2.1 Language

We describe a simple message-passing language MINIMP with syntax in Fig. 1. There is one datatype: integers; 0 is interpreted as *false* and any non-zero integer as *true*. A program consists of global variable declarations followed by (mutually recursive) procedure definitions. Global variables may start with arbitrary values. Each procedure takes a sequence of formal parameters. The procedure body consists of local variable declarations followed by a sequence of statements. Local variables are initially 0. Assignment, branch, loop, call, and compound statements have the usual semantics. Operations have the usual meaning and always

$$program ::= (\ \text{int } x \ ; \ )* \ procdef+$$
$$procdef ::= contract? \ \text{void } f \ (\ (\ \text{int } x \ (\ , \text{int } x \ )* \ )? \ ) \ \{ \ (\ \text{int } x \ ; \ )* \ s* \ \}$$
$$s \in stmt ::= x = e \ ; \ | \ f \ (\ (\ e \ (\ , e \ )* \ )? \ ) \ ; \ | \ \text{if } (e) \ s \ (\ \text{else } s \ )? \ | \ \text{while } (e) \ s$$
$$| \ \{ \ s* \ \} \ | \ \text{send } e \ \text{to } e \ ; \ | \ \text{recv } x \ \text{from } e \ ;$$
$$e \in expr ::= c \ | \ x \ | \ \text{nprocs} \ | \ \text{pid} \ | \ \ominus e \ | \ e \odot e \ | \ \backslash\text{on}(e,e) \ | \ \backslash\text{old}(e)$$
$$contract ::= \text{/*@ requires } e; \text{ ensures } e; \text{ assigns } (x(,x)*)?;$$
$$\text{waitsfor } \{ \ e \ | \ \text{int } x \ ; \ e \ \}; \text{ */}$$

$$c \in \mathbb{Z} \qquad x, f \in ID \qquad \ominus \in \{ \ \text{-}, \ ! \ \} \qquad \odot \in \{ \ \text{+}, \ \text{-}, \ *, \ /, \ \%, \ ==, \ <, \ <=, \ \&\&, \ || \ \}$$

Fig. 1. MINIMP syntax

return some value—even if the second argument of division is 0, e.g. Operators with '\', described below, occur only in the optional contract.

A procedure is executed by specifying a positive integer n, the number of processes. Each process executes its own "copy" of the code; there is no shared memory. Each process has a unique ID number in $\mathsf{PID} = \{0, \ldots, n-1\}$. A process can obtain its ID using the primitive pid; it can obtain n using nprocs.

The command "send *data* to *dest*" sends the value of *data* to the process with ID *dest*. There is one FIFO message buffer for each ordered pair of processes $p \to q$ and the effect of send is to enqueue the message on the buffer for which p is the ID of the sender and q is *dest*. The buffers are unbounded, so send never blocks. Command "recv *buf* from *source*" removes the oldest buffered message originating from *source* and stores it in variable *buf*; this command blocks until a message becomes available. A *dest* or *source* not in PID results in a no-op.

A procedure f with a contract is a *collective procedure*. The contract encodes a claim about executions of f: if f is called collectively (by all processes), in such a way that the precondition (specified in the requires clause) holds, then all of the following hold for each process p: p will eventually return; p's postcondition (specified in the ensures clause) will hold at the post-state; all variables not listed in p's assigns clause will have their pre-state values at the post-state; and if q is in p's waitsfor set then p will not return before q enters the call. These notions will be made precise below.

Global variables and the formal parameters of the procedure are the only variables that may occur free in a contract; only globals may occur in the *assigns* clause. A postcondition may use $\backslash\text{old}(e)$ to refer to the value of expression e in the pre-state; $\backslash\text{old}$ may not occur in this e. Pre- and postconditions can use $\backslash\text{on}(e,i)$ to refer to the value of e on process i. These constructs allow contracts to relate the state of different processes, and the state before and after the call.

Example 1. The program of Fig. 2 has two procedures, both collective. Procedure g accepts an argument k and sends its value for global variable x to its right neighbor, in a cyclic ordering. It then receives into local variable y from its left neighbor q, adds k to the received value, and stores the result in x. The contract for g states that when p exits (returns), the value of x on p is the sum of k and the original value of x on q. It also declares p cannot exit until q has entered. Procedure f calls g nprocs times. Its contract requires that all processes call f

```
int x;
/*@ requires 1;   ensures x == \on(\old(x), (pid+nprocs-1)%nprocs) + k;
    assigns x;   waitsfor { j | int j; j == (pid+nprocs-1)%nprocs }; */
void g(int k) {
  int y;
  send x to (pid+1)%nprocs;
  recv y from (pid+nprocs-1)%nprocs;
  x = y+k;
}
/*@ requires k == \on(k,0);   ensures x == \old(x) + nprocs*k;
    assigns x;   waitsfor { j | int j; 0<=j && j<nprocs }; */
void f(int k) { int i; i = 0; while (i<nprocs) { g(k); i = i+1; } }
```

Fig. 2. cyc: a MINIMP program

with the same value for k. It ensures that upon return, the value of x is the sum of its original value and the product of nprocs and k. It also declares that no process can exit until every process has entered.

2.2   Semantics

Semantics for procedural programs are well-known (e.g., [2]), so we will only summarize the standard aspects of the MINIMP semantics. Fix a program P and an integer $n \geq 1$ for the remainder of this section. Each procedure in P may be represented as a *program graph*, which is a directed graph in which nodes correspond to locations in the procedure body. Each program graph has a designated start node. An edge is labeled by either an expression ϕ (a *guard*) or one of the following kinds of statements: *assignment, call, return, send* or *receive*. An edge labeled *return* is added to the end of each program graph, and leads to the terminal node, which has no outgoing edges.

A *process state* comprises an assignment of values to global variables and a call stack. Each entry in the stack specifies a procedure f, the values of the local variables (including formal parameters) for f, and the program counter, which is a node in f's program graph. A *state* specifies a process state for each process, as well as the state of channel $p \rightarrow q$ for all $p, q \in \mathsf{PID}$. The channel state is a finite sequence of integers, the buffered messages sent from p to q.

An *action* is a pair $a = \langle e, p \rangle$, where e is an edge $u \xrightarrow{\alpha} v$ in a program graph and $p \in \mathsf{PID}$. Action a is *enabled* at state s if the program counter of the top entry of p's call stack in s is u and one of the following holds: α is a guard ϕ and ϕ evaluates to *true* in s; α is an assignment, call, return, or send; or α is a receive with source q and channel $q \rightarrow p$ is nonempty in s. The execution of an enabled action from s results in a new state s' in the natural way. In particular, execution of a call pushes a new entry onto the stack of the calling process; execution of a return pops the stack and, if the resulting stack is not empty, moves the caller to the location just after the call. The triple $s \xrightarrow{a} s'$ is a *transition*.

Let f be a procedure and s_0 a state with empty channels, and in which each process has one entry on its stack, the program counter of which is the start location for f. An n-process *execution* ζ of f is a finite or infinite chain of transitions $s_0 \xrightarrow{a_1} s_1 \xrightarrow{a_2} \cdots$. The *length* of ζ, denoted $\mathsf{len}(\zeta)$, is the number of transitions in ζ. An execution must be *fair*: if a process p becomes enabled at some point in an infinite execution, then eventually p will execute. Note that, once p becomes enabled, it will remain enabled until it executes, as no process other than p can remove a buffered message with destination p.

A process p *terminates* in ζ if for some i, the stack for p is empty in s_i. We say ζ *terminates* if p terminates in ζ for all $p \in \mathsf{PID}$. The execution *deadlocks* if it is finite, does not terminate, and ends in a state with no enabled action.

It is often convenient to add a "driver" to P when reasoning about executions of a collective procedure f. Say f takes m formal parameters. Form a program P^f by adding fresh global variables $x_1, \ldots, x_m$ to P, and adding a procedure

$$\text{void main() } \{ \ f(x_1, \ldots, x_m); \ \}.$$

By "execution of P^f," we mean an execution of main in this new program.

2.3   Collective Correctness

In this section, we formulate conditions that correct collective procedures are expected to satisfy. Some of these reflect standard practice, e.g., collectives should be called in the same order by all processes, while others specify how a procedure conforms to various clauses in its contract. Ultimately, these conditions will be used to ensure that a simple "stub" can stand in for a collective call, which is the essential point of our main result, Theorem 1.

In formulating these conditions, we focus on the negative, i.e., we identify the earliest possible point in an execution at which a violation occurs. For example, if a postcondition states that on every process, x will be 0 when the function returns, then a postcondition violation occurs as soon as one process returns when its x has a non-zero value. There is no need to wait until every process has returned to declare that the postcondition has been violated. In fact, this allows us to declare a postcondition violation even in executions that do not terminate because some processes never return.

Fix a program P and integer $n \geq 1$. Let $\mathcal{C}$ be the set of names of collective procedures of P. Let ζ be an execution $s_0 \xrightarrow{a_1} s_1 \xrightarrow{a_2} \cdots$ of a procedure in P. For $i \in 1..\mathsf{len}(\zeta)$, let ζ^i denote the prefix of ζ of length i, i.e., the execution $s_0 \xrightarrow{a_1} \cdots \xrightarrow{a_i} s_i$.

Collective Consistency. The first correctness condition for ζ is *collective consistency*. To define this concept, consider strings over the alphabet consisting of symbols of the form e^f and x^f, for $f \in \mathcal{C}$. Given an action a and $p \in \mathsf{PID}$, define string $T_p(a)$ as follows:

– if a is a call by p to some $f \in \mathcal{C}$, $T_p(a) = \mathsf{e}^f$ (a is called an *enter* action)

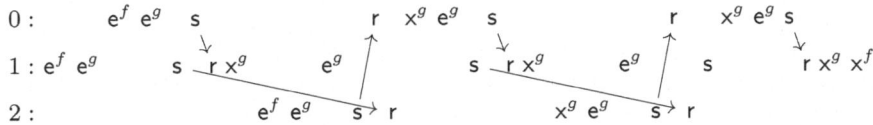

Fig. 3. Representation of a 3-process execution of cyc^f of Fig. 2. $\mathsf{e}^f =$ enter (call) f; $\mathsf{x}^f =$ exit (return from) f; $\mathsf{s} =$ send; $\mathsf{r} =$ receive. The execution has no collective errors and ends in a state with one buffered message sent from process 1 to process 2.

- if a is a return by p from some $f \in \mathcal{C}$, $T_p(a) = \mathsf{x}^f$ (a is called an *exit* action)
- otherwise, $T_p(a)$ is the empty string.

Now let $T_p(\zeta)$ be the concatenation $T_p(a_1)T_p(a_2)\cdots$. Hence $T_p(\zeta)$ records the sequence of collective actions—enter or exit actions—taken by p.

Definition 1. *An execution ζ is* collective consistent *if there is some $p \in$ PID such that for all $q \in$ PID, $T_q(\zeta)$ equals or is a prefix of $T_p(\zeta)$. We say ζ commits a consistency violation at step i if ζ^{i-1} is collective consistent but ζ^i is not.*

For the rest of this section, assume ζ is collective consistent.

The sequence of actions performed by p in ζ is divided into segments whose boundaries are the collective actions of p. More precisely, given $i \in 0..\mathsf{len}(\zeta)$ and $p \in$ PID, define $k = \mathsf{seg}_p(\zeta, i)$ to be the number of collective actions of p in $a_1, \ldots, a_i$. We say *p is in segment k at state i*.

Example 2. In program cyc of Fig. 2, there is a 3-process execution ζ of P^f illustrated in Figure 3. The execution is collective consistent: $T_p(\zeta)$ is a prefix of $T_1(\zeta) = \mathsf{e}^f\mathsf{e}^g\mathsf{x}^g\mathsf{e}^g\mathsf{x}^g\mathsf{e}^g\mathsf{x}^g\mathsf{x}^f$ for all $p \in \{0, 1, 2\}$. A process is in segment 0 at any point before it executes e^f; it is in segment 1 after executing e^f but before executing its first e^g; and so on. At a given state in the execution, processes can be in different segments; e.g., when process 2 is in segment 1, process 1 is in segment 3 and process 0 is in segment 2.

Precondition and Postcondition Violations. We now turn to the issue of evaluation of pre- and postconditions. Let f be a collective procedure in P with precondition $\mathsf{pre}(f)$ and postcondition $\mathsf{post}(f)$. Let V_f be the union of the set of formal parameters of f and the global variables of P. As noted above, these are the only variables that may occur free in $\mathsf{pre}(f)$ and $\mathsf{post}(f)$. An *f-valuation* is a function $\alpha\colon$ PID $\to (V_f \to \mathbb{Z})$. For each process, α specifies a value for each free variable that may occur in $\mathsf{pre}(f)$ or $\mathsf{post}(f)$.

For any expression e that may occur as a sub-expression of $\mathsf{pre}(f)$, and $p \in$ PID, define $[\![e]\!]_{\alpha,p} \in \mathbb{Z}$ as follows:

$$\llbracket c \rrbracket_{\alpha,p} = c$$
$$\llbracket x \rrbracket_{\alpha,p} = \alpha(p)(x)$$
$$\llbracket \texttt{nprocs} \rrbracket_{\alpha,p} = n$$
$$\llbracket \texttt{pid} \rrbracket_{\alpha,p} = p$$

$$\llbracket \ominus e \rrbracket_{\alpha,p} = \ominus \llbracket e \rrbracket_{\alpha,p}$$
$$\llbracket e_1 \odot e_2 \rrbracket_{\alpha,p} = \llbracket e_1 \rrbracket_{\alpha,p} \odot \llbracket e_2 \rrbracket_{\alpha,p}$$
$$\llbracket \texttt{\textbackslash on}(e_1, e_2) \rrbracket_{\alpha,p} = \llbracket e_1 \rrbracket_{\alpha,q}, \text{ where } q = \llbracket e_2 \rrbracket_{\alpha,p}.$$

This is the result of evaluating e in process p. Note how \on shifts the evaluation context from process p to the process specified by e_2, allowing the precondition to refer to the value of an expression on another process.

Evaluation of an expression involving \old, which may occur only in post(f), requires a second f-valuation β specifying values in the pre-state. The definition of $\llbracket \cdot \rrbracket_{\alpha,\beta,p}$ repeats the rules above, replacing each subscript "α" with "α, β", and adds one rule:

$$\llbracket \texttt{\textbackslash old}(e) \rrbracket_{\alpha,\beta,p} = \llbracket e \rrbracket_{\beta,p}.$$

Say $1 \leq i \leq \mathsf{len}(\zeta)$ and a_i is an e^f action in process p. Let $r = \mathsf{seg}_p(\zeta, i)$ and

$$Q = \{q \in \mathsf{PID} \mid \mathsf{seg}_q(\zeta, i) \geq r\}, \qquad \alpha' \colon Q \to (V_f \to \mathbb{Z}),$$

where $\alpha'(q)(v)$ is the value of v on process q in state $s_{j(q)}$, and $j(q)$ is the unique integer in $1..i$ such that $a_{j(q)}$ is the r-th collective action of q in ζ. (As ζ is collective consistent, $a_{j(q)}$ is also an e^f action.) In other words, α' uses the values of process q's variables just after q entered the call. Now, α' is not an f-valuation unless $Q = \mathsf{PID}$. Nevertheless, we can ask whether α' can be extended to an f-valuation α such that $\llbracket \mathsf{pre}(f) \rrbracket_{\alpha,q}$ holds for all $q \in \mathsf{PID}$. If no such α exists, we say a *precondition violation* occurs at step i.

Example 3. Consider program cyc of Fig. 2. Suppose process 1 calls $f(1)$ and process 2 calls $f(2)$. Then a precondition violation of f occurs with the second call, because there is no value that can be assigned to k on process 0 for which $1 = \texttt{\textbackslash on}(k, 0)$ and $2 = \texttt{\textbackslash on}(k, 0)$ both hold.

If a_i is an x^f action, define Q and $j(q)$ as above; for any $q \in Q$, $a_{j(q)}$ is also an x^f action. Let $\alpha'(q)(v)$ be the value of v in q at state $s_{j(q)-1}$, i.e., just before q exits. Define $k(q) \in 1..j(q)-1$ so that $a_{k(q)}$ is the e^f action in q corresponding to $a_{j(q)}$, i.e., $a_{k(q)}$ is the call that led to the return $a_{j(q)}$. Define $\beta' \colon Q \to (V_f \to \mathbb{Z})$ so that $\beta'(q)(v)$ is the value of v on q in state $s_{k(q)}$, i.e., in the pre-state. A *postcondition violation* occurs if it is not the case that there are extensions of α' and β' to f-valuations α and β such that $\llbracket \mathsf{post}(f) \rrbracket_{\alpha,\beta,q}$ holds for all $q \in \mathsf{PID}$.

Waitsfor Violations. We now explain the *waitsfor* contract clause. Assume again that a_i is an x^f action in process p, and that k is the index of the corresponding e^f action in p. The expression in the waitsfor clause is evaluated at the pre-state s_k to yield a set $W \subseteq \mathsf{PID}$. A *waitsfor violation* occurs at step i if there is some $q \in W$ such that $\mathsf{seg}_q(\zeta, i) < \mathsf{seg}_p(\zeta, k)$, i.e., p exits a collective call before q has entered it.

Correct Executions and Conformance to Contract. We can now encapsulate all the ways something may go wrong with collective procedures and their contracts:

Definition 2. *Let P be a program, $\zeta = s_0 \xrightarrow{a_1} s_1 \cdots$ an execution of a procedure in P, and $i \in 1..\mathsf{len}(\zeta)$. Let p be the process of a_i and $r = \mathsf{seg}_p(\zeta, i)$. We say ζ commits* a collective error *at step i if any of the following occur at step i:*

1. *a consistency, precondition, postcondition, or* waitsfor *violation,*
2. *an* assigns violation*: a_i is an exit action and the value of a variable not in p's assigns set differs from its pre-state value,*
3. *a segment boundary violation: a_i is a receive of a message sent from a process q at a_j $(j < i)$ and $\mathsf{seg}_q(\zeta, j) > r$; or a_i is a send to q and $\mathsf{seg}_q(\zeta, i) > r$, or*
4. *an* unreceived message violation*: a_i is a collective action and there is an unreceived message sent to p from q at a_j $(j < i)$, and $\mathsf{seg}_q(\zeta, j) = r - 1$.*

The last two conditions imply that a message that crosses segment boundaries is erroneous. In particular, if an execution terminates without collective errors, every message sent within a segment is received within that same segment.

Definition 3. *An execution of a procedure is* correct *if it is finite, does not deadlock, and has no collective errors.*

We can now define what it means for a procedure to conform to its contract. Let f be a collective procedure in P. By a $pre(f)$-state, we mean a state of P^f in which (i) every process has one entry on its call stack, pointing to the start location of main, (ii) all channels are empty, and (iii) for all processes, the assignment to the global variables satisfies the precondition of f.

Definition 4. *A collective procedure f* conforms *(to its contract) if all executions of P^f from $pre(f)$-states are correct.*

Note that any maximal non-deadlocking finite execution terminates. So a conforming procedure will always terminate if invoked from a $pre(f)$-state, i.e., ours is a "total" (not "partial") notion of correctness in the Hoare logic sense.

2.4   Simulation

In the sequential theory, one may verify properties of a procedure f using only the contracts of the procedures called by f. We now generalize that approach for collective procedures. We will assume from now on that P has no "collective recursion." That is, in the call graph for P—the graph with nodes the procedures of P and an edge from f to g if the body of f contains a call to g—there is no cycle that includes a collective procedure. This simplifies reasoning about termination.

If $f, g \in \mathcal{C}$, we say f *uses* g if there is a path of positive length in the call graph from f to g on which any node other than the first or last is not in $\mathcal{C}$.

Given $f \in \mathcal{C}$, we construct a program $\overline{P^f}$ which abstracts away the implementation details of each collective procedure g used by f, replacing the body of g with a stub that simulates g's contract. The stub consists of two new statements. The first may be represented with pseudocode

```
havoc(assigns(g)); assume(post(g));
```

This nondeterministic statement assigns arbitrary values to the variables specified in the *assigns* clause of g's contract, as long as those values do not commit
a postcondition violation for g. The second statement may be represented

```
wait(\old(waitsfor(g)));
```

and blocks the calling process p until all processes in p's wait set (evaluated in
p's pre-state) reach this statement. This ensures the stub will obey g's *waitsfor*
contract clause. Now $\overline{P^f}$ is a program with the same set of collective procedure
names, and same contracts, as P^f. A *simulation* of f is an execution of $\overline{P^f}$.

Theorem 1 *Let P be a program with no collective recursion. Let f be a collective
procedure in P and assume all collective procedures used by f conform. If all
simulations of f from a pre(f)-state are correct then f conforms.*

Theorem 1 is the basis for the contract-checking tool described in Sect. 4.2.
The tool consumes a C/MPI program annotated with procedure contracts. The
user specifies a single procedure f and the tool constructs a CIVL-C program
that simulates f by replacing the collective procedures called by f with stubs
derived from their contracts. It then uses symbolic execution and model checking
techniques to verify that all simulations of f behave correctly. By Theorem 1,
one can conclude that f conforms.

A detailed proof of Theorem 1 is given in [43]. Here we summarize the main
ideas of the proof. We assume henceforth that P is a collective recursion-free
program.

Two actions from different processes commute as long as the second does
not receive a message sent by the first. Two executions are *equivalent* if one can
be obtained from the other by a finite number of transpositions of commuting
adjacent transitions. We first observe that equivalence preserves most violations:

Lemma 1 *Let ζ and η be equivalent executions of a procedure f in P. Then*

1. *ζ commits a consistency, precondition, postcondition, assigns, segment boundary, or unreceived message violation iff η commits such a violation.*
2. *ζ deadlocks iff η deadlocks.*
3. *ζ is finite iff η is finite.*

If ζ commits a collective error when control is not inside a collective call
made by f (i.e., when f is the only collective function on the call stack), we
say the error is *observable*. If the error is not observable, it is *internal*. We say
ζ is *observably correct* if it is finite, does not deadlock, and is free of observable
collective errors.

We are interested in observable errors because those are the kind that will
be visible in a simulation, i.e., when each collective function g called by f is
replaced with a stub that mimics g's contract.

When ζ has no observable collective error, it can be shown that a collective call to g made within ζ can be *extracted* to yield an execution of g. The idea behind the proof is to transpose adjacent transitions in ζ until all of the actions inside the call to g form a contiguous subsequence of ζ. The resulting execution ξ is equivalent to ζ. Using Lemma 1, it can be shown that ξ is also observably correct and the segment involving the call to g can be excised to yield an execution of g. The next step is to show that extraction preserves internal errors:

Lemma 2 *Assume ζ is an observably correct execution of collective procedure f in P. Let $g_1, g_2, \ldots$ be the sequence of collective procedures called from f. If a transition in region r (i.e., inside the call to g_r) of ζ commits an internal collective error then the execution of P^{g_r} extracted from region r of ζ is incorrect.*

A corollary of Lemma 2 may be summarized as "conforming + observably correct = correct". More precisely,

Lemma 3 *Let f be a collective procedure of P. Assume all collective procedures used by f conform. Let ζ be an execution of P^f. Then ζ is correct if and only if ζ is observably correct.*

To see this, suppose ζ is observably correct but commits an internal collective error. Let r be the region of the transition committing the first internal collective error of ζ. Let g be the associated collective procedure used by f, and χ the execution of P^g extracted from region r of ζ. By Lemma 2, χ is incorrect, contradicting the assumption that g conforms.

Next we show that observable errors will be picked up by some simulation. The following is proved using extraction and Lemma 3:

Lemma 4 *Suppose f is a collective procedure of P, all collective procedures used by f conform, and ζ is an execution of P^f. If ζ has an observable collective error or ends in deadlock then there exists an incorrect simulation of f.*

Since infinite executions are also considered erroneous, we must ensure they are detected by simulation:

Lemma 5 *Suppose f is a collective procedure of P, and all collective procedures used by f conform. If ζ is an infinite execution of P^f with no observable collective error then there exists an incorrect simulation of f.*

Finally, we prove Theorem 1. Assume f is a collective procedure in P and all collective procedures used by f conform. Suppose f does not conform; we must show there is an incorrect simulation of f. As f does not conform, there is an incorrect execution ζ of P^f from a *pre(f)*-state. By Lemma 3, ζ is not observably correct. If ζ is finite or commits an observable collective error, Lemma 4 implies an incorrect simulation exists. Otherwise, Lemma 5 implies such a simulation exists. This completes the proof.

3   Collective Contracts for C/MPI

In Sect. 3.1, we summarize the salient aspects of C/MPI needed for a contract system. Section 3.2 describes the overall grammar of MPI contracts and summarizes the syntax and semantics of each new contract primitive.

3.1   Background from MPI

In the toy language of Sect. 2, every collective procedure was invoked by all processes. In MPI, a collective procedure is invoked by all processes in a *communicator*, an abstraction representing an ordered set of processes and an isolated communication universe.[1] Programs may use multiple communicators. The *size* of a communicator is the number of processes. Each process has a unique *rank* in the communicator, an ID number in $0..size - 1$.

In Sect. 2, a receive always selects the oldest message in a channel. In MPI, a point-to-point send operation specifies a *tag*, an integer attached to the "message envelope." A receive can specify a tag, in which case the oldest message in the channel with that tag is removed, or the receive can use `MPI_ANY_TAG`, in which case the oldest message is. MPI collective functions do not use tags.

MPI communication operations use *communication buffers*. A buffer b is specified by a pointer p, *datatype* d (an object of type `MPI_Datatype`), and nonnegative integer *count*. There are constants of type `MPI_Datatype` corresponding to the C basic types: `MPI_INT`, `MPI_DOUBLE`, etc. MPI provides functions to build aggregate datatypes. Each datatype specifies a *type map*: a sequence of ordered pairs (t, m) where t is a basic type and m is an integer displacement in bytes. A type map is *nonoverlapping* if the memory regions specified by distinct entries in the type map do not intersect. A receive operation requires a nonoverlapping type map; no such requirement applies to sends. For example, the type map $\{(\texttt{int}, 0), (\texttt{double}, 8)\}$, together with p, specifies an `int` at p and a `double` at `(char*)p+8`. As long as `sizeof(int)` ≤ 8, this type map is nonoverlapping.

The *extent* of d is the distance from its lowest to its highest byte, including possible padding bytes at the end needed for alignment; the precise definition is given in the MPI Standard. The type map of b is defined to be the concatenation of $T_0, \ldots, T_{count-1}$, where T_i is the type map obtained by adding $i * extent(d)$ to the displacements of the entries in the type map of d. For example, if *count* is 2, `sizeof(double)` $= 8$ and `int`s and `double`s are aligned at multiples of 8 bytes, the buffer type map in the example above is

$$\{(\texttt{int}, 0), (\texttt{double}, 8), (\texttt{int}, 16), (\texttt{double}, 24)\}.$$

A message is created by reading memory specified by the send buffer, yielding a sequence of basic values. The message has a *type signature*—the sequence of basic types obtained by projecting the type map onto the first component. The receive operation consumes a message and writes the values into memory according to the receive buffer's type map. Behavior is undefined if the send and receive buffers do not have the same type signature.

---

[1] We consider only *intra-communicators* in this paper.

function-contract ::= *requires-clause*∗ *terminates-clause*∗ *decreases-clause*?
   simple-clause∗ *comm-clause*∗ *named-behavior*∗ *completeness-clause*∗
   collective-contract∗
simple-clause ::= *assigns-clause* | *ensures-clause* | *allocation-clause* | *abrupt-clause*
named-behavior ::= **behavior** id : *assumes-clause*∗ *requires-clause*∗
   simple-clause∗ *comm-clause*∗
comm-clause ::= **mpi uses** term (, term)∗ ;
collective-contract ::= **mpi collective**(term) : *requires-clause*∗ *simple-clause*∗
   waitsfor-clause∗ *mpi-named-behavior*∗ *completeness-clause*∗
mpi-named-behavior ::= **behavior** id :   *assumes-clause*∗ *requires-clause*∗
   simple-clause∗ *waitsfor-clause*∗

Fig. 4. Grammar for ACSL function contracts, extended for MPI. Details for standard ACSL clauses can be found in [10].

3.2 Contract Structure

We now describe the syntax and semantics for C/MPI function contracts. A contract may specify either an MPI collective function, or a user-defined collective function. A user function may be implemented using one or more communicators, point-to-point operations, and MPI collectives.

The top level grammar is given in Fig. 4. A function contract begins with a sequence of distinct behaviors, each with an assumption that specifies when that behavior is active. Clauses in the global contract scope preceding the first named behavior are thought of as comprising a single behavior with a unique name and assumption *true*. The behaviors may be followed by `disjoint behaviors` and `complete behaviors` clauses, which encode claims that the assumptions are pairwise disjoint, and their disjunction is equivalent to *true*, respectively. All of this is standard ACSL, and we refer to it as the *sequential part* of the contract.

A new kind of clause, the *comm-clause*, may occur in the sequential part. A comm-clause begins "`mpi uses`" and is followed by a list of terms of type `MPI_Comm`. Such a clause specifies a guarantee that no communication will take place on a communicator *not* in the list. When multiple comm-clauses occur within a behavior, it is as if the lists were appended into one.

Collective contracts appear after the sequential part. A collective contract begins "`mpi collective`" and names a communicator c which provides the context for the contract; c must occur in a comm-clause from the sequential part. A collective contract on c encodes the claim that the function conforms to its contract (Definition 4) with the adjustment that all of the collective errors defined in Definition 2 are interpreted with respect to c only.

A collective contract may comprise multiple behaviors. As with the sequential part, clauses occurring in the collective contract before the first named behavior are considered to comprise a behavior with a unique name and assumption *true*.

Type Signatures. The new logic type `mpi_sig_t` represents MPI type signatures. Its domain consists of all finite sequences of basic C types. As with all ACSL types, equality is defined and `==` and `!=` can be used on two such values

in a logic specification. If t is a term of integer type and s is a term of type
mpi_sig_t, then t*s is a term of type mpi_sig_t. If the value of t is n and
$n \geq 0$, then t*s denotes the result of concatenating the sequence of s n times.

Operations on Datatypes. Two logic functions and one predicate are defined:

```
int \mpi_extent(MPI_Datatype datatype);
mpi_sig_t \mpi_sig(MPI_Datatype datatype);
\mpi_nonoverlapping(MPI_Datatype datatype);
```

The first returns the extent (in bytes) of a datatype. The second returns the type
signature of the datatype. The predicate holds iff the type map of the datatype is
nonoverlapping, a requirement for any communication buffer that receives data.

Value Sequences. The domain of type mpi_seq_t consists of all finite
sequences of pairs (t, v), where t is a basic C type and v is a value of type
t. Such a sequence represents the values stored in a communication buffer or
message. Similar to the case with type signatures, we define multiplication of an
integer with a value of type mpi_seq_t to be repeated concatenation.

Communication Buffers. Type mpi_buf_t is a struct with fields base (of
type void*), count (int), and datatype (MPI_Datatype). A value of this type
specifies an MPI communication buffer and is created with the logic function

```
mpi_buf_t \mpi_buf(void * base, int count, MPI_Datatype datatype);
```

The ACSL predicate \valid is extended to accept arguments of type mpi_buf_t
and indicates that the entire extent of the buffer is allocated memory; predicate
\valid_read is extended similarly.

Buffer Arithmetic. An integer and a buffer can be added or multiplied. Both
operations are commutative. These are defined by

```
n * \mpi_buf(p, m, dt) == \mpi_buf(p, n * m, dt)
n + \mpi_buf(p, m, dt) == \mpi_buf((char*)p + n*\mpi_extent(dt), m, dt)
```

Multiplication corresponds to multiplying the size of a buffer by n. It is meaningful only when both n and m are nonnegative. Addition corresponds to shifting a
buffer by n units, where a unit is the extent of the datatype dt. It is meaningful
for any integer n.

Buffer Dereferencing. The dereference operator * may take an mpi_buf_t b
as an argument. The result is the value sequence (of type mpi_seq_t) obtained
by reading the sequence of values from the buffer specified by b.

The term *b used in an assigns clause specifies that any of the memory
locations associated to b may be modified; these are the bytes in the range $p + m$
to $p + m + \text{sizeof}(t) - 1$, for some entry (t, m) in the type map of b.

The ACSL predicate \separated takes a comma-separated list of expressions, each of which denotes a set of memory locations. It holds if those sets are

pairwise disjoint. We extend the syntax to allow expressions of type mpi_buf_t in the list; these expressions represent sets of memory locations as above.

Terms. The grammar for ACSL *terms* is extended:

term ::= \mpi_comm_rank | \mpi_comm_size | \mpi_on(*term*, *term*)

The term \mpi_comm_size is a constant, the number of processes in the communicator; \mpi_comm_rank is the rank of "this" process. In the term \mpi_on(t,r), r must have integer type and is the rank of a process in the communicator. Term t is evaluated in the state of the process of rank r. For convenience, we define a macro \mpi_agree(x) which expands to x==\mpi_on(x,0). This is used to say the value of x is the same on all processes.

Reduction. A predicate for reductions is defined:

```
\mpi_reduce(mpi_seq_t out, integer lo, integer hi,
           MPI_Op op, (integer)->mpi_seq_t in);
```

The predicate holds iff the value sequence out on this process is a point-wise reduction, using operator op, of the $hi - lo$ value sequences in(lo), in(lo + 1), ..., in(hi − 1). Note in is a function from integer to mpi_seq_t. We say a reduction, and not *the* reduction, because op may not be strictly commutative and associative (e.g., floating-point addition).

4 Evaluation

In this section we describe a prototype tool we developed for MPI collective contract verification, and experiments applying it to various example codes. All experimental artifacts, including the tool source code, are available online [43].

4.1 Collective Contract Examples

The first part of our evaluation involved writing contracts for a variety of collective functions. We started with the 17 MPI blocking collective functions specified in [45, Chapter 5]. These represent the most commonly used message-passing patterns, such as broadcast, scatter, gather, transpose, and reduce (fold). The MPI Standard is a precisely written natural language document, similar to the C Standard. We scrutinized each sentence in the description of each function and checked that it was reflected accurately in the contract.

Figure 5 shows the contract for the MPI collective function MPI_Allreduce. This function "combines the elements provided in the input buffer of each process... using the operator op" and "the result is returned to all processes" [45]. This guarantee is reflected in line 13. "The 'in place' option ... is specified by passing the value MPI_IN_PLACE to the argument sendbuf at all processes. In this case, the input data is taken at each process from the receive buffer, where it

```
1 #define SBUF \mpi_buf(sbuf, count, dt)
2 #define RBUF \mpi_buf(rbuf, count, dt)
3 /*@ mpi uses comm; mpi collective(comm):
4   requires \valid(RBUF) && \mpi_nonoverlapping(dt);
5   requires \mpi_agree(count) && \mpi_agree(dt) && \mpi_agree(op) && count >= 0;
6   requires \separated(RBUF, {SBUF |int i; sbuf != MPI_IN_PLACE});
7   assigns *RBUF;
8   ensures \mpi_agree(*RBUF);
9   waitsfor { i | int i; 0 <= i < \mpi_comm_size && count > 0};
10  behavior not_in_place:
11    assumes sbuf != MPI_IN_PLACE;
12    requires \mpi_agree(sbuf != MPI_IN_PLACE) && \valid_read(SBUF);
13    ensures \mpi_reduce(*RBUF, 0, \mpi_comm_size, op, \lambda integer t; \mpi_on(*SBUF, t));
14  behavior in_place:
15    assumes sbuf == MPI_IN_PLACE;
16    requires \mpi_agree(sbuf == MPI_IN_PLACE);
17    ensures
18      \mpi_reduce(*RBUF, 0, \mpi_comm_size, op, \lambda integer t; \mpi_on(\old(*RBUF), t));
19  disjoint behaviors; complete behaviors; */
20 int MPI_Allreduce(const void *sbuf, void *rbuf, int count, MPI_Datatype dt, MPI_Op op,
21                   MPI_Comm comm);
```

Fig. 5. The contract of the `MPI_Allreduce` function.

will be replaced by the output data." This option is represented using two behaviors. These are just a few examples of the tight mapping between the natural language and the contract.

The only ambiguity we could not resolve concerned synchronization. The Standard is clear that collective operations may or may not impose barriers. It is less clear on whether certain forms of synchronization are implied by the semantics of the operation. For example, many users assume that a non-root process must wait for the root in a broadcast, or that all-reduce necessarily entails a barrier. But these operations could be implemented with no synchronization when count is 0. (Similarly, a process executing all-reduce with *logical and* could return immediately if its contribution is *false*.) This issue has been discussed in the MPI Forum [17]. Our `MPI_Allreduce` contract declares, on line 9, that barrier synchronization occurs if count > 0, but other choices could be encoded.

In addition to the MPI collectives, we wrote contracts for a selection of user-defined collectives from the literature, including:

1. `exchange`: "ghost cell exchange" in 1d-diffusion solver [58]
2. `diff1dIter`: computes one time step in 1d-diffusion [58]
3. `dotProd`: parallel dot-product procedure from Hypre [23]
4. `matmat`: matrix multiplication using a block-striped decomposition [52]
5. `oddEvenIter`: odd-even parallel sorting algorithm [30,41].

We also implemented `cyc` of Fig. 2 in MPI with contracts.

Figure 6 shows the contract and the implementation for `dotProd`. The functions `hypre_MPI*` are simple wrappers for the corresponding MPI functions. The input vectors are block distributed. Each process gets its blocks and computes their inner product. The results are summed across processes with an all-reduce. The contract uses the ACSL `\sum` function to express the local result on a process (line 3) as well as the global result (line 13). Thus the contract is only

```
1 #define hypre_ParVectorComm(vector) ((vector) -> comm)
2 #define PAR_SIZE x->local_vector->size * x->local_vector->num_vectors
3 #define LOCAL_RESULT  \sum(0, PAR_SIZE-1, \lambda int t; \
4   x->local_vector->data[t] * y->local_vector->data[t])
5 /*@ requires \valid_read(x) && \valid_read(x->local_vector);
6     requires \valid_read(y) && \valid_read(y->local_vector);
7     requires \valid_read(x->local_vector->data + (0 .. PAR_SIZE-1));
8     requires \valid_read(y->local_vector->data + (0 .. PAR_SIZE-1));
9     requires x->local_vector->size > 0 && x->local_vector->num_vectors > 0;
10    mpi uses hypre_ParVectorComm(x);
11    mpi collective(hypre_ParVectorComm(x)):
12      assigns \nothing;
13      ensures \result == \sum(0, \mpi_comm_size-1,
14                          \lambda integer k; \mpi_on(LOCAL_RESULT, k));
15      waitsfor {i | int i; 0 <= i < \mpi_comm_size}; */
16 HYPRE_Real hypre_ParVectorInnerProd(hypre_ParVector *x, hypre_ParVector *y) {
17    MPI_Comm comm = hypre_ParVectorComm(x);
18    hypre_Vector *x_local = hypre_ParVectorLocalVector(x);
19    hypre_Vector *y_local = hypre_ParVectorLocalVector(y);
20    HYPRE_Real result = 0.0;
21    HYPRE_Real local_result = hypre_SeqVectorInnerProd(x_local, y_local);
22    hypre_MPI_Allreduce(&local_result, &result, 1, hypre_MPI_REAL,
23                        hypre_MPI_SUM, comm);
24    return result;
25 }
```

Fig. 6. The parallel dotProd function from Hypre [23], with contract.

valid if a real number model of arithmetic is used. This is a convenient and commonly-used assumption when specifying numerical code. We could instead use our predicate \mpi_reduce for a contract that holds in the floating-point model.

4.2   Bounded Verification of Collective Contracts

For the second part of our evaluation, we developed a prototype tool for verifying that C/MPI collective procedures conform to their contracts. We used CIVL, a symbolic execution and model checking framework [57] written in Java, because it provides a flexible intermediate verification language and it already has strong support for concurrency and MPI [44]. We created a branch of CIVL and modified the Java code in several ways, which we summarize here.

We modified the front-end to accept contracts in our extended version of ACSL. This required expanding the grammar, adding new kinds of AST nodes, and updating the analysis passes. Our prototype can therefore parse and perform basic semantic checks on contracts.

We then added several new primitives to the intermediate language to support the formal concepts described in Sect. 2. For example, in order to evaluate pre- and postconditions using \mpi_on expressions, we added a type for *collective state*, with operations to take a "snapshot" of a process state and merge snapshots into a program state, in order to check collective conditions.

Finally, we implemented a *transformer*, which consumes a C/MPI program annotated with contracts and the name of the function f to be verified. It generates a program similar to $\overline{P^f}$ (Sect. 2.4). This program has a driver that initializes the global variables and arguments for f to arbitrary values constrained only

function	states	prover	time(s)
g (cyc)	3,562	7	4
allreduceDR	7,390	15	5
f (cyc)	7,913	16	15
oddEvenIter	14,216	91	8
bcast	29,256	80	16
allreduce	14,174	64	16
dotProd	4,690	102	40
diff1dIter	4,762	130	100

function	states	prover	time(s)
allgather	14,606	356	32
reduce	118,278	54	46
scatter	125,900	394	69
gather	126,724	259	71
matmat	8,345	275	188
reduceScatterNC	264,215	259	214
reduceScatter	211,541	499	505
exchange	896,869	9659	478

Fig. 7. Verification performance for nprocs $\leq$ 5.

by f's precondition, using CIVL's $assume statement. The body of a collective function g used by f is replaced by code of the form

```
wait(waitsfor(g)); $assert(precondition); $havoc(assigns(g));
wait(waitsfor(g)); $assume(postcondition);
```

where wait is implemented using CIVL primitive $when, which blocks until a condition holds. When the CIVL verifier is applied to this program, it explores all simulations of f, verifying they terminate and are free of collective errors. By Thm. 1, the verifier can prove, for a bounded number of processes, f conforms.

Our prototype has several limitations. It assumes no wildcard is used in the program. It does not check *assigns violation* for the verifying function. It assumes all communication uses standard mode blocking point-to-point functions and blocking MPI collective functions. Nevertheless, it can successfully verify a number of examples with nontrivial bounds on the number of processes.

For the experiment, we found implementations for several of the MPI collective functions. Some of these are straightforward; e.g., the implementation of MPI_Allreduce consists of calls to MPI_Reduce followed by a call to MPI_Bcast. Two of these implementations are more advanced: allreduceDR implements MPI_Allreduce using a double recursive algorithm; reduceScatterNC implements MPI_Reduce_scatter using an algorithm optimized for noncommutative reduction operations [12].

We applied our prototype to these collective implementations, using the contracts described in Sect. 4.1. We also applied it to the 5 user-defined collectives listed there. We were able to verify these contracts for up to 5 processes (no other input was bounded), using a Mac Mini with an M1 chip and 16GB memory. For the CIVL configuration, we specified two theorem provers to be used in order: (1) CVC4 [8] 1.8, and (2) Z3 [49] 4.8.17, each with a timeout of two seconds.

Results are given in Fig. 7. For each problem, we give the number of states saved by CIVL, the number of calls to the theorem provers, and the total verification time in seconds, rounded up to the nearest second.

The times range from 4 seconds to 8 and a half minutes. In general, time increases with the number of states and prover calls. Exceptions to this pattern occur when prover queries are very complex and the prover times out—two seconds in our case. For example, `matmat`, whose queries involve integer multiplications and uninterpreted functions, times out often. It is slower than most of the test cases despite a smaller state space.

Comparing `reduceScatter` with `reduceScatterNC`, it is noteworthy that verifying the simple implementation takes significantly longer than the advanced version. This is because the simple implementation re-uses verified collective functions. Reasoning about the contracts of those functions may involve expensive prover calls.

For `exchange`, nearly one million states are saved though its implementation involves only two MPI point-to-point calls. This is due to the generality of its contract. A process communicates with its left and right "neighbors" in this function. The contract assumes that the neighbors of a process can be any two processes—as long as each pair of processes agree on whether they are neighbors. Hence there is combinatorial explosion generating the initial states.

For each example, we made erroneous versions and confirmed that CIVL reports a violation or "unknown" result.

5   Related Work

The ideas underlying code contracts originate in the work of Floyd on formal semantics [26], the proof system of Hoare [29], the specification system Larch [27], and Meyer's work on Eiffel [46,47]. Contract systems have been developed for many other languages, including Java [25,32,38], Ada [5], C# [7], and C [10,18].

Verification condition generation (VCG) [6,25,39] and symbolic execution [35,36,51] are two techniques used to verify that code conforms to a contract. *Extended static checking* is an influential VCG approach for Java [25,32,39]. Frama-C's WP plugin [9,18] is a VCG tool for ACSL-annotated C programs, based on the Why platform [24]. The Kiasan symbolic execution platform [20] has been applied to both JML and Spark contracts [11].

Several contract systems have been developed for shared memory concurrency. The VCC verifier [15,16,48] takes a contract approach, based on object invariants in addition to pre- and postconditions, to shared-memory concurrent C programs. VeriFast is a deductive verifier for multithreaded C and Java programs [31]. Its contract language is based on concurrent separation logic [14]. These systems focus on issues, such as ownership and permission, that differ from those that arise in distributed computing.

For distributed concurrency, type-theoretic approaches based on *session types* [50,54,59] are used to describe communication protocols; various techniques verify an implementation conforms to a protocol. ParTypes [40] applies this approach to C/MPI programs using a user-written protocol that specifies the sequence of messages transmitted in an execution. Conformance guarantees deadlock-freedom for an arbitrary number of processes. However, ParTypes protocols cannot specify programs with wildcards or functional correctness, and they serve a different purpose than our contracts. Our goal is to provide a public contract for a collective procedure—the messages transmitted are an implementation detail that should remain "hidden" to the extent possible.

Several recent approaches to the verification of distributed systems work by automatically transforming a message-pasing program to a simplified form. One of these takes a program satisfying *symmetric nondeterminism* and converts it to a sequential program, proving deadlock-freedom and enabling verification of other safety properties [4]. Another does the same for a more general class of distributed programs, but requires user-provided information such as an "invariant action" and an abstraction function [37]. A related approach converts an asynchronous *round-based* message-passing program, with certain user-provided annotations, to a synchronous form [19]. This technique checks that each round is *communication-closed*, a concept that is similar to the idea of collective-style procedures. It is possible that these approaches could be adapted to verify that collective-style procedures in an MPI program conform to their contracts.

There are a number of correctness tools for MPI programs, including the dynamic model checkers ISP [60] and DAMPI [61], the static analysis tool MPI-Checker [22], and the dynamic analysis tool MUST [28]. These check for certain pre-defined classes of defects, such as deadlocks and incorrectly typed receive statements; they are not used to specify or verify functional correctness.

Ashcroft introduced the idea of verifying parallel programs by showing every atomic action preserves a global invariant [3]. This approach is applied to a simple message-passing program in [42] using Frama-C+WP and ghost variables to represent channels. The contracts are quite complicated; they are also a bespoke solution for a specific problem, rather than a general language. However, the approach applies to non-collective as well as collective procedures.

A parallel program may also be specified by a functionally equivalent sequential version [56]. This works for whole programs which consume input and produce output, but it seems less applicable to individual collective procedures.

Assume-Guarantee Reasoning. [1, 21, 33, 34] is another approach that decomposes along process boundaries. This is orthogonal to our approach, which decomposes along procedure boundaries.

6   Discussion

We have summarized a theory of contracts for collective procedures in a toy message-passing language. We have shown how this theory can be realized for C programs that use MPI using a prototype contract-checking tool. The approach is applicable to programs that use standard-mode blocking point-to-point operations, blocking MPI collective functions, multiple communicators, user-defined datatypes, pointers, pointer arithmetic, and dynamically allocated memory. We have used it to fully specify all of the MPI blocking collective functions, and several nontrivial user-defined collective functions.

MPI's nonblocking operations are probably the most important and widely-used feature of MPI not addressed here. In fact, there is no problem specifying a collective procedure that uses nonblocking operations, as long as the procedure completes all of those operations before returning. For such procedures, the nonblocking operations are another implementation detail that need not be mentioned in the public interface. However, some programs may use one procedure to post nonblocking operations, and another procedure to complete them; this is in fact the approach taken by the new MPI "nonblocking collective" functions [45, Sec. 5.12]. The new "neighborhood collectives" [45, Sec. 7.6] may also require new abstractions and contract primitives.

Our theory assumes no use of `MPI_ANY_SOURCE` "wildcard" receives. It is easy to construct counterexamples to Theorem 1 for programs that use wildcards. New conceptual elements will be required to ensure a collective procedure implemented with wildcards will always behave as expected.

Our prototype tool for verifying conformance to a contract uses symbolic execution and bounded model checking techniques. It demonstrates the feasibility of this approach, but can only "verify" with small bounds placed on the number of processes. It would be interesting to see if the verification condition generation (VCG) approach can be applied to our contracts, so that they could be verified without such bounds. This would require a kind of Hoare calculus for message-passing parallel programs, and/or a method for specifying and verifying a global invariant.

One could also ask for runtime verification of collective contracts. This is an interesting problem, as the assertions relate the state of multiple processes, so checking them would require communication.

Acknowledgements. We are grateful to the anonymous reviewers for providing valuable advice on the presentation of the results in this paper and for pointing out important related work. This material is based upon work by the RAPIDS Institute, supported by the U.S. Department of Energy, Office of Science, Office of Advanced Scientific Computing Research, Scientific Discovery through Advanced Computing (SciDAC) program, under award DE-SC0021162. Support was also provided by U.S. National Science Foundation awards CCF-1955852, CCF-1319571, and CCF-2019309.

References

1. Abadi, M., Lamport, L.: Conjoining specifications. ACM Trans. Program. Lang. Syst. **17**(3), 507–535 (1995). https://doi.org/10.1145/203095.201069
2. Alur, R., Bouajjani, A., Esparza, J.: Model Checking Procedural Programs, chap. 17, pp. 541–572. Springer, Cham (2018).https://doi.org/10.1007/978-3-319-10575-8_17
3. Ashcroft, E.A.: Proving assertions about parallel programs. J. Comput. Syst. Sci. **10**(1), 110–135 (1975). https://doi.org/10.1016/S0022-0000(75)80018-3
4. Bakst, A., Gleissenthall, K.v., Kıcı, R.G., Jhala, R.: Verifying distributed programs via canonical sequentialization. Proc. ACM Program. Lang. **1**(OOPSLA) (2017). https://doi.org/10.1145/3133934
5. Barnes, J.: High Integrity Software: The SPARK Approach to Safety and Security. Addison-Wesley, Boston (2003)
6. Barnett, M., Chang, B.Y.E., DeLine, R., Jacobs, B., Leino, K.R.M.: Boogie: a modular reusable verifier for object-oriented programs. In: de Boer, F.S., Bonsangue, M.M., Graf, S., de Roever, W.P. (eds.) FMCO 2005. LNCS, vol. 4111, pp. 364–387. Springer, Heidelberg (2005). https://doi.org/10.1007/11804192_17

7. Barnett, M., Fähndrich, M., Leino, K.R.M., Müller, P., Schulte, W., Venter, H.: Specification and verification: the Spec# experience. Commun. ACM **54**(6), 81–91 (2011). https://doi.org/10.1145/1953122.1953145
8. Barrett, C., et al.: CVC4. In: International Conference on Computer Aided Verification, pp. 171–177. Springer, Heidelberg (2011). http://dl.acm.org/citation.cfm?id=2032305.2032319
9. Baudin, P., Bobot, F., Correnson, L., Dargaye, Z., Blanchard, A.: WP plug-in manual: frama-C 22.0 (Titanium) (2020). https://frama-c.com/download/frama-c-wp-manual.pdf
10. Baudin, P., et al.: ACSL: ANSI/ISO C Specification Language, version 1.16 (2020). http://frama-c.com/download/acsl-1.16.pdf
11. Belt, J., Hatcliff, J., Robby, Chalin, P., Hardin, D., Deng, X.: Bakar Kiasan: flexible contract checking for critical systems using symbolic execution. In: Bobaru et al. [13], pp. 58–72.https://doi.org/10.1007/978-3-642-20398-5_6
12. Bernaschi, M., Iannello, G., Lauria, M.: Efficient implementation of reduce-scatter in MPI. In: Proceedings of the 10th Euromicro Conference on Parallel, Distributed and Network-Based Processing (EUROMICRO-PDP 2002), pp. 301–308. IEEE Computer Society, Washington (2002). http://dl.acm.org/citation.cfm?id=1895489.1895529
13. Bobaru, M.G., Havelund, K., Holzmann, G.J., Joshi, R. (eds.): NASA Formal Methods - Third International Symposium, NFM 2011, Pasadena, 18–20 April 2011. Proceedings, LNCS, vol. 6617. Springer, Heidelberg (2011). https://doi.org/10.1007/978-3-642-20398-5
14. Brookes, S.: A semantics for concurrent separation logic. Theoret. Comput. Sci. **375**(1), 227–270 (2007). https://doi.org/10.1016/j.tcs.2006.12.034. Festschrift for John C. Reynolds's 70th Birthday
15. Cohen, E., et al.: VCC: a practical system for verifying concurrent C. In: Berghofer, S., Nipkow, T., Urban, C., Wenzel, M. (eds.) Theorem Proving in Higher Order Logics, LNCS, vol. 5674, pp. 23–42. Springer, Heidelberg (2009). https://doi.org/10.1007/978-3-642-03359-9_2
16. Cohen, E., Moskal, M., Schulte, W., Tobies, S.: Local verification of global invariants in concurrent programs. In: Touili, T., Cook, B., Jackson, P. (eds.) CAV 2010. LNCS, vol. 6174, pp. 480–494. Springer, Heidelberg (2010). https://doi.org/10.1007/978-3-642-14295-6_42
17. Community, M.: Collective Synchronization (2020). https://github.com/mpi-forum/mpi-issues/issues/257. Accessed 13 Aug 2021
18. Cuoq, P., Kirchner, F., Kosmatov, N., Prevosto, V., Signoles, J., Yakobowski, B.: Frama-C—a software analysis perspective. In: Eleftherakis, G., Hinchey, M., Holcombe, M. (eds.) SEFM 2012. LNCS, vol. 7504, pp. 233–247. Springer, Heidelberg (2012). https://doi.org/10.1007/978-3-642-33826-7_16
19. Damian, A., Drăgoi, C., Militaru, A., Widder, J.: Communication-closed asynchronous protocols. In: Dillig, I., Tasiran, S. (eds.) Computer Aided Verification,pp. 344–363. Springer, Cham (2019). https://doi.org/10.1007/978-3-030-25543-5_20
20. Deng, X., Lee, J., Robby: Bogor/Kiasan: a k-bounded symbolic execution for checking strong heap properties of open systems. In: 21st IEEE/ACM International Conference on Automated Software Engineering (ASE 2006), 18–22 September 2006, Tokyo, pp. 157–166. IEEE Computer Society, USA (2006). https://doi.org/10.1109/ASE.2006.26
21. Dingel, J.: Computer-assisted assume/guarantee reasoning with VeriSoft. In: Proceedings of the 25th International Conference on Software Engineering (ICSE

2003), pp. 138–148. IEEE Computer Society, Washington (2003).https://doi.org/10.1109/ICSE.2003.1201195

22. Droste, A., Kuhn, M., Ludwig, T.: MPI-checker: static analysis for MPI. In: Proceedings of the Second Workshop on the LLVM Compiler Infrastructure in HPC (LLVM 2015), pp. 3:1–3:10. ACM, New York (2015). https://doi.org/10.1145/2833157.2833159

23. Falgout, R.D., Yang, U.M.: *hypre*: a library of high performance preconditioners. In: Sloot, P.M.A., Hoekstra, A.G., Tan, C.J.K., Dongarra, J.J. (eds.) Computational Science—ICCS 2002, pp. 632–641. Springer, Heidelberg (2002). https://doi.org/10.1007/3-540-47789-6_66

24. Filliâtre, J.C., Paskevich, A.: Why3: where programs meet provers. In: Felleisen, M., Gardner, P. (eds.) Proceedings of the 22nd European Conference on Programming Languages and Systems (ESOP 2013), pp. 125–128. Springer, Heidelberg (2013). https://doi.org/10.1007/978-3-642-37036-6_8

25. Flanagan, C., Leino, K.R.M., Lillibridge, M., Nelson, G., Saxe, J.B., Stata, R.: Extended static checking for Java. In: Knoop, J., Hendren, L.J. (eds.) Proceedings of the 2002 ACM SIGPLAN Conference on Programming Language Design and Implementation (PLDI), Berlin, 17–19 June 2002, pp. 234–245. Association for Computing Machinery, New York (2002). https://doi.org/10.1145/512529.512558

26. Floyd, R.W.: Assigning meanings to programs. Math. Aspects Comput. Sci. **19**, 19–32 (1967)

27. Guttag, J.V., Horning, J.J., Wing, J.M.: The Larch family of specification languages. IEEE Softw. **2**(5), 24–36 (1985). https://doi.org/10.1109/MS.1985.231756

28. Hilbrich, T., Protze, J., Schulz, M., de Supinski, B.R., Müller, M.S.: MPI runtime error detection with MUST: advances in deadlock detection. In: Hollingsworth, J.K. (ed.) International Conference on High Performance Computing Networking, Storage and Analysis, SC 2012, Salt Lake City, 11–15 November 2012, pp. 30:1–30:11. IEEE Computer Society Press, Los Alamitos (2012). https://doi.org/10.1109/SC.2012.79

29. Hoare, C.A.R.: An axiomatic basis for computer programming. Commun. ACM **12**(10), 576–580 (1969). https://doi.org/10.1145/363235.363259

30. Huisman, M., Monahan, R., Müller, P., Mostowski, W., Ulbrich, M.: VerifyThis 2017: A Program Verification Competition. Tech. Rep. Karlsruhe Reports in Informatics 2017, 10, Karlsruhe Institute of Technology, Faculty of Informatics (2017). https://doi.org/10.5445/IR/1000077160

31. Jacobs, B., Piessens, F.: Expressive modular fine-grained concurrency specification. In: Proceedings of the 38th Annual ACM SIGPLAN-SIGACT Symposium on Principles of Programming Languages (POPL 2011), pp. 271–282. Association for Computing Machinery, New York (2011). https://doi.org/10.1145/1926385.1926417

32. James, P.R., Chalin, P.: Faster and more complete extended static checking for the Java Modeling Language. J. Automat. Reason. **44**, 145–174 (2010). https://doi.org/10.1007/s10817-009-9134-9

33. Jones, C.B.: Tentative steps toward a development method for interfering programs. ACM Trans. Program. Lang. Syst. **5**(4), 596–619 (1983). https://doi.org/10.1145/69575.69577

34. Jones, C.B.: Specification and design of (parallel) programs. In: Mason, R.E.A. (ed.) Information Processing 83, Proceedings of the IFIP 9th World Computer Congress, Paris, 19–23 September 1983, pp. 321–332. North-Holland/IFIP, Newcastle University (1983)

35. Khurshid, S., Păsăreanu, C.S., Visser, W.: Generalized symbolic execution for model checking and testing. In: Garavel, H., Hatcliff, J. (eds.) Tools and Algorithms for the Construction and Analysis of Systems, 9th International Conference, TACAS 2003, Held as Part of the Joint European Conferences on Theory and Practice of Software, ETAPS 2003, Warsaw, 7–11 April 2003, Proceedings. LNCS, vol. 2619, pp. 553–568. Springer, Heidelberg (2003). https://doi.org/10.1007/3-540-36577-X_40

36. King, J.C.: Symbolic execution and program testing. Commun. ACM **19**(7), 385–394 (1976). https://doi.org/10.1145/360248.360252

37. Kragl, B., Enea, C., Henzinger, T.A., Mutluergil, S.O., Qadeer, S.: Inductive sequentialization of asynchronous programs. In: Proceedings of the 41st ACM SIGPLAN Conference on Programming Language Design and Implementation (PLDI 2020), pp. 227–242. Association for Computing Machinery, New York (2020). https://doi.org/10.1145/3385412.3385980

38. Leavens, G.T., Baker, A.L., Ruby, C.: Preliminary design of JML: a behavioral interface specification language for Java. SIGSOFT Softw. Eng. Notes **31**(3), 1–38 (2006). https://doi.org/10.1145/1127878.1127884

39. Leino, K.R.M.: Extended static checking: a ten-year perspective. In: Wilhelm, R. (ed.) Informatics - 10 Years Back. 10 Years Ahead. LNCS, vol. 2000, pp. 157–175. Springer, Heidelberg (2001). https://doi.org/10.1007/3-540-44577-3_11

40. López, H.A., et al.: Protocol-based verification of message-passing parallel programs. In: Aldrich, J., Eugster, P. (eds.) Proceedings of the 2015 ACM SIGPLAN International Conference on Object-Oriented Programming, Systems, Languages, and Applications, OOPSLA 2015, Part of SPLASH 2015, Pittsburgh, 25–30 October 2015, pp. 280–298. ACM, New York (2015). https://doi.org/10.1145/2814270.2814302

41. Luo, Z., Siegel, S.F.: Symbolic execution and deductive verification approaches to VerifyThis 2017 challenges. In: Margaria, T., Steffen, B. (eds.) Leveraging Applications of Formal Methods, Verification and Validation (ISoLA 2018), Proceedings, Part II: Verification. LNCS, vol. 11245, pp. 160–178. Springer, Heidelberg (2018). https://doi.org/10.1007/978-3-030-03421-4_12

42. Luo, Z., Siegel, S.F.: Towards deductive verification of message-passing parallel programs. In: Laguna, I., Rubio-González, C. (eds.) 2018 IEEE/ACM 2nd International Workshop on Software Correctness for HPC Applications (Correctness), pp. 59–68. IEEE (2018). https://doi.org/10.1109/Correctness.2018.00012

43. Luo, Z., Siegel, S.F.: Artifact of "Collective contracts for message-passing parallel programs" (2024). https://doi.org/10.5281/zenodo.10938740

44. Luo, Z., Zheng, M., Siegel, S.F.: Verification of MPI programs using CIVL. In: Proceedings of the 24th European MPI Users' Group Meeting (EuroMPI 2017), pp. 6:1–6:11. ACM, New York (2017). https://doi.org/10.1145/3127024.3127032

45. Message-Passing Interface Forum. MPI: A Message-Passing Interface standard, version 3.1 (2015). https://www.mpi-forum.org/docs/mpi-3.1/mpi31-report.pdf

46. Meyer, B.: Applying "Design by Contract." IEEE Comput. **25**(10), 40–51 (1992). https://doi.org/10.1109/2.161279

47. Meyer, B., Nerson, J.M., Matsuo, M.: EIFFEL: object-oriented design for software engineering. In: Nichols, H.K., Simpson, D. (eds.) ESEC 1987. LNCS, vol. 289, pp. 221–229. Springer, Heidelberg (1987). https://doi.org/10.1007/BFb0022115

48. Moskal, M.: Verifying functional correctness of C programs with VCC. In: Bobaru et al. [13], pp. 56–57 (2011). https://doi.org/10.1007/978-3-642-20398-5_5

49. de Moura, L., Bjørner, N.: Z3: an efficient SMT solver. In: Ramakrishnan, C.R., Rehof, J. (eds.) Tools and Algorithms for the Construction and Analysis of Systems, pp. 337–340. Springer, Heidelberg (2008). https://doi.org/10.1007/978-3-540-78800-3_24

50. Ng, N., Yoshida, N., Honda, K.: Multiparty session C: safe parallel programming with message optimisation. In: Furia, C.A., Nanz, S. (eds.) Objects, Models, Components, Patterns. LNCS, vol. 7304, pp. 202–218. Springer, Heidelberg (2012). https://doi.org/10.1007/978-3-642-30561-0_15

51. Păsăreanu, C., Visser, W.: A survey of new trends in symbolic execution for software testing and analysis. Int. J. Softw. Tools Techol. Transf. 11(4), 339–353 (2009). https://doi.org/10.1007/s10009-009-0118-1

52. Quinn, M.: Parallel Programming in C with MPI and OpenMP. McGraw-Hill (2004)

53. Romano, P.K., Horelik, N.E., Herman, B.R., Nelson, A.G., Forget, B., Smith, K.: OpenMC: a state-of-the-art Monte Carlo code for research and development. Ann. Nucl. Energy 82, 90–97 (2015). https://doi.org/10.1016/j.anucene.2014.07.048

54. Scalas, A., Yoshida, N., Benussi, E.: Verifying message-passing programs with dependent behavioural types. In: Proceedings of the 40th ACM SIGPLAN Conference on Programming Language Design and Implementation (PLDI 2019), pp. 502–516. Association for Computing Machinery, New York (2019).https://doi.org/10.1145/3314221.3322484

55. Siegel, S.F., Avrunin, G.S.: Modeling wildcard-free MPI programs for verification. In: Proceedings of the Tenth ACM SIGPLAN Symposium on Principles and Practice of Parallel Programming (PPoPP 2005), pp. 95–106. Association for Computing Machinery, New York (2005).https://doi.org/10.1145/1065944.1065957

56. Siegel, S.F., Mironova, A., Avrunin, G.S., Clarke, L.A.: Combining symbolic execution with model checking to verify parallel numerical programs. ACM Trans. Softw. Eng. Methodol. 17(2), 1–34 (2008). https://doi.org/10.1145/1348250.1348256

57. Siegel, S.F., et al.: CIVL: the Concurrency Intermediate Verification Language. In: Proceedings of the International Conference for High Performance Computing, Networking, Storage and Analysis (SC 2015), pp. 61:1–61:12. ACM, New York (2015). http://doi.acm.org/10.1145/2807591.2807635

58. Siegel, S.F., Zirkel, T.K.: FEVS: a functional equivalence verification suite for high performance scientific computing. Math. Comput. Sci. 5(4), 427–435 (2011). https://doi.org/10.1007/s11786-011-0101-6

59. Takeuchi, K., Honda, K., Kubo, M.: An interaction-based language and its typing system. In: Halatsis, C., Maritsas, D., Philokyprou, G., Theodoridis, S. (eds.) PARLE 1994 Parallel Architectures and Languages Europe. LNCS, vol. 817, pp. 398–413. Springer, Heidelberg (1994). https://doi.org/10.1007/3-540-58184-7_118

60. Vakkalanka, S., Gopalakrishnan, G., Kirby, R.M.: Dynamic verification of MPI programs with reductions in presence of split operations and relaxed orderings. In: Gupta, A., Malik, S. (eds.) CAV 2008. LNCS, vol. 5123, pp. 66–79. Springer, Heidelberg (2008). https://doi.org/10.1007/978-3-540-70545-1_9

61. Vo, A., Aananthakrishnan, S., Gopalakrishnan, G., Supinski, B.R.d., Schulz, M., Bronevetsky, G.: A scalable and distributed dynamic formal verifier for MPI programs. In: Proceedings of the 2010 ACM/IEEE International Conference for High Performance Computing, Networking, Storage and Analysis (SC 2010), pp. 1–10. IEEE Computer Society, Washington (2010). https://doi.org/10.1109/SC.2010.7

62. Yang, U., Falgout, R., Park, J.: Algebraic Multigrid Benchmark, Version 00 (2017). https://www.osti.gov/servlets/purl/1389816

Distributed Systems

mypyvy: A Research Platform for Verification of Transition Systems in First-Order Logic

James R. Wilcox[1], Yotam M. Y. Feldman[2], Oded Padon[3], and Sharon Shoham[2]([✉])

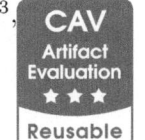

[1] University of Washington, Seattle, USA
[2] Tel Aviv University, Tel Aviv-Yafo, Israel
sharon.shoham@gmail.com
[3] VMware Research, Palo Alto, USA

Abstract. mypyvy is an open-source tool for specifying transition systems in first-order logic and reasoning about them. mypyvy is particularly suitable for analyzing and verifying distributed algorithms. mypyvy implements key functionalities needed for safety verification and provides flexible interfaces that make it useful not only as a verification tool but also as a research platform for developing verification techniques, and in particular invariant inference algorithms. Moreover, the mypyvy input language is both simple and general, and the mypyvy repository includes several dozen benchmarks—transition systems that model a wide range of distributed and concurrent algorithms. mypyvy has supported several recent research efforts that benefited from its development framework and benchmark set.

1 Introduction

mypyvy is an open-source[1] research platform for automated reasoning about symbolic transition systems expressed in first-order logic. A chief design goal for mypyvy is to lower the barrier to entry for developing new techniques for solver-aided analysis and verification of transition systems. As a result, mypyvy's modeling language is simple and close to the underlying logical foundation, and the tool is designed as a collection of reusable components, making it easy to experiment with new verification techniques.

The main application domain of mypyvy is verification of complex distributed algorithms. Following prior work [32,33], transition systems in mypyvy are expressed in uninterpreted first-order logic (i.e., without theories). Using uninterpreted first-order logic is motivated by the experience that solvers often struggle when theories (e.g., arithmetic, arrays, or algebraic data types) are combined with quantifiers. Quantifiers are essential for describing distributed algorithms (e.g., to state properties about all messages in the network), but theories can often be avoided, yielding improved automation.

---

[1] https://github.com/wilcoxjay/mypyvy.

© The Author(s) 2024
A. Gurfinkel and V. Ganesh (Eds.): CAV 2024, LNCS 14682, pp. 71–85, 2024.
https://doi.org/10.1007/978-3-031-65630-9_4

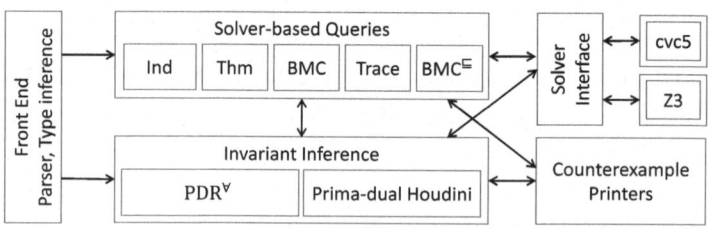

Fig. 1. Main components of mypyvy.

mypyvy consists of a language for expressing transition systems directly as logical formulas but in a convenient manner (Sect. 2), a tool for reasoning about such systems, and a collection of benchmarks accumulated over the last few years (Sect. 2.1). Figure 1 depicts mypyvy's components, which are divided to solver-based queries (Sect. 3) and invariant inference algorithms (Sect. 4). Solver-based queries such as inductiveness checking and bounded model checking are answered by translating them into satisfiability checks that are sent to external first-order solvers. These queries are used as basic building blocks for developing invariant inference algorithms. mypyvy includes an implementation of two such algorithms: PDR$^\forall$ [21] and Primal-dual Houdini [34]. mypyvy's internals are designed with the goal of making it easy to build on (Sect. 5). mypyvy interacts with multiple solvers, and currently supports Z3 [13] and cvc5 [2]. To present counterexamples (states, transitions, or traces) in a user-friendly way, mypyvy supports custom printers that simplify and improve readability of counterexamples.

mypyvy is not just the sum of the analyses currently available; it is a platform for doing research in automated verification. Several projects (including ongoing ones) use the mypyvy foundation and benchmark suite to build new invariant inference techniques, user interfaces for verification and exploration, and, most recently, liveness verification techniques (Sect. 6).

mypyvy's first-order modeling is inspired by Ivy [30,33], which promoted the idea of modeling distributed systems in the EPR decidable fragment of first-order logic. Ivy includes a rich and modular high-level imperative specification language, as well as mechanisms for creating executable implementations, specification-based testing, liveness verification, and more. As a result, Ivy's syntax, semantics, and code base are more complicated than what would be ideal for enabling rapid exploration of new techniques. In contrast, mypyvy's focus on transition systems, with a simple syntax and semantics, makes it especially suited for enabling verification research.[2] Moreover, mypyvy's code base is intentionally designed, documented, and typed (using Python's support for type annotations), to make it easy to build on and extend.

---

[2] There are current open-source efforts to automatically translate Ivy to mypyvy [9,36], which would allow Ivy users to benefit from mypyvy's algorithms.

Broadly, mypyvy has three target audiences:

1. Researchers interested in modeling and verifying distributed algorithms. mypyvy offers a user-friendly input language, several queries that assist in developing models of distributed algorithms, readable counterexamples, and access to a variety of automatic verification algorithms.
2. Researchers developing verification techniques, and invariant inference in particular. mypyvy offers a starting point for implementing new algorithms on top of a developer-friendly code base. mypyvy includes many useful building blocks, and has already been successfully used in several research projects.
3. Researchers looking for benchmarks for various verification tasks. mypyvy includes a significant set of transition systems (and their invariants), which can serve as benchmarks for invariant inference or other verification tasks.

2 Modeling Language

We present mypyvy through a simple example of modeling and analyzing a toy consensus protocol.[3] To get started, the user first expresses a transition system in mypyvy's input language, which is a convenient syntax for (many-sorted) uninterpreted first-order logic. A mypyvy model of the toy consensus protocol is shown in Fig. 2. In this protocol, each node *votes* for a single value, and once a majority or *quorum* of nodes vote for the same value a *decision* takes place. Because majorities intersect, the protocol ensures that at most one value is decided on. Modeling an algorithm or system of interest as a transition system in first-order logic may involve some abstraction, e.g., modeling majorities as abstract quorums such that every two quorums intersect [31].

States. The first step is to choose the types over which the transition system is defined. In the fashion of first-order logic, the basic types are *uninterpreted sorts* (mypyvy does not use SMT theories). In the example, we use the sorts node, value, and quorum to represent the nodes that participate in the distributed system, the values they choose from, and the sets of nodes that suffice for a decision (we abstract majorities following [4,32]). The state of the system is modeled by variables which can be *constants* (individuals), *relations*, or *functions*, whose domains are constructed from the aforementioned sorts. Each state variable is either immutable, which means it does not change throughout an execution of the system, or mutable, which means it may change with each transition. In the example, all state variables are relations. An immutable relation member denotes membership of a node in a quorum. The other relations are mutable: v records votes of nodes for values, b tracks which nodes already voted, and d records decisions.

---

[3] While not useful as a consensus protocol, this example does illustrate important aspects from proofs of complex, widely used consensus protocols like Paxos [25].

```
1   sort node
2   sort value
3   sort quorum
4
5   immutable relation member(node, quorum)
6   axiom forall Q1, Q2. exists N.
7           member(N, Q1) & member(N, Q2)
8
9   mutable relation v(node, value)
10  mutable relation b(node)
11  mutable relation d(value)
12
13  init forall N, V. !v(N,V)
14  init forall N. !b(N)
15  init forall V. !d(V)
16
17  transition vote(n: node, x: value)
18    modifies v, b
19    !b(n) &
20    (forall N, V.
21      v'(N, V) <-> v(N, V) | (N = n & V = x)) &
22    (forall N. b'(N) <-> b(N) | N = n)
23
24  transition decide(x: value)
25    modifies d
26    (exists Q. forall N. member(N, Q) -> v(N, x)) &
27    (forall V. d'(V) <-> d(V) | V = x)
28
29  safety [agreement] forall X, Y. d(X) & d(Y) -> X = Y
30  invariant [decision_quorums] forall X. d(X) ->
31    exists Q. forall N. member(N, Q) -> v(N, X)
32  invariant [unique_votes] forall N, X, Y.
33      v(N, X) & v(N, Y) -> X = Y
34  invariant [voting_bit] forall N, X. v(N, X) -> b(N)
35
36  zerostate theorem forall Q. exists N. member(N, Q)
37  onestate theorem unique_votes & decision_quorums -> agreement
38  twostate theorem forall N, X.
39        voting_bit & vote(N, X) -> voting_bit'
40
41  unsat trace {
42    vote
43    vote
44    vote
45    decide
46    decide
47    assert !safety
48  }
49
50  sat trace {
51    any transition
52    assert exists N, V. v(N,V)
53    decide
54    assert exists V. d(V)
55  }
```

Fig. 2. The toy consensus example in mypyvy.

```
> mypyvy verify consensus.pyv

checking init:
  implies invariant agreement..ok.
checking transition vote:
  preserves invariant agreement..ok.
checking transition decide:
  preserves invariant agreement..no!

counterexample:
  universes:
    sort node (1): node0
    sort quorum (1): quorum0
    sort value (2): value0 value1

  immutable:
    member(node0,quorum0)

  state 0:
    d(value1)
    v(node0,value0)

  state 1:
    d(value0)
    d(value1)
    v(node0,value0)

error consensus.pyv: invariant
agreement is not preserved by
transition decide
```

Fig. 3. A counterexample to induction (CTI) for the toy consensus protocol's safety property without additional invariants.

Axioms. mypyvy allows the user to define a "background theory" over the immutable symbols, which restricts the state space, via **axiom** declarations. In the example, the property that any two quorums intersect (abstracting majorities) is expressed as an axiom for the **member** relation (line 6). (The sorts of quantified variables are omitted in formulas since mypyvy infers them automatically.) Another common background theory that is useful when modeling distributed protocols in mypyvy is a total order, which can be used to abstract the natural numbers in first-order logic (e.g., to model rounds or indices).

Initial States. The initial states are defined as those that satisfy all **init** declarations. In the example, these declare that all mutable relations are initially empty (lines 13 to 15).

Transitions. The transitions of the system are expressed by **transition** declarations. The semantics is that each transition executes atomically and can modify the system's state. Transitions can have parameters, which are local variables that are assigned nondeterministically whenever the transition is executed. The example has two transitions: vote(n, x) and decide(x) (lines 17 to 27). An important design choice of **mypyvy** is that the user specifies transitions by explicitly writing logical formulas. Each transition is defined over two states: variables in the usual notation refer to the state *before* the transition is applied (*pre-state*), and primed variables refer to the state *after* the transition (*post-state*). Pre-conditions are encoded as conjuncts in the formula about the pre-state; for example, vote requires that the node has not already voted by specifying !b(n). Post-conditions are encoded as conjuncts about the post-state, relating it to the pre-state; for example, vote specifies that the relation b is updated to include exactly the same nodes as before in addition to n. Writing transitions directly through formulas offers great flexibility, but in order to write these formulas succinctly, a transition starts with a **modifies** clause that declares which mutable state variables are changed by it. For any mutable state component *not* in the modifies clause, **mypyvy** implicitly adds a conjunct encoding that the component does not change. Formally, the transition relation is the disjunction of the formulas from each of the transitions, where parameters are existentially quantified.

Safety. Finally, the user may specify safety properties using first-order formulas in **safety** declarations. The agreement safety property in the example (line 29) states that at most one value is decided. A safety property holds if it is satisfied by every state that is reachable from an initial state via a sequence of transitions.

2.1 Benchmarks

The **mypyvy** repository includes over 30 transition systems collected over the years. Some of these were translated from Ivy, while others were directly modeled in **mypyvy**. The benchmarks model a variety of distributed and concurrent algorithms, including consensus algorithms, networking algorithms, and cache coherence protocols. The variety of benchmarks, which also vary in complexity, is useful for evaluating and experimenting with new verification techniques. Additional details can be found in the paper's artifact [39].

3   Satisfiability-Based Queries

Once a transition system is specified, **mypyvy** supports several satisfiability-based queries over it, which are directly translated to satisfiability checks and handed off to solvers (currently Z3 [13] and cvc5 [2] are supported). These queries are useful building blocks for developing more advanced solver-aided algorithms, and for users who are interested in analyzing specific systems (especially during the model development process). For most queries, mypyvy provides counterexamples based on satisfying models obtained from solvers. And while solvers are not guaranteed to terminate, mypyvy makes it easy to follow the EPR fragment restrictions, which ensures termination.

3.1   Queries

Inductiveness Checking. mypyvy allows the user to add invariant declarations to prove safety by induction. These are first-order formulas, whose conjunction (together with the safety properties) forms a candidate inductive invariant. Figure 2 lists three supporting invariants (lines 30 to 34). The most common query in mypyvy is to check if the candidate invariant is inductive. When translating an inductiveness check to the solver, mypyvy splits it into one solver query per (transition, invariant) pair. In our experience, splitting the disjunction outside the solver improves performance and reliability, and, best of all, improves transparency for the user when one of the cases is more problematic (e.g., takes a long time).

Theorems. In addition to invariants, which are meant to hold in all reachable states of the transition system, mypyvy supports checking theorem declarations, which specify first-order formulas that are expected to be valid modulo the background theory (i.e., axioms). zerostate theorems refer to immutable state variables only, onestate theorems may refer to the mutable state variables as well, and twostate theorems involve two states, similarly to transition declarations. In the toy consensus example, a zerostate theorem (line 36) is used to state that quorums cannot be empty (follows from the quorum intersection axiom); a onestate theorem (line 37) is used to state that, given the background theory, the unique_votes and decision_quorums invariants imply the agreement safety property; and a twostate theorem (line 39) is used to check that the voting_bit invariant is preserved by the vote transition.

Bounded Model Checking (BMC). It is often useful to explore (un)reachability of a safety violation via BMC. Given a transition system and a safety property, BMC asks, "Is there a counterexample trace with $\leq k$ transitions?" BMC is implemented in the usual way, by unrolling the transition relation.

Trace Queries. Trace queries allow the user to explore the possible executions of the system in a more targeted way than BMC. This is useful both when the user is interested only in specific scenarios, and when BMC does not scale to sufficient depth. As an illustration, in a model of a distributed system with many protocol steps, BMC may only reasonably scale to a small depth, say 5 transitions, but many interesting behaviors of the system may not occur until at least 10 or 15 transitions. In Fig. 2, lines 41 to 48 show a query for the nonexistence of an execution trace that starts with three vote transitions, followed by two decide transitions, and then reaches a safety violation. mypyvy translates such a query to a first-order formula that is checked for unsatisfiability.

As a complement of trace queries that are expected to be unsatisfiable (specified by the unsat keyword), it is also useful to make sat trace queries that are expected to be satisfiable, demonstrating that some behaviors are indeed possible.[4] For example, lines 50 to 54 show a query expecting the existence of a trace that starts with any transition after which there exists a vote, followed by a decide transition after which there exists a decision. (That is possible when the number of nodes is 1.) Such satisfiable trace queries are especially useful for detecting *vacuity bugs*, where, due to a modeling error, some transitions mistakenly cannot execute, potentially making the system erroneously safe.

Relaxed Bounded Model Checking ($BMC^{\sqsubseteq}$). So far we discussed *concrete* traces. mypyvy can also search for *relaxed* counterexample traces of a bounded depth. A relaxed trace consists of a sequence of interleaved transitions and "relaxation steps", where some elements get deleted from the structure. As shown in [21], a relaxed counterexample trace that starts at an initial state and ends in a safety violation *proves* that there is no universally quantified inductive invariant that implies safety. This is the case in the toy consensus example—a relaxed counterexample trace found by mypyvy for this example is provided in the paper's artifact [39]. The key to implementing relaxed BMC queries is encoding universe reduction between states. mypyvy does so by introducing a mutable unary relation active for each sort and using it as a guard in every quantifier, effectively restricting the universe in each state to the "active" part. Relaxation steps are then modeled by adding a relax transition where each active relation in the post-state is a subset of the corresponding one in the pre-state (expressed as a universally quantified formula); all other state variables are unmodified over the active part. Finally, a relaxed BMC query is encoded similarly to a BMC query (with the added relax transitions), except that, due to the use of different active universes, the axioms are asserted not only at the beginning of the trace but also after every (relaxation) step, together with assertions requiring that the active universe contains the constants and is closed under functions.

3.2 Counterexamples

When a query fails (except for a sat trace query), it is because the formula sent to the solver was satisfiable. In such cases, mypyvy obtains a model from the solver and displays a *counterexample*—which can be a state, a transition, or a trace, depending on the failing query. For example, when inductiveness checking fails, it returns either a 1-state model demonstrating a violation of safety at an initial state, or a 2-state model demonstrating a counterexample to induction (CTI). As

---

[4] mypyvy uses solver queries to generate executions of the transition system. A solver is needed due to mypyvy's flexible and abstract modeling language. More imperative modeling languages, e.g. that of Ivy, admit execution/simulation without solvers, which can be useful for invariant inference as well [40,42]. Such simulation can also be implemented for a fragment of mypyvy's language.

another example, when BMC finds an execution that violates safety, it returns a k-state model providing a counterexample trace. Figure 3 shows a CTI (2-state model) for the toy consensus protocol when the invariants supporting the safety property are omitted. In general, mypyvy displays a k-state model by first listing the universe of each sort and the interpretations of the immutable symbols (member in our example). Then, for each of the k states, the interpretations of the mutable symbols in that state are printed. For relations, by default mypyvy only prints positive literals, i.e., the tuples that are in the relation.

Annotations, Plugins, and Custom Printers. In some cases, the default counterexample printing of mypyvy is not as readable as it could be. For example, if one of the sorts in the transition system is totally ordered (using a binary relation and suitable axioms), it would make sense to name the elements of that sort according to the total order. To improve the readability of counterexamples, mypyvy supports custom formatting via *printer plugins* and *annotations*. Every declaration in mypyvy can be tagged with *annotations*, which have no inherent meaning, but can be detected by plugins, e.g., to cause things to be printed differently. For example, the declaration sort round @printed_by(ordered_by_printer, le) invokes the ordered_by_printer plugin and tells mypyvy that the sort round should be printed in the order given by the le relation. mypyvy provides several other custom printers, including one for printing sorts that represent sets of elements coming from another sort. Users can also implement their own custom printing plugins in Python.

mypyvy also supports a handful of other annotations. @no_print instructs mypyvy not to print a sort, relation, constant, or function at all, which can be useful either because of a custom printer for another symbol, or temporarily because the model is large and the symbol is irrelevant to the current debugging session. @no_minimize is used to instruct mypyvy's model minimizer not to minimize elements of a certain sort or relation. The annotation framework is extensible, and we expect more uses for it to come up.

3.3   Decidability and Finite Counterexamples via EPR

In general, mypyvy does not restrict the quantifier structure used in formulas, nor the signatures of state variables. As a result, the first-order formulas that encode different queries in mypyvy are not guaranteed to reside in any decidable fragment and solvers may diverge. However, a common practice when working with mypyvy is to use the effectively propositional (EPR) [35,37] fragment of first-order logic, which imposes certain restrictions on functions and quantifier alternations. To encode a system in EPR (i.e., ensure that formulas generated for all queries are in EPR), the user can rely on recently developed methodologies [32,38]. For example, the toy consensus example of Fig. 2 is in EPR. Satisfiability of EPR is decidable, and reliably checked by solvers. EPR enjoys a small-model property, which implies queries have finite counterexamples (if any). Solver reliability and finite counterexamples are key enablers for more advanced algorithms (e.g., invariant inference) that make thousands of solver queries and employ model-based techniques. mypyvy's language is close to the underlying logic used in queries, making it relatively easy to follow the EPR restrictions.

4   Invariant Inference

mypyvy's design aims to make it easy to implement complex solver-aided analysis algorithms on top of the simpler queries. Two such algorithms, for automatically finding inductive invariants, are included in mypyvy: PDR$^\forall$ and Primal-dual Houdini.

*Universal Property-Directed Reachability (*PDR$^\forall$ *).* mypyvy includes an implementation of PDR$^\forall$ [21], which infers universally quantified inductive invariants in first-order logic. Like IC3/PDR [7], PDR$^\forall$ constructs invariants incrementally by finding backwards reachable states and "blocking" them relative to a "frame". To block a state, PDR$^\forall$ computes a "forbidden sub-state" that rules out all states containing a certain pattern. If PDR$^\forall$ succeeds, it returns the inductive invariant in the form of a conjunction of universally quantified clauses. Otherwise, it either loops forever or returns a relaxed trace, proving that no universally quantified inductive invariant exists for the property. On the toy consensus example, PDR$^\forall$ returns a relaxed trace similar to the one obtained by BMC$^\sqsubseteq$. mypyvy's implementation is the state-of-the-art implementation of PDR$^\forall$, and was used for comparison with PDR$^\forall$ in various papers [23,34,40]. The results demonstrate the success of mypyvy's PDR$^\forall$ implementation in solving benchmarks that only require universally quantified invariants.

Primal-Dual Houdini. Primal-dual Houdini [34] is a recent invariant inference algorithm based on a formal duality between reachability in transition systems and a notion of incremental induction proofs. mypyvy includes an implementation of Primal-dual Houdini for universally quantified invariants. Primal-dual Houdini works best for transition systems where the inductive invariant can be constructed incrementally, adding one universally quantified clause at a time. Several complex distributed algorithms have this feature. In cases where the invariant cannot be constructed incrementally, Primal-dual Houdini can find a witness for that fact. See [34] for more details and an empirical evaluation. Primal-dual Houdini was prototyped using mypyvy's infrastructure, and its development is an example of the usefulness of mypyvy for research in invariant inference.

5   Designing mypyvy's Internals

We designed mypyvy's internals with the goal of making it easy to build on. The most important aspects of the internals from the developer's perspective are (1) using typed Python,(2) the design of the abstract syntax trees (ASTs), and (3) the interface to the underlying first-order solver. mypyvy is written in statically typed Python using the mypy type checker. Types not only help catch bugs, but also document the interfaces available to the developer. In our experience, types allow developers to get up to speed more quickly on the code base and facilitate communication.

The ASTs for representing logical formulas in mypyvy were designed to support symbolic manipulation, as is common in solver-aided algorithms. This led us to avoid any additional intermediate representations between the ASTs representing the user-level formulas and the ASTs representing the input to solvers. We also structured the ASTs so that it is easy to (re)compute any analysis performed. For example, instead of using a traditional (mutable, long-lived) symbol table to resolve names, mypyvy uses a purely functional context to track scopes during AST traversals. The context is thrown away and recomputed every time the AST is traversed. This makes it easy to traverse programmatically generated ASTs, without needing to update any symbol tables or other global data structures, and the extra run time overhead is negligible.

Developers who use mypyvy often want to make many queries to the underlying solvers (currently Z3 and cvc5). We expose two interfaces for this. First, many common primitives, such as those discussed in Sect. 3.1, are exposed as a library. Second, mypyvy has a lower-level solver interface, where developers can issue their own satisfiability queries, and also gain access to minimized models and minimized unsat cores. Furthermore, developers of sophisticated invariant inference algorithms may have many thousands of queries to run, so mypyvy supports running many solvers in parallel.

6   Works Using mypyvy

One of mypyvy's goals is to serve the research community and enable research on verification, and invariant inference in particular. Indeed, in recent years several works have built on mypyvy or used it to various extents.

Phase-PDR$^\forall$ [14] is a user-guided invariant inference technique. The user provides a *phase structure* to convey temporal intuition, and suitable *phase invariants* are found using an adaptation of PDR$^\forall$. Phase-PDR$^\forall$ was developed on top of the mypyvy code base and mypyvy's PDR$^\forall$ implementation, and its evaluation uses benchmarks available from mypyvy augmented with phase structures.

SWISS [18] is an invariant inference algorithm that finds quantified invariants, including quantifier alternations, using explicit search. While SWISS does not use the mypyvy code base (it is implemented in C++), it accepts mypyvy's input files and its evaluation uses benchmarks available from mypyvy.

P-FOL-IC3 [23] is a variant of IC3/PDR that can find invariants with arbitrary quantification using *quantified separation* [22]. P-FOL-IC3 was implemented using mypyvy's code, and also benefited from mypyvy's benchmark set.

IC3PO [15,16] is an IC3/PDR variant that finds quantified invariants for protocols by analyzing finite instances. It does not use mypyvy's code, but is evaluated on some of mypyvy's benchmarks, manually translated to its input format.

LVR [41] develops a methodology for proving liveness properties. It uses mypyvy "twice": first, as a modeling language and a source of benchmarks, and second, as an invariant inference engine (using P-FOL-IC3) to find invariants that are required to support a liveness proof based on ranking functions.

7 Related Work

Several tools promote specification and verification of systems and algorithms using first-order logic, dating back to Abstract State Machines [6,17]. Alloy [20] is a relational modeling language and a tool that performs bounded verification, i.e., bounding the size of the universe of each sort. Alloy goes beyond first-order logic and has concepts such as transitive closure, but it shares mypyvy's emphasis on using uninterpreted relations and quantifiers, rather than SMT theories. Electrum [8,29] is an extension of Alloy that was recently integrated into Alloy 6 [1]; it essentially turns Alloy into a modeling language for transition systems. When universe sizes are bounded, Electrum/Alloy 6 can use finite-state model checkers to verify safety as well as liveness properties.

Ivy [30,33] is a multi-modal verification tool that supports modeling using first-order logic and EPR as well as some decidable SMT theories, modular reasoning, extracting executable implementations, liveness verification, specification-based testing, and more. Unlike Alloy, Ivy is not restricted to bounded verification; instead, it relies on user-provided inductive invariants and restricts the quantifier-alternation structure of verification conditions to ensure decidability of unbounded verification queries.

Verification of transition systems is also the focus of the TLA$^+$ toolbox [26], where transition systems are expressed in a very rich logic (based on set theory). As a result, verification is restricted to model checking bounded instances [24,43] similar to Alloy, or manually writing detailed machine-checked proofs [10].

The IronFleet project [19] verifies distributed systems by formalizing transition systems and refinement in Dafny [27], a general-purpose deductive verification language. In IronFleet, transition systems are expressed using the rich Dafny type system, which is based on SMT combined with quantifiers. But as a result, queries to Z3, the underlying SMT solver, suffer from instability, especially when quantifiers—which are handled using triggers—are involved [28].

Compared to the aforementioned systems, mypyvy takes a similar approach to Ivy in using first-order logic without theories and aiming for unbounded verification, but unlike Ivy it focuses on automatically finding inductive invariants, and enabling research in that direction. We note that automated invariant inference depends on the reliability of invariant checking and related queries, which is absent from Dafny, TLA+, or Alloy (for the unbounded case), and obtained in mypyvy by using EPR in the style of [32].

Another related line of research is developing intermediate representation languages for invariant inference. VMT [11] is a format that extends SMT-LIB [3] to a transition system semantics. Constrained Horn Clauses (CHCs) [5,12] is another SMT-LIB extension that is similar to transition systems but more general (it captures, e.g., recursive programs). Both VMT and CHCs are typically used with rich SMT theories, whereas **mypyvy**'s logic is centered around uninterpreted first-order logic and quantifiers.

Acknowledgements. The research leading to these results has received funding from the European Research Council under the European Union's Horizon 2020 research and innovation programme (grant agreement No [759102-SVIS]). This research was partially supported by the Israeli Science Foundation (ISF) grant No. 2117/23.

References

1. Alloy 6 announcement (2021). https://alloytools.org/alloy6.html. Accessed 03 Feb 2023
2. Barbosa, H., et al.: cvc5: A versatile and industrial-strength SMT solver. In: Fisman, D., Rosu, G. (eds.) ETAPS 2022, Part I. LNCS, vol. 13243, pp. 415–442. Springer, Cham (2022). https://doi.org/10.1007/978-3-030-99524-9_24
3. Barrett, C., Stump, A., Tinelli, C.: The SMT-LIB standard: version 2.0. In: Gupta, A., Kroening, D. (eds.) Proceedings of the 8th International Workshop on Satisfiability Modulo Theories (Edinburgh, UK) (2010)
4. Berkovits, I., Lazić, M., Losa, G., Padon, O., Shoham, S.: Verification of threshold-based distributed algorithms by decomposition to decidable logics. In: Dillig, I., Tasiran, S. (eds.) CAV 2019. LNCS, vol. 11562, pp. 245–266. Springer, Cham (2019). https://doi.org/10.1007/978-3-030-25543-5_15
5. Bjørner, N., Gurfinkel, A., McMillan, K., Rybalchenko, A.: Horn clause solvers for program verification. In: Beklemishev, L.D., Blass, A., Dershowitz, N., Finkbeiner, B., Schulte, W. (eds.) Fields of Logic and Computation II. LNCS, vol. 9300, pp. 24–51. Springer, Cham (2015). https://doi.org/10.1007/978-3-319-23534-9_2
6. Börger, E., Stärk, R.F.: Abstract State Machines. A Method for High-Level System Design and Analysis. Springer, Heidelberg (2003). http://www.springer.com/computer/swe/book/978-3-540-00702-9
7. Bradley, A.R.: SAT-based model checking without unrolling. In: Jhala, R., Schmidt, D. (eds.) VMCAI 2011. LNCS, vol. 6538, pp. 70–87. Springer, Heidelberg (2011). https://doi.org/10.1007/978-3-642-18275-4_7
8. Brunel, J., Chemouil, D., Cunha, A., Macedo, N.: The electrum analyzer: model checking relational first-order temporal specifications. In: Huchard, M., Kästner, C., Fraser, G. (eds.) Proceedings of the 33rd ACM/IEEE International Conference on Automated Software Engineering. ASE 2018, Montpellier, France, 3–7 September 2018, pp. 884–887. ACM (2018). https://doi.org/10.1145/3238147.3240475
9. Chajed, T.: Ivy to mypyvy translator (2023). https://github.com/tchajed/ivy-to-mypyvy
10. Chaudhuri, K., Doligez, D., Lamport, L., Merz, S.: The TLA+ proof system: building a heterogeneous verification platform. In: Cavalcanti, A., Deharbe, D., Gaudel, M.-C., Woodcock, J. (eds.) ICTAC 2010. LNCS, vol. 6255, pp. 44–44. Springer, Heidelberg (2010). https://doi.org/10.1007/978-3-642-14808-8_3
11. Cimatti, A., Griggio, A., Tonetta, S.: The VMT-LIB language and tools. CoRR abs/2109.12821 (2021). https://arxiv.org/abs/2109.12821

12. De Angelis, E., Hari Govind, V.K.: CHC-COMP 2022: competition report. In: Hamilton, G.W., Kahsai, T., Proietti, M. (eds.) Proceedings 9th Workshop on Horn Clauses for Verification and Synthesis and 10th International Workshop on Verification and Program Transformation. HCVS/VPT@ETAPS 2022, and 10th International Workshop on Verification and Program TransformationMunich, Germany, 3 April 2022. EPTCS, vol. 373, pp. 44–62 (2022). https://doi.org/10.4204/EPTCS.373.5

13. de Moura, L., Bjørner, N.: Z3: an efficient SMT solver. In: Ramakrishnan, C.R., Rehof, J. (eds.) TACAS 2008. LNCS, vol. 4963, pp. 337–340. Springer, Heidelberg (2008). https://doi.org/10.1007/978-3-540-78800-3_24

14. Feldman, Y.M.Y., Wilcox, J.R., Shoham, S., Sagiv, M.: Inferring inductive invariants from phase structures. In: Dillig, I., Tasiran, S. (eds.) CAV 2019. LNCS, vol. 11562, pp. 405–425. Springer, Cham (2019). https://doi.org/10.1007/978-3-030-25543-5_23

15. Goel, A., Sakallah, K.: On symmetry and quantification: a new approach to verify distributed protocols. In: Dutle, A., Moscato, M.M., Titolo, L., Muñoz, C.A., Perez, I. (eds.) NFM 2021. LNCS, vol. 12673, pp. 131–150. Springer, Cham (2021). https://doi.org/10.1007/978-3-030-76384-8_9

16. Goel, A., Sakallah, K.A.: Towards an automatic proof of Lamport's paxos. In: Formal Methods in Computer Aided Design. FMCAD 2021, New Haven, CT, USA, 19–22 October 2021, pp. 112–122. IEEE (2021). https://doi.org/10.34727/2021/isbn.978-3-85448-046-4_20

17. Gurevich, Y.: Evolving Algebras 1993: Lipari Guide, pp. 9–36. Oxford University Press, Specification and Vgalidation Methods edn. (1995). https://arxiv.org/pdf/1808.06255.pdf

18. Hance, T., Heule, M., Martins, R., Parno, B.: Finding invariants of distributed systems: it's a small (enough) world after all. In: Mickens, J., Teixeira, R. (eds.) 18th USENIX Symposium on Networked Systems Design and Implementation. NSDI 2021, 12–14 April 2021, pp. 115–131. USENIX Association (2021). https://www.usenix.org/conference/nsdi21/presentation/hance

19. Hawblitzel, C., et al.: IronFleet: proving practical distributed systems correct. In: Proceedings of the 25th ACM Symposium on Operating Systems Principles (SOSP), pp. 1–17. Monterey, CA (2015)

20. Jackson, D.: Software Abstractions: Logic, Language, and Analysis. MIT Press, Cambridge (2012)

21. Karbyshev, A., Bjørner, N., Itzhaky, S., Rinetzky, N., Shoham, S.: Property-directed inference of universal invariants or proving their absence. J. ACM **64**(1), 7:1–7:33 (2017)

22. Koenig, J.R., Padon, O., Immerman, N., Aiken, A.: First-order quantified separators. In: Donaldson, A.F., Torlak, E. (eds.) Proceedings of the 41st ACM SIGPLAN International Conference on Programming Language Design and Implementation. PLDI 2020, London, UK, 15–20 June 2020, pp. 703–717. ACM (2020). https://doi.org/10.1145/3385412.3386018

23. Koenig, J.R., Padon, O., Shoham, S., Aiken, A.: Inferring invariants with quantifier alternations: taming the search space explosion. In: TACAS 2022. LNCS, vol. 13243, pp. 338–356. Springer, Cham (2022). https://doi.org/10.1007/978-3-030-99524-9_18

24. Konnov, I., Kukovec, J., Tran, T.: TLA+ model checking made symbolic. Proc. ACM Program. Lang. **3**(OOPSLA), 123:1–123:30 (2019). https://doi.org/10.1145/3360549

25. Lamport, L.: The part-time parliament. ACM Trans. Comput. Syst. **16**(2), 133–169 (1998)
26. Lamport, L.: Specifying Systems: The TLA$^+$ Language and Tools for Hardware and Software Engineers. Addison-Wesley Professional, Boston (2002)
27. Leino, K.R.M.: Dafny: an automatic program verifier for functional correctness. In: Clarke, E.M., Voronkov, A. (eds.) LPAR 2010. LNCS (LNAI), vol. 6355, pp. 348–370. Springer, Heidelberg (2010). https://doi.org/10.1007/978-3-642-17511-4_20
28. Leino, K.R.M., Pit-Claudel, C.: Trigger selection strategies to stabilize program verifiers. In: Chaudhuri, S., Farzan, A. (eds.) CAV 2016. LNCS, vol. 9779, pp. 361–381. Springer, Cham (2016). https://doi.org/10.1007/978-3-319-41528-4_20
29. Macedo, N., Brunel, J., Chemouil, D., Cunha, A., Kuperberg, D.: Lightweight specification and analysis of dynamic systems with rich configurations. In: Zimmermann, T., Cleland-Huang, J., Su, Z. (eds.) Proceedings of the 24th ACM SIGSOFT International Symposium on Foundations of Software Engineering. FSE 2016, Seattle, WA, USA, 13–18 November 2016, pp. 373–383. ACM (2016). https://doi.org/10.1145/2950290.2950318
30. McMillan, K.L., Padon, O.: Ivy: a multi-modal verification tool for distributed algorithms. In: Lahiri, S.K., Wang, C. (eds.) CAV 2020, Part II. LNCS, vol. 12225, pp. 190–202. Springer, Cham (2020). https://doi.org/10.1007/978-3-030-53291-8_12
31. Padon, O.: Deductive verification of distributed protocols in first-order logic. Ph.D. thesis, Tel Aviv University (2018)
32. Padon, O., Losa, G., Sagiv, M., Shoham, S.: Paxos made EPR: decidable reasoning about distributed protocols. PACMPL **1**(OOPSLA), 108:1–108:31 (2017)
33. Padon, O., McMillan, K.L., Panda, A., Sagiv, M., Shoham, S.: Ivy: safety verification by interactive generalization. In: Proceedings of the 2016 ACM SIGPLAN Conference on Programming Language Design and Implementation (PLDI), pp. 614–630. Santa Barbara, CA (2016)
34. Padon, O., Wilcox, J.R., Koenig, J.R., McMillan, K.L., Aiken, A.: Induction duality: Primal-dual search for invariants. Proc. ACM Program. Lang. **6**(POPL), 1–29 (2022).https://doi.org/10.1145/3498712
35. Piskac, R., de Moura, L.M., Bjørner, N.S.: Deciding effectively propositional logic using DPLL and substitution sets. J. Autom. Reason. **44**(4), 401–424 (2010)
36. Pîrlea, G.: Translation from ivy to mypyvy (2024). https://github.com/kenmcmil/ivy/pull/76
37. Ramsey, F.P.: On a problem of formal logic. Proc. Lond. Math. Soc. **s2–30**(1), 264–286 (1930). https://doi.org/10.1112/plms/s2-30.1.264, https://londmathsoc.onlinelibrary.wiley.com/doi/abs/10.1112/plms/s2-30.1.264
38. Taube, M., et al.: Modularity for decidability of deductive verification with applications to distributed systems. In: Proceedings of the 2018 ACM SIGPLAN Conference on Programming Language Design and Implementation (PLDI). Philadelphia, PA (2018)
39. Wilcox, J.R., Feldman, Y.M.Y., Padon, O., Shoham, S.: mypyvy: A Research Platform for Verification of Transition Systems in First-Order Logic (Artifact) (2024). https://doi.org/10.5281/zenodo.10948110
40. Yao, J., Tao, R., Gu, R., Nieh, J.: Duoai: fast, automated inference of inductive invariants for verifying distributed protocols. In: Aguilera, M.K., Weatherspoon, H. (eds.) 16th USENIX Symposium on Operating Systems Design and Implementation. OSDI 2022, Carlsbad, CA, USA, 11–13 July 2022, pp. 485–501. USENIX Association (2022). https://www.usenix.org/conference/osdi22/presentation/yao

41. Yao, J., Tao, R., Gu, R., Nieh, J.: Mostly automated verification of liveness properties for distributed protocols with ranking functions. Proc. ACM Program. Lang. **8**(POPL) (2024). https://doi.org/10.1145/3632877
42. Yao, J., Tao, R., Gu, R., Nieh, J., Jana, S., Ryan, G.: Distai: data-driven automated invariant learning for distributed protocols. In: Brown, A.D., Lorch, J.R. (eds.) 15th USENIX Symposium on Operating Systems Design and Implementation. OSDI 2021, 14–16 July 2021, pp. 405–421. USENIX Association (2021). https://www.usenix.org/conference/osdi21/presentation/yao
43. Yu, Y., Manolios, P., Lamport, L.: Model checking TLA$^+$ specifications. In: Pierre, L., Kropf, T. (eds.) CHARME 1999. LNCS, vol. 1703, pp. 54–66. Springer, Heidelberg (1999). https://doi.org/10.1007/3-540-48153-2_6

Efficient Implementation of an Abstract Domain of Quantified First-Order Formulas

Eden Frenkel[1]([✉]) [iD], Tej Chajed[2] [iD], Oded Padon[3] [iD], and Sharon Shoham[1] [iD]

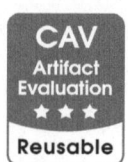

[1] Tel Aviv University, Tel Aviv, Israel
edenfrenkel@mail.tau.ac.il
[2] University of Wisconsin-Madison, Madison, WI, USA
[3] VMware Research, Palo Alto, CA, USA

Abstract. This paper lays a practical foundation for using abstract interpretation with an abstract domain that consists of sets of quantified first-order logic formulas. This abstract domain seems infeasible at first sight due to the complexity of the formulas involved and the enormous size of sets of formulas (abstract elements). We introduce an efficient representation of abstract elements, which eliminates redundancies based on a novel syntactic subsumption relation that under-approximates semantic entailment. We develop algorithms and data structures to efficiently compute the join of an abstract element with the abstraction of a concrete state, operating on the representation of abstract elements. To demonstrate feasibility of the domain, we use our data structures and algorithms to implement a symbolic abstraction algorithm that computes the least fixpoint of the best abstract transformer of a transition system, which corresponds to the strongest inductive invariant. We succeed at finding, for example, the least fixpoint for Paxos (which in our representation has 1,438 formulas with $\forall^*\exists^*\forall^*$ quantification) in time comparable to state-of-the-art property-directed approaches.

Keywords: Abstract interpretation · First-order logic · Symbolic abstraction · Invariant inference · Quantifier alternation · Least fixpoint

1 Introduction

Recent years have seen significant progress in automated verification based on first-order logic. In particular, quantified first-order formulas have been used to model many systems, their properties and their inductive invariants [1,6,9–11,13–18,20,22,24,26,28,30,31]. Automatic verification in this domain is challenging because of the combination of the complexity of first-order reasoning performed by solvers and the enormous search space of formulas, especially due to the use of quantifiers. Despite these challenges, there are impressive success stories of automatically inferring quantified inductive invariants for complex distributed and concurrent algorithms [9–11,14,15,17,26,30,31].

© The Author(s) 2024
A. Gurfinkel and V. Ganesh (Eds.): CAV 2024, LNCS 14682, pp. 86–108, 2024.
https://doi.org/10.1007/978-3-031-65630-9_5

Previous works on invariant inference for first-order logic search for invariants in the form of sets of formulas (interpreted conjunctively) from some language of quantified first-order formulas. Each approach fixes some restricted, typically finite (but extremely large) language $\mathcal{L}$, and searches for a set of $\mathcal{L}$-formulas that form an inductive invariant using sophisticated heuristics and algorithmic techniques, such as property-directed reachability (IC3) [14,15], incremental induction [11,26], generalization from finite instances [9,17], and clever forms of pruning and exploration [30,31]. While prior techniques can successfully handle some challenging examples, the accumulation of specially-tailored techniques makes the results computed by these techniques unpredictable, and makes it hard to extend or improve them.

Abstract interpretation [4,5] suggests a more systematic approach for the development of verification algorithms based on logical languages, where we consider sets of $\mathcal{L}$-formulas as elements in an abstract domain. The abstraction of a set of states S in this domain is given by $\alpha(S) = \{\varphi \in \mathcal{L} \mid \forall s \in S.\ s \models \varphi\}$, i.e., the formulas that are satisfied by all states in the set. Algorithms based on abstract interpretation are better understood and are easier to combine, extend, and improve. However, an abstract domain of quantified first-order formulas seems infeasible: for interesting systems, the abstract elements involved in proofs would contain an astronomical number of formulas.

The main contribution of this work is to develop algorithms and data structures that make an abstract domain based on quantified first-order formulas feasible. Working with this abstract domain introduces two main challenges: (i) efficiently storing and manipulating abstract elements comprising of many formulas, and (ii) overcoming solver limitations when reasoning over them. This work focuses on the first challenge and adopts ideas from prior work [15] to deal with the second. Our techniques lay a practical foundation for using an abstract interpretation approach to develop new analyses in the domain of quantified first-order formulas. We demonstrate feasibility of the abstract domain by applying it to an analysis of several intricate distributed protocols.

Our first key idea is to design a *subsumption relation* for quantified first-order formulas and use it to represent abstract elements (sets of formulas) more compactly, pruning away some formulas that are redundant since they are equivalent to or are entailed by another formula. Subsumption over propositional clauses (disjunctions of literals) is traditionally used for similar pruning purposes (e.g., [19]), but the generalization to first-order formulas, which include disjunction, conjunction, and quantification, is novel.

The second key ingredient of our approach is a way to manipulate abstract elements in our representation. Rather than implementing the standard operations of α (abstraction) and $\sqcup$ (abstract join), we observe that our subsumption-based representation makes it more natural to directly implement an operation that computes the join of an abstract element a with the abstraction of a given concrete state s, i.e., $a \sqcup \alpha(\{s\})$. This operation can be used to compute the abstraction of a set of states, and can also be used to compute the least fixpoint of the best abstract transformer (in the style of symbolic abstraction [27]). The crux of computing $a \sqcup \alpha(\{s\})$ is to *weaken* the formulas in the representation of a to formulas that are subsumed by them and that s satisfies.

Finally, the third key ingredient of our approach is a data structure for storing a set of formulas, with efficient filters for (i) formulas that a given state does not satisfy, and (ii) formulas that subsume a given formula. This data structure is then used to store abstract elements, and the filters make the implementation of $a \sqcup \alpha(\{s\})$ more efficient.

While the paper presents the ingredients of our approach (subsumption, weakening, and the data structure) sequentially, they are interconnected; they all affect each other in subtle ways, and must be designed and understood together. Specifically, there is an intricate tradeoff between the precision of subsumption, which determines the extent of pruning (and therefore the compactness of the representation), and the complexity of abstract domain operations such as weakening (e.g., for computing $a \sqcup \alpha(\{s\})$). The definitions, algorithms, and data structures we present are carefully crafted to balance these considerations. Our subsumption relation, which approximates entailment, is cheap to compute, eliminates enough redundancy to keep the representation of abstract elements compact, and enables an efficient implementation of the weakening operation.

To evaluate our implementation of the abstract domain, we use it to implement a symbolic abstraction [27] procedure that computes the least fixpoint of the best abstract transformer of a transition system (i.e., the strongest inductive invariant for the transition system in the given language). Our evaluation uses benchmarks from the literature, mostly from safety verification of distributed protocols. While our fixpoint computation algorithm is not fully competitive with property-directed invariant inference approaches that exploit various sophisticated heuristics and optimizations, it does demonstrate that fixpoint computation in our abstract domain is feasible, which is quite surprising given the amount of quantified formulas the domain considers. Our approach successfully computes the least fixpoint for transition systems that previously could only be analyzed using property-directed, heuristic techniques (which do not compute the least fixpoint, but an unpredictable heuristic fixpoint). For example, we succeed at finding the strongest inductive invariant of Paxos as modeled in [24] (which in our representation has 1,438 formulas with $\forall^*\exists^*\forall^*$ quantification, representing orders of magnitude more subsumed formulas).

In summary, this paper makes the following contributions:

1. We develop a compact representation of sets of formulas based on a novel syntactic *subsumption relation*. We make a tradeoff here between the extent of pruning and efficiency, accepting some redundant formulas in exchange for practical algorithms. (Sect. 3)
2. We show how to implement a key operation of *weakening* a formula to be satisfied by a given state, and leverage it to compute the join of an abstract element and the abstraction of a state, when abstract elements are represented using our subsumption-based representation. (Sect. 4)
3. We present a data structure that provides an efficient implementation of operations used in the join computation described above. (Sect. 5)

4. We evaluate the approach by applying it to compute the least fixpoint of the best abstract transformer for several distributed and concurrent protocols from the literature, demonstrating the promise of our approach. (Sect. 6)

The rest of this paper is organized as follows: Sect. 2 introduces definitions and notation, Sects. 3 to 6 present the main contributions outlined above, Sect. 7 discusses related work, and Sect. 8 concludes. The proofs of all theorems stated in the paper are given in [8].

2   Background

First-Order Logic. For simplicity of the presentation, we present our approach for single-sorted first-order logic, although in practice we consider many-sorted logic. The generalization of our methods to many-sorted logic is straightforward.

Given a first-order signature Σ that consists of constant, function and relation symbols, the sets of terms and formulas are defined in the usual way: a *term t* is either a variable x, a constant c or a function application $f(t_1, \ldots, t_n)$ on simpler terms; a *formula* is either an equality between terms $t_1 = t_2$, a relation application $r(t_1, \ldots, t_n)$ on terms, or the result of applying Boolean connectives or quantification. We also include $\bot$ as a formula (that is never satisfied).

Terms and formulas are interpreted over first-order structures and assignments to the (free) variables. Given a first-order signature Σ, a structure $\sigma = (\mathcal{U}, \mathcal{I})$ consists of a *universe* $\mathcal{U}$ and an *interpretation* $\mathcal{I}$ to the symbols in Σ. We denote by **structs**$[\Sigma]$ the set of structures of Σ whose universe is a finite set.[1] When considering formulas with free variables V, and given some structure $\sigma = (\mathcal{U}, \mathcal{I})$, an *assignment* $\mu : V \to \mathcal{U}$ maps each variable to an element of the structure's universe. We write $(\sigma, \mu) \models \varphi$ to mean that a structure σ with an assignment μ satisfies a formula φ, and $\psi \models \varphi$ to mean that a formula ψ semantically entails φ, i.e., $(\sigma, \mu) \models \psi$ whenever $(\sigma, \mu) \models \varphi$.

Abstract Interpretation. Abstract interpretation [4,5] is a framework for approximating the semantics of systems. It assumes a concrete domain and an abstract domain, each given by a partially ordered set, $(\mathcal{C}, \sqsubseteq_\mathcal{C})$ and $(\mathcal{A}, \sqsubseteq_\mathcal{A})$, respectively. These are related via a Galois connection consisting of a monotone abstraction function $\alpha : \mathcal{C} \to \mathcal{A}$ and a monotone concretization function $\gamma : \mathcal{A} \to \mathcal{C}$ satisfying $\alpha(c) \sqsubseteq_\mathcal{A} a \iff c \sqsubseteq_\mathcal{C} \gamma(a)$ for all $a \in \mathcal{A}$ and $c \in \mathcal{C}$.

In this work we consider logical abstract domains parameterized by a finite first-order language $\mathcal{L}$ of closed formulas over signature Σ. In this context, concrete elements are sets of states from $\mathbb{S} = \mathbf{structs}[\Sigma]$,[2] i.e., $\mathcal{C} = \mathcal{P}(\mathbb{S})$, ordered by $\sqsubseteq_\mathcal{C} = \subseteq$ (set inclusion). Abstract elements are sets of formulas from $\mathcal{L}$, i.e., $\mathcal{A} = \mathcal{P}(\mathcal{L})$, ordered by $\sqsubseteq_\mathcal{A} = \supseteq$, and the Galois connection is given by $\alpha(S) = \{\varphi \in \mathcal{L} \mid \forall s \in \mathbb{S}.\ s \models \varphi\}$ and $\gamma(F) = \{s \in \mathbb{S} \mid \forall \varphi \in F.\ s \models \varphi\}$. That is, abstraction in this domain consists of all $\mathcal{L}$-formulas that hold on a given

---

[1] We restrict our attention to FOL fragments that have a finite-model property.

[2] Later we consider non-closed formulas and let $\mathbb{S}$ denote structures with assignments.

concrete set, and concretization consists of all states that satisfy a given set of formulas. Note that sets of formulas are interpreted conjunctively in this context.

This logical abstract domain forms a join-semilattice (meaning every two elements have a least upper bound) with a least element. The least element, denoted $\perp_{\mathcal{A}}$ (not to be confused with the formula $\perp$), is $\mathcal{L}$, and join, denoted $\sqcup$, corresponds to set intersection. For example, $F \sqcup \alpha(\{s\}) = F \cap \{\varphi \in \mathcal{L} \mid s \models \varphi\} = \{\varphi \in F \mid s \models \varphi\}$, and can be understood as *weakening* F by eliminating from it all formulas that are not satisfied by s.

3   Subsumption-Based Representation of Sets of Formulas

In this section we develop an efficient representation for elements in the abstract domain $\mathcal{A} = \mathcal{P}(\mathcal{L})$ induced by a finite first-order language $\mathcal{L}$. The abstract elements are sets of formulas, interpreted conjunctively, which may be extremely large (albeit finite). Our idea is to reduce the size and complexity of such sets by avoiding redundancies that result from semantic equivalence and entailment. For example, when representing a set of formulas we would like to avoid storing both φ and ψ when they are semantically equivalent ($\varphi \equiv \psi$). Similarly, if $\varphi \models \psi$ then instead of keeping both φ and ψ we would like to keep only φ.

In practice, it is not possible to remove all such redundancies based on semantic equivalence and entailment, since, as we shall see in Sect. 4, performing operations over the reduced representation of abstract elements involves recovering certain subsumed formulas, and finding these in the case of entailment essentially requires checking all formulas in the language. This is clearly infeasible for complex languages such as the ones used in our benchmarks (see Table 1), and is exacerbated by the fact that merely checking entailment is expensive for formulas with quantifiers. Instead, our key idea is to remove redundancies based on a cheap-to-compute subsumption relation, which approximates semantic entailment, and enables efficient operations over abstract elements such as joining them with an abstraction of a concrete state.

We start the section with an inductive definition of a family of finite first-order languages that underlies all of our developments (Sect. 3.1). We then introduce a syntactic *subsumption* relation for first-order formulas (Sect. 3.2), which we leverage to develop an efficient *canonicalization* of formulas, effectively determining a single representative formula for each subsumption-equivalence class (Sect. 3.3). We then use antichains of canonical formulas, i.e., sets of canonical formulas where no formula is subsumed by another, to represent sets of formulas (Sect. 3.4). Sects. 4 and 5 develop ways to effectively manipulate this representation in order to accommodate important operations for abstract interpretation algorithms, such as weakening an abstraction to include a given concrete state.

3.1   Bounded First-Order Languages

At core of our approach is an inductively-defined family of first-order languages, termed *bounded first-order languages*. These languages are all finite and bound various syntactic measures of formulas (e.g., number of quantifiers, size of the Boolean structure), which, in turn, determine the precision of the abstract domain. The inductive definition of bounded languages facilitates efficient recursive implementations of our developments.

We fix a signature Σ and a variable set V. Definition 1 provides the inductive definition of the family of bounded first-order languages (over Σ and V), where each language $\mathcal{L}$ is also equipped with a bottom element $\bot_{\mathcal{L}}$ (equivalent to false). We use $\mathfrak{S}_X$ to denote the set of permutations over a set of variables X, and use $\varphi\pi$ to denote the formula obtained by substituting free variables in a formula φ according to $\pi \in \mathfrak{S}_X$. A set of formulas F is $\mathfrak{S}_X$-closed if $\varphi\pi \in F$ for every $\varphi \in F, \pi \in \mathfrak{S}_X$. All bounded first-order languages will be $\mathfrak{S}_V$-closed; this will be important for canonicalization. We use $\bar{\varphi} = \langle \varphi_1, \ldots, \varphi_n \rangle$ to denote a sequence of formulas, φ_{-i} to denote the formula φ_{n-i+1} in the sequence, $|\bar{\varphi}|$ for the length of $\bar{\varphi}$, and $[\bar{\varphi}]$ for its set of indices $\{1, \ldots, |\bar{\varphi}|\}$. We use $\mathcal{L}^*$ for the set of all (finite) sequences of formulas from $\mathcal{L}$, and ϵ for the empty sequence ($|\epsilon| = 0$).

Definition 1 (Bounded First-Order Languages). *A bounded first-order language is one of the following, where $X \subseteq V$ denotes a finite set of variables, and $\mathcal{L}$, $\mathcal{L}_1$ and $\mathcal{L}_2$ denote bounded first-order languages:*

$$\mathcal{L}_A = A \cup \{\bot\} \text{ with } \bot_{\mathcal{L}_A} = \bot, \text{ where } A \text{ is any finite } \mathfrak{S}_V\text{-closed set of formulas}$$
$$\vee[\mathcal{L}_1, \mathcal{L}_2] = \{\varphi_1 \vee \varphi_2 \mid \varphi_1 \in \mathcal{L}_1, \varphi_2 \in \mathcal{L}_2\} \text{ with } \bot_{\vee[\mathcal{L}_1, \mathcal{L}_2]} = \bot_{\mathcal{L}_1} \vee \bot_{\mathcal{L}_2}$$
$$\wedge[\mathcal{L}_1, \mathcal{L}_2] = \{\varphi_1 \wedge \varphi_2 \mid \varphi_1 \in \mathcal{L}_1, \varphi_2 \in \mathcal{L}_2\} \text{ with } \bot_{\wedge[\mathcal{L}_1, \mathcal{L}_2]} = \bot_{\mathcal{L}_1} \wedge \bot_{\mathcal{L}_2}$$
$$\vee_k[\mathcal{L}] = \{\bigvee \bar{\varphi} \mid \bar{\varphi} \in \mathcal{L}^* \text{ and } |\bar{\varphi}| \leq k\} \text{ with } \bot_{\vee_k[\mathcal{L}]} = \bigvee \epsilon, \text{ where } k \in \mathbb{N}$$
$$\wedge_\omega[\mathcal{L}] = \{\bigwedge \bar{\varphi} \mid \epsilon \neq \bar{\varphi} \in \mathcal{L}^*\} \text{ with } \bot_{\wedge_\omega[\mathcal{L}]} = \bigwedge \langle \bot_{\mathcal{L}} \rangle$$
$$\exists_X[\mathcal{L}] = \{\exists X.\varphi \mid \varphi \in \mathcal{L}\} \text{ with } \bot_{\exists_X[\mathcal{L}]} = \exists X.\bot_{\mathcal{L}}$$
$$\forall_X[\mathcal{L}] = \{\forall X.\varphi \mid \varphi \in \mathcal{L}\} \text{ with } \bot_{\forall_X[\mathcal{L}]} = \forall X.\bot_{\mathcal{L}}$$
$$\exists\!\forall_X[\mathcal{L}] = \{QX.\varphi \mid \varphi \in \mathcal{L}, Q \in \{\exists, \forall\}\} \text{ with } \bot_{\exists\!\forall_X[\mathcal{L}]} = \forall X.\bot_{\mathcal{L}}$$

The base case is any finite set of formulas (over Σ and V) that is closed under variable permutations, augmented by $\bot$ (denoting false). Typical examples include the set of all literals over Σ and V with a bounded depth of function applications. We introduce binary language constructors for disjunction and conjunction, each operating on two possibly different languages. We also introduce constructors for homogeneous disjunction of at most k disjuncts, as well as unbounded non-empty conjunction, over any single language. Finally, we introduce constructors for quantification ($\exists$ or $\forall$) over a finite set of variables and a language, as well as a constructor that includes both quantifiers for languages where both options are desired. Note that for the construction of a logical abstract domain, we are interested in languages where all formulas are closed (have no free variables), but the inductive definition includes languages with free variables.

The semantics of formulas in each language is defined w.r.t. states $\mathbb{S}$ that consist of first-order structures and assignments to the free variables, following the standard first-order semantics, extended to conjunctions and disjunctions of finite sequences in the natural way, where $\bigvee \epsilon \equiv \bot$. (We do not allow $\bigwedge \epsilon$, which would have been equivalent to "true", since it is not useful for our developments.)

Observe that for a fixed language $\mathcal{L}$, the formulas $\varphi_1 \vee \varphi_2 \in \vee[\mathcal{L}, \mathcal{L}]$ and $\bigvee \langle \varphi_1, \varphi_2 \rangle \in \vee_2[\mathcal{L}]$ are syntactically different but semantically equivalent (and similarly for conjunctions). Nonetheless, we introduce homogeneous disjunction and conjunction since they admit a more precise subsumption relation, yielding a more efficient representation of sets of formulas. Also note that we consider bounded disjunction but unbounded conjunction; Sect. 4.3 explains this choice.

Example 1. $\mathcal{L} = \forall_{\{x,y\}}[\vee_2[\mathcal{L}_A]]$ with $A = \{p(x), \neg p(x), p(y), \neg p(y)\}$ is a bounded first-order language over signature Σ that has one unary predicate p and variables $V = \{x, y\}$. Formulas in this language are universally quantified homogeneous disjunctions of at most two literals. For instance, $\mathcal{L}$ includes $\forall\{x,y\}. \bigvee \epsilon$, which is also $\bot_{\mathcal{L}}$, as well as $\forall\{x,y\}. \bigvee \langle p(x) \rangle$, $\forall\{x,y\}. \bigvee \langle p(x), \neg p(y) \rangle$, etc.

3.2 Syntactic Subsumption

Next, we define a *subsumption* relation for each bounded first-order language. The subsumption relation serves as an easy-to-compute under-approximation for entailment between formulas from the same language. We use $\sqsubseteq_{\mathcal{L}}$ to denote the subsumption relation for language $\mathcal{L}$, or simply $\sqsubseteq$ when $\mathcal{L}$ is clear from context. When $\varphi \sqsubseteq \psi$ we say φ *subsumes* ψ, and then we will also have $\varphi \models \psi$.

Definition 2 (Subsumption). *We define $\sqsubseteq_{\mathcal{L}}$ inductively, following the definition of bounded first-order languages, as follows, where $\circ \in \{\vee, \wedge\}$, $k \in \mathbb{N}$, $Q, Q' \in \{\exists, \forall\}$, X is a finite set of variables, and $\mathcal{L}$, $\mathcal{L}_1$ and $\mathcal{L}_2$ are bounded first-order languages:*

$$\varphi \sqsubseteq_{\mathcal{L}_A} \psi \text{ iff } \varphi = \bot \text{ or } \varphi = \psi$$

$$\varphi_1 \circ \varphi_2 \sqsubseteq_{\circ[\mathcal{L}_1, \mathcal{L}_2]} \psi_1 \circ \psi_2 \text{ iff } \varphi_1 \sqsubseteq_{\mathcal{L}_1} \psi_1 \text{ and } \varphi_2 \sqsubseteq_{\mathcal{L}_2} \psi_2 \quad \text{(pointwise extension)}$$

$$\bigvee \bar{\varphi} \sqsubseteq_{\vee_k[\mathcal{L}]} \bigvee \bar{\psi} \text{ iff } \exists m \colon [\bar{\varphi}] \to [\bar{\psi}]. \forall i \in [\bar{\varphi}]. \varphi_i \sqsubseteq \psi_{m(i)} \text{ and } m \text{ is injective}$$

$$\bigwedge \bar{\varphi} \sqsubseteq_{\wedge_\omega[\mathcal{L}]} \bigwedge \bar{\psi} \text{ iff } \exists m \colon [\bar{\psi}] \to [\bar{\varphi}]. \forall i \in [\bar{\psi}]. \varphi_{m(i)} \sqsubseteq \psi_i$$

$$(QX.\varphi) \sqsubseteq_{Q_X[\mathcal{L}]} (QX.\psi) \text{ iff } \exists \pi \in \mathfrak{S}_X. \varphi \sqsubseteq_{\mathcal{L}} \psi\pi$$

$$(QX.\varphi) \sqsubseteq_{\exists_X[\mathcal{L}]} (Q'X.\psi) \text{ iff } \exists \pi \in \mathfrak{S}_X. \varphi \sqsubseteq_{\mathcal{L}} \psi\pi, \text{ and } Q = \forall \text{ or } Q' = \exists$$

The subsumption relation of a bounded first-order language $\mathcal{L}$ is composed, hierarchically, from the subsumption relations of the bounded first-order languages that $\mathcal{L}$ is composed from. For example, the languages participating in the composition of $\mathcal{L} = \forall_{\{x,y\}}[\vee_2[\mathcal{L}_A]]$ defined in Example 1 are $\mathcal{L}_A$, $\vee_2[\mathcal{L}_A]$, and $\forall_{\{x,y\}}[\vee_2[\mathcal{L}_A]]$, and each is equipped with its own subsumption relation.

In the base case, formulas in $\mathcal{L}_A$ are only subsumed by themselves or by $\bot$. For example, considering Example 1, $p(x) \not\sqsubseteq_{\mathcal{L}_A} p(y)$. Subsumption is lifted to languages obtained by binary conjunctions and disjunctions in a pointwise manner. For the languages obtained by homogeneous constructors, a mapping over indices determines which element of one sequence subsumes which element of the other. To approximate entailment, the mapping in the disjunctive case maps each element of $\bigvee \bar{\varphi}$ to one in $\bigvee \bar{\psi}$ that it subsumes, and in the conjunctive case maps each element of $\bigwedge \bar{\psi}$ to one in $\bigwedge \bar{\varphi}$ that subsumes it. As a result, subsumption is more precise in the homogeneous case than in the binary one. For example, considering A from Example 1, $p(x) \vee p(y) \not\sqsubseteq_{\vee[\mathcal{L}_A, \mathcal{L}_A]} p(y) \vee p(x)$, even though the formulas are semantically equivalent. On the other hand, $\bigvee\langle p(x), p(y)\rangle \sqsubseteq_{\vee_2[\mathcal{L}_A]} \bigvee\langle p(y), p(x)\rangle$

In the case of quantifiers, subsumption is lifted from the language of the body while considering permutations over the quantified variables. For example, in Example 1, $\forall\{x, y\}. \bigvee\langle p(x)\rangle \sqsubseteq_{\mathcal{L}} \forall\{x, y\}. \bigvee\langle p(y)\rangle$ due to variable permutations, even though $\bigvee\langle p(x)\rangle \not\sqsubseteq_{\vee_2[\mathcal{L}_A]} \bigvee\langle p(y)\rangle$. When both quantifiers are considered, a universal quantifier can subsume an existential one.

The injectivity requirement for $\sqsubseteq_{\vee_k[\mathcal{L}]}$ can be dropped without damaging any of the definitions or theorems in this section, but it enables a simpler definition of the weakening operator in Sect. 4 (as discussed further in Sect. 4.3).

The following theorem establishes the properties of $\sqsubseteq_{\mathcal{L}}$.

Theorem 1 (Properties of $\sqsubseteq_{\mathcal{L}}$). *For any bounded first-order language $\mathcal{L}$, $\sqsubseteq_{\mathcal{L}}$ is a preorder (i.e., reflexive and transitive) such that for any $\varphi, \psi \in \mathcal{L}$, if $\varphi \sqsubseteq \psi$ then $\varphi \models \psi$. Moreover, $\bot_{\mathcal{L}} \sqsubseteq_{\mathcal{L}} \varphi$ for any $\varphi \in \mathcal{L}$.*

As with entailment, where two distinct formulas can entail each other (i.e., be semantically equivalent), there can be distinct formulas $\varphi, \psi \in \mathcal{L}$ with $\varphi \sqsubseteq_{\mathcal{L}} \psi$ and $\psi \sqsubseteq_{\mathcal{L}} \varphi$ (since $\sqsubseteq_{\mathcal{L}}$ is not always a partial order, i.e., not antisymmetric). We call such formulas *subsumption-equivalent*, and denote this by $\varphi \equiv_{\sqsubseteq_{\mathcal{L}}} \psi$. ($\equiv_{\sqsubseteq_{\mathcal{L}}}$ is clearly an equivalence relation.) The existence of subsumption-equivalent formulas is a positive sign, indicating that our subsumption relation manages to capture nontrivial semantic equivalences. This is thanks to the definition of subsumption for homogeneous disjunction and conjunction, as well as for quantification. For example, $\bigvee\langle \varphi, \psi\rangle \equiv_{\sqsubseteq} \bigvee\langle \psi, \varphi\rangle$ (and similarly for conjunction), and if $\varphi \sqsubseteq \psi$ then $\bigwedge\langle \varphi, \psi\rangle \equiv_{\sqsubseteq} \bigwedge\langle\varphi\rangle$. For quantifiers, $QX.\varphi \equiv_{\sqsubseteq} QX.\varphi\pi$ for any $\pi \in \mathfrak{S}_X$ and $Q \in \{\exists, \forall\}$. (In contrast, $\sqsubseteq_{\mathcal{L}_A}$ is always antisymmetric, and the definitions of $\vee[\mathcal{L}_1, \mathcal{L}_2]$ and $\wedge[\mathcal{L}_1, \mathcal{L}_2]$ preserve antisymmetry.)

3.3 Canonicalization

As a first step towards an efficient representation of sets of formulas, we use a canonicalization of formulas w.r.t. $\equiv_{\sqsubseteq}$, which allows us to only store canonical formulas as unique representatives of their (subsumption-) equivalence class. In general, a *canonicalization* w.r.t. an equivalence relation $\equiv$ over a set S is a function $c: S \to S$ such that $\forall x \in S. c(x) \equiv x$ (representativeness) and $\forall x, y \in S. x \equiv y \iff c(x) = c(y)$ (decisiveness). We say that x is *canonical* if $c(x) = x$. When the equivalence relation is derived from a preorder (as $\equiv_{\sqsubseteq}$ is derived from $\sqsubseteq$) then the preorder is a partial order over the set of canonical elements. For our case, that means that $\sqsubseteq_{\mathcal{L}}$ is a partial order over the set of canonical $\mathcal{L}$-formulas.

It is useful, both for the algorithms developed in the sequel and for the definition of canonicalization for $Q_X[\mathcal{L}]$ ($Q \in \{\exists, \forall, \nexists\}$), to define a total order

$\leq_{\mathcal{L}}$ over canonical $\mathcal{L}$-formulas that extends $\sqsubseteq_{\mathcal{L}}$. We thus define the canonicalization function $c_{\mathcal{L}}$ and the total order $\leq_{\mathcal{L}}$ over canonical $\mathcal{L}$-formulas by mutual induction. For a set of canonical $\mathcal{L}$-formulas F, we use $\min_{\sqsubseteq_{\mathcal{L}}} F$ to denote the set of formulas in F not subsumed by others, i.e., $\min_{\sqsubseteq_{\mathcal{L}}} F = \{\varphi \in F \mid \forall \psi \in F \setminus \{\varphi\}. \, \psi \not\sqsubseteq \varphi\}$, and use $\min_{\leq_{\mathcal{L}}} F$ to denote the minimal element of a non-empty set F w.r.t. the total order $\leq_{\mathcal{L}}$. Finally, we use $\langle \bar{\varphi} \rangle_{\leq}$ for the sequence obtained by sorting $\bar{\varphi}$ according to $\leq$ in ascending order, and similarly $\langle F \rangle_{\leq}$ for the sequence obtained by sorting the elements of a set F.

Definition 3 (Canonicalization). *For every bounded first-order language $\mathcal{L}$, we define the* canonicalization function $c_{\mathcal{L}} \colon \mathcal{L} \to \mathcal{L}$ *and a total order* $\leq_{\mathcal{L}}$ *over canonical $\mathcal{L}$-formulas by mutual induction (where $\circ \in \{\vee, \wedge\}$ and $Q \in \{\exists, \forall\}$):*

$$c_{\mathcal{L}_A}(\varphi) = \varphi$$
$$c_{\circ[\mathcal{L}_1, \mathcal{L}_2]}(\varphi_1 \circ \varphi_2) = c_{\mathcal{L}_1}(\varphi_1) \circ c_{\mathcal{L}_2}(\varphi_2) \; \textit{(pointwise)}$$
$$c_{\vee_k[\mathcal{L}]}\left(\bigvee \bar{\varphi}\right) = \bigvee \langle c_{\mathcal{L}}(\varphi_1), \ldots, c_{\mathcal{L}}(\varphi_{|\bar{\varphi}|}) \rangle_{\leq_{\mathcal{L}}}$$
$$c_{\wedge_\omega[\mathcal{L}]}\left(\bigwedge \bar{\varphi}\right) = \bigwedge \langle \min_{\sqsubseteq_{\mathcal{L}}} \{c_{\mathcal{L}}(\varphi_1), \ldots, c_{\mathcal{L}}(\varphi_{|\bar{\varphi}|})\} \rangle_{\leq_{\mathcal{L}}}$$
$$c_{Q_X[\mathcal{L}]}(QX.\varphi) = QX. \min_{\leq_{\mathcal{L}}} \{c_{\mathcal{L}}(\varphi\pi) \mid \pi \in \mathfrak{S}_X\}$$
$$c_{\exists\!\forall_X[\mathcal{L}]}(QX.\varphi) = c_{Q_X[\mathcal{L}]}(QX.\varphi)$$

and

$$\leq_{\mathcal{L}_A} \textit{ is an arbitrary total order extending } \sqsubseteq_{\mathcal{L}_A}$$
$$\varphi_1 \circ \varphi_2 \leq_{\circ[\mathcal{L}_1, \mathcal{L}_2]} \psi_1 \circ \psi_2 \iff \varphi_1 <_{\mathcal{L}_1} \psi_1, \textit{ or } \varphi_1 = \psi_1 \textit{ and } \varphi_2 \leq_{\mathcal{L}_2} \psi_2$$
$$\bigvee \bar{\varphi} \leq_{\vee_k[\mathcal{L}]} \bigvee \bar{\psi} \iff \bar{\varphi} \textit{ is a suffix of } \bar{\psi},$$
$$\textit{or } \exists i \in [\bar{\varphi}] \cap [\bar{\psi}]. \; \varphi_{-i} <_{\mathcal{L}} \psi_{-i} \wedge \forall j < i. \; \varphi_{-j} = \psi_{-j}$$
$$\bigwedge \bar{\varphi} \leq_{\wedge_\omega[\mathcal{L}]} \bigwedge \bar{\psi} \iff \bar{\psi} \textit{ is a prefix of } \bar{\varphi},$$
$$\textit{or } \exists i \in [\bar{\varphi}] \cap [\bar{\psi}]. \; \varphi_i <_{\mathcal{L}} \psi_i \wedge \forall j < i. \; \varphi_j = \psi_j$$
$$QX.\varphi \leq_{Q_X[\mathcal{L}]} QX.\psi \iff \varphi \leq_{\mathcal{L}} \psi$$
$$QX.\varphi \leq_{\exists\!\forall_X[\mathcal{L}]} Q'X.\psi \iff Q = Q' \textit{ and } \varphi \leq_{\mathcal{L}} \psi, \textit{ or } Q = \forall \textit{ and } Q' = \exists$$

where $\varphi <_{\mathcal{L}} \psi$ is shorthand for "$\varphi \leq_{\mathcal{L}} \psi$ and $\varphi \neq \psi$".

Our inductive definition of canonicalization in Definition 3 recognizes the only possible sources of nontrivial subsumption-equivalence in our construction: non-canonicity of subformulas, ordering of sequences, internal subsumption in $\wedge_\omega[\cdot]$-sequences, and permuting of quantified variables. To address these, we canonicalize all subformulas, order their sequences w.r.t $\leq_{\mathcal{L}}$ in $\vee_k[\mathcal{L}]$ and $\wedge_\omega[\mathcal{L}]$, minimize $\wedge_\omega[\mathcal{L}]$-sequences w.r.t $\sqsubseteq_{\mathcal{L}}$, and in $Q_X[\mathcal{L}]$, $Q \in \{\exists, \forall, \exists\!\forall\}$, choose the permutation yielding the $\leq_{\mathcal{L}}$-least (canonical) body. For the total order in the cases of Boolean connectives, we use lexicographic-like orderings carefully designed to extend their associated subsumption relations (e.g., homogeneous disjunction uses a right-to-left lexicographic ordering). For quantification, the total order is directly lifted from the total order for canonical bodies.

As an example, consider $\mathcal{L} = \forall_{\{x,y\}}[\vee_2[\mathcal{L}_A]]$ from Example 1. To obtain a canonicalization for $\mathcal{L}$, we provide an arbitrary total order $\leq_{\mathcal{L}_A}$, say $p(x) <_{\mathcal{L}_A} \neg p(x) <_{\mathcal{L}_A} p(y) <_{\mathcal{L}_A} \neg p(y)$ (recall that $\bot \in \mathcal{L}_A$ is least). This uniquely determines the total order and canonicalization of $\mathcal{L}$ and all of its sub-languages. For example, canonicalization of both $\forall\{x,y\}. \bigvee\langle p(x)\rangle$ and $\forall\{x,y\}. \bigvee\langle p(y)\rangle$, which are $\sqsubseteq_{\mathcal{L}}$-equivalent, is $\forall\{x,y\}. \bigvee\langle p(x)\rangle$. This is because $p(x) <_{\mathcal{L}_A} p(y)$, and thus $c_{\vee_2[\mathcal{L}_A]}(\bigvee\langle p(x)\rangle) = \bigvee\langle p(x)\rangle <_{\vee_2[\mathcal{L}_A]} \bigvee\langle p(y)\rangle = c_{\vee_2[\mathcal{L}_A]}(\bigvee\langle p(y)\rangle)$. Note that $\bigvee\langle p(x)\rangle$ and $\bigvee\langle p(y)\rangle$ are both canonical, but adding quantifiers merges the two formulas into the same subsumption-equivalence class, necessarily making the quantified version of one of them non-canonical. Similarly, the $\sqsubseteq_{\vee_2[\mathcal{L}_A]}$-equivalent formulas $\bigvee\langle p(x), p(y)\rangle$ and $\bigvee\langle p(y), p(x)\rangle$ are both canonicalized into $\bigvee\langle p(x), p(y)\rangle$ (by sorting the sequences of literals according to $\leq_{\mathcal{L}_A}$).

The properties of $c_{\mathcal{L}}$ and $\leq_{\mathcal{L}}$ defined above are established by the following theorem, which ensures that Definition 3 is well-defined (e.g., that whenever $\min_{\leq_{\mathcal{L}}}$ is used, $\leq_{\mathcal{L}}$ is a total order).

Theorem 2. *For any bounded language $\mathcal{L}$, $c_{\mathcal{L}}$ is a canonicalization w.r.t. $\equiv_{\sqsubseteq_{\mathcal{L}}}$, that is, it is representative ($c_{\mathcal{L}}(\varphi) \equiv_{\sqsubseteq_{\mathcal{L}}} \varphi$) and decisive ($\varphi \equiv_{\sqsubseteq_{\mathcal{L}}} \psi \iff c_{\mathcal{L}}(\varphi) = c_{\mathcal{L}}(\psi)$); $\sqsubseteq_{\mathcal{L}}$ is a partial order over canonical $\mathcal{L}$-formulas; and $\leq_{\mathcal{L}}$ is a total order over canonical $\mathcal{L}$-formulas that extends $\sqsubseteq_{\mathcal{L}}$.*

Corollary 1. *For any $\varphi, \psi \in \mathcal{L}$, if $\varphi \sqsubseteq_{\mathcal{L}} \psi$ then $c_{\mathcal{L}}(\varphi) \leq_{\mathcal{L}} c_{\mathcal{L}}(\psi)$.*

Henceforth, we use $\mathbf{\mathcal{L}}$ to denote the set of canonical $\mathcal{L}$-formulas.

3.4 Representing Sets of Formulas

We utilize the subsumption relation and canonicalization to efficiently represent sets of formulas which are interpreted conjunctively as antichains of canonical formulas, where an *antichain* is a set of formulas incomparable by subsumption.

Definition 4 (Set Representation). *Given a set of formulas $F \subseteq \mathbf{\mathcal{L}}$, we define its* representation *as the set $R_F = \min_{\sqsubseteq_{\mathcal{L}}}\{c(\varphi) \mid \varphi \in F\}$.*

The representation combines two forms of redundancy elimination: the use of canonical formulas eliminates redundancies due to subsumption-equivalence, and the use of $\sqsubseteq_{\mathcal{L}}$-minimal elements reduces the size of the set by ignoring subsumed formulas. Observe that the more permissive the subsumption relation is, the smaller the set representations are, because more formulas will belong to the same equivalence class and more formulas will be dropped by $\min_{\sqsubseteq_{\mathcal{L}}}$.

This representation preserves the semantics of a set of formulas (interpreted conjunctively). For sets that are upward-closed w.r.t. subsumption (e.g., $\alpha(S)$ for some set of states S), the representation is lossless as a set can be recovered by taking the upward closure of its representation. For a set $F \subseteq \mathbf{\mathcal{L}}$, we use $\uparrow F$ to denote its *upward closure* (w.r.t. $\sqsubseteq_{\mathcal{L}}$), given by $\uparrow F = \{\varphi \in \mathbf{\mathcal{L}} \mid \exists \psi \in F. \psi \sqsubseteq_{\mathcal{L}} \varphi\}$.

Theorem 3 (Antichain Representation). *For $F \subseteq \mathbf{\mathcal{L}}$ and $R_F = \min_{\sqsubseteq_{\mathcal{L}}}\{c(\varphi) \mid \varphi \in F\}$ its representation, $\bigwedge R_F \equiv \bigwedge F$ and $\uparrow R_F = \uparrow F$.*

Corollary 2. *If $F \subseteq \mathcal{L}$ is upward closed w.r.t. $\sqsubseteq_{\mathcal{L}}$ then $F = \uparrow R_F$.*

In particular, Corollary 2 applies to any set that is closed under entailment.

4 The Weaken Operator

This section develops an algorithm that computes a *weaken* operator, which takes a representation of an upward-closed set $F \subseteq \mathcal{L}$ and a state s and computes a representation of $F \cap \alpha(\{s\}) = \{\varphi \in F \mid s \models \varphi\}$. When F is viewed as an abstract element, this operation corresponds to computing $F \sqcup \alpha(\{s\})$. While it is not a general abstract join operator, joining an abstract element with the abstraction of a single concrete state is a powerful building block that can be used, for example, to compute the abstraction of a set of states or even the least fixpoint of the best abstract transformer (*á la* symbolic abstraction [27]).

In an explicit representation of F, computing $F \sqcup \alpha(\{s\})$ would amount to removing from F all the formulas that are not satisfied by s. However, in the subsumption-based representation R_F, simply removing said formulas is not enough. Instead, we must *weaken* them, i.e., replace them by formulas they subsume that are satisfied by s. To this end, Sect. 4.1 develops an appropriate weakening operator for a single formula, and Sect. 4.2 then lifts it to antichains used as representations.

4.1 Weakening a Single Canonical Formula

Given a canonical formula φ and a state s such that $s \not\models \varphi$, the weaken operator computes the set of minimal canonical formulas that are subsumed by φ and satisfied by s, which can be understood as a representation of $\uparrow\{\varphi\} \cap \alpha(\{s\})$.

Definition 5 (The Weaken Operator). *The* weaken operator *of $\mathcal{L}$ is the function $\mathcal{W}_{\mathcal{L}} \colon \mathcal{L} \times \mathbb{S} \to \mathcal{P}(\mathcal{L})$ defined as follows:*

$$\mathcal{W}_{\mathcal{L}}(\varphi, s) = \min_{\sqsubseteq_{\mathcal{L}}} \{c_{\mathcal{L}}(\psi) \mid \psi \in \mathcal{L}, \varphi \sqsubseteq \psi, \text{ and } s \models \psi\}.$$

Note that $\mathcal{W}_{\mathcal{L}}(\varphi, s)$ returns a set of formulas, since there may be different incomparable ways to weaken φ such that it is satisfied by s.

While Definition 5 does not suggest a way to compute $\mathcal{W}_{\mathcal{L}}(\varphi, s)$, the following theorem provides a recursive implementation of $\mathcal{W}_{\mathcal{L}}(\varphi, s)$ that follows the inductive structure of bounded languages. For the quantification cases, we weaken according to all assignments of variables in $X \subseteq V$. Recall that a state can be unpacked as $s = ((\mathcal{U}, \mathcal{I}), \mu)$ where $(\mathcal{U}, \mathcal{I})$ is a first-order structure (universe and interpretation) and μ is an assignment to variables (into $\mathcal{U}$). For assignments μ and ν, we use $\mu \overleftarrow{\sqcup} \nu$ to denote the assignment obtained from μ by updating (possibly extending) it according to ν.

Theorem 4 (Implementation of Weaken). *Let $\varphi \in \mathcal{L}$ be a canonical formula in a bounded first-order language $\mathcal{L}$ and $s \in \mathbb{S}$ a state. If $s \models \varphi$ then $\mathcal{W}_{\mathcal{L}}(\varphi, s) = \{\varphi\}$. If $s \not\models \varphi$, then $\mathcal{W}_{\mathcal{L}}(\varphi, s)$ is given by:*

$$\mathcal{W}_{\mathcal{L}_A}(\varphi, s) = \begin{cases} \{\psi \in A \mid s \models \psi\}, & \text{if } \varphi = \bot \\ \emptyset, & \text{if } \varphi \neq \bot \end{cases}$$

$$\mathcal{W}_{\vee[\mathcal{L}_1, \mathcal{L}_2]}(\varphi_1 \vee \varphi_2, s) = \{\varphi_1 \vee \varphi_2 \mid \psi \in \mathcal{W}_{\mathcal{L}_1}(\varphi_1, s)\} \cup \{\varphi_1 \vee \psi \mid \psi \in \mathcal{W}_{\mathcal{L}_2}(\varphi_2, s)\}$$

$$\mathcal{W}_{\wedge[\mathcal{L}_1, \mathcal{L}_2]}(\varphi_1 \wedge \varphi_2, s) = \{\psi_1 \wedge \psi_2 \mid \psi_1 \in \mathcal{W}_{\mathcal{L}_1}(\varphi_1, s), \psi_2 \in \mathcal{W}_{\mathcal{L}_2}(\varphi_2, s)\}$$

$$\mathcal{W}_{\vee_k[\mathcal{L}]}\left(\bigvee \bar{\varphi}, s\right) = \min{}_{\sqsubseteq_{\vee_k[\mathcal{L}]}}\left(W_{|\bar{\varphi}|} \cup W_{|\bar{\varphi}|+1}\right) \; where$$

$$W_{|\bar{\varphi}|} = \left\{\bigvee\langle\varphi_1, \ldots, \varphi_{i-1}, \psi, \varphi_{i+1}, \ldots, \varphi_{|\bar{\varphi}|}\rangle_{\leq_{\mathcal{L}}} \mid i \in [\bar{\varphi}], \psi \in \mathcal{W}_{\mathcal{L}}(\varphi_i, s)\right\} \; and$$

$$W_{|\bar{\varphi}|+1} = \left\{\bigvee\langle\varphi_1, \ldots, \varphi_{|\bar{\varphi}|}, \psi\rangle_{\leq_{\mathcal{L}}} \mid \psi \in \mathcal{W}_{\mathcal{L}}(\bot_{\mathcal{L}}, s) \; and \; |\bar{\varphi}| < k\right\}$$

$$\mathcal{W}_{\wedge_\omega[\mathcal{L}]}\left(\bigwedge \bar{\varphi}, s\right) = \left\{\bigwedge\langle\min{}_{\sqsubseteq_{\mathcal{L}}} \mathcal{W}_{\mathcal{L}}(\varphi_1, s) \cup \cdots \cup \mathcal{W}_{\mathcal{L}}(\varphi_{|\bar{\varphi}|}, s)\rangle_{\leq_{\mathcal{L}}}\right\}$$

$$\mathcal{W}_{\exists_X[\mathcal{L}]}(\exists X.\varphi, ((\mathcal{U}, \mathcal{I}), \mu)) = \min{}_{\sqsubseteq_{\exists_X[\mathcal{L}]}}\{c(\exists X.\psi) \mid \nu : X \to \mathcal{U}, \psi \in \mathcal{W}_{\mathcal{L}}\left(\varphi, ((\mathcal{U}, \mathcal{I}), \mu \overline{\cup} \nu)\right)\}$$

$$\mathcal{W}_{\forall_X[\mathcal{L}]}(\forall X.\varphi, ((\mathcal{U}, \mathcal{I}), \mu)) = \min{}_{\sqsubseteq_{\forall_X[\mathcal{L}]}}\{c(\forall X.\psi) \mid \psi \in \Omega_\varphi\left(\{((\mathcal{U}, \mathcal{I}), \mu \overline{\cup} \nu) \mid \nu : X \to \mathcal{U}\}\right)\}$$

$$where \; \Omega_{\varphi_0}(\{s_1, \ldots, s_n\}) = \{\varphi_n \mid \varphi_1 \in \mathcal{W}_{\mathcal{L}}(\varphi_0, s_1), \ldots, \varphi_n \in \mathcal{W}_{\mathcal{L}}(\varphi_{n-1}, s_n)\}$$

$$\mathcal{W}_{\exists\forall_X[\mathcal{L}]}(\exists X.\varphi, s) = \mathcal{W}_{\exists_X[\mathcal{L}]}(\exists X.\varphi, s)$$

$$\mathcal{W}_{\exists\forall_X[\mathcal{L}]}(\forall X.\varphi, s) = \min{}_{\sqsubseteq_{\exists\forall_X[\mathcal{L}]}}\left(\mathcal{W}_{\exists_X[\mathcal{L}]}(\exists X.\varphi, s) \cup \mathcal{W}_{\forall_X[\mathcal{L}]}(\forall X.\varphi, s)\right)$$

When $s \models \varphi$, no weakening of φ is needed for s to satisfy it. In the case of $\mathcal{L}_A$, only $\bot$ can be weakened to make s satisfy it, yielding the set of formulas from A that are satisfied by s. (For $\mathcal{L}_A$, weakening anything except $\bot$ that is not satisfied by s yields the empty set.) In the case of disjunction, it suffices for one of the disjuncts to be satisfied by s. Therefore, weakening is done by (i) weakening exactly one of the existing disjuncts, which applies to both $\vee[\mathcal{L}_1, \mathcal{L}_2]$ and $\vee_k[\mathcal{L}]$; or by (ii) adding a disjunct that weakens $\bot_{\mathcal{L}}$, which applies only to $\bigvee \bar{\varphi} \in \vee_k[\mathcal{L}]$ when $|\bar{\varphi}| < k$. In the case of homogeneous disjunction, each resulting disjunction needs to be sorted to restore canonicity; moreover, some of the resulting disjunctions may be subsumed by others, so $\min{}_{\sqsubseteq_{\vee_k[\mathcal{L}]}}$ is applied to the set of weakened disjunctions. In the case of conjunction, all conjuncts need to be weakened to be satisfied by s. In the binary case, this leads to all pairs that combine weakened conjuncts. But in the homogeneous case a single conjunction can accumulate all weakened conjuncts, so weakening always yields a singleton set; filtering the weakened conjuncts using $\min{}_{\sqsubseteq_{\mathcal{L}}}$ is required to ensure canonicity, as one weakened conjunct may subsume another. To satisfy an existentially quantified formula, it suffices for the body to be satisfied by a single assignment. Therefore, each possible assignment ν contributes to the result of weakening. In contrast, for a universally quantified formula the body must be satisfied by all assignments. Therefore, the body of the formula is iteratively weakened by *all* assignments. In both cases, formulas are re-canonicalized and non-minimal elements are removed. The case of $\exists\forall_X[\mathcal{L}]$ combines the two quantified cases.

Example 2. Consider applying the weaken operator of $\mathcal{L} = \forall_{\{x,y\}}[\vee_2[\mathcal{L}_A]]$ from Example 1 to the bottom element $\bot_{\mathcal{L}} = \forall\{x, y\}.\bigvee \epsilon$, with the state $s = ((\mathcal{U}, \mathcal{I}), \mu)$ where $\mathcal{U} = \{a, b\}$, $p^{\mathcal{I}} = \{a, b\}$, and μ is an empty assignment. To weaken the universally quantified formula, we first iteratively weaken its body,

$\varphi_0 = \bigvee \epsilon$, with the states $s_1, \ldots, s_4$, each of which extends s with one of the 4 possible assignments to x, y. Since all of these states satisfy $p(x)$ and $p(y)$, the first weakening (with s_1) results in $\{\bigvee \langle p(x) \rangle, \bigvee \langle p(y) \rangle\}$, and no formula is weakened further in later iterations (since both of them are already satisfied by s_2, s_3, s_4). As we have seen in Sect. 3.3, both formulas are canonical; however, they become subsumption-equivalent when the quantifier prefix is added, demonstrating the need for additional canonicalization in the computation of weaken for $\forall_X[\cdot]$. The result is the antichain of canonical formulas $\{\forall\{x, y\}. \bigvee \langle p(x) \rangle\}$. Note that the weakened formula $\perp_{\mathcal{L}}$ has 21 formulas in its $\sqsubseteq_{\mathcal{L}}$-upward closure, and its weakening has 14 formulas (see [8] for the lists of formulas); yet throughout the weakening process we only dealt with at most two formulas.

Algorithm 1: In-place Weaken for LSet[$\mathcal{L}$]

Input: An antichain of canonical $\mathcal{L}$-formulas R stored in the LSet[$\mathcal{L}$] data structure and a state $s \in \mathbb{S}$

Output: R modified in place to store $\mathcal{W}_{\mathcal{L}}(R, s)$

1 $U := R|_{\not\vDash s}$;
2 **for** $\varphi \in U$ **do** $R.\text{remove}(\varphi)$;
3 $W := \bigcup_{\varphi \in U} \mathcal{W}_{\mathcal{L}}(\varphi, s)$;
4 **for** $\varphi \in W$ *sorted by* $\leq_{\mathcal{L}}$ **do**
5 $\quad$ **if** $R|_{\sqsubseteq \varphi} = \emptyset$ **then** $R.\text{insert}(\varphi)$;

4.2 Weakening Sets of Formulas

We lift the weaken operator to sets of canonical formulas. For a set $R \subseteq \mathcal{L}$, we define $\mathcal{W}_{\mathcal{L}}(R, s) = \min_{\sqsubseteq} \bigcup_{\varphi \in R} \mathcal{W}_{\mathcal{L}}(\varphi, s)$, motivated by the following theorem.

Theorem 5 (From Weaken to Join). *Let $F \subseteq \mathcal{L}$ be upward-closed w.r.t. $\sqsubseteq$, R_F its representation ($R_F = \min_{\sqsubseteq}\{c(\varphi) \mid \varphi \in F\}$), and s a state. The representation of $F \sqcup \alpha(\{s\})$ is given by $\mathcal{W}_{\mathcal{L}}(R_F, s) = \min_{\sqsubseteq} \bigcup_{\varphi \in R_F} \mathcal{W}_{\mathcal{L}}(\varphi, s)$.*

Corollary 3 (Weaken for a Set of States). *Let $F \subseteq \mathcal{L}$ be upward-closed w.r.t. $\sqsubseteq$, R_F its representation, and $s_1, \ldots, s_n$ states. The representation of $F \sqcup \alpha(\{s_1, \ldots, s_n\})$ is given by $\mathcal{W}_{\mathcal{L}}(\mathcal{W}_{\mathcal{L}}(\cdots \mathcal{W}_{\mathcal{L}}(\mathcal{W}_{\mathcal{L}}(R_F, s_1), s_2), \cdots s_{n-1}), s_n)$.*

Corollary 4 (Abstraction of a Set of States). *The representation of $\alpha(S)$ for a set of states S The representation of $\alpha(\{s_1, \ldots, s_n\})$ is given by $\mathcal{W}_{\mathcal{L}}(\mathcal{W}_{\mathcal{L}}(\cdots \mathcal{W}_{\mathcal{L}}(\mathcal{W}_{\mathcal{L}}(\{\perp_{\mathcal{L}}\}, s_1), s_2), \cdots s_{n-1}), s_n)$.*

Theorem 5 and Corollary 3 show that weakening of a single formula can be lifted to compute join between an upward-closed set of formulas (represented using its minimal elements w.r.t. $\sqsubseteq$) and the abstraction of one or more states.

Next, we observe that we can implement $\mathcal{W}_{\mathcal{L}}(R, s)$ by (i) focusing only on formulas that actually need weakening, i.e., formulas in R that are not satisfied by s, without iterating over formulas that s satisfies; and (ii) leveraging the $\leq_{\mathcal{L}}$ total order to accumulate the set of minimal elements more efficiently.

Algorithm 1 presents our implementation of $\mathcal{W}_{\mathcal{L}}(R, s)$ for an antichain R of canonical formulas and a state s. It updates R to $\mathcal{W}_{\mathcal{L}}(R, s)$ in place, which is useful for computing an abstraction of a set of states (Corollary 3) or even for fixpoint computation (Sect. 6). The algorithm uses a data structure LSet[$\mathcal{L}$] (whose implementation is explained in Sect. 5) that stores a set of canonical $\mathcal{L}$-formulas and supports two efficient filters: one for formulas that are not satisfied by a given state s, denoted by $R|_{\not\models s}$; and one for formulas that subsume a given formula φ, denoted by $R|_{\sqsubseteq \varphi}$. Formally: $R|_{\not\models s} = \{\psi \in R \mid s \not\models \psi\}$ and $R|_{\sqsubseteq \varphi} = \{\psi \in R \mid \varphi \sqsupseteq \psi\}$.

To weaken R, Algorithm 1 first identifies all formulas that need weakening using the $R|_{\not\models s}$ filter. It then removes these formulas, weakens them, and adds the weakened formulas back to the set, while filtering out formulas that are not $\sqsubseteq_{\mathcal{L}}$-minimal. For the minimality filtering, we leverage $\leq_{\mathcal{L}}$ to ensure that if $\varphi \sqsubseteq_{\mathcal{L}} \psi$ then φ is added before ψ. As a result, when inserting a formula φ we only need to check that it is not already subsumed by another formula in the set, which is done by checking if $R|_{\sqsubseteq \varphi}$ is empty[3]. Importantly, a formula $\varphi \in R \setminus R|_{\not\models s}$ cannot be subsumed by a formula from $\mathcal{W}_{\mathcal{L}}(\psi, s)$ for $\psi \in R|_{\not\models s}$. (If we assume the contrary we easily get that $\psi \sqsubseteq \varphi$, contradicting the fact that R is an antichain.)

4.3   Design Consideration and Tradeoffs

We are now in a position to discuss the tradeoffs and considerations that arise in our framework in the design of languages and their subsumption relations, explaining the design choices behind Definitions 1 and 2.

There is a tradeoff between the precision of the subsumption relation $\sqsubseteq_{\mathcal{L}}$ and the complexity of implementing the weaken operator $\mathcal{W}_{\mathcal{L}}$. From a representation perspective, a more precise $\sqsubseteq_{\mathcal{L}}$ is desirable (i.e., relating more formulas), since it means that the upward closure $\uparrow\{\varphi\}$ of a formula φ is larger, and (upward-closed) sets of formulas can be represented using less minimal formulas. On the other hand, when $\uparrow\{\varphi\}$ is larger, computing $\mathcal{W}_{\mathcal{L}}(\varphi, s)$ is generally more complicated. As an extreme case, if $\sqsubseteq_{\mathcal{L}}$ is trivial (i.e., a formula only subsumes itself), we get no pruning in the representation, but computing $\mathcal{W}_{\mathcal{L}}(\varphi, s)$ is very easy, since it is either $\{\varphi\}$ or $\emptyset$. As another example, compare $\vee[\mathcal{L}, \mathcal{L}]$ with $\vee_2[\mathcal{L}]$. The subsumption relation of $\vee[\mathcal{L}, \mathcal{L}]$ is a pointwise extension, while that of $\vee_2[\mathcal{L}]$ allows swapping the two formulas, which is more precise. (E.g., $\bigvee\langle\varphi, \psi\rangle \sqsubseteq_{\vee_2[\mathcal{L}]} \bigvee\langle\psi, \varphi\rangle$ always holds but we might have $\varphi \vee \psi \not\sqsubseteq_{\vee[\mathcal{L},\mathcal{L}]} \psi \vee \varphi$.) Accordingly, weakening of $\vee_2[\mathcal{L}]$-formulas is slightly more involved.

As opposed to reordering of disjuncts, $\sqsubseteq_{\vee_k[\mathcal{L}]}$ does not allow multiple disjuncts to subsume the same one, e.g., $\bigvee\langle\varphi, \psi\rangle \not\sqsubseteq_{\vee_k[\mathcal{L}]} \bigvee\langle\psi\rangle$ even if $\varphi \sqsubseteq_{\mathcal{L}} \psi$ (recall that the mapping between disjuncts must be injective). This choice makes the

---

[3] While the implementation of the weaken operator only checks the emptiness of $R|_{\sqsubseteq \varphi}$, the full set is used in the recursive implementation of $R|_{\sqsubseteq \varphi}$ (Sect. 5).

computation of $\mathcal{W}_{\vee_k[\mathcal{L}]}$ simpler, as it only needs to consider individually weakening each disjunct or adding a new one, but not merging of disjuncts (to "make space" for a new disjunct). For example, when computing $\mathcal{W}_{\vee_2[\mathcal{L}]}(\bigvee\langle \varphi_1, \varphi_2 \rangle, s)$, we do not have to consider formulas of the form $\bigvee\langle \varphi, \psi \rangle$ where $s \models \psi$ and $\varphi_1, \varphi_2 \sqsubseteq_{\mathcal{L}} \varphi$, which we would need to include if the mapping was not required to be injective. One seemingly undesirable consequence of the injectivity requirement is that canonical formulas may contain redundant disjuncts, e.g., $\bigvee\langle \varphi, \psi \rangle$ when $\varphi \sqsubseteq \psi$ (or even $\bigvee\langle \varphi, \varphi \rangle$). However, when formulas are obtained by iterative weakening, as in the computation of the representation of $\alpha(S)$ for a set of concrete states S, formulas with such redundancies will be eliminated as they are always subsumed by a canonical formula without redundancies.

Our design of bounded first-order languages uses bounded disjunction but unbounded conjunction. The reason is that we obtain formulas by weakening other formulas, starting from $\bot_{\mathcal{L}}$. In this scenario, bounding the size of conjunctions would have replaced one conjunction by all of its subsets smaller than the bound, causing an exponential blowup in the number of formulas, without contributing much to generalization. On the other hand, bounding the size of disjunctions yields generalization without blowing up the number of formulas (in fact, it reduces the number of formulas compared to unbounded disjunction).

5 Data Structure for Sets of Formulas

The implementation of $\mathcal{W}_{\mathcal{L}}(R, s)$ presented in Algorithm 1 uses the filters $R|_{\not\models s}$ and $R|_{\sqsubseteq \varphi}$. Since the sets may be very large, a naive implementation that iterates over R to find formulas that are not satisfied by s ($R|_{\not\models s}$) or formulas that subsume φ ($R|_{\sqsubseteq \varphi}$) may become inefficient. We therefore introduce a data structure for bounded first-order languages, which we call LSet[$\mathcal{L}$], that stores a set of canonical $\mathcal{L}$-formulas R (not necessarily an antichain), and implements $R|_{\not\models s}$ and $R|_{\sqsubseteq \varphi}$ without iterating over all formulas in R. The key idea is to define the LSet[$\mathcal{L}$] data structure recursively, following the structure of $\mathcal{L}$, and to use auxiliary data to implement the $R|_{\not\models s}$ and $R|_{\sqsubseteq \varphi}$ filters more efficiently.

For example, to implement LSet[$\vee[\mathcal{L}_1, \mathcal{L}_2]$], we store a set of $\vee[\mathcal{L}_1, \mathcal{L}_2]$-formulas and two auxiliary data fields: an LSet L : LSet[$\mathcal{L}_1$] and a map M : Map[$\mathcal{L}_1$, LSet[$\mathcal{L}_2$]]. We maintain the invariant that $\varphi_1 \vee \varphi_2$ is in the set iff $\varphi_2 \in M[\varphi_1]$, and that L contains the same $\mathcal{L}_1$-formulas as the keys of M. Then, to find formulas that are not satisfied by a state s, i.e., formulas where both disjuncts are not satisfied by s, we first query L to find φ_1's that are not satisfied by s, and for each such φ_1 we query the LSet $M[\varphi_1]$ to find φ_2's that are not satisfied by s. Implementing the subsumption filter follows a similar logic.

Our implementation of LSet[$\vee_k[\mathcal{L}]$] uses a trie data structure that generalizes the binary case. Each edge is labeled by an $\mathcal{L}$-formula, and each node represents an $\vee_k[\mathcal{L}]$-formula that is the disjunction of the edge labels along the path from the root to the node. The outgoing edges of each node are stored using an LSet[$\mathcal{L}$] that can be used to filter only the edges whose label is not satisfied by a given state, or subsumes a given formula. Then, the $R|_{\not\models s}$ and $R|_{\sqsubseteq \bigvee \bar\varphi}$ filters are implemented by recursive traversals of the tree that only traverse filtered edges.

The recursive implementation for the other language constructors is simpler, and follows a similar intuition to that of the cases presented above. The base case LSet[$\mathcal{L}_A$] is implemented without any auxiliary data using straightforward iteration. The full details of the LSet[$\mathcal{L}$] data structure appear in [8].

6 Implementation and Evaluation

To evaluate our abstract domain implementation, we used it to implement a symbolic abstraction [27, 29] algorithm that computes the least fixpoint of the best abstract transformer of a transition system. We evaluated our implementation on 19 distributed protocols commonly used as benchmarks in safety verification and obtained promising results.

6.1 Implementation

We implemented our abstract domain and the symbolic abstraction algorithm in Flyvy,[4] an open-source verification tool written in Rust, whose implementation leverages parallelism and the optimizations detailed below. The implementation and benchmarks used, as well as the log files and raw results from the experiments reported, are publicly available in this paper's artifact [7].

Our implementation receives as input (i) a first-order transition system (ι, τ) over signature Σ, where ι is a closed first-order formula over Σ specifying the initial states and τ is a closed first-order formula over two copies of Σ specifying the transitions, and (ii) a specification of a bounded first-order language $\mathcal{L}$ over Σ that defines the abstract domain $\mathcal{P}(\mathcal{L})$. The reachable states of the system are the least fixpoint of a concrete transformer $\mathcal{T} : \mathcal{P}(\mathbb{S}) \rightarrow \mathcal{P}(\mathbb{S})$ given by $\mathcal{T}(S) = \{s' \in \mathbb{S} \mid s' \models \iota \vee \exists s \in S.\ \langle s, s' \rangle \models \tau\}$, where $\langle s, s' \rangle \models \tau$ indicates that the pair of states satisfies the two-vocabulary formula τ, i.e., that s' is a successor of s w.r.t the transition relation defined by τ. For more details on this style of modeling distributed systems in first-order logic, see [23–25].

The Galois connection (α, γ) between $\mathcal{P}(\mathbb{S})$ and $\mathcal{P}(\mathcal{L})$ induces a *best abstract transformer* $\mathcal{T}^\sharp : \mathcal{P}(\mathcal{L}) \rightarrow \mathcal{P}(\mathcal{L})$ defined by $\mathcal{T}^\sharp = \alpha \circ \mathcal{T} \circ \gamma$. Any fixpoint of $\mathcal{T}^\sharp$, i.e., a set $F \subseteq \mathcal{L}$ such that $\mathcal{T}^\sharp(F) = F$, is an *inductive invariant* of (ι, τ) (when sets are interpreted conjunctively), and the least fixpoint, lfp$\mathcal{T}^\sharp$, is the strongest inductive invariant in $\mathcal{L}$. The strongest inductive invariant is useful for verifying safety properties of the system, or showing that they cannot be proven in $\mathcal{L}$ (if the strongest inductive invariant in $\mathcal{L}$ cannot prove safety, neither can any other inductive invariant expressible in $\mathcal{L}$).

Symbolic abstraction computes lfp$\mathcal{T}^\sharp$ without computing $\mathcal{T}^\sharp$ explicitly: beginning with $F = \mathcal{L}$ (the least element in $\mathcal{P}(\mathcal{L})$), and as long as $F \neq \mathcal{T}^\sharp(F)$, a *counterexample to induction* (CTI) of F is sampled, i.e., a state $s' \not\models \bigwedge F$ that is either an initial state or the successor of a state s with $s \models \bigwedge F$, and F is updated to $F \sqcup \alpha(\{s'\})$. Our implementation uses the representation R_F and

---

[4] Flyvy's code is available at https://github.com/vmware-research/temporal-verifier.

Algorithm 1 to compute the join (more details in [8]). To find CTIs or determine that none exist we use SMT solvers (Z3 [21] and cvc5 [2]), with queries restricted to the EPR fragment (following [24]), which ensures decidability and the existence of finite counterexamples. Solvers still struggle in some challenging benchmarks, and we employ several optimizations detailed in [8] to avoid solver timeouts.

6.2   Experiments

To evaluate our techniques, we computed the least fixpoints (strongest inductive invariants) of 19 distributed protocols commonly used as benchmarks in safety verification, in a language expressive enough to capture their human-written safety invariants. We used all EPR benchmarks from [15], except for universally quantified Paxos variants. To evaluate the utility of the LSet data structure described in Sect. 5, we ran each experiment twice, once using LSet and once using a naive (but parallelized) implementation for the filters $R|_{\neq_{s}}$ and $R|_{\sqsubseteq\varphi}$.

To specify the bounded first-order language for each example, we provide the tool with a quantifier prefix (using $\exists_X[\cdot]$, $\forall_X[\cdot]$, and $\exists\forall_X[\cdot]$) composed on top of a quantifier-free bounded language that captures k-pDNF (following [15]). A k-pDNF formula has the structure $c_1 \rightarrow (c_2 \vee \cdots \vee c_k)$, where $c_1, c_2, \ldots, c_k$ are cubes (conjunctions of literals). We specify such formulas as $\vee[\vee_n[\mathcal{L}_{A_1}], \vee_{k-1}[\wedge_{\omega}[\mathcal{L}_{A_2}]]]$, where k and n are parameters, and A_1 and A_2 are sets of literals. Inspired by [30], we observe that we can restrict the variables used in A_1 and A_2 to reduce the size of the language without losing precision.[5] For additional details see [8]. The list of examples with their language parameters appears in Table 1. For each example, we report the quantifier structure, the k and n parameters of the k-pDNF quantifier-free matrix, and the approximate size of the language $\mathcal{L}$. Recall that the size of the abstract domain is $2^{|\mathcal{L}|}$.

All experiments were performed on a 48-threaded machine with 384 GiB of RAM (AWS's z1d.metal) and a three-hour time limit. For each example we also provide runtimes of two state-of-the-art safety verification tools, DuoAI [30] and P-FOL-IC3 [15]. Note that, unlike our technique, these tools look for *some* inductive invariant proving safety, not necessarily the strongest, but are also given fewer explicit language constraints. Moreover, the runtimes of DuoAI and P-FOL-IC3 are sourced from their respective papers, and reflect different architectures and time limits. Thus, the inclusion of their results is not intended as a precise comparison to our tool, but as a reference for the difficulty of the invariant inference task of each example, as evidenced by state-of-the-art techniques.

---

[5] One of the language reductions used by [30] relies on an overly generalized lemma [30, Lemma 6]; we confirmed this with the authors of [30]. We prove and use a correct (but less general) variant of this lemma, see [8] for details.

6.3   Results

The results of the symbolic abstraction computation are presented in Table 1. For each experiment we report the runtime of our tool and the following statistics: the percentage of time spent weakening formulas (as opposed to searching for CTIs), the number of formulas in the representation of the fixpoint (if reached), and the maximal number of formulas in the representation of an abstract element throughout the run. Each experiment was run five times, unless it timed out, in which case it was run only once. We aggregate the results of each statistic across multiple runs as *median ± deviation*, where *deviation* is the maximal distance between the median value and the value of the statistic in any given run.

For simple examples, the fixpoint computation terminates very quickly, often faster than the other tools, and maintains only tens or hundreds of formulas throughout its run. Some of the larger examples, such as `ticket`, `paxos-epr`, `flexible-paxos-epr`, and `cache` also terminate after similar times to the other tools. In fact, this is the first work to compute least fixpoints for any Paxos variant or `cache`. (DuoAI, for instance, has a component that attempts to compute a precise fixpoint, but [30] reports that it times out on all Paxos variants.)

Unsurprisingly, there is a significant gap between the runtimes of examples with and without quantifier alternation, mostly due to the time spent in SMT solvers. For example, in `ticket` we spend about 43% of the runtime performing weakenings, but this percentage drops to 1% and 4% for `paxos-epr` and `flexible-paxos-epr`, respectively. This causes the runtime of `paxos-epr` to exceed that of `ticket` by more than an order of magnitude, although its fixpoint computation considers fewer formulas and actually spends less time weakening. Similarly, in `cache` we manage to prove a fixpoint of a hundred thousand formulas in about an hour and spend a third of it weakening formulas, while `multi-paxos-epr` and `fast-paxos-epr` time out, although they consider far fewer formulas and spend a negligible amount of time weakening.

Next, we observe that the use of LSet significantly reduces time spent in weakening, leading to more than an order of magnitude difference even in moderate examples, e.g., `ticket` and `paxos-epr`. In terms of the *total* fixpoint computation time, in examples where the runtime is small or dominated by the SMT solvers, the effect might be negligible, but otherwise the speedup is significant. For example, `cache` is not solved within the 3-hour limit with a naive data structure; it gets stuck after reaching ∼ 20,000 formulas in the abstraction, whereas using LSet it is solved in about an hour while handling more than ten times the number of formulas. Similarly, in the two unsolved examples where SMT calls seem to be the bottleneck (`multi-paxos-epr` and `fast-paxos-epr`), using a naive data structure causes weakening to become the bottleneck and time out.

Finally, the remaining timeouts, `learning-switch`, `stoppable-paxos-epr`, and `vertical-paxos-epr`, are the only examples where the weakening process itself is the bottleneck. These are cases where the language induced by the human-written invariant, using the constraining parameters of bounded languages, create a inefficient weakening process. The cause for this is either a profusion of literals in the basis language (>600 in `learning-switch` and

Table 1. Symbolic abstraction over invariant inference benchmarks with a time limit of 3 h (10800 s). We describe the bounded language underlying the abstract domain of each example, including its approximate size, and report the runtime of our technique—with and without using LSet—along with some statistics. For reference, we provide runtimes of two state-of-the-art safety-verification tools. 'T/O' indicates a timeout, and 'N/A' indicates that the example was not reported by the respective tool.

Example	Language				Runtime (sec)	LSet	% in $\mathcal{W}$	Lfp. Size	Max. Size	Safety (sec)	
	quant	k	n	size						P-FOL-IC3	DuoAI
lockserv	$\forall^2$	1	3	10^4	$\mathbf{0.4 \pm 0.1}$	✓	6 ± 1 %	12	28 ± 7	19	1.9
					0.5 ± 0.1	–	6 ± 1 %		29 ± 3		
toy-consensus-forall	$\forall^3$	1	3	10^3	$\mathbf{0.2 \pm 0.0}$	✓	9 ± 2 %	5	18 ± 5	4	1.9
					0.2 ± 0.0	–	7 ± 1 %		18 ± 4		
ring-id	$\forall^3$	1	3	10^5	$\mathbf{1.6 \pm 0.1}$	✓	16 ± 1 %	97	182 ± 22	7	3.5
					1.9 ± 0.1	–	20 ± 1 %		189 ± 22		
sharded-kv	$\forall^5$	1	3	10^4	$\mathbf{0.5 \pm 0.1}$	✓	8 ± 0 %	20	26 ± 2	8	1.9
					0.5 ± 0.0	–	8 ± 1 %		26 ± 4		
ticket	$\forall^4$	1	5	10^9	$\mathbf{32.6 \pm 3.3}$	✓	43 ± 7 %	2621	8531 ± 119	23	23.9
					862.2 ± 21.9	–	97 ± 0 %		8533 ± 121		
learning-switch	$\forall^4$	1	4	10^{11}	$\mathbf{T/O}$	✓	98 %	–	9576194	76	52.4
					T/O	–	100 %		5998		
consensus-wo-decide	$\forall^3$	1	3	10^6	$\mathbf{3.0 \pm 0.2}$	✓	19 ± 1 %	41	717 ± 109	50	3.9
					4.0 ± 0.6	–	38 ± 4 %		724 ± 43		
consensus-forall	$\forall^4$	1	3	10^6	$\mathbf{3.5 \pm 0.4}$	✓	21 ± 2 %	51	740 ± 114	1980	11.9
					5.1 ± 0.9	–	40 ± 6 %		708 ± 82		
cache	$\forall^6$	1	5	10^{11}	$\mathbf{4029.4 \pm 220.7}$	✓	30 ± 2 %	106348	271255 ± 13081	2492	N/A
					T/O	–	100 ± 0 %		19183 ± 9466		
sharded-kv-no-lost-keys	$\forall^1 (\exists\forall)^2$	1	2	10^2	$\mathbf{0.3 \pm 0.0}$	✓	3 ± 0 %	4	4 ± 0	4	2.1
					0.3 ± 0.0	–	2 ± 0 %		4 ± 0		
toy-consensus-epr	$\forall^2 (\exists\forall)^1 \forall^1$	1	3	10^4	$\mathbf{0.3 \pm 0.0}$	✓	9 ± 1 %	5	18 ± 4	4	2.6
					0.3 ± 0.0	–	7 ± 1 %		19 ± 3		
consensus-epr	$(\exists\forall)^1 \forall^4$	1	3	10^6	$\mathbf{5.1 \pm 0.7}$	✓	17 ± 2 %	51	800 ± 137	37	4.8
					8.8 ± 1.7	–	46 ± 8 %		783 ± 88		
client-server-ae	$\forall^2 (\exists\forall)^1$	2	1	10^3	$\mathbf{0.2 \pm 0.0}$	✓	4 ± 1 %	2	5 ± 0	4	1.5
					0.2 ± 0.1	–	3 ± 1 %		5 ± 0		
paxos-epr	$\forall^4 (\exists\forall)^2$	2	3	10^{11}	$\mathbf{621.5 \pm 246.8}$	✓	1 ± 1 %	1438	1693 ± 203	920	60.4
					789.6 ± 285.5	–	11 ± 3 %		1737 ± 168		
flexible-paxos-epr	$\forall^4 (\exists\forall)^2$	2	3	10^{11}	$\mathbf{166.7 \pm 29.3}$	✓	4 ± 1 %	964	1622 ± 177	418	78.7
					235.6 ± 31.7	–	35 ± 8 %		1575 ± 196		
multi-paxos-epr	$\forall^5 (\exists\forall)^3$	2	3	10^{30}	$\mathbf{T/O}$	✓	2 %	–	27508	4272	1549
					T/O	–	100 %		6400		
fast-paxos-epr	$\forall^4 (\exists\forall)^3$	2	4	10^{14}	$\mathbf{T/O}$	✓	1 %	–	16290	9630	26979
					T/O	–	99 %		13683		
stoppable-paxos-epr	$\forall^7 (\exists\forall)^3$	2	5	10^{155}	$\mathbf{T/O}$	✓	100 %	–	37529	>18297	4051
					T/O	–	100 %		3331		
vertical-paxos-epr	$\forall^4 (\exists\forall)^3$	3	5	10^{54}	$\mathbf{T/O}$	✓	100 %	–	112990	T/O	T/O
					T/O	–	100 %		2576		

`stoppable-paxos-epr`, less than 200 in all other examples), or a very expressive language (e.g., `vertical-paxos-epr` uses 3-pDNF, whereas all other examples use 1- and 2-pDNF). For these examples, it might be necessary to restrict the languages in additional ways, e.g., as was done in [30]. Our experience, however, is that the more significant bottleneck for computing least fixpoints for the most complicated examples is the SMT queries.

7 Related Work

Many recent works tackle invariant inference in first-order logic [9–11,14,15,17, 26,30,31]. These works are all property-guided and employ sophisticated heuristics to guide the search for invariants. Of these works, the most closely related to ours are [30,31]. DistAI [31] is restricted to universally quantified invariants, while DuoAI [30] infers invariants with quantifier alternations. DuoAI defines a "minimum implication graph" enumerating all formulas in a first-order logical language, whose transitive closure can be understood as a specific subsumption relation, and where replacing a node with its successors can be understood as a form of weakening. DuoAI's "top-down refinement" precisely computes the strongest invariant in the logical domain. However, this computation does not scale to complex examples such as all Paxos variants, in which case "bottom-up refinement" is used—a property-guided process that does not compute the strongest invariant. Our approach based on a generic subsumption relation is both more principled and more scalable, as it succeeds in computing the least fixpoint for some Paxos variants.

Another work concerning a least-fixpoint in a logical domain is [19], which computes the set of propositional clauses up to length k implied by a given formula, minimized by the subsumption relation $\sqsubseteq = \subseteq$; a trie-based data structure is used to maintain the formulas, weaken them, and check subsumption of a formula by the entire set. Both that data structure and LSet$[\vee_k[\cdot]]$ bear similarity to UBTrees [12], also employed in [3], which store sets and implement filters for subsets and supersets. However, while UBTrees and LSets always maintain ordered tree paths, these are unordered in [19], which allows [19] to perform weakening directly on the data structure, whereas we need to remove the unsatisfied disjunctions, weaken, and insert them. On the other hand, this makes filtering for subsets in UBTrees and LSets more efficient. Also note that LSet is more general than both, since it supports a more general subsumption relation.

8 Conclusion

We have developed key algorithms and data structures for working with a logical abstract domain of quantified first-order formulas. Our fundamental idea is using a well-defined subsumption relation and a *weaken* operator induced by it. This idea makes the abstract domain feasible, and it is also extensible: while we explored one possible subsumption relation and its associated weaken operator, future work may explore others, representing different tradeoffs between pruning and weakening. We demonstrated the feasibility of our approach by computing the least abstract fixpoint for several distributed protocols modeled in first-order logic—a challenging application domain where previously only property-directed heuristics have been successful. For some of the examples in our evaluation, the computation still times out. In some of these cases, SMT queries (for computing CTIs) become the bottleneck. Dealing with this bottleneck is an orthogonal problem that we leave for future work. For the examples with the largest logical languages, abstract domain operations remain the bottleneck, and future work may either scale the abstract domain implementation to such languages or explore combinations with property-directed approaches.

Acknowledgments. We thank Alex Fischman and James R. Wilcox for their contributions to the Flyvy verification tool. We thank Raz Lotan, Kenneth McMillan, and the anonymous reviewers for their helpful and insightful comments.

The research leading to these results has received funding from the European Research Council under the European Union's Horizon 2020 research and innovation programme (grant agreement No [759102-SVIS]). This research was partially supported by the Israeli Science Foundation (ISF) grant No. 2117/23.

References

1. Ball, T., et al.: Vericon: towards verifying controller programs in software-defined networks. In: O'Boyle, M.F.P., Pingali, K. (eds.) ACM SIGPLAN Conference on Programming Language Design and Implementation, PLDI 2014, Edinburgh, United Kingdom, 09–11 June 2014, pp. 282–293. ACM (2014). https://doi.org/10.1145/2594291.2594317

2. Barbosa, H., et al.: cvc5: a versatile and industrial-strength SMT solver. In: TACAS 2022. LNCS, vol. 13243, pp. 415–442. Springer, Cham (2022). https://doi.org/10.1007/978-3-030-99524-9_24

3. Cadar, C., Dunbar, D., Engler, D.R., et al.: Klee: unassisted and automatic generation of high-coverage tests for complex systems programs. In: OSDI, vol. 8, pp. 209–224 (2008)

4. Cousot, P., Cousot, R.: Abstract interpretation: a unified lattice model for static analysis of programs by construction or approximation of fixpoints. In: Graham, R.M., Harrison, M.A., Sethi, R. (eds.) Conference Record of the Fourth ACM Symposium on Principles of Programming Languages, Los Angeles, California, USA, January 1977, pp. 238–252. ACM (1977). https://doi.org/10.1145/512950.512973

5. Cousot, P., Cousot, R.: Systematic design of program analysis frameworks. In: Aho, A.V., Zilles, S.N., Rosen, B.K. (eds.) Conference Record of the Sixth Annual ACM Symposium on Principles of Programming Languages, San Antonio, Texas, USA, January 1979, pp. 269–282. ACM Press (1979). https://doi.org/10.1145/567752.567778

6. Feldman, Y.M.Y., Padon, O., Immerman, N., Sagiv, M., Shoham, S.: Bounded quantifier instantiation for checking inductive invariants. In: Legay, A., Margaria, T. (eds.) TACAS 2017. LNCS, vol. 10205, pp. 76–95. Springer, Heidelberg (2017). https://doi.org/10.1007/978-3-662-54577-5_5

7. Frenkel, E., Chajed, T., Padon, O., Shoham, S.: Efficient implementation of an abstract domain of quantified first-order formulas (artifact) (2024). https://doi.org/10.5281/zenodo.10938367

8. Frenkel, E., Chajed, T., Padon, O., Shoham, S.: Efficient implementation of an abstract domain of quantified first-order formulas (extended version) (2024). https://doi.org/10.48550/arXiv.2405.10308

9. Goel, A., Sakallah, K.: On symmetry and quantification: a new approach to verify distributed protocols. In: Dutle, A., Moscato, M.M., Titolo, L., Muñoz, C.A., Perez, I. (eds.) NFM 2021. LNCS, vol. 12673, pp. 131–150. Springer, Cham (2021). https://doi.org/10.1007/978-3-030-76384-8_9

10. Goel, A., Sakallah, K.A.: Towards an automatic proof of Lamport's Paxos. In: FMCAD, pp. 112–122. IEEE (2021). https://doi.org/10.34727/2021/isbn.978-3-85448-046-4_20

11. Hance, T., Heule, M., Martins, R., Parno, B.: Finding invariants of distributed systems: It's a small (enough) world after all. In: Mickens, J., Teixeira, R. (eds.) 18th USENIX Symposium on Networked Systems Design and Implementation, NSDI 2021, 12–14 April 2021, pp. 115–131. USENIX Association (2021). https://www.usenix.org/conference/nsdi21/presentation/hance

12. Hoffmann, J., Koehler, J.: A new method to index and query sets. In: IJCAI, vol. 99, pp. 462–467 (1999)

13. Itzhaky, S., Banerjee, A., Immerman, N., Nanevski, A., Sagiv, M.: Effectively-propositional reasoning about reachability in linked data structures. In: Sharygina, N., Veith, H. (eds.) CAV 2013. LNCS, vol. 8044, pp. 756–772. Springer, Heidelberg (2013). https://doi.org/10.1007/978-3-642-39799-8_53

14. Karbyshev, A., Bjørner, N.S., Itzhaky, S., Rinetzky, N., Shoham, S.: Property-directed inference of universal invariants or proving their absence. J. ACM **64**(1), 7:1–7:33 (2017). https://doi.org/10.1145/3022187

15. Koenig, J.R., Padon, O., Shoham, S., Aiken, A.: Inferring Invariants with quantifier alternations: taming the search space explosion. In: TACAS 2022. LNCS, vol. 13243, pp. 338–356. Springer, Cham (2022). https://doi.org/10.1007/978-3-030-99524-9_18

16. Löding, C., Madhusudan, P., Peña, L.: Foundations for natural proofs and quantifier instantiation. Proc. ACM Program. Lang. **2**(POPL), 10:1–10:30 (2018). https://doi.org/10.1145/3158098

17. Ma, H., Goel, A., Jeannin, J., Kapritsos, M., Kasikci, B., Sakallah, K.A.: I4: incremental inference of inductive invariants for verification of distributed protocols. In: SOSP, pp. 370–384. ACM (2019). https://doi.org/10.1145/3341301.3359651

18. Mathur, U., Madhusudan, P., Viswanathan, M.: What's decidable about program verification modulo axioms? In: TACAS 2020. LNCS, vol. 12079, pp. 158–177. Springer, Cham (2020). https://doi.org/10.1007/978-3-030-45237-7_10

19. McMillan, K.: Don't-care computation using k-clause approximation. In: Proceedings of the IWLS 2005, pp. 153–160 (2005)

20. McMillan, K.L., Padon, O.: Deductive verification in decidable fragments with ivy. In: Podelski, A. (ed.) SAS 2018. LNCS, vol. 11002, pp. 43–55. Springer, Cham (2018). https://doi.org/10.1007/978-3-319-99725-4_4

21. de Moura, L., Bjørner, N.: Z3: an efficient SMT solver. In: Ramakrishnan, C.R., Rehof, J. (eds.) TACAS 2008. LNCS, vol. 4963, pp. 337–340. Springer, Heidelberg (2008). https://doi.org/10.1007/978-3-540-78800-3_24

22. Murali, A., Peña, L., Blanchard, E., Löding, C., Madhusudan, P.: Model-guided synthesis of inductive lemmas for FOL with least fixpoints. Proc. ACM Program. Lang. **6**(OOPSLA2), 1873–1902 (2022). https://doi.org/10.1145/3563354

23. Padon, O.: Deductive Verification of Distributed Protocols in First-Order Logic. Ph.D. thesis, Tel Aviv University (2019)
24. Padon, O., Losa, G., Sagiv, M., Shoham, S.: Paxos made EPR: decidable reasoning about distributed protocols. Proc. ACM Program. Lang. **1**(OOPSLA), 108:1–108:31 (2017). https://doi.org/10.1145/3140568
25. Padon, O., McMillan, K.L., Panda, A., Sagiv, M., Shoham, S.: Ivy: safety verification by interactive generalization. In: PLDI, pp. 614–630. ACM (2016). https://doi.org/10.1145/2908080.2908118
26. Padon, O., Wilcox, J.R., Koenig, J.R., McMillan, K.L., Aiken, A.: Induction duality: primal-dual search for invariants. Proc. ACM Program. Lang. **6**(POPL), 1–29 (2022). https://doi.org/10.1145/3498712
27. Reps, T., Sagiv, M., Yorsh, G.: Symbolic implementation of the best transformer. In: Steffen, B., Levi, G. (eds.) VMCAI 2004. LNCS, vol. 2937, pp. 252–266. Springer, Heidelberg (2004). https://doi.org/10.1007/978-3-540-24622-0_21
28. Taube, M., et al.: Modularity for decidability of deductive verification with applications to distributed systems. In: PLDI, pp. 662–677. ACM (2018). https://doi.org/10.1145/3192366.3192414
29. Thakur, A.V.: Symbolic abstraction: algorithms and applications. Ph.D. thesis, The University of Wisconsin-Madison (2014)
30. Yao, J., Tao, R., Gu, R., Nieh, J.: DuoAI: fast, automated inference of inductive invariants for verifying distributed protocols. In: Aguilera, M.K., Weatherspoon, H. (eds.) 16th USENIX Symposium on Operating Systems Design and Implementation, OSDI 2022, Carlsbad, CA, USA, 11–13 July 2022, pp. 485–501. USENIX Association (2022). https://www.usenix.org/conference/osdi22/presentation/yao
31. Yao, J., Tao, R., Gu, R., Nieh, J., Jana, S., Ryan, G.: Distai: data-driven automated invariant learning for distributed protocols. In: OSDI, pp. 405–421. USENIX Association (2021)

Verifying Cake-Cutting, Faster

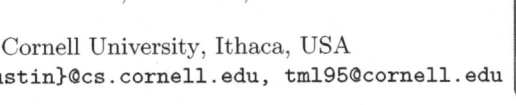

Noah Bertram[✉], Tean Lai, and Justin Hsu

Cornell University, Ithaca, USA
{nbertram,justin}@cs.cornell.edu, tml95@cornell.edu

Abstract. Envy-free cake-cutting protocols procedurally divide an infinitely divisible good among a set of agents so that no agent prefers another's allocation to their own. These protocols are highly complex and difficult to prove correct. Recently, Bertram, Levinson, and Hsu introduced a language called Slice for describing and verifying cake-cutting protocols. Slice programs can be translated to formulas encoding envy-freeness, which are solved by SMT. While Slice works well on smaller protocols, it has difficulty scaling to more complex cake-cutting protocols.

We improve Slice in two ways. First, we show any protocol execution in Slice can be replicated using piecewise uniform valuations. We then reduce Slice's constraint formulas to formulas within the theory of linear real arithmetic, showing that verifying envy-freeness is efficiently decidable. Second, we design and implement a linear type system which enforces that no two agents receive the same part of the good. We implement our methods and verify a range of challenging examples, including the first nontrivial four-agent protocol.

Keywords: Fair division · Automated verification · Type system

1 Introduction

How would you divide a piece of cake between two children? Classic wisdom would say to have one child cut the piece into two, and have the other take their preferred slice. Procedures that divide an infinitely divisible good amongst a set of agents are called *cake-cutting protocols*. If the protocol ensures no agent prefers what another received, it is called *envy-free*. While classic wisdom gives an envy-free protocol for two agents, a three-agent envy-free protocol was not discovered until 1960, and a four-agent envy-free protocol that does not dispose any cake was only proposed in 2015 by Aziz and Mackenzie [2]. Modern cake-cutting protocols are highly complex, and proving envy-freeness requires checking an enourmous number of cases.

Verifying Envy-Freeness. To make cake-cutting protocols easier to verify, Bertram et al. [4] introduced a language called Slice that can describe cake-cutting protocols, and encode envy-freeness as a logical formula that can be

© The Author(s) 2024
A. Gurfinkel and V. Ganesh (Eds.): CAV 2024, LNCS 14682, pp. 109–129, 2024.
https://doi.org/10.1007/978-3-031-65630-9_6

dispatched to an SMT solver. While Slice can verify envy-freeness fully automatically, it has some drawbacks. First, it is not able to verify that agents receive non-overlapping pieces. This basic property, known as *disjointness*, is crucial for correctness.

Another drawback of Slice is the SMT instances encoding envy-freeness for complicated protocols are difficult to solve, and only scale to some three-agent protocols—non-trivial algorithms, but relatively simple compared to modern cake-cutting protocols. One reason the instances are difficult is they are *higher order*: they quantify over *valuations*, which are functions that describe the agents' preferences.

Our Work: Verifying Disjointness and Envy-Freeness, Faster. We address these weaknesses in Slice. To verify disjointness, we develop an affine type system for Slice which restricts usage of the cake and then prove that well-typed programs are disjoint. Typechecking is straightforward and syntax-directed, requiring no use of SMT.

To verify envy-freeness more efficiently, we reduce Slice constraints into linear real arithmetic formulas, removing the need to quantify over valuations. This reduction leverages a key observation: the behavior of a protocol on any valuation can be replicated by a piecewise uniform valuation, which enables envy-freeness to be encoded as a first-order formula in linear real arithmetic. As a side benefit, our work shows that verifying envy-freeness of Slice protocols is decidable.

Finally, we implement both our affine type system and formula reduction procedure on top of the Slice implementation and transcribe two significantly more complicated protocols into Slice, including the first nontrivial four agent cake-cutting protocol [16]. For all Slice protocols, our type system establishes disjointness and our constraints encoding envy-freeness can be verified in substantially less time than in the previous version of Slice.

Outline. After describing the cake-cutting model (Sect. 2), we present the Slice language and our new linear type system for verifying disjointness (Sect. 3). We then review Slice's constraints (Sect. 4) and describe our new constraint translation (Sect. 5). We discuss our implementation and evaluation (Sect. 6), and then conclude with related work and future directions (Sect. 7).

2   Cake-Cutting Preliminaries

In this section, we introduce the basics of cake-cutting protocols; the reader can consult a standard text for more background [14].

We begin by fixing a finite set of agents $\mathbb{A}$. The cake or good is modeled by the unit interval $[0, 1]$. A *piece* P is a finite union of intervals from the cake: $P = [r_1, r'_1] \cup \cdots \cup [r_n, r'_n]$ where $r_1 \leq r'_1 < r_2 \leq r'_2 < \cdots < r_n \leq r'_n$; the points r_i and r'_i are *boundary points* of P, and we write ∂P for the set of all boundary points. Two pieces P_1 and P_2 are *disjoint* if $(P_1 \setminus \partial P_1) \cap (P_2 \setminus \partial P_2) = \emptyset$, that is, P_1 and P_2 only share possibly their boundary points.

Cake-cutting protocols produce an *allocation* of pieces to agents, i.e., an $\mathbb{A}$-tuple of pieces $(P_a \mid P_a \in \mathbb{P}, a \in \mathbb{A})$. Protocols produce allocations based on agent preferences, which are typically modelled by functions $V : \mathbb{P} \to [0,1]$ called *valuations*. We assume that valuations satisfy five standard assumptions: (1) Additivity: $V(P \cup P') = V(P) + V(P')$ provided P and P' are disjoint; (2) Non-negativity: $V(P) \geq 0$; (3) Continuity: $V([r, r'])$ is continuous in both r and r'; (4) Monotonicity: $V(P) \geq V(P')$ if $P' \subseteq P$; and (5) Normalization: $V([0,1]) = 1$. We will often write $V[r, r']$ for $V([r, r'])$. A *valuation set* $\overline{V}$ is an $\mathbb{A}$-tuple of valuations $(V_a \mid a \in \mathbb{A})$. We write $\overline{V}_a$ for agent a's valuation.

Cake-cutting protocols aim to produce fair allocations where no agent prefers another agent's piece. More precisely, if A is an allocation and $\overline{V}$ is a valuation set, we say A is *envy-free* (with respect to $\overline{V}$) if $\overline{V}_a(A_a) \geq \overline{V}_a(A_{a'})$ for all $a, a' \in \mathbb{A}$.

Protocols are assumed to have indirect access to agent valuations through specific kinds of *agent queries*. Slice implements the Robertson-Webb (RW) query model [15], which is the typical query model in the cake-cutting literature and captures most protocols. In the RW model, there are two kinds of queries. An *eval query* takes as input an agent and a piece and reports the agent's value of that piece:

$$\mathsf{eval}_a(P) \text{ reports } \overline{V}_a(P).$$

A *mark query*, when supplied an interval and a value, reports how much of the interval is needed to attain that value:

$$\mathsf{mark}_a([\ell, r], v) \text{ reports } r' \text{ where } \overline{V}_a[\ell, r'] = v, \text{ provided that } v \leq \overline{V}_a[\ell, r].$$

This query enables us to find intervals within the cake which have a specified value for a certain agent. For example, $\mathsf{mark}_a([0,1], 1/2)$ will output a point r' such that $\overline{V}_a[0, r'] = 1/2 = \overline{V}_a[r', 1]$. The assumption $v \leq \overline{V}_a[\ell, r]$ is required since $\overline{V}_a$ is monotone: if $v > \overline{V}_a[\ell, r]$, no such point exists. Note that if multiple points r' are a valid answer to a mark query, then mark can report any of them.

3 Language and Type System

We review the language [4] before describing our novel affine type system. Full details for this section can be found in the full paper [3].

3.1 Syntax of Base Slice

The set of all basic Slice expressions $\mathcal{E}$ is given by the grammar shown in Fig. 1. The expression v is a value and $\mathcal{X}$ is an infinite set of variables. We can form tuples and, through the split expression, extract their components. We have standard if-then-else expression, and a set $\mathcal{O}$ consisting of primitive operations like $+, \geq$, etc.

The remaining expressions are cake-cutting specific. The expression cake represents the whole cake, divide takes an interval and a point, splitting the interval into two at the point, and piece takes in a list of intervals and forms a piece out of them. The expression eval_a implements the eval query by taking in an interval or piece, and producing its value according to agent a. The expression mark_a implements the mark query by taking in an interval and the target value, returning any point satisfying the query.

$$
\begin{aligned}
e ::= {}& v \mid x \in \mathcal{X} \mid (e_1, \ldots, e_n) \mid \text{let } x_1, \ldots, x_n = \text{ split } e_1 \text{ in } e_2 \\
& \mid \text{ if } e_1 \text{ then } e_2 \text{ else } e_3 \mid o(e_1, \ldots, e_n) \qquad (o \in \mathcal{O}) \\
& \mid \text{ cake} \mid \text{divide}(e_1, e_2) \mid \text{piece}(e_1, \ldots, e_n) \\
& \mid \text{mark}_a(e_1, e_2) \mid \text{eval}_a(e) \qquad (a \in \mathbb{A})
\end{aligned}
$$

$$
\begin{aligned}
v ::= {}& \text{true} \mid \text{false} \mid r\#\text{Pt} \mid [r, r'] \qquad (r \le r') \\
& \mid (v_1, \ldots, v_n) \mid P\,[r_1, r_1']\,, \ldots, [r_n, r_n'] \qquad (r_i \le r_i') \\
& \mid r_1 \cdot V_{a_1}(P_1) + \cdots + r_n \cdot V_{a_n}(P_n)
\end{aligned}
$$

Fig. 1. The grammar for Slice expressions (top) and values (bottom).

The set of all values is denoted by $\mathcal{V}$. We have boolean constants, *points* $r\#\text{Pt}$, and *intervals* $[r, r']$. Points represent positions within the cake. Intervals describe contiguous pieces of the cake. Tuple values enable us to describe allocations.

Values of the form $P[r_1, r_1'], \ldots, [r_n, r_n']$ and $r_1 \cdot V_{a_1}(P_1) + \cdots + r_n \cdot V_{a_n}(P_n)$ are referred to as *pieces* and *valuations*, respectively. Note that for piece values, we do not assume that $[r_i, r_i']$ is disjoint from $[r_j, r_j']$ if $i \ne j$. We sometimes write piece values as $P_{i=1}^n[r_i, r_i']$, or $P_i[r_i, r_i']$, where i ranges over a finite set. Within the valuation value, $P_1, \ldots, P_n$ are interval or piece values, $a_1, \ldots, a_n$ are agents, and $r_1, \ldots, r_n$ are real numbers. We sometimes write $\sum_{i=1}^n r_i \cdot V_{a_i}(P_i)$, or $\sum_i r_i \cdot V_{a_i}(P_i)$ for short.

Figure 2 shows the two agent protocol described in Sect. 1 implemented in Slice; for now, we can ignore the bars over variables. This protocol uses the eval and mark queries to divide the cake into two pieces equally preferred by agent 1, and then uses eval queries for agent 2's comparison.

```
let p = split cake in
let p₁, p₂ = split divide(p, mark₁(p̄, 1/2 · eval₁(p̄))) in
if eval₂(p̄₁) ≥ eval₂(p̄₂) then
    (piece(p₂), piece(p₁))
else
    (piece(p₁), piece(p₂))
```

Fig. 2. Cut-choose in SLICE.

3.2   A Linear Type System for Slice

In this section, we develop a new, affine type system for Slice. At a high level, our type system ensures that no two agents receive overlapping pieces in the allocation. In order to accomplish this, it suffices to ensure that any duplicated variable bound to an interval or piece cannot be used either make further cuts or form more pieces. After all, you can't have your cake and eat it too!

Types. Slice types include affine types τ and non-affine types $\hat{\tau}$:

$$\hat{\tau} ::= \mathsf{Bool} \mid \mathsf{Point} \mid \mathsf{Vltn} \mid \overline{\mathsf{Intvl}} \mid \overline{\mathsf{Piece}}$$

$$\tau ::= \mathsf{Intvl} \mid \mathsf{Piece} \mid \hat{\tau}_1 \times \cdots \times \hat{\tau}_n \times \tau_1 \times \cdots \times \tau_n$$

Any non-linear type can be viewed as a linear type (i.e., as a unary product). We treat Intvl and Piece as affine types to prevent their values from being duplicated. However, restricting interval and piece types poses a problem: protocols often query an agent before using the same interval or piece for division or allocation. For example, in the second line in Fig. 2, p needs to be used to mark itself appropriately before being divided. To address this issue, we include two new base non-affine types, $\overline{\mathsf{Intvl}}$ and $\overline{\mathsf{Piece}}$, called "read only" types. Since these types are non-affine, variables of these types can be freely used in queries. However, dividing or forming pieces from read-only types is not allowed. This restriction ensures we can only create disjoint pieces.

Values and Expressions. We extend Slice with values of read-only type:

$$v ::= \cdots \mid \overline{[r, r']} \mid \overline{P[r_1, r_1'], \ldots, [r_n, r_n']}$$

The overline syntax is also extended to notation on other values and types, e.g. $\overline{r} = r$, $\overline{(v_1, v_2)} = (\overline{v_1}, \overline{v_2})$, $\overline{\mathsf{Vltn}} = \mathsf{Vltn}$, and $\overline{\tau_1 \times \tau_2} = \overline{\tau_1} \times \overline{\tau_2}$. Next, we extend Slice expressions with two new classes of variables. Affine variables are drawn from $\mathcal{W}$, while read-only variables are drawn from $\overline{\mathcal{W}}$. Finally, we extend the syntax of the split expression to bind these variables:

$$\mathsf{let}\ x_1, \ldots, x_n, w_1, \ldots, w_{n'} = \mathsf{split}\ e_1\ \mathsf{in}\ e_2$$

This expression implicitly binds read-only variables $\overline{w_1}, \ldots, \overline{w_{n'}}$ corresponding to the affine variables $w_1, \ldots, w_n$. For example, in Fig. 2, $\overline{p}$ is bound in the first line and both $\overline{p_1}$ and $\overline{p_2}$ are bound in the second line.

Affine Typing Rules. Our typing judgements are of the form $\Gamma; \Delta \vdash e : \tau$, for Γ a partial map from $\mathcal{X} \cup \overline{\mathcal{W}}$ to non-affine types, and Δ a partial map from $\mathcal{W}$ to linear types. We present a selection of rules in Fig. 3. For affine type contexts Δ_1 through Δ_n, the concatenation $\Delta_1, \ldots, \Delta_n$ denotes the union of *disjoint* contexts: $\mathrm{dom}(\Delta_i) \cap \mathrm{dom}(\Delta_j) = \emptyset$ if $i \neq j$.

The variable rules [T-VAR] and [T-AFFVAR] type the given variable based on its context. The rule [T-PIECE] shows the role of affine variables. The premise has

$$\frac{}{\Gamma, x : \hat{\tau}; \Delta \vdash x : \hat{\tau}} \; \text{T-Var} \qquad\qquad \frac{}{\Gamma; w : \tau \vdash w : \tau} \; \text{T-AffVar}$$

$$\frac{\Gamma; \Delta_1 \vdash e_1 : \text{Intvl} \quad \cdots \quad \Gamma; \Delta_n \vdash e_n : \text{Intvl}}{\Gamma; \Delta_1, \ldots, \Delta_n \vdash \text{piece}(e_1, \ldots, e_n) : \text{Piece}} \; \text{T-Piece}$$

$$\frac{\Gamma; \Delta_1 \vdash e_1 : \text{Intvl} \quad \Gamma; \Delta_2 \vdash e_2 : \text{Point}}{\Gamma; \Delta_1, \Delta_2 \vdash \text{divide}(e_1, e_2) : \text{Intvl} \times \text{Intvl}} \; \text{T-Div}$$

$$\frac{\Gamma; \Delta_1 \vdash e_1 : \overline{\text{Intvl}} \quad \Gamma; \Delta_2 \vdash e_2 : \text{Vltn}}{\Gamma; \Delta_1, \Delta_2 \vdash \text{mark}_a(e_1, e_2) : \text{Point}} \; \text{T-Mark} \qquad \frac{\Gamma; \Delta \vdash e : \overline{\text{Piece}}}{\Gamma; \Delta \vdash \text{eval}_a(e) : \text{Vltn}} \; \text{T-EvalPc}$$

$$\frac{\Gamma; \Delta_1 \vdash e_1 : \hat{\tau}_1 \times \cdots \times \hat{\tau}_n \times \tau_1 \times \cdots \times \tau_{n'} \quad \Gamma, x_1 : \hat{\tau}_1, \ldots, x_n : \hat{\tau}_n, \overline{w_1} : \overline{\tau_1}, \ldots, \overline{w_{n'}} : \overline{\tau_{n'}}; \Delta_2, w_1 : \tau_1, \ldots, w_{n'} : \tau_{n'} \vdash e_2 : \tau}{\Gamma; \Delta_1, \Delta_2 \vdash \text{let } x_1, \ldots, x_n, w_1, \ldots, w_{n'} = \text{split } e_1 \text{ in } e_2 : \tau} \; \text{T-Split}$$

Fig. 3. Select typing rules for Slice expressions.

expressions e_i under linear type contexts Δ_i, while the conclusion has the combined affine type context $\Delta_1, \ldots, \Delta_n$. Since the Δ_i must have disjoint domain, the expressions e_i cannot share affine variables. In particular, it is not possible for the same interval variable to appear more than once in a piece.

The rules [T-Piece], [T-Div], [T-Mark], and [T-EvalPc] highlight the difference between affine types and their read-only variants. [T-Piece] requires its subexpressions have type Intvl as it is forming a piece. [T-Div] requires the first argument have type Intvl since it is forming new pieces. In contrast, [T-Mark] requires the first argument to have type $\overline{\text{Intvl}}$ as it is querying a valuation, not forming a piece, and similarly for [T-EvalPc].

The most complicated rule is [T-Split], which binds multiple variables at once by pattern matching on tuples.

3.3   Semantics

We present a big-step style semantics, defined by a relation $\Downarrow_{\overline{V}} \subseteq \mathcal{E} \times \mathcal{V}$ indexed by a valuation set $\overline{V}$, so our judgments are of the form $e \Downarrow_{\overline{V}} v$. We omit $\overline{V}$ when clear from context. Our big-step rules are straightforward. We present a few rules in Fig. 4 and discuss them here.

The rule [E-Tup] forms a tuple out of a collection of values. [E-Mark] implements the mark query; since the equation $\overline{V}_a[r_1, r] = \sum_i r_i \overline{V}_{a_i}(P_i)$ can be satisfied by more than one r, the big-step semantics is non-deterministic. [E-EvalPc] implements the eval query. [E-Div] splits an interval into two, requiring the interval to contain the split point. Both this condition and the condition for [E-Mark] mean that some well-typed protocols may become stuck: they may not evaluate to values. Lastly, [E-Split] binds the variables $x_1, \ldots, x_n, w_1, \ldots, w_{n'}$ to the values $v_1, \ldots, v_n, \ldots, v_{n+n'}$, and binds $\overline{w_1}, \ldots, \overline{w_n}$ to read-only versions

$$\frac{e_1 \Downarrow v_1 \quad \cdots \quad e_n \Downarrow v_n}{(e_1, \ldots, e_n) \Downarrow (v_1, \ldots, v_n)} \text{ E-TUP}$$

$$\frac{e_1 \Downarrow \overline{[r_1, r_1']} \quad e_2 \Downarrow \sum_i r_i V_{a_i}(P_i) \quad V_a([r_1, r]) = \sum_i r_i \cdot V_{a_i}(P_i)}{\mathsf{mark}_a(e_1, e_2) \Downarrow r} \text{ E-MARK}$$

$$\frac{e \Downarrow \overline{P\,[r_1, r_1'], \ldots, [r_n, r_n']}}{\mathsf{eval}_a(e) \Downarrow V_a(P[r_1, r_1'], \ldots, [r_n, r_n'])} \text{ E-EVALPC}$$

$$\frac{e_1 \Downarrow [r_1, r_1'] \quad e_2 \Downarrow r_2 \quad r_1 \leq r_2 \leq r_1'}{\mathsf{divide}(e_1, e_2) \Downarrow ([r_1, r_2], [r_2, r_1'])} \text{ E-DIV}$$

$$\frac{e_1 \Downarrow (v_1, \ldots, v_{n+n'}) \qquad e_2\{x_i \mapsto v_i \mid 1 \leq i \leq n\}\{\overline{w_i} \mapsto \overline{v_{i+n}}, w_i \mapsto v_{i+n} \mid 1 \leq i \leq n'\} \Downarrow v}{\mathsf{let}\ x_1, \ldots, x_n, w_1, \ldots, w_{n'} = \mathsf{split}\ e_1\ \mathsf{in}\ e_2 \Downarrow v} \text{ E-SPLIT}$$

Fig. 4. Select evaluation rules for Slice expressions.

$\overline{v_{n+1}}, \ldots, \overline{v_{n+n'}}$ of the affine values. It is straightforward to show that evaluation preserves types:

Proposition 1 (Type soundness). *If* $\cdot \vdash e : \tau$ *and* $e \Downarrow v$, *then* $\cdot \vdash v : \tau$.

3.4   Disjointness

Our affine type system is designed to ensure that well-typed programs produce only disjoint allocations, i.e., tuples of pieces that do not overlap. To prove this claim, we generalize and define disjointness for values and general expressions, and then show that a well-typed disjoint program can only evaluate to a disjoint value.

Informally, an expression is disjoint if all interval values within it, excluding read-only versions, are disjoint from each other. Disjointness ignores read-only values since well-typed programs are allowed to duplicate them; this does not affect disjointness verification since we are only concerned with programs that return allocations, i.e., values of type $\mathsf{Piece}^{\mathbb{A}}$.

Since our type system prevents multiple uses of variables with type Intvl and Piece, they cannot be duplicated so programs cannot construct pieces and intervals with overlapping components. This invariant enables us to show that disjoint expressions only evaluate to disjoint values.

Proposition 2. *If* $\cdot \vdash e : \tau$ *and* e *is disjoint, then* $e \Downarrow v$ *implies* v *is disjoint.*

Checking that a well-typed protocol is disjoint is easily done syntactically, and in the protocols we are concerned with, amounts to ensuring cake is only used once.

Example 1. We illustrate our type system with the two-agent *Surplus* protocol. In brief, both agents are asked to mark the cake at half the value of the whole cake. The agent that marked furthest to the left is given all the cake to the left of their own mark. Symmetrically, the other agent is given everything to the right of their own mark, leaving the cake lying between the marks un-allocated. The Slice programs shown in Fig. 5 both correctly implement the Surplus protocol, however, the left program is not well-typed, while the right one is. The left program does not type check because it divides the whole cake twice (highlighted in red), leaving either p_1 and p_4 or p_2 and p_3 to overlap. Disjointness cannot be verified in this instance since there are intermediate expressions that will not be in its evaluation. The right program avoids this issue by only dividing the cake once it is known where the marks lie in relation to each other. □

```
let p = split cake in
let m1 = mark1(p̄, 1/2 · eval1(p̄)) in
let m2 = mark2(p̄, 1/2 · eval2(p̄)) in
let p1, p2 = split divide(p, m1) in
let p3, p4 = split divide(p, m2) in
if m2 ≥ m1 then
    (piece(p1), piece(p4))
else
    (piece(p2), piece(p3))
```

```
let p = split cake in
let m1 = mark1(p̄, 1/2 · eval1(p̄)) in
let m2 = mark2(p̄, 1/2 · eval2(p̄)) in
if m2 ≥ m1 then
    let p1, p2 = split divide(p, m1) in
    let p2, p3 = split divide(p2, m2)in
    (piece(p1), piece(p3))
else
    let p1, p2 = split divide(p, m2) in
    let p2, p3 = split divide(p2, m1)in
    (piece(p3), piece(p1))
```

(a) Not well-typed.   (b) Well-typed.

Fig. 5. The Surplus protocol written in two ways. (Color figure online)

4   Constraints

Now that we've seen the Slice language, we review the original Slice constraint translation. For full details see the full paper [3].

Paths. As is standard, we consider each path through a program separately. Paths b are Slice expressions (Sect. 3) with an assert expression assert b_1 in b_2 in place of if-then-else.

Logical syntax Protocol paths are translated into a multi-sorted first order logic. The logic is standard, so most details are omitted, though we make note of select function symbols:

– $[\_, \_]$, $\cup$ for forming intervals and pieces respectively

- 1, r for obtaining the left and right endpoints of an interval respectively
- V_a for each $a \in \mathbb{A}$ for representing agent valuations
- π_i for the ith component of a tuple
- O which contains logical counterparts to the primitive operations O (e.g. +, $\geq$)

Through the function symbols and constants, any program value v can be encoded as a logical term v. Throughout, the typewriter font designates logical counterparts to program objects. We also include a special set of variables $\mathcal{Y}$, disjoint from $\mathcal{X}$, which will only be used to represent points in our formulas.

With our logic, we can express envy-freeness, where x represents allocation:

$$E(x) \triangleq \bigwedge_{a,a' \in \mathbb{A}} V_a(\pi_a x) \geq V_a(\pi_{a'} x). \tag{1}$$

Logical Semantics. Formula semantics are given by an interpretation $\mathcal{A}$ and variable assignment μ. An interpretation associates sorts with sets and function symbols with functions on these sets. A variable assignment is a map from variables to elements of these sets. For our purposes, we fix a base interpretation that interprets everything but the symbols V_a for all a, and all full interpretations agree with the base. The base interprets objects as one would expect, e.g. $[\![1]\!]([r, r']) = r$. For full interpretations, the symbols V_a are interpreted over all possible valuations. Thus, full interpretations are uniquely determined by the choice of valuation set, and we write $\mathcal{A}_{\overline{V}}$ for the interpretation such that $[\![V_a]\!]_{\mathcal{A}_{\overline{V}}} = \overline{V}_a$.

For a logical term t, we let $[\![t]\!]^\mu_{\mathcal{A}}$ denote the interpretation of t according to $\mathcal{A}$, with variable values determined by μ, defined in the usual way (e.g., $[\![V_a([y, y'])]\!]^\mu_{\mathcal{A}_{\overline{V}}} = \overline{V}_a[\mu(y), \mu(y')]$). Likewise, for a formula φ, we write $\mathcal{A}, \mu \vDash \varphi$ if φ is true when interpreted through $\mathcal{A}$ with variable values determined by μ, also defined in the usual way. We write $\mathcal{A} \vDash \varphi$ if for all assignments μ we have $\mathcal{A}, \mu \vDash \varphi$. If t is a term containing no V_a symbols, then for a fixed assignment μ, the term t is always interpreted the same way and we write just $[\![t]\!]^\mu$.

If v is an allocation, $\mathcal{A}_{\overline{V}}, \mu \vDash E(v)$ states that $[\![v]\!]^\mu_{\mathcal{A}_{\overline{V}}}$ is an envy-free allocation. If e is a expression, we say that e *satisfies* $E(x)$ and write $e \vDash E(x)$ if for all valuation sets $\overline{V}$, $e \Downarrow_{\overline{V}} v$ implies $\mathcal{A}_{\overline{V}} \vDash E(v)$. Thus $e \vDash E(x)$ means e is envy-free.

In order to verify envy-freeness, Slice translates programs e to logical formulas ensuring $e \vDash E(x)$. We review this constraint translation next, before describing our improved translation.

Constraints. To translate protocols to formulas, we translate each path in a protocol to a formula consisting of a logical term $\rho(b)$ and a formula $c(b)$. Intuitively, $\rho(b)$ is the logical term representation of the value that b evaluates to assuming that the formula $c(b)$ holds. We give some cases of the definition in Fig. 6.

It is informative to compare these definitions to the big-step semantics shown in Sect. 3. For instance, $\rho(\mathsf{divide}(b_1, b_2))$ is a logical encoding of the original interval being split into two, $\rho(\mathsf{mark}_a(b_1, b_2))$ is a variable that represents the mark, $\rho(\mathsf{eval}_a(b))$ is the value of the interval or piece provided.

$$\rho(\overline{v}) \triangleq \mathsf{v} \qquad \rho(v) \triangleq \mathsf{v} \qquad \rho(x) \triangleq x \qquad \rho(w) \triangleq w \qquad \rho(\overline{w}) \triangleq \overline{w}$$

$$\rho(\mathsf{divide}(b_1, b_2)) \triangleq ([\mathbf{1}(\rho(b_1)), \rho(b_2)], [\rho(b_2), \mathbf{r}(\rho(b_1))]) \qquad \rho(\mathsf{mark}_a(b_1, b_2)) \triangleq y \in \mathcal{Y}$$

$$\rho(\mathsf{eval}_a(b)) \triangleq \mathsf{V}_a(\rho(b)) \qquad \rho(\mathsf{assert}\ b_1\ \mathsf{in}\ b_2) \triangleq \rho(b_2)$$

$$c(\mathsf{divide}(b_1, b_2)) \triangleq c(b_1) \wedge c(b_2) \wedge \mathbf{1}(\rho(b_1)) \leq \rho(b_2) \leq \mathbf{r}(\rho(b_1)) \qquad c(\mathsf{eval}_a(b)) \triangleq c(b)$$

$$c(\mathsf{mark}_a(b_1, b_2)) \triangleq c(b_1) \wedge c(b_2) \wedge (\mathsf{V}_a([\mathbf{1}(\rho(b_1)), \rho(\mathsf{mark}_a(b_1, b_2))]) = \rho(b_2))$$

$$c(\mathsf{assert}\ b_1\ \mathsf{in}\ b_2) \triangleq (\rho(b_1) = \mathsf{true}) \wedge c(b_1) \wedge c(b_2)$$

Fig. 6. $\rho(b)$ and $c(b)$ for select path expressions b.

The formula $c(b)$ is referred to as the *constraint of b*. Roughly, the formula corresponds to the side conditions shown in the big-step semantics. The most interesting cases of the definition are in Fig. 6. All constraints conjoin the conditions from their subexpressions. The constraint for divide encodes that the point dividing the interval must be within. The constraint of eval has no additional conditions to satisfy, so it is just the constraint of its subexpression. The constraint of mark ensures that the new point has the required property and the constraint of assert asserts that the guard must hold.

Example 2. Consider the following path, denoted b, from Cut-Choose (Fig. 2):

> let p = split cake in
> let p_1, p_2 = split divide$(p, \mathsf{mark}_1(\overline{p}, 1/2 \cdot \mathsf{eval}_1(\overline{p})))$ in
> assert $\mathsf{eval}_2(\overline{p_1}) \geq \mathsf{eval}_2(\overline{p_2})$ in $(\mathsf{piece}(p_2), \mathsf{piece}(p_1))$

The path b gives the following (simplified) constraint:

$$c(b) = (\mathsf{V}_1([0, y]) = 1/2 \cdot \mathsf{V}_1([0, 1])) \wedge (\mathsf{V}_2([0, y]) \geq \mathsf{V}_2([y, 1]))$$
$$\rho(b) = (\cup[y, 1], \cup[0, y])$$

The first conjunct in $c(b)$ is from the expression $\mathsf{mark}_1(\overline{p}, 1/2 \cdot \mathsf{eval}_1(\overline{p}))$, while the second is from $\mathsf{eval}_2(\overline{p_1}) \geq \mathsf{eval}_2(\overline{p_2})$. The term $\rho(b)$ is a logical encoding of b's evaluation. □

The following result, akin to Corollary 4.8 for Slice [4], characterizes paths in terms of their constraints.

Theorem 1. *Suppose $\cdot \vdash b : \tau$. Then $b \Downarrow_{\overline{V}} v$ if and only if there is a variable assignment μ such that $\mathcal{A}_{\overline{V}}, \mu \vDash c(b)$ and $[\![\rho(b)]\!]_{\mathcal{A}_{\overline{V}}}^{\mu} = |v|$.*

With our constraint translation being sound and complete, we look to use constraints to verify envy-freeness only by checking the validity of certain formulas involving the constraint. For the following, let $\mathcal{Y}_b$ be the set of free variables contained in $c(b)$, and let $B(e)$ be the set of paths within e. The following theorem forms the basis for automated verification in Slice.

Theorem 2. *Suppose that* e *is a well-formed expression and* $\cdot \vdash e : \mathsf{Piece}^{\mathbb{A}}$. *Then*

$$\mathcal{A}_{\overline{V}} \vDash \bigwedge_{b \in B(e)} \forall \mathcal{Y}_b.(c(b) \Rightarrow E(\rho(b))) \tag{2}$$

for all $\overline{V}$ *if and only if* $e \vDash E(x)$.

The formal definition for a well-formed expression can be found within the full paper [3], though the imposed conditions are mild; any typical cake-cutting protocol is well-formed. This theorem can be generalized from $E(x)$ to general formulas $F(x)$ satisfying mild conditions.

We stress that in order to apply this theorem to conclude $e \vDash E(x)$, Formula (2) needs to be valid *for all* valuation sets. Our logic is not rich enough to quantify over valuations and their axioms, so for verification, these formulas must be embedded in a richer theory (e.g., from a modern SMT solver).

5 Piecewise Uniform Reduction

Now that we have seen how the existing constraint translation works in Slice, we show how to produce a result similar to Theorem 2, but instead with a formula in the theory of linear real arithmetic. Formula (2) contains terms like $\mathbb{1}([t_1, t_2])$, $\pi_k(t_1, \ldots, t_n)$, and $\mathsf{V}_a(t)$, which all need to be reduced to linear sums of real variables. Most terms can be reduced via syntactic simplifications, but reducing valuation terms $\mathsf{V}_a(t)$ is much more challenging.

The broad approach is to show a protocol execution on any valuation set can be replicated with a *piecewise uniform valuation* set, then replace terms $\mathsf{V}_a(t)$ with sums of differences of real variables that represent $\mathsf{V}_a(t)$. We discuss conditions under which protocol executions can be replicated, then show there are always piecewise uniform valuations meeting these conditions. Then, we describe how to construct the formula reduction, prove that it preserves validity, and then apply it to obtain an analog to Theorem 2. Our approach is inspired by Theorem 1 from Kurokawa, Lai, and Procaccia [9].

For this section only, we will assume that the operations $\mathcal{O}$ consist only of boolean operators, comparisons, constant multiplication and addition. These operations are sufficient for describing cake-cutting protocols. A more detailed description of $\mathcal{O}$ is shown in the full paper [3].

5.1 Replicating Protocol Executions

In this subsection, we give a condition when the same evaluation judgement holds for two possibly different valuation sets. For this, we define the following relationship between valuation sets.

Definition 1. *Let* $M \supseteq \{0, 1\}$ *a finite set of points. We say that valuation sets* $\overline{U}$ *and* $\overline{V}$ *agree on* M *if for any piece* P *with boundary points in* M, $V_a(P) = U_a(P)$ *for all* $a \in \mathbb{A}$.

The following theorem says that we can identically derive an evaluation judgement with a different valuation set, as long as the valuation set agrees with the original on all pieces formed from points in the derivation.

Theorem 3. *Let $\overline{U}$ and $\overline{V}$ be valuation sets, and suppose $e \Downarrow_{\overline{V}} v$. If $\overline{U}$ and $\overline{V}$ agree on all points considered in the derivation of $e \Downarrow_{\overline{V}} v$, then $e \Downarrow_{\overline{U}} v$.*

There is an analog for formulas.

Theorem 4. *If valuation sets $\overline{U}$ and $\overline{V}$ agree on the set of points considered in a formula φ under variable assignment μ, then $\mathcal{A}_{\overline{V}}, \mu \vDash \varphi \iff \mathcal{A}_{\overline{U}}, \mu \vDash \varphi$.*

5.2   Piecewise Uniform Valuations

Now that we have seen what is required for replication, we show that there is always a special piecewise uniform valuation set that meets the requirements.

We first formally define piecewise uniform valuations. It is easiest to define these valuations in terms of their *density*. For our purposes, a *density* is a function $w : [0,1] \to \mathbb{R}_{\geq 0}$, and a valuation W *has density* w if $W(P) = \int_P w$ for all $P \in \mathbb{P}$.

Definition 2. *We say that a valuation U is* piecewise uniform *if U has density u for which there exists a piece $P \in \mathbb{P}$ and a constant c such that*

$$u(x) = \begin{cases} c & \text{if } x \in P \\ 0 & \text{if } x \notin P. \end{cases}$$

We let $P(U)$ denote P and $c(U)$ denote c.

Because valuations are normalized, the constant associated with a piecewise uniform valuation U is the reciprocal length of $P(U)$. Therefore, any piece P uniquely determines a piecewise uniform valuation U_P, where $P(U_P) = P$.

Much of the advantage of these valuations lies in how we can represent their values on specific pieces. For intervals built from right endpoints of $P(U)$, the valuation reduces to a simple sum of differences between real numbers. If we write out $P(U) = [l_1, r_1] \cup \cdots \cup [l_n, r_n]$ where $l_1 \leq r_1 < \cdots < l_n \leq r_n$, then

$$U[r_i, r_{i'}] = c(U) \cdot \sum_{i' \geq j > i} (r_j - l_j). \tag{3}$$

This formula is key for our reduction, as it enables us to convert valuations applied to intervals (left) to sums of differences of real numbers (right).

We call a valuation set a *piecewise uniform valuation* set if all valuations within it are piecewise uniform. Our formula reduction will benefit from the following key conditions on piecewise uniform valuation sets.

Definition 3. *Let $\overline{U}$ be a piecewise uniform valuation set and let $M \supseteq \{0,1\}$ be a finite set of points. We say that $\overline{U}$ is* easily replaceable *on M if*

1. *For each $a \in \mathbb{A}$, and for each $m \in M^{\setminus 0} \triangleq M \setminus \{0\}$, there exists $l_a(m)$ such that if $l_a(m) < m'$ for $m' \in M^{\setminus 0}$, then $m \leq m'$ and*

$$P(\overline{U}_a) = \bigcup_{m \in M^{\setminus 0}} [l_a(m), m].$$

2. *For each $a, a' \in \mathbb{A}$, $c(\overline{U}_a) = c(\overline{U}_{a'})$.*

The first part is valuable for the reduction as it removes the need to keep track of distinct right endpoints for each agent. The second part means that the coefficient in Eq. (3) can be ignored when comparing these valuations with each other, which will be important later for the formulas to be in real linear arithmetic.

Theorem 5. *For any valuation set $\overline{V}$ and any finite set of points $M \supseteq \{0, 1\}$, there exists a piecewise uniform valuation set that both agrees with $\overline{V}$ on M and is easily replaceable on M.*

The proof constructs a specific piecewise uniform valuation set that satisfies these properties. The construction is a slightly more general version of the construction shown in Theorem 1 by Kurokawa, Lai, and Procaccia [9].

A consequence of the theorem is that any protocol execution can be replicated by the specific piecewise uniform valuation set, and any formulas that hold for the original valuation set that only consider points from the execution will also hold for this specific valuation set.

Example 3. We illustrate the construction for $\mathbb{A} = \{1, 2\}$ with valuation $\overline{V}_1$ being the uniform valuation over the cake, and $\overline{V}_2$ having density $x \mapsto 2x$, and the set of points $M = \{0, 1/2, 1\}$. Set $\overline{U}_1 = U_{P_1(d)}$ and $\overline{U}_2 = U_{P_2(d)}$ for pieces

$$P_1(d) = [1/2 - 1/2 \cdot 1/d, 1/2] \cup [1 - 1/2 \cdot 1/d, 1]$$
$$P_2(d) = [1/2 - 1/4 \cdot 1/d, 1/2] \cup [1 - 3/4 \cdot 1/d, 1]$$

for $d \geq 3/2$. Clearly both pieces have interval right endpoints of $\{1/2, 1\} = M^{\setminus 0}$. Also, it is easily to calculate that $c(U_{P_1}) = c(U_{P_2}) = d$. Thus, $\overline{U}$ is easily replaceable on M. We additionally have

$$\overline{U}_1[0, 1/2] = d \cdot (1/2 - (1/2 - 1/2 \cdot 1/d)) = 1/2 = \overline{V}_1[0, 1/2],$$
$$\overline{U}_1[1/2, 1] = d \cdot (1 - (1 - 1/2 \cdot 1/d)) \quad = 1/2 = \overline{V}_1[1/2, 1],$$
$$\overline{U}_2[0, 1/2] = d \cdot (1/2 - (1/2 - 1/4 \cdot 1/d)) = 1/4 = \overline{V}_2[0, 1/2],$$
$$\overline{U}_2[1/2, 1] = d \cdot (1 - (1 - 3/4 \cdot 1/d)) \quad = 3/4 = \overline{V}_2[1/2, 1],$$

so $\overline{U}$ replicates $\overline{V}$ on M.   □

5.3   Piecewise Uniform Replacement

We leverage the above results to produce a reduction on protocol constraints. At a high level, for any formula having only variables for points, we can simplify it to be a disjunction of inequalities in terms of the form $\sum_i r_i \cdot V_{a_i}(P_i)$ for real

r_i and logical pieces and intervals P_i. We then replace terms of the form $V_a(P)$ with sums of differences of real variables. Using Theorem 4 and Theorem 5 we can show that the original formula holds if and only if the replaced formula holds for a piecewise uniform valuation set.

Simplified terms are the terms within the following sets, indexed by sort:

$$R_{\texttt{Point}} \triangleq \mathcal{Y} \cup \{r \# \mathsf{Pt} \mid r \in \mathbb{R}\} \qquad R_{\texttt{Piece}} \triangleq \{\cup(t_1, \ldots, t_i) \mid t_i \in R_{\texttt{Intvl}}\}$$

$$R_{\texttt{Intvl}} \triangleq \{[t, t'] \mid t, t' \in R_{\texttt{Point}}\} \qquad R_{\texttt{Vltn}} \triangleq \{\textstyle\sum_i r_i \cdot V_{a_i}(P_i) \mid P_i \in R_{\texttt{Intvl}} \cup R_{\texttt{Piece}}\}$$

For any well-sorted term t containing only variables in $\mathcal{Y}$, we can produce an equivalent simplified version of it, which we denote by $R(t)$. The notion of simplified and the simplification operation R easily extends to whole formulas as well. For further details of this step, see the full paper [3]. For further use, if t is a simplified term or formula, we let $\#\mathsf{Pt}(t)$ denote the subset of $R_{\texttt{Point}}$ contained as subterms of t.

Proceeding with the reduction, we introduce a new set of logical variables, $\mathcal{Z}$ and we assume for each $y \in \mathcal{Y} \cup \{1\}$, and $a \in \mathbb{A}$, there is a unique $z_{a,y} \in \mathcal{Z}$. To understand the purpose of $\mathcal{Z}$, consider a piecewise uniform valuation set $\overline{U}$ that is easily replaceable on M. Then $P(\overline{U}_a)$, the piece corresponding to agent a's valuation, is the union of intervals of the form $[l_a(m), m]$ for $m \in M^{\backslash 0}$. If the variable y represents the variable m, then the variable $z_{a,y}$ then represents the left endpoint $l_a(m)$.

Definition 4. *A piecewise uniform replacement is a finite totally ordered subset* $(S, >_S)$ *of* $\mathcal{Y} \cup \{0, 1\}$ *such that* $\{0, 1\} \subseteq S$ *and* $0 \leq_S y \leq_S 1$ *for all* $y \in S$. *For* $y, y' \in S$, *we define* $S|_y^{y'} \triangleq \{y'' \in S \mid y' \geq_S y'' >_S y\}$. *We let* $S|_t \triangleq S|_y^{y'}$ *if* $t = [y, y']$ *and* $S|_t \triangleq S|_{y_1}^{y'_1} \cup \cdots \cup S|_{y_n}^{y'_n}$ *if* $t = \cup[y_1, y'_1], \ldots, [y_n, y'_n]$.

The piecewise uniform replacement packages neatly all the data needed to replace valuation symbols in formulas. The order on S represents the ordering of real numbers, since variables from $\mathcal{Y}$ represent points. A replacement is applied to terms:

Definition 5. *The application of a piecewise uniform substitution S on a term* $t \in R_S$ *for which* $\#\mathsf{Pt}(t) \subseteq S$ *is as follows:*

$$S(V_a(t)) \triangleq \sum_{y \in S|_t} (y - z_{a,y}) \quad S(\textstyle\sum_i r_i \cdot t_i) \triangleq \sum_i r_i \cdot S(t_i) \quad S(t) \triangleq t \ otherwise.$$

S *can be applied to formulas by passing itself down to its terms. When* $S|_t$ *is empty, we replace the term with* 0.

The piecewise uniform replacement syntactically applies Eq. (3) (ignoring the constant) to valuation terms for valuations of the form shown in Definition 3. The following example illustrates this concretely.

Example 4. Returning to the path b shown in Example 2, consider the piecewise uniform replacement $S = \{0, y, 1\}$ where $0 <_S y <_S< 1$. Then $V_a([0, y])$ and

$V_a([y, 1])$ are replaced with $y - z_{a,y}$ and $1 - z_{a,1}$ respectively. The formula $c(b)$ simplifies to

$$S(c(b)) = (y - z_{1,y} = 1/2 \cdot (y - z_{1,y} + 1 - z_{1,1})) \wedge (y - z_{2,y} \geq 1 - z_{2,1}),$$

and the encoding of envy-freeness becomes

$$S(E(\rho(b))) = (y - z_{2,y} \geq 1 - z_{2,1}) \wedge (y - z_{1,y} \geq 1 - z_{1,1}).$$

Both are clearly linear inequalities in real variables.   □

Piecewise uniform replacements are used to reduce simplified formulas to linear real inequalities:

Proposition 3. *Let f be a simplified formula. Let S be a piecewise uniform replacement such that $\#\mathsf{Pt}(f) \subseteq S$. Then $S(f)$ consists only of conjunctions and disjunctions of linear inequalities of real variables.*

To apply piecewise uniform replacements in a sound way, the variable assignment must properly line it up with the valuation set; the precise conditions for this are given in the following definition.

Definition 6. *Let $\overline{U}$ be a piecewise uniform valuation set. Let S is a piecewise uniform replacement and μ a variable assignment. We write $S \xrightarrow{\mu} \overline{U}$ if*

1. *$\overline{U}$ is easily replaceable on $\mu(S)$ (by convention $\mu(0) = 0$ and $\mu(1) = 1$)*
2. *$\mu(z_{a,y}) = l_a(\mu(y))$ if $y = \min\{y' \in S \mid \mu(y') = \mu(y)\}$*
3. *$\mu(z_{a,y}) = \mu(y)$ if $y \neq \min\{y' \in S \mid \mu(y') = \mu(y)\}$*
4. *If $\mu(y) < \mu(y')$ then $y <_S y'$.*

This definition formalizes how we think of variables in a piecewise uniform replacement. Condition (1) says that $\mu(S)$ captures the right endpoints of $P(\overline{U}_a)$ correctly, (2) and (3) together ensure that we don't repeat values in our sums, and (4) ensures that the variable ordering is compatible with the real ordering given by μ.

Example 5. Let $S = \{0, y, 1\}$, and let $\overline{U}$ be the piecewise uniform valuation set described in Example 3. Set $\mu(y) = 1/2$, and

$$\mu(z_{1,y}) = 1/2 - 1/2 \cdot 1/d \quad \mu(z_{1,1}) = 1 - 1/2 \cdot 1/d$$
$$\mu(z_{2,y}) = 1/2 - 1/4 \cdot 1/d \quad \mu(z_{2,1}) = 1 - 3/4 \cdot 1/d.$$

Then $\mu(S) = \{0, 1/2, 1\}$ and Example 3 illustrates that $\overline{U}$ is easily replaceable on $\mu(S)$. Also, $z_{a,y}$ is the left endpoint, $l_a(1/2)$, of the left interval for $P_a(d)$, and $z_{a,1}$ is the left endpoint, $l_a(1)$, of the right interval for $P_a(d)$, hence condition (2) is satisfied. Condition (3) is vacuous here. Clearly, $0 < 1/2 < 1$ and $0 <_S y <_S 1$ so condition (4) is satisfied. Thus we have that $S \xrightarrow{\mu} \overline{U}$.   □

Piecewise uniform replacements preserve validity when the conditions in Definition 6 are met.

Theorem 6. *Let f be a simplified formula and let S be a piecewise uniform replacement such that $\#\mathsf{Pt}(f) \subseteq S$. Let μ be an assignment and $\overline{U}$ a piecewise uniform valuation set. If $S \xrightarrow{\mu} \overline{U}$ then $\mathcal{A}_{\overline{U}}, \mu \vDash f \iff \mathcal{A}_{\overline{U}}, \mu \vDash S(f)$.*

Example 6. We illustrate the theorem by applying it with $S = \{0, y, 1\}$ for the formula $c(b)$ Example 2 reproduced here:

$$c(b) = (\mathsf{V}_1([0, y]) = 1/2 \cdot \mathsf{V}_1([0, 1])) \wedge (\mathsf{V}_2([0, y]) \geq \mathsf{V}_2([y, 1])).$$

Supposing $S \xrightarrow{\mu} \overline{U}$, this formula is equivalent to its reduced version from Example 4:

$$S(c(b)) = (y - z_{1,y} = 1/2 \cdot (y - z_{1,y} + 1 - z_{1,1})) \wedge (y - z_{2,y} \geq 1 - z_{2,1}).$$

One can verify this equivalence for the example $\overline{U}$ and μ shown in Example 5.

Associated with each piecewise uniform replacement S, is a formula $\psi(S)$.

Definition 7. *Let S be a piecewise uniform replacement, written $S = \{y_1, \ldots, y_n\}$ so that $y_1 <_S \cdots <_S y_n$. We let $\psi(S)$ denote the conjunction of the following formulas for all agents $a, a' \in \mathbb{A}$:*

$$0 \leq z_{a,y_1} \leq y_1 \leq \cdots \leq z_{a,y_n} \leq y_n \leq 1, \qquad \sum_{y \in S} y - z_{a,y} = \sum_{y \in S \setminus \{0\}} y - z_{a',y}.$$

Whenever the above formula holds for some variable assignment μ, a piecewise uniform valuation set $\overline{U}$ that is easily replaceable on $\mu(S)$ can be constructed:

$$P(\overline{U}_a) = \bigcup_{y \in S \setminus \{0\}} [\mu(z_{a,y}), \mu(y)], \qquad c(\overline{U}_a) = \sum_{y \in S \setminus \{0\}} \mu(y) - \mu(z_{a,y}).$$

This assists us in showing that our constraint reduction procedure is complete.

We now state our main theorem. For a path b, let S_b be the set of piecewise uniform replacements on $\mathcal{Y}_b \cup \{0, 1\}$—note that this set is *finite*.

Theorem 7. *Suppose e is well-formed and $\cdot \vdash e : \mathsf{Piece}^{\mathbb{A}}$. Then $e \vDash E(x)$ if and only if*

$$\vDash \bigwedge_{b \in B(e)} \bigwedge_{S \in S_b} \forall \mathcal{Y}_b. S(\mathsf{R}(c(b) \wedge \psi(S) \Rightarrow E(\rho(b)))). \tag{4}$$

In contrast to Theorem 2, we no longer need to quantify over valuations—a valuation set is baked into the formula through $\psi(S)$. This also gives a valuation set witness whenever Formula (4) does not hold.

Similar to Theorem 2, this theorem can be extended to more general formulas $F(x)$.

Proof (sketch). For the forward direction, we assume that $e \Downarrow_{\overline{V}} v$ and apply Theorems 5 to 3 to obtain a piecewise uniform valuation set $\overline{U}$ for which $e \Downarrow_{\overline{U}} v$. Then it is a matter of applying Theorem 6 and Theorem 4 to obtain that $E(\mathrm{v})$ is satisfied. For the backward direction, we suppose that Formula (4) doesn't hold for some b and S_b, and use $\psi(S)$ to construct a piecewise uniform valuation set that evaluates to v yet $E(\mathrm{v})$ is not satisfied.

According to Proposition 3, Formula (4) consists entirely of linear inequalities of real variables. Thus, we have the following corollary.

Corollary 1. *Let e be a well-formed and well-typed Slice protocol. Checking if e is envy-free is decidable.*

6   Implementation and Evaluation

We implemented our type system and formula reduction on top of the Slice implementation. Protocols are first type-checked following our linear typing rules, and then compiled to linear real arithmetic constraints encoding envy-freeness, which are dispatched to Z3 [12].

Benchmark Protocols. In our benchmarks, we include all original protocols implemented in Slice [4]; we briefly describe them here. *Cut-choose* is the classic 2 agent protocol where one agent cuts and the other picks. *Surplus* is a two agent protocol which leaves a "surplus" piece of the cake in the center. *Selfridge-Conway-Full* is the classic three agent protocol [6]. *Selfridge-Conway-Surplus* is a variant of Selfridge-Conway-Full that disposes the trimming, and *Waste-Makes-Haste-3* [16] effectively is a minor variant on Selfridge-Conway-Surplus.

We also implement two new, more complicated protocols. The first, *Aziz-Mackenzie-3*, is the three-agent variant of the first bounded envy-free four agent protocol with no free disposal [2]. Briefly, this protocol obtains an envy-free allocation by first obtaining a partial allocation where one agent does not care how the rest is allocated amongst the others. Cut-Choose is then applied. The second, *Waste-Makes-Haste-4*, is the four-agent connected variant of the Waste-Makes-Haste free disposal protocol [16, Section 6]. This protocol relies on *equalize* queries: Equalize$_a(n)$ has agent a divide the cake to produce n equally most preferred (according to a) pieces of the cake. It can be shown using Hall's marriage theorem that an envy-free allocation can be made from a set of pieces following some sequence of equalize queries among the agents (for 4 agents, $n \leq 5$), although the allocation must be found through exhaustive search. This protocol exhaustively tries certain sequences of equalize queries until an envy-free allocation is obtained. Notably, this is the first four agent envy-free cake-cutting protocol to be implemented and verified.

Evaluation. Table 1 presents some statistics from verifying envy-freeness for each of our benchmark protocols. Our experiments were conducted on an M1 MacBook Pro with 16 GB of RAM. We measured the time both to compile protocols to constraints, and the actual time Z3 took to solve. We also record here the number of paths in each protocol, as well as the number of lines for the protocol implementation and the constraint formula. Each path corresponds to a distinct disjunct in the constraint. We measure this against the solving time for the original Slice constraints (Old), which uses non linear real arithmetic formulas. Our results demonstrate a reduction in solving time compared with the old constraints. The four-agent protocol is significantly more complex than the others, though Z3 can still solve the constraints efficiently.

Table 1. Verifying envy-freeness (averaged over 5 runs).

Protocol	#Paths	Size (lines)		Time (seconds)		
		Program	Constraints	Compile	Z3	Z3 (Old)
Cut-Choose	2	6	35	1.31	0.00	0.02
Surplus	2	11	56	1.23	0.00	0.02
Waste-Makes-Haste-3	24	8	924	0.85	0.02	0.84
Selfridge-Conway-Surplus	216	19	7726	1.09	0.01	0.82
Selfridge-Conway-Full	1800	21	98292	9.20	0.46	19.38
Aziz-Mackenzie-3	93384	23	8086180	2m4	6.82	n/a
Waste-Makes-Haste-4	1953792	290	157553237	37m02	1m22	n/a

7   Related and Future Work

Cake Cutting Verification. In recent work, Lester [11] proposes a system called Crumbs to verify and disprove envy-freeness, using C bounded model checker (CBMC) instead of SMT. While performance on correct (envy-free) protocols is similar to the prior version of Slice, Lester [11] shows that Crumbs is much more effective at finding counterexamples for incorrect protocols. By using our new constraint reduction, our current work significantly outperforms Slice and Crumbs for correct protocols, and we can efficiently construct counterexamples for incorrect protocols (details in the full paper [3]). In terms of expressivity, Crumbs supports a more restrictive, higher-level query model, enabling constraint solving over bounded integer arithmetic. In contrast, our work supports all protocols written in the standard Robertson-Webb model. Our system also establishes disjointness, which Crumbs does not consider.

Substructural Type Systems. Our type system is an example of a *substructural type system*, which originate from substructural logics. In brief, substructural logics restrict the application of assumptions in proofs. Likewise, substructural type systems restrict the usage of variables, enabling computational resource usage to be restricted. A classic example is *linear logic*, due to Girard [8], which led to *linear type systems* [1,10,17,18]. Walker [19] provides a resource for learning about substructural type systems. Our type system is designed to ensures *physical disjointness* of parts of the cake; we are not aware of prior work that uses substructural types for a single divisible good, though there are similar ideas in separation logic (e.g., [5]).

Formal Methods and Social Choice. Cake-cutting protocols belong to a broader literature on social choice theory, which has had many fruitful interactions with formal methods. In one direction, formal methods researchers have used interactive theorem provers to verify classical protocols and impossibility theorems in social choice theory (e.g., [13]). In the other direction, social choice researchers have used computer-aided solvers to prove novel theorems in social choice theory (e.g., [7]).

Conclusions and Future Work. Our work makes progress in cake-cutting protocol verification, through an affine type system for disjointness and a formula reduction that enables much more efficient envy-freeness checking. However, there are envy-free cake-cutting protocols even more complex than what we can verify here. The complexity of these protocols makes it difficult to even write them down in Slice, let alone the constraint compiling and solving time involved. New Slice language features may be needed to address transcription effort, while improvements to the Slice implementation and early pruning of unreachable paths could significantly decrease both compile and solving time. The most notable of these protocols is the four agent version of Aziz-Mackenzie-*3* [2], which does not discard any cake, unlike Waste-Makes-Haste-4. By making our affine type system instead linear, it could be used to verify no cake is discarded for that protocol, and others already implemented.

Acknowledgments. We thank Cornell's PL discussion group (PLDG) and Martin Lester for discussions about this work. We also thank the anonymous reviewers for their close reading and detailed feedback. This work is partially supported by NSF grant CCF-2319186.

References

1. Abramsky, S.: Computational interpretations of linear logic. Theoret. Comput. Sci. **111**(1), 3–57 (1993). https://doi.org/10.1016/0304-3975(93)90181-R
2. Aziz, H., Mackenzie, S.: A discrete and bounded envy-free cake cutting protocol for four agents. In: ACM SIGACT Symposium on Theory of Computing (STOC), Cambridge, Massachusetts, pp. 454–464 (2016).https://doi.org/10.1145/2897518. 2897522
3. Bertram, N., Lai, T., Hsu, J.: Verifying cake-cutting, faster (2024). https://arxiv. org/abs/2405.14068
4. Bertram, N., Levinson, A., Hsu, J.: Cutting the cake: a language for fair division. In: ACM SIGPLAN Conference on Programming Language Design and Implementation (PLDI), Orlando, Florida (2023). https://doi.org/10.1145/3591293
5. Boyland, J.: Fractional permissions. In: Clarke, D., Noble, J., Wrigstad, T. (eds.) Aliasing in Object-Oriented Programming. Types, Analysis and Verification. LNCS, vol. 7850, pp. 270–288. Springer, Heidelberg (2013). https://doi.org/ 10.1007/978-3-642-36946-9_10

6. Brams, S.J., Jones, M.A., Klamler, C.: Better ways to cut a cake. Not. AMS **53**(11), 1314–1321 (2006). https://www.ams.org/cgi-bin/notices/

7. Geist, C.: Generating insights in social choice theory via computer-aided methods. Ph.D. thesis, Technical University Munich, Germany (2016). https://nbn-resolving.org/urn:nbn:de:bvb:91-diss-20160906-1296898-1-8

8. Girard, J.Y.: Linear logic. Theoret. Comput. Sci. **50**(1), 1–101 (1987). https://doi.org/10.1016/0304-3975(87)90045-4

9. Kurokawa, D., Lai, J., Procaccia, A.: How to cut a cake before the party ends. In: AAAI Conference on Artificial Intelligence, Bellevue, Washington (2013). https://doi.org/10.1609/aaai.v27i1.8629

10. Lafont, Y.: The linear abstract machine. Theoret. Comput. Sci. **59**(1), 157–180 (1988). https://doi.org/10.1016/0304-3975(88)90100-4

11. Lester, M.M.: Cutting the cake into crumbs: verifying envy-free cake-cutting protocols using bounded integer arithmetic. In: Practical Aspects of Declarative Languages (PADL), London, England (2024). https://doi.org/10.1007/978-3-031-52038-9_7

12. de Moura, L., Bjørner, N.: Z3: an efficient SMT solver. In: International Conference on Tools and Algorithms for the Construction and Analysis of Systems (TACAS), Budapest, Hungary (2008). https://doi.org/10.1007/978-3-540-78800-3_24

13. Nipkow, T.: Social choice theory in HOL. J. Autom. Reason. **43**(3), 289–304 (2009). https://doi.org/10.1007/S10817-009-9147-4

14. Procaccia, A.D.: Cake cutting algorithms. In: Brandt, F., Conitzer, V., Endriss, U., Lang, J., Procaccia, A.D. (eds.) Handbook of Computational Social Choice, pp. 311–330, Cambridge University Press (2016). https://doi.org/10.1017/CBO9781107446984.014

15. Robertson, J., Webb, W.: Cake-Cutting Algorithms: Be Fair If You Can. A K Peters/CRC Press, Boca Raton (1998). https://doi.org/10.1201/9781439863855

16. Segal-Halevi, E., Hassidim, A., Aumann, Y.: Waste makes haste: bounded time algorithms for envy-free cake cutting with free disposal. ACM Trans. Algorithms **13**(1), 1–32 (2016). https://doi.org/10.1145/2988232

17. Wadler, P.: Linear types can change the world! In: Programming Concepts and Methods, Sea of Galilee, Israel (1990)

18. Wadler, P.: Is there a use for linear logic? In: ACM SIGPLAN Symposium on Partial Evaluation and Semantics-Based Program Manipulation (PEPM), New Haven, Connecticut, USA (1991). https://doi.org/10.1145/115865.115894

19. Walker, D.: Substructural type systems. In: Pierce, B.C. (ed.) Advanced Topics in Types and Programming Languages. The MIT Press (2004). https://doi.org/10.7551/mitpress/1104.003.0003

Runtime Verification and Monitoring

General Anticipatory Runtime Verification

Raik Hipler[1] , Hannes Kallwies[1]([envelope]) , Martin Leucker[1] ,
and César Sánchez[2]

[1] University of Lübeck, Lübeck, Germany
{hipler,kallwies,leucker}@isp.uni-luebeck.de
[2] IMDEA Software Institute, Madrid, Spain
cesar.sanchez@imdea.org

Abstract. Runtime verification is a technique for monitoring a system's behavior against a formal specification. Monitors must produce verdicts that are sound with respect to the specification. Anticipation is the ability to immediately produce verdicts when the monitor can confidently predict the inevitability of the verdict.

Stream runtime verification is a specialized form of runtime verification tailored to the monitoring and verification of data streams. In this paper we study anticipatory monitoring for stream runtime verification. More specifically, we present an algorithm with anticipation for monitoring of Lola specifications, which we then extend to exploit assumptions and tolerate uncertainties. As perfect anticipation is in general not computable, we use techniques from abstract interpretation, especially widening, to approximate anticipatory monitoring verdicts. Finally, we report on three empirical cases studies using a prototype implementation of a symbolic instantiation of our approach.

1   Introduction

In its simplest definition, *runtime verification (RV)* [26] solves the word problem: whether a certain property (for example, expressed as an LTL formula) is satisfied for a system run, given the run or a prefix of it. In recent years, advanced RV paradigms have emerged, such as *stream runtime verification (SRV)*, extending the traditional notion of runtime verification. First, SRV allows computations and outputs over arbitrary data domains, not only atomic Boolean propositions and verdicts like for LTL. Second, they specify "point-wise properties", which assign outputs to every position of the trace (instead of a single verdict for the trace as a whole). This is especially useful to identify points in a trace, e.g. an error location.

This work was funded in part by PRODIGY Project (TED2021-132464B-I00)—funded by MCIN/AEI/10.13039/501100011033/ and the European Union NextGenerationEU/PRTR—by DECO Project (PID2022-138072OB-I00)—funded by MCIN/AEI/10.13039/501100011033 and by the ESF+—and by a research grant from Nomadic Labs and the Tezos Foundation.

A. Gurfinkel and V. Ganesh (Eds.): CAV 2024, LNCS 14682, pp. 133–155, 2024.
https://doi.org/10.1007/978-3-031-65630-9_7

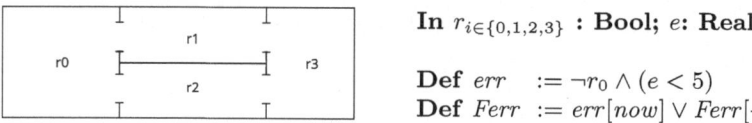

In $r_{i \in \{0,1,2,3\}}$: **Bool;** e: **Real**

Def err $:= \neg r_0 \wedge (e < 5)$
Def $Ferr$ $:= err[now] \vee Ferr[+1 \mid false]$

Fig. 1. Example Lola specification and room map for a vacuum cleaner robot.

Figure 1 shows an SRV specification in the pioneering formalism Lola [9] (see Sect. 2), which we will use as a running example. The scenario models a vacuum cleaner robot in a house with four rooms, connected by open doors. The charging station is located in room r_0. We want to check the following property: "*The robot may not enter rooms if its battery is not charged enough to be able to reach the base station.*" The Lola specification for this property defines four input streams of type Boolean $r_0, \ldots, r_3$ and one stream e of type real. A stream is a sequence of data values over time. The input streams originate from the robot system and are incrementally passed to the monitor. The values (events) of streams $r_0, \ldots, r_3$ encode the current location of the robot while e contains the battery charge (between 0% and 100%). The Lola specification defines a Boolean output stream err that defines the error: the robot is not in room 0 and its battery has run below 5%. Output streams contain events in synchrony with input streams, so the values at each input stream instant produce a value of err, revealing whether the system has run into an error. That is, this specification is a point-wise property. The specification also defines $Ferr$, which is true if either err is true now or in the future (by referring to $Ferr$ at the next instant, with default value false at the trace end).

Monitoring can be performed *online* or *offline*. In offline monitoring the input trace is completely known upfront, for example as a log file. On the other hand, an online monitor receives the trace event by event while the observed system is running. In this paper we deal with online runtime verification. There is a significant difference between both kinds of monitoring when the specification contains future references (as stream $Ferr$ above). Future references are not a problem in offline RV, because future input values can be easily accessed, but future values are unknown in online monitoring. In general there are two strategies for future references in online RV: (1) stalling calculations until all relevant input events are accessible [9]; (2) cast at each step an output as precise as possible with the information available (e.g. a set/interval of possible values). For a Boolean stream these outputs could be $\top = \{tt\}$, $\bot = \{ff\}$ or ? $= \{tt, ff\}$ when both values are possible, depending on future inputs. This strategy is used in LTL$_3$ monitoring [2], but not for point-wise properties. The online monitoring of point-wise properties—while emitting the best possible sets of valuations—is called *perfect recurrent monitoring* in [20,21].

A stream being defined using future references does not necessarily imply that a ? verdict has to be cast. Consider $Ferr$ above: if the value of err is true at some instant then $Ferr$ is true now, independently of future events. Moreover, additional knowledge about the monitored system available in the form of *assumptions* [4, 18, 24] allows to reduce the set of possible valuations. Consider again our running example and assume that the robot consumes 3% of energy when passing from one room to the next. We may conclude that room 0 is not reachable without dropping below 5% battery before (and thus *Ferr* is *true*), if the robot is in room 3 with an energy level below 8%. This kind of monitoring is called *anticipatory* [3].

In this paper we study the problem of anticipatory monitoring for Lola under assumptions and also uncertainties (missed or imprecise sensor values) in the input trace. While for a propositional logic, whether a prefix satisfies or violates a property in all continuations can be modeled using (Büchi) automata, whose emptiness can be effectively determined, the problem is more complex for richer domains. They require reasoning about satisfiability and validity in richer theories—which are computationally expensive or even undecidable—and require reasoning about all futures as finite formulas (instead of automata).

Related Work. Early RV research focused mostly on the monitoring of LTL [29] properties. The LTL_3 monitoring approach [2] was the first to consider anticipation, by reasoning about all possible trace continuations. More expressive RV formalisms were later introduced adding notions of time or complex data values in the traces. Examples include signal temporal logic (STL) [27], mission time LTL [31], Eagle [14] or metric first order temporal logic (MFOTL) [1]. A prominent class of extended RV approaches is SRV, pioneered by Lola [9], and later extended in asynchronous languages like RTLola [11,12], TeSSLa [6,22] and Striver [15,16]. Many RV formalisms can be encoded in Lola [20]. Recurrent monitoring [21] was first studied in [17] for past LTL and later extended with resets [4,5], and also for Lola [20]. The use of symbolic representations for monitoring (also to handle uncertainty) has recently been studied [4,5,10,13,34] and also applied to Lola [19]. Considering assumptions during monitoring was first proposed in [24] (under different wording) and later successfully adapted and extended [4,5,19,35]. The topic is theoretically studied in [18]. The approach that we present in this paper is based on the theory of abstract interpretation [7,8], which was used in RV to handle uncertainties in [25].

The works closest to this paper are [5,13] which study symbolic anticipatory LTL monitoring with linear arithmetic sub-formulas. The former [5] also considers uncertainties and assumptions.

In this paper we first introduce variations of the original Lola semantics: We give *monitoring semantics* which define the perfect monitoring results for uncertain stream prefixes. Based on this we define the *instant* and then (more importantly) *transformer semantics*, which also capture perfect monitoring outputs but discard unnecessary information about relations to all past and future events and can be deterministically computed. We then introduce a general abstraction framework for the effective computation of the transformer semantics and derive an efficient, anticipatory Lola monitoring algorithm. Provided with a sound or perfect abstraction for the stream values (e.g. one from the various literature on abstract interpretation) we present a general algorithm to monitor Lola specifications with future references. We give a criterion for the existence of perfect monitoring, and present a technique based on widening to produce a sound monitor if perfect monitoring is impossible. Then, we instantiate our general framework for linear real arithmetic specifications using symbolic computation. Finally, we report on an empirical evaluation of a prototype implementation of our approach on three complex case studies.

Contributions. Compared to previous works (esp. [5,13]) the main contributions of our approach are:

– The anticipated monitor outputs may be of richer data types than Boolean.
– The monitor is able to produce arbitrarily many outputs per time step.
– Instead of unrolling a specification from the beginning to handle anticipation, we unroll from the back until an invariant is found which is then used to efficiently look ahead during the actual monitoring.
– If no perfect anticipation exists, we provide sound over-approximations instead.
– We are not restricted to symbolic reasoning but provide a general abstraction-based monitoring framework.

2 Lola Monitoring Revisited

2.1 Recurrent Monitoring

Recurrent monitoring starts from a point-wise property, which assigns to every position of a trace a *valuation*. Traditionally, valuations are Boolean or other truth domains [33]. Here, we consider valuations from an arbitrary data domain.

Definition 1 (Point-wise property). *A point-wise property $\mathcal{P}$ of words of length n over domain Γ into domain $\mathbb{D}$ is a function $\mathcal{P} : \Gamma^n \times \{1, 2, \ldots, n\} \to \mathbb{D}$.*

In online monitoring of point-wise properties, the input $w \in \Gamma^n$ is not available at once but provided incrementally, and the monitor produces an output after each input letter. A monitor may output several possible values from $\mathbb{D}$, which in practice is encoded as an interval or ? (for all values). We identify a monitor with its characteristic function $\overline{M} : \Gamma^{\leq n} \to 2^{\mathbb{D}}$ which maps prefixes of inputs to sets of possible outputs. After the first k letters of the input, a recurrent monitor [21] tries to evaluate the corresponding property at position k. A *sound* recurrent monitor outputs a super set of the possible verdicts at the current instant (compatible with all possible future input continuations). The monitor is *perfect* if it casts exactly the set of possible property valuations.

Definition 2 (Sound/perfect recurrent monitor). *Given a point-wise property $\mathcal{P}$ and a non-empty input prefix $w \in \Gamma^{\leq n}$, the set of possible verdicts after w is $pos(w) = \{\mathcal{P}(wv, |w|) \mid v \in \Gamma^{n-|w|}\}$. A recurrent monitor M for $\mathcal{P}$ is sound whenever for every w, $\overline{M}(w) \supseteq pos(w)$. M is perfect if $\overline{M}(w) = pos(w)$.*

2.2 Lola

A Lola specification defines a transformation from a tuple of input streams to a tuple of output streams. A finite stream of type $\mathbb{D}$ over a time domain $\mathbb{T} = \{0, 1, \ldots, t_{max}\}$ is a function $s : \mathcal{S}_\mathbb{D} := \mathbb{T} \to \mathbb{D}$ that assigns a data value to every instant in $\mathbb{T}$. In this work we fix t_{max} and thus $\mathbb{T}$. We use sequences to represent streams and their prefixes. Given $s = \langle 3, 4, 2 \rangle$ we use $s(0) = 3$, $s(1) = 4$, $s(2) = 2$.

A Lola specification [9] is given as an equation system, which defines output streams in terms of input and other output streams. The set of Lola expressions over a set of stream identifiers S, $Expr_S$, is recursively defined as

$$Expr_S := c \mid f(Expr_S, \ldots, Expr_S) \mid s[o|c]$$

where $s \in S$ is a stream identifier, c a constant value, f a function symbol, and $o \in \mathbb{Z}$ is an integer offset. A constant expression is interpreted as a stream with that constant value at all instants; a function application as the stream which results from the application of the function on the argument stream events at every instant. The operator $s[o|c]$, called the offset operator, describes a stream which carries the values of stream s, shifted o instants. To refer to past events o can be chosen to be negative. If the accessed instant does not exist because it is beyond the trace ends (beginning or end) the default value c is used instead. For offset operators with offset 0, the default value does not play a role, thus we use the notation $s[now]$ or simply s for $s[0|c]$ for arbitrary constant c.

Syntax. A Lola specification $\varphi = (I, S, E)$ is a 3-tuple where I is a finite set of input stream identifiers; S is finite set of output stream identifiers with $I \cap S = \emptyset$; $E : S \to Expr_{I \cup S}$ assigns a defining expression to every output steam. For the rest of the paper, we assume that specifications are *flat*, i.e. they only contain offsets $-1, 0, +1$. Every specification can be flattened by introducing additional streams and splitting greater offsets to a chain of ± 1 offsets.

Semantics. The formal semantics of a Lola specification $\varphi = (I, S, E)$ with input streams $I = \{i_1, \ldots, i_n\}$ and output streams $S = \{s_1, \ldots, s_m\}$ maps a tuple of concrete input streams to the corresponding tuple of concrete output streams as follows. Given a tuple of input streams $\Sigma = (\sigma_1, \ldots, \sigma_n)$ the semantics $[\![e]\!]_\Sigma \in \mathcal{S}_\mathbb{D}$ of an expression $e \in Expr_{I \cup S}$ of type $\mathbb{D}$ is:

- $[\![c]\!]_\Sigma(t) = c$
- $[\![f(e_1, \ldots, e_n)]\!]_\Sigma(t) = f([\![e_1]\!]_\Sigma(t), \ldots, [\![e_n]\!]_\Sigma(t))$
- $[\![i_j[o|c]]\!]_\Sigma(t) = \begin{cases} \sigma_j(t + o) & \text{if } t + o \in \mathbb{T} \\ c & \text{otherwise} \end{cases}$
- $[\![s_j[o|c]]\!]_\Sigma(t) = \begin{cases} [\![E(s_j)]\!](t + o) & \text{if } t + o \in \mathbb{T} \\ c & \text{otherwise} \end{cases}$

The semantics of φ, $[\![\varphi]\!] : \mathcal{S}_{\mathbb{D}_1} \times \cdots \times \mathcal{S}_{\mathbb{D}_n} \to \mathcal{S}_{\mathbb{D}'_1} \times \cdots \times \mathcal{S}_{\mathbb{D}'_m}$ is given as

$$[\![\varphi]\!](\Sigma) = ([\![E(s_1)]\!]_\Sigma, \ldots, [\![E(s_m)]\!]_\Sigma)$$

This Lola semantics is well-defined if the value of no stream event is dependent on itself. This is the case when the graph of the specification contains no self-loops, which can easily be checked [9]. We assume that all Lola specifications are well-defined. With $\mathbf{D} := \mathbb{D}_1 \times \cdots \times \mathbb{D}_n$ and $\mathbf{D}' := \mathbb{D}'_1 \times \cdots \times \mathbb{D}'_m$, the *induced pointwise* property of a specification φ is the function $\mathcal{P}_\varphi : \mathbf{D}^{t_{max}} \times \mathbb{T} \to \mathbf{D}'$ defined as

$$\mathcal{P}_\varphi(w, t) = (s_1(t), \ldots, s_m(t))$$

where $(s_1, \ldots, s_m) = [\![\varphi]\!](w)$. Thereby we implicitly understand w as a tuple of streams.

Assumptions. Assumptions are knowledge about system and environment [18], which allow to restrict the actual set of possible input and output traces. Consider again Fig. 1. First, the robot can only be in one room at a time, so exactly one of r_0, r_1, r_2, r_3 must be true at any instant. The map also limits the transitions, so if r_1 is true at some instant, only r_0, r_1, r_3 can be true at the next instant, but not r_2. We can also make assumptions about energy consumption (for example at least 3% of energy is used at every instant). We follow [19] and encode assumptions in Lola, using a special stream Λ which we assume to be true at every instant. The assumptions above are e.g. encoded as follows:

$$\textbf{Def } \Lambda := (r_0[now] \leftrightarrow \neg(r_1[now] \lor r_2[now] \lor r_3[now])) \land \cdots \land$$
$$(r_0[now] \to (r_0[1|tt] \lor r_1[1|tt] \lor r_2[1|tt])) \land \cdots \land$$
$$(e[now] \leq e[-1|103] - 3)$$

Given a specification φ with assumption Λ and a tuple of input streams $\Sigma = (\sigma_1, \ldots, \sigma_n)$ we write $\Sigma \models_\Lambda \varphi$ if $[\![\varphi]\!](\Sigma)$ yields an output that only contains tt events for Λ.

Recurrent Lola Monitoring. Based on Definition 2 we define a sound and perfect recurrent Lola monitor as a recurrent monitor for the induced point-wise property of a specification, taking assumptions into account.

Given a Lola specification φ over input data types $\mathbf{D}$ and given assumption Λ, the set of possible verdicts after a non-empty input prefix $w \in \mathbf{D}^{\leq t_{max}}$ is $pos_\varphi(w) = \{\mathcal{P}_\varphi(wv, |w| - 1) \mid wv \in \mathbf{D}^{t_{max}+1} \land wv \models_\Lambda \varphi\}$.

Definition 3 (Sound/perfect recurrent Lola monitor). *A recurrent Lola monitor M is:*

- sound *iff for every non-empty $w \in \mathbf{D}^{\leq t_{max}}$, $\overline{M}(w) \supseteq pos_\varphi(w)$.*
- perfect *iff for every non-empty $w \in \mathbf{D}^{\leq t_{max}}$, $\overline{M}(w) = pos_\varphi(w)$.*

Lola monitors receive input streams instant by instant and, per input, cast the set (or an over-approximation) of the possible output stream value tuples.

Several monitoring approaches can be reduced to recurrent monitoring by modification of the specification. For example, consider a Boolean stream b representing a property. The initial value of this property (the value of b at position 0) can iteratively be monitored by introduction of an additional stream **Def** $s = $ **if** *first* **then** $b[now]$ **else** $s[-1|ff]$. Note that s at instant 0 takes the value of b and otherwise takes the previous value of s. A recurrent monitor for s outputs increasingly precise verdicts about the initial property b. This monitor simulates the typical initial monitor, for example for LTL_3 [2]. Recurrent Lola monitors further subsume monitoring with reset [4]; monitoring instants with a fixed offset of k to the current instant, or a fixed size window around the current instant; monitoring the distance to the next instant where a violation of a property occurs (see [21]) or counting of violations, etc. All these notions can be solved with recurrent monitoring by introducing additional streams in the specification.

Perfect recurrent monitoring requires reasoning about possible future continuations of a trace. This ability however, especially together with the presence of assumptions makes recurrent monitors very powerful. The vacuum cleaning robot example above could include the following four stream definitions:

$$\textbf{Def } enter_{i \in \{0,1,2,3\}} := r_i[+1|false] \land \neg Ferr[now]$$

Note that if a recurrent monitor yields the verdict $\perp = \{ff\}$ for one of these streams, entering the corresponding room will inevitably cause *Ferr* to be true, which means that the base station cannot be reached anymore with the remaining battery energy. On the other hand, the verdict $? = \{tt, ff\}$ implies that it is possible that *Ferr* is false when the corresponding room is entered. This way a higher level planning system an use the information that the monitor provides to steer and prevent the robot from going into rooms which will inevitably cause an error. If the robot always follows a path where $?$ verdicts are obtained it will eventually end up in room 0 if the battery level is critical. In this example anticipatory verdicts are possible if assumptions that are included in the specification reveal information about where the robot can drive and how much energy it consumes.

3   Lola Recurrent Online Monitoring Semantics

We now introduce a novel Lola semantics for recurrent online monitoring. While the original semantics from Sect. 2 describes a relation between fully known input and output streams (i.e. an offline semantics), we now give a semantics that relates prefixes of input streams with partially known output streams. We base our definition on monitoring stream tuples (inspired by [32]) which represent a set of possible (complete and fully known) stream tuples:

Definition 4 (Monitoring stream tuple). *A monitoring stream tuple of n streams of types $\mathbb{D}_1, \ldots, \mathbb{D}_n$ is an element from $\mathcal{T}_{\mathbb{D}_1,\ldots,\mathbb{D}_n} := 2^{S_{\mathbb{D}_1} \times \cdots \times S_{\mathbb{D}_n}}$.*

We will use monitoring stream tuples in two ways: (1) to define input stream prefixes, which are only known up to a certain instant $t \in \mathbb{T}$; and (2) to encode uncertain input readings. (Note that the first case is a special case of the second, where all events after t are fully unknown.) The idea is that the monitoring stream tuple is the set of all complete and fully known input streams that are compatible with the (uncertain) input readings received so far.

Example 1. Consider again the robot example from Fig. 1 for $\mathbb{T} = \{0, 1, 2, 3, 4\}$ and where the received trace prefix is known up to instant 3. Assume that the robot started at room r_0 and moved to r_1 and then to r_3; then it is uncertain whether the robot remained in r_3 or moved back to r_1 again. Furthermore, the energy started at 100% and was reduced by 3% per step, but the sensor has an uncertainty of $\pm 1\%$. This input would be encoded by the following monitoring stream tuple, where the streams follow the order r_0, r_1, r_2, r_3, e:

$$s = \{(\langle tt, f\!\!f, f\!\!f, f\!\!f, r_0^4 \rangle, \langle f\!\!f, tt, f\!\!f, r_1^3, r_1^4 \rangle, \langle f\!\!f, f\!\!f, f\!\!f, f\!\!f, r_2^4 \rangle, \langle f\!\!f, f\!\!f, tt, r_3^3, r_3^4 \rangle,$$
$$\langle e^0, e^1, e^2, e^3, e^4 \rangle) \mid$$
$$r_1^3 \leftrightarrow \neg r_3^3, e^0 \in [99, 101], e^1 \in [96, 98], e^2 \in [93, 95], e^3 \in [90, 92]\}$$

Given a monitoring stream tuple $s \in \mathcal{T}_{\mathbb{D}_1 \times \cdots \times \mathbb{D}_n}$ we use $s(t)$ for $t \in \mathbb{T}$ to denote the set of all value tuples at position t. In the example above $s(3) = \{(f\!\!f, r_1^3, f\!\!f, r_3^3, e_3) \mid r_1^3 \leftrightarrow \neg r_3^3, e_3 \in [90, 92]\}$.

In this paper we restrict to "instant-wise uncertainty": our monitoring streams only encode uncertain values which are independent from the values at other instants. That is, we can encode that the robot is in room 3 iff it is not in room 0, but not that the robot is in room 3 if it was in room 0 in the previous instant. In many cases relations among instants can still be encoded as assumptions.

To simplify the definitions, for the rest of the paper we fix a Lola specification $\varphi = (I, S, E)$ with n input streams of type $\mathbb{D}_{1 \leq i \leq n}$ and m output streams of type $\mathbb{D}'_{1 \leq i \leq m}$. A monitoring stream tuple Σ for the input is then $\Sigma \in \mathcal{T}_{\mathbb{D}_1, \ldots, \mathbb{D}_n}$. We define the *monitoring semantics* of a Lola specification as the application of the standard Lola semantics on all streams from the input monitoring stream tuple.

Definition 5 (Lola monitoring semantics). *Let φ be a specification and Σ the monitoring stream tuple for the inputs. The monitoring semantics of φ, Σ is defined as:*

$$[\![\varphi]\!]^{mon} : \mathcal{T}_{\mathbb{D}_1, \ldots, \mathbb{D}_n} \to \mathcal{T}_{\mathbb{D}_1, \ldots, \mathbb{D}_n, \mathbb{D}'_1, \ldots, \mathbb{D}'_m}$$
$$[\![\varphi]\!]^{mon}(\Sigma) = \{(\sigma_1, \ldots, \sigma_n) \circ [\![\varphi]\!](\sigma_1, \ldots, \sigma_n) \mid (\sigma_1, \ldots, \sigma_n) \in \Sigma\}$$

We handle assumptions by adding the condition $(\sigma_1, \ldots, \sigma_n) \models_A \varphi$ which restrict the input streams considered. The Lola monitoring semantics is closely related to a perfect recurrent Lola monitor: the output of a perfect recurrent Lola monitor after receiving input Σ at monitoring step t is $[\![\varphi]\!]^{mon}(\Sigma)(t)$. Receiving tuples $\Sigma_0, \Sigma_1, \Sigma_2 \ldots$ with growing information about input readings a monitor could compute $[\![\varphi]\!]^{mon}(\Sigma_0)$, $[\![\varphi]\!]^{mon}(\Sigma_1)$, $[\![\varphi]\!]^{mon}(\Sigma_2)$, $\ldots$ and generate the outputs $[\![\varphi]\!]^{mon}(\Sigma_0)(0)$, $[\![\varphi]\!]^{mon}(\Sigma_1)(1)$, $[\![\varphi]\!]^{mon}(\Sigma_2)(2), \ldots$. This monitor, however, computes a monitoring stream tuple of all inputs and outputs so it contains information about all events of all streams, which makes semantics costly. Note that for recurrent monitoring we are actually only interested in the events at the current instant. Therefore, in the following we introduce a variation of the Lola monitoring semantics which produces sets of possible stream value combinations (called *configurations*) for every instant, with no information relating different instants.

We first introduce some additional notation. Given a flat specification $\varphi = (I, S, E)$ for input stream types $\mathbb{D}_1, \ldots, \mathbb{D}_n$ and output stream types $\mathbb{D}'_1, \ldots, \mathbb{D}'_m$, we use $\mathbf{D}^\varphi = \mathbb{D}_1 \times \cdots \times \mathbb{D}_n \times \mathbb{D}'_1 \times \cdots \times \mathbb{D}'_m$ to denote the product of all stream types. Given $d \in \mathbf{D}^\varphi$ and $s \in I \cup S$ we use $d(s)$ to denote the entry of stream s in d. Elements from $2^{\mathbf{D}^\varphi}$, i.e. sets of stream value tuples, are called *configuration sets*. Given an expression $e \in Expr_{I \cup S}$ of type $\mathbb{D}$, the following three functions $[\![e]\!]_\varphi^\triangleright$ and $[\![e]\!]_\varphi^\triangleleft$ (with type $\mathbf{D}^\varphi \times \mathbf{D}^\varphi \to \mathbb{D}$), and $[\![e]\!]_\varphi^\bowtie$ (with type $\mathbf{D}^\varphi \times \mathbf{D}^\varphi \times \mathbf{D}^\varphi \to \mathbb{D}$) compute the value of e at the beginning, at the end and in the middle of the trace. $[\![e]\!]_\varphi^\triangleright$ receives the configuration for the current and subsequent instant, $[\![e]\!]_\varphi^\triangleleft$ receives the current and previous instant, and $[\![e]\!]_\varphi^\bowtie$ the configuration for the previous, current and subsequent instant. This semantics are:

$$[\![d]\!]_\varphi^\bowtie(b, c, a) = d$$
$$[\![f(e_1, \ldots, e_n)]\!]_\varphi^\bowtie(b, c, a) = f([\![e_1]\!]_\varphi^\bowtie(b, c, a), \ldots, [\![e_n]\!]_\varphi^\bowtie(b, c, a))$$
$$[\![s[-1|d]]\!]_\varphi^\bowtie(b, c, a) = b(s)$$
$$[\![s[now]]\!]_\varphi^\bowtie(b, c, a) = c(s)$$
$$[\![s[+1|d]]\!]_\varphi^\bowtie(b, c, a) = a(s)$$

for constant $d \in \mathbb{D}$, stream identifier $s \in I \cup S$ and sub-expressions $e_1, \ldots, e_n \in Expr_{I \cup S}$. Here, b denotes the valuation at the previous instant, c at the current instant and a at the successor instant. The definitions for $[\![e]\!]_\varphi^\triangleright$ and $[\![e]\!]_\varphi^\triangleleft$ are analogous, but these use the default value for -1 and +1 references (resp.). Let $\varphi = (I, S, E)$ and let $S = \{s_1, \ldots, s_n\}$ be the output stream identifiers. We use

$$[\![\varphi]\!]^\triangleleft(b, c) = ([\![E(s_1)]\!]_\varphi^\triangleleft(b, c), \quad \ldots, [\![E(s_n)]\!]_\varphi^\triangleleft(b, c))$$
$$[\![\varphi]\!]^\triangleright(c, a) = ([\![E(s_1)]\!]_\varphi^\triangleright(c, a), \quad \ldots, [\![E(s_n)]\!]_\varphi^\triangleright(c, a))$$
$$[\![\varphi]\!]^\bowtie(b, c, a) = ([\![E(s_1)]\!]_\varphi^\bowtie(b, c, a), \quad \ldots, [\![E(s_n)]\!]_\varphi^\bowtie(b, c, a))$$

to denote the application of the given functions on all defining expressions of φ.

We can finally define an alternative fixed point semantics which can serve as the basis for recurrent monitoring.

Definition 6 (Lola instant semantics). *Let φ be a specification and Σ a monitoring stream tuple of the input streams. The instant semantics fixed point equation of φ, Σ is:*

$$[\![\varphi]\!]_\Sigma^{inst} : (2^{\mathbf{D}^\varphi})^{|\mathbb{T}|} \to (2^{\mathbf{D}^\varphi})^{|\mathbb{T}|}$$
$$[\![\varphi]\!]_\Sigma^{inst}(V) = (V'_0, \ldots, V'_{t_{max}})$$

with

$$V'_0 = \{c \mid c = \sigma \circ [\![\varphi]\!]^\triangleright(c, a), \sigma \in \Sigma(0), a \in V(1)\}$$
$$V'_t = \{c \mid c = \sigma \circ [\![\varphi]\!]^\bowtie(b, c, a), \sigma \in \Sigma(t), b \in V(t-1), a \in V(t+1)\}$$
$$V'_{t_{max}} = \{c \mid c = \sigma \circ [\![\varphi]\!]^\triangleleft(b, c), \sigma \in \Sigma(t_{max}), b \in V(t_{max} - 1)\}.$$

The instant semantics *of φ is given as the greatest fixed point of $[\![\varphi]\!]_{\Sigma}^{inst}$ w.r.t.
the point-wise $\subseteq$ order on the $(2^{\boldsymbol{D}^{\varphi}})^{|\mathbb{T}|}$ structure:*

$$[\![\varphi]\!]^{inst} \quad : \; \mathcal{T}_{\mathbb{D}_1,\dots,\mathbb{D}_n} \rightarrow (2^{\boldsymbol{D}^{\varphi}})^{|\mathbb{T}|}$$
$$[\![\varphi]\!]^{inst}(\Sigma) = \nu([\![\varphi]\!]_{\Sigma}^{inst})$$

The instant semantics fixed point equation takes a structure of configuration
sets for every trace position, and returns a homogeneous structure consisting
of the possible inputs and the semantics of the output stream expressions for
the corresponding positions (based on the argument structure). Consequently, a
fixed point of this equation is a solution of the Lola specification. We define the
instant semantics as the greatest fixed point of the instant semantics fixed point
equation. One structure is greater or equal than another if at every instant it
contains at least the same configurations, i.e. is the point-wise application of $\subseteq$.
Note that the instant semantics of φ is equivalent to the monitoring semantics
with respect to the stream events at every instant, that is

$$\forall t \in \mathbb{T}. \nu([\![\varphi]\!]_{\Sigma}^{inst})(t) = \{T(t) \mid T \in [\![\varphi]\!]^{mon}(\Sigma)\}$$

Hence, this semantics can also be used as basis for recurrent monitoring.
Computing this semantics, however, is rather complex—requiring a fixed point
iteration—and it must be recomputed every time new inputs are received (since
Σ changes). Therefore, we slightly adjust this semantics again. Instead of computing the possible value combinations (configurations sets) we now compute
them *parametric in the values of the previous instant*, using the structure
$(\boldsymbol{D}^{\varphi} \rightarrow 2^{\boldsymbol{D}^{\varphi}})^{|\mathbb{T}|}$ instead of $(2^{\boldsymbol{D}^{\varphi}})^{|\mathbb{T}|}$. We call the elements of this structure *transformers* as they transform the configurations from the previous instant to those
of the current instant. Transformers receive a configuration $b \in \boldsymbol{D}^{\varphi}$ at $t \in \mathbb{T}$ and
return the set of all possible configurations at $t + 1 \in \mathbb{T}$, provided b.

Definition 7 (Lola transformer semantics). *Let φ be a specification and Σ
an input stream tuple. The transformer semantics fixed-point equation of φ and
Σ is given as:*

$$[\![\varphi]\!]_{\Sigma}^{tra} \quad : \; (\boldsymbol{D}^{\varphi} \rightarrow 2^{\boldsymbol{D}^{\varphi}})^{|\mathbb{T}|} \rightarrow (\boldsymbol{D}^{\varphi} \rightarrow 2^{\boldsymbol{D}^{\varphi}})^{|\mathbb{T}|}$$
$$[\![\varphi]\!]_{\Sigma}^{tra}(V) = (V_0', \dots, V_{t_{max}}')$$

with

$$V_0'(b) \quad = \{c \mid c = \sigma \circ [\![\varphi]\!]^{\triangleright}(c, a), \sigma \in \Sigma(0), a \in V(1)(c)\}$$
$$V_t'(b) \quad = \{c \mid c = \sigma \circ [\![\varphi]\!]^{\bowtie}(b, c, a), \sigma \in \Sigma(t), a \in V(t+1)(c)\}$$
$$V_{t_{max}}'(b) = \{c \mid c = \sigma \circ [\![\varphi]\!]^{\triangleleft}(b, c), \sigma \in \Sigma(t_{max})\}.$$

The transformer semantics of φ is the (only) fixed point of $[\![\varphi]\!]_{\Sigma}^{tra}$:

$$[\![\varphi]\!]^{tra} \quad : \; \mathbb{T}_{\mathbb{D}_1,\dots,\mathbb{D}_n} \rightarrow (2^{\boldsymbol{D}^{\varphi}})^{|\mathbb{T}|}$$
$$[\![\varphi]\!]^{tra}(\Sigma) = \mu([\![\varphi]\!]_{\Sigma}^{tra})$$

This semantics is basically equivalent to the instant semantics except that V_t' is no longer dependent on $V(t-1)$, as the generated transformers are parameterized in the configuration of their previous instant. Therefore, b is now a parameter of the single structure entries and a is still received from the argument structure of the fixed point equation, by applying the current configuration on the subsequent transformer $(V(t+1)(c))$.

This new semantics has several advantages for online monitoring. First, the fixed point of the upper semantics is unique and can (as opposed to monitoring and instant semantics) be deterministically computed from the back, as the single transformer elements only depend on the subsequent transformer. Second, this semantics can still conveniently be used for recurrent monitoring. One can mutually compute the current monitor state (i.e. the currently possible stream configurations) and the transformer to the subsequent instant and apply the current state on the transformer (see Sect. 5). However, one caveat is that computing with $(\mathbf{D}^\varphi \rightarrow 2^{\mathbf{D}^\varphi})^{|\mathbb{T}|}$ is complex, as it is unclear how to represent the elements in $\mathbf{D}^\varphi \rightarrow 2^{\mathbf{D}^\varphi}$ and in $2^{\mathbf{D}^\varphi}$. Furthermore, the recursively defined sets V_i' are hard to determine. Therefore, we introduce a framework for abstract computation of this semantics.

4 An Abstraction Framework for Lola Monitoring

We borrow concepts from abstract interpretation to efficiently implement the transformer semantics. The main element is an abstract domain which is a perfect representation (or a sound over-approximation) of the transformer or configuration set domain. An appropriate abstract domain must be easy to represent in memory and enable efficient computations.

We introduce two domains: A, whose elements abstract concrete configuration sets from Sect. 3, and $\tilde{A}$ that contains abstractions of the transformers. We require that $(A, \sqsubseteq^A)$ and $(\tilde{A}, \sqsubseteq^{\tilde{A}})$ are complete lattices, that is, partial orders where every subset has a least upper bound and a greatest lower bound. The relation $a \sqsubseteq^A b$ indicates that b over-approximates a, i.e. that every configuration represented by a is also represented by b. The same holds for $\sqsubseteq^{\tilde{A}}$. We demand the existence of functions:

$$\gamma^A : A \rightarrow 2^{\mathbf{D}^\varphi} \qquad\qquad \alpha^A : 2^{\mathbf{D}^\varphi} \rightarrow A$$
$$\gamma^{\tilde{A}} : \tilde{A} \rightarrow (\mathbf{D}^\varphi \rightarrow 2^{\mathbf{D}^\varphi}) \qquad\qquad \alpha^{\tilde{A}} : (\mathbf{D}^\varphi \rightarrow 2^{\mathbf{D}^\varphi}) \rightarrow \tilde{A}$$

which are able to translate from the concrete configuration set or transformer domain to the abstract counterpart and back. We require that these function pairs are Galois connections:

$$\forall a \in A, c \in 2^{\mathbf{D}^\varphi} \qquad : \alpha^A(c) \sqsubseteq^A a \leftrightarrow c \subseteq \gamma^A(a)$$
$$\forall a \in A, c \in (\mathbf{D}^\varphi \rightarrow 2^{\mathbf{D}^\varphi}) : \alpha^{\tilde{A}}(c) \sqsubseteq^{\tilde{A}} a \leftrightarrow c \unlhd \gamma^{\tilde{A}}(a)$$

Here, $\unlhd$ denotes the pointwise application of $\subseteq$ on all corresponding configurations sets where the functions from $(\mathbf{D}^\varphi \rightarrow 2^{\mathbf{D}^\varphi})$ map to. Galois connections ensure that a translation from the concrete to the abstract domain and back leads to an over-approximation, so abstract computations in the abstract domain produce sound monitor outputs.

We say that A is a *perfect configuration set abstraction* if for all $c \in 2^{\mathbf{D}^\varphi}$, $\gamma^A(\alpha^A(c)) = c$. Analogously $\tilde{A}$ is a *perfect transformer abstraction* if for all $c \in (\mathbf{D}^\varphi \to 2^{\mathbf{D}^\varphi})$, $\gamma^{\tilde{A}}(\alpha^{\tilde{A}}(c)) = c$.

Symbolic Abstraction. We introduce now a perfect abstract transformer and configuration set abstract domain based on symbolic constraints, which will be later used for an anticipatory Lola monitoring algorithm in Sect. 6. For the symbolic abstraction we use symbolic constraints (i.e. quantifier-free first order logic expressions) that perfectly describe the relation among all possible values of a configuration or transformer.

We start with the symbolic representation of the configuration sets. We use a symbolic constraint where every stream value is represented by its own variable. For example, $C = \{(tt, 3), (ff, 5)\}$—for two streams b (of type bool) and r (of type real)—captures values that can either be tt and 3 or ff and 5, This configuration set can be expressed as $(b \to (r = 3)) \land (\neg b \to (r = 5))$. Our symbolic computation is restricted to those configuration sets which are symbolically representable, thus the theory of choice (e.g. Boolean algebra or linear real arithmetic) determines the capabilities of the monitor. We assume that the chosen algebra can encode all monitor inputs and operations in the specification.

The concretization function of a symbolic constraint ψ is:

$$\gamma(\psi) = \{v \in \mathbf{D}^\varphi \mid \big(\bigwedge_{s \in I \cup S} s = v(s) \big) \models \psi\}$$

Recall that $v(s)$ denotes the value of stream s in a configuration $v \in \mathbf{D}^\varphi$. We implicitly define α s.t. for any configuration set $C \in 2^{\mathbf{D}^\varphi}$, $\gamma(\alpha(C)) = C$. That is, every configuration set C has a canonical symbolic encoding. In the algorithm we only require α for translating uncertain input readings to symbolic representations. Note that by the given definition of α the symbolic domain is a perfect configuration set abstraction. Also note that while our symbolic domain is defined as abstraction of configuration sets over all streams, it is also possible to encode only sets of sub-configurations, e.g. only input stream values.

Consider for example Fig. 1 and the following configuration set $v = \{(ff, r_1^3, ff, r_3^3, e_3) \mid \neg(r_1^3 \leftrightarrow r_3^3), e_3 \in [90, 92]\}$, which represents the uncertain input for instant 3 from the example above. A symbolic representation of this configuration set is $\alpha(v) = \neg r_0 \land \neg r_2 \land \neg(r_1 \leftrightarrow r_3) \land (90 \leq e \leq 92)$.

We also encode transformers symbolically, extending the variables of our constraints to $I \cup S \cup \{s^{-1} \mid s \in I \cup S\}$, where s^{-1} represent the stream values at the previous instant in which the transformer is parametric. The corresponding concretization function for transformers is given as $\gamma(\psi) = \tau$ s.t.

$$\forall v \in \mathbf{D}^\varphi : \tau(v) = \{u \in \mathbf{D}^\varphi \mid \big(\bigwedge_{s \in I \cup S} ((s^{-1} = v(s)) \land (s = u(s))) \big) \models \psi\}.$$

Abstract Transformer Semantics Computation. We now present the computation of an alternative, abstract transformer semantics, related to the concrete semantics given in Definition 7. This semantics is computed in an $\tilde{A}^{|\mathbb{T}|}$ structure where each entry contains the abstract transformer for the corresponding trace position.

We fix an abstract transformer domain $\tilde{A}$ with translation functions $\gamma^{\tilde{A}} : \tilde{A} \to (\mathbf{D}^{\varphi} \to 2^{\mathbf{D}^{\varphi}})$ and $\alpha^{\tilde{A}} : (\mathbf{D}^{\varphi} \to 2^{\mathbf{D}^{\varphi}}) \to \tilde{A}$.

Definition 8 (Abstract Lola transformer semantics). *A fixed point equation for φ, Σ is called* abstract Lola transformer fixed point equation *if*

$$[\![\varphi]\!]_{\Sigma}^{\sharp} \quad : \tilde{A}^{|\mathbb{T}|} \to \tilde{A}^{|\mathbb{T}|}$$
$$[\![\varphi]\!]_{\Sigma}^{\sharp}(V) = (\tau_{\varphi,\Sigma}^{0}(V(1)), \tau_{\varphi,\Sigma}^{1}(V(2)), \ldots, \tau_{\varphi,\Sigma}^{t_{max}})$$

with $\tau_{\varphi,\Sigma}^{t_{max}} : \tilde{A}$ and $\tau_{\varphi,\Sigma}^{t} : \tilde{A} \to \tilde{A}$ for $t \in \{0, \ldots, t_{max} - 1\}$ s.t.

$$\tau_{\varphi,\Sigma}^{0}(V_1) \quad \sqsupseteq^{\tilde{A}} \alpha^{\tilde{A}}(b \mapsto \{c \mid c = \sigma \circ [\![\varphi]\!]^{\triangleright}(c, a) \mid \sigma \in \Sigma(0), a \in \gamma^{\tilde{A}}(V_1)(c)\})$$
$$\tau_{\varphi,\Sigma}^{t}(V_{t+1}) \sqsupseteq^{\tilde{A}} \alpha^{\tilde{A}}(b \mapsto \{c \mid c = \sigma \circ [\![\varphi]\!]^{\bowtie}(b, c, a) \mid \sigma \in \Sigma(t), a \in \gamma^{\tilde{A}}(V_{t+1})(c)\})$$
$$\tau_{\varphi,\Sigma}^{t_{max}} \quad \sqsupseteq^{\tilde{A}} \alpha^{\tilde{A}}(b \mapsto \{c \mid c = \sigma \circ [\![\varphi]\!]^{\triangleleft}(b, c) \mid \sigma \in \Sigma(t_{max})\}).$$

This corresponds to a computation in the abstract structure $\tilde{A}^{|\mathbb{T}|}$ where all the entries are over-approximations of the transformers of the concrete Lola transformer semantics. If the $\sqsupseteq^{\tilde{A}}$ relation in the above definitions is an equality then $[\![\varphi]\!]_{\Sigma}^{\sharp}$ is called a *perfect abstract Lola transformer fixed point equation*. We will later in Sect. 6 provide the abstract transformer constructors $\tau_{\varphi,\Sigma}^{t}$ for the symbolic abstract domain introduced above.

As in the concrete case, the abstract transformer fixed point equation above has a unique fixed point $\mu([\![\varphi]\!]_{\Sigma}^{\sharp})$, as it can be computed deterministically from back to front given a particular input Σ. We say that our abstract transformer semantics is sound in relation to the concrete semantics if for all $t \in \mathbb{T}$, $\mu([\![\varphi]\!]_{\Sigma}^{tra})(t) \subseteq \gamma^{\tilde{A}}(\mu([\![\varphi]\!]_{\Sigma}^{\sharp})(t))$ and perfect if $\mu([\![\varphi]\!]_{\Sigma}^{tra})(t) = \gamma^{\tilde{A}}(\mu([\![\varphi]\!]_{\Sigma}^{\sharp})(t))$. By properties of abstract interpretation the following holds:

Theorem 1. *Let $\mu([\![\varphi]\!]_{\Sigma}^{\sharp})$ be an abstract transformer semantics for φ. Then:*

– *$\mu([\![\varphi]\!]_{\Sigma}^{\sharp})$ is sound.*
– *$\mu([\![\varphi]\!]_{\Sigma}^{\sharp})$ is perfect if $[\![\varphi]\!]_{\Sigma}^{\sharp}$ is a perfect abstract Lola transformer fixed point equation and $\tilde{A}$ is a perfect transformer abstraction.*

This justifies that we can build a sound or perfect recurrent Lola monitor based on this abstract semantics. Consider the computation of the fixed point $\mu([\![\varphi]\!]_{\top}^{\sharp})$, where $\top$ is the maximal element in $\mathcal{T}_{\mathbb{D}_1,\ldots,\mathbb{D}_n}$ (i.e. the input monitoring stream tuple where no information about any input streams is available). The abstract transformer structure chosen for the abstract semantics has one significant advantage in terms of the computation of this fixed point: As soon as a single element in $S = \mu([\![\varphi]\!]_{\top}^{\sharp})$ repeats, all entries of the structure (except the one for instant 0) are known. This is because if $S(t) = S(t + k)$ for $k > 0$, $t \in \mathbb{T}$, then also $S(t - 1) = S(t + k - 1)$ are equal (as no input information is available with $\Sigma = \top$). Therefore, all entries in S can be filled up to instant 1 without new computations being required. Hence, $\mu(\llbracket\varphi\rrbracket^\sharp_\top)$ can be computed back to front until the first instant at which $\mu(\llbracket\varphi\rrbracket^\sharp_\top)(t) = \mu(\llbracket\varphi\rrbracket^\sharp_\top)(t+k)$ occurs, and then the values at all instants are determined (except for the first entry). If the number of elements in the abstract domain $\tilde{A}$ is bounded by c, (e.g. Boolean specifications) then after at most c iterations a loop in $\mu(\llbracket\varphi\rrbracket^\sharp_\top)$ is found. There are domains beyond Booleans for which finite perfect representations exist [13].

For abstract domains where $|\tilde{A}|$ is unbounded one can use a widening operator [7,8]. For example, using $\mu(\llbracket\varphi\rrbracket^\sharp_\top)(t) \triangledown \mu(\llbracket\varphi\rrbracket^\sharp_\top)(t-1)$ instead of $\mu(\llbracket\varphi\rrbracket^\sharp_\top)(t-1)$ in the fixed point computation where the operator $\triangledown : \tilde{A} \times \tilde{A} \to \tilde{A}$ yields an over-approximation of the arguments by taking all unstable components of the abstractions directly to the extreme limits and thus enforcing a loop in $\mu(\llbracket\varphi\rrbracket^\sharp_\top)$.

Based on these observations we build in the next section an efficient sound (or perfect) recurrent Lola monitoring algorithm.

5   Abstraction-Based Recurrent Lola Monitoring

We introduce our monitor construction based on the abstract structure from the previous section. At runtime the monitor receives information incrementally, so there is a sequence of extending input monitoring stream tuples $\Sigma_0, \Sigma_1, \ldots, \Sigma_{t_{max}}$ where in Σ_t all streams are fully unknown for instants larger than t and equal to Σ_{t-1} for instants smaller than t. Based on this observation we introduce the online monitoring algorithm Algorithm 1.

Algorithm 1. Abstract Lola monitoring algorithm

Compute (over-approximation of) $\mu(\llbracket\varphi\rrbracket^\sharp_\top)$
$s^\sharp \leftarrow \top^A$
foreach $t \in \mathbb{T}$ **do**
  Read inputs for t
  Compute $\mu(\llbracket\varphi\rrbracket^\sharp_{\Sigma_t})(t) = \tau^t_{\varphi, \Sigma_t}(\mu(\llbracket\varphi\rrbracket^\sharp_\top)(t + 1))$
  $s^\sharp \leftarrow \mu(\llbracket\varphi\rrbracket^\sharp_{\Sigma_t})(t)(s^\sharp)$
  Output $\gamma(s^\sharp)$
end

The algorithm first determines $\mu(\llbracket\varphi\rrbracket^\sharp_\top)$, which is not dependent on inputs and can thus be computed statically as part of the monitor synthesis (as described at the end of the previous section). Then, at runtime the monitor receives iteratively the (possibly uncertain) inputs for the current instant t and computes $\mu(\llbracket\varphi\rrbracket^\sharp_{\Sigma_t})(t)$. By definition

$$\mu(\llbracket\varphi\rrbracket^\sharp_{\Sigma_t})(t) = \tau^t_{\varphi, \Sigma_t}(\mu(\llbracket\varphi\rrbracket^\sharp_{\Sigma_t})(t + 1)).$$

However, $\mu(\llbracket \varphi \rrbracket_{\Sigma_t}^{\sharp})(t+1) = \mu(\llbracket \varphi \rrbracket_{\top}^{\sharp})(t+1)$ because for all $t' > t$ no inputs are available yet. This can be taken from the pre-computed $\mu(\llbracket \varphi \rrbracket_{\top}^{\sharp})$, and hence $\mu(\llbracket \varphi \rrbracket_{\Sigma_t}^{\sharp})(t)$ can be efficiently determined by applying $\tau_{\varphi, \Sigma_t}^t$ once without requiring a full computation of the fixed point $\mu(\llbracket \varphi \rrbracket_{\Sigma_t}^{\sharp})$ from the end.

Then, the algorithm applies the abstracted configuration set from the previous step, stored in $s^{\sharp}$ (of type A) on the computed transformer $\mu(\llbracket \varphi \rrbracket_{\Sigma_t}^{\sharp})(t)$ and assigns the result to $s^{\sharp}$ again. In this manner $s^{\sharp}$ represents the monitor state: the set of possible stream configurations at the current instant t. Note that $s^{\sharp}$ is not available for $t = 0$ as there is no previous instant and thus also no monitor state. Yet $\mu(\llbracket \varphi \rrbracket_{\Sigma_0}^{\sharp})(0)$ yields (by definition) a transformer which is independent of the predecessor argument. The concrete representation of $s^{\sharp}$ is $\gamma(s^{\sharp})$ which consists of a set of possible value tuples for all streams, and serves as the monitor output. This output is perfect if and only if the chosen abstract domains A and $\tilde{A}$ are perfect configuration set and transformer abstractions and the abstract transformer semantics is also perfect (see Theorem 1).

The application of an abstract transformer $T \in \tilde{A}$ on a configuration set abstraction $s \in A$ is technically defined as $T(s) = \alpha^A(\{\gamma^{\tilde{A}}(T)(c) \mid c \in \gamma^A(s)\})$. Depending on the concrete abstractions there may be easier ways to achieve the application, for example using symbolic constraints, as we will see in the next section.

The size of $s^{\sharp}$ may grow over time, so for a constant-size monitor it may be necessary to find an over-approximation. In conclusion the following holds:

Theorem 2. *Let φ be a Lola specification let $\Sigma_0, \Sigma_1, \ldots, \Sigma_{t_{max}}$ be an extending sequence of input monitoring stream tuples where Σ_t contains the input readings for instant t. Algorithm 1 yields a sound recurrent Lola monitor and a perfect recurrent Lola monitor if $\llbracket \varphi \rrbracket_{\Sigma}^{\sharp}$ is a perfect abstract Lola transformer fixed point equation and $\tilde{A}$ is a perfect transformer abstraction.*

6 Symbolic Recurrent Lola Monitoring

We now show a symbolic monitoring strategy under assumptions that tolerates uncertainty, for linear real arithmetic Lola specifications based on the general framework from the previous section. This theory supports real and Boolean streams, and the common Boolean operations, additions, constant multiplications and comparisons among real streams.

We will use the symbolic abstract domain to symbolically represent configurations and transformers. For convenience we use instant variables formed by stream names with the corresponding instant in the exponent of the symbolic variables. For example, s^3 indicates the value of the event in stream s at instant 3. Abstractions of configuration sets only contain variables of a single instant, transformer abstractions those of the current and previous instant.

Example 2. Consider a specification with a single stream e of type real. The configuration set that states the value of e at instant 3 is between 90 and 92 (both inclusive) would be represented by the constraint $90 \leq e^3 \leq 92$. To express that the value of e at instant 4 is at least 3 less than the value one instant before, that is, the transformer $T(e) = \{e' \mid e' \leq e - 3\}$, we could use $e^4 \leq e^3 - 3$.

A perfect monitoring procedure requires—besides perfect abstract domains $\tilde{A}$ and A—perfect symbolic constructions for the transformers $\tau^t_{\varphi,\Sigma}$. This can be achieved in a straight forward manner as follows. To compute the transformer at instant t we take the symbolic representation of the subsequent transformer in the structure, and conjunct it with the symbolic instantiation of the specification at the current instant and the input readings for the current instant. This works because we required the input values of different instants to be independent of each other. For $t = 0$ or $t = t_{max}$ we use the default values.

Example 3. Consider again the specification from Fig. 1 (for this example without the parts added later like assumptions) and the situation where no inputs are known, which can be encoded by the symbolic constraint tt, and $\mathbb{T} = \{0, \ldots, 10\}$. The symbolic transformer $\tau^{t_{max}}_{\varphi,\mathbb{T}}$ for $t_{max} = 10$ is:

$$\mu(\llbracket \varphi \rrbracket^{\sharp}_{\mathbb{T}})(10) = \tau^{10}_{\varphi,\mathbb{T}} = (err^{10} = \neg r^{10}_0 \wedge (e^{10} < 5)) \wedge (Ferr^{10} = err^{10})$$

and $\tau^9_{\varphi,\mathbb{T}}$ applied on $\mu(\llbracket \varphi \rrbracket^{\sharp}_{\mathbb{T}})(10)$ is

$$\mu(\llbracket \varphi \rrbracket^{\sharp}_{\mathbb{T}})(9) = \tau^9_{\varphi,\mathbb{T}}(\mu(\llbracket \varphi \rrbracket^{\sharp}_{\mathbb{T}})(10)) = (err^{10} = \neg r^{10}_0 \wedge (e^{10} < 5)) \wedge (Ferr^{10} = err^{10})$$
$$\wedge (err^9 = \neg r^9_0 \wedge (e^9 < 5)) \wedge (Ferr^9 = err^9 \vee Ferr^{10}).$$

Applying this strategy, the resulting formulas can grow and ultimately involve all instant variables from the current instant up to the trace end. Likewise instant variables from later instants are included, which are actually not allowed to be included in the transformers because their presence could prevent finding a repeated element in $\tilde{A}$ and result in full unrolling of the specification. The fully computed transformers would express relations among all the instant variables to the stream end. In contrast, our online monitoring only preserves the relation among the variables for the current and previous instant, so we search for an alternative representation of the formula above which is equivalent w.r.t. the instant variables at the current and previous time points. This is equivalent to existentially quantifying over the variables to be removed and apply quantifier elimination if it can be used.

Example 4. Revisiting the previous example, real linear arithmetic quantifier elimination determines that $\mu(\llbracket \varphi \rrbracket^{\sharp}_{\mathbb{T}})(9)$ is

$$\mu(\llbracket \varphi \rrbracket^{\sharp}_{\mathbb{T}})(9) = \exists r^{10}_0, err^{10}, Ferr^{10}, e^{10}.(err^{10} = \neg r^{10}_0 \wedge (e^{10} < 5)) \wedge$$
$$(Ferr^{10} = err^{10}) \wedge (err^9 = \neg r^9_0 \wedge (e^9 < 5)) \wedge (Ferr^9 = err^9 \vee Ferr^{10})$$
$$= (err^9 = \neg r^9_0 \wedge (e^9 < 5)) \wedge (err^9 \rightarrow Ferr^9)$$

Following this strategy for $\mu(\llbracket \varphi \rrbracket^{\sharp}_{\mathbb{T}})(8)$:

$$\mu(\llbracket \varphi \rrbracket^{\sharp}_{\mathbb{T}})(8) = \exists \neg r^9_0, err^9, Ferr^9, e^9.(err^9 = \neg r^9_0 \wedge (e^9 < 5)) \wedge$$
$$(err^9 \rightarrow Ferr^9) \wedge (err^8 = \neg r^8_0 \wedge (e^8 < 5)) \wedge (Ferr^8 = err^8 \vee Ferr^9)$$
$$= (err^8 = \neg r^8_0 \wedge (e^8 < 5)) \wedge (err^8 \rightarrow Ferr^8)$$

Thus $\mu(\llbracket\varphi\rrbracket_\top^\sharp)(9)$ and $\mu(\llbracket\varphi\rrbracket_\top^\sharp)(8)$ are (modulo instant variable timestamps) equal to each other and consequently also to $\mu(\llbracket\varphi\rrbracket_\top^\sharp)(7), \ldots, \mu(\llbracket\varphi\rrbracket_\top^\sharp)(1)$. Hence, after three computation steps $\mu(\llbracket\varphi\rrbracket_\top^\sharp)$ is fully computed, independent of the concrete t_{max} (except for the entry at instant 0).

If the specification contains assumptions, we also add $\ldots \wedge \Lambda^t$ to each symbolic transformer. Unfortunately, quantifier elimination does not guarantee to reach a stabilized formula as above. Therefore, we propose the following three stage strategy for the computation of the initial fixed point, which may ultimately lead to an over-approximation of $\mu(\llbracket\varphi\rrbracket_\top^\sharp)$:

1. Compute the elements of $\mu(\llbracket\varphi\rrbracket_\top^\sharp)$ from back to front applying quantifier elimination for k steps.
2. If no repeating entry is found for l steps, the elements of $\mu(\llbracket\varphi\rrbracket_\top^\sharp)$ are determined but besides variables of future instants all real variables are eliminated. For the current instant real variables' maximal and minimal bounds are determined based on the computed symbolic representation and added to the final symbolic representation (see [19]).
3. If still no repeating element is found, the strategy is applied again but with widening [7] on the bounds of two subsequent instants interval. For example, let $[a, b]$ be the previously computed interval and $[a', b']$ the new one. The lower widened interval bound is $-\infty$ if $a' < a$ and a otherwise. Dually, the upper widened interval bound is ∞ if $b' > b$ and b otherwise.

As all constraints over a fixed number of Boolean variables can be represented in a formula of constant length and the bounds of all real variables either stabilize or are brought to $\pm\infty$ by widening, it is guaranteed that a repeating element will be found in the third stage. Note that eliminating real variables and replacing their constraints with bounds leads to an over-approximation. The resulting transformer and monitor are still sound but not necessarily perfect.

For the monitoring we finally recompute $\mu(\llbracket\varphi\rrbracket_{\Sigma^t}^\sharp)(t)$ for each timestamp t. We do this analogously to the initial fixed point computation before, but also add the new input constraints $\alpha(\Sigma^t)\backslash\alpha(\Sigma^{t-1})$ (i.e. the input readings of the current instant).

When it comes to the application of the computed transformer to the current monitor state we can simply conjunct the constraints of the transformer and the current monitor state and again use quantifier elimination to eliminate the variables from the previous instant.

Example 5. Take again the transformer $\tau = (e^4 \leq e^3 - 3)$ from Example 2 and the monitoring state $s^\sharp = (90 \leq e^3 \leq 92)$ from above, we get $\tau(s) = \exists e^3.(e^4 \leq e^3 - 3) \wedge (90 \leq e^3 \leq 92)$. After application of quantifier elimination this would lead to state $s^\sharp = e^4 \leq 89$.

If the monitor state grows too large we can also apply the second stage of the above strategy to reduce its size at the cost of making the monitor state less precise. As a further optimization, note that from the first fixed point (for

$\Sigma = \top$), we only need the relation between those variables that are referenced by $+1$ offsets in the specification. Therefore, during quantifier elimination for the initial fixed point we can also remove all variables from the current instant which are not referenced in this way.

7   Empirical Evaluation

We developed a prototype for symbolic recurrent Lola monitoring in Scala using Z3 [28] as backend solver for symbolic reasoning and quantifier elimination. We evaluated our tool on three case studies running on a 64-bit Linux machine with an Intel Core i7-1365U CPU and 32GB of RAM.

Path Planning. The first case study examines a variation of the vacuum cleaning robot from Fig. 1. The example was extended such that the output does not only specify whether a room can be safely entered but also with how much surplus or missing energy. This information could then be used to control the robot's behavior, e.g. switching to a power-saving mode, showing the advantages of a monitoring approach which is able to compute richer verdicts than just Booleans.

We analyzed the monitor's synthesis time (i.e. the time for the computation of the initial fixed point), and the monitor time per instant at runtime for a variable number of rooms by simulating a random walk according to the monitor's output. In this case study, the initial semantics could be fully determined without widening, as a repeating symbolic transformer element was found after a few computations. As Fig. 2a shows, the synthesis time grows non-linearly. This is because the backwards calculation becomes more expensive with longer paths. This can be remedied by simplifying the symbolic representation of formulas during computation. However, Z3 is rather optimized for satisfiability checks but not for simplifying symbolic constraints. We will explore the benefits of specialized simplifiers and further optimizations for reducing the synthesis time as future work.

More important than synthesis time is the execution time of the monitors. The average computation time per instant during the monitor execution, measured with different degrees of induced uncertainty, is shown in Fig. 2b. Runtime increases when uncertainty is introduced but the time-per-event is still small (384 ms) in the worst case.

Collision Avoidance. In the second case study a robot uses a Lola monitor to navigate through an area with obstacles. The robot receives a set of waypoints from the user and tries to follow them while avoiding the obstacles. The monitor receives as inputs the distance $dist$ to the closest obstacle in front of the robot, as well as its leftmost and rightmost points $left$ and $right$. The monitor outputs the possible steering angles to avoid collisions in the future (see Fig. 3a). Assumptions define parameters like the maximum possible steering angle and the bounding box of the robot (see b and d in Fig. 3a).

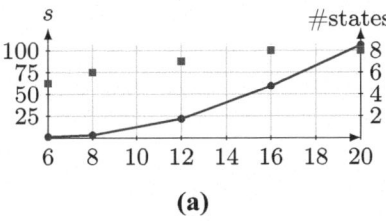 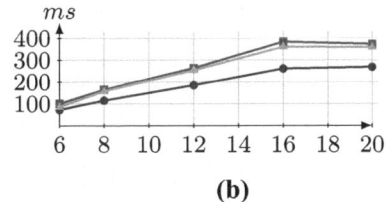

(a)   **(b)**

Fig. 2. a: Monitor synthesis per number of rooms. Synthesis time in seconds (•) and number of computed states (■). b: Avg. runtime (ms) per instant for different room numbers. Full certain (•), 30% noisy (■) and 15% entirely unknown (▲).

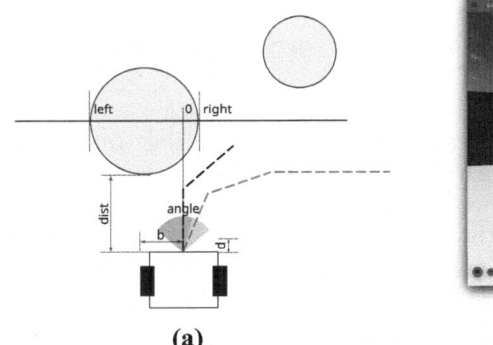 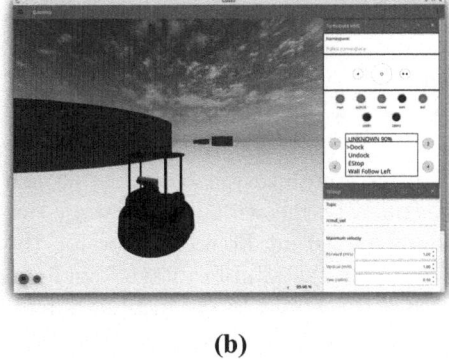

(a)   **(b)**

Fig. 3. a: Collision avoidance (scheme). b: Screenshot of the simulation in Gazebo.

The study was qualitatively evaluated by integrating our Lola monitoring tool with the robot operating system ROS [30] running on a turtlebot[1] inside the simulation environment Gazebo [23] (see Fig. 3b). The robot follows a user defined path, periodically calling the monitor for the closest obstacle in front obtaining safe steering angles, from which the robot chooses the one closest to the defined path. The monitor was able to steer the robot without collision with an uncertainty margin of up to 30%. We additionally extracted execution traces and evaluated the performance of the monitor offline. Figure 4 shows the runtime per instant, which increases with growing input uncertainty due to the increasing complexity of the constraint states.

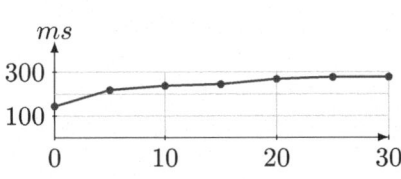

Fig. 4. Average runtime (ms) for uncertainty margins from 0% to 30%.

Program Monitoring. In the third case study we use our approach for traditional program monitoring. An excerpt of the monitored program is shown

---

[1] https://www.turtlebot.com/.

below on the left.

```
1  x = getInput();
2  [...]
3  y = 0;
4  while (x > 0) {
5      x--;
6      y += 2;
7  }
8  assert y >= 15;
```

At the end of the program we wanted to ensure that the value of variable y which is previously computed in a while loop does exceed 15. We have created a Lola specification which receives the current variable values as input streams and the current program line. Furthermore the program behavior itself was encoded in a straight-forward manner as assumption in the Lola specification. With its anticipation capabilities the monitor was able to compute legal values for the variables at certain program positions s.t. the assertion at the end is satisfied. Thus, it was able to detect program failures at an early stage during program execution.

Since the valid variable values depend on the number of while loop executions in the program (and thus the remaining trace length), the initial transformer semantics computation of our approach did not find a repeating transformer. Consequently the widening strategy described above has been applied to yield a sound recurrent Lola monitor for the specification. In the particular example however the simple interval widening was still able to capture that before entering the while loop variable x has to be at least 8, yet some other variable connections have been over-approximated. Yet, when in line 1 an input was entered which ultimately lead to $x < 8$ in line 3 the monitor was able to detect the failure right there. Altogether this provides an illustrative example how the approach from this paper could be used for a mixture of static and dynamic program analysis, which in a large scale however would require more sophisticated widening techniques than in the current implementation.

8   Conclusion

In this paper we have studied general anticipatory monitoring of Lola specifications under uncertainties and assumptions. We have introduced a hierarchy of monitoring semantics and presented an abstraction based framework for monitoring, from which we developed a general sound or perfect online monitoring algorithm for Lola. This algorithm considers future continuations of the received input, provided an abstraction of stream data values. Finally, we have presented an instantiation of this algorithm based on a symbolic representation. and evaluated the approach in three practical scenarios. Due to Lola's universality, our theory can also serve a general framework for anticipatory monitoring of synchronous RV formalisms.

Future work includes a more efficient implementation, especially improving the simplification of the symbolic constraints applied during monitoring, and applications to other Lola fragments beyond linear arithmetic. We also plan to extend the approach to infinite traces and asynchronous SRV formalisms.

Disclosure of Interests. The authors have no competing interests to declare that are relevant to the content of this article.

References

1. Basin, D., Harvan, M., Klaedtke, F., Zălinescu, E.: MONPOLY: monitoring usage-control policies. In: Khurshid, S., Sen, K. (eds.) RV 2011. LNCS, vol. 7186, pp. 360–364. Springer, Heidelberg (2012). https://doi.org/10.1007/978-3-642-29860-8_27

2. Bauer, A., Leucker, M., Schallhart, C.: Monitoring of real-time properties. In: Arun-Kumar, S., Garg, N. (eds.) FSTTCS 2006. LNCS, vol. 4337, pp. 260–272. Springer, Heidelberg (2006). https://doi.org/10.1007/11944836_25

3. Bauer, A., Leucker, M., Schallhart, C.: Comparing LTL semantics for runtime verification. J. Log. Comput. **20**(3), 651–674 (2010). https://doi.org/10.1093/logcom/exn075

4. Cimatti, A., Tian, C., Tonetta, S.: Assumption-based runtime verification with partial observability and resets. In: Finkbeiner, B., Mariani, L. (eds.) RV 2019. LNCS, vol. 11757, pp. 165–184. Springer, Cham (2019). https://doi.org/10.1007/978-3-030-32079-9_10

5. Cimatti, A., Tian, C., Tonetta, S.: Assumption-based runtime verification of infinite-state systems. In: Feng, L., Fisman, D. (eds.) RV 2021. LNCS, vol. 12974, pp. 207–227. Springer, Cham (2021). https://doi.org/10.1007/978-3-030-88494-9_11

6. Convent, L., Hungerecker, S., Leucker, M., Scheffel, T., Schmitz, M., Thoma, D.: TeSSLa: temporal stream-based specification language. In: Massoni, T., Mousavi, M.R. (eds.) SBMF 2018. LNCS, vol. 11254, pp. 144–162. Springer, Cham (2018). https://doi.org/10.1007/978-3-030-03044-5_10

7. Cousot, P.: Principles of Abstract Interpretation. The MIT Press (2021)

8. Cousot, P., Cousot, R.: Abstract interpretation: a unified lattice model for static analysis of programs by construction or approximation of fixpoints. In: Proceedings of the 4th ACM Symposium on Principles of Programming Languages (POL 1977), pp. 238–252. ACM (1977). https://doi.org/10.1145/512950.512973

9. D'Angelo, B., et al.: LOLA: runtime monitoring of synchronous systems. In: Proceedings of the 12th International Symposium of Temporal Representation and Reasoning (TIME 2005), pp. 166–174. IEEE Computer Society (2005). https://doi.org/10.1109/TIME.2005.26

10. Decker, N., Leucker, M., Thoma, D.: Monitoring modulo theories. Int. J. Softw. Tools Technol. Transf. **18**(2), 205–225 (2016). https://doi.org/10.1007/s10009-015-0380-3

11. Faymonville, P., et al.: StreamLAB: stream-based monitoring of cyber-physical systems. In: Dillig, I., Tasiran, S. (eds.) CAV 2019. LNCS, vol. 11561, pp. 421–431. Springer, Cham (2019). https://doi.org/10.1007/978-3-030-25540-4_24

12. Faymonville, P., Finkbeiner, B., Schwenger, M., Torfah, H.: Real-time stream-based monitoring. CoRR abs/1711.03829 (2017). http://arxiv.org/abs/1711.03829

13. Felli, P., Montali, M., Patrizi, F., Winkler, S.: Monitoring arithmetic temporal properties on finite traces. In: Proceedings of the 37th AAAI Conference on Artificial Intelligence (AAAI 2023), pp. 6346–6354. AAAI Press (2023). https://doi.org/10.1609/aaai.v37i5.25781

14. Goldberg, A., Havelund, K.: Automated runtime verification with eagle. In: Proceedings of the 3rd International Workshop on Modelling, Simulation, Verification and Validation of Enterprise Information Systems, (MSVVEIS 2005). INSTICC Press (2005)

15. Gorostiaga, F., Sánchez, C.: Striver: stream runtime verification for real-time event-streams. In: Colombo, C., Leucker, M. (eds.) RV 2018. LNCS, vol. 11237, pp. 282–298. Springer, Cham (2018). https://doi.org/10.1007/978-3-030-03769-7_16

16. Gorostiaga, F., Sánchez, C.: Stream runtime verification of real-time event streams with the Striver language. Int. J. Softw. Tools Technol. Transfer **23**, 157–183 (2021). https://doi.org/10.1007/s10009-021-00605-3

17. Havelund, K., Roşu, G.: Synthesizing monitors for safety properties. In: Katoen, J.-P., Stevens, P. (eds.) TACAS 2002. LNCS, vol. 2280, pp. 342–356. Springer, Heidelberg (2002). https://doi.org/10.1007/3-540-46002-0_24

18. Henzinger, T.A., Saraç, N.E.: Monitorability under assumptions. In: Deshmukh, J., Ničković, D. (eds.) RV 2020. LNCS, vol. 12399, pp. 3–18. Springer, Cham (2020). https://doi.org/10.1007/978-3-030-60508-7_1

19. Kallwies, H., Leucker, M., Sánchez, C.: Symbolic runtime verification for monitoring under uncertainties and assumptions. In: Bouajjani, A., Holík, L., Wu, Z. (eds.) ATVA 2022. LNCS, vol. 13505, pp. 117–134. Springer, Cham (2022). https://doi.org/10.1007/978-3-031-19992-9_8

20. Kallwies, H., Leucker, M., Sánchez, C.: General anticipatory monitoring for temporal logics on finite traces. In: Katsaros, P., Nenzi, L. (eds.) RV 2023. LNCS, vol. 14245, pp. 106–125. Springer, Cham (2023). https://doi.org/10.1007/978-3-031-44267-4_6

21. Kallwies, H., Leucker, M., Sánchez, C., Scheffel, T.: Anticipatory recurrent monitoring with uncertainty and assumptions. In: Dang, T., Stolz, V. (eds.) RV 2022. LNCS, vol. 13498, pp. 181–199. Springer, Cham (2022). https://doi.org/10.1007/978-3-031-17196-3_10

22. Kallwies, H., Leucker, M., Schmitz, M., Schulz, A., Thoma, D., Weiss, A.: TeSSLa - an ecosystem for runtime verification. In: Dang, T., Stolz, V. (eds.) RV 2022. LNCS, vol. 13498, pp. 314–324. Springer, Cham (2022). https://doi.org/10.1007/978-3-031-17196-3_20

23. Koenig, N.P., Howard, A.: Design and use paradigms for Gazebo, an open-source multi-robot simulator. In: Proceedings of the 2004 IEEE/RSJ International Conference on Intelligent Robots and Systems (IROS 2004), vol. 3, pp. 2149–2154. IEEE (2004). https://doi.org/10.1109/IROS.2004.1389727

24. Leucker, M.: Sliding between model checking and runtime verification. In: Qadeer, S., Tasiran, S. (eds.) RV 2012. LNCS, vol. 7687, pp. 82–87. Springer, Heidelberg (2013). https://doi.org/10.1007/978-3-642-35632-2_10

25. Leucker, M., Sánchez, C., Scheffel, T., Schmitz, M., Thoma, D.: Runtime verification for timed event streams with partial information. In: Finkbeiner, B., Mariani, L. (eds.) RV 2019. LNCS, vol. 11757, pp. 273–291. Springer, Cham (2019). https://doi.org/10.1007/978-3-030-32079-9_16

26. Leucker, M., Schallhart, C.: A brief account of runtime verification. J. Log. Algebraic Methods Program. **78**(5), 293–303 (2009). https://doi.org/10.1016/j.jlap.2008.08.004

27. Maler, O., Nickovic, D.: Monitoring temporal properties of continuous signals. In: Lakhnech, Y., Yovine, S. (eds.) FORMATS/FTRTFT -2004. LNCS, vol. 3253, pp. 152–166. Springer, Heidelberg (2004). https://doi.org/10.1007/978-3-540-30206-3_12

28. de Moura, L., Bjørner, N.: Z3: an efficient SMT solver. In: Ramakrishnan, C.R., Rehof, J. (eds.) TACAS 2008. LNCS, vol. 4963, pp. 337–340. Springer, Heidelberg (2008). https://doi.org/10.1007/978-3-540-78800-3_24

29. Pnueli, A.: The temporal logic of programs. In: Proceedings of the 18th IEEE Symposium on the Foundations of Computer Science (FOCS-1977), pp. 46–57. IEEE Computer Society Press (1977). https://doi.org/10.1109/SFCS.1977.32

30. Quigley, M., et al.: ROS: an open-source robot operating system. In: Workshops at the IEEE International Conference on Robotics and Automation (ICRA90), vol. 3 (2009)

31. Reinbacher, T., Rozier, K.Y., Schumann, J.: Temporal-logic based runtime observer pairs for system health management of real-time systems. In: Ábrahám, E., Havelund, K. (eds.) TACAS 2014. LNCS, vol. 8413, pp. 357–372. Springer, Heidelberg (2014). https://doi.org/10.1007/978-3-642-54862-8_24

32. Schmitz, M.: Efficient implementation of stream transformations. Ph.D. thesis, University of Lübeck, Germany (2024). https://www.zhb.uni-luebeck.de/epubs/ediss3011.pdf

33. Shoham, S., Grumberg, O.: A game-based framework for CTL counterexamples and 3-valued abstraction-refinement. In: Hunt, W.A., Somenzi, F. (eds.) CAV 2003. LNCS, vol. 2725, pp. 275–287. Springer, Heidelberg (2003). https://doi.org/10.1007/978-3-540-45069-6_28

34. Waga, M., André, É., Hasuo, I.: Symbolic monitoring against specifications parametric in time and data. In: Dillig, I., Tasiran, S. (eds.) CAV 2019. LNCS, vol. 11561, pp. 520–539. Springer, Cham (2019). https://doi.org/10.1007/978-3-030-25540-4_30

35. Waga, M., André, É., Hasuo, I.: Model-bounded monitoring of hybrid systems. ACM Trans. Cyber-Phys. Syst. **6:4**(30), 1–26 (2021). https://doi.org/10.1145/3529095

Proactive Real-Time First-Order Enforcement

François Hublet[1], Leonardo Lima[2(✉)], David Basin[1], Srđan Krstić[1], and Dmitriy Traytel[2]

[1] ETH Zürich, Zurich, Switzerland
{francois.hublet,basin,srdan.krstic}@inf.ethz.ch
[2] University of Copenhagen, Copenhagen, Denmark
{leonardo,traytel}@di.ku.dk

Abstract. Modern software systems must comply with increasingly complex regulations in domains ranging from industrial automation to data protection. Runtime enforcement addresses this challenge by empowering systems to not only observe, but also actively control, the behavior of target systems by modifying their actions to ensure policy compliance. We propose a novel approach to the proactive real-time enforcement of policies expressed in metric first-order temporal logic (MFOTL). We introduce a new system model, define an expressive MFOTL fragment that is enforceable in that model, and develop a sound enforcement algorithm for this fragment. We implement this algorithm in a tool called WHYENF and carry out a case study on enforcing GDPR-related policies. Our tool can enforce all policies from the study in real-time with modest overhead. Our work thus provides the first tool-supported approach that can proactively enforce expressive first-order policies in real time.

Keywords: runtime enforcement · temporal logic · obligations

1 Introduction

As modern software systems become increasingly complex, they are required to comply with a myriad of growingly intricate regulations. The ability to monitor and control such systems is an important, technically challenging task.

Runtime *enforcement* [58] tackles this problem by observing and controlling a target system under scrutiny (SuS), so that its actions, possibly modified, comply with a given policy. Runtime enforcement is performed by a component called *enforcer*, which observes the SuS and influences its behavior as permitted by the system model, e.g., by suppressing or causing SuS actions. Enforcement is thus an inherently *online* problem performed during the SuS's execution. When time constraints are involved, enforcement is called *real-time*. This is a more difficult problem than runtime *monitoring* [8], where the SuS is only observed and policy violations are reported, but not prevented. Applications of runtime enforcement are manifold, ranging from safety protocols in industrial automation

© The Author(s) 2024
A. Gurfinkel and V. Ganesh (Eds.): CAV 2024, LNCS 14682, pp. 156–181, 2024.
https://doi.org/10.1007/978-3-031-65630-9_8

to regulatory compliance and it is closely related to the problem of controller synthesis [1,56].

Policies can be decomposed into provisions and obligations [37]. Compliance with provisions depends on past and present SuS behavior, and it is sufficient for an enforcer to react to the current SuS action. Compliance with obligations, on the other hand, depends on future SuS behavior, requiring the enforcer to account for this behavior and *proactively act* [11] to prevent violations.

In existing approaches to proactive runtime enforcement [11], policies are typically propositional: they regard every system action as either true or false. In practice, however, actions are often parameterized with data values coming from an infinite domain, like strings or integers, and first-order policies are used to formulate dependencies between such actions' parameters. To the best of our knowledge, no previous work supports proactive enforcement of first-order policies: Hublet et al.'s [39] enforcement is real-time, but not proactive; Aceto et al. [5] similarly support only the *reactive* runtime enforcement of first-order provisions.

In this paper, we propose an approach for proactively enforcing metric first-order temporal logic (MFOTL) [18] policies. Our approach features a realistic system model that supports proactive real-time enforcement *in the nick of time* [11,12], i.e., the enforcer can act at least once per clock tick. Our model includes causable, suppressable, and only-observable SuS actions. Due to its proactivity, our enforcer supports an expressive MFOTL fragment with past and future operators.

Our enforcer is *sound* (modified SuS behavior complies with a given policy) for an enforceable MFOTL fragment (EMFOTL), and *transparent* (if SuS behavior is already policy-compliant, then it is not modified) for a fragment of EMFOTL. Our enforcer relies on the runtime *monitoring* tool WHYMON [49] as a backend. After reviewing MFOTL and WHYMON (Sect. 2) we describe our approach and evaluate the associated implementation. Our work makes the following contributions:

- We introduce a new system model for the proactive real-time enforcement of metric first-order policies (Sect. 3).
- We present an enforceable MFOTL fragment (called EMFOTL) with past and future operators that we characterize using a type system (Sect. 4).
- We develop an enforcement algorithm for EMFOTL and prove its soundness. We also prove its transparency for a fragment of EMFOTL (Sect. 5).
- We implement the type system and the algorithm into a new tool, called WHYENF. We carry out a case study on monitoring core GDPR provisions [7], using WHYENF to enforce the monitored policies. We find that WHYENF can seamlessly enforce all monitorable policies from this case study in real time with modest runtime overhead (Sect. 6).

To our knowledge, WHYENF (available at [43]) is the first proactive first-order policy enforcer (Sect. 7). All proofs can be found in our extended report [42].

2   Preliminaries

We introduce traces that model system executions, metric-first order temporal logic (MFOTL), and WHYMON, a monitor for an expressive MFOTL fragment.

Let $x, y, z \in \mathbb{V}$ be variables and $c, d \in \mathbb{D}$ be values from an infinite domain $\mathbb{D}$ of constant symbols, like integers or strings. Terms $t \in \mathbb{V} \cup \mathbb{D}$ are either variables or constants. Finite sequences of terms $t_1, \ldots, t_n$ are written as $\bar{t}$. Let $\mathbb{E}$ denote a finite set of *event names*, and the function $\iota : \mathbb{E} \to \mathbb{N}$ map event names to arities. An *event* is a pair $(e, (d_1, \ldots, d_{\iota(e)})) \in \mathbb{E} \times \mathbb{D}^{\iota(e)}$ of an event name e and $\iota(e)$ arguments. We fix a *signature* $\Sigma = (\mathbb{D}, \mathbb{E}, \iota)$ and define the set $\mathbb{DB}$ of *databases* over Σ as $\mathcal{P}(\{(e, \bar{d}) \mid e \in \mathbb{E}, \bar{d} \in \mathbb{D}^{\iota(e)}\})$. The subset of all databases with event names in $E \subseteq \mathbb{E}$ is $\mathsf{DB}(E) := \{D \in \mathbb{DB} \mid \forall (e, (d_1, \ldots, d_{\iota(e)})) \in D. \; e \in E\}$.

Example 1. Consider a system logging GDPR-relevant events defined with the signature $\Sigma_0 = (\mathbb{N}, \mathbb{E}_0, \iota_0)$, where $\mathbb{E}_0 = \{\mathsf{use}, \mathsf{consent}, \mathsf{delete}, \mathsf{deletion\_request}, \mathsf{legal\_ground}\}$, $\iota_0(\mathsf{use}) = \iota_0(\mathsf{delete}) = \iota_0(\mathsf{deletion\_request}) = 3$, and $\iota_0(\mathsf{consent}) = \iota_0(\mathsf{legal\_ground}) = 2$. The events' denotations are: $\mathsf{use}(c, d, u)$ means 'system uses user u's data d from category c', $\mathsf{delete}(c, d, u)$ means 'user u's data d from category c is deleted', $\mathsf{deletion\_request}(c, d, u)$ means 'user u requests deletion of data d from category c', $\mathsf{consent}(u, c)$ means 'user u provides consent for category c', and $\mathsf{legal\_ground}(u, d)$ means 'legal ground was claimed to process user u's data d'.

A *trace* σ is a sequence $\langle (\tau_i, D_i) \rangle_{0 \leq i \leq k}$, $k \in \mathbb{N} \cup \{\infty\}$ of timestamps $\tau_i \in \mathbb{N}$ and finite databases $D_i \in \mathbb{DB}$, where timestamps grow *monotonically* ($\forall i < |\sigma|. \; \tau_i \leq \tau_{i+1}$) and *progress* (if $|\sigma| = \infty$, then $\forall \tau. \; \exists i. \; \tau < \tau_i$). An index $0 \leq i < |\sigma|$, in a trace σ is called a *time-point*. The empty trace is denoted by ε, the set of all traces by $\mathbb{T}$, and the set of finite (resp. infinite) traces by $\mathbb{T}_f$ (resp. $\mathbb{T}_\omega$). For traces $\sigma \in \mathbb{T}_f$ and $\sigma' \in \mathbb{T}$, $\sigma \cdot \sigma'$ denotes their concatenation. A *property* is a subset $P \subseteq \mathbb{T}_\omega$.

Example 2. Consider two infinite traces of a data management system

$$\sigma_1 = (10, \{\mathsf{consent}(1,1), \mathsf{consent}(1,2)\}), (50, \{\mathsf{use}(1,3,1), \mathsf{use}(2,1,1)\}), \ldots$$
$$\sigma_2 = (10, \{\mathsf{deletion\_request}(2,1,1)\}), (50, \{\mathsf{use}(1,3,1)\}), \ldots$$

In σ_1, user 1 provides consent for categories 1 and 2 at time-point 0 with timestamp 10; at time-point 1 with timestamp 50, the system uses user 1's data 3 (with category 1) and user 1's data 1 (with category 2). In σ_2, user 1 requests deletion of data 1 with category 2, and then the system uses data 3 with category 1.

MFOTL formulae are defined by the following grammar

$$\varphi ::= \; \top \mid e(\bar{t}) \mid \neg\varphi \mid \varphi \wedge \varphi \mid \exists x. \; \varphi \mid \bigcirc_I \varphi \mid \bullet_I \varphi \mid \varphi \, \mathsf{U}_I \, \varphi \mid \varphi \, \mathsf{S}_I \, \varphi,$$

where $e \in \mathbb{E}$, $x \in \mathbb{V}$, and $I \in \mathbb{I}$ ranges over non-empty intervals in $\mathbb{N}$. We use the standard abbreviations $\bot := \neg\top$, $\varphi \vee \psi := \neg(\neg\varphi \wedge \neg\psi)$, $\varphi \to \psi := \neg\varphi \vee \psi$, $\varphi \leftrightarrow \psi := (\varphi \to \psi) \wedge (\psi \to \varphi)$, $\forall x. \; \varphi := \neg(\exists x. \; \neg\varphi)$, $\Diamond_I \varphi := \top \, \mathsf{U}_I \, \varphi$ (eventually),

$v, i \vDash e(\bar{t})$ iff $(e, [\![\bar{t}]\!]_v) \in D_i$ $v, i \vDash \top$

$v, i \vDash \exists x. \; \varphi$ iff $v[x \mapsto d], i \vDash \varphi$ for some $d \in \mathbb{D}$ $v, i \vDash \neg \varphi$ iff $v, i \nvDash \varphi$

$v, i \vDash \bigcirc_I \varphi$ iff $v, i+1 \vDash \varphi$ and $\tau_{i+1} - \tau_i \in I$ $v, i \vDash \varphi \wedge \psi$ iff $v, i \vDash \varphi$ and $v, i \vDash \psi$

$v, i \vDash \bullet_I \varphi$ iff $i > 0$ and $v, i-1 \vDash \varphi$ and $\tau_i - \tau_{i-1} \in I$

$v, i \vDash \varphi \, \mathsf{U}_I \, \psi$ iff $v, j \vDash \psi$ for some $j \geq i$ with $\tau_j - \tau_i \in I$ and $v, k \vDash \varphi$ for all $i \leq k < j$

$v, i \vDash \varphi \, \mathsf{S}_I \, \psi$ iff $v, j \vDash \psi$ for some $j \leq i$ with $\tau_i - \tau_j \in I$ and $v, k \vDash \varphi$ for all $j < k \leq i$

Fig. 1. MFOTL semantics for a fixed, infinite trace σ

$\blacklozenge_I \varphi := \top \mathsf{S}_I \varphi$ (once), $\square_I \varphi := \neg \lozenge_I \neg \varphi$ (always), and $\blacksquare_I \varphi := \neg \blacklozenge_I \neg \varphi$ (historically). A *polarity* $p \in \{+, -\}$ acts upon a formula φ by $+\varphi := \varphi$ and $-\varphi := \neg\varphi$. We omit intervals of the form $[0, \infty)$ from the temporal operators' subscript. We write $\varphi[d/x]$ for the formula resulting from substituting the free variable x with the constant d in the formula φ. The notation $\varphi[v]$ generalizes such a unary substitution to applying a full *valuation* $v : \mathbb{V} \to \mathbb{D}$, i.e., a mapping from variables to domain values.

Example 3. Suppose that the time unit is *days*. Consider the formulae

$$\varphi_{\mathsf{law}} \equiv \square \left(\forall c, d, u. \, \mathsf{use} \, (c, d, u) \to \blacklozenge \left(\mathsf{consent} \, (u, c) \vee \mathsf{legal\_grounds} \, (u, d) \right) \right)$$

$$\varphi_{\mathsf{del}} \equiv \square \left(\forall c, d, u. \, \mathsf{deletion\_request} \, (c, d, u) \to \lozenge_{[0,30]} \mathsf{delete} \, (c, d, u) \right)$$

The formula φ_{law} formalizes *lawfulness of processing*: 'whenever data d with category c belonging to user u is processed, then either u has consented to her data with category c being used, or the controller has claimed a legal ground to process d.' The formula φ_{del} formalizes the GDPR's *right to erasure*: 'whenever a user u requests the deletion of data d of category c, then d must be deleted within 30 d'.

We write $\mathsf{fv}(\varphi)$ and $\mathsf{cs}(\varphi)$ for the set of free variables and constants of a formula φ, respectively. We define the *active domain* $\mathsf{AD}_i(\varphi)$ of a formula φ at time-point i as $\mathsf{cs}(\varphi) \cup \left(\bigcup_{j \leq i} \{ d \mid d \text{ is one of } d_k \text{ in } e(d_1, \ldots, d_{\iota(e)}) \in D_j \} \right)$. The active domain of φ at i contains all constants occurring in φ together with all constants occurring as event arguments in the trace up to time-point i.

Example 4. As $\mathsf{cs}(\varphi_{\mathsf{law}}) = \mathsf{cs}(\varphi_{\mathsf{del}}) = \emptyset$, we have $\mathsf{AD}_0(\varphi_{\mathsf{law}}) = \mathsf{AD}_0(\varphi_{\mathsf{del}}) = \{1, 2\}$ and $\mathsf{AD}_1(\varphi_{\mathsf{law}}) = \mathsf{AD}_1(\varphi_{\mathsf{del}}) = \{1, 2, 3\}$ for σ_1.

MFOTL's semantics (Fig. 1) is defined over infinite traces. Given a valuation v, we define the interpretation of terms as $[\![x]\!]_v = v(x)$ (for variables) and $[\![c]\!]_v = c$ (for constants). We lift this operation straightforwardly to lists of terms. A valuation update is denoted as $v[d/x]$. Each sequent $v, i \vDash_\sigma \varphi$ denotes that φ is satisfied at time-point i of trace σ under valuation v. We omit σ whenever it is clear from the context. The *language* of a formula φ is $\mathcal{L}(\varphi) = \{ \sigma \in \mathbb{T}_\omega \mid \exists v. \, v, 0 \vDash_\sigma \varphi \}$.

Lima et al. [49] present an algorithm and a tool, called WHYMON, that can monitor an expressive safety fragment of MFOTL both online and offline. This

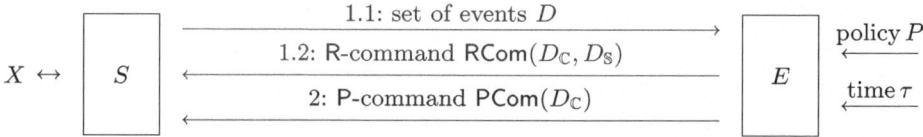

Fig. 2. System model for proactive real-time first-order enforcement

fragment contains *all* formulae with future-bounded until operators. Thus, it strictly extends the fragments supported by other tools like MonPoly [13] and VeriMon [9], which only support formulas in relational algebra normal form [20], and DejaVu [35], which is restricted to past temporal operators.

Abstractly, WHYMON implements a function $\text{SAT}(v, \varphi, i) = v, i \vDash \varphi$ that checks if a valuation satisfies the formula φ on a (fixed) trace σ at time-point i. Internally, it manipulates objects representing proofs of φ's subformulae. This technique additionally allows WHYMON to output *explanations* [48] of its verdicts (satisfactions or violations) in the form of proofs that can be checked using a proof checker. We refer to Lima et al.'s work [49] for further details.

3 Proactive, Real-Time, First-Order Enforcement

Our system model (Sect. 3.1) is inspired by Basin et al.'s model for proactive *propositional* enforcement [11, 12] and Hublet et al.'s model for (non-proactive) *first-order* enforcement [39]. Within this model, we define enforcers (Sect. 3.2).

3.1 System Model

Figure 2 shows a system S supervised by an enforcer E described using a communication diagram [32]. The system S interacts with an environment X that E cannot control. The enforcer E must ensure that the sequence of actions executed by S complies with a given policy P. To this end, S reports to E sets of events (from $\mathbb{E}$) that capture the system's observable actions. The enforcer E can send commands to S, whereby it instructs S to cause or suppress the actions corresponding to specific events. There are two kinds of such commands, R-commands and P-commands, which will be described below. We assume that the set of events is partitioned into a set of *causable* events $\mathbb{C}$ capturing actions that E can instruct S to cause, a set of *suppressable* events $\mathbb{S}$ capturing actions that E can instruct S to suppress, and a set of *only-observable* events $\mathbb{O} = \mathbb{E} \setminus (\mathbb{S} \cup \mathbb{C})$ capturing actions that can be neither caused nor suppressed.

Example 5. Suppose that the system from Example 1 can be instrumented so that an enforcer can (observe and) prevent data usage and cause data deletion, but can only observe the remaining actions. The corresponding event sets are then $\mathbb{C} = \{\text{delete}\}$, $\mathbb{S} = \{\text{use}\}$, and $\mathbb{O} = \{\text{consent}, \text{legal\_ground}, \text{deletion\_request}\}$.

More specifically, we assume that E interacts with S in three modes: (1) *Before* performing any suppressable actions, S sends the corresponding set of (suppressable) events $D \in \mathbb{DB}$ to E. The enforcer inspects D and *reactively* responds with an R-command $\mathsf{RCom}(D_\mathbb{C}, D_\mathbb{S})$, where $D_\mathbb{C} \in \mathsf{DB}(\mathbb{C})$ is a set of causable events and $D \supseteq D_\mathbb{S} \in \mathsf{DB}(\mathbb{S})$ is a set of suppressable events. S then performs the actions corresponding to the events in $(D \setminus D_\mathbb{S}) \cup D_\mathbb{C}$, i.e., all actions corresponding to events in $D_\mathbb{C}$ (resp. $D_\mathbb{S}$) are caused (resp. suppressed). (2) *After* performing actions that are *not suppressable*, S sends the corresponding set of events $D \in \mathbb{DB}$ to E. The enforcer inspects D and responds with an R-command $\mathsf{RCom}(D_\mathbb{C}, \emptyset)$. As no suppressable actions are to be performed and the events are sent after the actions, the enforcer can only instruct S to cause actions, but not to suppress them. (3) *Before* any clock tick ('in the nick of time' [12]), E can *proactively* send a P-command $\mathsf{PCom}(D_\mathbb{C})$ with $D_\mathbb{C} \in \mathsf{DB}(\mathbb{C})$ to S. The system S then performs the actions corresponding to the events in $D_\mathbb{C}$. Note that sending a P-command before a tick is always possible, but the enforcer may instead choose not to send any command.

These modes of interaction cover different enforcement scenarios. In mode (1), E *reacts* to suppressable events by possibly suppressing or causing events. E.g., the formula φ_{law} from Example 3 can be enforced by suppressing data usage (the use events) if no appropriate event has previously occurred. In mode (2), E reacts to only-observable events (e.g., the consent events) by possibly causing events corresponding to corrective actions after the executed action. Finally, mode (3) enforces policies by causing events at times when the SuS does not, on its own, send any observable events. This is the case, e.g., when enforcing φ_{del} on σ_2: data 1 with category 2 must be deleted between timestamps 10 and 40.

Discussion. Assume that the enforcer E can ensure that the sequence of actions it observes complies with P. When does this guarantee that the system actually complies with P? Basin et al. [12] state two conditions for achieving soundness: (a) the system and enforcer must be synchronized and (b) the enforcer must be fast enough to keep up with the real-time system behavior. These conditions also apply in our model. Condition (a) ensures that the order of events observed by E reflect the order of S's actions. Condition (b) ensures that the timestamps of events reflect the time at which the corresponding actions are performed by S. The interval t between two clock ticks must satisfy the *real-time condition* $t > \delta_S + 2\delta_{S \leftrightarrow E} + \delta_E$, where δ_S is the worst-case time needed by S to create events before performing observable actions and process the enforcer's reactions, $\delta_{S \leftrightarrow E}$ is the worst-case communication time between S and E, and δ_E is the worst-case latency of the enforcer. Threats to the model's validity may thus stem from high communication time, or poor SuS or enforcer performance.

```
1: run(s, σ, σ′, τ) = case σ′ of
2: | ε ⇒ ε
3: | (τ′, D) · σ″ when τ′ > τ ⇒ let (o, s′) = μ(σ, s, τ) in
4:     case o of | PCom(D_C) ⇒ (τ, D_C) · run(s′, σ · (τ, D_C), σ′, τ + 1)
5:                | NoCom ⇒ run(s′, σ, σ′, τ + 1)
6: | (τ′, D) · σ″ when τ′ = τ ⇒ let (o, s′) = μ(σ · (τ′, D), s, ⊥); D′ = (D \ D_S) ∪ D_C)
   in
7:     case o of | RCom(D_C, D_S) ⇒ (τ′, D′) · run(s′, σ · (τ′, D′), σ″, τ + 1)
8: ℰ(σ) = run(s_0, ε, σ, if σ = ε then 0 else fts(σ))
```

Algorithm 1: Enforced trace

3.2   Enforcers

An enforcer reads the consecutive prefixes of an SuS's trace and returns commands:

Definition 1. *A* command *is any element of the form* $\mathsf{RCom}(D_\mathbb{C}, D_\mathbb{S})$ *('R-command'),* $\mathsf{PCom}(D_\mathbb{C})$ *('P-command'), or* NoCom *('no command'), where* $D_\mathbb{C} \in \mathsf{DB}(\mathbb{C})$ *and* $D_\mathbb{S} \in \mathsf{DB}(\mathbb{S})$. *The set of commands is denoted by* $\mathcal{C}$.

Definition 2. *An* enforcer *$\mathcal{E}$ is a triple* $(\mathcal{S}, s_0, \mu)$, *where $\mathcal{S}$ is a set of states, $s_0 \in \mathcal{S}$ is an initial state, and $\mu : \mathbb{T}_f \times \mathcal{S} \times (\mathbb{N} \cup \{\bot\}) \to \mathcal{C} \times \mathcal{S}$ is a computable* update *function such that the following two conditions hold:*

$$\forall \sigma, \tau, D, s. \; \exists D_\mathbb{C}, D_\mathbb{S}, s'. \; \mu(\sigma \cdot (\tau, D), s, \bot) = (\mathsf{RCom}(D_\mathbb{C}, D_\mathbb{S}), s') \wedge D_\mathbb{S} \subseteq D$$
$$\forall \sigma, s, \tau \in \mathbb{N}. \; \exists D_\mathbb{C}, s'. \; \mu(\sigma, s, \tau) \in \{(\mathsf{PCom}(D_\mathbb{C}), s'), (\mathsf{NoCom}, s')\}.$$

If μ's third argument is $\bot$, then μ returns an R-command. The set of events to be suppressed contained in this command is a subset of the last set of events reported by the SuS. On the other hand, if μ's third argument is an integer timestamp, then μ returns either a P-command for the corresponding timestamp, or no command. Any enforcer induces the following trace transduction:

Definition 3. *For any $\sigma \in \mathbb{T}$ and enforcer $\mathcal{E} = (\mathcal{S}, s_0, \mu)$, the* enforced trace *$\mathcal{E}(\sigma)$ is defined co-recursively in Algorithm 1, where $\mathsf{fts}(\sigma)$ is the first timestamp in σ.*

Algorithm 1 formalizes the interaction described in Sect. 3.1: the enforcer is called once at every time-point in the input trace σ to generate an R-command (lines 6–7), and once before each clock tick to (possibly) generate a P-command (lines 3–5). The generated commands are executed sequentially to produce the enforced trace $\mathcal{E}(\sigma)$, which thus reflects the actions performed by the SuS when composed with the enforcer as in Sect. 3.1.

To be considered *correct* with respect to a given property P, enforcers are typically required to fulfill two properties: *soundness* and *transparency* [47]. Soundness states that any trace modified by the enforcer must be compliant with P, while transparency states that the enforcer does not alter a trace that already complies with the policy. A transparent enforcer modifies the system's behavior *only when necessary*. The following definition formalizes these notions.

Definition 4. *An enforcer $\mathcal{E}$ is* sound *with respect to a property P iff for any $\sigma \in \mathbb{T}_\omega$, we have $\mathcal{E}(\sigma) \in P$. An enforcer $\mathcal{E} = (\mathcal{S}, s_0, \mu)$ is* transparent *with respect to a property P iff for all $\sigma \in P$, $\mathcal{E}(\sigma) = \sigma$. A property P (resp. a formula φ) is* enforceable *iff there exists a sound enforcer with respect to P (resp. $\mathcal{L}(\varphi)$).*

4 Enforceable MFOTL Formulae

In this section, we present EMFOTL, an expressive and enforceable fragment of MFOTL. An enforcer for EMFOTL formulae will be presented in Sect. 5.

EMFOTL is defined using the typing rules in Fig. 3. These consist of sequents of the form $\Gamma \vdash \varphi : \alpha$, reading '$\varphi$ types to α under Γ'. Here, context $\Gamma : \mathbb{E} \to \{\mathbb{C}, \mathbb{S}\}$ is a mapping from event names to either of the symbols $\mathbb{C}$ or $\mathbb{S}$, φ is an MFOTL formula, and α is a type in $\{\mathbb{C}, \mathbb{S}\}$. The type names $\mathbb{C}$ and $\mathbb{S}$ overload the names of the sets of suppressable and causable events in a natural way: any event $e_c(\bar{t})$ with $e_c \in \mathbb{C}$ (resp. $e_s \in \mathbb{S}$) has type $\mathbb{C}$ (resp. $\mathbb{S}$) under the context $\{e_c \mapsto \mathbb{C}\}$ (resp. $\{e_s \mapsto \mathbb{S}\}$). EMFOTL is defined as the set of all φ for which $\exists \Gamma. \Gamma \vdash \varphi : \mathbb{C}$. Intuitively, a formula types to $\mathbb{C}$ under Γ ('φ is causable under Γ') if it can be enforced by causing events $e_c(\bar{t})$ such that $\Gamma(e_c) = \mathbb{C}$ and suppressing events $e_s(\bar{t})$ such that $\Gamma(e_s) = \mathbb{S}$. It types to $\mathbb{S}$ under Γ ('φ is suppressable under Γ') if $\neg\varphi$ can be enforced under the same conditions on Γ.

We now review the typing rules presented in Fig. 3. Our approach for enforcing temporal operators is illustrated in Fig. 4.

Constants and predicates (Rules $\top^\mathbb{C}$, $\bot^\mathbb{S}$, $\mathbb{E}^\mathbb{C}$, $\mathbb{E}^\mathbb{S}$). The constant $\top$ (resp. $\bot$) is causable (resp. suppressable). Event $e(t_1, \ldots, t_k)$ is causable (resp. suppressable) under Γ if $e \in \mathbb{C}$ and $\Gamma(e) = \mathbb{C}$ (resp. $e \in \mathbb{S}$ and $\Gamma(e) = \mathbb{S}$).

Negation (Rules $\neg^\mathbb{C}$, $\neg^\mathbb{S}$). Negation exchanges $\mathbb{C}$ and $\mathbb{S}$: a formula is causable iff its negation is suppressable; it is suppressable iff its negation is causable.

Conjunction (Rules $\wedge^\mathbb{C}$, $\wedge^\mathrm{SL}$, $\wedge^\mathrm{SR}$). A conjunction is causable if both of its conjuncts are causable; it is suppressable if either of its conjuncts is suppressable.

Quantifiers (Rules $\exists^\mathbb{C}$, $\exists^\mathbb{S}$). The formula $\varphi' = \exists x.\ \varphi$ is causable if φ is causable: it is enough to set x to some value v and cause $\varphi[x/v]$ to cause φ'. In contrast, to suppress φ' at i, we must ensure that *no value of* $v \in \mathbb{D}$ can satisfy φ. If φ depends on the future, then values of v satisfying φ' may only be discovered *strictly after* i. Then, it may not be possible to decide which $\varphi[x/v]$ to suppress at i. Our fragment rules this case out by requiring that x be *past-guarded* in φ, i.e., that any value of x that satisfies φ is a constant or present in the trace up until i. Formally:

$$\frac{}{\vdash e(\ldots,x,\ldots): \mathsf{PG}(x)^+}\ \mathbb{E}_{\mathrm{PG}}^+ \qquad \frac{\vdash \varphi: \mathsf{PG}(x)^{\neg p}}{\vdash \neg\varphi: \mathsf{PG}(x)^p}\ \neg_{\mathrm{PG}} \qquad \frac{x \neq z \quad \vdash \varphi: \mathsf{PG}(z)^p}{\vdash \exists x.\ \varphi: \mathsf{PG}(z)^p}\ \exists_{\mathrm{PG}}$$

$$\frac{\vdash \varphi: \mathsf{PG}(x)^+}{\vdash \varphi \wedge \psi: \mathsf{PG}(x)^+}\ \wedge_{\mathrm{PG}}^{\mathrm{L+}} \qquad \frac{\vdash \psi: \mathsf{PG}(x)^+}{\vdash \varphi \wedge \psi: \mathsf{PG}(x)^+}\ \wedge_{\mathrm{PG}}^{\mathrm{R+}} \qquad \frac{\vdash \varphi: \mathsf{PG}(x)^- \quad \vdash \psi: \mathsf{PG}(x)^-}{\vdash \varphi \wedge \psi: \mathsf{PG}(x)^-}\ \wedge_{\mathrm{PG}}^-$$

$$\frac{0 \notin I \quad \vdash \varphi: \mathsf{PG}(x)^+}{\vdash \varphi\, \mathsf{S}_I\, \psi: \mathsf{PG}(x)^+}\ \mathsf{S}_{\mathrm{PG}}^{\mathrm{L+}} \qquad \frac{\vdash \psi: \mathsf{PG}(x)^+}{\vdash \varphi\, \mathsf{S}_I\, \psi: \mathsf{PG}(x)^+}\ \mathsf{S}_{\mathrm{PG}}^{\mathrm{R+}} \qquad \frac{0 \in I \quad \vdash \psi: \mathsf{PG}(x)^-}{\vdash \varphi\, \mathsf{S}_I\, \psi: \mathsf{PG}(x)^-}\ \mathsf{S}_{\mathrm{PG}}^-$$

$$\frac{0 \notin I \quad \vdash \varphi: \mathsf{PG}(x)^+}{\vdash \varphi\, \mathsf{U}_I\, \psi: \mathsf{PG}(x)^+}\ \mathsf{U}_{\mathrm{PG}}^{\mathrm{L+}} \qquad \frac{\vdash \varphi: \mathsf{PG}(x)^+ \quad \vdash \psi: \mathsf{PG}(x)^+}{\vdash \varphi\, \mathsf{U}_I\, \psi: \mathsf{PG}(x)^+}\ \mathsf{U}_{\mathrm{PG}}^{\mathrm{LR+}}$$

| Past-guardedness | $\dfrac{0 \in I \quad \vdash \psi: \mathsf{PG}(x)^-}{\vdash \varphi\, \mathsf{U}_I\, \psi: \mathsf{PG}(x)^-}\ \mathsf{U}_{\mathrm{PG}}^-$ | $\dfrac{\vdash \varphi: \mathsf{PG}(x)^+}{\vdash \blacklozenge_I\, \varphi: \mathsf{PG}(x)^+}\ \blacklozenge_{\mathrm{PG}}^+$ |

$$\frac{}{\Gamma \vdash \top: \mathbb{C}}\ \top^{\mathbb{C}} \qquad \frac{}{\Gamma \vdash \bot: \mathbb{S}}\ \bot^{\mathbb{S}} \qquad \frac{e \in \mathbb{C} \quad \Gamma(e) = \mathbb{C}}{\Gamma \vdash e(t_1,\ldots,t_k): \mathbb{C}}\ \mathbb{E}^{\mathbb{C}} \qquad \frac{e \in \mathbb{S} \quad \Gamma(e) = \mathbb{S}}{\Gamma \vdash e(t_1,\ldots,t_k): \mathbb{S}}\ \mathbb{E}^{\mathbb{S}}$$

$$\frac{\Gamma \vdash \varphi: \mathbb{S}}{\Gamma \vdash \neg\varphi: \mathbb{C}}\ \neg^{\mathbb{C}} \qquad \frac{\Gamma \vdash \varphi: \mathbb{C}}{\Gamma \vdash \neg\varphi: \mathbb{S}}\ \neg^{\mathbb{S}} \qquad \frac{\Gamma \vdash \varphi: \mathbb{C}}{\Gamma \vdash \exists x.\ \varphi: \mathbb{C}}\ \exists^{\mathbb{C}} \qquad \frac{\Gamma \vdash \varphi: \mathbb{S} \quad \vdash \varphi: \mathsf{PG}(x)^+}{\Gamma \vdash \exists x.\ \varphi: \mathbb{S}}\ \exists^{\mathbb{S}}$$

$$\frac{\Gamma \vdash \varphi: \mathbb{C} \quad \Gamma \vdash \psi: \mathbb{C}}{\Gamma \vdash \varphi \wedge \psi: \mathbb{C}}\ \wedge^{\mathbb{C}} \qquad \frac{\Gamma \vdash \varphi: \mathbb{S}}{\Gamma \vdash \varphi \wedge \psi: \mathbb{S}}\ \wedge^{\mathrm{SL}} \qquad \frac{\Gamma \vdash \psi: \mathbb{S}}{\Gamma \vdash \varphi \wedge \psi: \mathbb{S}}\ \wedge^{\mathrm{SR}}$$

$$\frac{0 \in I \quad \Gamma \vdash \psi: \mathbb{C}}{\Gamma \vdash \varphi\, \mathsf{S}_I\, \psi: \mathbb{C}}\ \mathsf{S}^{\mathbb{C}} \qquad \frac{0 \notin I \quad \Gamma \vdash \varphi: \mathbb{S}}{\Gamma \vdash \varphi\, \mathsf{S}_I\, \psi: \mathbb{S}}\ \mathsf{S}^{\mathrm{SL}} \qquad \frac{0 \in I \quad \Gamma \vdash \varphi: \mathbb{S} \quad \Gamma \vdash \psi: \mathbb{S}}{\Gamma \vdash \varphi\, \mathsf{S}_I\, \psi: \mathbb{S}}\ \mathsf{S}^{\mathrm{SLR}}$$

$$\frac{\Gamma \vdash \psi: \mathbb{S}}{\Gamma \vdash \varphi\, \mathsf{U}_I\, \psi: \mathbb{S}}\ \mathsf{U}^{\mathbb{S}} \qquad \frac{b \neq \infty \quad \Gamma \vdash \psi: \mathbb{C}}{\Gamma \vdash \varphi\, \mathsf{U}_{[0,b]}\, \psi: \mathbb{C}}\ \mathsf{U}^{\mathrm{CR}} \qquad \frac{b \neq \infty \quad \Gamma \vdash \varphi: \mathbb{C} \quad \Gamma \vdash \psi: \mathbb{C}}{\Gamma \vdash \varphi\, \mathsf{U}_{[a,b]}\, \psi: \mathbb{C}}\ \mathsf{U}^{\mathrm{CLR}}$$

| Typing of formulae as causable/suppressable | $\dfrac{\Gamma \vdash \varphi: \mathbb{C} \quad b > 0}{\Gamma \vdash \bigcirc_{[0,b)}\, \varphi: \mathbb{C}}\ \bigcirc^{\mathbb{C}}$ | $\dfrac{\Gamma \vdash \varphi: \mathbb{S}}{\Gamma \vdash \bigcirc_I\, \varphi: \mathbb{S}}\ \bigcirc^{\mathbb{S}}$ |

Fig. 3. Typing rules for EMFOTL

Definition 5. (Past-guardedness). *A variable x is past-guarded in φ iff*
$$\forall v, i.\ v, i \vDash \varphi \wedge x \in \mathrm{dom}\, v \implies v(x) \in \mathsf{AD}_i(\varphi).$$

Past-guardedness can be soundly overapproximated using the type system in the upper half of Fig. 3. The PG typing rules define sequents of the form $\vdash \varphi: \mathsf{PG}(x)^p$, where $p \in \{+, -\}$. In our extended report [42], we prove

Lemma 1. *For $p \in \{+, -\}$, if $\vdash \varphi: \mathsf{PG}(x)^p$, then x is past-guarded in $p\varphi$.*

Since (Rules $\mathsf{S}^{\mathbb{C}}$, S^{SL}, $\mathsf{S}^{\mathrm{SLR}}$). As enforcers cannot affect the past, causation of $\varphi' = \varphi\, \mathsf{S}_I\, \psi$ is only possible when $0 \in I$ and ψ is enforceable. In this case, φ' is caused by causing ψ in the present (Fig. 4, a). To suppress φ', we consider two scenarios. If $0 \notin I$, then to suppress φ', it suffices to suppress φ in the present (Fig. 4, b). If $0 \in I$, both φ and ψ may need to be suppressed (Fig. 4, c).

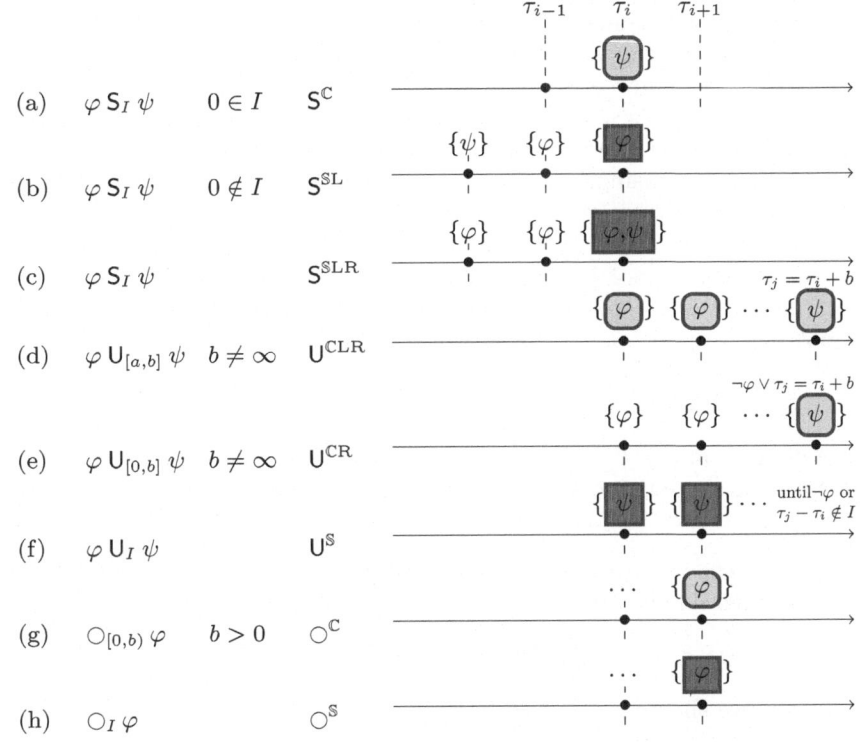

Fig. 4. Enforcement for temporal operators: $\boxed{\varphi}$ = cause φ and $\blacksquare\varphi$ = suppress φ

Until (Rules $\mathsf{U}^{\mathbb{S}}$, U^{CR}, $\mathsf{U}^{\mathrm{CLR}}$). The formula $\varphi' = \varphi\,\mathsf{U}_I\,\psi$ is causable if both φ and ψ are causable: one can cause φ until the interval I has elapsed, and then cause ψ 'in the nick of time' (Fig. 4, d). This requires a finite upper bound for I; otherwise, the enforcer may wait indefinitely to cause ψ, producing a non-compliant trace. (For $I = [a, \infty)$, we could enforce φ' non-transparently by causing ψ after an arbitrary, finite interval $[a, b)$. In this case, the user could have as well specified $\varphi\,\mathsf{U}_{[a,b)}\,\psi$. Hence, our type system requires a finite I.) Alternatively, if $0 \in I$, then φ' can be caused when ψ is causable, with the enforcer causing ψ as soon as φ ceases to hold or the interval has elapsed (Fig. 4, e). In contrast, φ' can be suppressed whenever ψ is suppressable (Fig. 4, f). This also applies when I is unbounded: if necessary, the formula ψ can be suppressed indefinitely. Enforcement can thus be performed for formulae that are generally not supported by existing monitors [18]. Namely, monitors exclude non-future-bounded formulae, for which compliance cannot be guaranteed by observing a finite prefix of the trace and hence verdicts cannot be given in finite time. However, an enforcer can ensure compliance at every time-point.

Previous. The formula $\varphi' = \bullet_I \varphi$ can neither be caused nor suppressed without editing databases of events that happened strictly in the past. This goes beyond the enforcer's capabilities in our model.

Next (Rules $\bigcirc^{\mathbb{C}}$, $\bigcirc^{\mathbb{S}}$). If φ is suppressable, the formula $\varphi' = \bigcirc_I \varphi$ is also suppressable: φ' is suppressed by suppressing φ at the next time-point (Fig. 4, g). In contrast, causing φ' is not possible for arbitrary I. If $I = [a, b)$ with $a > 0$, then, to cause φ' at i, one must ensure $\tau_{i+1} \geq \tau_i + a$. But the next time-point in the input trace might be $\tau_{i+1} < \tau_i + a$ (e.g., $\tau_{i+1} = \tau_i$), and this timestamp cannot be suppressed. If $I = [0, 0]$, then enforcing $\varphi'' = \Box\varphi'$ is not possible, since no trace satisfies φ'' (a trace must satisfy progress): one cannot both support $I = [0, 0]$ in rule $\bigcirc^{\mathbb{C}}$ and use the previous definition of $\mathsf{U}^{\mathbb{S}}$. Therefore, our fragment only supports causation of $\bigcirc_I \varphi$ for intervals I of the form $[0, b)$, $b > 0$ (Fig. 4, h).

Our use of the context Γ is inspired by Hublet et al. [39]. By ensuring that all events with the same name are only caused or only suppressed, we exclude non-enforceable formulae such as $e \wedge \neg e$, where e is both causable and suppressable.

Example 6. We show that φ_{del} presented in Example 3 is in EMFOTL. We work with the "desugared" variant of φ_{del} (instead of using abbreviations like $\Diamond$):

$$\varphi'_{\mathsf{del}} \equiv \neg\left(\top \mathsf{U}\left(\exists c, d, u.\, \mathsf{deletion\_request}\,(c, d, u) \wedge \left(\neg\left(\top \mathsf{U}_{[0,30]}\, \mathsf{delete}\,(c, d, u)\right)\right)\right)\right)$$

Furthermore, we shorten $\varphi'_{\mathsf{del}} \equiv \neg(\top \mathsf{U}\, \varphi_{\exists_1})$, where:

$$\varphi_{\exists_1} \equiv \exists c.\, \varphi_{\exists_2} \qquad \varphi_{\exists_2} \equiv \exists d.\, \varphi_{\exists_3} \qquad \varphi_{\exists_3} \equiv \exists u.\, \varphi_\wedge \qquad \varphi_\wedge \equiv \varphi_{\wedge_1} \wedge \varphi_{\wedge_2}$$
$$\varphi_{\wedge_1} \equiv \mathsf{deletion\_request}\,(c, d, u) \qquad \varphi_{\wedge_2} \equiv \neg\varphi_{\mathsf{U}} \qquad \varphi_{\mathsf{U}} \equiv \top \mathsf{U}_{[0,30]}\, \mathsf{delete}\,(c, d, u)$$

Lastly, we use the typing rules presented in Fig. 3 to show that φ'_{del} types to $\mathbb{C}$:

$$
\cfrac{
P_1 \quad \cfrac{
P_2 \quad \cfrac{
P_3 \quad \cfrac{
\cfrac{
\cfrac{
\cfrac{\mathsf{delete} \in \mathbb{C}}{\{\mathsf{delete} \mapsto \mathbb{C}\} \vdash \mathsf{delete}(c, d, u) : \mathbb{C}}\ \mathbb{E}^{\mathbb{C}}
}{\{\mathsf{delete} \mapsto \mathbb{C}\} \vdash \varphi_{\mathsf{U}} \equiv \top \mathsf{U}_{[0,30]}\, \mathsf{delete}\,(c, d, u) : \mathbb{C}}\ \mathsf{U}^{\mathbb{CR}}
}{\{\mathsf{delete} \mapsto \mathbb{C}\} \vdash \varphi_{\wedge_2} \equiv \neg\varphi_{\mathsf{U}} : \mathbb{S}}\ \neg^{\mathbb{S}}
}{\{\mathsf{delete} \mapsto \mathbb{C}\} \vdash \varphi_\wedge \equiv \varphi_{\wedge_1} \wedge \varphi_{\wedge_2} : \mathbb{S}}\ \wedge^{\mathbb{SR}}
}{\{\mathsf{delete} \mapsto \mathbb{C}\} \vdash \varphi_{\exists_3} \equiv \exists u.\, \varphi_\wedge : \mathbb{S}}\ \exists^{\mathbb{S}}
}{\{\mathsf{delete} \mapsto \mathbb{C}\} \vdash \varphi_{\exists_2} \equiv \exists d.\, \varphi_{\exists_3} : \mathbb{S}}\ \exists^{\mathbb{S}}
}{\{\mathsf{delete} \mapsto \mathbb{C}\} \vdash \varphi_{\exists_1} \equiv \exists c.\, \varphi_{\exists_2} : \mathbb{S}}\ \exists^{\mathbb{S}}
}{
\cfrac{\{\mathsf{delete} \mapsto \mathbb{C}\} \vdash \top \mathsf{U}\, \varphi_{\exists_1} : \mathbb{S}}{\{\mathsf{delete} \mapsto \mathbb{C}\} \vdash \varphi'_{\mathsf{del}} \equiv \neg(\top \mathsf{U}\, \varphi_{\exists_1}) : \mathbb{C}}\ \neg^{\mathbb{C}}
}\ \mathsf{U}^{\mathbb{S}}
$$

where $P_{1,2,3}$ respectively stand for:

$$
\cfrac{
\cfrac{
\cfrac{\vdash \varphi_{\wedge_1} : \mathsf{PG}(c)^+}{\vdash \varphi_\wedge : \mathsf{PG}(c)^+}\ \mathbb{E}^+_{\mathsf{PG}} \atop \wedge^{\mathsf{L}+}_{\mathsf{PG}} \quad u \neq c
}{\vdash \varphi_{\exists_3} : \mathsf{PG}(c)^+}\ \exists_{\mathsf{PG}}
}{\vdash \varphi_{\exists_2} : \mathsf{PG}(c)^+}\ \exists_{\mathsf{PG}} \quad d \neq c
\qquad\qquad
\cfrac{
\cfrac{\vdash \varphi_{\wedge_1} : \mathsf{PG}(d)^+}{\vdash \varphi_\wedge : \mathsf{PG}(d)^+}\ \mathbb{E}^+_{\mathsf{PG}} \atop \wedge^{\mathsf{L}+}_{\mathsf{PG}} \quad u \neq d
}{\vdash \varphi_{\exists_3} : \mathsf{PG}(d)^+}\ \exists_{\mathsf{PG}}
$$

$$
\cfrac{\vdash \varphi_{\wedge_1} : \mathsf{PG}(u)^+}{\vdash \varphi_\wedge : \mathsf{PG}(u)^+}\ \mathbb{E}^+_{\mathsf{PG}} \atop \wedge^{\mathsf{L}+}_{\mathsf{PG}}
$$

$$\mathsf{fo}_{\mathsf{init},\varphi_1} = \lambda_{\_}.\, \varphi_1$$

$$\mathsf{fo}_{\tau,\bigcirc,I,\varphi_1} = \lambda\tau'.\, \text{if } \tau' - \tau \le \sup I \text{ then } (\neg\mathsf{TP})\, \mathsf{U}_{I-(\tau'-\tau)}\, (\mathsf{TP} \wedge \varphi_1) \text{ else } \bot$$

$$\mathsf{fo}_{\tau,\mathsf{U},I,\varphi_1,\varphi_2} = \lambda\tau'.\, \text{if } \tau' - \tau \le \sup I \text{ then } (\mathsf{TP} \to \varphi_1)\, \mathsf{U}_{I-(\tau'-\tau)}\, (\mathsf{TP} \wedge \varphi_2) \text{ else } \bot$$

Fig. 5. Mappings in the first component of future obligations

The formula φ_{law} is also in EMFOTL (see our extended report [42]).

5   Enforcing EMFOTL

We now describe our enforcement algorithm. First, we present the enforcer's state, which consists of a set of *obligations* (Sect. 5.1). We then explain how Lima et al.'s monitoring algorithm [49] can be extended to check the satisfaction of a formula φ *under assumptions* about the future (Sect. 5.2). Finally, we present our algorithm (Sect. 5.3) and prove its soundness and transparency (Sect. 5.4).

5.1   Obligations

Our algorithm manipulates sets of *obligations* that encode the formulae to be caused or suppressed in the future. There are two types of obligations, *present* and *future obligations*. A *present obligation* is a triple (φ, v, p) of an MFOTL formula φ, a valuation v, and a polarity $p \in \{+, -\}$ such that $p\varphi \in \text{EMFOTL}$. After reading a new time-point, our enforcer's state will contain a finite set of such present obligations. Some of these obligations will be immediately discharged via causation or suppression. Others will be processed to generate simpler present obligations and new *future obligations* that will then be propagated to the next time-point. Future obligations are triples (ξ, v, p) where $\xi : \mathbb{N} \to \text{MFOTL}$ maps timestamps to EMFOTL formulae and v and p are as before. The set of future obligations is denoted by FO. The mapping ξ is evaluated with the next timestamp to generate present obligations at the next time-point in the trace.

In some cases (e.g., φ_{del}), the enforcer must insert a time-point. In other cases (e.g., φ_{law}), the enforcer can modify the events at existing time-points. To insert a time-point *only when necessary*, we use a special, causable TP event encoding the existence of a time-point. When processing a time-point already present in the trace (l. 6 in Algorithm 1), the enforcer receives the additional present obligation $(\mathsf{TP}, \emptyset, +)$, as the time-point cannot be suppressed. When computing P-commands (l. 3 in Algorithm 1), this obligation is *not* given to the enforcer, but TP may be generated from other obligations, in which case a time-point is inserted.

Figure 5 shows the mappings used in the first component of future obligations. There are three types of mappings, corresponding to the obligations passed to the enforcer in the initial state and those generated from unrolling $\bigcirc$ and U.

$$\frac{(\text{fo}_{\tau,\bigcirc,I,\varphi_1},v,+) \in X}{v,i,X \vdash^+ \bigcirc_I \varphi_1} \;\; \bigcirc^+_{\text{assm}} \quad \frac{v,i,X \vdash^+ \varphi_1 \quad (\text{fo}_{\tau,\mathsf{U},I,\varphi_1,\varphi_2},v,+) \in X}{v,i,X \vdash^+ \varphi_1 \, \mathsf{U}_I \, \varphi_2} \;\; \mathsf{U}^+_{\text{assm}}$$

$$\frac{(\text{fo}_{\tau,\bigcirc,I,\varphi_1},v,-) \in X}{v,i,X \vdash^- \bigcirc_I \varphi_1} \;\; \bigcirc^-_{\text{assm}} \quad \frac{0 \in I \implies v,i,X \vdash^- \varphi_2 \quad (\text{fo}_{\tau,\mathsf{U},I,\varphi_1,\varphi_2},v,-) \in X}{v,i,X \vdash^- \varphi_1 \, \mathsf{U}_I \, \varphi_2} \;\; \mathsf{U}^-_{\text{assm}}$$

Fig. 6. Additional proof rules

5.2 Checking Satisfaction of MFOTL Formulae Under Assumptions

Our enforcer uses WHYMON's monitoring algorithm to check the satisfaction of formulae. Unlike Lima et al. [49], we must however compute satisfactions under assumptions encoding future obligations. To guarantee, e.g., that causing φ in the present and satisfying $fo = (\lambda\tau'. \top \,\mathsf{U}\, (\text{TP} \wedge \neg\varphi), \emptyset, -)$ guarantees $\Box\varphi$, one must be able to check that after causing φ, $\Box\varphi$ is satisfied at i *assuming* that fo is satisfied at $i+1$. Since the enforcer will suppress all time-points not containing TP, future time-points can be assumed to all contain TP.

Let $\{\mathbb{C}\}_+ := \mathbb{C}$, $\{\mathbb{C}\}_- := \mathbb{S}$, and $\overline{\sigma}^{\text{TP}} = \langle(\tau_i, D_i \cup \{\text{TP}\})\rangle_{i\in\mathbb{N}}$ for the trace $\sigma = \langle(\tau_i, D_i)\rangle_{i\in\mathbb{N}}$. Consider $\varphi \in \text{EMFOTL}$, and obtain Γ such that $\Gamma \vdash \varphi : \mathbb{C}$. Our satisfiability checker under assumptions is a function

$$\text{SAT} : (\mathbb{V} \to \mathbb{D}) \times \text{MFOTL} \times \mathbb{T}_f \times \mathcal{P}(\text{FO}) \to \{\top, \bot\}$$

. The implementation of the checker must ensure that, for any $p \in \{+,-\}$, φ such that $\Gamma \vdash \varphi : \{\mathbb{C}\}_p$, and $X \subseteq \text{FO}$, $\text{SAT}(v,\varphi,\sigma',X)$ implies

$$\forall ts \in \mathbb{N}, D \in \mathbb{DB}, \sigma'' \in \mathbb{T}_\omega. \, (\forall(\xi,v',p') \in X. \, v', |\sigma'| \models_{\overline{\sigma'\cdot(ts,D)\cdot\sigma''}^{\text{TP}}} p'\xi(ts))$$
$$\implies v, |\sigma'| - 1 \models_{\overline{\sigma'\cdot(ts,D)\cdot\sigma''}^{\text{TP}}} \varphi. \qquad (\star)$$

Intuitively, this condition expresses that whenever $\text{SAT}(v,\varphi,\sigma',X)$ is true and the (infinite) trace $\sigma = \overline{\sigma' \cdot (ts,D) \cdot \sigma''}^{\text{TP}}$ satisfies all the future obligations in X at time-point $|\sigma'|$, then φ holds over σ at time-point $|\sigma'| - 1$.

For our algorithm to eventually recognize satisfaction and terminate, one must ensure that for large enough X, the implication $(\star)$ is an equivalence. This guarantees that after generating a finite set of reactions and future obligations, the algorithm can use SAT to assess that no more immediate actions are needed.

To support assumptions about the future, we extend Lima et al's algorithm [49] with the proof rules in Fig. 6. In our extended report [42], we show

Lemma 2. *The proof system of [49] extended with the rules from Fig. 6 yields a decision procedure* SAT *that satisfies* $(\star)$.

Lemma 3. *There exists a set* $\text{FO}^+_{i,ts}(\varphi)$ *such that whenever* $X \supseteq \text{FO}^+_{|\sigma|,\tau_{|\sigma|}}(\varphi)$, *the converse of* $(\star)$ *also holds for* SAT *constructed as in Lemma 2.*

5.3   The Enforcement Algorithm

Our enforcer's update function enf is shown in Algorithm 2. It is used to define an enforcer $\mathcal{E}_\varphi = (\mathcal{S}, s_\varphi, \text{enf})$, where $\mathcal{S} = \mathcal{P}(\text{FO})$ and $s_\varphi = \{(\text{fo}_{\text{init},\varphi}, \emptyset, +)\}$. In the algorithm and its description below, we annotate operators that fulfill the typing conditions in Fig. 3 with the respective typing rule names. For example, we write $\varphi \, \mathsf{U}^{\text{CLR}}_{[a,b]} \, \psi$ to denote $\varphi \, \mathsf{U}_{[a,b]} \, \psi$ where $b \neq \infty$, $\Gamma \vdash \varphi : \mathbb{C}$, and $\Gamma \vdash \psi : \mathbb{C}$ under some Γ.

As required by Definition 2, the function enf takes a trace σ, a set of future obligations X, and a timestamp ts as input. If $ts = \bot$, i.e., the enforcer processes a time-point already present in the trace, then ts is set to the latest timestamp $\tau_{|\tau|}$ (line 4). The enforcer computes a (closed) formula Φ that summarizes all obligations at the present time-point (line 5). Then Φ, σ, an empty set of future obligations, and an empty valuation are passed to $\text{enf}^+_{ts,\bot}$ (line 6). The function $\text{enf}^+_{ts,b}$ takes a formula φ, a trace σ, a set of (new) future obligations X, and a valuation v as input, and returns a triple (D_C, D_S, X') such that D_C is a set of events to cause, D_S is a set of events to suppress, and X' is an updated version of X. The function is parameterized by the current timestamp ts and a Boolean b that is true iff the current time-point is the last one with the current timestamp. The definition of enf^+ (resp. enf^-) guarantees that if we update D_i according to D_S and D_C and assume that all obligations in X' are satisfied at time-point $i + 1$, then φ is always (resp. never) satisfied under v at i on the new trace.

After computing D_S, D_C, and X', an R-command $\text{RCom}(D_C, D_S)$ is returned (line 7) and the state is updated to X'. If $ts \neq \bot$, a similar approach is followed, but now TP is not conjoined with Φ (line 9) and the boolean b is set to $\top$ as enforcement happens 'in the nick of time.' If TP is part of the set D_C returned by enf^+, then a P-command $\text{PCom}(D_C)$ and a new state X' are returned. Otherwise, NoCom is returned and the state is not updated.

The functions enf^+ and enf^- recurse over the structure of φ. The traversal of φ is guided by the typing: the function enf^+ (resp. enf^-) is only called on subformulae of type $\mathbb{C}$ (resp. $\mathbb{S}$). The algorithm implements the approach described in Sect. 4. For space reasons, we only explain the more complex cases: $\varphi = \varphi_1 \wedge^{\mathbb{C}} \varphi_2$, $\varphi = \exists^{\mathbb{S}} x. \, \varphi_1$, and $\varphi = \varphi_1 \, \mathsf{U}^{\text{CLR}}_I \, \varphi_2$.

Causing $\varphi_1 \wedge \varphi_2$ (Algorithm 2, enf^+ l. 9). Causing $\varphi_1 \wedge \varphi_2$ where both φ_1 and φ_2 are causable requires a fixed-point computation [39]. Consider, e.g., the EMFOTL formula $\varphi = \psi \wedge (\psi \to \chi)$, where ψ and χ both type to $\mathbb{C}$. If neither ψ nor χ are satisfied, then the right conjunct of φ is satisfied; however, to satisfy the left conjunct, ψ must be caused. But after causing ψ, the right conjunct is not satisfied, and χ must be caused too. In general, the two conjuncts are repeatedly enforced until both are satisfied. This is achieved by combining the function fp (performing a fixed-point computation) and $\text{enf}^+_{\text{and},\varphi_1,\varphi_2,v,ts}$ that calls the function enf^+ on both φ_1 and φ_2 if none of these formulae is satisfied. In our extended report [42], we prove the termination of this fixed-point computation

Suppressing $\exists x. \, \varphi_1$ (Algorithm 2, enf^- l. 13). The suppression of $\exists$ follows a similar pattern, but this time there are $\text{AD}_{|\sigma|}(\varphi_1)$ rather than just 2 cases to consider, corresponding to all potential values of the (past-guarded) variable x. Similar to the previous case, we prove termination in our extended report [42]. **Causing** $\varphi_1 \cup_{[a,b]} \varphi_2$, $b \neq \infty$ (Algorithm 2, enf$^+$ l. 17–22). There are two cases for causing $\varphi_1 \cup_I \varphi_2$: we cause φ_1 and generate the future obligation $\mathsf{fo}_{\tau,\cup,I,\varphi_1,\varphi_2}$ if $I \neq [0,0]$ or $b = \bot$; otherwise, we cause φ_2 and TP.

Example 7. Let us enforce φ_{del} on σ_2. Consider the following abbreviations:

$$\varphi_{\mathsf{del}} \equiv \Box \varphi_\forall \qquad \varphi_\forall \equiv \forall c, d, u.\, \mathsf{deletion\_request}\,(c, d, u) \to \Diamond_{[0,30]} \mathsf{delete}\,(c, d, u)$$

$$\varphi_\cup \equiv (\mathsf{TP} \to \top)\, \cup\, (\mathsf{TP} \wedge \neg\varphi_\forall) \quad E_1 \equiv \mathsf{deletion\_request}(2,1,1) \quad E_1' \equiv \mathsf{delete}(2,1,1)$$

$$\mathsf{fo}_2^{x,y} \equiv (\lambda\tau'.\, \Diamond_{[0,x]-(y-\tau')}\,(\mathsf{TP} \wedge \mathsf{delete}\,(c,d,u))\,, \{c \mapsto 2, d \mapsto 1, u \mapsto 1\}, +)$$

Figure 7 shows our algorithm's execution.

Initially, enf decomposes its goal $\Phi = \mathsf{TP} \wedge \varphi_{\mathsf{del}}$ into the present obligations $(\mathsf{TP}, \emptyset, +)$ and $(\varphi_{\mathsf{del}}, \emptyset, +)$. The former is discharged by causing TP; the latter is unrolled into the present obligation $(\varphi_\forall, \emptyset, +)$ and the future obligation $\mathsf{fo}_1 = (\mathsf{fo}_{10,\cup,[0,\infty),\top,\neg\varphi_\forall}, \emptyset, -) = (\lambda\_.\, \varphi_\cup, \emptyset, -)$. The present obligation $(\varphi_\forall, \emptyset, +)$ is violated, since $\mathsf{deletion\_request}(2,1,1)$ is satisfied but at this point there is no corresponding delete. In this case, enf$^+_{10,\bot}$ generates the future obligation $\mathsf{fo}_2^{30,10}$. Satisfying this future obligation guarantees the satisfaction of Φ, hence the algorithm proceeds. Next, the algorithm processes the timestamp 10 'in the nick of time'. The function enf computes $\Phi = \mathsf{fo}_1(10) \wedge \mathsf{fo}_2^{30,10}(10) = \varphi_\cup \wedge \Diamond_{[0,30]}(\mathsf{TP} \wedge E_1')$ and calls enf$^+_{10,\top}$ on Φ. First, it decomposes Φ into the present obligations $po_1 = (\varphi_\forall, \emptyset, +)$ and $po_2 = (\Diamond_{[0,30]}(\mathsf{TP} \wedge E_1'), \emptyset, +)$ and the future obligation fo_1. The present obligation po_1 is vacuously satisfied, since no deletion_request takes place. In contrast, the satisfaction of po_2 can rely on the satisfaction of the future obligation $(\mathsf{fo}_2^{30,10}, \emptyset, +)$ at the next time-point. Hence, the enforcer emits NoCom and propagates the future obligations $X' = \{\mathsf{fo}_1, \mathsf{fo}_2^{30,10}\}$ to the next time-point. The timestamp 11 is also processed 'in the nick of time'. The goal $\Phi = \mathsf{fo}_1(11) \wedge \mathsf{fo}_2^{30,10}(11) = \varphi_\cup \wedge \Diamond_{[0,29]}(\mathsf{TP} \wedge E_1')$ is computed, and reduced to the future obligations $X' = \{\mathsf{fo}_1, \mathsf{fo}_2^{29,11}\}$. Similar iterations occur until timestamp 40, when the goal becomes $\Phi = \mathsf{fo}_1(40) \wedge \mathsf{fo}_2^{1,39}(40) = \varphi_\cup \wedge \Diamond_{[0,0]}(\mathsf{TP} \wedge E_1')$. Here, enf$^+_{40,\top}$ produces the present obligations $(\mathsf{TP}, \emptyset, +)$ and $(E_1', \emptyset, +)$, which are discharged by causing TP and E_1', respectively. Thus, $D_C = \{\mathsf{TP}, E_1'\}$ and the command $\mathsf{PCom}(\{E_1'\})$ is emitted, resulting in $(40, \{E_1'\})$ being inserted into the trace. The future obligations $X' = \{\mathsf{fo}_1\}$ are propagated to the next timestamp. Similar iterations occur until timestamp 50. At this point, $b = \bot$ and the trace is already compliant, so the enforcer responds with $\mathsf{RCom}(\emptyset, \emptyset)$.

5.4   Correctness

Let φ be a closed formula to be enforced. The proofs of all lemmata are given in our extended report [42]. First, recall the following standard definition of safety [6]:

```
1: function enf(σ, X, ts)
2:     let ⟨τ⟩, ⟨D⟩ = unzip(σ) in
3:     if ts = ⊥ then
4:         let ts = τ_{|τ|} in
5:         let Φ = TP ∧ ⋀_{(ξ,v,⊤)∈X} ξ(ts)[v] ∧ ⋀_{(ξ,v,⊥)∈X} ¬ξ(ts)[v] in
6:         let (D_C, D_S, X') = enf⁺_{ts,⊥}(Φ, σ, ∅, ∅) in
7:         (RCom(C \ {TP}, S), X')
8:     else
9:         let Φ = ⋀_{(ξ,v,⊤)∈X} ξ(ts)[v] ∧ ⋀_{(ξ,v,⊥)∈X} ¬ξ(ts)[v] in
10:        let (D_C, D_S, X') = enf⁺_{ts,⊤}(Φ, σ · (ts, ∅), ∅, ∅) in
11:        if TP ∈ D_C then (PCom(D_C \ {TP}), X') else (NoCom, X)
12:    end if
13: end function
```

```
1: function enf⁺_{ts,b}(φ, σ, X, v)
2:     if φ = ⊤^C then
3:         (∅, ∅, ∅)
4:     else if φ = p(t̄) then
5:         ({(p, ([[t̄]]_v))}, ∅, ∅)
6:     else if φ = ¬^C φ_1 then
7:         enf⁻_{ts,b}(φ_1, σ, X, v)
8:     else if φ = φ_1 ∧^C φ_2 then
9:         fp(σ, X, enf⁺_{and,φ_1,φ_2,v,ts})
10:    else if φ = ∃^C x. φ_1 then
11:        enf⁺_{ts,b}(φ_1, σ, X, v[0/x])
12:    else if φ = ○_I^C φ_1 then
13:        (∅, ∅, {(fo_{τ,○,I,φ_1}, v, +)})
14:    else if φ = φ_1 S_I^C φ_2 then
15:        enf⁺_{ts,b}(φ_2, σ, X, v)
16:    else if φ = φ_1 U_I^{CLR} φ_2 then
17:        if I = [0,0] ∧ b then
18:            enf⁺_{ts,b}(φ_2, σ, X, v) ⊎ ({TP}, ∅, ∅)
19:        else
20:            enf⁺_{ts,b}(φ_1, σ, X, v) ⊎
21:                (∅, ∅, {(fo_{τ,U,I,φ_1,φ_2}, v, +)})
22:        end if
23:    else if φ = φ_1 U_I^{CR} φ_2 then
24:        if I = [0,0] ∧ b then
25:            enf⁺_{ts,b}(φ_2, σ, X, v) ⊎ ({TP}, ∅, ∅)
26:        else if ¬Sat(v, φ_1, σ, X) then
27:            enf⁺_{ts,b}(φ_2, σ, X, v)
28:        else
29:            (∅, ∅, {(fo_{τ,U,I,φ_1,φ_2}, v, +)})
30:        end if
31:    end if
32: end function
```

```
1: function fp(σ · ⟨(τ, D)⟩, X, f)
2:     (D_C, D_S) ← (∅, ∅)
3:     r ← None
4:     while (D_C, D_S, X) ≠ r do
5:         r ← (D_S, D_C, X)
6:         let D' = (D \ D_S) ∪ D_C in
7:         (D_C, D_S, X) ← r ⊎ f(σ · ⟨(τ, D')⟩, X)
8:     end while
9:     (D_C, D_S, X)
10: end function
```

```
1: function enf⁻_{ex,φ_1,v,ts,b}(σ, X)
2:     r ← (∅, ∅, ∅)
3:     for d ∈ AD_{|σ|}(φ_1) do
4:         if ¬Sat(v[d/x], ¬φ_1, σ, X) then
5:             r ← r ⊎ enf⁻_{ts,b}(φ_1, σ, X, v[d/x])
6:         end if
7:     end for
8:     r
9: end function
```

```
1: function enf⁻_{ts,b}(φ, σ, X, v)
2:     if φ = ⊥^S then
3:         (∅, ∅, ∅)
4:     else if φ = p(t̄) then
5:         (∅, {(p, ([[t̄]]_v))}, ∅)
6:     else if φ = ¬^S φ_1 then
7:         enf⁺_{ts,b}(φ_1, σ, X, v)
8:     else if φ = φ_1 ∧^{SL} φ_2 then
9:         enf⁻_{ts,b}(φ_1, σ, X, v)
10:    else if φ = φ_1 ∧^{SR} φ_2 then
11:        enf⁻_{ts,b}(φ_2, σ, X, v)
12:    else if φ = ∃^S x. φ_1 then
13:        fp(σ, X, enf⁻_{ex,φ_1,v,ts,b})
14:    else if φ = ○_I^S φ_1 then
15:        (∅, ∅, {(fo_{τ,○,I,φ_1}, v, -)})
16:    else if φ = φ_1 S_I^{SL} φ_2 then
17:        enf⁻_{ts,b}(φ_1, σ, X, v)
18:    else if φ = φ_1 S_I^{SR} φ_2 then
19:        let φ' =
20:            ¬(φ_1 ∧^{SL} (φ_1 S_I φ_2)) in
21:        fp(σ, X, enf⁺_{and,φ',¬φ_2,v,ts,b})
22:    else if φ = φ_1 U_I^S φ_2 then
23:        fp(σ, X, enf⁻_{until,I,φ_1,φ_2,v,ts,b})
24:    end if
25: end function
```

```
1: function enf⁻_{until,I,φ_1,φ_2,v,ts,b}(σ, X)
2:     r ← (∅, ∅, ∅)
3:     if 0 ∈ I ∧ ¬Sat(v, ¬φ_2, σ, X) then
4:         r ← enf⁻_{ts,b}(φ_2, σ, X, v)
5:     end if
6:     if ¬Sat(v, ¬φ_1, σ, X) then
7:         r ← r ⊎ (∅, ∅, {(fo_{τ,U,I,φ_1,φ_2}, v, -)}
8:     end if
9:     r
10: end function
```

```
1: function enf⁺_{and,φ_1,φ_2,v,ts,b}(σ, X)
2:     r ← (∅, ∅, ∅)
3:     if ¬Sat(v, φ_1, σ, X) then
4:         r ← r ⊎ enf⁺_{ts,b}(φ_1, σ, X, v)
5:     end if
6:     if ¬Sat(v, φ_2, σ, X) then
7:         r ← r ⊎ enf⁺_{ts,b}(φ_2, σ, X, v)
8:     end if
9:     r
10: end function
```

Algorithm 2: Proactive real-time first-order enforcement algorithm

tp	ts	b	X	Φ	D_C	D_S	X'	Response
0	10	⊥	$\{(\lambda_{\_} \cdot \varphi_{del}, \emptyset, +)\}$	$\mathsf{TP} \wedge \varphi_{del}$	$\{\mathsf{TP}\}$	$\emptyset$	$\{fo_1, fo_2^{30,10}\}$	$\mathsf{RCom}(\emptyset, \emptyset)$
–	10	⊤	$\{fo_1, fo_2^{30,10}\}$	$\varphi_U \wedge \Diamond_{[0,30]}(\mathsf{TP} \wedge E'_1)$	$\emptyset$	$\emptyset$	$\{fo_1, fo_2^{30,10}\}$	NoCom
–	11	⊤	$\{fo_1, fo_2^{30,10}\}$	$\varphi_U \wedge \Diamond_{[0,29]}(\mathsf{TP} \wedge E'_1)$	$\emptyset$	$\emptyset$	$\{fo_1, fo_2^{29,11}\}$	NoCom
...	...	...	...	...	...	...	...	...
–	39	⊤	$\{fo_1, fo_2^{2,38}\}$	$\varphi_U \wedge \Diamond_{[0,1]}(\mathsf{TP} \wedge E'_1)$	$\emptyset$	$\emptyset$	$\{fo_1, fo_2^{1,39}\}$	NoCom
–	40	⊤	$\{fo_1, fo_2^{1,39}\}$	$\varphi_U \wedge \Diamond_{[0,0]}(\mathsf{TP} \wedge E'_1)$	$\{\mathsf{TP}, E'_1\}$	$\emptyset$	$\{fo_1\}$	$\mathsf{PCom}(\{E'_1\})$
–	41	⊤	$\{fo_1\}$	φ_{del}	$\emptyset$	$\emptyset$	$\{fo_1\}$	NoCom
...	...	...	...	...	...	...	...	...
–	49	⊤	$\{fo_1\}$	φ_{del}	$\emptyset$	$\emptyset$	$\{fo_1\}$	NoCom
1	50	⊥	$\{fo_1\}$	$\mathsf{TP} \wedge \varphi_{del}$	$\{\mathsf{TP}\}$	$\emptyset$	$\{fo_1\}$	$\mathsf{RCom}(\emptyset, \emptyset)$

Fig. 7. Enforcement of the formula φ_{del} on trace σ_2

Definition 6. *P is a* safety property *iff for any* $\sigma \in \mathbb{T}_\omega \setminus P$, *there exists a finite prefix* $\sigma' \in \mathbb{T}_f$ *of* σ *such that for all* $\sigma'' \in \mathbb{T}_\omega$, *we have* $\sigma \cdot \sigma'' \notin P$. *A formula* φ *is a* safety formula *when* $\mathcal{L}(\varphi)$ *is a safety property.*

Our algorithm can enforce formulae that are *not* safety formulae. This is the case, e.g., for any $\psi \vee \Diamond\chi \equiv \neg(\neg\psi \wedge \neg(\top \mathbin{U} \chi))$, where ψ types to $\mathbb{C}$. In this case, enforcement is performed greedily: if the monitor cannot construct a proof of $\Diamond\chi$ (which occurs whenever χ cannot be satisfied in the present), then ψ is caused. Thus our algorithm actually enforces a stronger formula, which we denote by $[\psi \vee \Diamond\chi]_+ \equiv \neg(\neg\psi \wedge^{R\omega} \neg(\top \mathbin{U} \chi))$, where $\wedge^{R\omega}$ has the semantics

$$v, i \vDash_\sigma \varphi \wedge^{R\omega} \psi \qquad \text{iff } v, i \vDash_\sigma \varphi \text{ and } \exists\sigma'. v, i \vDash_{\sigma|_{..i}\cdot\sigma'} \psi.$$

This semantics states that $\varphi \wedge^{R\omega} \psi$ holds whenever φ holds on σ at time-point i and there exists at least one extension of the prefix $\sigma|_{..i}$ on which ψ holds. The formula $[\psi \vee \Diamond\chi]_+$ thus requires than ψ holds on σ at time-point i and $\Diamond\psi$ holds on σ at time-point i for any extension of $\sigma|_{..i}$. The formula $[\psi \vee \Diamond\chi]_+$, unlike $\psi \vee \Diamond\chi$, is safety. In our extended report [42], we define a similar transformation $[\bullet]_p$, $p \in \{+, -\}$ for all operators and prove

Lemma 4. *For any* φ *such that* $\Gamma \vdash \varphi : \{\mathbb{C}\}_p$, *we have* $v, i \vDash_\sigma p[\varphi]_p \implies v, i \vDash_\sigma p\varphi$. *In particular,* $\mathcal{L}([\varphi]_+) \subseteq \mathcal{L}(\varphi)$.

We prove that $\mathcal{E}_\varphi$ soundly enforces $[\varphi]_+$, and hence φ:

Theorem 1. (Soundness). *If* $\varphi \in EMFOTL$, *the enforcer* $\mathcal{E}_\varphi$ *is sound with respect to* $\mathcal{L}([\varphi]_+) \subseteq \mathcal{L}(\varphi)$. *As a consequence,* φ *is enforceable.*

In our model, *transparent* enforcement of non-safety formulae such as $\psi \vee \Diamond\chi$ is generally not possible, since the necessity to cause ψ depends on future events:

Lemma 5. *If a property admits a transparent enforcer, it is a safety formula.*

Thus, when enforcing a non-safety formula φ, one can at best achieve transparency with respect to some sound safety approximation φ' of φ. We prove:

$\text{collect}(c,d,u)^{699}$ $\text{use}(c,d,u)\text{-}^{2316}$ $\quad$ $\text{consent}(u,c)^{699}$ $\quad$ $\text{legal\_grounds}(u,d)^{397}$ $\quad$ $\text{revoke}(u,c)\text{+}^{8}$

$\text{inform}(u)\text{+}^{0}$ $\quad$ $\text{deletion\_request}(c,d,u)^{8}$ $\quad$ $\text{delete}(c,d,u)\text{+}^{521}$ $\quad$ $\text{share}(p,d)^{982}$ $\quad$ $\text{notify}(p,d)\text{+}^{0}$

"Minimization" $\quad$ $\varphi_{\mathsf{min}} = \Box(\forall c,d,u.\, \text{collect}(c,d,u) \rightarrow \Diamond\, \text{use}(c,d,u))$

"Limitation" $\quad$ $\varphi_{\mathsf{lim}} = \Box(\forall c,d,u.\, \text{collect}(c,d,u) \rightarrow \Diamond\, \text{delete}(c,d,u))$

"Lawfulness" $\quad$ $\varphi_{\mathsf{law}} = \Box(\forall c,d,u.\, \text{use}(c,d,u) \rightarrow \blacklozenge(\text{consent}(u,c) \vee \text{legal\_grounds}(u,d)))$

"Consent" $\quad$ $\varphi_{\mathsf{con}} = \Box(\forall c,d,u.\, \text{use}(c,d,u) \rightarrow (\blacklozenge\, \text{legal\_grounds}(u,d)) \vee (\neg\text{revoke}(u,c)\, \mathsf{S}\, \text{consent}(u,c)))$

"Information" $\quad$ $\varphi_{\mathsf{inf}} = \Box(\forall c,d,u.\, \text{collect}(c,d,u) \rightarrow ((\bigcirc\, \text{inform}(u)) \vee (\blacklozenge\, \text{inform}(u))))$

"Deletion" $\quad$ $\varphi_{\mathsf{del}} = \Box(\forall c,d,u.\, \text{deletion\_request}(c,d,u) \rightarrow \Diamond_{[0,30]}\, \text{delete}(c,d,u))$

"Sharing" $\quad$ $\varphi_{\mathsf{sha}} = \Box(\forall c,d,u,p.\, \text{deletion\_request}(c,d,u) \wedge (\blacklozenge\, \text{share}(p,d)) \rightarrow \Diamond_{[0,30]}\, \text{notify}(p,d))$

c: data category; d: data ID; u: user ID; p: processor ID; -: suppressable; +: causable

Fig. 8. Selected events and policies from Arfelt et al. [7]

Theorem 2. (Transparency). *If $\varphi \in EMFOTL$, the enforcer $\mathcal{E}_\varphi$ is transparent with respect to $\mathcal{L}([\varphi]_+)$.*

By imposing more constraints on the formulae (e.g., the formula χ must not depend on the future in $\psi \wedge^{\mathrm{SL}} \chi$), one can obtain an EMFOTL fragment for which $[\varphi]_+ = \varphi$ and the enforcer $\mathcal{E}_\varphi$ is transparent (see our extended report [42]).

6 Evaluation

We implemented our type system and enforcement algorithm in a tool, called WHYENF, consisting of 2 800 lines of OCaml code. WHYENF uses a modified version of WHYMON [49], which we call WHYMON*. It ignores the explanations' structures (not required by our algorithm) and returns only Boolean verdicts.

Our evaluation aims to answer the following research questions:

RQ1. Is EMFOTL expressive enough to formalize real-world policies?
Is manual formula rewriting necessary, as in previous works [14,40]?
RQ2. At what maximum event rate can WHYENF perform real-time enforcement?
RQ3. Do WHYENF's performance and capabilities improve upon the state-of-the-art?

The notion of 'real-world policies' in RQ1 is domain-dependent. In the following, we demonstrate our approach's effectiveness in the case of privacy regulations.

Case study. Arfelt et al. [7] define events and MFOTL formulae formalizing core GDPR provisions that they monitor on a trace produced by a real-world system [24]. Relevant events (superscripted by their number of occurrences in the trace) and formulae are shown in Fig. 8 and Examples 1 and 3. We pre-process the trace to obtain 3 846 time-points containing 5 630 system events distributed over 515 d. We interpret the 'Lawyer review' and 'Architect review' events as both use and share (sharing with third-parties) events, and the 'Abort' events as both revoke (revoking consent) and deletion_request. Otherwise, we follow Arfelt et al.'s pre-processing. We make the following assumptions [40]: use events are suppressable, while delete, inform (informing the user), and notify (notifying a third-party) events are causable. All metric constraints are specified in days.

RQ1: Expressiveness. Except for φ_{min}, all formulae are in EMFOTL. Unlike in previous works [15,18,40], no further policy engineering (e.g., manual rewriting to equivalent formulae in supported fragments) is needed. For all enforceable formulae except φ_{lim}, our algorithm guarantees *transparent* enforcement. For φ_{lim}, which contains an unbounded $\Diamond$ operator, non-transparent enforcement is possible by enforcing the stronger formula $\varphi_{\mathsf{lim}}^b = \Box(\forall c, d, u. \, \mathsf{collect}(c, d, u) \rightarrow \Diamond_{[0,b]}\mathsf{delete}(c, d, u))$ for any $b \in \mathbb{N}$. The formula φ_{min}, capturing *data minimization*, is intrinsically non-enforceable, as a sound $\mathcal{E}_{\varphi_{\mathsf{min}}}$ must either always suppress collect, or eventually cause use, which is only suppressable.

WHYENF's type system helps determine appropriate suppressible and causable events. For instance, if use was marked as only-observable, the type checker would state that φ_{law} is not enforceable and suggest to make use suppressible, or otherwise make either consent or legal_ground causable. Since use actually is suppressable, the type checker concludes that φ_{law} is transparently enforceable.

RQ2: Maximum event rate. We enforce the enforceable formulae from Fig. 8, i.e., all but φ_{min}. As we do not have access to the SuS, we simulate online enforcement by reproducing [45] the events from the above trace to WHYENF at the speed specified by the trace's timestamps. We also consider different accelerations of the original trace's real-time behavior to challenge WHYENF. We measure WHYENF's latency ℓ and processing time t for each time-point. Latency is the time delay between the emission of a time-point to WHYENF and the reception of the corresponding command, whereas processing time is the time WHYENF effectively takes to process the time-point. We report the average latency ($\mathsf{avg}_\ell(a)$) and maximum latency ($\mathsf{max}_\ell(a)$) given an acceleration a, as well as the average processing time (avg_t), and the maximum processing time (max_t) all computed over the entire trace. If $\mathsf{max}_\ell(a)$ is smaller than the interval $\frac{1}{a}$ between two timestamps in the accelerated trace, then the real-time condition (Sect. 3.1) is met assuming that the SuS's and communication latency are small enough.

All measurements were performed on a 2.4 GHz Intel i5-1135G7 CPU with 32 GB RAM. For each formula and acceleration $a \in \{10^5 \cdot 2^0, \ldots, 10^5 \cdot 2^9\}$, we plot $\mathsf{max}_\ell(a)$, the function $\frac{1}{a}$ (right y-axis), and the corresponding average event rate $\mathsf{avg}_{er}(a)$ (left y-axis) in Fig. 9. We include similar plots for WHYMON* and ENFPOLY and latency profiles for individual runs in our extended report [42].

As presented in Fig. 9, for all formulae, WHYENF meets the real-time condition for all accelerations up to $4 \cdot 10^5$, which corresponds to a maximum latency of 96 ms and an average event rate of 51 events/s. Hence, even though the analyzed trace specifies time intervals in days, the real-time enforcement of the same trace can in fact be performed for sub-second intervals. Note that the average

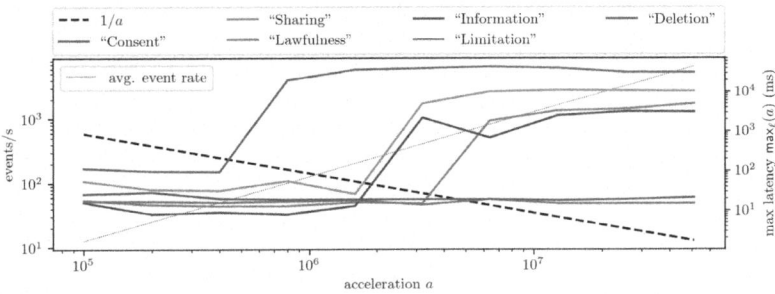

Fig. 9. RQ2: Maximum latency of WHYENF and event rate for the formulae in Fig. 8.

latency is much lower (20 ms for the most challenging policy), with the maximum latency occurring when many events occur within a short time span. The two formulae that only define future obligations, φ_{lim} and φ_{del}, have much lower maximum latency, of 14 and 19 ms, respectively, corresponding to an average event rate of about 600 events/s. Due to proactivity, the enforcer does not need to keep the history of past events for these formulae. Overall, our experiments show that WHYENF can efficiently enforce a real-world SuS.

RQ3: Comparison with the state of the art. We compare WHYENF's performance to its two most closely related tools: WHYMON*, which provides similar expressiveness as WHYENF but no enforcement, and ENFPOLY [39], the only tool supporting non-proactive enforcement of an MFOTL fragment. In addition to the real-world log [24], we generate synthetic traces with $n \in \{100 \cdot 2^0, \ldots, 100 \cdot 2^8\}$ time-points each containing $k \in \{2^0, \ldots, 2^8\}$ random events. We report avg_t for the three tools and six formulae in Fig. 11, imposing a 10-minute timeout (t.o.).

WHYMON* cannot monitor φ_{lim}, as the formula has an unbounded $\Diamond$ operator. For all other formulae, WHYMON* satisfies the real-time condition for accelerations $a \leq 10^5$. WHYENF's latency is at most twice WHYMON*'s for φ_{law} and φ_{con} as the enforcer calls the monitor at least once per iteration and also performs fixed-point computations (Fig. 10). In contrast, WHYENF can enforce φ_{lim} and has significantly (up to 22 times) lower latency for φ_{inf}, φ_{sha}, and φ_{del}. Unlike WHYMON*, WHYENF is able to lazily evaluate implications involving future obligations, which improves its runtime performance. WHYENF's processing time also scales better than WHYMON*'s for large values of n and k (Fig. 11).

Only φ_{law} and φ_{con} are transparently enforceable without proactivity. We enforce them using ENFPOLY after manually rewriting them into equivalent formulae in ENFPOLY's fragment. WHYENF's average and maximum latencies are higher than ENFPOLY's, but WHYENF's algorithm covers a much larger fragment of MFOTL than ENFPOLY, which makes computating verdicts more costly. The same behavior is observed in terms of average processing time (Fig. 11).

Policy	WhyEnf						WhyMon*						EnfPoly					
	a	avg_ℓ	max_ℓ	avg_t	max_t	avg_{er}	a	avg_ℓ	max_ℓ	avg_t	max_t	avg_{er}	a	avg_ℓ	max_ℓ	avg_t	max_t	avg_{er}
φ_{lim}	3.2e6	0.19	14	0.22	1.0	632	has unbounded future						requires proactivity					
φ_{law}	3.2e6	2.6	15	2.6	15	405	3.2e6	2.5	12	2.5	12	405	5.1e7	0.10	1.0	0.14	1.0	6479
φ_{con}	4e5	20	96	20	96	51	8e5	9.3	51	9.3	52	101	5.1e7	0.10	1.0	0.14	1.0	6479
φ_{inf}	1.6e6	2.9	13	3.0	13	202	3.2e6	0.16	16	0.19	1.0	405	requires proactivity					
φ_{del}	3.2e6	0.19	19	0.22	1.0	632	1e5	42	434	42	434	13	requires proactivity					
φ_{sha}	1.6e6	4.6	26	4.7	26	202	1e5	69	289	69	299	13	requires proactivity					

Fig. 10. RQ2–3: Latency and processing time for the largest a such that $max_\ell(a) \leq 1/a$.

	WhyEnf					WhyMon*					EnfPoly				
$k = 10$	$n:$ 100	400	1.6e3	6.4e3	2.6e4	$n:$ 100	400	1.6e3	6.4e3	2.6e4	$n:$ 100	400	1.6e3	6.4e3	2.6e4
φ_{lim}	.29	.28	.28	.30	.30	has unbounded future					requires proactivity				
φ_{law}	.73	1.3	2.0	2.2	2.7	.26	.57	1.4	3.5	15	.16	.16	.16	.16	.16
φ_{con}	1.8	4.9	9.1	11	12	.53	1.7	7.4	11	t.o.	.19	.16	.18	.17	.17
φ_{inf}	.78	1.0	1.2	1.1	1.2	.22	.31	.51	1.0	2.2	requires proactivity				
φ_{del}	.17	.24	.26	.28	.56	.40	1.2	2.9	4.4	4.9	requires proactivity				
φ_{sha}	.86	2.3	5.3	7.6	7.0	.54	2.3	13	56	t.o.	requires proactivity				
$n = 1000$	$k:$ 1	4	16	64	256	$k:$ 1	4	16	64	256	$k:$ 1	4	16	64	256
φ_{lim}	.24	.24	.35	.83	4.7	has unbounded future					requires proactivity				
φ_{law}	.61	1.2	2.2	2.9	6.1	.38	.71	1.3	1.6	2.3	.14	.19	.18	.22	.38
φ_{con}	1.4	4.1	9.5	11.5	13.3	1.2	4.3	5.3	4.2	4.9	.14	.16	.16	.20	.32
φ_{inf}	.48	.79	1.4	4.8	24	.21	.28	.44	.78	1.1	requires proactivity				
φ_{del}	.23	.24	.32	.40	1.0	.44	1.1	3.0	4.8	6.3	requires proactivity				
φ_{sha}	.78	3.2	7.4	7.1	12	1.2	4.3	9.7	14	16	requires proactivity				

Fig. 11. RQ3: Average processing time (ms) for different trace and time-point sizes.

7   Related Work

Security automata [26,58] were first used for enforcement by terminating the SuS. Fredrikson et al. [31] also terminate the SuS upon violation detection, but use symbolic automata which allow policies to refer to the SuS's state. Bauer et al. [21] investigate enforcers that can cause and suppress events, as do Ligatti et al. [47], who use edit automata with the ability to buffer events. Ngo et al. [51] study policy enforcement for reactive systems for which they disallow the enforcer to buffer events or inspect SuS code. Basin et al. [15] distinguish between suppressable and only-observable events, without considering causation. More complex bidirectional enforcement [3,4] and enforcement through delaying events [27,54] have also been proposed. Pinisetty et al. [55] further allow the enforcer to inspect the SuS's code to perform *predictive* enforcement.

Most runtime enforcement approaches (and tools [28,29]) rely on automata as policies. Metric interval temporal logic formulae can be enforced via translation to timed automata [53,57]. Basin et al. [11,12] use dynamic condition response graphs [36] to formalize and enforce obligations in real time by suppressing and (proactively) causing events. Finally, controller synthesis tools for LTL [25,44,60], Timed CTL [22,52], or MTL [38,46] can generate enforcement mechanisms.

To the best of our knowledge, only a few approaches enforce *first-order temporal* policies. Hallé and Villemaire [33,34] develop a monitor for LTL-FO$^+$, a first-order variant of future-only linear temporal logic. They use the monitor to block the system in case of detected policy violations, in the spirit of the work on security automata [26,58]. Hublet et al. [39–41] developed the ENFPOLY tool that enforces policies from a fragment of MFOTL that can contain future operators, but only nested with past ones such that the formula overall does not refer to the future. Independently, Aceto et al. [2–5] consider the safety fragment of Hennessy-Milner Logic (HML) with recursion as their policy language. They generalize HML to allow quantification over event parameters, but do not support time constraints. They also focus on instrumentation scenarios where all events are suppressable.

A satisfiability checking tool [30] and many runtime monitoring tools support (different fragments of) MFOTL [23], including MONPOLY [13,17–19], VeriMon [9,10,59] and DejaVu [35]. Lima et al. [48] recently introduced EXPLANATOR2, an MTL monitor that outputs explanations. They later extended their work to MFOTL with the WHYMON tool [49], upon which our enforcer relies. WHYMON supports a large fragment of MFOTL as it uses partitioned decision trees to represent variable assignments. To the best of our knowledge, all existing monitoring tools only support safety formulae of the form $\Box\varphi$. Our work additionally supports (non-transparent) enforcement of some non-safety formulae.

8   Conclusion

We have presented the first proactive real-time enforcement algorithm and an efficient tool, WHYENF, for metric first-order temporal logic. Our approach lends itself to a number of extensions. For instance, WHYMON's runtime performance can be optimized for large formulae. Features like complex data types [50], let bindings [61], and aggregations [16] would further improve our enforcer's expressiveness. Finally, refinements of the type system when the same event can be both caused and suppressed in different contexts would be a useful addition.

Acknowledgement. Hublet is supported by the Swiss National Science Foundation grant"Model-driven Security & Privacy" (204796). Lima and Traytel are supported by a Novo Nordisk Fonden start package grant (NNF20OC0063462). We thank the anonymous reviewers for their insightful feedback.

References

1. Abadi, M., Lamport, L., Wolper, P.: Realizable and unrealizable specifications of reactive systems. In: Ausiello, G., Dezani-Ciancaglini, M., Rocca, S.R.D. (eds.) 16th International Colloquium on Automata, Languages and Programming (ICALP). LNCS, vol. 372, pp. 1–17. Springer (1989). https://doi.org/10.1007/BFB0035748
2. Aceto, L., Cassar, I., Francalanza, A., Ingólfsdóttir, A.: On runtime enforcement via suppressions. In: 29th International Conference on Concurrency Theory (2018)
3. Aceto, L., Cassar, I., Francalanza, A., Ingólfsdóttir, A.: On bidirectional runtime enforcement. In: Peters, K., Willemse, T.A.C. (eds.) FORTE 2021. LNCS, vol. 12719, pp. 3–21. Springer, Cham (2021). https://doi.org/10.1007/978-3-030-78089-0_1

4. Aceto, L., Cassar, I., Francalanza, A., Ingolfsdottir, A.: Bidirectional runtime enforcement of first-order branching-time properties. Logical Methods Comput. Sci. **19** (2023)
5. Aceto, L., Cassar, I., Francalanza, A., Ingólfsdóttir, A.: On first-order runtime enforcement of branching-time properties. Acta Inform., 1–67 (2023)
6. Alpern, B., Schneider, F.B.: Defining liveness. Inform. Process. Lett. **21**(4), 181–185 (1985)
7. Arfelt, E., Basin, D., Debois, S.: Monitoring the GDPR. In: Sako, K., Schneider, S., Ryan, P.Y.A. (eds.) ESORICS 2019. LNCS, vol. 11735, pp. 681–699. Springer, Cham (2019). https://doi.org/10.1007/978-3-030-29959-0_33
8. Bartocci, E., Falcone, Y. (eds.): Lectures on Runtime Verification. LNCS, vol. 10457. Springer, Cham (2018). https://doi.org/10.1007/978-3-319-75632-5
9. Basin, D., et al.: VeriMon: a formally verified monitoring tool. In: Seidl, H., Liu, Z., Pasareanu, C.S. (eds.) 19th International Colloquium on Theoretical Aspects of Computing (ICTAC). LNCS, vol. 13572, pp. 1–6. Springer (2022). https://doi.org/10.1007/978-3-031-17715-6_1
10. Basin, D., et al.: A formally verified, optimized monitor for metric first-order dynamic logic. In: Peltier, N., Sofronie-Stokkermans, V. (eds.) IJCAR 2020. LNCS (LNAI), vol. 12166, pp. 432–453. Springer, Cham (2020). https://doi.org/10.1007/978-3-030-51074-9_25
11. Basin, D., Debois, S., Hildebrandt, T.T.: In the nick of time: proactive prevention of obligation violations. In: 29th Computer Security Foundations Symposium (CSF), pp. 120–134. IEEE (2016)
12. Basin, D., Debois, S., Hildebrandt, T.: Proactive enforcement of provisions and obligations. J. Comput/ Sec. (to appear)
13. Basin, D., Harvan, M., Klaedtke, F., Zălinescu, E.: MONPOLY: monitoring usage-control policies. In: Khurshid, S., Sen, K. (eds.) RV 2011. LNCS, vol. 7186, pp. 360–364. Springer, Heidelberg (2012). https://doi.org/10.1007/978-3-642-29860-8_27
14. Basin, D., Harvan, M., Klaedtke, F., Zalinescu, E.: Monitoring data usage in distributed systems. IEEE Trans. Softw. Eng. **39**(10), 1403–1426 (2013)
15. Basin, D., Jugé, V., Klaedtke, F., Zălinescu, E.: Enforceable security policies revisited. ACM Trans. Inf. Syst. Secur. **16**(1), 1–26 (2013)
16. Basin, D., Klaedtke, F., Marinovic, S., Zălinescu, E.: Monitoring of temporal first-order properties with aggregations. Formal Methods Syst. Des. **46**, 262–285 (2015)
17. Basin, D., Klaedtke, F., Müller, S., Pfitzmann, B.: Runtime monitoring of metric first-order temporal properties. In: IARCS Annual Conference on Foundations of Software Technology and Theoretical Computer Science. Schloss Dagstuhl-Leibniz-Zentrum für Informatik (2008)
18. Basin, D., Klaedtke, F., Müller, S., Zălinescu, E.: Monitoring metric first-order temporal properties. J. ACM (JACM) **62**(2), 1–45 (2015)
19. Basin, D., Klaedtke, F., Zalinescu, E.: The MonPoly monitoring tool. RV-CuBES **3**, 19–28 (2017)
20. Basin, D., Krstić, S., Schneider, J., Traytel, D.: Correct and efficient policy monitoring, a retrospective. In: 21st International Symposium on Automated Technology for Verification and Analysis (ATVA), pp. 3–30. Springer (2023). https://doi.org/10.1007/978-3-031-45329-8_1
21. Bauer, L., Ligatti, J., Walker, D.: More enforceable security policies. In: Workshop on Foundations of Computer Security (FCS). Citeseer (2002)

22. Behrmann, G., Cougnard, A., David, A., Fleury, E., Larsen, K.G., Lime, D.: UPPAAL-tiga: time for playing games! In: Damm, W., Hermanns, H. (eds.) CAV 2007. LNCS, vol. 4590, pp. 121–125. Springer, Heidelberg (2007). https://doi.org/10.1007/978-3-540-73368-3_14

23. Chomicki, J.: Efficient checking of temporal integrity constraints using bounded history encoding. ACM Trans. Database Syst. (TODS) 20(2), 149–186 (1995)

24. Debois, S., Slaats, T.: The analysis of a real life declarative process. In: 2015 IEEE Symposium Series on Computational Intelligence, pp. 1374–1382. IEEE (2015)

25. Ehlers, R.: Unbeast: symbolic bounded synthesis. In: Abdulla, P.A., Leino, K.R.M. (eds.) TACAS 2011. LNCS, vol. 6605, pp. 272–275. Springer, Heidelberg (2011). https://doi.org/10.1007/978-3-642-19835-9_25

26. Erlingsson, Ú., Schneider, F.: SASI enforcement of security policies: a retrospective. In: Kienzle, D., Zurko, M.E., Greenwald, S., Serbau, C. (eds.) Workshop on New Security Paradigms, pp. 87–95. ACM (1999)

27. Falcone, Y., Jéron, T., Marchand, H., Pinisetty, S.: Runtime enforcement of regular timed properties by suppressing and delaying events. Sci. Comput. Program. 123, 2–41 (2016)

28. Falcone, Y., Krstić, S., Reger, G., Traytel, D.: A taxonomy for classifying runtime verification tools. Int. J. Softw. Tools Technol. Transf. 23(2), 255–284 (2021)

29. Pinisetty, S., Falcone, Y., Jéron, T., Marchand, H., Rollet, A., Nguena Timo, O.L.: Runtime enforcement of timed properties. In: Qadeer, S., Tasiran, S. (eds.) RV 2012. LNCS, vol. 7687, pp. 229–244. Springer, Heidelberg (2013). https://doi.org/10.1007/978-3-642-35632-2_23

30. Feng, N., Marsso, L., Sabetzadeh, M., Chechik, M.: Early verification of legal compliance via bounded satisfiability checking. In: Enea, C., Lal, A. (eds.) CAV 2023. LNCS, vol. 13966, pp. 374–396. Springer (2023). https://doi.org/10.1007/978-3-031-37709-9_18

31. Fredrikson, M., et al.: Efficient runtime policy enforcement using counterexample-guided abstraction refinement. In: Madhusudan, P., Seshia, S.A. (eds.) CAV 2012. LNCS, vol. 7358, pp. 548–563. Springer, Heidelberg (2012). https://doi.org/10.1007/978-3-642-31424-7_39

32. Gomaa, H.: Software modeling and design: UML, use cases, patterns, and software architectures. Cambridge University Press (2011)

33. Hallé, S., Villemaire, R.: Browser-based enforcement of interface contracts in web applications with beepbeep. In: Bouajjani, A., Maler, O. (eds.) CAV 2009. LNCS, vol. 5643, pp. 648–653. Springer, Heidelberg (2009). https://doi.org/10.1007/978-3-642-02658-4_50

34. Hallé, S., Villemaire, R.: Runtime enforcement of web service message contracts with data. IEEE Trans. Serv. Comput. 5(2), 192–206 (2012)

35. Havelund, K., Peled, D., Ulus, D.: First-order temporal logic monitoring with bdds. Formal Methods Syst. Des. 56(1–3), 1–21 (2020)

36. Hildebrandt, T., Mukkamala, R.R., Slaats, T., Zanitti, F.: Contracts for cross-organizational workflows as timed dynamic condition response graphs. J. Logic Algebraic Program. 82(5–7), 164–185 (2013)

37. Hilty, M., Basin, D., Pretschner, A.: On obligations. In: di Vimercati, S.C., Syverson, P., Gollmann, D. (eds.) ESORICS 2005. LNCS, vol. 3679, pp. 98–117. Springer, Heidelberg (2005). https://doi.org/10.1007/11555827_7

38. Murphy, L., Viger, T., Sandro, A.D., Shahin, R., Chechik, M.: Validating safety arguments with lean. In: Calinescu, R., Păsăreanu, C.S. (eds.) SEFM 2021. LNCS, vol. 13085, pp. 23–43. Springer, Cham (2021). https://doi.org/10.1007/978-3-030-92124-8_2

39. Hublet, F., Basin, D., Krstić, S.: Real-time policy enforcement with metric first-order temporal logic. In: European Symposium on Research in Computer Security. pp. 211–232. Springer (2022). https://doi.org/10.1007/978-3-031-17146-8_11

40. Hublet, F., Basin, D., Krstić, S.: Enforcing the GDPR. In: Tsudik, G., Conti, M., Liang, K., Smaragdakis, G. (eds.) Computer Security – ESORICS 2023. LNCS, vol. 14344. Springer (2023). https://doi.org/10.1007/978-3-031-51476-0_20

41. Hublet, F., Basin, D., Krstić, S.: User-controlled privacy: Taint, track, and control. Proc. Priv. Enhancing Technol. **2024**(1), 597–616 (2024)

42. Hublet, F., Lima, L., Basin, D., Krstić, S., Traytel, D.: Proactive real-time first-order enforcement (extended report) (2024). https://github.com/runtime-enforcement/whyenf/blob/main/docs/cav24-extended.pdf

43. Hublet, F., Lima, L., Basin, D., Krstić, S., Traytel, D.: WHYENF (2024). https://github.com/runtime-enforcement/whyenf

44. Jobstmann, B., Bloem, R.: Optimizations for LTL synthesis. In: International Conference Formal Methods in Computer-Aided Design (FMCAD), pp. 117–124. IEEE (2006)

45. Krstić, S., Schneider, J.: A benchmark generator for online first-order monitoring. In: Deshmukh, J., Ničković, D. (eds.) RV 2020. LNCS, vol. 12399, pp. 482–494. Springer, Cham (2020). https://doi.org/10.1007/978-3-030-60508-7_27

46. Li, G., Jensen, P., Larsen, K., Legay, A., Poulsen, D.: Practical controller synthesis for $MTL_{0,\infty}$. In: Erdogmus, H., Havelund, K. (eds.) ACM SIGSOFT International SPIN Symposium on Model Checking of Software, pp. 102–111. ACM (2017)

47. Ligatti, J., Bauer, L., Walker, D.: Edit automata: enforcement mechanisms for run-time security policies. Int. J. Inf. Secur. **4**, 2–16 (2005)

48. Lima, L., Herasimau, A., Raszyk, M., Traytel, D., Yuan, S.: Explainable online monitoring of metric temporal logic. In: International Conference on Tools and Algorithms for the Construction and Analysis of Systems (TACAS), pp. 473–491. Springer (2023). https://doi.org/10.1007/978-3-031-30820-8_28

49. Lima, L., Huerta y Munive, J.J., Traytel, D.: Explainable online monitoring of metric first-order temporal logic. In: International Conference on Tools and Algorithms for the Construction and Analysis of Systems, pp. 288–307. Springer (2024). https://doi.org/10.1007/978-3-031-57246-3_16

50. Lima Graf, J., Krstić, S., Schneider, J.: Metric first-order temporal logic with complex data types. In: International Conference on Runtime Verification. pp. 126–147. Springer (2023). https://doi.org/10.1007/978-3-031-44267-4_7

51. Ngo, M., Massacci, F., Milushev, D., Piessens, F.: Runtime enforcement of security policies on black box reactive programs. In: Rajamani, S.K., Walker, D. (eds.) 42nd ACM SIGPLAN-SIGACT Symposium on Principles of Programming Languages (POPL), pp. 43–54. ACM (2015)

52. Peter, H.-J., Ehlers, R., Mattmüller, R.: Synthia: verification and synthesis for timed automata. In: Gopalakrishnan, G., Qadeer, S. (eds.) CAV 2011. LNCS, vol. 6806, pp. 649–655. Springer, Heidelberg (2011). https://doi.org/10.1007/978-3-642-22110-1_52

53. Pinisetty, S., Falcone, Y., Jéron, T., Marchand, H.: TiPEX: a tool chain for timed property enforcement during execution. In: International Conference on Runtime Verification (RV), pp. 306–320. Springer (2015)

54. Pinisetty, S., Falcone, Y., Jéron, T., Marchand, H., Rollet, A., Nguena Timo, O.: Runtime enforcement of timed properties revisited. Formal Methods Syst. Des. **45**, 381–422 (2014)

55. Pinisetty, S., Preoteasa, V., Tripakis, S., Jéron, T., Falcone, Y., Marchand, H.: Predictive runtime enforcement. Formal Methods Syst. Des. **51**(1), 154–199 (2017)

56. Pnueli, A., Rosner, R.: On the synthesis of a reactive module. In: 16th ACM Symposium on Principles of Programming Languages (POPL), pp. 179–190. ACM Press (1989)
57. Renard, M., Rollet, A., Falcone, Y.: GREP: games for the runtime enforcement of properties. In: Yevtushenko, N., Cavalli, A.R., Yenigün, H. (eds.) ICTSS 2017. LNCS, vol. 10533, pp. 259–275. Springer, Cham (2017). https://doi.org/10.1007/978-3-319-67549-7_16
58. Schneider, F.: Enforceable security policies. ACM Trans. Inf. Syst. Secur. **3**(1), 30–50 (2000)
59. Schneider, J., Basin, D., Krstić, S., Traytel, D.: A formally verified monitor for metric first-order temporal logic. In: Finkbeiner, B., Mariani, L. (eds.) RV 2019. LNCS, vol. 11757, pp. 310–328. Springer, Cham (2019). https://doi.org/10.1007/978-3-030-32079-9_18
60. Zhu, S., Tabajara, L.M., Li, J., Pu, G., Vardi, M.Y.: A symbolic approach to safety LTL synthesis. In: HVC 2017. LNCS, vol. 10629, pp. 147–162. Springer, Cham (2017). https://doi.org/10.1007/978-3-319-70389-3_10
61. Zingg, S., Krstić, S., Raszyk, M., Schneider, J., Traytel, D.: Verified first-order monitoring with recursive rules. In: TACAS 2022. LNCS, vol. 13244, pp. 236–253. Springer, Cham (2022). https://doi.org/10.1007/978-3-030-99527-0_13

Predictive Monitoring with Strong Trace Prefixes

Zhendong Ang$^{(\boxtimes)}$ ⓘ and Umang Mathur ⓘ

National University of Singapore, Singapore, Singapore
zhendong.ang@u.nus.edu, umathur@comp.nus.edu.sg

Abstract. Runtime predictive analyses enhance coverage of traditional dynamic analyses based bug detection techniques by identifying a space of feasible reorderings of the observed execution and determining if any reordering in this space witnesses the violation of some desired safety property. The most popular approach for modelling the space of feasible reorderings is through Mazurkiewicz's trace equivalence. The simplicity of the framework also gives rise to efficient predictive analyses, and has been the de facto means for obtaining space and time efficient algorithms for monitoring concurrent programs.

In this work, we investigate how to enhance the predictive power of trace-based reasoning, while still retaining the algorithmic benefits it offers. Towards this, we extend trace theory by naturally embedding a class of prefixes, which we call *strong trace prefixes*. We formally characterize strong trace prefixes using an enhanced dependence relation, study its predictive power and establish a tight connection to the previously proposed notion of synchronization-preserving correct reorderings developed in the context of data race and deadlock prediction. We then show that despite the enhanced predictive power, strong trace prefixes continue to enjoy the algorithmic benefits of Mazurkiewicz traces in the context of prediction against co-safety properties, and derive new algorithms for synchronization-preserving data races and deadlocks with better asymptotic space and time usage. We also show that strong trace prefixes can capture more violations of pattern languages. We implement our proposed algorithms and our evaluation confirms the practical utility of reasoning based on strong prefix traces.

Keywords: concurrency · runtime verification · dynamic analysis · trace languages

1 Introduction

Dynamic analysis has emerged as a popular class of techniques for ensuring reliability of large scale software, owing to their scalability and soundness (no false positives). At a high level, such techniques solve the membership problem — given an execution σ, typically modelled as a sequence of events, does σ belong to L_{bug}, a chosen set of executions that exhibit some undesired behaviour.

© The Author(s) 2024
A. Gurfinkel and V. Ganesh (Eds.): CAV 2024, LNCS 14682, pp. 182–204, 2024.
https://doi.org/10.1007/978-3-031-65630-9_9

In the context of concurrent software, however, such a naive testing paradigm suffers from poor coverage, since even under the ideal input, the execution σ observed at the time of testing, may not reveal the presence of bug (membership in L_{bug}), because of the non-determinism due to thread scheduling. Runtime prediction, which is also the subject of this work, has emerged as a systematic approach to enhance vanilla dynamic analyses [15,21,40]. Instead of solving the vanilla membership problem ($\sigma \in L_{\mathsf{bug}}$), runtime predictive techniques solve the *predictive membership* or *predictive monitoring* problem — they generalize the observed execution σ to a larger set of executions S_σ and check if there is some execution in S_σ that belongs to L_{bug}.

The predictive power (how often real bugs are identified) as well as the speed of a runtime predictive analysis (or predictive monitoring), often conflicting goals, crucially depend upon the space of S_σ that the analysis reasons about. In the most general case, S_σ can be the set of all executions that preserve the control and data flow of σ, namely *correct reorderings* [38] of σ. Analyses that exhaustively reason about the entire space of correct reorderings have the highest prediction power in theory [35], but quickly become intractable even for very simple classes of bugs [21,25]. On the other extreme is the class of trivial analyses which consider $S_\sigma = \{\sigma\}$ but offer no predictive power. Analyses based on Mazurkiewicz's *trace equivalence* theory [28] opt for middleground and balance predictive power with moderate computational complexity of the predictive monitoring question.

In the framework of trace theory, one fixes a concurrent alphabet $(\Sigma, \mathbb{D})$ consisting of a finite set of labels Σ, and a symmetric, reflexive dependence relation $\mathbb{D} \subseteq \Sigma \times \Sigma$. Now, each string $w \in \Sigma^*$ can be generalized to its equivalence class $[\![w]\!]_{\mathbb{D}}$, comprising all those strings w' which can be obtained from w by repeatedly swapping neighbouring events when their labels are not dependent. The corresponding predictive monitoring question under trace equivalence then translates to the disjointness check $[\![\sigma]\!]_{\mathbb{D}} \cap L_{\mathsf{bug}} \neq \varnothing$. Consider the *sound* dependence relation $\mathbb{D}_{\mathsf{RWL}}$ that marks pairs of events of the same thread, and pairs of events that write to the same memory location or the same lock as dependent. Here, we say $\mathbb{D}$ is sound if one can only infer correct reorderings from $\mathbb{D}$, i.e., for every well-formed execution σ, $[\![\sigma]\!]_{\mathbb{D}} \subseteq \mathsf{CReorderings}(\sigma)$. Then consider, for example, the execution σ_1 in Fig. 1a consisting of 6 events $\{e_i\}_{i \leq 6}$ performed by threads t_1 and t_2. It is easy to conclude that σ_1 is equivalent to the reordering $\rho_1 = e_1 e_4 e_2 e_3 e_5 e_6$, i.e., $\rho_1 \in [\![\sigma]\!]_{\mathbb{D}_{\mathsf{RWL}}}$ and thus $[\![\sigma]\!]_{\mathbb{D}_{\mathsf{RWL}}}$ is not disjoint from the set of executions where two $\mathsf{w}(x)$ events are consecutive. For a large class of languages L_{bug} [30], this question can, in fact, be answered in a one pass streaming constant-space algorithm, the holy grail of runtime monitoring, and has been instrumental in the success of industrial strength concurrency bug detectors [17,29,36].

Despite the simplicity and algorithmic efficiency of reasoning with commutativity of *individual events*, trace theory falls short in accurately reasoning about commutativity of *atomic* blocks of events in executions of concurrent programs. Consider, for example, the execution σ_2 from Fig. 1b. Here, under the depen-

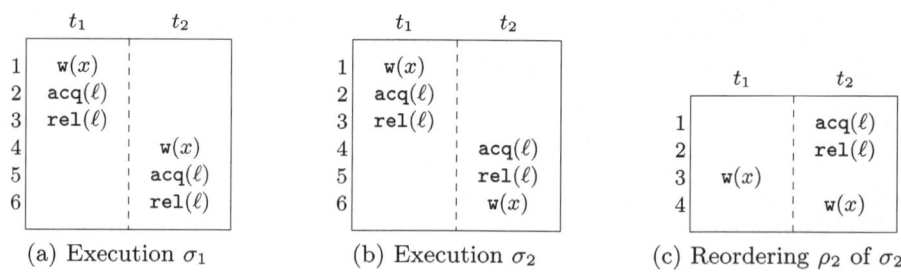

Fig. 1. Execution σ_1 has a predictable data race, and can be exposed with trace equivalence. Execution σ_2 has a predictable data race (witnessed by ρ_2) which cannot be exposed under trace equivalence, but can be exposed by strong trace prefixes.

dence $\mathbb{D}_{\text{RWL}}$ described above, the events $e_1 = \text{w}(x)^{t_1}$ and $e_6 = \text{w}(x)^{t_2}$ are ordered through the chain of dependence $(e_1, e_3), (e_3, e_4), (e_4, e_6)$. However, the reordering $\rho_2' = e_4 e_5 e_1 e_6 e_2 e_3$ is a correct reordering of σ_2 and also witnesses the two write events consecutively. In other words, the equivalence induced by a dependence relation can be conservative since commutativity on individual events maybe insufficient to determine when two blocks commute. Observe that simply relaxing the dependence relation $\mathbb{D}_{\text{RWL}}$ to a smaller set (say by removing dependence on locks) may be detrimental to soundness as one may infer that the ill-formed execution $\rho_2'' = e_1 e_2 e_4 e_3 e_5 e_6$ is equivalent to σ_2. Indeed, one can show that $\mathbb{D}_{\text{RWL}}$ is the most relaxed sound dependence relation. At the same time, we remark that the efficiency of the algorithms based on trace equivalence [9,11,13,16,27] crucially stems from reasoning about commutativity of individual events (instead of blocks of events).

In this work, we propose taking a different route for enhancing the predictive power of trace-based reasoning. Instead of allowing flexibility for commuting individual *blocks* of events, we observe that we can nevertheless enhance predictive power by sticking to commutativity of events but allowing for *greater flexibility in selecting events that participate in these reorderings*. Consider, for example, the execution ρ_2 in Fig. 1c, which is a correct reordering of σ_2 and also witnesses that the two write events are consecutive. Intuitively, one can obtain ρ_2 from σ_2 by first dropping the earlier critical section in t_1, thereby unblocking the critical section in t_2 so that it can commute to the beginning of the execution using event based commutativity.

In this work, we argue that the above style of reasoning can be formalized as a simple extension of the classic trace theory and no sophisticated algebraic formulation may be required. The dependence relation $\mathbb{D}$ plays a dual role — (**downward-closure**) for each event e in some reordering, all events dependent before e must be present in the reordering, and (**order-preservation**) amongst the set of events present in the reordering, the relative order of all dependent events must be preserved. Towards this, we propose to make this distinction explicit. Reflecting on the example above, a key tool we employ here is to *stratify* the dependence in $\mathbb{D}_{\text{RWL}}$ based on their strength. On one hand, we have *strong* dependencies, such as program order, for which both the roles (**downward-closure**) and (**order-preservation**) must be respected and cannot be relaxed. On the other hand, we have dependence between lock events, for which (**order-preservation**) must be kept intact, but nevertheless the first role (**downward-closure**) can be relaxed. We formalize this notion, in Sect. 3, using two sets of dependence relations, a strong dependence $\mathbb{S}$ and a weak one $\mathbb{W}$, and the resulting notion of a *strong trace prefix* of an execution, whose set of events is downward closed with respect to $\mathbb{S}$ and further, the relative order on the residual events in it respects the order induced by $\mathbb{S} \cup \mathbb{W}$.

Our generalization of traces to strong trace prefixes has important advantages. First, and the most obvious one, is the enhanced predictive power when monitoring against a language L_{bug}, as we illustrated above. The second consequence of the explicit stratification of the dependence relation, is that we can predict against new, previously impossible, languages such as those for deadlock prediction [40]. Third, the simplicity of our strong trace prefixes framework and its proximity to the original trace-theoretic framework implies that the predictive monitoring question in this new setting is solvable in essentially the same time and space complexity as in the trace-theory setting, despite the enhanced predictive power it unveils. We present a unified scheme, in Sect. 4, to translate any predictive algorithm that works under trace equivalence against some language L_{bug} to one that works under strong trace prefixes (for the same language L_{bug}) with additional non-determinism (but similar time and space usage) or alternatively with a polynomial multiplicative blowup in time. Thus, when the predictive question can be answered in constant space for Mazurkiewicz traces (as with data races [1]), it continues to be solvable in constant space for strong trace prefixes.

In Sect. 5 we further shorten the gap between commutativity style reasoning (aka strong trace prefixes) and the full semantic space (aka correct reorderings). In particular, we show that we can further relax the dependence on conflicting memory locations $((\mathbf{r}, \mathbf{w}), (\mathbf{w}, \mathbf{r}))$, that otherwise ensure soundness, and regain soundness back by baking in extra *reads-from* constraints in the prefixes. We define *strong reads-from prefixes* to formalize the resulting space of reorderings, and show that predictive monitoring under them can also be done with same time and space complexity as with strong trace prefixes. Next, in Sect. 6 we draw an interesting connection between strong reads-from prefixes and the class of *synchronization-preserving* data races [26] and deadlocks [40] which are the fastest and most predictive practical algorithms for detecting these concurrency bugs. We show that while synchronization-preserving reorderings are a larger class of reorderings, strong reads-from prefixes are nevertheless sufficient to capture the corresponding class of data races and deadlocks. As a consequence, we obtain constant-space algorithms for predicting classes of bugs, improving the previously known linear-space algorithms.

We put the new formalism to test by implementing the algorithms that follow from our results, for various specifications such as data races, deadlocks, and pattern languages [1]. We evaluated them on benchmark program traces derived from real world software applications and demonstrate the effectiveness of our formalism through its enhanced prediction power.

2 Predictive Monitoring and Trace Theory

Here we discuss some preliminary background on the predictive monitoring problem, trace theory and some limitations when applying the latter in the context of the former.

Events, Executions and Monitoring. We model an execution as a finite sequence $\sigma = e_1, e_2, \ldots, e_k$ of events where each event e_i is labelled with a letter $a_i = \mathsf{lab}(e_i) \in \Sigma$ from a fixed alphabet Σ. We will use Events_σ to denote the set of events of σ and use the notation $e_1 <_\sigma e_2$ to denote that the event e_1 appears before e_2 in the sequence σ. We will often use the custom alphabet Σ_{RWL} to label events of shared memory multithreaded programs. For this, we fix sets $\mathcal{T}$, $\mathcal{L}$ and $\mathcal{X}$ of thread, lock, and memory location identifiers. Then, $\Sigma_{\mathsf{RWL}} = \{\mathsf{op}(d)^t \mid t \in \mathcal{T}, \mathsf{op}(d) \in \{\mathsf{r}(x), \mathsf{w}(x), \mathsf{acq}(\ell), \mathsf{rel}(\ell)\}_{x \in \mathcal{X}, \ell \in \mathcal{L}}\}$ consists of labels denoting read/write of memory locations $\mathcal{X}$ or acquire/release of locks $\mathcal{L}$, each being performed by some thread $t \in \mathcal{T}$. Executions of multithreaded programs are assumed to be well-formed, i.e., belong to the regular language $L_{\mathsf{WF}} \subseteq \Sigma_{\mathsf{RWL}}^*$ that contains all strings where each release event e has a unique matching acquire event e' on the same lock and same thread, and no two critical sections on the same lock overlap. In addition, we only consider sequential consistency memory model in this paper. Our focus here is the runtime monitoring problem against a property $L \subseteq \Sigma^*$ — 'given an execution σ, does $\sigma \in L$?'

Predictive Monitoring and Correct Reorderings. Vanilla dynamic analyses that answer the membership question '$\sigma \in L$?' often miss bugs thanks to non-deterministic thread interleaving. Nevertheless, even when an execution σ does not belong to the target language L, it may still be possible to *predict* bugs in alternate executions that can be inferred from σ. Here, one first defines the set $\mathsf{CReorderings}(\sigma)$ of *correct reorderings* [35,38] of σ comprising executions similar to σ in the following precise sense — every program P that can generate σ, will also generate all executions in $\mathsf{CReorderings}(\sigma)$. For an execution $\sigma \in L_{\mathsf{WF}} \subseteq \Sigma_{\mathsf{RWL}}^*$ of a multithreaded program, $\mathsf{CReorderings}(\sigma)$ can be defined to be the set of all executions ρ of σ such that (1) $\mathsf{Events}_\rho \subseteq \mathsf{Events}_\sigma$, (2) ρ is well-formed, i.e., $\rho \in L_{\mathsf{WF}}$, (3) ρ is downward-closed with respect to the *program-order* of σ, i.e., for any two events e_1, e_2 performed by the same thread and $e_1 <_\sigma e_2$, if $e_2 \in \mathsf{Events}_\rho$, then $e_1 \in \mathsf{Events}_\rho$, and (4) for any read event e_r labelled $\mathsf{r}(x)^t$, the write event e_w that e_r reads-from ($e_\mathsf{r} \in \mathsf{rf}_\sigma(e_\mathsf{w})$) must also be in ρ. Here, we say that $e_\mathsf{r} \in \mathsf{rf}_\sigma(e_\mathsf{w})$ if e_r and e_w access the same memory location x and there is no other write event e_w' such that $e_\mathsf{w} <_\sigma e_\mathsf{w}' <_\sigma e_\mathsf{r}$. The *predictive monitoring* question against a language L can now be formalized as 'given an execution σ, is $\mathsf{CReorderings}(\sigma) \cap L \neq \varnothing$?'. Observe that any witness $\rho \in \mathsf{CReorderings}(\sigma) \cap L$ is a true positive since every execution in $\mathsf{CReorderings}(\sigma)$ passes the same control flow as σ and thus can be generated by any program that generates σ. In general, this predictive monitoring question does not admit a tractable solution, even for the simplest class of (regular) languages, such as the class of executions that contain a data race [25], and has been shown to admit super-linear-space hardness even for 2 threads [12]. Practical and sound algorithms for solving the predictive monitoring problem [21, 24, 26, 31, 38] often weaken predictive power in favour of soundness by considering a smaller space S_σ of reorderings. A set $S_\sigma \subseteq \Sigma^*_{\mathsf{RWL}}$ is said to be <u>sound</u> for a given execution $\sigma \in L_{\mathsf{WF}}$ if $S_\sigma \subseteq \mathsf{CReorderings}(\sigma)$, an algorithm that restricts its search of reorderings to S_σ will not report false positives.

Mazurkiewicz Traces. Trace theory, proposed by Antoni Mazurkiewicz [28], offers a tractable solution to the otherwise intractable predictive monitoring problem, by characterizing a simpler subclass of reorderings. Here, one identifies a reflexive and symmetric *dependence* relation $\mathbb{D} \subseteq \Sigma \times \Sigma$, and deems an execution ρ equivalent to σ if one can obtain ρ from σ by repeatedly swapping neighbouring events when they are not dependent. Together, $(\Sigma, \mathbb{D})$ constitute a *concurrent alphabet*. Formally, the *trace equivalence* $\sim_\mathbb{D}$ of the concurrent alphabet $(\Sigma, \mathbb{D})$ is the smallest equivalence on Σ^* such that for every $w_1, w_2 \in \Sigma^*$ and for every $(a, b) \in \Sigma \times \Sigma \setminus \mathbb{D}$, we have $w_1 \cdot a \cdot b \cdot w_2 \sim_\mathbb{D} w_1 \cdot b \cdot a \cdot w_2$. We use $[\![w]\!]_\mathbb{D} = \{w' \mid w \sim_\mathbb{D} w'\}$ to denote the equivalence class of $w \in \Sigma^*$.

Model Shared-Memory Concurrency Using Traces. Let us see how traces can (conservatively) model a class of correct reorderings, with an appropriate choice of dependence over Σ_{RWL}. The dependence $\mathbb{D}_\mathcal{L} = \{(\mathsf{op}_1(\ell)^{t_1}, \mathsf{op}_2(\ell)^{t_2}) \mid \ell \in \mathcal{L}\}$ can be used enforce mutual exclusion of critical sections — for every $\rho \in [\![\sigma]\!]_{\mathbb{D}_\mathcal{L}}$, the order of locking events is the same as in σ, and thus if σ is well-formed, then so is ρ. Likewise, the dependence $\mathbb{D}_\mathcal{T} = \{(\mathsf{op}_1(d_1)^t, \mathsf{op}_2(d_2)^t) \mid t \in \mathcal{T}\}$ is such that every $\rho \in [\![\sigma]\!]_{\mathbb{D}_\mathcal{T}}$ preserves the program order of σ. Indeed, the dependence $\mathbb{D}_{\mathsf{HB}} = \mathbb{D}_\mathcal{T} \cup \mathbb{D}_\mathcal{L}$ is the classic *happens-before* dependence employed in modern data race detectors such as THREADSANITIZER [36]. Finally, the dependence $\mathbb{D}_{\mathsf{RWL}} = \mathbb{D}_\mathcal{T} \cup \mathbb{D}_\mathcal{L} \cup \mathbb{D}_{\mathsf{conf}}$, where $\mathbb{D}_{\mathsf{conf}} = \{(\mathsf{op}_1(x)^{t_1}, \mathsf{op}_2(x)^{t_2}) \mid x \in \mathcal{X}, (\mathsf{op}_1, \mathsf{op}_2) \in \{(\mathsf{w}, \mathsf{r}), (\mathsf{r}, \mathsf{w}), (\mathsf{w}, \mathsf{w})\}\}$, ordering all conflicting memory accesses, ensures that for a well-formed execution σ, we have $[\![\sigma]\!]_{\mathbb{D}_{\mathsf{RWL}}} \subseteq \mathsf{CReorderings}(\sigma)$. The inclusion of $\mathbb{D}_\mathcal{T}$ ensures that program order is preserved, $\mathbb{D}_\mathcal{L}$ ensures well-formedness, while the remaining dependencies preserve the order of all conflicting pairs of events, and thus the reads-from relation. Indeed, $\mathbb{D}_{\mathsf{RWL}}$ is the smallest dependence that ensures soundness. Here, we say that $\mathbb{D} \subseteq \Sigma_{\mathsf{RWL}} \times \Sigma_{\mathsf{RWL}}$ is sound if for every $\sigma \in \Sigma^*$, $[\![\sigma]\!]_\mathbb{D} \subseteq \mathsf{CReorderings}(\sigma)$,

Predictive Monitoring with Traces. The predictive monitoring question under trace equivalence induced by a generic concurrent alphabet $(\Sigma, \mathbb{D})$ becomes — 'given an execution σ, is $[\![\sigma]\!]_\mathbb{D} \cap L \neq \varnothing$?'. In general, even when L is regular, this problem cannot be solved faster than $O(|\sigma|^\alpha)$. Here, α is the degree of concurrency in $\mathbb{D}$, or the size of the largest set without containing pairwise dependent events [1]. For the subclass of *star-connected* regular languages [30], this problem can be solved using a constant-space linear-time algorithm. Star-connected

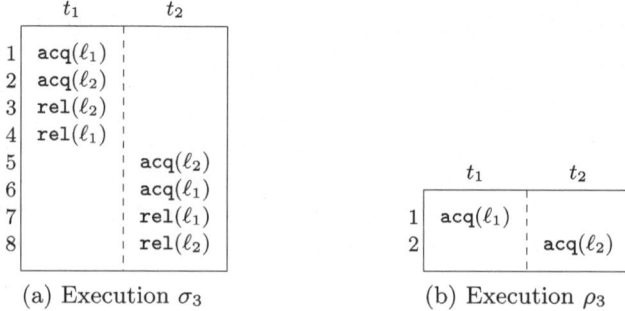

(a) Execution σ_3 (b) Execution ρ_3

Fig. 2. Execution σ_3 has a predictable deadlock, as witnessed by the correct reordering ρ_3, but cannot be exposed by without violating $\mathbb{D}_{\mathcal{L}}$.

languages include the class of languages that can encode data races [9,16], and the class of *pattern languages* [1] that capture other temporal bugs.

Example 1. Let $L_{\mathsf{race}} = \Sigma^*_{\mathsf{RWL}} \mathsf{w}(x)^{t_1} \mathsf{w}(x)^{t_2} \Sigma^*_{\mathsf{RWL}}$ be the set of executions that witness a race between two write accesses on memory location x between threads t_1 and t_2. Consider the execution σ_1 illustrated in Fig. 1a and recall from Sect. 1 that $\llbracket \sigma_1 \rrbracket_{\mathsf{D_{RWL}}} \cap L_{\mathsf{race}} \neq \varnothing$. Further, recall that for the trace σ_2 from Fig. 1b, we have $\llbracket \sigma_2 \rrbracket_{\mathsf{D_{RWL}}} \cap L_{\mathsf{race}} = \varnothing$, even though $\mathsf{CReorderings}(\sigma_2) \cap L_{\mathsf{race}} \neq \varnothing$. In other words, data race prediction based on trace equivalence may have strictly less predictive power than prediction based on correct reorderings.

Example 2. While trace equivalence can expose some data races (as with σ_1 from Fig. 1a), it can fundamentally not model deadlock prediction. Consider the execution σ_3 in Fig. 2a. It consists of two nested critical sections in inverted order of acquisition. Any program that generates σ_3 is prone to a deadlock, as witnessed by the correct reordering ρ_3 in Fig. 2b that acquires ℓ_1 in t_1 and then immediately switches context to t_2 in which lock ℓ_2 is acquired. Clearly, the underlying program is deadlocked at this point. Since $(\mathsf{lab}(e_3), \mathsf{lab}(e_5))$ and $(\mathsf{lab}(e_4), \mathsf{lab}(e_6)) \in \mathbb{D}_{\mathcal{L}}$, trace equivalence cannot predict this deadlock. Indeed, nested critical sections, acquired in a cyclic order, can never be reordered to actually expose the deadlock without violating the dependence between earlier release events and later acquire events induced by $\mathbb{D}_{\mathcal{L}}$.

3   Strong Trace Prefixes

Observe that for both the executions σ_2 (Example 1) and σ_3 (Example 2), the correct reordering that exposes the bug in question can be obtained by relaxing the order of two events that were otherwise ordered by the dependence relation, in particular $\mathbb{D}_{\mathcal{L}}$. Since the dependence $\mathbb{D}_{\mathcal{L}}$ enforces mutual exclusion, it cannot be ignored altogether without compromising soundness. For example, setting $\mathbb{D}_{\mathcal{L}} = \varnothing$, would deem $\rho'_2 = \mathsf{w}(x)^{t_1} \mathsf{acq}(\ell)^{t_1} \mathsf{acq}(\ell)^{t_2} \mathsf{rel}(\ell)^{t_1} \mathsf{rel}(\ell)^{t_2} \mathsf{w}(x)^{t_2}$ to be equivalent to σ_2, even though $\rho_2' \notin \mathsf{CReorderings}(\sigma_2)$. Nevertheless, both these examples illustrate a key insight behind how we generalize the trace-theoretic framework — the dependence due to locks is *weak*. That is, let $e_1 = \mathtt{rel}(\ell)^{t_1} <_\sigma$ $e_2 = \mathtt{acq}(\ell)^{t_2}$ be events of an execution σ. If they both appear in a reordering ρ of σ, then, under commutativity-style reasoning, we demand that their relative order must be $e_1 <_\rho e_2$. However, reorderings that drop the entire critical section of e_1 may nevertheless be allowed and may not compromise well-formedness. This is in contrast with *strong* dependence such as those induced due to $\mathbb{D}_\mathcal{T}$ or *reads-from* — any reordering must be downward closed with respect to them.

Building on these insights, we formalize strong trace prefixes by distinguishing dependencies that are absolutely necessary, i.e., *strong* dependence, from *weak* dependence, which do not affect *causality*, but only offer convenience for modelling constructs like mutual exclusion in a swap-based equivalence like trace equivalence. We present the formal definition of strong trace prefixes next.

Definition 1 (Dual Concurrent Alphabet). *A* dual concurrent alphabet *is a tuple* $(\Sigma, \mathbb{S}, \mathbb{W})$, *where* Σ *is a finite alphabet,* $\mathbb{S} \subseteq \Sigma \times \Sigma$ *is a reflexive and symmetric strong dependence relation, and* $\mathbb{W} \subseteq \Sigma \times \Sigma$ *is an irreflexive symmetric weak dependence relation.*

Definition 2 (Strong Trace Prefix). *The* strong trace prefix order *induced by the dual alphabet* $(\Sigma, \mathbb{S}, \mathbb{W})$, *denoted* $\preceq_\mathbb{S}^\mathbb{W}$, *is the smallest reflexive and transitive binary relation on* Σ^* *that satisfies:*

1. $\sim_{\mathbb{S}\cup\mathbb{W}} \subseteq \preceq_\mathbb{S}^\mathbb{W}$, *and*
2. *for every* $u, v \in \Sigma^*$ *and for every* $a \in \Sigma$, *if for every* $b \in v$, $(a, b) \notin \mathbb{S}$, *then we have* $u \cdot v \preceq_\mathbb{S}^\mathbb{W} u \cdot a \cdot v$

We say that $w' \in \Sigma^*$ *is a* strong trace prefix *of* w *if* $w' \preceq_\mathbb{S}^\mathbb{W} w$. *We use* $\langle\!\langle w |\!|_\mathbb{S}^\mathbb{W} = \{w' \in \Sigma^* \mid w' \preceq_\mathbb{S}^\mathbb{W} w\}$ *to denote the* strong downward closure *of* w.

Let us also recall the classical notion of ideal based prefixes using the above. For a reflexive symmetric dependence relation $\mathbb{D} \subseteq \Sigma \times \Sigma$, we use the notation $\sqsubseteq_\mathbb{D}$ to denote the *ideal prefix* relation $\preceq_\mathbb{D}^\varnothing$, and call w_1 an ideal prefix of w_2 if $w_1 \sqsubseteq_\mathbb{D} w_2$. We use $[\![w]\!]_\mathbb{D} = \{w' \in \Sigma^* \mid w' \sqsubseteq_\mathbb{D} w\}$ to denote the ideal downward closure of w.

A few observations about Definition 2 are in order. First, the relations $\preceq_\mathbb{S}^\mathbb{W}$ and $\sqsubseteq_\mathbb{D}$ defined here are not equivalence relations (unlike $\sim_\mathbb{D}$) but only quasi orders and relate executions of different lengths (namely strong (or ideal) prefixes). Second, in the case $\mathbb{W} \subseteq \mathbb{S}$, the strong trace prefix order gives the ideal prefix order $\sqsubseteq_{\mathbb{S}\cup\mathbb{W}}$. Third, in general, strong prefixes are more permissive than ideal prefixes, i.e., $\preceq_{\mathbb{S}\cup\mathbb{W}}^\varnothing \subseteq \preceq_\mathbb{S}^\mathbb{W}$, and is key to enhancing the predictive power of commutativity-style reasoning.

Example 3. Consider the alphabet $\Sigma = \{a, b, c\}$. Fix the strong dependence relation $\mathbb{S} = \{(a, a), (b, b), (c, c), (b, c), (c, b)\}$ and the weak dependence relation $\mathbb{W} = \{(a, b), (b, a)\}$. Let $\mathbb{D} = \mathbb{S} \cup \mathbb{W}$ be a traditional Mazurkiewicz-style dependence. Now, consider the string $w = abacba$. First, observe the simple equivalence $w \sim_\mathbb{D}$ $w' = abcaba$. Indeed, no other strings in Σ^* are $\sim_\mathbb{D}$-equivalent to w. The ideal prefixes of w $[\![w]\!]_{\mathbb{D}} = \{\epsilon, a, ab, aba, abac, abacb, abacba, abc, abca, abcab, abcaba\}$ is precisely the set of (string) prefixes of the two strings w and w'. The set of strong trace prefixes induced by $(\Sigma, \mathbb{S}, \mathbb{W})$ is larger though. First, consider the string $w_1 = abcb$ and observe that $w_1 \preccurlyeq_{\mathbb{S}}^{\mathbb{W}} w$. This follows because (1) $w' = abcab \cdot a \cdot \epsilon$, and thus $abcab \preccurlyeq_{\mathbb{S}}^{\mathbb{W}} w$, (2) $abcab = abc \cdot a \cdot b$ and $(a, b) \notin \mathbb{S}$ and thus $abcb \preccurlyeq_{\mathbb{S}}^{\mathbb{W}} abcab$, and finally (3) due to transitivity, we have $w_1 \preccurlyeq_{\mathbb{S}}^{\mathbb{W}} w$. Consider now the string $w_2 = bcb$, and observe that $abcb = \epsilon \cdot a \cdot bcb$, giving us $w_2 \preccurlyeq_{\mathbb{S}}^{\mathbb{W}} w_1$ since $\{(a, b), (a, c)\} \cap \mathbb{S} = \varnothing$. Thus, $w_2 \preccurlyeq_{\mathbb{S}}^{\mathbb{W}} w$. On the other hand, observe that $w_1 \not\preccurlyeq_{\mathbb{D}} w$ and $w_2 \not\preccurlyeq_{\mathbb{D}} w$.

3.1   Modelling Correct Reorderings with Strong Trace Prefixes

Recall that $\mathbb{D}_{\mathsf{RWL}}$ ordered events of the same thread, same locks and conflicting events of a given memory location allowing us to soundly represent a class of correct reorderings of an execution σ as the equivalence class $[\![\sigma]\!]_{\mathbb{D}_{\mathsf{RWL}}}$. Here, we identify a finer gradation of $\mathbb{D}_{\mathsf{RWL}}$, to allow for a larger subset of correct reorderings. Specifically, we define the strong and weak dependence on Σ_{RWL} as:

$$\mathbb{W}_{\mathsf{w}} = \{(\mathsf{w}(x)^{t_1}, \mathsf{w}(x)^{t_2}) \mid x \in \mathcal{X}, t_1 \neq t_2 \in \mathcal{T}\}, \quad \mathbb{W}_{\mathcal{L}} = \{(a^{t_1}, b^{t_2}) \in \mathbb{D}_{\mathcal{L}} \mid t_1 \neq t_2\}$$
$$\mathbb{W}_{\mathsf{RWL}} = \mathbb{W}_{\mathcal{L}} \cup \mathbb{W}_{\mathsf{w}}, \qquad \mathbb{S}_{\mathsf{RWL}} = \mathbb{D}_{\mathsf{RWL}} \setminus \mathbb{W}_{\mathsf{RWL}} \tag{1}$$

In other words, the dual concurrent alphabet $(\Sigma_{\mathsf{RWL}}, \mathbb{S}_{\mathsf{RWL}}, \mathbb{W}_{\mathsf{RWL}})$ relaxes the 'hard ordering' between writes to the same memory location (i.e., 'conflicting writes') as well as that between critical sections of the same lock (i.e., 'conflicting lock events'). We next explain the intuition behind the above relaxations.

Weakening Dependence on Writes. Let us begin by arguing about $\mathbb{W}_{\mathsf{w}}$. When an execution contains two *consecutive* write events e_1, e_2 with $\mathsf{lab}(e_1) = \mathsf{w}(x)^{t_1}$ and $\mathsf{lab}(e_2) = \mathsf{w}(x)^{t_2}$ on the same memory location $x \in \mathcal{X}$, then, clearly, there is no event reading from the first write event e_1 since it is immediately overwritten by e_2. In this case, while flipping the order of e_1 and e_2 may violate the read-from relation of a read event reading from e_2, observe that e_1 can be completely *dropped* (in absence of later $\mathbb{S}_{\mathsf{RWL}}$-dependent events after e_1) without dropping e_2 and without affecting any control flow. In other words, the presence of e_2 does not mandate the presence of e_1, but when both are present, the conservative choice of placing e_1 before e_2 ensures that the reads-from relation is preserved.

Weakening Dependence on Lock Events. Recall that the primary role of the dependence $\mathbb{D}_{\mathcal{L}}$ was to ensure mutual exclusion, i.e., two critical sections of the same lock do not overlap in any execution obtained by repeatedly swapping neighboring independent events. We identify that this is not a strong dependence, in that one can possibly *drop* an earlier critical section entirely, while retaining a later critical section on the same lock in a candidate correct reordering. The correct reordering ρ_2 of σ_2 in Fig. 1c can be obtained by leveraging this insight. Indeed, $\rho_2 \in \langle\!\langle \sigma_2 \|_{\mathbb{S}_{\mathsf{RWL}}}^{\mathbb{W}_{\mathsf{RWL}}}$ because $(o_1(\ell)^{t_1}, o_2(\ell)^{t_2}) \in \mathbb{W}_{\mathsf{RWL}}$ for $o_1, o_2 \in \{\mathsf{acq}, \mathsf{rel}\}$.

Moreover, in the deadlock example (Fig. 2), $\rho_3 \in \langle\!\langle \sigma_3 \|^{\mathbb{W}_{\mathsf{RWL}}}_{\mathbb{S}_{\mathsf{RWL}}}$, since the critical section of l_2 in thread t_1 can be completely dropped without affecting the presence of $\mathtt{acq}(l_2)^{t_2}$.

Well-Formedness. The weak dependence $\mathbb{W}_{\mathcal{L}}$ ensures that no two *complete* critical sections on the same lock overlap in a strong trace prefix (provided they did not overlap in the original execution). However, simply marking lock dependencies as *weak* still does not forbid strong trace prefixes where an earlier *incomplete* critical section overlaps with a later *complete* critical section. Consider for example, the (ill-formed) execution $\rho'_2 = \mathtt{w}(x)^{t_1}\mathtt{acq}(\ell)^{t_1}\mathtt{acq}(\ell)^{t_2}\mathtt{rel}(\ell)^{t_2}\mathtt{w}(x)^{t_2}$. Observe that ρ'_2 is a strong trace prefix of σ_2 under $\mathbb{S}_{\mathsf{RWL}}$ and $\mathbb{W}_{\mathsf{RWL}}$. As we will show in Sect. 4.3, we can remedy this mild peculiarity in the predictive monitoring algorithm.

Soundness and Precision Power. Strong trace prefixes retain soundness (as long as they are well-formed) while enjoying higher predictive power:

Theorem 1 (Soundness and Precision Power). *For each well-formed execution $\sigma \in L_{\mathsf{WF}}$, we have:*

$$[\![\sigma]\!]_{\mathbb{S}_{\mathsf{RWL}} \cup \mathbb{W}_{\mathsf{RWL}}} \subseteq [\![\sigma]\!]_{\mathbb{S}_{\mathsf{RWL}} \cup \mathbb{W}_{\mathsf{RWL}}} \subseteq \langle\!\langle \sigma \|^{\mathbb{W}_{\mathsf{RWL}}}_{\mathbb{S}_{\mathsf{RWL}}} \cap L_{\mathsf{WF}} \subseteq \mathit{CReorderings}(\sigma).$$

Moreover, there is a $\sigma \in L_{\mathsf{WF}}$ for which each of the subset relationships are strict.

Maximality. Our choice of the dual concurrent alphabet $(\Sigma_{\mathsf{RWL}}, \mathbb{S}_{\mathsf{RWL}}, \mathbb{W}_{\mathsf{RWL}})$ is also the best one amongst the space of sound dual concurrent alphabets obtained by stratifying $\mathbb{D}_{\mathsf{RWL}}$. Formally,

Theorem 2 (Maximality). *Let $(\Sigma_{\mathsf{RWL}}, \mathbb{S}, \mathbb{W})$ be a dual concurrent alphabet such that $\mathbb{D}_{\mathsf{RWL}} \subseteq \mathbb{S} \cup \mathbb{W}$, and, for every $\sigma \in \Sigma^*_{\mathsf{RWL}}$, $\langle\!\langle \sigma \|^{\mathbb{W}}_{\mathbb{S}} \cap L_{\mathsf{WF}} \subseteq \mathit{CReorderings}(\sigma)$. Then, $\mathbb{S}_{\mathsf{RWL}} \subseteq \mathbb{S}$, and thus, for every σ, $\langle\!\langle \sigma \|^{\mathbb{W}}_{\mathbb{S}} \subseteq \langle\!\langle \sigma \|^{\mathbb{W}_{\mathsf{RWL}}}_{\mathbb{S}_{\mathsf{RWL}}}$*

The formal proof of the theorems in this paper can be found in the extended version of our paper [2].

4 Complexity of Predictive Monitoring

In this section we investigate the impact of generalizing Mazurkiewicz traces to strong trace prefixes, on the predictive monitoring question. We present two *schemes* to translate arbitrary Turing machines for predictive monitoring under trace equivalence against a language L to one for predictive monitoring under strong trace prefixes against the same language L. The first scheme (Sect. 4.1), uses additional non-determinism (but same time and space usage), and the second (Sect. 4.2) employs polynomial multiplicative blow-up in time complexity.

4.1 Non-deterministic Predictive Monitoring

We first show that an algorithm that solves the vanilla predictive monitoring problem ($\llbracket\sigma\rrbracket_\mathbb{D} \cap L \neq \varnothing$) can be transformed into an algorithm for predictive monitoring against strong trace prefixes with similar resource (time and space) usage, albeit with use of non-determinism.

Theorem 3. *Let $L \subseteq \Sigma^*$ and let M be a deterministic Turing machine, that uses time $T(|w|)$ and space $S(|w|)$, such that $L(M) = \{w \mid \llbracket w \rrbracket_\mathbb{D} \cap L \neq \varnothing\}$. There is a nondeterministic Turing machine M' that uses time $T(|w|) + O(|w|)$ and space $S(|w|) + O(|w|)$, such that $L(M') = \{w \mid \langle\!\langle w \rangle\!\rangle_\mathbb{S}^\mathbb{W} \cap L \neq \varnothing\}$. Moreover, if M runs in one-pass, then M' uses space $S(|w|) + c$ (for some constant c).*

Observe that, in the above, we have $S(|w|) + c \in O(S(|w|))$. Further, when $T(|w|) \in \Omega(|w|)$, then $T(|w|) + O(|w|) \in O(T(|w|))$. Thus, the time and space usage of the non-deterministic machine M' in Theorem 3 are essentially the same as those of M.

The proof of Theorem 3 relies on the observation that any strong prefix u of a string w is equivalent (according to trace equivalence using $\sim_{\mathbb{S}\cup\mathbb{W}}$) to a subsequence w' of w, such that w' is downward closed with respect to strong dependencies. The non-deterministic Turing machine M' first non-deterministically guesses a subsequence w' of the input execution w, then, using constant space and an additional forward streaming pass, ensures that w' is downward closed with respect to $\mathbb{S}$, and finally invokes the Turing machine M on the string w'.

It follows from Theorem 3 that when the language of M is regular, so is the language of M'. This means, that when a language L can be predictively monitored in constant space under trace equivalence (for example data races, deadlocks, or pattern languages [1]), then it can also be predictively monitored in constant space, yet with higher predictive power, under strong trace prefixes!

4.2 Deterministic Predictive Monitoring

While Theorem 3 illustrates that the predictive monitoring question with strong trace prefixes becomes decidable (when assuming the analogous problem for Mazurkiewicz traces is decidable), we remark that the use of nondeterminism may lead to exponential blow-ups in time and space when translating it to a deterministic machine that can then be used in a practical predictive testing setup. Here, in this section, we establish that one can tactfully avoid this blow-up. In fact, we show that only allowing a polynomial multiplicative blow-up is sufficient to do predictive monitoring under strong prefixes starting with a deterministic Turing machine for that works under trace equivalence.

Our result is inspired by prior works on predictive monitoring under trace languages [3]. Here, one identifies strong ideals[1], i.e., sets of events that are downward closed with respect to the *strong* dependence relation, and checks

---

[1] A strong ideal X of an execution $\sigma = e_1, \ldots, e_k$ is a subset of $\{e_1, e_2, ..., e_k\}$ such that for every $i < j$, if $(\mathsf{lab}(e_i), \mathsf{lab}(e_j)) \in \mathbb{S}$ and if $e_j \in X$, then $e_i \in X$.

whether there is a linearization of one of them that respects both strong and weak dependence and also belongs to the target language L. A parameter that crucially determines the time complexity here is the *width* of the concurrency alphabet. In our setting, the width $\alpha_{\mathbb{S}}$ is the size of the largest subset of Σ, that contains no two letters which are dependent according to $\mathbb{S}$.

Theorem 4. *Fix a language L. Let M be a deterministic Turing machine that uses time $T(|w|)$ and space $S(|w|)$, such that $L(M) = \{w \mid [\![w]\!]_{\mathbb{D}} \cap L \neq \varnothing\}$. Then, there exists a deterministic Turing machine M' that runs in time $O((|w| + T(|w|)) \cdot n^{\alpha_{\mathbb{S}}})$ and uses space $S(|w|) + O(|w|)$, such that $L(M') = \{w \mid \langle\!\langle w |\!|_{\mathbb{S}}^{\mathbb{W}} \cap L \neq \varnothing\}$.*

The above complexity bounds follow because one can systematically enumerate those subsequences of the input w which are downward closed with respect to $\mathbb{S}$, by in turn enumerating the space of strong ideals. The set of strong ideals is, in turn, bounded by $|w|^{\alpha_{\mathbb{S}}}$.

4.3   Ensuring Well-Formedness and Soundness

Recall that the dual concurrent alphabet $(\Sigma_{\mathsf{RWL}}, \mathbb{S}_{\mathsf{RWL}}, \mathbb{W}_{\mathsf{RWL}})$ is not sufficient by itself for ensuring that the strong trace prefixes of an execution $\sigma \in L_{\mathsf{WF}}$ are also well-formed. Well-formedness can nevertheless be retrofitted in the predictive monitoring algorithm with same additional time, space and non-determinism. Theorem 5 formalizes this and follows from the observation that the set L_{WF} is (a) regular, and (b) closed under trace equivalence, i.e., for every $\sigma \in L_{\mathsf{WF}}$, we have $[\![\sigma]\!]_{\mathbb{D}_{\mathsf{RWL}}} \subseteq L_{\mathsf{WF}}$, and algorithms for predictive monitoring can be easily augmented to reason about the set $\langle\!\langle \sigma |\!|_{\mathbb{S}_{\mathsf{RWL}}}^{\mathbb{W}_{\mathsf{RWL}}} \cap L_{\mathsf{WF}}$.

Theorem 5. *Let $L \subseteq \Sigma_{\mathsf{RWL}}^*$ and let M be a deterministic Turing machine, that uses time $T(|w|)$ and space $S(|w|)$, such that $L(M) = \{\sigma \in L_{\mathsf{WF}} \mid [\![\sigma]\!]_{\mathbb{D}_{\mathsf{RWL}}} \cap L_{\mathsf{WF}} \cap L \neq \varnothing\}$. There is a nondeterministic Turing machine M' (resp. deterministic Turing machine M'') that uses time $T(|w|) + O(|w|)$ (resp. $O((|w| + T(|w|)) \cdot n^{\alpha_{\mathbb{S}}}))$ and space $S(|w|) + O(|w|)$ such that $L(M')(= L(M'')) = \{\sigma \in L_{\mathsf{WF}} \mid \langle\!\langle \sigma |\!|_{\mathbb{S}}^{\mathbb{W}} \cap L_{\mathsf{WF}} \cap L \neq \varnothing\}$. Moreover, if M runs in one-pass, M' uses space $S(|w|) + c$ (for some constant c).*

5   Strong Reads-From Prefixes

Strong trace prefixes generalize Mazurkiewicz traces and can enhance precision of predictive monitoring algorithms. In this section, we propose further generalizations in the context of Σ_{RWL}, bringing the power of trace-based reasoning further close to correct reorderings. Towards this, we observe that the key constraints that correct reorderings must satisfy are only thread-order and reads-from relation, and thus $\mathbb{S}_{\mathsf{RWL}}$ may be relaxed further by removing the dependence between writes and reads.

Consider the trace σ_4 in Fig. 3. Here, the only strong prefixes of σ (under $\mathbb{S}_{\mathsf{RWL}}$ and $\mathbb{W}_{\mathsf{RWL}}$) are its own (string) prefixes. That is, strong trace prefixes

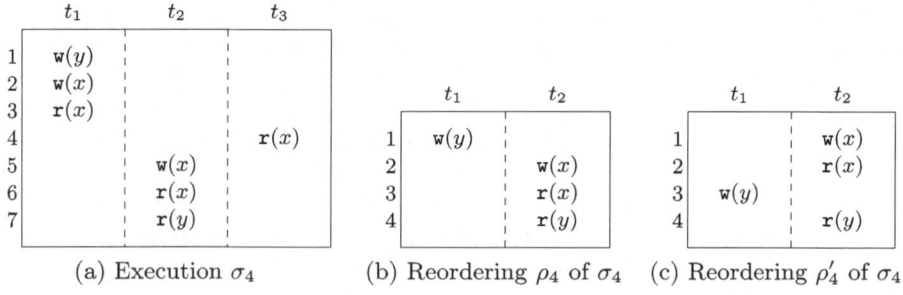

(a) Execution σ_4 (b) Reordering ρ_4 of σ_4 (c) Reordering ρ_4' of σ_4

Fig. 3. Execution σ_4 has a predictable data race, and can be exposed with strong reads-from prefixes in ρ_4', but cannot be exposed by strong trace prefixes.

cannot be used to argue that there is a reordering (namely ρ_4' in Fig. 3c) in which $\mathtt{w}(y)$ and $\mathtt{r}(y)$ are next to each other. Intuitively, one can first obtain the intermediate ρ_4 (Fig. 3b) from σ_4 by dropping all events in the block of events containing e_2 labelled $\mathtt{w}(x)^{t_1}$ together with all its read events $\mathtt{rf}_{\sigma_4}(e_2) = \{e_3, e_4\}$, and then obtain ρ_4' from ρ_4 using Mazurkiewicz between independent events. We remark however that, neither ρ_4 nor ρ_3' is a strong trace prefix of σ_4 because $(\mathtt{r}(x)^{t_3}, \mathtt{w}(x)^{t_2}) \in \mathbb{S}_{\mathsf{RWL}}$. However, observe that one cannot obtain this reordering ρ_4 in the presence of $\mathbb{S}_{\mathsf{RWL}}$.

The above example illustrates the possibility of relaxing $\mathbb{S}_{\mathsf{RWL}}$ by removing the dependencies between reads and writes. However, an incautious relaxation (such as removing $(\mathtt{w}(x)^{t_1}, \mathtt{r}(x)^{t_3})$ from $\mathbb{S}_{\mathsf{RWL}}$) may result into a prefix like $\rho_4'' = \mathtt{w}(y)^{t_1} \mathtt{r}(x)^{t_3} \mathtt{w}(x)^{t_2} \mathtt{r}(x)^{t_2} \mathtt{r}(y)^{t_2}$ which is not a correct reordering of σ_4. In other words, while $(\mathtt{r}, \mathtt{w})$ and $(\mathtt{w}, \mathtt{r})$ dependencies can be relaxed, the stronger semantic dependence due to reads-from must still be retained. As a reminder, such a relaxation cannot accurately be modelled under strong prefixes alone since $(\Sigma_{\mathsf{RWL}}, \mathbb{S}_{\mathsf{RWL}}, \mathbb{W}_{\mathsf{RWL}})$ is already the weakest alphabet (Theorem 2). We instead model this as *strong reads-from prefixes* defined below:

Definition 3 (Strong Reads-from Prefix). *The* strong reads-from prefix order *induced by* $(\Sigma_{\mathsf{RWL}}, \mathbb{S}_{\mathsf{RWL}}, \mathbb{W}_{\mathsf{RWL}})$, *denoted* $\trianglelefteq_{\mathsf{rf}}$, *is the smallest reflexive and transitive binary relation on* Σ_{RWL}^* *that satisfies:*

1. $\preccurlyeq_{\mathbb{S}_{\mathsf{RWL}}}^{\mathbb{W}_{\mathsf{RWL}}} \subseteq \trianglelefteq_{\mathsf{rf}}$, *and*
2. *let* $\sigma = \sigma_1 \cdot e \cdot \sigma_2$, *if* $\forall e' \in \sigma_2$, *we have* $(e, e') \notin \mathbb{D}_{\mathcal{T}}$ *and* $e' \notin \mathsf{rf}_\sigma(e)$, *then* $\sigma_1 \cdot \sigma_2 \trianglelefteq_{\mathsf{rf}} \sigma_1 \cdot e \cdot \sigma_2$.

We say $w' \in \Sigma_{\mathsf{RWL}}^*$ *is a* strong reads-from prefix *of* w *if* $w' \trianglelefteq_{\mathsf{rf}} w$. *We use* $\langle\!\langle w \rangle\!\rangle_{\mathsf{rf}} = \{w' \in \Sigma_{\mathsf{RWL}}^* \mid w' \trianglelefteq_{\mathsf{rf}} w\}$ *to denote the* strong reads-from downward closure *of* w.

In the above example, ρ_4 and ρ_4' now can be modelled as strong reads-from prefixes of σ_4, i.e., $\rho_4, \rho_4' \in \langle\!\langle \sigma_4 \rangle\!\rangle_{\mathsf{rf}}$, since $\mathtt{w}(x)^{t_1}$ and $\mathtt{r}(x)^{t_1}$ are not strong dependent with and not in the reads-from relation with any subsequent events. The soundness and precision power of strong-reads from prefixes are clear:

Theorem 6 (Soundness and Precision Power). *For each well-formed execution $\sigma \in L_{\mathsf{WF}}$, we have:*

$$[\![\sigma]\!]_{\mathbb{S}_{\mathsf{RWL}} \cup \mathbb{W}_{\mathsf{RWL}}} \subseteq [\![\sigma]\!]_{\mathbb{S}_{\mathsf{RWL}} \cup \mathbb{W}_{\mathsf{RWL}}} \subseteq \langle\!\langle\sigma|\!|_{\mathbb{S}_{\mathsf{RWL}}}^{\mathbb{W}_{\mathsf{RWL}}} \cap L_{\mathsf{WF}} \subseteq \langle\!\langle\sigma|\!|_{\mathsf{rf}} \cap L_{\mathsf{WF}} \subseteq \mathit{CReorderings}(\sigma).$$

Moreover, there is a $\sigma \in L_{\mathsf{WF}}$ for which each of the subset relationships are strict.

We now discuss the algorithmic impact of this further relaxation to strong reads-from prefixes. Here we obtain results which are analogue to Theorem 3 and Theorem 4. These follow because one can guess and check whether a prefix preserves thread order and reads-from relations.

Theorem 7. *Let $L \subseteq \Sigma^*$ and let M be a deterministic Turing machine, that uses time $T(n)$ and space $S(n)$, such that $L(M) = \{w \mid [\![w]\!]_{\mathbb{D}} \cap L \neq \varnothing\}$. There is a nondeterministic Turing machine M' (resp. deterministic Turing machine M'') that uses time $T(n) + O(n)$ (resp. $O((n+T(n)) \cdot n^{\alpha_{\mathbb{S}_{\mathsf{RWL}}}}))$ and space $S(n) + O(n)$ such that $L(M')(= L(M'')) = \{w \mid \langle\!\langle w|\!|_{\mathsf{rf}} \cap L \neq \varnothing\}$. Moreover, if M runs in one-pass, then M' uses space $S(n) + c$ (for some constant c).*

In next section, we will show that such a relaxation allows us to obtain a previously known class of synchronization-preserving data races and deadlocks.

6   Strong Prefixes Versus Synchronization Preservation

Recall the execution σ_2 in Fig. 1, where (e_1, e_6) is a data race, but cannot be detected using a happens-before style detector, i.e., using the dependence $\mathbb{D}_L$. On the other hand, trace ρ_2 demonstrates that this can be captured using strong prefixes (i.e., under $\mathbb{S}_{\mathsf{RWL}}$ and $\mathbb{W}_{\mathsf{RWL}}$). Indeed, this is a classic example of a *synchronization-preserving* data race proposed in [26] and characterizes a large class of predictable data races that can also be detected in linear time. The analogous notion of synchronization-preserving deadlocks captures a large class of predictable deadlocks [40], and can be detected efficiently. Both these classes of bugs can be predicted by looking for *synchronization-preserving correct reorderings*, and in this section we investigate the relationship between them and strong reads-from prefixes.

Synchronization-Preserving Reorderings, Data Races and Deadlocks. An execution $\rho \in \Sigma^*_{\mathsf{RWL}}$ is a synchronization-preserving correct reordering of execution $\sigma \in \Sigma^*_{\mathsf{RWL}}$ if (a) ρ is a correct reordering of σ, and (b) for each pair of acquire events $a_1 \neq a_2$ (alternatively, critical sections) of σ on the same lock ℓ, such that both a_1 and a_2 are present in ρ, we have, $a_1 <_\rho a_2$ iff $a_1 <_\sigma a_2$. We use $\mathsf{SyncP}(\sigma)$ to denote the set of all synchronization-preserving correct reordering of σ. A sync(hronization)-preserving data races are a pair of conflicting events (e_1, e_2), such that there is a synchronization-preserving correct reordering ρ in which e_1 and e_2 are ρ-enabled. Likewise, a sync-preserving deadlock of length k is a deadlock pattern[2] $(e_1, \ldots, e_k)$, such that there is a synchronization-preserving correct reordering ρ in which $e_1, \ldots, e_k$ are σ-enabled. This class of data races and deadlocks can be detected in linear time and space [26, 40].

We observe that the algorithmic efficiency in predicting sync-preserving data races (resp. deadlocks) stems from the fact that whenever (e_1, e_2) is a data race (resp. $(e_1, \ldots, e_k)$ is a deadlock), it can be witnessed by a reordering which is not only synchronization-preserving, but *also preserves the order of conflicting read and write events*, i.e., through a *conflict-preserving reordering*:

Definition 4. *(Conflict-preserving Correct Reordering) A reordering ρ of an execution σ is a conflict-preserving correct reordering if (a) ρ is the correct reordering of σ, (b) for every lock ℓ and for any two acquire event a_1, a_2 labelled* $\mathsf{acq}(\ell)$ *in ρ, $a_1 <_\rho a_2$ iff $a_1 <_\sigma a_2$, and (c) for every two conflicting events e_1 and e_2 in ρ, $e_1 <_\rho e_2$ iff $e_1 <_\sigma e_2$.*

Here, we say (e_1, e_2) is a conflicting pair of events if $(\mathsf{lab}(e_1), \mathsf{lab}(e_2)) \in \mathbb{D}_{\mathsf{conf}}$. We use $\mathtt{ConfP}(\sigma)$ to denote all conflict-preserving correct reorderings of σ. Observe that every conflict-preserving correct reordering of σ is also a synchronization-preserving correct reordering of σ.

Proposition 1. *For any execution $\sigma \in \Sigma_{\mathsf{RWL}}^*$, we have $\mathtt{ConfP}(\sigma) \subseteq \mathtt{SyncP}(\sigma)$.*

We now formalize our observation: We identify that in fact every synchronization-preserving data race (deadlock) is also a conflict-preserving data race (deadlock).

Lemma 1. *Let $\sigma \in \Sigma_{\mathsf{RWL}}^*$ be an execution. A sequence of events $(e_1, \ldots, e_k)$ is σ-enabled in some synchronization-preserving reordering of σ iff they are σ-enabled in some conflict-preserving reordering of σ. Thus, sync-preserving data races and deadlocks can also be witnessed using conflict-preserving reorderings.*

The connection between synchronization-preserving and strong reads-from prefixes is now straightforward because the class of conflict-preserving races or conflict-preserving deadlocks can be accurately modelled in our framework:

Lemma 2. *Let $\sigma \in \Sigma_{\mathsf{RWL}}^*$ be an execution. We have $\langle\!\langle \sigma \|_{\mathsf{rf}} \cap L_{\mathsf{WF}} = \mathtt{ConfP}(\sigma)$.*

According to Lemma 1 and Lemma 2, we build the connection between sync-preserving data race (deadlock) and our strong reads-from prefixes: a sequence of events $(e_1, \ldots, e_k)$ is σ-enabled in some synchronization-preserving reordering of σ iff they are σ-enabled in a well-formed strong reads-from prefix. Consequently, we get algorithms for detecting sync-preserving data races and deadlocks with improved space bound and same time:

---

[2] A deadlock pattern of size k is a sequence of acquire events $D = (e_1, \ldots, e_k)$ performed by k distinct threads $t_1, \ldots, t_k$, acquiring k distinct locks $\ell_1, \ldots, \ell_k$ such that $\ell_i \in \mathtt{HeldLks}(e_{i\%k+1})$, and further, the locks held at e_i and e_j are disjoint $(i \neq j)$. The set $\mathtt{HeldLks}(e)$ is the set of locks which have been acquired in thread of e, before e, but not released until after e is performed.

Theorem 8. *Synchronization-preserving races and deadlocks can be detected in linear time and constant space.*

Even though, in the context of data races and deadlocks, it suffices to look at conflict-preserving correct reorderings, in general, the class of synchronization-preserving reorderings is much more expressive. As a consequence, when one goes beyond data races and deadlocks to a slightly different class of specifications, the predictive monitoring question under synchronization-preserving reorderings quickly becomes hard. In particular, we demonstrate this in the context of predicting if two events can be reordered in a certain order. Under Mazurkiewicz's trace equivalence, this problem can be decided in linear time and constant space, and thus also for strong trace prefixes (Theorem 3). However, in the context of synchronization-preserving reorderings, we show that this problem cannot be solved in linear time and constant space.

Theorem 9. *Let $\sigma \in \Sigma_{\mathsf{RWL}}^*$ be an execution, and $e_1, e_2 \in \mathsf{Events}_\sigma$ be two events. Any streaming algorithm that checks if there is an execution $\rho \in \mathsf{SyncP}(\sigma)$ such that $e_1 <_\rho e_2$ uses linear space.*

Indeed, the above problem (checking if two events can be flipped) is an example of the level $1/2$ in the Straubing-Thérien hierarchy[3] [32], or pattern languages[4] [1], whose predictive monitoring can be solved in linear time and constant space under Mazurkiewicz traces, and thus also under strong prefixes. However, Theorem 9 indicates that any streaming algorithm deciding this problem against pattern languages under synchronization-preserving reorderings has a linear-space lower bound. We therefore remark that, strong prefixes lie at the horizon of tractability in the context of predictive monitoring.

7   Experimental Evaluation

We evaluate the effectiveness of strong prefixes and strong reads-from prefixes for the purpose of predictive monitoring of executions (over Σ_{RWL}^*) of shared memory multi-threaded programs. The goal of our evaluation is two-folds. First, we want to empirically gauge the enhanced predictive power of strong reads-from prefixes over prediction based on trace equivalence. We demonstrate this using prediction against pattern languages proposed in [1]. For data races, strong reads-from prefixes can capture sync-preserving races, which have already been shown to have more empirical predictive power over trace-based reasoning [26]. Second, we want to evaluate how our, not-so-customized but constant space, algorithm for synchronization-preserving data races and deadlocks (Theorem 8) performs against the linear-space algorithm due to [26,40].

---

[3] The level $1/2$ in the Straubing-Thiérin hierarchy contains languages of Σ^* that are finite union of languages in the form of $L_0 a_0 L_1 \ldots L_{n-1} a_{n-1} L_n$, where $a_0, \ldots, a_{n-1} \in \Sigma$ and $L_0, \ldots, L_n \in \{\Sigma^*, \varnothing\}$.

[4] Pattern languages are regular languages of the form $\Sigma^* a_1 \Sigma^* \ldots \Sigma^* a_d \Sigma^*$, where $a_1, \ldots, a_d \in \Sigma$.

Table 1. Predictive monitoring against pattern languages, grouped by pattern length. Column 3 (Column 6) reports the total time taken under trace equivalence (strong reads-from prefixes). Column 2 (Column 4) reports the number of successful matches under trace equivalence (strong reads-from prefixes). Column 5 reports the number of times prediction based on strong reads-from prefixes reports an earlier match.

1	2	3	4	5	6
Length of Pattern	#Match in Maz	Time Maz	#Match in Strong RF	#Earlier Match in Strong RF	Time Strong RF.
3	230	10 h 23 m	249	7	10 h 55 m
5	197	9 h 6 m	209	12	10 h 17 m
Total	427	19 h 29 m	458	19	21 h 12 m

Implementation and Setup. We implemented our predictive monitoring algorithms for data races, deadlocks and pattern languages, in Java, obtained by determinizing the non-deterministic monitors obtained from Theorem 7. We evaluate against benchmarks derived from [1, 26, 40], consisting of concurrent programs from a variety of suites: (a) the IBM Contest suite [10], (b) the DaCapo suite [5], (c) the Java Grande suite [39], (d) the Software Infrastructure Repository suite [8], and (e) others [6, 18–20, 23]. For each benchmark program, we generated an execution log using RV-Predict [33] and evaluate all competing algorithms on the same execution. Our experiments were conducted on a 64-bit Linux machine with Java 19 and 400GB heap space. Throughout, we set a timeout of 3 hours for each run of every algorithm. We present brief summary of our results here, and the full result can be found in [2].

7.1 Enhanced Predictive Power of Strong Prefixes

We demonstrate the enhanced predictive power due to our proposed formalism in the context of predictive monitoring against pattern languages [1]. Pattern language specifications take the form $\Sigma^* a_1 \Sigma^* \ldots \Sigma^* a_d \Sigma^*$, and thus include all executions that contain $a_1, \ldots, a_d$ as a sub-sequence. Predictive monitoring against pattern languages can be performed in constant space and linear time under trace equivalence [1].

Implementation and Methodology. M (under trace equivalence) proposed in [1]. To perform predictive monitoring under strong reads-from prefixes, our algorithm M' guesses an appropriate prefix and invokes the predictive monitor M (under trace equivalence) proposed in [1], . Since M consumes constant space, in theory, simulating M' also requires constant space (see also Theorem 7). The resulting space complexity, however, can be prohibitive in practice. For scalability, we employ randomization to select a subset of prefixes, and only inspect these. Our results show that, despite this compromise, the predictive power under strong reads-from prefixes is higher than under trace equivalence. We use 30 benchmark executions, and for each execution, we isolate 20 patterns (of size 3 and 5), from randomly chosen sub-executions of length 5000, following [1]. For each pair of benchmark and pattern, we run the two streaming algorithms (trace equivalence v/s strong reads-from prefixes), on the sub-execution from which the pattern is extracted, allowing us to optimize memory usage. Both algorithms terminate as soon as the pattern is matched, otherwise the algorithms process the entire sub-execution. We use the publicly available implementation of [1].

Evaluation Results. Our results are summarized in Table 1. First, all matches reported under trace equivalence were also reported under strong reads-from prefixes, as expected based on Theorem 6 . Second, out of the 30×20 combinations of executions and patterns, trace equivalence based prediction reports 33 fewer matches as compared to prediction based on strong reads-from prefixes (466 vs 499). The enhancement in prediction power spans patterns of both sizes — 15 extra matches were found for patterns of size 3 and 18 extra matches were found for patterns of size 5. Third, we also collect more fine-grained information — amongst the 466 combinations reported by both, 18 were reported earlier (in a shorter execution prefix) under strong reads-from prefixes, and thus are new violations. Finally, the total time taken for prediction under reads-from prefixes is higher, as expected, but only by 6%. In summary, strong reads-from prefixes offer higher prediction power in practice, with moderate additional overhead.

Table 2. Synchronization-preserving v/s conflict-preserving data races. $\mathcal{N}$ and $\mathcal{T}$ denote the number of events and threads in the executions.

1	2	3	4	5	6	7
Benchmark	$\mathcal{N}$	$\mathcal{T}$	SyncP		ConfP	
			Race	Time	Race	Time
lang	6K	8	400	0.25 s	400	0.96 s
readerswriters	11K	6	199	0.70 s	199	1.10 s
raytracer	15K	4	8	0.16 s	8	0.27 s
ftpserver	49K	12	85	5.70 s	85	7984 s
moldyn	200K	4	103	0.65 s	103	3.24 s
derby	1M	5	29	12.99 s	29	29.3 s
jigsaw	3M	12	6	1.16 s	6	2.76 s
xalan	122M	9	37	149.39 s	37	1075
lufact	134M	5	21951	45.80 s	21951	29.78 s
batik	157M	7	10	0.11 s	10	0.37 s
lusearch	217M	8	232	7.57 s	232	2685 s
tsp	307M	10	143	115.8 s	143	631.8 s
luindex	397M	3	15	0.73 s	15	0.70 s
Total	1338M			341.01 s		12444.28 s

7.2 Strong Reads-From Prefixes v/s Sync-Preservation

We implemented the constant-space linear-time algorithm for sync-preserving data races and deadlocks (Theorem 8) and compare it against the linear-space algorithms due to [26,40], solving the same problem.

Implementation and Methodology. The algorithm guesses strong reads-from prefixes and checks whether the enabled events in them constitute a data race or a deadlock. Following [26,40], we filtered out thread-local events to reduce the space usage of all algorithms. We compare our predictive monitoring algorithm under strong reads-from prefixes (conflict-preserving reorderings) with SyncP [26] and SyncPD [40] under synchronization-preserving prefixes. We use the publicly available implementation of [26,40]. We run all algorithms on the entire executions. For the case of data races, we report the number of events e_2 for which there is an earlier event e_1 such that (e_1, e_2) is a sync-preserving data race. For the case of deadlocks, we report the number of tuples of program locations corresponding to events reported to be in deadlock.

Evaluation Results. We present our results in Table 2 and Table 3. First, observe that the precision of data race and deadlock prediction based on strong reads-from prefixes is exactly the same as the prediction based on synchronization-preservation (compare columns 4 and 6 in both tables). Next, we observe that our implementations (even though constant space) is slower than the optimized algorithms proposed [26]. We conjecture this is because the constants appearing after determinization, are large (of the order of $O(2^{\mathsf{poly}(|\mathcal{X}|+|\mathcal{T}|+|\mathcal{L}|)})$), also resulting in out-of-memory exceptions on some large benchmarks.

Table 3. Synchronization-preserving v/s conflict-preserving deadlocks. $\mathcal{N}$ and $\mathcal{T}$ denote the number of events and threads in the executions.

1	2	3	4	5	6	7
Benchmark	$\mathcal{N}$	$\mathcal{T}$	SyncP		ConfP	
			Deadlock	Time	Deadlock	Time
JDBCMySQL-1	442K	3	2	0.48 s	2	4.45 s
JDBCMySQL-2	442K	3	1	0.43 s	1	0.35 s
ArrayList	2.63M	801	3	2.47 s	–	OOM
IdentityHashMap	2.71M	801	1	1.95 s	1	3.79 s
Stack	2.93M	801	3	3.77 s	3	261 s
LinkedList	3.40M	801	3	3.02 s	3	1174 s
HashMap	3.43M	801	2	2.34 s	–	OOM
WeakHashMap	3.48M	801	2	2.60 s	–	OOM
VecOOMr	3.80M	3	1	2.58 s	1	7.59 s
LinkedHashMap	4.20M	801	2	2.42 s	–	OOM
TreeMap	9.03M	801	2	2.44 s	2	1564 s
Total	36M			24.50 s		>3015.18 s

8   Related Work and Conclusions

Our work is inspired from runtime predictive analysis for testing concurrent programs, where the task is to enhance the coverage of naive dynamic analysis techniques to a larger space of correct reorderings [15,34,35]. A key focus here is to improve the scalability of prediction techniques for concurrency bugs such as data races [21,24,26,31,37,38], deadlocks [20,40], atomicity violations [4,11,27] and more general properties [1,14] for an otherwise intractable problem [25]. The theme of our work is to develop efficient algorithms for predictive concurrency bug detection. We start with the setting of trace theory [28], where questions such as checking whether two events can be flipped, which are intractable in general [12,22,25], can be answered in constant space. The problem of relaxing Mazurkiewicz traces has been studied [7]. Recent work [12] has focused on reasoning about commutativity of *grains* of events.

In contrast, our work takes an orthogonal angle and proposes that, for co-safety properties, one might be able to perform relaxations by exploiting semantic properties of programming constructs in multithreaded shared-memory programs. To this end, strong trace prefixes and its extension on a concrete alphabet Σ_{RWL}, strong reads-from prefixes, where the commutativity between events can be stratified into strong and weak dependencies. This simple relaxation allows us to capture a larger class of concurrency bugs, while still retaining the algorithmic simplicity that event based commutativity offers. We also show connections between prior algorithms for (sync-preserving) data race and deadlock prediction and our formalism, and arrive at asymptotically faster algorithms for them. We envision that combining commutativity based on groups of events [12] and prefix based prediction may be an interesting avenue for future research.

Acknowledgement. We thank the anonymous reviewers for several comments that helped improve the paper. Some initial ideas of this work originated from the discussion with Mahesh Viswanathan and Andreas Pavlogiannis. This work is partially supported by a Singapore Ministry of Education (MoE) Academic Research Fund (AcRF) Tier 1 grant.

References

1. Ang, Z., Mathur, U.: Predictive monitoring against pattern regular languages. Proc. ACM Program. Lang. **8**(POPL) (2024). https://doi.org/10.1145/3632915, https://doi.org/10.1145/3632915
2. Ang, Z., Mathur, U.: Predictive monitoring with strong trace prefixes (2024). https://arxiv.org/abs/2405.10499
3. Bertoni, A., Mauri, G., Sabadini, N.: Membership problems for regular and context-free trace languages. Inf. Comput. **82**(2), 135–150 (1989). https://doi.org/10.1016/0890-5401(89)90051-5, https://www.sciencedirect.com/science/article/pii/0890540189900515
4. Biswas, S., Huang, J., Sengupta, A., Bond, M.D.: Doublechecker: efficient sound and precise atomicity checking. ACM SIGPLAN Not. **49**(6), 28–39 (2014)

5. Blackburn, S.M., et al.: The dacapo benchmarks: java benchmarking development and analysis. In: OOPSLA (2006)

6. Cai, Y., Yun, H., Wang, J., Qiao, L., Palsberg, J.: Sound and efficient concurrency bug prediction. In: Proceedings of the 29th ACM Joint Meeting on European Software Engineering Conference and Symposium on the Foundations of Software Engineering, pp. 255–267 (2021)

7. Diekert, V.: A partial trace semantics for petri nets. Theor. Comput. Sci. **134**(1), 87–105 (1994). https://doi.org/10.1016/0304-3975(94)90280-1

8. Do, H., Elbaum, S.G., Rothermel, G.: Supporting controlled experimentation with testing techniques: An infrastructure and its potential impact. Empir. Softw. Eng. **10**(4), 405–435 (2005). https://doi.org/10.1007/S10664-005-3861-2

9. Elmas, T., Qadeer, S., Tasiran, S.: Goldilocks: a race and transaction-aware java runtime. In: Proceedings of the 28th ACM SIGPLAN Conference on Programming Language Design and Implementation, PLDI 2007, pp. 245-255. Association for Computing Machinery, New York (2007). https://doi.org/10.1145/1250734.1250762

10. Farchi, E., Nir, Y., Ur, S.: Concurrent bug patterns and how to test them. In: 17th International Parallel and Distributed Processing Symposium (IPDPS 2003), 22-26 April 2003, Nice, France, CD-ROM/Abstracts Proceedings, pp. 286. IEEE Computer Society (2003). https://doi.org/10.1109/IPDPS.2003.1213511

11. Farzan, A., Madhusudan, P.: Monitoring atomicity in concurrent programs. In: Gupta, A., Malik, S. (eds.) CAV 2008. LNCS, vol. 5123, pp. 52–65. Springer, Heidelberg (2008). https://doi.org/10.1007/978-3-540-70545-1_8

12. Farzan, A., Mathur, U.: Coarser equivalences for causal concurrency. Proc. ACM Program. Lang. **8**(POPL) (2024). https://doi.org/10.1145/3632873

13. Flanagan, C., Freund, S.N.: Fasttrack: efficient and precise dynamic race detection. In: Proceedings of the 30th ACM SIGPLAN Conference on Programming Language Design and Implementation, PLDI 2009, pp. 121-133. Association for Computing Machinery, New York (2009). https://doi.org/10.1145/1542476.1542490, https://doi.org/10.1145/1542476.1542490

14. Huang, J., Luo, Q., Rosu, G.: Gpredict: generic predictive concurrency analysis. In: Proceedings of the 37th International Conference on Software Engineering, ICSE 2015, vol. 1. pp. 847-857. IEEE Press (2015)

15. Huang, J., Meredith, P.O., Rosu, G.: Maximal sound predictive race detection with control flow abstraction. In: Proceedings of the 35th ACM SIGPLAN Conference on Programming Language Design and Implementation, PLDI 2014, pp. 337-348. Association for Computing Machinery, New York (2014). https://doi.org/10.1145/2594291.2594315

16. Itzkovitz, A., Schuster, A., Zeev-Ben-Mordehai, O.: Toward integration of data race detection in dsm systems. J. Parallel Distributed Comput. **59**(2), 180–203 (1999). https://doi.org/10.1006/jpdc.1999.1574, https://www.sciencedirect.com/science/article/pii/S0743731599915745

17. Jannesari, A., Bao, K., Pankratius, V., Tichy, W.F.: Helgrind+: an efficient dynamic race detector. In: 2009 IEEE International Symposium on Parallel & Distributed Processing, pp. 1–13. IEEE (2009)

18. Joshi, P., Park, C.S., Sen, K., Naik, M.: A randomized dynamic program analysis technique for detecting real deadlocks. ACM Sigplan Not. **44**(6), 110–120 (2009)

19. Jula, H., Tralamazza, D.M., Zamfir, C., Candea, G.: Deadlock immunity: Enabling systems to defend against deadlocks. In: Draves, R., van Renesse, R. (eds.) 8th USENIX Symposium on Operating Systems Design and Implementation, OSDI 2008, 8-10 December 2008, San Diego, California, USA, Proceedings, pp. 295–308. USENIX Association (2008). http://www.usenix.org/events/osdi08/tech/full_papers/jula/jula.pdf

20. Kalhauge, C.G., Palsberg, J.: Sound deadlock prediction. Proc. ACM Program. Lang. 2(OOPSLA) (2018). https://doi.org/10.1145/3276516

21. Kini, D., Mathur, U., Viswanathan, M.: Dynamic race prediction in linear-time. In: Proceedings of the 38th ACM SIGPLAN Conference on Programming Language Design and Implementation, PLDI 2017, pp. 157-170, Association for Computing Machinery, New York (2017). https://doi.org/10.1145/3062341.3062374

22. Kulkarni, R., Mathur, U., Pavlogiannis, A.: Dynamic data-race detection through the fine-grained lens. In: Haddad, S., Varacca, D. (eds.) 32nd International Conference on Concurrency Theory (CONCUR 2021). Leibniz International Proceedings in Informatics (LIPIcs), vol. 203, pp. 16:1–16:23. Schloss Dagstuhl – Leibniz-Zentrum für Informatik, Dagstuhl, Germany (2021). https://doi.org/10.4230/LIPIcs.CONCUR.2021.16, https://drops.dagstuhl.de/entities/document/10.4230/LIPIcs.CONCUR.2021.16

23. Legunsen, O., Hassan, W.U., Xu, X., Roşu, G., Marinov, D.: How good are the specs? a study of the bug-finding effectiveness of existing java api specifications. In: 2016 31st IEEE/ACM International Conference on Automated Software Engineering (ASE), pp. 602–613 (2016)

24. Mathur, U., Kini, D., Viswanathan, M.: What happens-after the first race? enhancing the predictive power of happens-before based dynamic race detection. Proc. ACM Program. Lang. 2(OOPSLA) (2018). https://doi.org/10.1145/3276515

25. Mathur, U., Pavlogiannis, A., Viswanathan, M.: The complexity of dynamic data race prediction. In: Proceedings of the 35th Annual ACM/IEEE Symposium on Logic in Computer Science, LICS 2020, pp. 713-727. Association for Computing Machinery, New York (2020). https://doi.org/10.1145/3373718.3394783

26. Mathur, U., Pavlogiannis, A., Viswanathan, M.: Optimal prediction of synchronization-preserving races. Proc. ACM Program. Lang. 5(POPL) (2021). https://doi.org/10.1145/3434317

27. Mathur, U., Viswanathan, M.: Atomicity checking in linear time using vector clocks. In: Proceedings of the Twenty-Fifth International Conference on Architectural Support for Programming Languages and Operating Systems, pp. 183–199 (2020)

28. Mazurkiewicz, A.: Trace theory. In: Brauer, W., Reisig, W., Rozenberg, G. (eds.) Petri Nets: Applications and Relationships to Other Models of Concurrency, pp. 278–324. Springer, Berlin Heidelberg, Berlin, Heidelberg (1987). https://doi.org/10.1007/978-0-387-09766-4_491

29. Müehlenfeld, A., Wotawa, F.: Fault detection in multi-threaded c++ server applications. In: Proceedings of the 12th ACM SIGPLAN Symposium on Principles and Practice of Parallel Programming, pp. 142–143 (2007)

30. Ochmański, E.: Regular behaviour of concurrent systems. Bull. EATCS 27, 56–67 (1985)

31. Pavlogiannis, A.: Fast, sound, and effectively complete dynamic race prediction. Proc. ACM Program. Lang. 4(POPL) (2019). https://doi.org/10.1145/3371085

32. Pin, J.-E., Weil, P.: Polynomial closure and unambiguous product. In: Fülöp, Z., Gécseg, F. (eds.) ICALP 1995. LNCS, vol. 944, pp. 348–359. Springer, Heidelberg (1995). https://doi.org/10.1007/3-540-60084-1_87

33. Roșu, G., Viswanathan, M.: Testing extended regular language membership incrementally by rewriting. In: Nieuwenhuis, R. (ed.) Rewriting Tech. Appli., pp. 499–514. Springer, Berlin Heidelberg, Berlin, Heidelberg (2003)
34. Said, M., Wang, C., Yang, Z., Sakallah, K.: Generating data race witnesses by an smt-based analysis. In: Proceedings of the Third International Conference on NASA Formal Methods, NFM 2011, pp. 313–327. Springer-Verlag, Berlin (2011). http://dl.acm.org/citation.cfm?id=1986308.1986334
35. Șerbănuță, T.F., Chen, F., Roșu, G.: Maximal causal models for sequentially consistent systems. In: Qadeer, S., Tasiran, S. (eds.) Runtime Verification, pp. 136–150. Springer, Berlin Heidelberg, Berlin, Heidelberg (2013). https://doi.org/10.1007/978-3-642-35632-2_16
36. Serebryany, K., Iskhodzhanov, T.: Threadsanitizer: data race detection in practice. In: WBIA 2009 (2009)
37. Shi, Z., Mathur, U., Pavlogiannis, A.: Optimistic prediction of synchronization-reversal data races. In: Proceedings of the IEEE/ACM 46th International Conference on Software Engineering, ICSE 2024, Association for Computing Machinery, New York (2024). https://doi.org/10.1145/3597503.3639099
38. Smaragdakis, Y., Evans, J., Sadowski, C., Yi, J., Flanagan, C.: Sound predictive race detection in polynomial time. In: Proceedings of the 39th Annual ACM SIGPLAN-SIGACT Symposium on Principles of Programming Languages, POPL 2012, pp. 387-400. Association for Computing Machinery, New York (2012). https://doi.org/10.1145/2103656.2103702, https://doi.org/10.1145/2103656.2103702
39. Smith, L.A., Bull, J.M., Obdržálek, J.: A parallel java grande benchmark suite. In: Proceedings of the 2001 ACM/IEEE Conference on Supercomputing, SC 2001, p. 8. ACM, New York (2001). https://doi.org/10.1145/582034.582042
40. Tunç, H.C., Mathur, U., Pavlogiannis, A., Viswanathan, M.: Sound dynamic deadlock prediction in linear time. Proc. ACM Program. Lang. 7(PLDI), 1733–1758 (2023)

Case Studies and Tools

Monitoring Unmanned Aircraft: Specification, Integration, and Lessons-Learned

Jan Baumeister[1]([✉])[iD], Bernd Finkbeiner[1][iD], Florian Kohn[1][iD], Florian Löhr[2], Guido Manfredi[2], Sebastian Schirmer[3][iD], and Christoph Torens[3][iD]

[1] CISPA Helmholtz Center for Information Security, Saarbrücken, Germany
{jan.baumeister,finkbeiner,florian.kohn}@cispa.de
[2] Volocopter GmbH, Bruchsal, Germany
{florian.loehr,guido.manfredi}@volocopter.com
[3] German Aerospace Center (DLR), Cologne, Germany
{sebastian.schirmer,christoph.torens}@dlr.de

Abstract. This paper reports on the integration of runtime monitoring into fully-electric aircraft designed by Volocopter, a German aircraft manufacturer of electric multi-rotor helicopters. The runtime monitor recognizes hazardous situations and system faults. Since the correct operation of the monitor is critical for the safety of the aircraft, the development of the monitor must follow strict aeronautical standards. This includes the integration of the monitor into different development environments, such as log-file analysis, hardware/software-in-the-loop testing, and test flights. We have used the stream-based monitoring framework RTLola to generate monitors for a range of requirements. In this paper, we present representative monitoring specifications and our lessons learned from integrating the generated monitors. Our main finding is that the specification and the integration need to be decoupled, because the specification remains stable throughout the development process, whereas the different development stages require a separate integration of the monitor into each environment. We achieve this decoupling with a novel abstraction layer in the monitoring framework that adapts the monitor to each environment without affecting the core component generated from the specification. The decoupling of the integration has also allowed us to react quickly to the frequent changes in the hardware and software environment of the monitor due to the fast-paced development of the aircraft in a startup company.

Keywords: Runtime Verification · Stream Monitoring · Autonomous Aircraft

This work was partially supported by the Aviation Research Program LuFo of the German Federal Ministry for Economic Affairs and Energy as part of "Volocopter Sicherheitstechnologie zur robusten eVTOL Flugzustandsabsicherung durch formales Monitoring"(No. 20Q1963C).

A. Gurfinkel and V. Ganesh (Eds.): CAV 2024, LNCS 14682, pp. 207–218, 2024.
https://doi.org/10.1007/978-3-031-65630-9_10

1   Introduction

The new generation of fully-electric aircraft pioneered by companies like Volocopter promises a revolution in urban air mobility. Fully-electric aircraft air taxis, cargo drones, and longer-range passenger aircraft will provide transit solutions that are emission-free and thus more sustainable and efficient than traditional forms of air transport. A critical part of the safety engineering of such aircraft is to analyze log-files and tests, as well as the real-time data obtained during the actual flight, so that the health status of the system can be assessed and mitigation procedures can be initiated when needed. In this paper, we report on the design and integration of formally specified monitors into aircraft developed by Volocopter, based on the monitoring framework RTLola. The goal of our collaboration over the past three years has been to explore the benefits and challenges of applying formal runtime verification within the strict aeronautical standards of aircraft development.

Volocopter specializes in the design, manufacturing, and operations of electric Vertical Takeoff and Landing (eVTOL) vehicles. The company targets Urban Air Mobility (UAM) operations, i.e., passenger and cargo transportation above and around cities. These operations involve high population density on the ground and high traffic density in the air. Consequently, all developments must meet the highest level of safety similar to airliners: one failure for every billion hours flown. To ensure such a level of safety, the design of the vehicles follows aeronautical standards, especially SAE's ARP4754b [14] to ensure the coherency between the concept of operation, requirements, design, and implementation. The development cycle described in this standard uses a layered approach with multiple verification and validation steps.

RTLola [3,8] is a formal monitoring framework that consists of a stream-based specification language for real-time properties, an interpreter, and compilers into software- and hardware-based execution platforms. An RTLola specification of hazardous situations and system failures is statically analyzed in terms of consistency and resource usage and then automatically translated into an FPGA-based monitor. This approach leads to highly efficient, parallelized monitors with formal guarantees on the noninterference of the monitor with the normal operation of the monitored system.

Previous case studies with RTLola [2] and similar frameworks, such as R2U2 [10] and Copilot [12], have already shown that properties that are critical for the safety of the aircraft can readily be expressed in such formal languages and that the resulting monitors can be integrated into real systems. Our ambition has been to go beyond such one-time applications, and integrate the specified monitors into the complete development process. This means that the generated monitors are not only integrated into the specific setup of the case study, but rather are continuously adapted according to the needs of the development process.

We consider monitoring in all stages of the development process. Initially, the role of the monitor is to annotate log-files and guide the user during an offline analysis, e.g. these annotations split a test flight into flight-phases for separate inspection. Next, the monitor validates data from test-benches that check that external components conform to their specifications, such as delivering data within deadlines. Finally, the monitor validates safety requirements during test flights. The monitoring specifications are based on the requirements of the various regulatory authorities and cover a range of safety-critical requirements from single-component checks to system-level health.

Our main finding is that the specification and the integration need to be decoupled, because the specification remains stable throughout the development process, whereas the different development stages require a separate integration of the monitor into each environment. We achieve this decoupling with a novel abstraction layer in the monitoring framework that adapts the monitor to each environment without affecting the core component generated from the specification. In the abstraction layer, the monitor is framed with two new components, the *event conversion* and the *verdict converison*. The decoupling of the integration has also allowed us to react quickly to the frequent changes in the hardware and software environment of the monitor due to the fast-paced development of the aircraft in a startup company.

1.1   Related Work

Runtime monitoring is a scalable dynamic verification approach that has been applied to a variety of domains [9,11]. For cyber-physical systems, many monitoring tools exist [1,2,12], but despite integration being an important part of the usage of monitoring   [7], tools are often specific to certain environments and leave embedding in different environments to the user, i.e., the user needs to establish a connection, parse received events, and forward it to the monitor. For some specific environments, these user efforts are reduced. For instance, SOTER [4] a specification language that is based on the P language [5], was recently extended [16] to produce code for the Robot Operating System (ROS), which allows to just specify which ROS topics are subscribed and published. Similarly, TeSSLa features keywords to subscribe and publish ROS topics [16]. A more generic approach is pursued by R2U2 Version 3.0 [10] which allows to specify C-like structs. This makes it easy for engineers to receive structs and just forward them to the monitor unit. In this work, we foster this kind of generalization by providing an automatic mapping of the received and the forwarded events.

2   Stream-Based Monitoring

RTLOLA is a real-time monitoring framework [8] aimed at, but not exclusively applicable to, cyber-physical systems. At its core is a stream-based specification language that distinguishes between two kinds of streams: Input streams represent sensor readings from the system under observation. Output streams perform computations over these input streams and other output streams. Special kinds of output streams, called triggers, define violations based on boolean conditions.

Equipped with a message, they notify the system operator when a violation is detected. Consider the following example:

```
1  input altitude: Float
2  output average_alt @1Hz := altitude.aggregate(over: 60s, using: avg).defaults(to: 0.0)
3  trigger average_alt > 300.0
```

In this example, the monitor observes the altitude of the system through the input stream `altitude`. The output stream `average_alt` aggregates all values of this input stream over the last minute and computes the average of these values. It also highlights the real-time capabilities of RTLOLA. By explicitly annotating the output stream with a frequency, the monitor cannot only react to events but also proactively perform computations. More concretely, the output stream evaluates at a fixed frequency of 1 Hz. The final defined trigger then notifies an operator if the average altitude is above 300.

3 Setup

All components that are integrated into aircrafts designed by Volocopter need to follow aeronautical standards, especially SAE's ARP4754b [14]. This standard ensures that the concept of operation, requirements, design, and implementation are coherent. In general, it describes a development cycle using a layered approach with multiple verification and validation steps, i.e., new components are validated in different environments that get closer to the operation with each step.

Integrating a monitor in this setup is two-folded: 1. the monitor verifies the behavior of new components and 2. the monitor itself needs to be verified The monitor can provide valuable feedback when new components undergo the aforementioned validation steps. This feedback includes statistical assessments or violations of given requirements. Yet, the monitor as a safety-critical component needs to be evaluated in the same manner.

3.1 Monitoring Applications

This section presents four applications that highlight the benefit of the monitors feedback during the development of new components:

1. *Debugging.* A monitor is developed alongside the component giving full information about its internal state. During the execution of the system, the monitor checks whether the component works as intended by the developer used as a white-box testing component.
2. *Validation.* The monitor is developed independently of the component and checks its behavior based on the inputs and outputs of defined test cases. Hence, the monitor functions as a black-box testing component. The monitor output on these test cases is then used as a report for internal validation, validation of components by external companies, or as proof of conformity for aviation authorities.

3. *Pre-Post-Flight Analysis.* Before the flight, the monitor checks whether all necessary components are operational. After the flight, the monitor computes more sophisticated information to better evaluate the flight and detect irregularities that were not detected during the flight.

4. *In-Flight Analysis/Safe Integration.* The monitor communicates with the remote operator. e.g., through the User Interface of the ground control station, to provide feedback about the safety of the drone. It validates the correctness of individual components to ensure a safe flight or monitors the flight operation. For instance, it supports the pilot by checking that the drone stays within safe flight parameters such as a geofence.

Before presenting concrete specifications for each application in Sect. 5, we elaborate on the validation of a monitor.

3.2 Development Cycle for the Monitor

This section introduces the four environments into which the monitor must be integrated to validate its correctness.

1. *Log-File Analysis.* This step evaluates the functional correctness of the specification. We test the generated monitors against traces that violate or satisfy the specification and analyze the output of the monitor.

2. *Software-in-the-Loop (SiL).* The monitor interacts with simulated systems and environments. This step is crucial for a runtime monitor since most temporal behaviors are not visible until these tests.

3. *Hardware-in-the-loop (HiL).* This step is similar to the SiL environment. However, the monitor and the system run on the actual resource-constrained hardware used in the aircraft. This setup brings even more time-related effects to the evaluation and allows an evaluation with replayed flight data.

4. *Flight Testing.* Running the monitor in parallel with the flying aircraft allows for assessing the impact of all effects coming from the aircraft, the ground system, and the environment.

The integration of the monitors in the different validation environments poses new challenges for the monitoring framework. In our experience, each step in the development process relies on different ways of communication. For instance, in the log-file analysis, events are processed in CSV-format, while during test flights, the communication with the monitor uses a custom protocol over TCP. Yet, the changes in the monitor should be as minimal as possible to simplify its validation. Specifically, the specification has to remain unchanged after the *Log-file Analysis* as otherwise its functional correctness is not guaranteed anymore.

4   Abstract Integration

In this section, we present our approach integrating the RTLOLA framework [8] into the different environments described in Sect. 3.

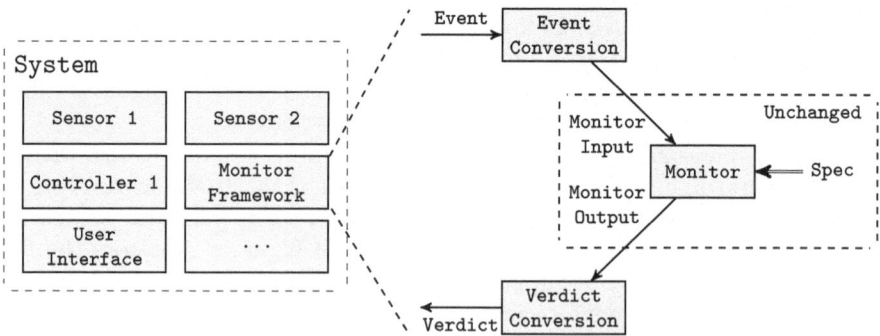

Fig. 1. Overview of the Generalization

Figure 1 shows an overview of this approach. The system on the left side represents the UAV under development. From a monitoring perspective, the current step in the development cycle does not influence the underlying monitor, only its integration into the system. This is depicted on the right side of Fig. 1. The monitor framework receives or requests incoming data from the different components of the system (Event), analyses this data, and produces an output (Verdict). In the center of the monitoring framework is a fixed monitor generated from a formal specification. This monitor has a fixed representation of the Monitor Input and Monitor Output that are independent of the integration.

To bridge the communication gap between the system and the monitor, we propose an abstraction layer that translates system outputs to monitor inputs and vice versa. This abstraction also generalizes the monitor's interface such that no expert knowledge about the concrete monitor is necessary to integrate the monitor. This abstraction layer can vary depending on the specific integration into the development cycle but allows the monitor to remain unchanged following the idea of decoupling the specification from the integration.

Our approach introduces two translation components: the Event Conversion and the Verdict Conversion. Each component is again split into two parts: *data-acquisition/data-dispatch* and *data-conversion* to allow a generic implementation of the *data-acquisition/data-dispatch*. This results in reusable and maintainable implementation while keeping the changes between the development stages minimal.

In the following, we elaborate on the data-acquisition and data-conversion of the *Event Conversion* in more detail. The results are transferable to the *Verdict Conversion*.

4.1   Common Interfaces

The Event Conversion is a generic translation layer between the systems output and the monitor input. During instantiation it validates the mapping between the system output and the monitor input, representing the input streams in the specification. Hence, it checks that the Events are a superset of the Monitor Input avoiding any runtime errors resulting from an invalid mapping. The *data-acquisition* part of the Event Conversion is handled through the *Event Source* interface, while the *data-conversion* is handled by an *Event Factory*. Both interfaces are defined in Fig. 2.

```
1 | pub trait EventSource {
2 |   fn next_event(&mut self)
3 |     -> Result<Event, Error>;
4 | }
```

(a) Event Source Interface

```
1 | pub trait EventFactory {
2 |   fn new(map: &InputStreams, cfg: Config)
3 |     -> Result<Self, Error>;
4 |   fn create(&mut self, ev: Event)
5 |     -> Result<MonitorInput, Error>;
6 | }
```

(b) Event Factory Interface

Fig. 2. Common interfaces for the Event Conversion.

The *Event Source* consists of a single function called next_event. It is used to communicate to the system that the monitor is ready to accept the next event. The *Event Factory* as a counterpart has two functions: The new function gets a description of the input streams derived from the specification and the configuration of the *Event Source*. It then checks if each input in the specification can be matched with the data provided by the Event Factory implementation. If successful, it computes a static mapping for each input stream to a data segment in an incoming Event. The second function create is called for every Event and creates the internal event structure Monitor Input, given the input mapping.

Implementation. We implemented the approach from this section in the RTLOLA framework and were able to provide implementations for a variety of *Event Sources* that are independent of the data format they receive. These include basic file-based input methods such as reading from stdin or a local file, up to network protocols that receive data over UDP, TCP, or MQTT. We also provide ready-to-use *Event Factories* to parse, for example, data in CSV or PCAP format as well as a binary data parser derived from a user-provided configuration.

Yet, implementing a custom *Event Factory* still requires knowledge about the structure of the Monitor Input that is undesired for a successful integration in real-production where implementations need to be maintained by non-monitoring experts. In the RTLOLA framework, we provide further abstractions over the interfaces presented in Fig. 2 to reduce the required knowledge about the monitoring framework.

```
1 | #[derive(ValueFactory)]
2 | #[factory(prefix)]
3 | struct GPS {
4 |   lat: Float64,
5 |   lon: Float64
6 | }
```

Fig. 3. Interfacing a custom data structure.

These abstractions range from helper implementations encapsulating common functionality to procedural macros that automatically generate implementations

Validation Environments			
Log-File	SiL	HiL	Test Flight

Debugging	Flight-Phase-Detection
Validation	Remote-Control-System
Pre-Post-Flight	System Checks
In-Flight	Flight-Phase-Detection, Geofence
Safe-Intergration	Detect-And-Avoid

Fig. 4. Overview of the concrete integrations that have been performed in the research project

of these interfaces. Figure 3 shows an example of the macro application. It demonstrates a simplified version of a GPS-Package, exposing the fields of the struct to input streams named GPS_lat and GPS_lon.

5   Concrete Integration of Representative Specifications

This section provides a set of representative specifications to validate our approach presented in Sect. 4. The specifications have been obtained by collaborating with flight engineers or from official RTCA [13] standards and cover all monitoring applications.

Figure 4 provides an overview of the concrete specifications and the integration of the generated monitors. The x-axis in this graph visualizes the different environments in which the monitor was integrated, labeled at the top of the figure. The y-axis of the graph in Fig. 4 maps the specifications to their application from Sect. 3.1.

In our setup, log-files are usually given in the csv-format, the SiL is a Matlab Simulation or a simplified replay of log-files and the Hil is a concrete replay of the simulated data or flights on the actual hardware. The test flights were performed on the VoloDrone, a cargo transportation drone that offers highly automated flights with a range of 40km and a payload of up to 200kg. Not all monitors could be validated up to a flight test, but we validated our approach in at least two environments presented in Sect. 3.2. In our experience, the provided *Event Sources* are sufficient for all environments. We either used the *Event Source* to access data stored in files or used the implementations for the different network protocols from Sect. 4. For the concrete implementation of the *Event Factories*, we either use the ready-to-use *CSV Event Factory* or create new implementations using the macros shown in Fig. 3. These implementations do not require any internal knowledge of the monitoring tool as intended by our approach.

We published the specifications on Github[1] after replacing some sensitive information, e.g., by replacing some streams with arbitrary constants.

The rest of the section describes the general idea of the specifications and refers to the concrete monitoring application.

---

[1] https://github.com/reactive-systems/rtlola-uav-specifications.

```
1   input rpm : Int64
2   input src : UInt8
3   output rpm_1 eval when src == ROTOR_1 with abs(rpm)
4   output rpm_2 eval when src == ROTOR_2 with abs(rpm)
5   ...
6   output rpm_on_check := avg(rpm_1.hold(or: 0), rpm_2.hold(or: 0), ...) > ε_rpm_on
7   output rpm_on @1s := rpm_on_check.aggregate(over: 1s, using: avg, or: 0.0) > ε_rpm_on_per
8   ...
9   output phase_1 := ¬take_off ∧ ¬landed ∧ rpm_on ∧ ¬rpm_in_air
```

Fig. 5. Excerpt of the specification of the Flight-Phase-Detection

```
1   /// Property 1: Log message increment
2   output valid_seq_number := seq_number = seq_number.offset(by: -1, or: -1) + 1
3   /// Property 7: RC fallback test
4   output main_fallback_valid_dyn
5       spawn when lost_connection_to_master
6       close when switch_to_secondary ∨ both_rc_disconnected
7       eval @200ms with false
8   output main_fallback_valid @true := main_fallback_valid_dyn.hold(or: true)
```

Fig. 6. Excerpt of the requirements specific to one RCC

Flight-Phase-Detection (FPD). The FPD specification detects different flight phases, helping the debugging of correct automated flights. In the log-file analysis, the monitor annotates previous test flights pointing the engineer to critical points, e.g., when no clear phase could be detected. In the software and hardware simulation, we evaluate the handling of asynchronous inputs and the timing of the monitor. For a final flight test, the monitor was integrated into the ground station to check if a flight phase is always detected moving the monitor also to the in-flight application.

Figure 5 presents partially the specification for the FPD. It gets data from several sensors and computes binary flags describing the current state of the drone. One example is the rpm_one_check flag that compares the average rotations per minute of all rotors against a threshold. In general, a simple state machine then decides based on these flags if a flight phase is detected and which one. However, the data of the sensors arrives asynchronously with different frequencies and we need to synchronize the flags for the comparison. For this synchronization, the streams rpm_on aggregate over the corresponding flags, computing the percentage of how often the condition is satisfied during the last second. This value is then used in phase_1 stream for the flight phase detection instead of asynchronous rpm_one_check flag.

Remote-Control System (RCS). Assuring a safe development is especially challenging when combining in-house products with commercial off-the-shelf hardware or software products. In our example, we validated the correctness of an RCS that receives flight commands from different sources and dependent on the configuration decides which source should be used by the system. More concretely, we used RTLoLA to validate that the requirements given to the company developing the RCS are satisfied by the resulting product. Besides the in-house validation, this approach comes with certification evidence that can be submitted to the safety agency for the certification process.

As a redundant system, the RCS runs several instances of remote control computers (RCCs) and unions their output. Figure 6 presents some stream-declarations for requirements validating each RCC individually. This specification includes checks of simple invariants such as property one that validates if the sequence number increments, but also includes complex real-time properties exemplified with property seven. The stream declarations for this property implement a watchdog. It reports a violation in the case that the connection to the main controller is lost and the RCC does not switch from the main to the secondary controller in a time frame of 200ms.

System Checks. We developed a specification to validate the system parameters of different sensors. This specification included requirements monitoring the battery level and voltage drops, pre-flight sensor inconsistencies, and accelerations bound. Due to the sensible information of this specification that requires knowledge of the complete system, we cannot publish this specification.

Geofence. Defining a geography volume and a contingency volume, where the UAV will operate and can be used to maneuver in case of a problem, is part of a risk assessment required for a flight permit in the specific category [6]. This risk assessment also requires a runtime validation that the position of the UAV is within these bounds for which we use the monitors generated from an RTLOLA specification. Similar to the FPD, we integrated the monitor in the ground station to communicate with the remote pilot. We used the geofence specification from previous case-studies with RTLola [2,15] describing the intersection between the flight vehicle line and the geofence polygon. Further, this paper extends the specification to predict a possible breach of the geofence by computing the minimum distance to each polygon line and to approximate the time until that breach.

Detect-And-Avoid (DAA). We use the validation of the DAA function as a representative specification for the safe integration monitoring application. This function is essential for any UAV flying beyond visual line of sight and ensures that the UAV avoids any collision with the surrounding traffic. One of the most common sensors in commercial aviation is the ADS-B in receiver which can sense all surrounding aircraft equipped with ADS-B out emitters. However, this sensor is susceptible to attacks by spoofing, so the RTCA standard [13] demands a safe integration in which this sensor needs to be supported by a secondary sensor, usually an "active surveillance" sensor. Instead of merging both signals, it is common practice to use the active surveillance sensor data to check if parts or all of the ADS-B in signal have been compromised. The challenges for the RTLOLA specification are similar to the flight phase detection. The specification compares data from sensors with different frequencies and validates these frequencies. Compared to the FPD, the standard assumes in its validation these frequencies, so a comparison with the last values is sufficient instead of aggregating the data.

6 Conclusion

This paper presents the results of our research project investigating the use of runtime monitors implemented in the RTLOLA framework for the development of unmanned aircraft systems. We demonstrate the benefits of decoupling the specification and integration when the monitor has to undergo the same development as other safety-critical components, in this safety-critical environment. To keep the changes for the monitor during the development as minimal as possible, we presented an abstraction for monitoring frameworks. This abstraction introduces two layers that translate between system outputs and monitoring inputs and vice versa. We conducted a large case study to validate our approach and presented representative specifications for different monitoring applications derived from aeronautical safety standards and internal requirements from Volocopter. In a final step, we performed a test flight where the monitor reported its feedback to the ground control station used by the remote pilot. From a monitoring perspective, this approach can be used to start the development of automatic contingencies triggered by the monitor instead of notifying the pilot.

References

1. Bartocci, E., et al.: Specification-based monitoring of cyber-physical systems: a survey on theory, tools and applications. In: Bartocci, E., Falcone, Y. (eds.) Lectures on Runtime Verification. LNCS, vol. 10457, pp. 135–175. Springer, Cham (2018). https://doi.org/10.1007/978-3-319-75632-5_5
2. Baumeister, J., Finkbeiner, B., Schirmer, S., Schwenger, M., Torens, C.: RTLola cleared for take-off: monitoring autonomous aircraft. In: Lahiri, S.K., Wang, C. (eds.) CAV 2020. LNCS, vol. 12225, pp. 28–39. Springer, Cham (2020). https://doi.org/10.1007/978-3-030-53291-8_3
3. Baumeister, J., Finkbeiner, B., Schwenger, M., Torfah, H.: FPGA stream-monitoring of real-time properties. CoRR abs/ arXiv: 2003.12477 (2020)
4. Desai, A., Ghosh, S., Seshia, S.A., Shankar, N., Tiwari, A.: SOTER: a runtime assurance framework for programming safe robotics systems. In: 49th Annual IEEE/IFIP International Conference on Dependable Systems and Networks, DSN 2019, Portland, OR, USA, 24-27 June 2019, pp. 138–150. IEEE (2019) https://doi.org/10.1109/DSN.2019.00027
5. Desai, A., Gupta, V., Jackson, E.K., Qadeer, S., Rajamani, S.K., Zufferey, D.: P: safe asynchronous event-driven programming. In: Boehm, H., Flanagan, C. (eds.) ACM SIGPLAN Conference on Programming Language Design and Implementation, PLDI 2013, Seattle, WA, USA, 16-19 June 2013, pp. 321–332. ACM (2013) https://doi.org/10.1145/2491956.2462184
6. European Union Aviation Safety Agency (EASA): Specific operations risk assessment (sora) (2019). https://www.easa.europa.eu/en/domains/civil-drones-rpas/specific-category-civil-drones/specific-operations-risk-assessment-sora

7. Falcone, Y., Krstic, S., Reger, G., Traytel, D.: A taxonomy for classifying runtime verification tools. Int. J. Softw. Tools Technol. Transf. **23**(2), 255–284 (2021). https://doi.org/10.1007/S10009-021-00609-Z

8. Faymonville, P., et al.: StreamLAB: stream-based monitoring of cyber-physical systems. In: Dillig, I., Tasiran, S. (eds.) CAV 2019. LNCS, vol. 11561, pp. 421–431. Springer, Cham (2019). https://doi.org/10.1007/978-3-030-25540-4_24

9. Henzinger, T.A., Karimi, M., Kueffner, K., Mallik, K.: Monitoring algorithmic fairness. In: Enea, C., Lal, A. (eds.) Computer Aided Verification, pp. 358–382. Springer Nature Switzerland, Cham (2023). https://doi.org/10.1007/978-3-031-37703-7_17

10. Johannsen, C., Jones, P., Kempa, B., Rozier, K.Y., Zhang, P.: R2u2 version 3.0: Reimagining a toolchain for specification, resource estimation, and optimized observer generation for runtime verification in hardware and software. In: Enea, C., Lal, A. (eds.) Computer Aided Verification, pp. 483–497. Springer Nature Switzerland, Cham (2023). https://doi.org/10.1007/978-3-031-37709-9_23

11. Junges, S., Torfah, H., Seshia, S.A.: Runtime monitors for markov decision processes. In: Silva, A., Leino, K.R.M. (eds.) CAV 2021. LNCS, vol. 12760, pp. 553–576. Springer, Cham (2021). https://doi.org/10.1007/978-3-030-81688-9_26

12. Perez, I., Dedden, F., Goodloe, A.: Copilot 3. Tech. rep. (2020). https://ntrs.nasa.gov/citations/20200003164

13. Radio Technical Commission for Aeronautics (RTCA): Minimum operational performance standards (mops) for detect and avoid (daa) systems (2022). https://my.rtca.org/productdetails?id=a1B36000003FXGyEAO

14. S-18 Aircraft and Sys Dev and Safety Assessment Committee: Guidelines for development of civil aircraft and systems arp4754b (2023). https://doi.org/10.4271/ARP4754B

15. Schirmer, S., Torens, C.: Safe Operation Monitoring for Specific Category Unmanned Aircraft, pp. 393–419. Springer International Publishing, Cham (2022). https://doi.org/10.1007/978-3-030-83144-8_16

16. Shivakumar, S., Torfah, H., Desai, A., Seshia, S.A.: Soter on ros: a run-time assurance framework on the robot operating system. In: Deshmukh, J., Ničković, D. (eds.) Runtime Verification, pp. 184–194. Springer International Publishing, Cham (2020). https://doi.org/10.1007/978-3-030-60508-7_10

Testing the Migration from Analog to Software-Based Railway Interlocking Systems

Anna Becchi[1,2]([✉]) , Alessandro Cimatti[2] , and Giuseppe Scaglione[3]

[1] University of Trento, Trento, Italy
[2] Fondazione Bruno Kessler, Trento, Italy
{abecchi,cimatti}@fbk.eu
[3] RFI Rete Ferroviaria Italiana, Roma, Italy
g.scaglione@rfi.it

Abstract. We work in the context of a tool set developed for the Italian Railway Network supporting the migration of legacy relay-based interlocking systems to a new software-based implementation. We propose to generate test cases from the analog implementation in a way that they are significant for a comparison with a cycle-based computational model, by leveraging stable states abstraction. Our methodology found actual bugs in the new code that were missed by other analyses, and aids in documenting the expected differences with the legacy behaviors.

Keywords: railway interlockings systems · model-based testing · legacy systems · relay-based circuits · model checking

1 Introduction

Railway Interlocking Systems (RIS) implement the controlling logic that regulates train traffic and prevents collisions in stations and railroad crossings. In Italy, RIS were first implemented decades ago with electro-mechanical circuits based on relays. Although this solution is working safely, the adopted technology limits flexibility and makes maintenance difficult. For these reasons, the Italian Railway Network (RFI) is migrating to a new software-based solution.

A tool-supported methodology for the specification, implementation, and verification of interlocking systems has been recently developed in an ongoing project between Fondazione Bruno Kessler (FBK) and RFI [5]. Here, C code is automatically generated starting from standardized requirements written in Controlled Natural Language (CNL) by railway experts. Given the critical nature of the application, the project involves support for formal verification and testing of the produced code against the specifications it was generated from.

A key observation is that the legacy relay-based circuits are considered to be the golden specification of what RIS should implement and guarantee: hence, the formalized requirements that the new software originates from must be checked to be compliant with the old implementation, and the project includes a strategy for *validating the migration* to the new development.

A. Gurfinkel and V. Ganesh (Eds.): CAV 2024, LNCS 14682, pp. 219–232, 2024.
https://doi.org/10.1007/978-3-031-65630-9_11

The comparison between the new software (SwRIS) and the old circuits (ReRIS) faces several difficulties. First, ReRIS were engineered and optimized several years ago[1], and a formal collection of requirements applicable to a software development process is missing. Moreover, they are available only as handwritten drawings on paper, making the inspection and their understanding even more limited to a handful of people.

Second, SwRIS define generic types and classes that can be instantiated to generate the code for a given train station by assigning values to parameters. Such parameters define the topology of the station (e.g., the number and orientation of routes, switches, etc.) and their instantiation is called a *configuration*. Instead, ReRIS exist only in their concrete form, for specific train stations.

Third, SwRIS and ReRIS differ in the set of variables used and, most importantly, in the computational model. While the software is cycle-based, with a discrete interpretation of time, the circuits depend on their intrinsic continuous aspects (flowing of electrical current, delays in capacitors charging, ...).

Finally, a complete equivalence between ReRIS and SwRIS is *not* expected. On one hand, the new software is specified to cover *more* functionalities than before. On the other hand, ReRIS's safety relies on several normative rules that the railway operators should respect when interacting with the system: many of these rules are now integrated into the controlling logic of the new software, therefore preventing human errors by blocking illicit signals. Hence, it is expected to have different behaviors under certain stimuli, e.g., a scenario that is possible in ReRIS cannot be simulated in the SwRIS if it breaks the normative ReRIS rules. Moreover, it would be important to properly document which assumptions, that were implicit in the ReRIS, have been embedded in the SwRIS.

In this paper, we describe our strategy to address these difficulties when pursuing the goal of testing SwRIS against test cases extracted from ReRIS.

For making available ReRIS in a format that is amenable to formal analyses, we leverage the tool NORMA [4] developed for RFI to digitalize and compile in timed transition systems the drawings of the relay-based circuits. We benefit from the NORMA's functionality that allows the user to analyze a portion of the whole ReRIS[2], and inject constraints and assumptions on the open inputs and environment. By combining a part of the ReRIS with a stub that summarizes in an abstract way the surrounding circuits, we are able to symbolically handle a set of concrete configurations simultaneously.

Facing the comparison of two different computational models, we build on the Abstraction Modulo Stability (AMS) framework [7]. AMS allows the user to isolate the stable states traversed when accomplishing an action, disregarding the internal transient steps needed. Applied in this context, by filtering the stable

---

[1] The circuits were developed for different train stations throughout the 20th century, roughly until the 1980s.

[2] The transition system for the entire station is huge and likely to encounter scalability issues if analyzed monolithically. Besides, the activity of collecting and digitalizing the available circuits is still ongoing and some parts may be yet to be compiled.

states, we obtain scenarios that should be shared by the two implementations although they are internally working differently.

Guided by different coverage criteria we extract a set of stable scenarios, i.e., sequences of stable states, from the ReRIS. In contrast with classic model-based testing, where test cases are extracted from the abstract model of the system's specifications, we derive test cases from a different concrete implementation used as a reference. With a mapping provided by domain experts, every ReRIS scenario (expressed in terms of electrical variables) is then translated in a SwRIS test case (expressed in terms of software variables). Due to the generality of the stub added to the ReRIS transition system, the obtained tests can be instantiated in multiple configurations. After running the tests on the corresponding configured code, we analyze the failing cases and distinguish (1) scenarios that have been deliberately excluded in the SwRIS (and that must be documented), or (2) scenarios witnessing real bugs in the SwRIS.

We show the benefits of integrating such an activity in the ongoing deployment of the new software. We extract scenarios from the relay-based implementation of a railroad switch and run the tests on the new code for a number of real train stations. The analysis of the failed tests reported more than 10 real bugs originating from errors in the specifications the new model-based development starts with: although compliant with its requirements, the new software was unintentionally behaving differently from the legacy reference implementation. Other failed tests produced documentation about expected differences between SwRIS and ReRIS.

The rest of the paper is structured as follows: Sect. 2 gives a high-level description of the legacy and the new development processes; Sect. 3 focuses on the extraction of scenarios from ReRIS and their translation in tests for SwRIS; Sect. 4 studies related works; Sect. 5 shows the results of including this testing strategy in the development of SwRIS; we conclude in Sect. 6.

2 Operational Setting

Let p represent a configuration for a train station assigning parameters such as the number of railway switches, the number and disposition of routes passing through the station, etc.

On the left-hand side of Fig. 1, it is described how relay-based RIS had been developed decades ago (see label *legacy development*). Starting from laws and regulations documented in official books, a human modeler drew the schematics of one train station at a time by combining copies of basic "general-purpose" circuits (e.g., the one for a generic railroad switch) and linking their terminals. Only these final results, named ReRIS[p] in Fig. 1, are now available.

On the right-hand side of Fig. 1, the label *new development* points at the main phases of the new methodology for the definition of *software-based* RIS.

AIDA is the part taking care of the generation of the new code. The new process starts with Functional Requirements Specifications (FRS), written by domain experts in Controlled Natural Language. From these, SysML diagrams

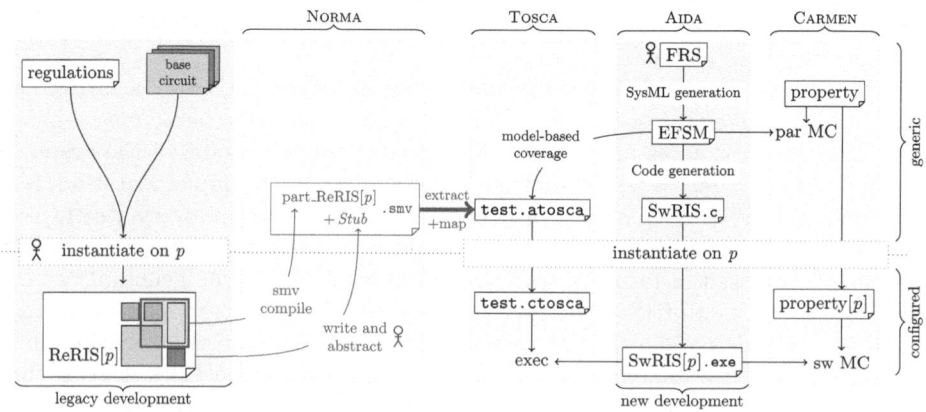

Fig. 1. Legacy development of relay-based RIS (on the left), tool set supporting the development of a software-based implementation (on the right).

(and documentation) are automatically produced: such diagrams model in the form of an Extended Finite State Machine (EFSM) how the main railway entities interact with each other from a general (or abstract) perspective, i.e., without referring to a specific station. Generic C code (SwRIS.c) is automatically generated from the diagrams: a configured version of the logic is obtained by plugging the parameters of a specific configuration p, hence obtaining an executable SwRIS[p].

The *new development* in AIDA is supported by other tools: CARMEN, providing both parametric [12] and software model-checking [18], and TOSCA, providing testing functionalities. Interestingly, abstract test cases (.atosca files) are written by the user in Controlled Natural Language, or generated covering the EFSM models. These tests are called abstract since they specify general constraints on the declared variables which may identify multiple configurations. TOSCA allows for instantiating an abstract test case to concrete and executable versions (.ctosca) for all the known configurations p that are consistent with the declarations. An execution environment, including a simulator of the physical yard and a simulator of the operator interface, then executes the test running the corresponding configured logic SwRIS[p].

Finally, the tool NORMA [4,25] completes the picture: it allows for the digitalization of the ReRIS[p] and their translation in timed transition systems (in Timed SMV language). This step is fundamental to enable standard analyses, such as simulations and reverse-engineering, on the circuits, otherwise available only as handwritten drawings on paper.

3   Bridging the Gap Between ReRIS and SwRIS

In this section, we describe the process of extraction of test cases from ReRIS corresponding to the red part in Fig. 1. In Sect. 3.1 we show how to collect simulations from a generic transition system according to a given coverage criterion. In Sect. 3.2 we describe how the transition system compiled from a subset of circuits can be combined with a handwritten *Stub* for the missing parts, and obtain a model that abstracts multiple configured schemas. In Sect. 3.3 we show how to map a simulation into an abstract test case, and in Sect. 3.4 we discuss the outcomes of the analysis of the failing cases.

Background. We assume familiarity with Satisfiability Modulo Theory (SMT) [6] and Linear Temporal Logic (LTL) [11,24]. We use capital letters X, Y for sets of variables, X', Y' for their next versions, and x, y for their interpretations. We abuse the notation and write $P = Q$ for $P \leftrightarrow Q$ when P and Q are Boolean variables. Similarly for $P = p$, where $p \in 2^P$. We work with timed transition systems $\mathcal{S} = \langle X, Y, C, I(X), T(X, Y, X') \rangle$, where X are the Boolean and theory state variables, Y are the Boolean input variables, C are the real-valued clock variables, $I(X)$ and $T(X, Y, X')$ are the initial and discrete transition formulae. We denote with $\Pi(\mathcal{S})$ the set of paths of $\mathcal{S}$.

We work in the context of Abstraction Modulo Stability (AMS) [7], where σ is a stability criterion defined by the user. While the AMS framework comes with a number of suggestions for the stability definition, in this paper, we fix σ as the *non-urgency* condition: a σ-stable state is a state where time can elapse, while a transient (or urgent) state is forced to move with a discrete transition. Urgent states are often introduced to model causal relations between components: intuitively, they correspond to states traversed when accomplishing a complex – but instantaneous – action. For example, an (instantaneous) relay is an electrical component that immediately closes a remote electrical switch when traversed with current: it follows that the activation of a relay may trigger the activation of several relays in sequence, until all effects are propagated. By choosing σ as the non-urgency condition, all intermediate steps in this chain of activations are seen as transient states (satisfying $\neg\sigma$), leading to the final σ-state. Such a σ definition was chosen by domain experts among the ones suggested in [7]. The use of other more aggressive stability definitions (e.g., considering as transient the states that are traversed in a "short" time as well) is future work.

3.1   Simulations Extractor

We consider the problem of extracting a set of simulations[3] from a transition system according to a *coverage criterion*. The coverage criterion defines a set of test targets, i.e., features to be stressed by at least one test in the test suite. When leveraging model checking for tests extraction, the target to be covered is considered a *trap property* [17] or a never-claim [15] for which a counter-example is looked for. A counter-example for a trap property is a path of the model that shows how the target under consideration is reached, i.e., covered.

Let $\mathcal{S}$ be a transition system on X variables and Y inputs, V, W be sets of Boolean variables, with $V \subseteq X$, $W \subseteq X \cup Y$. For a coverage criterion *cov.crit*,

---

[3]   In this context, simulations will be also called test cases, and the obtained set of simulations will be also called test suite [16].

let $\mathrm{Targ}(cov.crit)$ return the corresponding targets, and for a $t \in \mathrm{Targ}(cov.crit)$, let $[\![t]\!]$ return the corresponding LTL trap property. We consider three coverage criteria:

- states(V): the targets to cover are the possible assignments to V variables: $\mathrm{Targ}(\mathrm{states}(V)) \doteq 2^V$, and for each $v \in \mathrm{Targ}(\mathrm{states}(V))$, $[\![v]\!] \doteq (V = v)$.
- trans(V): the targets to cover are the possible transitions on V variables: $\mathrm{Targ}(\mathrm{trans}(V)) \doteq 2^V \times 2^V$, and for each $(v_1, v_2) \in \mathrm{Targ}(\mathrm{trans}(V))$, $[\![(v_1, v_2)]\!] \doteq (V = v_1 \wedge V' = v_2)$.
- trans$_\sigma(V, W)$: the targets to cover are the possible σ-stable transitions on V variables, with W inputs: $\mathrm{Targ}(\mathrm{trans}_\sigma(V, W)) \doteq 2^V \times 2^W \times 2^V$, and for each $(v_1, w, v_2) \in \mathrm{Targ}(\mathrm{trans}_\sigma(V, W))$,

$$[\![(v_1, w, v_2)]\!] \doteq (\sigma \wedge V = v_1) \wedge \mathrm{G}(W = w) \wedge \mathrm{X}((\neg\sigma)\mathrm{U}(\sigma \wedge V = v_2)).$$

Intuitively, a path covering the trap property $[\![(v_1, w, v_2)]\!]$ witnesses that with the reception of only input w a σ-state where v_1 holds moves to a σ-stable state where v_2 holds, possibly passing through a sequence of transient steps.

The test suite extracted from $\mathcal{S}$ according to $cov.crit$ is a finite set $\mathrm{TS}(\mathcal{S}, cov.crit) \subseteq \Pi(\mathcal{S})$ such that:

$$\forall t \in \mathrm{Targ}(cov.crit) . \exists \pi \in \mathrm{TS}(\mathcal{S}, cov.crit) . \pi \models \mathrm{F}([\![t]\!]).$$

Namely, the test suite includes the simulations π for the system that show how the candidate targets can be reached. In practice, the path π is obtained as a counter-example of the model-checking query $\mathcal{S} \models \neg\mathrm{F}([\![t]\!])$. For the candidate traps that are not covered in $\mathrm{TS}(\mathcal{S}, cov.crit)$, there is a proof of the fact that $\mathcal{S} \models \neg\mathrm{F}[\![t]\!]$, i.e., that they are unreachable.

The understandability and readability of the generated tests are important for the engagement of domain experts in the process. Notably, the coverage criterion of trans$_\sigma(V, W)$ allows for extracting test cases that are similar to the ones that an engineer would manually write by looking at the circuits. By using as V the variables representing the status of some relays and as W the variables representing the switches connected to them, we obtain scenarios showing that under certain inputs the relays will change configuration, and that under others the relays will stay still. Considering stable transitions, instead of one-step ones, is crucial to visualize the stable effects of a change in the inputs, and to disregard the internal transient steps needed by the relays to propagate their signals. Our method is designed to support this engineers' standard practice of test case extraction in an automated and complete way.

3.2   Working with a Partial ReRIS Model

For a parametrization p, let $\mathcal{S}_p$ be the entire corresponding ReRIS, which consists of many tables and schematics that may be very large or not yet fully translated in transition systems by NORMA. Let $\mathcal{R}$ be the subset of circuits that are available in the form of a transition system. We consider the composition of $\mathcal{R}$ with a system *Stub*, introduced to mock the behaviors of the non-available circuits with respect to $\mathcal{R}$'s inputs. Writing an adequate *Stub* is a hard task since it should summarize many circuits and let $\mathcal{R}$ receive only the correct input sequences. In our process, a domain expert is directly involved in this phase, supported by verifying a set of properties as sanity checks on the produced model. The *Stub* is also validated by checking the TS extracted from the model. If a missing (resp, spurious) target was noticed by the expert, they could fix the *Stub* implementation by enlarging (resp, refining) its constraints.

The definition of the *Stub* attempts to generalize the concrete configuration p of the schematics where $\mathcal{R}$ was taken from. It symbolically includes all the parametrizations that might share the $\mathcal{R}$ part. We denote with $p^\sharp$ such an abstract parametrization, and with $\mathcal{S}_{p^\sharp}$ the composition of $\mathcal{R}$ and *Stub*.

Example 1. Consider as the original $\mathcal{S}_p$ the interlocking logic of Trento supporting 20 routes (named A, B, C...) with 10 railroad switches (named r1, r2, r3...). Assume that the available part $\mathcal{R}$ is the one representing the switch r7, that is shared by 2 concurrent routes A and B, running left-to-right and right-to-left respectively. The safety logic ensures that switch is booked by one route at a time. Instead of considering a stub only for such A and B, we use a wider *Stub*, that mimics how *any* pair of routes interact with a similar switch, by treating symbolically their running direction.

3.3   Mapping a ReRIS Simulation into an Abstract SwRIS Test

Since $\mathcal{S}_{p^\sharp}$ is made of a generic *Stub*, its simulations induce *abstract* test cases, that can be concretized in multiple instantiations. In the middle of Fig. 2, we show the skeleton of a sample `test.atosca`, with placeholders (in `<..>`) to be filled with data read from the simulation π. While defining *Stub*, the domain expert collects the constraints defining the compatible instantiations. The abstract test starts with the declaration of the constraints on the used variables (see the "let" namespace), read from the abstract configuration $p^\sharp$. Based on these constraints, the expert also provides a dictionary where ReRIS expressions are mapped in SwRIS expressions. In Fig. 2 we denote such a rewriting with function map(). This is a key element that allows for translating a $\pi \in$ TS, i.e., a sequence of assignments to ReRIS variables, into a sequence of test steps. Specifically, each test step corresponds to a unique state of the simulation π and, except for the initialization one, it corresponds to a command (or stimulus), read from the π inputs (see keyword "do"). Each test step assume*s* the stub behavior, and assert*s* the system state, both read from the corresponding π state: for a state s, i.e., a complete assignment to the $\mathcal{S}_{p^\sharp}$ variables, we denote with $s|_{Stub}$ the assignments to *Stub* variables only.

As it is discussed in [7], ReRIS simulations show transient implementation-dependent states that are irrelevant from the perspective of high-level railway functionalities. After an input is received, the system reacts with a chain of internal steps, until stability is accomplished. We believe that in order to obtain

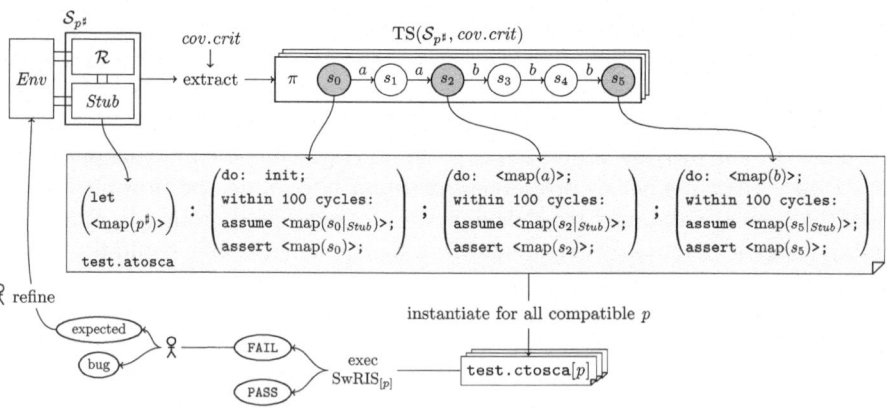

Fig. 2. Extraction and analysis of concrete test cases from $\mathcal{S}_{p\sharp}$. σ-stable states of $\mathcal{S}_{p\sharp}$ are colored in gray (i.e., s_0, s_2, s_5 satisfy σ, while s_1, s_3, s_4 do not).

a test scenario for a different implementation we have to disregard such internal steps, and consider only the stable ones. For this reason, the mapping of the π states into test steps is limited to the σ-*stable*, i.e., *non-urgent*, states (colored in gray in Fig. 2): we disregard the discrete steps that in the simulation are executed at the same time (in a super-dense time domain) and retain all the states where time elapses. In our models, we easily classify the states by checking the value of the δ variable (introduced by Timed nuXmv for synchronizing the clocks) that represents the time dwelling in each state.

The obtained sequence of test steps is about stable railway aspects only. Since the SwRIS execution will go through its implementation-dependent steps as well, we need to take stability into account in the test too, and allow for more internal steps between the stimuli and the assertions. For this, we leverage a TOSCA's syntactic construct specifying that the assertions should be verified *within N cycles* ("within 100 cycles", in Fig. 2).

In the .atosca file we also add traceability information mapping each test step back to the originating state in π. Finally, we minimize the resulting set of tests by removing the ones that are syntactically a prefix of another.

3.4   Test Execution

Each abstract test mapped from a $\pi \in \mathrm{TS}(\mathcal{S}_{p\sharp}, cov.crit)$ is then instantiated in a set of concrete tests by looking for a concrete p that is consistent with the variables declarations. Then, each test.ctosca[p] is executed on the corresponding code SwRIS[p]. If the test passes, then the scenario of π is reproducible in the SwRIS[p]. If the test fails, then ReRIS and SwRIS react in different ways to the same stimuli. A domain expert analyzes the failing case and decides whether it witnesses a bug of the SwRIS, or whether the inputs received in the ReRIS simulation are in fact not allowed by the rules that a human operator should follow when controlling the interlocking. The latter case corresponds to a spurious failed test case (the "expected" case in Fig. 2), that can be fixed by refining the environment Env around $\mathcal{S}_{p\sharp}$ before restarting the procedure. We highlight the importance of this iteration for reverse engineering and documentation purposes. As a matter of fact, there is no proper report of the rules that are *assumed* by the ReRIS and are instead implemented in the SwRIS.

4 Related Works

Several techniques exist for developing and verifying railway interlocking systems [9,14,20,21,23]. For relay-based RIS [1], tools for graphical modeling supporting verification exist [19,22]. In these works, the circuits are described with discrete formulae between the stable states of the components. In [3], CSP modeling is proposed to also represent transient states, which are fundamental for complete verification. Our work differs because our modeling format is electrically accurate and includes transient states by construction; since in this context we do not focus on verifying the circuits, we afterward formally select the stable states to obtain more significant scenarios in a reverse-engineering perspective. The importance of modeling the surrounding environment is also faced in [2].

Legacy systems migration is considered in [8], where the legacy and the new systems are tested to behave consistently on a common test suite. In [26], the migration of legacy systems to the cloud is validated, similarly to our case, by generating tests from the legacy implementation. The key difference is that in [26], the legacy system is manually abstracted and reverse-engineered into a requirements model, whose paths are then used as test cases. We instead extract simulations from the legacy model and abstract (i.e., remove transient states) in each of them individually, therefore avoiding computing an abstract state machine whose paths may be spurious.

5 Experimental Evaluation

We evaluate the benefits of including our approach in the development process of the new software-based RIS. We started with the (drawing of an) electrical circuit of a railroad switch. A domain expert wrote a generic *Stub*, able to cover symbolically every pair of routes interacting with the switch, for any running direction. Let $\mathcal{S}_{p\sharp}$ be the resulting transition system compiled by NORMA. We extracted 6 sets of simulations of $\mathcal{S}_{p\sharp}$, according to different coverage criteria: the criterion "states 8" (resp, "trans 4") induces the set of simulations covering all the reachable states (resp, transitions) of 8 (resp, 4) relays chosen by the domain expert as significant. The sets induced by the criteria "trans$_\sigma$-A", "trans$_\sigma$-B", "trans$_\sigma$-C", "trans$_\sigma$-D" are considered by the domain expert the most significant scenarios, because they show every way in which a specific relay changes (or does not change) position according to the controlling signals. The extraction of the simulations is performed with the model-checker NUXMV [10], leveraging IC3IA algorithm [13]. We mapped each simulation in an abstract test case (891 in total)

Table 1. Sizes of the test suites before (TS) and after refining the environment (TS$_{Env}$); FAIL percentages on original version of SwRIS (v0.1) and the one (v0.2) obtained by fixing the signalled bugs; FAIL cases for each concrete test instantiation.

cov.crit	size TS	v0.1 FAIL%	size TS$_{Env}$	v0.1 FAIL%	v0.2 FAIL%	v0.2 # of FAIL							
						S1:c1	S1:c2	S2:c1	S2:c2	S3:c1	S3:c2	S4:c1	S4:c2
states 8	81	91%	54	70%	**69%**	36	36	42	36	42	36	36	36
trans 4	41	58%	13	25%	**25%**	3	3	4	3	4	3	3	3
trans$_\sigma$-A	38	0%	26	0%	**0%**	0	0	0	0	0	0	0	0
trans$_\sigma$-B	52	54%	36	40%	**36%**	11	11	19	11	19	11	11	11
trans$_\sigma$-C	298	34%	228	17%	**13%**	31	33	32	31	32	31	31	31
trans$_\sigma$-D	381	50%	372	39%	**30%**	101	108	150	101	150	101	101	101

which we instantiated on 4 different railway stations (S1, S2, S3, S4), and on two different railroad switches each (c1, c2), hence obtaining 7128 concrete tests.

In the first three columns of Table 1, we show the size of the test suites and the FAIL percentage obtained on the current version of the code, denoted with v0.1. It's important to observe that this version already went through other tests and verifications foreseen in the new development process. By inspecting some of the failing tests, a railway expert recognized *expected* failures (as in Fig. 2), where the scenario was breaking the normative rules that a railway operator should follow. We documented such cases and consequently *refined* the model by adding an environment *Env* in the transition system. By restarting the procedure on $\mathcal{S}_{p\sharp} + Env$, we extracted new test suites (denoted as TS$_{Env}$ in Table 1) for each criterion (totaling 5832 concrete tests), with more significant scenarios.

In the remaining failures, the domain expert found *more than 10 actual bug sources* in the software logics, originating from errors in the Functional Requirements Specifications (FRS, the entry point of the new development, as in Fig. 1). Based on the produced bug report, the FRS were fixed and a new version of the code (denoted with v0.2) was generated. The "v0.2 FAIL%" column of Table 1 shows that the FAIL percentage actually decreases.

The remaining failures are currently under analysis and may lead to further refinements of the environment (and more documentation), or to new bug reports. The last 8 columns of Table 1 show how the remaining FAIL cases are divided in different instantiations of the abstract test cases (four stations, 2 concrete switches each). We see that a ReRIS simulation may induce tests failing only in some configurations of the parameters. This highlights the importance of generalizing the *Stub* and instantiating in multiple stations the abstract tests.

Between the considered *cov.crit*, "states 8" and "trans 4" induce longer simulations (50 states on average), while the "trans$_\sigma$-" criteria induce shorter ones (30 states on average): the latter are more significant and understandable for the domain expert, who chose to prioritize the analysis of these test suites.

We also evaluated the coverage on SwRIS (in terms of lines of code) with the execution of our tests. As expected, a good coverage level is limited to the code of the railroad switch (our system-under-test). Notably, a domain expert manually analyzed some of the uncovered lines and confirmed that they are related to functionalities added in the new implementation that did not exist in the legacy ReRIS. We plan to automatize this process and produce additional documentation on the migration.

6 Conclusions

We described our contribution within an ongoing industrial collaboration between Fondazione Bruno Kessler and the Italian Railway Network (RFI), currently migrating from analog to software-based railway interlocking systems. We applied test case generation via model-checking by using another concrete implementation as a reference model; we avoid building an abstract model for the legacy implementation, rather, we abstract each simulation into a scenario that is significant when comparing two different computational models (analog vs cycle-based), by skipping implementation-dependent transient states.

The approach we proposed in this paper is now integrated into the ongoing process of development and validation of the new code. Although the latter was already subject to substantial scrutiny in terms of other properties, this new methodology targets the comparison with the legacy functionalities. Our approach proved to be effective already from its first application on the railroad switch circuits, as it allowed RFI engineers (i.e., not formal-methods experts) to find more than 10 real bugs in the new software. As an additional feature, our pipeline supports the documentation of the expected differences between the two implementations due to changes in regulations.

We plan to apply the procedure to other circuits and analyze the bug reports on the newly developed versions of the software.

Acknowledgments. We thank the members of the FBK Software Engineering unit, Angelo Susi, Fitsum Meshesha Kifetew and Davide Prandi, for their support in using the official RFI tool set, and for their useful comments and suggestions. We also acknowledge the support of the PNRR project FAIR - Future AI Research (PE00000013), under the NRRP MUR program funded by the NextGenerationEU.

Disclosure of Interests. All authors are participating in the collaboration between RFI and FBK.

References

1. de Almeida Pereira, D.I.: Analysis and formal specification of relay-based railway interlocking systems. (Analyse et spécification formelle des systèmes d'enclenchement ferroviaire basés sur les relais). Ph.D. thesis, École centrale de Lille, Villeneuve-d'Ascq, France (2020)
2. de Almeida Pereira, D.I., Debbech, S., Perin, M., Bon, P., Collart-Dutilleul, S.: Formal specification of environmental aspects of a railway interlocking system based on a conceptual model. In: Laender, A.H.F., Pernici, B., Lim, E.-P., de Oliveira, J.P.M. (eds.) ER 2019. LNCS, vol. 11788, pp. 338–351. Springer, Cham (2019). https://doi.org/10.1007/978-3-030-33223-5_28

3. de Almeida Pereira, D.I., Oliveira, M.V.M., Bezerra, P.E.R., Bon, P., Dutilleul, S.C.: CSP specification and verification of relay-based railway interlocking systems. In: Hong, J., Bures, M., Park, J.W., Cerný, T. (eds.) The 37th ACM/SIGAPP Symposium on Applied Computing, SAC 2022, Virtual Event, 25–29 April 2022, pp. 97–106. ACM (2022). https://doi.org/10.1145/3477314.3507060

4. Amendola, A., et al.: NORMA: a tool for the analysis of Relay-based Railway Interlocking Systems. In: TACAS 2022. LNCS, vol. 13243, pp. 125–142. Springer, Cham (2022). https://doi.org/10.1007/978-3-030-99524-9_7

5. Amendola, A., et al.: A model-based approach to the design, verification and deployment of railway interlocking system. In: Margaria, T., Steffen, B. (eds.) ISoLA 2020. LNCS, vol. 12478, pp. 240–254. Springer, Cham (2020). https://doi.org/10.1007/978-3-030-61467-6_16

6. Barrett, C.W., Sebastiani, R., Seshia, S.A., Tinelli, C.: Satisfiability modulo theories. In: Handbook of Satisfiability, Frontiers in Artificial Intelligence and Applications, vol. 185, pp. 825–885. IOS Press (2009)

7. Becchi, A., Cimatti, A.: Abstraction modulo stability for reverse engineering. In: Shoham, S., Vizel, Y. (eds.) Proceedings of the 34th International Conference on Computer Aided Verification, CAV 2022, Part I, Haifa, Israel, 7–10 August 2022. LNCS, vol. 13371, pp. 469–489. Springer, Heidelberg (2022). https://doi.org/10.1007/978-3-031-13185-1_23

8. Bisbal, J., et al.: A survey of research into legacy system migration (2007). https://api.semanticscholar.org/CorpusID:5566249

9. Bougacha, R., Wakrime, A.A., Kallel, S., Ayed, R.B., Dutilleul, S.C.: A model-based approach for the modeling and the verification of railway signaling system. In: Damiani, E., Spanoudakis, G., Maciaszek, L.A. (eds.) Proceedings of the 14th International Conference on Evaluation of Novel Approaches to Software Engineering, ENASE 2019, Heraklion, Crete, Greece, 4–5 May 2019, pp. 367–376. SciTePress (2019).https://doi.org/10.5220/0007728403670376

10. Cavada, R., et al.: The NUXMV symbolic model checker. In: Biere, A., Bloem, R. (eds.) CAV 2014. LNCS, vol. 8559, pp. 334–342. Springer, Cham (2014). https://doi.org/10.1007/978-3-319-08867-9_22

11. Cimatti, A., Griggio, A., Magnago, E., Roveri, M., Tonetta, S.: SMT-based satisfiability of first-order LTL with event freezing functions and metric operators. Inf. Comput. **272**, 104–502 (2020). https://doi.org/10.1016/j.ic.2019.104502

12. Cimatti, A., Griggio, A., Redondi, G.: Verification of SMT systems with quantifiers. In: Bouajjani, A., Holík, L., Wu, Z. (eds.) Proceedings of the 20th International Symposium on Automated Technology for Verification and Analysis, ATVA 2022, Virtual Event, 25–28 October 2022. LNCS, vol. 13505, pp. 154–170. Springer, Heidelberg (2022). https://doi.org/10.1007/978-3-031-19992-9_10

13. Daniel, J., Cimatti, A., Griggio, A., Tonetta, S., Mover, S.: Infinite-state liveness-to-safety via implicit abstraction and well-founded relations. In: Chaudhuri, S., Farzan, A. (eds.) CAV 2016. LNCS, vol. 9779, pp. 271–291. Springer, Cham (2016). https://doi.org/10.1007/978-3-319-41528-4_15

14. Daskaya, I., Huhn, M., Milius, S.: Formal safety analysis in industrial practice. In: Salaün, G., Schätz, B. (eds.) FMICS 2011. LNCS, vol. 6959, pp. 68–84. Springer, Heidelberg (2011). https://doi.org/10.1007/978-3-642-24431-5_7

15. Engels, A., Feijs, L., Mauw, S.: Test generation for intelligent networks using model checking. In: Brinksma, E. (ed.) TACAS 1997. LNCS, vol. 1217, pp. 384–398. Springer, Heidelberg (1997). https://doi.org/10.1007/BFb0035401

16. Fraser, G., Wotawa, F., Ammann, P.: Testing with model checkers: a survey. Softw. Test. Verification Reliab. **19**(3), 215–261 (2009). https://doi.org/10.1002/STVR. 402

17. Gargantini, A., Heitmeyer, C.: Using model checking to generate tests from requirements specifications. In: Nierstrasz, O., Lemoine, M. (eds.) ESEC/SIGSOFT FSE -1999. LNCS, vol. 1687, pp. 146–162. Springer, Heidelberg (1999). https://doi.org/10.1007/3-540-48166-4_10

18. Griggio, A., Jonás, M.: Kratos2: an SMT-based model checker for imperative programs. In: Enea, C., Lal, A. (eds.) Proceedings of the 35th International Conference on Computer Aided Verification, CAV 2023, Paris, France, 17–22 July 2023, Part III. LNCS, vol. 13966, pp. 423–436. Springer, Heidelberg (2023). https://doi.org/10.1007/978-3-031-37709-9_20

19. Haxthausen, A.E., Kjær, A.A., Le Bliguet, M.: Formal development of a tool for automated modelling and verification of relay interlocking systems. In: Butler, M., Schulte, W. (eds.) FM 2011. LNCS, vol. 6664, pp. 118–132. Springer, Heidelberg (2011). https://doi.org/10.1007/978-3-642-21437-0_11

20. Haxthausen, A.E., Fantechi, A.: Compositional verification of railway interlocking systems. Formal Aspects Comput. **35**(1), 4:1–4:46 (2023). https://doi.org/10.1145/3549736

21. Hong, L.V., Haxthausen, A.E., Peleska, J.: Formal modelling and verification of interlocking systems featuring sequential release. Sci. Comput. Program. **133**, 91–115 (2017)

22. Karolak, J., Daszczuk, W.B., Grabski, W., Kochan, A.: Temporal verification of relay-based railway traffic control systems using the integrated model of distributed systems. Energies **15**(23) (2022). https://doi.org/10.3390/en15239041. https://www.mdpi.com/1996-1073/15/23/9041

23. Laursen, P.L., Trinh, V.A.T., Haxthausen, A.E.: Formal modelling and verification of a distributed railway interlocking system using UPPAAL. In: Margaria, T., Steffen, B. (eds.) ISoLA 2020, Part III. LNCS, vol. 12478, pp. 415–433. Springer, Cham (2020). https://doi.org/10.1007/978-3-030-61467-6_27

24. Pnueli, A.: The temporal logic of programs. In: 18th Annual Symposium on Foundations of Computer Science, Providence, Rhode Island, USA, 31 October—1 November 1977, pp. 46–57. IEEE Computer Society (1977). https://doi.org/10.1109/SFCS.1977.32

25. Stefenon, S.F., Cristoforetti, M., Cimatti, A.: Towards automatic digitalization of railway engineering schematics. In: Basili, R., Lembo, D., Limongelli, C., Orlandini, A. (eds.) Proceedings of the XXIInd International Conference of the Italian Association for Artificial Intelligence, AIxIA 2023, Advances in Artificial Intelligence. LNCS, Rome, Italy, 6–9 November 2023, vol. 14318, pp. 453–466. Springer (2023). https://doi.org/10.1007/978-3-031-47546-7_31

26. Wendland, M., Kranz, M., Hein, C., Ritter, T., Flaquer, A.G.: Model-based testing in legacy software modernization: an experience report. In: Carrozza, G., Pietrantuono, R., Manetti, V. (eds.) Proceedings of the 2013 International Workshop on Joining AcadeMiA and Industry Contributions to Testing Automation, JAMAICA 2013, Lugano, Switzerland, 15 July 2013, pp. 35–40. ACM (2013). https://doi.org/10.1145/2489280.2489291

soid: A Tool for Legal Accountability for Automated Decision Making

Samuel Judson[1]([✉]), Matthew Elacqua[1], Filip Cano[2], Timos Antonopoulos[1], Bettina Könighofer[2], Scott J. Shapiro[3], and Ruzica Piskac[1]

[1] Yale University, New Haven, USA
{samuel.judson,matt.elacqua,
timos.antonopoulos,ruzica.piskac}@yale.edu
[2] Graz University of Technology, Graz, Austria
{filip.cano,bettina.koenighofer}@iaik.tugraz.at
[3] Yale Law School and Yale University, New Haven, USA
scott.shapiro@yale.edu

Abstract. We present soid, a tool for interrogating the decision making of autonomous agents using SMT-based automated reasoning. Relying on the Z3 SMT solver and KLEE symbolic execution engine, soid allows investigators to receive rigorously proven answers to factual and counterfactual queries about agent behavior, enabling effective legal and engineering accountability for harmful or otherwise incorrect decisions. We evaluate soid qualitatively and quantitatively on a pair of examples, i) a buggy implementation of a classic decision tree inference benchmark from the explainable AI (XAI) literature; and ii) a car crash in a simulated physics environment. For the latter, we also contribute the soid-gui, a domain-specific, web-based example interface for legal and other practitioners to specify factual and counterfactual queries without requiring sophisticated programming or formal methods expertise.

1 Introduction

Recent advances in (often ML-based) artificial intelligence have led to a proliferation of algorithmic decision making (ADM) agents. The risk that these agents may cause harm – and the many demonstrated examples of them already doing so, ranging across numerous domains [3,8,19,30] – has led to a significant demand for technologies to enable their responsible use. In this work, we present soid, a tool based on Judson *et al.*'s method [16] to account for software systems using computational tools from the fields of formal methods and automated reasoning. The soid tool is primarily oriented towards supporting legal reasoning and analysis, in order to better understand the ultimate *purpose* of an agent's decision making – as is often relied upon by various bodies of law.

In particular, rather than traditional verification methods which aim towards proving a specific program property, soid instead aims to 'put the agent on the stand'. The design of soid enables factual and counterfactual querying – underlying a finding of fact – in support of human-centered assessment of the 'why' of the agent's decision making. Such an assessment can then in turn justify holding responsible an answerable owner or operator, like a person or company. We

© The Author(s) 2024
A. Gurfinkel and V. Ganesh (Eds.): CAV 2024, LNCS 14682, pp. 233–246, 2024.
https://doi.org/10.1007/978-3-031-65630-9_12

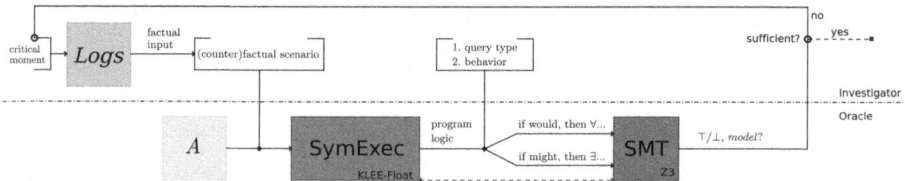

Fig. 1. Architecture of the soid tool.

describe the functioning of the soid tool itself as well as a pair of examples of its use on simulated harms. We also describe the soid-gui, a domain-specific interface for soid applied to autonomous vehicles, allowing for adaptive and interpretable analysis of driving decisions without requiring extensive programming skills or familiarity with formal logical reasoning.

The basic flow of soid, depicted in Fig. 1, is adaptive and requires a human in the loop. The human investigator – likely a practitioner such as a lawyer or regulator supported as necessary by engineers – uses soid to better understand the decision making of an agent program A. They do so by finding critical decision moments in the logs of A that transpired in the lead up to a harm, and then relaxing or perturbing the program inputs to specify a (family of) counterfactual scenario(s). The investigator then formulates a query asking what the behavior of A 'might' or 'would' have been [20] under that (family of) counterfactual(s). As we show in the design of our soid-gui, such questions can even be formulated in user-friendly interfaces that abstract away all of the formal logic and reasoning of soid for non-technical practitioners. Once a query is posed, a verification oracle using SMT-based automated reasoning – including constrained symbolic execution – gets the investigator a prompt answer. They can then continue to 'interrogate the witness' until they are satisfied they have a sufficient understanding of the purpose of A's decisions, and terminate the loop.

Contribution. In summary, we developed a command line tool and Python library soid, which uses symbolic execution (through Z3) and SMT solving (through KLEE) to enable rigorous interpretation of the decision-making logic of an autonomous agent. We demonstrate soid on a pair on instructive involving machine-learned agents. In both cases, we find soid able to resolve counterfactual queries with reasonable efficiency, even when adaptively posed through the interpretable soid-gui aimed at non-technical practitioners.

A Motivating Example. Consider a program A which computes a decision tree in order to classify the diabetes health risk status of an individual, a classic example in automated counterfactuals with legal implications due to [31]. The decision tree and code of A are shown in Fig. 2. However, the software system surrounding A creates an implicit unit conversion bug: A computes the body-mass-index (BMI) input to the decision tree, using height and weight parameters from its input. But, A expects metric inputs in kg and m and so computes the BMI without a necessary unit conversion, while the program inputs are instead

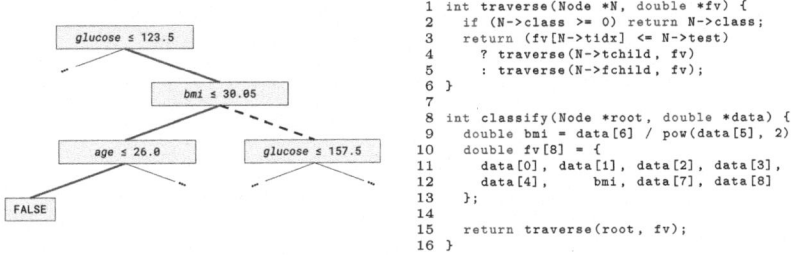

```
1  int traverse(Node *N, double *fv) {
2    if (N->class >= 0) return N->class;
3    return (fv[N->tidx] <= N->test)
4      ? traverse(N->tchild, fv)
5      : traverse(N->fchild, fv);
6  }
7
8  int classify(Node *root, double *data) {
9    double bmi = data[6] / pow(data[5], 2);
10   double fv[8] = {
11     data[0], data[1], data[2], data[3],
12     data[4],      bmi, data[7], data[8]
13   };
14
15   return traverse(root, fv);
16 }
```

Fig. 2. An incorrect decision tree classification. At left the decision subtree with the incorrect path in bolded red and the missed 'correct' branch in dashed blue. At right, the decision tree inference logic as implemented in C. (Color figure online)

provided in the imperial *in* and *lb*. Notably, A is 'correct' with respect to natural specifications – as is the decision tree in isolation. The flaw occurs due to a mistake in the composition of the software system as a whole. Nonetheless, the system misclassifies many inputs, as $(kg/m^2) \gg (lb/in^2)$ for the same quantities.

The goal of soid is to enable a legal practitioner to understand the presence of and conditions underlying a potential misclassification. Unlike statistical methods for counterfactual analysis which only analyze the (correct) decision model [31], the minimal assumptions underlying soid – namely, the lack of an assumption that the broader software system correctly uses the decision model – make it a more capable framework for analyzing this type of 'implicit conversion' failure. In §2.1 we run a small empirical analysis on A, showing how soid enables a user to specify concrete factual and counterfactual queries to understand the conditions under which the failure can occur and their implications.

1.1 Related Work

The explainable AI (XAI) and fairness, accountability, and transparency (FAccT) communities have developed numerous methods and tools for enabling accountability of ADMs, machine-learned or otherwise, for which [1,10,13] are recent surveys. The closest tool to soid of which we are aware is the VerifAI project [9,11]. Many of these tools and techniques focus on counterfactual reasoning in particular [7,14,15,24,31]. In comparison to the prevailing lines of this research, soid emphasizes i) after-the-fact (or *ex post*) analysis for algorithmic accountability in the style of with legal reasoning; ii) the use of SMT-based verification technologies capable of resolving counterfactual questions about whole families of scenarios; and iii) emphasis on the 'code as run', rather than evaluating a specific component like a particular decision model, or requiring an abstracted program representation or a formal model of the (often complex social and/or physical) environment the agent operates within.

2 soid Tool Architecture and Usage

Figure 1 illustrates the architecture of soid. The tool is implemented in Python, and invokes the Z3 SMT solver [26] for resolving queries.

```
1   @soid.register
2   def environmental(E):
3       return And(And(Equal(E.occupied_0_0, False)),
4                   ...      # omitted for brevity
5                   And(Equal(E.occupied_2_1, True), Equal(E.orient_2_1, cardinals['East'])),
6                   ... )    # omitted for brevity
7
8   @soid.register
9   def state(S):
10      return And(Equal(S.curr_direction, cardinals['North']),
11                 Equal(S.from,            cardinals['South']),
12                 ... ) # omitted for brevity
13
14  @soid.register
15  def F(E, S):
16      return ...        # omitted for brevity
17
18  @soid.register
19  def behavior(D):
20      return Equal(D.move, False)
```

Fig. 3. A counterfactual specified using soidlib for a simplified grid-based car crash implementation (also available within our codebase alongside our soid-gui). This query leaves the turn signal of the 'other' car at $(2, 1)$ unconstrained, defining a counterfactual family. The objects E , S , and D are user-specified in an omitted `declare` function, including datatype.

Before working with soid, the investigator must use their domain expertise to find and extract the critical moment they care about from the factual trace within the logging infrastructure of A. We assume some mechanism guarantees the authenticity of the trace, such as an accountable logging protocol, as has been previously proposed for cyberphysical systems [33]. After extracting the trace the investigator must specify the i) (counter)factual query defining the factual, counterfactual, or family of counterfactual scenarios the query concerns; as well as ii) some possible agent behavior. In the remainder of this section, we explain how the user does so using soid and a Python library interface it exposes called soidlib. Constraints are specified through an API similar to Z3Py, see Fig. 3, while queries can be written as independent Python scripts or generated dynamically within a Python codebase.

Upon invocation, soid symbolically executes A to generate a set of feasible program paths as constrained by the (counter)factual query. The constraints in that query must be provided directly to the symbolic execution engine – an integration API exposes the query to the symbolic execution in order to enable this communication, or the user can do so directly outside soid itself. After the symbolic execution completes, soid formulates the query formula and invokes Z3 to resolve it. It then outputs to the user the finding, as well as any model – which exists in the event of a failed 'would' or successful 'might' query.

Query API. The query API of soid is exposed as a Python library called soidlib. A query specified using soidlib is composed of a name and query type, as well as a set of functions. These functions return either soidlib variable declarations or constraints, which are in either case automatically encoded into a set of corresponding Z3Py constraints for use during SMT solving to establish the satisfiability or validity of the query. An example query is shown in Fig. 3. The main API function interfaces the user must define in order to encode their query are:

- `declare()` : A function that must return three dictionaries of soidlib variable declarations, enumerating the set of environmental inputs (E) and internal state inputs (S) over which the factual or (family of) counterfactual scenario(s) are defined, as well as the set of decision (D) variables over which the behavior is defined. In order to do this soidlib exposes a variety of variable types, which it then converts into Z3 statements with the appropriate logical sorts as required by the underlying SMT logic (*e.g.*, encoding an object of integer type as an object of the 32-bit bitvector sort).
- `environmental(E)` : A function that must return a soidlib constraint over E describing the environmental program inputs.
- `state(S)` : A function that must return a soidlib constraint over S describing the internal state program inputs.
- `falsified(E, S)` : An optional function, returns a soidlib constraint encoding a concrete factual to be negated from the query formula, and therefore excluded from the set of possible output models.
- `behavior(D)` : A function that must return a soidlib constraint over D describing the behavior being queried.

Language Support. Through a modular API soid extensively supports any symbolic execution engine that produces output in the SMT-LIB format [4]. An integrator needs only to write a Python class implementing an interface between soid and the engine. As such, soid supports agents written in any programming language for which a suitable symbolic execution engine is available. We use the KLEE family of symbolic execution engines throughout our benchmarks. At present, support is integrated into soid for C language programs with floating-point instructions using KLEE-Float [21], working over the SMT logic of QF_FPBV, the quantifier-free theory of floating-point and bitvectors. Support is also integrated for C and C++ language programs without floating-point using mainline KLEE [5], producing representations in QF_ABV, the quantifier-free theory of arrays and bitvectors.[1] KLEE can be further extended to analyze other LLVM-compilable languages such as Rust [22], while other engines exist for compiled binaries [29] and many other languages including Java [2] and Javascript [23].

Symbolic Execution API. Adding support for a new symbolic execution engine to soid requires specifying between two and five functions: `preprocess` , `execute` , `parse` , `clean` , and `postprocess` , which are all hooked into the main soid execution path. Only `execute` and `parse` are necessary – they must respectively invoke the symbolic execution and then process the output into a list of Z3Py statements capturing the possible path conditions. Optionally, `clean` provides a hook for cleaning up temporary or output files generated by the symbolic execution engine, while `preprocess` and `postprocess` are designed

---

[1] Adding support for floating-point instructions into mainline KLEE remains at present an open enhancement for the project, see: https://klee.github.io/projects/.

to automate additional steps that may be desirable for the symbolic execution – the former is given access to the query, the latter additionally to the set of variables declared along the path conditions. For example, KLEE-Float automatically converts arrays into bitvectors using a technique called Ackermannization [25], and renames any such variables in the process. The KLEE-Float `preprocess` function packaged with soid i) casts objects as necessary; and ii) constrains them to equal the corresponding input declarations in the `declare` function so that they alias those inputs, *e.g.*, adding the constraint `(= (fp.to_ieee_bv data) data_ackermann!0)` where `data_ackermann!0` is KLEE-Float's synthesized, Ackermannized representation of `data`.

Query to Symbolic Execution. One of the major benefits of the *ex post* method of soid is that the (counter)factual query specified by the user can be used to constrain what parts of the program A are relevant to the scenarios in question and therefore must be included in the formula being checked. However, in order to do so the query must also be exposed to the symbolic execution engine in order to limit the symbolic execution to just the (ideally small) set of program paths feasible under the (counter)factual scenario conditions. This can either be done independent of soid, *e.g.* by the code invoking soid when it is used as a library, or by using the `preprocess` hook in the symbolic execution framework. At present, our codebase exclusively uses the external method.

Invocation. There are two ways to use soid: through a command line script (the soidcli) or directly as a Python library. If the latter, the user calling the code must declare a `soid.Oracle` object and configure it with i) a `soid.Query`; ii) the path to the A; and iii) the identity of the symbolic execution engine. If using the soidcli, the CLI script declares the oracle object for the user, who must specify the path to where (a collection of) `soid.Query` objects can be found declared in independent Python scripts (as well as the same path to A and symbolic execution engine identity). In case multiple variants of A are required in order to specify different symbolic execution preconditions for different counterfactual families, soid passes an identifier corresponding to a `priority` index that the user can specify through the CLI interface. In the examples present in the soid codebase this identifier is passed to a Makefile, which is then used to invoke KLEE(-Float) on the correct variant.

2.1 Example #1: Decision Tree Inference

Using soid, we analyzed our decision tree misclassification motivating example. The results are summarized in Table 1, and were gathered on an Intel Xeon CPU E5-2650 v3 @ 2.30GHz workstation with 64 GB of RAM. We used scikit-learn [27] to train a decision tree over the Pima Indians dataset as used in [31]. We then implemented A as a C program that preprocesses the data – triggering the software system bug, as it does so without the necessary unit conversion – and then infers a binary classification using the decision tree. In order to create

Table 1. Benchmark results for our incorrect statistical inference example.

| model | output | timings (avg. $n = 10$) | | | paths |
		symbolic (s)	solving (s)	total (s)	
$\rightarrow$	φ_{fact}, *low risk?*				
dt	✔	0.746	4.896e-03	0.812	1
$\square \mapsto$	$\varphi^* \equiv \varphi_{fact}[(\text{weight} = 249.973) \mapsto \top]$, *ever high risk?*				
dt	✔	2.277	1.655	4.009	2

the factual basis for an investigation, we then invoked A on an example input where the unit conversion bug leads to the misclassification of the input as *low risk* instead of *high risk*.

We posed two queries:

1. Did the classification happen as described?
2. Does there exist a *weight* input parameter for which the instance is instead classified as *high risk* instead?

The former query provides a baseline for how much the counterfactual possibility of the latter query increases the cost of solving. It also fulfills the natural goal of many accountability processes to formally confirm apparent events and create a confirmed, end-to-end chain of analysis so that there is the highest possible societal confidence in any policy changes or punishments derived it. Both of these queries were resolved by soid in the positive, requiring at most a few seconds, even over a program structure in A that includes recursive invocations of floating-point comparison operations. Together, they demonstrate the weight input to A was causal for the classification, and establish its lack of unit conversion as contributory to the (harmful) misclassification decision.

Working with A, soid provides an adaptive oracle allowing the investigator to query its behavior and receive prompt and useful answers. The output of the program is also simple and interpretable. Without an intermediating GUI or developer tools, soid does require comfort with its API and the logical framework of expressing (counter)factuals and program outputs, but we do not expect a usable interface would be meaningfully difficult to integrate for this example.

3 soid-gui Architecture and Usage

The soid-gui is a web-based interactive interface for soid applied to the domain of autonomous vehicle accountability. It demonstrates that the use of soid can be managed by a high-level abstraction that exposes to non-technical practitioners the expressiveness and capacity of the tool, but none of its logical or technical complexity. We demonstrate the design and use of the soid-gui in Fig. 4.[2]

---

[2] The repositories for soid and soid-gui are available at https://github.com/sjudson/soid and https://github.com/mattelacqua/duckietown-soid, respectively.

Architecturally, the **soid-gui** is composed of three main components: i) a frontend written in React; ii) a backend server written in Python that operates a vehicle simulation using the Duckietown simulator for the OpenAI Gym (henceforce Gym-Duckietown [6]) and also interfaces with **soid**; and iii) a proxy server that manages communication between the browser frontend and the server backend. The Duckietown simulation is used as a stand-in for the real vehicle logs and instrumentation on which **soid** would be deployed in practice. We designed the crossroads intersection simulation interface to mimic the real-time driving context interface generated by contemporary autonomous vehicles, like those produced by Tesla. We stress that Gym-Duckietown is not exposed to **soid**, which operates exclusively over the program (and decision model) A. Gym-Duckietown is used only to simulate crashes and generate logfiles as the basis for **soid** queries.

Outside of the **soid** investigatory loop, the user can first use the **soid-gui** to design a car crash scenario by manipulating the location, destination, and other properties of the simulated car through menus and a drag and drop interface (see Fig. 4). The **soid-gui** also allows the user to select from among five different decision logics for the ego car: a directly programmed 'ideal' car, and four reinforcement-learned (specifically, Q-learned [32]) agents, colloquially the 'defensive', 'standard', 'reckless' and 'pathological' decision models. They are so named on the basis of the reward profiles used to train them.

After an iteration of the simulation (usually, after a crash occurs), the **soid-gui** allows the user to operate the **soid** investigatory loop. Using a slider the user can pick out a moment from the logs of the agent, and supported by detailed logging information about the inputs to A at each timestep can select the critical moment (see Step 1 in Fig. 4). They can then use car-specific dropdown menus to specify counterfactuals about any of the agents in the system in a user-friendly manner, which fully abstracts away the underlying logical formalism (Step 2 in Fig. 4). Finally, they can invoke **soid** on the query they have specified by asking whether the ego car 'might' or 'would' move or stop under the (family) of counterfactual scenario(s) they have defined (Step 3 in Fig. 4). After solving the **soid-gui** then presents an interpretable answer, including a valuation for any variables the counterfactual was stated over when one is available (Step 4 in Fig. 4). The user can then clear or adjust their counterfactual statement and ask further queries, until satisfied they have reached an understanding of the car's decision making under the selected decision model.

To use **soid**, the **soid-gui** first writes out a C language file with the necessary constraints for the KLEE-Float symbolic execution. It then creates the `soid.Query` and `soid.Oracle` objects, allowing it to invoke **soid** through the Python library interface. Once **soid** has invoked KLEE-Float and Z3 to determine the answer to the query the output is then processed. When applicable, this includes model parsing. The result is then passed back to the browser frontend to be shown to the user.

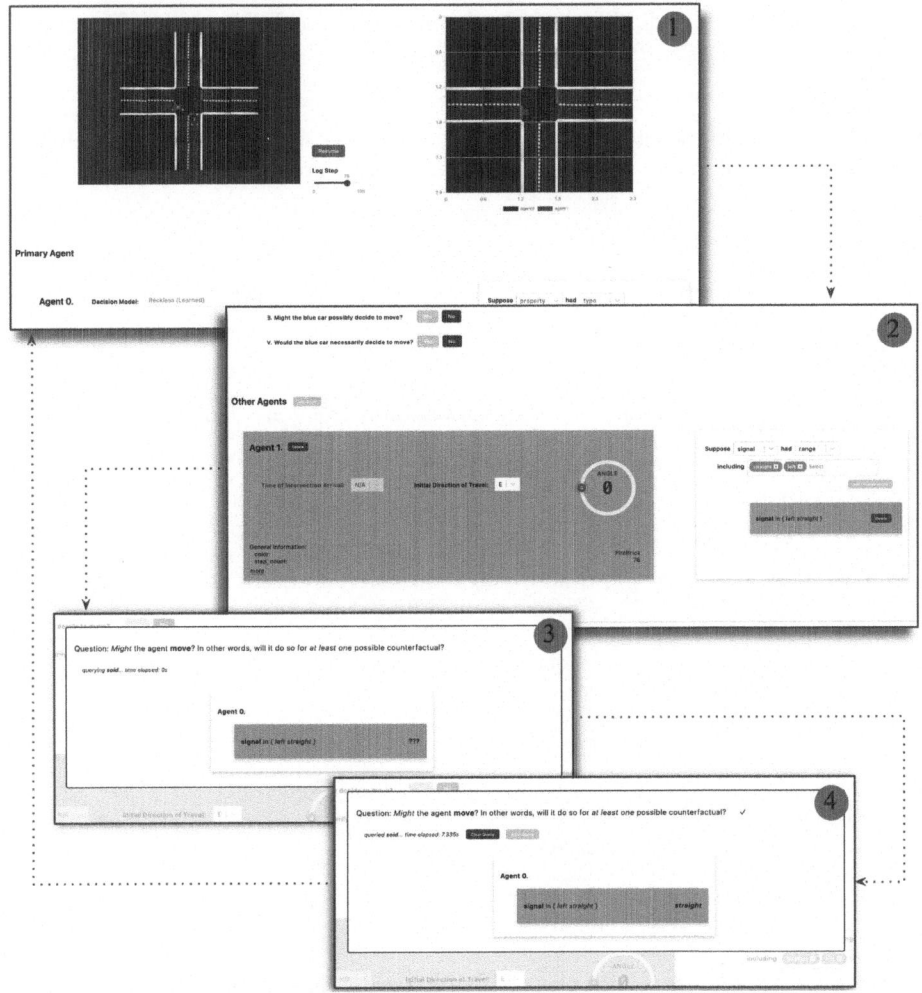

Fig. 4. After the (simulated) execution, the investigator (1) selects a critical moment; (2) poses a counterfactual query; (3) invokes the SMT solver; and (4) is presented with the response from the oracle.

3.1 Example #2: Three Cars on the Stand

We use the soid-gui to investigate a crash in Fig. 4. It is a simple intersection scenario, where the blue 'ego' car under investigation strikes the broadside of the red 'other' car which has indicated a right turn but proceeded straight nonetheless. As the red car possesses the right of way the fault lies with the blue car. We investigate 'to what purpose' the blue car entered in the intersection, in order to grade the severity of its misconduct in conjunction with legal norms that frequently apply the greatest possible penalties to purposeful action [16]. Notably, this crash occurs for all three of the 'standard', 'reckless', and 'pathological' decision models (but *not* the 'defensive' model).

Table 2. Benchmark results for our car crash example. For the final query, we phrased it as both a 'would' and a 'might' counterfactual for comparison.

model	output	timings (avg. $n = 10$)			paths
		symbolic (s)	solving (s)	total (s)	
$\rightarrow$	φ_{fact}, *moved?*				
standard	✔	3.575	4.290e-03	4.162	1
impatient	✔	3.607	4.317e-03	4.193	1
pathological	✔	3.626	4.249e-03	4.212	1
$\Box\rightarrow$	$\varphi^* \equiv \varphi_{fact}[(\text{agent1\_signal\_choice} = 2) \mapsto (\text{agent1\_signal\_choice} \in \{0, 1, 2\})]$, *always move?*				
standard	✗	3.979	2.371	7.754	3
impatient	✔	4.001	2.307	7.703	3
pathological	✔	3.958	2.326	7.681	3
$\Box\rightarrow$	$\varphi^*[(\text{agent1\_pos\_x} = 1.376) \mapsto (1.0 \leq \text{agent1\_pos\_x} \leq 1.5)]$, *always move?*				
standard	✗	154.7	17.14	179.7	19
impatient	✔	207.6	4.622	220.1	19
pathological	✗	141.1	17.34	166.1	19
$\Box\rightarrow$	$\varphi^* \wedge (\text{agent2\_pos\_x} = 1.316) \wedge (\text{agent2\_pos\_z} = 0.378) \wedge \cdots$, *always move?*				
standard	✗	8.995	4.111	16.74	3
impatient	✔	9.107	3.951	16.71	3
pathological	✔	9.037	3.913	16.54	3
$\Box\rightarrow$	$\varphi^* \wedge (\text{agent2\_pos\_x} = 1.316) \wedge (\text{agent2\_pos\_z} = 0.378) \wedge \cdots$, *ever not move?*				
standard	✔	8.483	4.029	16.33	3
impatient	✗	8.979	3.848	16.46	3
pathological	✗	9.087	3.941	16.70	3

We pose three queries about the blue car's decision making at the moment when it releases the brakes and enters the intersection (Step 1 in Fig. 4):

1. Did the blue car actually decide to move, as it appeared to?
2. Could a different turn signal have led the blue car to remain stationary?
3. If the blue car had arrived before the red car and the red car was not signaling a turn, might the blue car have waited to 'bait' the red car into entering the intersection and creating the opportunity for a crash?

Intuitively, the second question should distinguish the 'standard' car from the 'reckless' and 'pathological', which should continue to move into the intersection no matter what. The third question should then distinguish between the 'reckless' and 'pathological' cars, with the former taking the opportunity for a clean path through the intersection, while the latter lies in wait.

There are natural explanations for the behavior of the other decision models: the 'standard' car is undertaking common human driving behavior given the perception of an unobstructed path through the intersection, the 'reckless' car demonstrates a prioritization of individual speed over collective safe driving, while the 'pathological' car might be attempting to trigger a crash for insurance fraud. Notably, in the case of the 'reckless' car, we do not want to inherently describe that behavior as incorrect as verification methods might, such as any implementing [28]. It could be that exigent circumstances necessitate reckless behavior, and that the blue car not entering the intersection as fast as possible would trigger a greater harm than a minor crash.

The results of our benchmarks are summarized in Table 2. As before, all of the statistics were gathered on an Intel Xeon CPU E5-2650 v3 @ 2.30GHz workstation with 64 GB of RAM. Each heading in Table 2 describes a family of (counter)factual scenarios and behavior, as well as whether the query is a verification ('would...?') or counterfactual generation ('might...?') one. The rows list the decision model invoked within A, the answer as determined by the verification oracle, timings, and the total number of feasible paths.

We find that soid provides an interpretable and adaptive oracle allowing the investigator to query a sequence of counterfactuals without directly interacting with A or the machine learned-model underlying it. Most of our queries resolved within $< 20s$, providing effective usability. The results of the queries demonstrate the distinctive behaviors expected of the three conflicting purposes, allowing a capable investigator to distinguish them as desired.

4   Conclusion

We briefly conclude by considering some future directions for extensions to soid.

Supporting DNNs. Many modern machine-learned agents rely on models built out of deep neural network (DNN) architectures. Extending soid to support such agents – most likely by relying on recent innovations in symbolic execution for neural networks [12] and SMT-based neural network verifiers [17,18] – is a possible direction for increasing the utility of soid.

Programming Counterfactuals. Although soid is adaptive, that does not necessarily mean it needs to be interactive. A further possible direction would be to design a counterfactual calculus as the basis for a programming language that would invoke soid as part of its semantics. Such a language could potentially be the basis for formalizing legal regimes for which counterfactual analysis forms a critical component. A related direction would be to integrate with a scenario specification language like SCENIC from the VerifAI project [9,11] to add another layer of capability onto the specification of families of counterfactuals.

Acknowledgements. The authors thank Gideon Yaffe, Man-Ki Yoon, Cristian Cadar, and Daniel Liew. This work was supported by the Office of Naval Research (ONR) of the United States Department of Defense through a National Defense Science and Engineering Graduate (NDSEG) Fellowship, by the State Government of Styria, Austria - Department Zukunftsfonds Steiermark, by EPSRC grant no EP/R014604/1, and by NSF awards CCF-2131476, CCF-2106845, CCF-2219995, CCF-2318974, and CNS-2245344. The authors would also like to thank the Isaac Newton Institute for Mathematical Sciences, Cambridge, for support and hospitality during the programme Verified Software where work on this paper was undertaken.

References

1. Adadi, A., Berrada, M.: Peeking inside the black-box: a survey on Explainable Artificial Intelligence (XAI). IEEE Access **6**, 52138–52160 (2018)
2. Anand, S., Păsăreanu, C.S., Visser, W.: JPF–SE: a symbolic execution extension to Java PathFinder. In: Grumberg, O., Huth, M. (eds.) Tools and Algorithms for the Construction and Analysis of Systems, pp. 134–138. Springer Berlin Heidelberg, Berlin, Heidelberg (2007). https://doi.org/10.1007/978-3-540-71209-1_12
3. Angwin, J., Larson, J., Mattu, S., Kirchner, L.: Machine Bias. ProPublica (May 23rd, 2016). https://www.propublica.org/article/machine-bias-risk-assessments-in-criminal-sentencing
4. Barrett, C., Fontaine, P., Tinelli, C.: The SMT-LIB Standard: Version **2**, 6 (2021)
5. Cadar, C., Dunbar, D., Engler, D.R.: KLEE: Unassisted and automatic generation of high-coverage tests for complex systems programs. In: USENIX Symposium on Operating Systems Design and Implementation (OSDI '08), pp. 209–224 (2008)
6. Chevalier-Boisvert, M., Golemo, F., Cao, Y., Mehta, B., Paull, L.: Duckietown Environments for OpenAI Gym. https://github.com/duckietown/gym-duckietown (2018)
7. Chockler, H., Halpern, J.Y.: Responsibility and blame: a structural-model approach. J. Artif. Intell. Res. **22**, 93–115 (2004)
8. Dastin, J.: Amazon scraps secret AI recruiting tool that showed bias against women. Reuters (2018). https://www.reuters.com/article/us-amazon-com-jobs-automation-insight/amazon-scraps-secret-ai-recruiting-tool-that-showed-bias-against-women-idUSKCN1MK08G
9. Dreossi, T., et al.: VerifAI: a toolkit for the formal design and analysis of artificial intelligence-based systems. In: Intentional Conference on Computer Aided Verification (CAV '19), pp. 432–442. Springer (2019)
10. Feigenbaum, J., Jaggard, A.D., Wright, R.N.: Accountability in computing: Concepts and Mechanisms. Found. Trends® Privacy Security **2**(4), 247–399 (2020)
11. Fremont, D.J., Dreossi, T., Ghosh, S., Yue, X., Sangiovanni-Vincentelli, A.L., Seshia, S.A.: Scenic: a language for scenario specification and scene generation. In: ACM SIGPLAN Conference on Programming Language Design and Implementation (PLDI '19), pp. 63–78 (2019)
12. Gopinath, D., Wang, K., Zhang, M., Pasareanu, C.S., Khurshid, S.: Symbolic Execution for Deep Neural Networks. arXiv preprint arXiv:1807.10439 (2018)
13. Guidotti, R., Monreale, A., Ruggieri, S., Turini, F., Giannotti, F., Pedreschi, D.: A survey of methods for explaining black box models. ACM Comput. Surv. (CSUR) **51**(5), 1–42 (2018)
14. Halpern, J.Y., Pearl, J.: Causes and explanations: a structural-model approach. part i: causes. British J. Philos. Sci. **56**(4), 843–887 (2005)

15. Halpern, J.Y., Pearl, J.: Causes and explanations: a structural-model approach. part II: explanations. British J. Philos. Sci. **56**(4), 889–911 (2005)

16. Judson, S., Elacqua, M., Córdoba, F.C., Antonopoulos, T., Könighofer, B., Shapiro, S.J., Piskac, R.: 'Put the Car on the Stand': SMT-based Oracles for Investigating Decisions. In: ACM Symposium on Computer Science and Law (CSLAW '24) (2024). https://arxiv.org/abs/2305.05731 for an extended technical report

17. Katz, G., Barrett, C., Dill, D.L., Julian, K., Kochenderfer, M.J.: Reluplex: an efficient SMT solver for verifying deep neural networks. In: International Conference on Computer Aided Verification (CAV '17), pp. 97–117 (2017)

18. Katz, G.: The marabou framework for verification and analysis of deep neural networks. In: International Conference on Computer Aided Verification (CAV '19), pp. 443–452 (2019)

19. Kroll, J.A., et al.: Accountable algorithms. Univ. Pa. Law Rev. **165**(3), 633–705 (2017)

20. Lewis, D.: Counterfactuals. John Wiley & Sons (2013). originally published in 1973

21. Liew, D., Schemmel, D., Cadar, C., Donaldson, A.F., Zahl, R., Wehrle, K.: Floating-point symbolic execution: a case study in N-version programming. In: IEEE/ACM International Conference on Automated Software Engineering (ASE '17), pp. 601–612 (2017)

22. Lindner, M., Aparicius, J., Lindgren, P.: No panic! verification of rust programs by symbolic execution. In: 2018 IEEE 16th International Conference on Industrial Informatics (INDIN), pp. 108–114. IEEE (2018)

23. Loring, B., Mitchell, D., Kinder, J.: ExpoSE: practical symbolic execution of standalone JavaScript. In: International SPIN Symposium on Model Checking of Software (SPIN '17), pp. 196–199 (2017)

24. Mothilal, R.K., Sharma, A., Tan, C.: Explaining machine learning classifiers through diverse counterfactual explanations. In: ACM Conference on Fairness, Accountability, and Transparency (FAT* '20), pp. 607–617 (2020)

25. de Moura, L., Bjørner, N.: Model-based theory combination. Electron. Notes Theor. Comput. Sci. **198**(2), 37–49 (2008)

26. Moura, L.d., Bjørner, N.: Z3: An efficient SMT Solver. In: International Conference on Tools and Algorithms for the Construction and Analysis of Systems (TACAS '08), pp. 337–340 (2008)

27. Pedregosa, F., et al.: Scikit-learn: machine learning in Python. J. Mach. Learn. Res. **12**, 2825–2830 (2011)

28. Shalev-Shwartz, S., Shammah, S., Shashua, A.: On a Formal Model of Safe and Scalable Self-Driving Cars. arXiv preprint arXiv:1708.06374 (2017)

29. Shoshitaishvili, Y., et al.: SoK: (State of) The art of war: offensive techniques in binary analysis. In: IEEE Symposium on Security and Privacy (S&P '16) (2016)

30. Smiley, L.: 'I'm the Operator': The Aftermath of a Self-Driving Tragedy. Wired Magazine (2022). https://www.wired.com/story/uber-self-driving-car-fatal-crash/

31. Wachter, S., Mittelstadt, B., Russell, C.: Counterfactual explanations without opening the black box: automated decisions and the GDPR. Harvard J. Law Technolo. **31**, 841 (2017)

32. Watkins, C.J.C.H., Dayan, P.: Q-learning. Mach. Learn. **8**, 279–292 (1992)

33. Yoon, M.K., Shao, Z.: ADLP: accountable data logging protocol for publish-subscribe communication systems. In: International Conference on Distributed Computing Systems (ICDCS '19), pp. 1149–1160. IEEE (2019)

Machine Learning and Neural Networks

Marabou 2.0: A Versatile Formal Analyzer of Neural Networks

Haoze Wu[1(✉)], Omri Isac[2], Aleksandar Zeljić[1], Teruhiro Tagomori[1,3],
Matthew Daggitt[4], Wen Kokke[5], Idan Refaeli[2], Guy Amir[2], Kyle Julian[1],
Shahaf Bassan[2], Pei Huang[1], Ori Lahav[2], Min Wu[1], Min Zhang[6],
Ekaterina Komendantskaya[4], Guy Katz[2], and Clark Barrett[1]

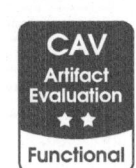

[1] Stanford University, Stanford, USA
haozewu@stanford.edu
[2] The Hebrew University of Jerusalem, Jerusalem, Israel
[3] NRI Secure, Palo Alto, USA
[4] Heriot-Watt University, Edinburgh, UK
[5] University of Strathclyde, Glasgow, UK
[6] East China Normal University, Shanghai, China

Abstract. This paper serves as a comprehensive system description of version 2.0 of the Marabou framework for formal analysis of neural networks. We discuss the tool's architectural design and highlight the major features and components introduced since its initial release.

1 Introduction

With the increasing pervasiveness of deep neural networks (DNNs), the formal analysis of DNNs has become a burgeoning research field within the formal methods community. Multiple DNN reasoners have been proposed in the past few years, including α-β-CROWN [56,65,69], ERAN [45–47], Marabou [32], MN-BaB [16], NNV [35,51], nnenum [4], VeriNet [24,25], and many others.

We focus here on the Marabou [32] tool, which has been used by the research community in a wide range of formal DNN reasoning applications (e.g., [9,12,17, 18,22,26,34,37,49,54,64,66], inter alia). Initially, Marabou was introduced as a from-scratch re-implementation of the Reluplex [31] decision procedure, with a native linear programming engine and limited support for DNN-level reasoning. Over the years, fundamental changes have been made to the tool, not only from an algorithmic perspective but also to its engineering and implementation.

This paper introduces version 2.0 of Marabou. Compared to its predecessor, Marabou 2.0: (i) employs a new build/test system; (ii) has an optimized core system architecture; (iii) runs an improved decision procedure and abstract interpretation techniques; (iv) handles a wider range of activation functions;(v) supports proof production; (vi) supports additional input formats; and (vii) contains a more powerful Python API. Due to these changes, the original system description [32] no longer gives an accurate account of the tool's current capabilities. Our goal in this paper is to close this gap and provide a comprehensive

© The Author(s) 2024
A. Gurfinkel and V. Ganesh (Eds.): CAV 2024, LNCS 14682, pp. 249–264, 2024.
https://doi.org/10.1007/978-3-031-65630-9_13

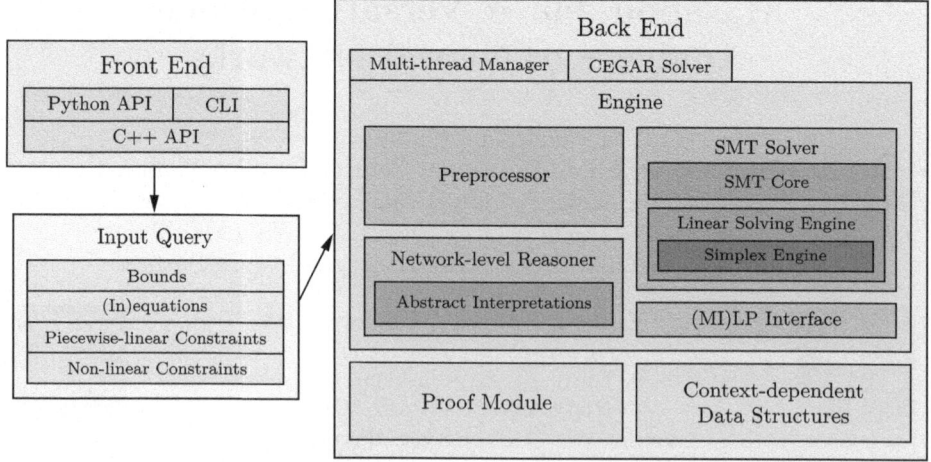

Fig. 1. High-level overview of Marabou 2.0's system architecture.

description of the current Marabou system. We highlight the major features introduced since the initial version, describe a few of its many recent uses, and report on its performance, as demonstrated by the VNN-COMP'23 results and additional runtime comparisons against an early version of Marabou.

2   Architecture and Core Components

In this section, we discuss the core components of Marabou 2.0. An overview of its system architecture is given in Fig. 1. At a high level, Marabou performs satisfiability checking on a set of linear and non-linear constraints, supplied through one of the front-end interfaces. The constraints typically represent a verification query over a neural network and are stored in an *InputQuery* object. We distinguish variable bounds from other linear constraints, and piecewise-linear constraints (which can be reduced to linear constraints via case analysis) from more general, non-linear constraints.

Variables are represented as consecutive indices starting from 0. (In)equations are represented as *Equation* objects. Piecewise-linear constraints are represented by objects of classes that inherit from the *PiecewiseLinearConstraint* abstract class. The abstract class defines the key interface methods that are implemented in each sub-class. This way, all piecewise-linear constraints are handled uniformly in the back end. Similarly, each other type of non-linear constraint is implemented as a sub-class of the new *NonlinearConstraint* abstract class. Initially, Marabou only supported the ReLU and Max constraints. In Marabou 2.0, over ten types of non-linear constraints (listed in the extended version of the paper [61]) are supported.

2.1   Engine

The centerpiece of Marabou is called the Engine, which reasons about the satisfiability of the input query. The engine consists of several components: the Preprocessor, which performs rewrites and simplifications; the Network-level Reasoner, which maintains the network architecture and performs all analyses that require this knowledge; the SMT Solver, which houses complete decision procedures for sets of linear and piecewise-linear constraints; and the (MI)LP Interface, which manages interactions with external (MI)LP solvers for certain optional solving modes as explained below.

Two additional modules are built on top of the Engine. The Multi-thread Manager spawns multiple Engine instances to take advantage of multiple processors. The CEGAR Solver performs incremental linearization [13,62] for nonlinear constraints that cannot be precisely handled by the SMT Solver.

Preprocessor. Every verification query first goes through multiple preprocessing passes, which *normalize, simplify,* and *rewrite* the query. One new normalizing pass introduces auxiliary variables and entailed linear constraints for each of the piecewise-linear constraints, so that case splits on the piecewise-linear constraints can be represented as bound updates and consequently do not require adding new equations.[1] This accelerates the underlying Simplex engine, as explained in the SMT Solver section below. Another significant preprocessing pass involves iterative bound propagation over all constraints. In this process, piecewise linear constraints might collapse into linear constraints and be removed. This pass was present in Marabou 1.0, but could become a runtime bottleneck; whereas Marabou 2.0 employs a data structure optimization that leads to a $\sim$60x speed up. Finally, the preprocessor merges any variables discovered to be equal to each other and also eliminates any constant variables. This results in updates to the variable indices, and therefore a mapping from old indices to new ones needs to be maintained for retrieving satisfying assignments.

SMT Solver. The SMT Solver module implements a sound and complete, lazy-DPLL(T)-based procedure for deciding the satisfiability of a set of linear and piecewise-linear constraints. It performs case analysis on the piecewise-linear constraints and, at each search state, employs a specialized procedure to iteratively search for an assignment satisfying both the linear and non-linear constraints.

Presently, the DeepSoI procedure [58] has replaced the Reluplex procedure [31,32] as Marabou's default procedure to run at each search state. The former provably converges to a satisfying assignment (if it exists) and empirically consistently outperforms the latter. DeepSoI extends the canonical

---

[1] For example, for a piece-wise linear constraint $y = \max(x_1, x_2)$, we would introduce $c_1 : y - x_1 = a_1 \wedge a_1 \geq 0 \wedge y - x_2 = a_2 \wedge a_2 \geq 0$, where a_1 and a_2 are fresh variables. This way, case splits on this constraint can be represented as $c_2 : a_1 \leq 0$ and $c_3 : a_2 \leq 0$, respectively. This preprocessing pass preserves satisfiability because the original constraint is equisatisfiable to $c_1 \wedge (c_2 \vee c_3)$.

sum-of-infeasibilities method in convex optimization [10], which determines the satisfiability of a set of linear constraints by minimizing a cost function that represents the total violation of the constraints by the current assignment. The constraints are satisfiable if and only if the optimal value is 0. Similarly, Deep-SoI formulates a cost function that represents the total violation of the current piecewise-linear constraints and uses a convex solver to stochastically minimize the cost function with respect to the convex relaxation of the current constraints. In addition, DeepSoI also informs the branching heuristics of the SMT Core, which performs a case split on the piecewise-linear constraint with the largest impact (measured by the *pseudocost* metric [58]) on the cost function. The Deep-SoI procedure is implemented for all supported piecewise-linear activation functions. The convex solver can be instantiated either with the native Simplex engine or with an external LP solver via the (MI)LP interface (detailed below). The latter can be more efficient but requires the use of external commercial solvers.

One optimization in Marabou 2.0's Simplex engine is that once the tableau has been initialized, it avoids introducing any new equations — a costly operation that requires re-computing the tableau from scratch. This is achieved by implementing case-splitting and backtracking as updates on variable bounds (as mentioned above), which only requires minimal updates to the tableau state. By our measure, this optimization reduces the runtime of the Simplex engine by over 50%. Moreover, the memory footprint of the solver is also drastically decreased, as the SMT Core no longer needs to save the entire tableau state during case-splitting (to be restored during backtracking).

Network-Level Reasoner. Over the past few years, numerous papers (e.g., [41,46,55,68,70], inter alia) have proposed abstract interpretation techniques that rely on network-level reasoning (e.g., propagating the input bounds layer by layer to tighten output bounds). These analyses can be viewed as a stand-alone, incomplete DNN verification procedure, or as in-processing bound tightening passes for the SMT Solver. Marabou 2.0 features a brand new *NetworkLevelReasoner* class that supports this type of analysis. The class maintains the neural network topology as a directed acyclic graph, where each node is a *Layer* object. The *Layer* class records key information such as weights, source layers, and mappings between neuron indices and variable indices. Currently, seven different analyses are implemented:[i] 1.interval bound propagation [20]; 2. symbolic bound propagation [55]; 3. DeepPoly/CROWN analysis [46,70]; 4. LP-based bound tightening [50]; 5. Forward-backward analysis [59]; 6.MILP-based bound tightening [50]; and 7. iterative propagation [57]. Analyses 2–7 are implemented in a parallelizable manner, and analyses 4–7 require calls to an external LP solver. By default, the DeepPoly/CROWN analysis is performed. The Network-level Reasoner tightly interleaves with the SMT Solver: the network-level reasoning is executed any time a new search state is reached (with the most up-to-date variable bounds), and the derived bound tightenings are immediately fed back to the search procedure.

It is noteworthy that the user does not have to explicitly provide the neural network topology to enable network-level reasoning. Instead, the network architecture is *automatically inferred* from the given set of linear and non-linear constraints, via the *constructNetworkLevelReasoner* method in the *InputQuery* class. The Network-level Reasoner is only initialized if such inference is successful. Apart from the abstract interpretation passes, the Network-level Reasoner can also evaluate concrete inputs. This is used to implement the LP-based bound tightening optimization introduced by the NNV tool [51].

(MI)LP Interface. Marabou can now optionally be configured to invoke the Gurobi Optimizer [23], a state-of-the-art Mixed Integer Linear Programming (MILP) solver. The *GurobiWrapper* class contains methods to construct a MILP problem and invoke the solver. The *MILPEncoder* class is in charge of encoding the current set of linear and non-linear constraints as (MI)LP constraints. Piecewise-linear constraints can either be encoded precisely, or replaced with a convex relaxation, resulting in a linear program. For other non-linear constraints, only the latter option is available. The (MI)LP interface presently has three usages in the code base. Two have already been mentioned, i.e., in some of the abstract interpretation passes and optionally in the DeepSoI procedure. Additionally, when Marabou is compiled with Gurobi, a `--milp` mode is available, in which the Engine performs preprocessing and abstract interpretation passes, and then directly encodes the verification problem as a MILP problem to be solved by Gurobi. The mode is motivated by the observation that the performance of Gurobi and the SMT Solver can be complementary [48,58].

Multi-thread Manager. Parallelization is an important way to improve verification efficiency. Marabou supports two modes of parallelization, both managed by the new *MultiThreadManager* class: the *split-and-conquer* mode [57] and the *portfolio* mode. In the split-and-conquer mode, the original query is dynamically partitioned and re-partitioned into independent sub-queries, to be handled by idle workers. The partitioning strategy is implemented as a sub-class of the *QueryDivider* abstract class. Currently, two strategies are available: one partitions the intervals of the input variables; the other splits on piecewise linear constraints. By default, the former is used only when the input dimension is less than or equal to ten. In the portfolio mode, each worker solves the same query with a different random seed, which takes advantage of the stochastic nature of the DeepSoI procedure. Developing an interface to define richer kinds of portfolios is work in progress.

CEGAR Solver. While the DNN verification community has by and large focused on piecewise-linear activation functions, other classes of non-linear connections exist and are commonly used for certain architectures [27,53]. Apart from introducing support for non-linear constraints in the Preprocessor and the Network-level Reasoner, the latest Marabou version also incorporates a counter-example guided abstraction refinement (CEGAR) solving mode [62], based on incremental linearization [13] to enable more precise reasoning about non-linear constraints that are not piecewise linear. Currently, the CEGAR solver only supports Sigmoid and Tanh, but the module can be extended to handle other activation functions.

2.2 Context-Dependent Data-Structures

When performing a case split or backtracking to a previous search state, the SMT Core needs to save or restore information such as variable bounds and the phase status of each piecewise-linear constraint (e.g., is a ReLU currently active, inactive, or unfixed). To efficiently support these operations, Marabou 2.0 uses the notion of a context level (borrowed from the CVC4 SMT solver [6]), and stores the aforementioned information in *context-dependent data structures*. These data structures behave similarly to their standard counterparts, except that they are associated with a context level and *automatically* save and restore their state as the context increases or decreases. This major refactoring has greatly simplified the implementation of saving and restoring solver states and is an important milestone in an ongoing effort to integrate a full-blown Conflict-Driven Clause-Learning (CDCL) mechanism into Marabou.

2.3 Proof Module

A proof module has recently been introduced into Marabou, enabling it to optionally produce proof certificates after an unsatisfiable (UNSAT) [29] result. This is common practice in the SAT and SMT communities and is aimed at ensuring solver reliability. Marabou produces proof certificates based on a constructive variant of the Farkas lemma [52], which ensures the existence of a *proof vector* that witnesses the unsatisfiability of a linear program. Specifically, the *proof vector* corresponds to a linear equation that is violated by the variable bounds [29]. The full certificate of UNSAT is comprised of a *proof tree*, whose nodes represent the search states explored during the solving. Each node may contain a list of *lemmas* that are used as additional constraints in its descendent nodes; and each leaf node contains the proof vector for the unsatisfiability of the corresponding sub-query. The lemmas encapsulate some of the variable bounds, newly derived by the piecewiese-linear constraints of the query, and require their own witnesses (i.e., proof vectors). The *BoundExplainer* class is responsible for constructing all proof vectors, for updating them during execution, and for appending them to the node. The proof tree itself is implemented using the *UnsatCertificateNode* class.

When the solver is run in proof-production mode, the Proof module closely tracks the steps of the SMT Solver module and constructs the proof tree on the fly: new nodes are added to the tree whenever a case split is performed; and a new proof vector is generated whenever a lemma is learned or UNSAT is derived for a sub-query. If the Engine concludes that the entire query is UNSAT, a proof checker (implemented as an instance of the *Checker* class) will be triggered to certify the proof tree. It does so by traversing the tree and certifying the

```
Q = Marabou.read_onnx("model.onnx")          Q = Marabou.read_onnx("model.onnx")
X, Y = Q.inputVars[0], Q.outputVars[0]       X, Y = Q.inputVars[0], Q.outputVars[0]
Q.setLowerBound(X[0], 0.1)                   Q.addConstraint(Var(X[0]) >= 0.1)
Q.addInequality([Y[0], Y[1]], [1, -0.5], 0)  Q.addConstraint(Var(Y[0]) <= 0.5 * Var(Y[1]))
Q.solve()                                    Q.solve()
```

(a) The base Python API   (b) The "Pythonic" API

Fig. 2. Two ways to define the same verification query through the Python API.

correctness of the lemmas and the unsatisfiability of the leaf nodes. A formally verified and precise proof-checker is currently under development [14]. Note that, currently, proof production mode is only compatible with a subset of the features supported by Marabou. Adding support for the remaining features (e.g., for the parallel solving mode) is an ongoing endeavor.

2.4 Front End

Marabou provides interfaces to prepare input queries and invoke the back-end solver in multiple ways. The Marabou executable can be run on the command line, taking in network/property/query files in supported formats. The Python and C++ APIs support this functionality as well, but also contain methods to add arbitrary linear and (supported) non-linear constraints. In addition, a layer on top of the Python API was added to Marabou 2.0 which allows users to define constraints in a more *Pythonic* manner, resulting in more succinct code. For example, suppose one wants to check whether the first output of a network (stored in the ONNX format) can be less than or equal to half of its second output, when the first input is greater than or equal to 0.1. Figure 2a shows how to perform this check with the base Python API, while Fig. 2b exhibits the "Pythonic" API.

Typically, a query consists of the encoding of (one or several) neural networks and the encoding of a property on the network(s). To encode a neural network, the user has two options: 1) pass in a neural network file to be parsed by one of the neural network parsers; or 2) manually add constraints to encode the neural network. The main network format for Marabou 2.0 is now ONNX, towards which the neural network verification community is converging. The NNet format and the Tensorflow protobuf format are still supported but will likely be phased out in the long run. To encode the property on top of the neural network encoding, the user can 1) pass in a property file to be parsed by one of the property parsers; or 2) manually encode the property. Currently Marabou has two property parsers, one for a native property file format [32], and a new one for the VNN-LIB format, supporting the standardization effort of the community.

In addition to the aforementioned network and property file formats, Marabou also supports a native query file format that describes a set of linear and non-linear constraints. This can be dumped/parsed from all interfaces.

2.5   Availability, License, and Installation

Marabou is available under the permissive modified BSD open-source license, and runs on Linux and macOS machines. The tool can be built from scratch using CMake. Marabou is now also available on The Python Package Index (PyPI) and can be installed through `pip`. The latest version of Marabou is available at: https://github.com/NeuralNetworkVerification/Marabou. The artifact associated with this tool description is archived on Zenodo [60].

3   Highlighted Features and Applications

In terms of performance, Marabou is on par with state-of-the-art verification tools. In the latest VNN-COMP [11], Marabou won the second place overall, and scored the highest among all CPU-based verifiers. We summarize the main results in the extended version of the paper [61]. In this section, we focus on the usability aspect of Marabou, and highlight some of its recent applications — as well as the features that make them possible. We believe this diverse set of use cases (as well as the relevant scripts in the artifact [60]) serve as valuable examples, which will inspire new ways to apply the solver. More use cases can be found in the extended version of the paper [61]. A runtime evaluation of Marabou 2.0 against an early version appears in Sect. 4.

Verifying the Decima Job Scheduler. Recently, Graph Neural Networks (GNNs) have been used to schedule jobs over multi-user, distributed-computing clusters, achieving state-of-the-art job completion time [38]. However, concerns remain over whether GNN-based solutions satisfy expected cost-critical properties beyond performance. Marabou has been used to verify a well-known fairness property called *strategy-proofness* [59] for a high-profile, state-of-the-art GNN-based scheduler called Decima [38]. The verified property states that "a user cannot get their job scheduled earlier by misrepresenting their resource requirement." While it is challenging to represent a GNN directly in ONNX [21], Marabou's Python API makes it possible to manually encode Decima and the specification as a set of linear and non-linear constraints. From these constraints, the Network-level Reasoner is able to automatically infer a feed-forward structure with residual connections and then use it for the purpose of abstract interpretation. Notably, Marabou was able to handle the *original* Decima architecture, proving that the property holds on the vast majority of the examined job profiles but can indeed be violated in some cases.

Formal XAI. Despite their prevalence, DNNs are considered "black boxes", uninterpretable to humans. *Explainable AI* (XAI) aims to understand DNN decisions to enhance trust. Most XAI methods are heuristic-based and lack formal correctness guarantees [36,43,44], which can be problematic for critical, regulation-heavy systems. Recent work showed that Marabou can be utilized as a sub-routine in procedures designed for producing *formal and provable* explanations for DNNs [7,8,26,37,63]. For instance, it can be used in constructing formal *abductive explanations* [8,28], which are subsets of input features that are, by themselves, provably sufficient for determining the DNN's output. This approach has been successfully applied to large DNNs in the domains of computer vision [8,63], NLP [37], and DRL robotic navigation [7]. These studies highlight the potential of Marabou in tasks that go beyond formal verification.

Analyzing Learning-Based Robotic Systems. Deep Reinforcement Learning has extensive application in robotic planning and control. Marabou has been applied in these settings to analyze different safety and liveness properties [2,3,15,54]. For example, Amir et al. [2] used Marabou to detect infinite loops in a real-world robotic navigation platform. This was achieved by querying whether there exists a state to which the robot will always return within a finite number of steps k, effectively entering an infinite loop. A multi-step property like this can be conveniently encoded in Marabou, by (i) encoding k copies of the control policy; (ii) for each time-step t, encoding the system transition as constraints over the current state (input to the policy at t), the decided action (output of the policy at t), and the next state (input to the policy at $t + 1$); and (iii) encoding the "loop" constraint that the initial state (t_1) is equal to the final state (t_k). From this set of constraints, the Network-level Reasoner can infer the structure of and perform abstract interpretations over a *concatenated network*, where the input is the initial state and the output is the final state. Moreover, due to the low input dimension, the split-and-conquer mode in the Multi-thread Manager can be used to perform input-splitting, effectively searching for such loops in independent input regions in parallel. Notably, Marabou can detect loops in the system for agents trained using state-of-the-art RL algorithms, in cases where gradient/optimization-based approaches fail to find any. Loops detected this way have also been observed in the real world [1].

Proof Production for the ACAS-Xu Benchmarks. A well-studied set of benchmarks in DNN verification derives from an implementation of the ACAS-Xu airborne system for collision avoidance [30]. Using Marabou, we were able to produce certificates of unsatisfiability for these benchmarks for the first time. Marabou was able to produce certificates for 113 out of the 180 tested benchmarks, with only mild overhead incurred by proof generation and certification. The proof certificates contained over 1.46 million proof-tree leaves, of which more than 99.99% were certified by the native proof checker, while the remaining were certified by a trusted SMT solver. Additional details are provided in [29].

Specifications on Neural Activation Patterns. Properties of hidden neurons garner increasing interest [67], as they shed light on the internal decision-making process of the neural network. Gopinath et al. [19] observed that for a fixed neural network, certain *neuron activation patterns* (NAPs) empirically entail a fixed prediction. More recently, Geng et al. [18] formally verified (using Marabou) the aforementioned property, along with a variety of other properties related to NAPs. Specifications related to NAPs can be conveniently encoded in Marabou. For example, specifying that a certain ReLU is activated amounts to setting the lower bound of the variable corresponding to the ReLU input to 0, using the general constraint-encoding methods in the Python/C++ API. Constraints on internal neurons, as with other constraints, can be propagated by the Preprocessor and Network-level Reasoner to tighten bounds.

Robustness Against Semantically Meaningful Perturbations. Considering specifications of perception networks, there is an ongoing effort in the verification community to go beyond *adversarial robustness* [5,33,39,40,62]. Marabou has been used to verify robustness against semantically meaningful perturbations that can be analytically defined/abstracted as linear constraints on the neural network inputs (e.g., brightness, uniform haze) [42]. More recently, Marabou has also been successfully applied in a neural symbolic approach, where the correct network behavior is defined with respect to that of another network [62,64]. For example, Wu et al. [62] considered the specification that an image classifier's prediction does not change with respect to outputs of an image generative model trained to capture a complex distribution shift (e.g., change in weather condition). A property like this can be conveniently defined in Marabou by loading the classifier and the generator through the Python API and adding the relevant constraints on/between their input and output variables.

4   Runtime Evaluation

We measure the performance improvement in Marabou 2.0 by comparing it against an early Marabou version (git commit 1c1c66), which can handle ReLU and Max constraints and supports symbolic bound propagation [55]. We collected four benchmark sets from the applications described in Section 3: Alternating Loop [2], DeepCert [42], NAP [18,19], and VeriX [63]. There are 745 instances in total. Details about the benchmarks can be found in the extended version of the paper [61].

Figure 3 compares the runtime of the two Marabou versions on all

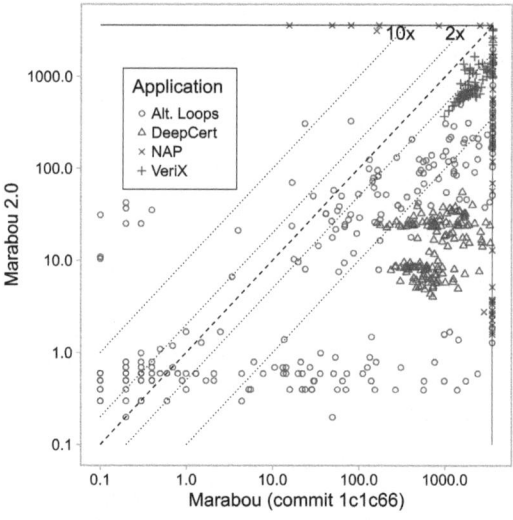

Fig. 3. Runtime performance of Marabou 2.0 and an early version of Marabou on four applications supported by both versions.

the benchmarks with a 1 h CPU timeout. Each configuration was given 1 core and 8GB of memory. Note that Marabou 2.0 was not configured with external solvers in this experiment. We see that Marabou 2.0 is significantly more efficient for a vast majority of the instances. Upon closer examination, an at-least $2\times$ speed-up is achieved on 428 instances and an at-least $10\times$ speed-up is achieved on 263 instances. Moreover, Marabou 2.0 is also significantly more memory efficient, with a median peak usage of 57MB (versus 604MB with the old version). Solvers'performance on individual benchmarks is reported in the extended version of the paper [61].

5   Conclusion and Next Steps

We have summarized the current state of Marabou, a maturing formal analyzer for neural-network-enabled systems that is under active development. In its current form, Marabou is a versatile and user-friendly toolkit suitable for a wide range of formal analysis tasks. Moving forward, we plan to improve Marabou in several dimensions. Currently, we are actively integrating a CDCL mechanism in the SMT Solver module. Given that many applications involve repeated invocation of the solver on similar queries, we also plan to support incremental solving in the style of pushing and popping constraints, leveraging the newly introduced context-dependent data structures. In addition, adding GPU support (in the Network-level Reasoner) and handling other types of non-linear constraints are also on the development agenda for Marabou.

Acknowledgment. The work of Wu, Zeljić, Tagomori, Huang and Wu was partially supported by the NSF (grant number 2211505), by the BSF (grant number 2020250), a Ford Alliance Project (199909), the Stanford Center for AI Safety, and the Stanford Institute for Human-Centered Artificial Intelligence (HAI). The work of Daggit, Kokke and Komendantskaya was partially supported by the EPSRC grant EP/T026952/1, AISEC: AI Secure and Explainable by Construction. The work of Isac, Refaeli, Amir, Bassan, Lahav and Katz was partially funded by the ISF (grant number 3420/21), by the BSF (grant numbers 2021769 and 2020250), and by the European Union (ERC,VeriDeL, 101112713). Views and opinions expressed are however those of the author(s) only and do not necessarily reflect those of the European Union or the European Research Council Executive Agency. Neither the European Union nor the granting authority can be held responsible for them. The work of Zhang was partially supported by the NSFC (grant number 62161146001).

References

1. Amir, G., et al.: Verifying Learning-Based Robotic Navigation Systems: Supplementary Video (2022). https://youtu.be/QIZqOgxLkAE
2. Amir, G., et al.: Verifying learning-based robotic navigation systems. In: Proceedings of the 29th International Conference on Tools and Algorithms for the Construction and Analysis of Systems (TACAS), pp. 607–627 (2023)

3. Amir, G., Schapira, M., Katz, G.: Towards scalable verification of deep reinforcement learning. In: Proceedings of the 21st International Conference on Formal Methods in Computer-Aided Design (FMCAD), pp. 193–203 (2021)
4. Bak, S., Tran, H.D., Hobbs, K., Johnson, T.T.: Improved geometric path enumeration for verifying ReLU neural networks. In: International Conference on Computer Aided Verification, pp. 66–96. Springer (2020)
5. Balunovic, M., Baader, M., Singh, G., Gehr, T., Vechev, M.: Certifying geometric robustness of neural networks. Adv. Neural Inf. Process. Syst. **32** (2019)
6. Barrett, C., et al.: CVC4. In: Gopalakrishnan, G., Qadeer, S. (eds.) CAV 2011. LNCS, vol. 6806, pp. 171–177. Springer, Heidelberg (2011). https://doi.org/10.1007/978-3-642-22110-1_14
7. Bassan, S., Amir, G., Corsi, D., Refaeli, I., Katz, G.: Formally explaining neural networks within reactive systems. In: Proceedings of the 23rd International Conference on Formal Methods in Computer-Aided Design (FMCAD), pp. 10–22 (2023)
8. Bassan, S., Katz, G.: Towards formal XAI: formally approximate minimal explanations of neural networks. In: Proceedings of the 29th International Conference on Tools and Algorithms for the Construction and Analysis of Systems (TACAS), pp. 187–207 (2023)
9. Bauer-Marquart, F., Boetius, D., Leue, S., Schilling, C.: SpecRepair: counterexample guided safety repair of deep neural networks. In: Legunsen, O., Rosu, G. (eds.) Model checking software: 28th International Symposium, SPIN 2022, Virtual Event, May 21, 2022, Proceedings, pp. 79–96. Springer, Cham (2022). https://doi.org/10.1007/978-3-031-15077-7_5
10. Boyd, S.P., Vandenberghe, L.: Convex Optimization. Cambridge University Press (2004)
11. Brix, C., Bak, S., Liu, C., Johnson, T.T.: The fourth international verification of neural networks competition (VNN-COMP 2023): summary and results. arXiv preprint arXiv:2312.16760 (2023)
12. Christakis, M., et al.: Automated safety verification of programs invoking neural networks. In: International Conference on Computer Aided Verification, pp. 201–224. Springer (2021)
13. Cimatti, A., Griggio, A., Irfan, A., Roveri, M., Sebastiani, R.: Incremental linearization for satisfiability and verification modulo nnlinear arithmetic and transcendental functions. ACM Trans. Computat. Logic **19**(3), 1–52 (2018)
14. Desmartin, R., Isac, O., Passmore, G., Stark, K., Komendantskaya, E., Katz, G.: Towards a certified proof checker for deep neural network verification. In: Proceedings of the 33rd International Symposium on Logic-Based Program Synthesis and Transformation (LOPSTR), pp. 198–209 (2023)
15. Eliyahu, T., Kazak, Y., Katz, G., Schapira, M.: Verifying learning-augmented systems. In: Proceedings of the Conference of the ACM Special Interest Group on Data Communication on the Applications, Technologies, Architectures, and Protocols for Computer Communication (SIGCOMM), pp. 305–318 (2021)
16. Ferrari, C., Mueller, M.N., Jovanović, N., Vechev, M.: Complete verification via multi-neuron relaxation guided branch-and-bound. In: International Conference on Learning Representations (2022)
17. Funk, N., Baumann, D., Berenz, V., Trimpe, S.: Learning event-triggered control from data through joint optimization. IFAC J. Syst. Control **16** (2021)
18. Geng, C., Le, N., Xu, X., Wang, Z., Gurfinkel, A., Si, X.: Towards reliable neural specifications. In: International Conference on Machine Learning, pp. 11196–11212. PMLR (2023)

19. Gopinath, D., Converse, H., Pasareanu, C., Taly, A.: Property inference for deep neural networks. In: 2019 34th IEEE/ACM International Conference on Automated Software Engineering (ASE), pp. 797–809. IEEE (2019)

20. Gowal, S., et al.: On the effectiveness of interval bound popagation for training verifiably robust models. arXiv preprint arXiv:1810.12715 (2018)

21. Graph Neural Networks support in ONNX (2022). https://github.com/microsoft/onnxruntime/issues/12103

22. Guidotti, D., Leofante, F., Pulina, L., Tacchella, A.: Verification of neural nNetworks: enhancing scalability through pruning. In: European Conference on Artificial Intelligence, pp. 2505–2512. IOS Press (2020)

23. Gurobi Optimization, LLC: Gurobi Optimizer Reference Manual (2023). https://www.gurobi.com

24. Henriksen, P., Lomuscio, A.: DEEPSPLIT: an eEfficient splitting method for neural network verification via indirect effect analysis. In: International Joint Conference on Artificial Intelligence, pp. 2549–2555. ijcai.org (2021)

25. Henriksen, P., Lomuscio, A.R.: Efficient neural network verification via adaptive refinement and adversarial search. In: Giacomo, G.D., et al. (eds.) European Conference on Artificial Intelligence, vol. 325, pp. 2513–2520. IOS Press (2020)

26. Huang, X., Marques-Silva, J.: From robustness to explainability and back again. arXiv preprint arXiv:2306.03048 (2023)

27. Huang, X., Liu, M.-Y., Belongie, S., Kautz, J.: Multimodal unsupervised image-to-image translation. In: Ferrari, V., Hebert, M., Sminchisescu, C., Weiss, Y. (eds.) ECCV 2018. LNCS, vol. 11207, pp. 179–196. Springer, Cham (2018). https://doi.org/10.1007/978-3-030-01219-9_11

28. Ignatiev, A., Narodytska, N., Marques-Silva, J.: Abduction-based explanations for machine learning models. In: AAAI Conference on Artificial Intelligence, vol. 33, pp. 1511–1519. AAAI Press (2019)

29. Isac, O., Barrett, C., Zhang, M., Katz, G.: Neural network verification with proof production. In: Proceedings of the 22nd International Conference on Formal Methods in Computer-Aided Design (FMCAD), pp. 38–48 (2022)

30. Julian, K., Kochenderfer, M., Owen, M.: Deep neural network compression for aircraft collision avoidance systems. J. Guid. Control. Dyn. 42(3), 598–608 (2019)

31. Katz, G., Barrett, C., Dill, D.L., Julian, K., Kochenderfer, M.J.: Reluplex: an efficient SMT solver for verifying deep neural networks. In: Majumdar, R., Kunčak, V. (eds.) CAV 2017. LNCS, vol. 10426, pp. 97–117. Springer, Cham (2017). https://doi.org/10.1007/978-3-319-63387-9_5

32. Katz, G., et al.: The Marabou framework for verification and analysis of deep neural networks. In: Dillig, I., Tasiran, S. (eds.) CAV 2019. LNCS, vol. 11561, pp. 443–452. Springer, Cham (2019). https://doi.org/10.1007/978-3-030-25540-4_26

33. Katz, S.M., Corso, A.L., Strong, C.A., Kochenderfer, M.J.: Verification of image-based neural network controllers using generative models. J. Aerosp. Inf. Syst. 19(9), 574–584 (2022)

34. Liu, C., Cofer, D., Osipychev, D. Verifying an aircraft collision avoidance neural network with Marabou. In: Rozier, K.Y., Chaudhuri, S. (eds.) NFM 2023. LNCS, pp. 79–85. Springer, Cham (2023). https://doi.org/10.1007/978-3-031-33170-1_5

35. Lopez, D.M., Choi, S.W., Tran, H.-D., Johnson, T.T.: NNV 2.0: the neural network verification tool. In: Enea, C., Lal, A. (eds.) CAV 2023, pp. 397–412. Springer, Cham (2023). https://doi.org/10.1007/978-3-031-37703-7_19

36. Lundberg, S.M., Lee, S.I.: A unified approach to interpreting model predictions. Adv. Neural Inf. Process. Syst. **30** (2017)

37. Malfa, E.L., Michelmore, R., Zbrzezny, A.M., Paoletti, N., Kwiatkowska, M.: On guaranteed optimal robust explanations for NLP models. In: International Joint Conference on Artificial Intelligence, pp. 2658–2665. ijcai.org (2021)
38. Matheson, R.: AI system optimally allocates workloads across thousands of servers to cut costs, save energy. Tech Xplore (2019). https://techxplore.com/news/2019-08-ai-optimally-allocates-workloads-thousands.html
39. Mirman, M., Hägele, A., Bielik, P., Gehr, T., Vechev, M.: Robustness certification with generative models. In: ACM SIGPLAN International Conference on Programming Language Design and Implementation, pp. 1141–1154 (2021)
40. Mohapatra, J., Weng, T.W., Chen, P.Y., Liu, S., Daniel, L.: Towards verifying robustness of neural networks against a family of semantic perturbations. In: IEEE/CVF Conference on Computer Vision and Pattern Recognition, pp. 244–252 (2020)
41. Müller, M.N., Makarchuk, G., Singh, G., Püschel, M., Vechev, M.: Prima: general and precise neural network certification via scalable convex hull approximations. Proc. ACM Program. Lang. 6(POPL), 1–33 (2022)
42. Paterson, C., et al.: DeepCert: verification of contextually relevant robustness for neural network image classifiers. In: Habli, I., Sujan, M., Bitsch, F. (eds.) SAFECOMP 2021. LNCS, pp. 3–17. Springer, Cham (2021). https://doi.org/10.1007/978-3-030-83903-1_5
43. Ribeiro, M.T., Singh, S., Guestrin, C.: Why should i trust you? Explaining the predictions of any classifier. In: ACM SIGKDD International Conference on Knowledge Discovery and Data Mining, pp. 1135–1144 (2016)
44. Ribeiro, M.T., Singh, S., Guestrin, C.: Anchors: high-precision model-agnostic explanations. In: AAAI Conference on Artificial Intelligence, vol. 32, pp. 1527–1535. AAAI Press (2018)
45. Singh, G., Ganvir, R., Püschel, M., Vechev, M.: Beyond the single neuron convex barrier for neural network certification. Adv. Neural. Inf. Process. Syst. 32, 15098–15109 (2019)
46. Singh, G., Gehr, T., Püschel, M., Vechev, M.: An abstract domain for certifying neural networks. Proc. ACM Program. Lang. 3(POPL), 1–30 (2019)
47. Singh, G., Gehr, T., Püschel, M., Vechev, M.: Boosting robustness certification of neural networks. In: International Conference on Learning Representations (2019)
48. Strong, C., et al.: Global optimization of objective functions represented by ReLU networks. J. Mach. Learn. 112(10), 3685–3712 (2021)
49. Sun, Y., Usman, M., Gopinath, D., Păsăreanu, C.S.: VPN: verification of poisoning in neural networks. In: Isac, O., Ivanov, R., Katz, G., Narodytska, N., Nenzi, L. (eds.) Software Verification and Formal Methods for ML-Enabled Autonomous Systems: 5th International Workshop, FoMLAS 2022, and 15th International Workshop, NSV 2022, Haifa, 31 July–1 August, and 11 August 2022, Proceedings, pp. 3–14. Springer, Cham (2022). https://doi.org/10.1007/978-3-031-21222-2_1
50. Tjeng, V., Xiao, K.Y., Tedrake, R.: Evaluating robustness of neural networks with mixed integer programming. In: International Conference on Learning Representations (2019)
51. Tran, H.D., et al.: NNV: the neural network verification tool for deep neural networks and learning-enabled cyber-physical systems. In: International Conference on Computer Aided Verification, pp. 3–17. Springer (2020)
52. Vanderbei, R.: Linear programming: foundations and extensions. J. Oper. Res. Soc. (1998)
53. Vaswani, A., et al.: Attention is all nou need. Adv. Neural Inf. Process. Syst. 30 (2017)

54. Vinzent, M., Sharma, S., Hoffmann, J.: Neural policy safety verification via predicate abstraction: CEGAR. In: AAAI Conference on Artificial Intelligence, pp. 15188–15196. AAAI Press (2023)
55. Wang, S., Pei, K., Whitehouse, J., Yang, J., Jana, S.: Efficient formal safety analysis of neural networks. Adv. Neural. Inf. Process. Syst. **31**, 6369–6379 (2018)
56. Wang, S., et al.: Beta-crown: efficient bound propagation with per-neuron split constraints for neural network robustness verification. Adv. Neural. Inf. Process. Syst. **34**, 29909–29921 (2021)
57. Wu, H., et al.: Parallelization techniques for verifying neural networks. In: Proceedings of the 20th International Conference on Formal Methods in Computer-Aided Design (FMCAD), pp. 128–137 (2020)
58. Wu, H., Zeljić, A., Katz, G., Barrett, C.: Efficient neural network analysis with sum-of-infeasibilities. In: Proceedings of the 28th International Conference on Tools and Algorithms for the Construction and Analysis of Systems (TACAS), pp. 143–163 (2022)
59. Wu, H., Barrett, C., Sharif, M., Narodytska, N., Singh, G.: Scalable verification of GNN-based job schedulers. Proc. ACM Program. Lang. **6**(OOPSLA), 1036–1065 (2022)
60. Wu, H., et al.: Artifact for Marabou 2.0: a versatile formal analyzer of neural networks (2022). https://doi.org/10.5281/zenodo.11116016
61. Wu, H., et al.: Marabou 2.0: a versatile formal analyzer of neural networks. arXiv preprint arXiv:2401.14461 (2024)
62. Wu, H., et al.: Toward certified robustness against real-world distribution shifts. In: IEEE Conference on Secure and Trustworthy Machine Learning, pp. 537–553. IEEE (2023)
63. Wu, M., Wu, H., Barrett, C.: VeriX: towards verified explainability of deep neural networks. Adv. Neural Inf. Process. Syst. (2022)
64. Xie, X., Kersting, K., Neider, D.: Neuro-symbolic verification of deep neural networks. In: International Joint Conferences on Artificial Intelligence, pp. 3622–3628. ijcai.org (2022)
65. Xu, K., et al.: Automatic perturbation analysis for scalable certified robustness and beyond. Adv. Neural. Inf. Process. Syst. **33**, 1129–1141 (2020)
66. Yerushalmi, R.: Enhancing deep reinforcement learning with executable specifications. In: International Conference on Software Engineering, pp. 213–217. IEEE (2023)
67. Yosinski, J., Clune, J., Nguyen, A., Fuchs, T., Lipson, H.: Understanding neural networks through deep visualization. arXiv preprint arXiv:1506.06579 (2015)
68. Zelazny, T., Wu, H., Barrett, C., Katz, G.: On reducing over-approximation errors for neural network verification. In: Proceedings of the 22nd International Conference on Formal Methods in Computer-Aided Design (FMCAD), pp. 17–26 (2022)
69. Zhang, H., et al.: General cutting planes for bound-propagation-based neural network verification. Adv. Neural. Inf. Process. Syst. **35**, 1656–1670 (2022)
70. Zhang, H., Weng, T.W., Chen, P.Y., Hsieh, C.J., Daniel, L.: Efficient neural network robustness certification with general activation functions. Adv. Neural. Inf. Process. Syst. **31**, 4944–4953 (2018)

– Applying a particular monitoring technology to a concrete NN involves significant tweaking and *hyperparameter tuning*, with no push-button technology available. OOD monitors typically compute a value from the input and the behavior of the NN. The input is considered OOD if this value is smaller than a configurable *threshold* τ (see Fig. 1)b. The value of this threshold has a significant influence on the performance of the monitors. More inputs would be classified as OOD if the threshold value is high, and vice versa. Moreover, OOD monitors generally have *multiple parameters* that require tuning, thereby aggravating the complexity of manual configuration.

– As OOD monitoring can currently be described as a search for a good heuristic, many more heuristics will appear, implying the need for streamlining their handling and fair comparison.

In this paper, we provide the infrastructure for users and developers of NN monitors aiming at detecting OOD inputs (onwards just "monitors").

Our contributions can be summarized as follows:

– We provide a modular tool called MONITIZER for automatic learning/constructing, optimizing, and evaluating monitors.

– MONITIZER supports (i) *easy practical use*, providing various recent monitors from the literature, which can directly be optimized and applied to user-given networks and datasets with no further inputs required; the push-button solution offers automatic choice of the best available monitor without requiring any knowledge on the side of the user; (ii) *advanced development use*, with the possibility of easily integrating a new monitor or new evaluation techniques. The framework also foresees and allows for the integration of monitoring other properties than OOD.

– We provide a library of 19 well-known monitors from the scientific literature to be used off-the-shelf, accompanied by 9 datasets and 15 NNs, which can be used for easy but rich automatic evaluation and comparison of monitors on various OOD categories.

– We demonstrate the functionality for principled use cases accompanied by examples and a case study comparing a few recent monitoring approaches.

Altogether, we are giving users the infrastructure for automatic creation of monitors, development of new methods, and their comparison to similar approaches.

2   Related Work

NN Monitoring Frameworks. OPENOOD [47,48] contains task-specific benchmarks for OOD detection that consist of an ID and multiple OOD datasets for specific tasks (e.g., Open Set Recognition and Anomaly Detection). Both OPENOOD and MONITIZER contain several different monitors and benchmarks. MONITIZER provides functionality to tune the monitors for the given objective, supports a comprehensive evaluation of monitors on a specific ID dataset by automatically providing generated OOD inputs by, e.g., the addition of noise, and can easily be extended with more datasets. OPENOOD, in contrast to MONITIZER, does not support hyperparameter tuning and generation of OOD inputs.

Samuels et al. propose a framework to optimize an OOD monitor during runtime on newly experienced OOD inputs [26]. While this contains optimization, the framework is specific to one monitor and is based on active learning. MONITIZER is meant to work in an offline setting and optimize a monitor before it is deployed. Additionally, MONITIZER is built for extensibility and reusability, which the other tool is not, e.g., it lacks an executable.

PYTORCH-OOD [27] is a library for OOD detection, yet despite its name, it is *not* part of the official PyTorch-library. It includes several monitors, datasets, and supports the evaluation of the integrated monitors. Both MONITIZER and PYTORCH-OOD provide a library of monitors and datasets. However, there are significant differences. MONITIZER supports optimization of monitors, allowing us to return monitors optimal for a chosen objective, provides a more structured view of the dataset, and provides a transparent and detailed evaluation showing how a monitor performs on different OOD classes. Besides, we provide a one-click solution to easily evaluate the whole set of monitors and automatically return the best available option, fine-tuned to the case. Consequently, MONITIZER is a tool that is much easier to use and extend. Last but not least, it is an alternative implementation that allows cross-checking outcomes, thereby making monitoring more trustworthy.

OOD Benchmarking. Various datasets have been published for OOD benchmarking [15,16,19,37,38], Breitenstein et al. present a classification for different types of OOD data in automated driving [5], and Ferreira et al. propose a benchmark set for OOD with several different categories [11].

3   Monitizer

MONITIZER aims to assist the developers and users of NN monitors and developers of new monitoring techniques by supporting optimization and transparent evaluation of their monitors. It structures OOD data in a hierarchy of classes, and a monitor can be tuned for any (combination) of these classes. It also provides a one-click solution to evaluate a set of monitors and return the best available option optimized for the given requirement.

3.1   Overview

MONITIZER offers two main building blocks, as demonstrated in Fig. 2: optimization and evaluation of NN monitors. NN monitors are typically parameterized and usually depend on the NN and dataset. Before one can evaluate them, they need to be configured and possibly tuned. We refer to monitors that are not yet configured as *monitor templates*. MONITIZER optimizes the monitor templates and evaluates them afterward on several different OOD classes, i.e., types of OOD data.

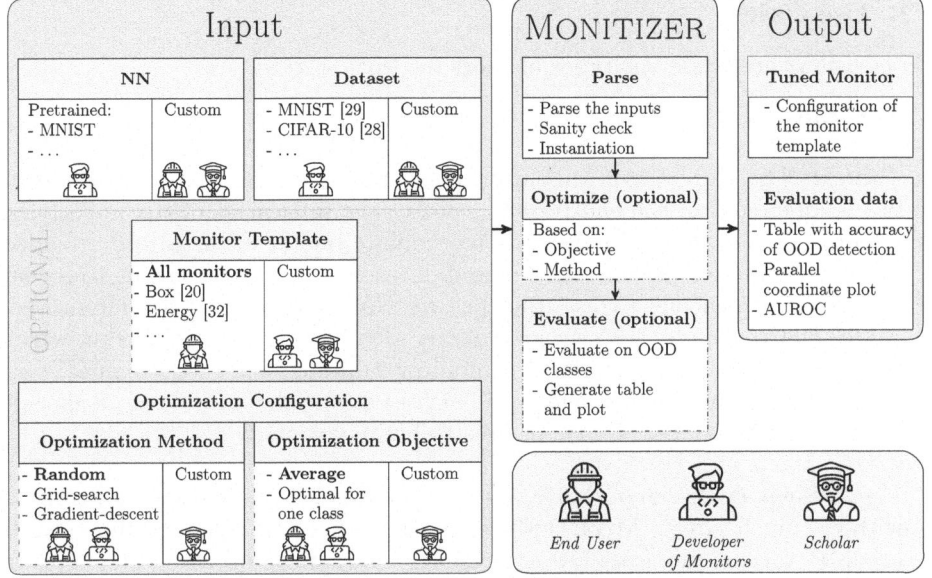

Fig. 2. Architecture of MONITIZER: The required inputs are an NN and the dataset (both can be chosen from existing options). The dashed area indicates optional inputs, and the bold-faced option indicates the default value. The icons(see footnote 1) indicate which types of users are expected to use each of the options.

MONITIZER needs at least two inputs (see Fig. 2): an NN, and an ID-dataset. The user can also provide a monitor template and an optimization configuration (consisting of an optimization objective and optimization method). If these are not provided, MONITIZER reverts to the default values (i.e., evaluating all monitors using the AUROC-score without optimization). For both inputs, the user can choose from the options we offer or provide a custom implementation.

MONITIZER optimizes the provided monitor based on the optimization objectives and method on the given ID dataset. An example of optimization would be:[1] maximize the detection accuracy on blurry images, but keep the accuracy on ID images at least 70%. Optimization is necessary to obtain a monitor that is ready to use. However, it is possible to evaluate a monitor template on its default values for the parameters using the *AUROC*-score (Area Under the Receiver Operating Characteristic Curve)[2].

On successful execution, MONITIZER provides the user with a configuration of the monitor template and the evaluation result. This can be either a table with the accuracy of OOD detection for each OOD dataset along with a parallel coordinate plot for the same (in case of optimization) or the AUROC score.

---

[1] Thanks to Flaticon.com for the Icons.

[2] The ROC (Receiver Operating Characteristic) curve shows the performance of a binary classifier with different decision thresholds. The AUROC computes the area under this curve. The best possible value is 1, indicating perfect prediction.

3.2   Use Cases

We envision three different types of users for MONITIZER:

1. **The End User**

   Context: The end user of a monitor, e.g., an engineer in the aviation industry, is interested in the end product, not in the intricacies of the underlying monitoring technique. She intends to evaluate one or all monitors provided by MONITIZER for her custom NN and dataset, and wants to come to a conclusion on which one to use. She has an NN that needs to be monitored. Additionally, she has her own proprietary ID dataset, e.g., the one on which the NN was trained. She wants a monitor fulfilling some requirement, e.g., one that is optimal on average for all classes or one that can detect a specific type of OOD that her NN is not able to handle properly.

   Usage: Such a user can obtain a monitor tuned to her needs using MONITIZER without much effort. MONITIZER supports this feature out of the box. It provides various monitors (19 at present) that can be optimized for a given network. In case she wants to use a custom NN or a dataset, she has to provide the NN as PyTorch-dump or in onnx-format [4] and add some lines of code to implement the interface for loading her data.

   Required Effort: After providing the interface for her custom dataset, the user only has to trigger the execution. The execution time depends on the hardware quality, the NN's size, the chosen monitor's complexity, and the dataset's size.

2. **The Developer of Monitors**

   Context: The developer of monitoring techniques, e.g., a researcher working in runtime verification of NNs, aims to create novel techniques and assess their performance in comparison to established methods.

   Usage: Such a user can plug their novel monitor into MONITIZER and evaluate it. MONITIZER directly provides the most commonly used NNs and datasets for academic evaluation.

   Required Effort: The code for the monitor needs to be in Python and should implement the functions specified in the interface for monitors in MONITIZER. Afterward, she can trigger the evaluation of her monitoring technique.

3. **The Scholar**

   Context: An expert in monitoring, e.g., an experienced researcher in NN runtime verification, intends to explore beyond the current boundaries. She might want to adapt an NN monitor to properties other than OOD, or to experiment with custom NNs or datasets.

Usage: MONITIZER provides interfaces, and instructions on how to integrate new NNs, datasets, monitors, custom optimization methods and objectives.

Required Effort: The required integration effort depends on the complexity of the concrete use case. For example, adding an NN would take much less time than developing a new monitor.

More detailed examples are available in [1].

3.3 Phases of MONITIZER

An execution of MONITIZER is typically a sequence of three phases: parse, optimize, and evaluate. As mentioned, the user can decide to skip the optimization or the evaluation.

Parse. This phase parses the input, loads the NN and dataset, and instantiates the monitor. It also performs sanity checks on the inputs, e.g., the datasets are available in the file system, the provided monitor is implemented correctly, etc.

Optimize. This phase tunes the parameters of a given monitor template to maximize an objective. It depends on two inputs, the optimization method and the optimization objective, that the user has to give.

An illustrative depiction of this process can be found in [1]. The optimization method defines the search space and generates a new candidate monitor by setting its parameters. MONITIZER then uses the optimization objective to evaluate this candidate. If the objective is to optimize at least one OOD class, MONITIZER evaluates the monitor on a validation set of this class, which is distinct from the test set used in the evaluation later. The optimization method obtains this result and decides whether to continue optimizing or stop and return the best monitor that it has found.

MONITIZER provides three optimization methods: random, grid-search, and gradient descent. Random search tries out a specified number of random sets of parameters and returns the monitor that worked best among these. Grid-search specifies a search grid by looking at the minimal and maximal values of the parameters. It then defines a grid on the search space. The monitor is infused with these parameters for each grid vertex and evaluated on the objective. Gradient-descent follows the gradient of the objective function towards the optimum.

MONITIZER supports multi-objective optimization of monitors. A user can specify a set of OOD classes to optimize for and the minimum required accuracy for ID detection. Single objective optimization is a special case when only one OOD class is specified for optimization. Based on a configuration value, MONITIZER would generate a set of different weight combinations for the objectives and create and evaluate a monitor for each of these combinations. If there are two objectives, MONITIZER generates a Pareto frontier plot; in the case of more than two objectives, the tool generates a table. The user obtains the performance of the optimized monitor for each weight-combination of objectives.

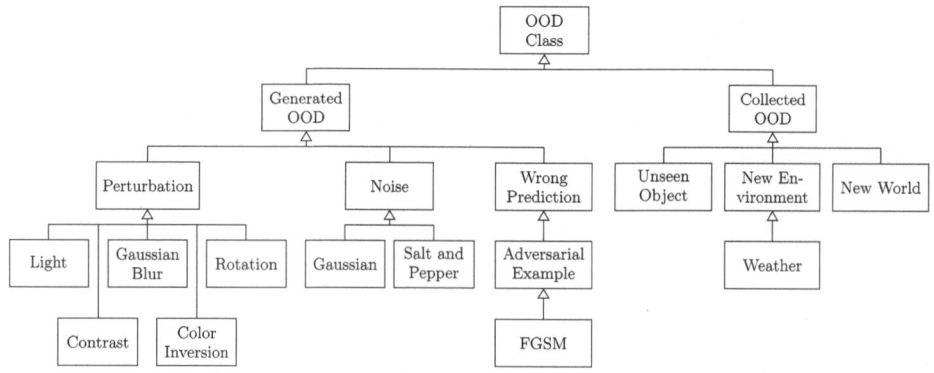

Fig. 3. Class diagram depicting the different types of OOD data.

Evaluate. The evaluation of NN monitors in MONITIZER is structured according to the OOD classification (detailed in the next section). We introduce this classification of OOD data to enable a clearer evaluation and gain knowledge about which monitor performs well on which particular class of OOD. Typically, no monitor performs well on every class of OOD [44]. We highlight this in our evaluation to ensure a fair and meaningful comparison between monitors rather than restricting to a non-transparent and possibly biased average score.

After evaluation, MONITIZER reports the detection accuracy for each OOD class and can also produce a parallel-coordinates-plot displaying the reported accuracy. MONITIZER can also provide confidence intervals for the evaluation quality, which is explained in [1].

3.4   Classification of Out-of-Distribution Data

We now introduce our classification of OOD data. At the top level, an OOD input can either be *generated*, i.e., obtained by distorting ID data [3,14,17,31,41], or it can be *collected* using data from some other available dataset.

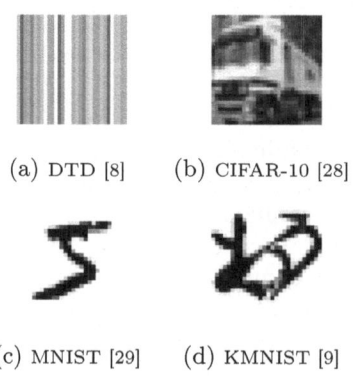

(a) DTD [8]   (b) CIFAR-10 [28]

(c) MNIST [29]   (d) KMNIST [9]

Fig. 4. Examples for OOD

The notion of generated OOD is straightforward. These classes are created by slightly distorting ID data, for example, by increasing the contrast or adding noise. An important factor is the amount of distortion, e.g., the amount of noise, as it influences the NN's performance and needs to be high enough to transform an ID into an OOD input.

We explain the idea of collected OOD with the help of an example shown in Fig. 4. Consider an ID dataset that consists of textures (Fig. 4a). Images containing objects (Fig. 4b) differ from images showing just a texture. But, when we consider a dataset of numbers as ID (Fig. 4c), it seems much more similar to a dataset of letters (Fig. 4d) than textures are to objects. In the first case, the datasets have no common meaning or concept, as if they were belonging to a *new world*. In the second case, the environment and the underlying concept are similar, but an *unseen object* is placed in it.

Figure 3 shows our classification of the OOD data. It is based on the kind of OOD data we found in the literature (discussed in Sect. 2). [1] contains a detailed description of each class and an illustrative figure.

OOD Benchmarks Implementation. Note that the generated OOD will be automatically created by MONITIZER for any given ID dataset. The collected OOD data has to be manually selected. We provide a few preselected datasets (for example, KMNIST [9] as unseen objects for MNIST [29]) in the tool. A user can easily add more when needed. However, for a user like the developer of monitors, MNIST and CIFAR-10 are often sufficient to test new monitoring methodologies, as related work has shown [13,20].

3.5 Library of Monitors, NNs, and Datasets

MONITIZER currently includes 19 monitors, accompanied by 9 datasets and 15 NNs. In the following, we give an overview of the available options.

Monitors. MONITIZER provides different highly cited monitors, which are also included in other tools such as OPENOOD/PYTORCH-OOD. We extended this list by adding monitors from the formal methods community (e.g., BOX monitor, GAUSSIAN monitor). The following monitors are available in MONITIZER: ASH-B,ASH-P,ASH-S [10], BOX-MONITOR [20], DICE [42], ENERGY [32], ENTROPY [33], GAUSSIAN [13], GRADNORM [23], KL MATCHING [15], KNN [43], MAXLOGIT [50], MDS [30], SOFTMAX [17], ODIN [31], REACT [41], MAHALANOBIS [39], SHE [49], TEMPERATURE [12] VIM [45].

Datasets. The following datasets are available in MONITIZER: CIFAR-10, CIFAR-100 [28], DTD [8], FashionMNIST [46], GTSRB [21], ImageNet [40], K-MNIST [9], MNIST [29], SVHN [36].

Neural Networks MONITIZER provides at least one pretrained NN for each available dataset. The library contains more NNs trained on commonly used datasets in academia, such as MNIST and CIFAR-10, allowing users to evaluate monitors on different architectures. [1] contains a detailed description of the pretrained NNs.

4   Summary of Evaluation by Case Study

We demonstrate the necessity of having a clear evaluation in Table 1. The full table containing all available OOD datasets can be found in [1]. We evaluate the

Table 1. Comparison of the AUROC-score of all implemented monitors on different OOD datasets multiplied by 100 (and rounded to the nearest integer). All monitors were evaluated on a fully connected network trained on MNIST. The cells are colored according to the relative performance of a monitor (column) in a specific OOD class (row). The monitors are divided in three ranks and the darker color represents better performance. If several monitors have the same score, they all belong to the better group.

Perturbations	ASH-B [10]	ASH-P [10]	ASH-S [10]	DICE [42]	Energy [32]	Entropy [33]	Gauss [13]	GradNorm [23]	KL Matching [15]	KNN [43]	MDS [30]	Mahalanobis [39]	MaxLogit [50]	ODIN [31]	ReAct [41]	SHE [49]	Softmax [17]	Temperature [12]	VIM [45]
Gaussian	64	65	65	65	65	37	48	89	35	48	62	66	35	50	56	38	61	65	46
Contrast	45	41	41	41	41	56	44	20	56	42	64	49	59	50	51	57	46	41	50
Invert	28	21	21	21	21	47	0	0	39	0	100	100	79	43	92	88	56	21	0
Rotate	60	62	62	61	61	38	43	79	39	41	69	67	39	50	59	41	62	61	41
KMNIST	64	82	81	81	82	18	16	84	18	10	98	97	18	54	84	30	82	82	14

available monitors on a network trained on the MNIST dataset on a GPU and depict the AUROC score. The values of MDS and Mahalanobis can differ when switching between CPU and GPU; refer to [1] for details. The BOX monitor [20] is not included as it does not have a single threshold and, therefore, no AUROC score can be computed. The table shows the ranking of the monitors for the detection of Gaussian noise, increased contrast, color inversion, rotation, and a new, albeit similar dataset (KMNIST). A darker color indicates a better ranking. One can see that there is barely any common behavior among the monitors. For example, while GRADNORM performs best on Gaussian noise, it performs worst on inverted images.

This also shows that it is important for the user to define her goal for the monitor. Not every monitor will be great at detecting a particular type of OOD, and she must carefully choose the right monitor for her setting. MONITIZER eases this task. In addition, it highlights the need for a clear evaluation of new monitoring methods in scientific publications.

We illustrate further features of MONITIZER using the following four monitors: ENERGY [32], ODIN [31], BOX [20], and GAUSSIAN [13]. The first two were proposed by the machine-learning community, and the latter two by the formal methods community.

The output produced by MONITIZER in the form of tables and plots (depicted in Fig. 5) helps the user see the effect of the choice of monitor, chosen objective, and dataset on the monitor's effectiveness. MONITIZER allows users to experiment with different choices and select the one suitable for their needs. Figure 5 shows the evaluation of the mentioned monitors with the MNIST dataset as ID

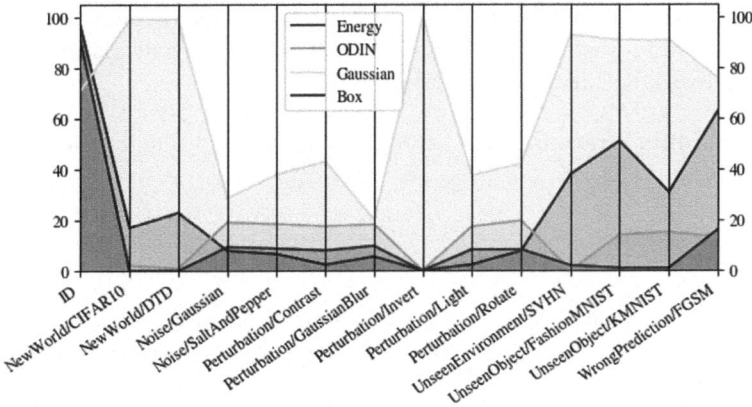

Fig. 5. The monitor templates were optimized on MNIST as ID and for detecting New-World / CIFAR-10 as OOD while keeping 70% accuracy on ID. All monitors were optimized randomly.

data and an optimization with the goal of detecting pre-selected images of the CIFAR-10 dataset as those are entirely unknown to the network. The optimization was performed randomly. This resulted in the GAUSSIAN monitor only correctly classifying around 70% of ID data, whereas the other monitors have higher accuracy on ID data. Consequently, the other monitors perform worse than the GAUSSIAN monitor in detecting OOD data, as there is a tradeoff between good performance on ID and OOD data. This highlights the necessity of proper optimization for each monitor. See [1] for a detailed evaluation where we report on the experiments with different monitors, optimization objectives, and datasets.

Our experiments show that different monitors have different strengths and limitations. One can tune a monitor for a specific purpose (e.g., detecting a particular OOD class with very high accuracy); however, this affects its performance in other OOD classes.

5   Conclusion

MONITIZER is a tool for automating the design and evaluation of NN monitors. It supports developers of new monitoring techniques, potential users of available monitors, and researchers attempting to improve the state of the art. In particular, it optimizes the monitor for the objectives specified by the user and thoroughly evaluates it.

MONITIZER provides a library of 19 monitors, accompanied by 9 datasets and 15 NNs (at least one for each dataset), and three optimization methods (random, grid-search, and gradient descent). Additionally, all these inputs can be easily customized by a few lines of Python code, allowing a user to provide their monitors, datasets, and networks. The framework is extensible so that the user can implement their custom optimization methods and objectives.

Monitizer is an open-source tool providing a freely available platform for new monitors and easing their evaluation. It is publicly available at https://gitlab.com/live-lab/software/monitizer.

Data Availability Statement. A reproduction package including all our results is available at Zenodo [2].

References

1. Azeem, M., Grobelna, M., Kanav, S., Křetínský, J., Mohr, S., Rieder, S.: Monitizer: Automating design and evaluation of neural network monitors. CoRR (2024). https://arxiv.org/abs/2405.10350
2. Azeem, M., Grobelna, M., Kanav, S., Křetínský, J., Mohr, S., Rieder, S.: Reproduction package for article 'monitizer: automating design and evaluation of neural network monitors. In: Proceedings of CAV 2024, Zenodo (2024). https://doi.org/10.5281/zenodo.10933013
3. Bai, H., Canal, G., Du, X., Kwon, J., Nowak, R.D., Li, Y.: Feed two birds with one scone: exploiting wild data for both out-of-distribution generalization and detection. In: ICML 2023. PMLR, vol. 202, pp. 1454–1471. PMLR (2023), https://proceedings.mlr.press/v202/bai23a.html
4. Bai, J., Lu, F., Zhang, K., et al.: ONNX: Open neural network exchange (2019). https://github.com/onnx/onnx
5. Breitenstein, J., Termöhlen, J., Lipinski, D., Fingscheidt, T.: systematization of corner cases for visual perception in automated driving. In: Proceedings of IV, pp. 1257–1264. IEEE (2020). https://doi.org/10.1109/IV47402.2020.9304789
6. Casadio, M., Komendantskaya, E., Daggitt, M.L., Kokke, W., Katz, G., Amir, G., Refaeli, I.: Neural network robustness as a verification property: a principled case study. In: Proceedings of CAV, pp. 219–231. Springer (2022). https://doi.org/10.1007/978-3-031-13185-1_11
7. Cheng, C., Nührenberg, G., Yasuoka, H.: Runtime monitoring neuron activation patterns. In: Proceedings of DATE, pp. 300–303. IEEE (2019). https://doi.org/10.23919/DATE.2019.8714971
8. Cimpoi, M., Maji, S., Kokkinos, I., Mohamed, S., , Vedaldi, A.: Describing textures in the wild. In: Proceedings of CVPR (2014). https://doi.org/10.1109/CVPR.2014.461
9. Clanuwat, T., Bober-Irizar, M., Kitamoto, A., Lamb, A., Yamamoto, K., Ha, D.: Deep learning for classical japanese literature. CoRR (2018). https://doi.org/10.48550/arXiv.1812.01718
10. Djurisic, A., Bozanic, N., Ashok, A., Liu, R.: Extremely simple activation shaping for out-of-distribution detection. In: Proceedings of ICLR. OpenReview.net (2023). https://openreview.net/forum?id=ndYXTEL6cZz
11. Ferreira, R.S., Arlat, J., Guiochet, J., Waeselynck, H.: Benchmarking safety monitors for image classifiers with machine learning. In: PRDC 2021, pp. 7–16. IEEE (2021). https://doi.org/10.1109/PRDC53464.2021.00012
12. Guo, C., Pleiss, G., Sun, Y., Weinberger, K.Q.: On calibration of modern neural networks. In: Proc. ICML, pp. 1321–1330. PMLR (2017). https://proceedings.mlr.press/v70/guo17a.html

13. Hashemi, V., Křetínský, J., Mohr, S., Seferis, E.: Gaussian-based runtime detection of out-of-distribution inputs for neural networks. In: Feng, L., Fisman, D. (eds.) RV 2021. LNCS, vol. 12974, pp. 254–264. Springer, Cham (2021). https://doi.org/10.1007/978-3-030-88494-9_14

14. Hashemi, V., Kretínský, J., Rieder, S., Schmidt, J.: Runtime monitoring for out-of-distribution detection in object detection neural networks. In: Proc. FM. LNCS, vol. 14000, pp. 622–634. Springer (2023). https://doi.org/10.1007/978-3-031-27481-7_36

15. Hendrycks, D., et al.: Scaling out-of-distribution detection for real-world settings. In: Proc. ICML. PMLR, vol. 162, pp. 8759–8773. PMLR (2022). https://proceedings.mlr.press/v162/hendrycks22a.html

16. Hendrycks, D., Dietterich, T.: Benchmarking neural network robustness to common corruptions and perturbations. In: ICLR. OpenReview.net (2019). https://openreview.net/forum?id=HJz6tiCqYm

17. Hendrycks, D., Gimpel, K.: A baseline for detecting misclassified and out-of-distribution examples in neural networks. In: Proc. ICLR. OpenReview.net (2017). https://openreview.net/forum?id=Hkg4TI9xl

18. Henriksen, P., Lomuscio, A.R.: Efficient neural network verification via adaptive refinement and adversarial search. In: Proceedings of ECAI. FAIA, vol. 325, pp. 2513–2520. IOS Press (2020). https://doi.org/10.3233/FAIA200385

19. Henriksson, J., et al.: Towards structured evaluation of deep neural network supervisors. In: Proceedings of AITest, pp. 27–34. IEEE (2019). https://doi.org/10.1109/AITest.2019.00-12

20. Henzinger, T.A., Lukina, A., Schilling, C.: Outside the box: abstraction-based monitoring of neural networks. In: Proceedings of ECAI, FAIA, vol. 325, pp. 2433–2440. IOS Press (2020). https://doi.org/10.3233/FAIA200375

21. Houben, S., Stallkamp, J., Salmen, J., Schlipsing, M., Igel, C.: Detection of traffic signs in real-world images: the german traffic sign detection benchmark. In: Proceedings of IJCNN. pp. 1–8. IEEE (2013). https://doi.org/10.1109/IJCNN.2013.6706807

22. Hsu, Y., Shen, Y., Jin, H., Kira, Z.: Generalized ODIN: detecting out-of-distribution image without learning from out-of-distribution data. In: Proceedings of CVPR, pp. 10948–10957. IEEE/CVF (2020). https://doi.org/10.1109/CVPR42600.2020.01096

23. Huang, R., Geng, A., Li, Y.: On the importance of gradients for detecting distributional shifts in the wild. In: NeurIPS, vol. 34, pp. 677–689 (2021), https://proceedings.neurips.cc/paper_files/paper/2021/hash/063e26c670d07bb7c4d30e6fc69fe056-Abstract.html

24. Katz, G., Barrett, C.W., Dill, D.L., Julian, K., Kochenderfer, M.J.: Reluplex: a calculus for reasoning about deep neural networks. FMSD **60**(1), 87–116 (2022). https://doi.org/10.1007/s10703-021-00363-7

25. Katz, G., et al.: The Marabou framework for verification and analysis of deep neural networks. In: Proceedings of CAV. LNCS, vol. 11561, pp. 443–452. Springer (2019). https://doi.org/10.1007/978-3-030-25540-4_26

26. Katz-Samuels, J., Nakhleh, J.B., Nowak, R.D., Li, Y.: Training OOD detectors in their natural habitats. In: Proc. ICML. PMLR, vol. 162, pp. 10848–10865. PMLR (2022). https://proceedings.mlr.press/v162/katz-samuels22a.html

27. Kirchheim, K., Filax, M., Ortmeier, F.: PyTorch-OOD: a library for out-of-distribution detection based on PyTorch. In: CVPR Workshops 2022, pp. 4350–4359. IEEE/CVF (2022). https://doi.org/10.1109/CVPRW56347.2022.00481

28. Krizhevsky, A., Hinton, G., et al.: Learning multiple layers of features from tiny images. Tech. rep., https://www.cs.toronto.edu/~kriz/learning-features-2009-TR.pdf
29. LeCun, Y., Cortes, C., Burges, C.: MNIST handwritten digit database **2**
30. Lee, K., Lee, K., Lee, H., Shin, J.: A simple unified framework for detecting out-of-distribution samples and adversarial attacks. In: NeurIPS, vol. 31, pp. 7167–7177 (2018). https://proceedings.neurips.cc/paper/2018/hash/abdeb6f575ac5c6676b747bca8d09cc2-Abstract.html
31. Liang, S., Li, Y., Srikant, R.: Enhancing the reliability of out-of-distribution image detection in neural networks. In: Proceedings of ICLR. OpenReview.net (2018). https://openreview.net/forum?id=H1VGkIxRZ
32. Liu, W., Wang, X., Owens, J., Li, Y.: Energy-based out-of-distribution detection. NeurIPS **33**, 21464–21475 (2020). https://proceedings.neurips.cc/paper_files/paper/2020/hash/f5496252609c43eb8a3d147ab9b9c006-Abstract.html
33. Macêdo, D., Ren, T.I., Zanchettin, C., Oliveira, A.L., Ludermir, T.: Entropic out-of-distribution detection. In: Proceedings of (IJCNN), pp. 1–8. IEEE (2021). https://doi.org/10.1109/IJCNN52387.2021.9533899
34. Müller, M.N., Brix, C., Bak, S., Liu, C., Johnson, T.T.: The third international verification of neural networks competition (VNN-COMP 2022): Summary and results. CoRR (2022). https://doi.org/10.48550/arXiv.2212.10376
35. Müller, M.N., Makarchuk, G., Singh, G., Püschel, M., Vechev, M.T.: PRIMA: general and precise neural network certification via scalable convex hull approximations. PACMPL **6**(POPL), 1–33 (2022). https://doi.org/10.1145/3498704
36. Netzer, Y., Wang, T., Coates, A., Bissacco, A., Wu, B., Ng, A.Y.: Reading digits in natural images with unsupervised feature learning
37. Olber, B., Radlak, K., Popowicz, A., Szczepankiewicz, M., Chachula, K.: Detection of out-of-distribution samples using binary neuron activation patterns. In: Proceedings of CVPR, pp. 3378–3387. IEEE/CVF (2023). https://doi.org/10.1109/CVPR52729.2023.00329
38. Pinggera, P., Ramos, S., Gehrig, S., Franke, U., Rother, C., Mester, R.: Lost and found: detecting small road hazards for self-driving vehicles. In: Proceedings of IROS, pp. 1099–1106. IEEE (2016). https://doi.org/10.1109/IROS.2016.7759186
39. Ren, J., Fort, S., Liu, J., Roy, A.G., Padhy, S., Lakshminarayanan, B.: A simple fix to mahalanobis distance for improving near-ood detection. CoRR (2021). https://doi.org/10.48550/arXiv.2106.09022
40. Russakovsky, O., et al.: ImageNet large scale visual recognition challenge. Int. J. Comput. Vis. **115**(3), 211–252 (2015). https://doi.org/10.1007/s11263-015-0816-y
41. Sun, Y., Guo, C., Li, Y.: ReAct: Out-of-distribution detection with rectified activations. In: NeurIPS. vol. 34, pp. 144–157 (2021). https://proceedings.neurips.cc/paper/2021/hash/01894d6f048493d2cacde3c579c315a3-Abstract.html
42. Sun, Y., Li, Y.: DICE: Leveraging sparsification for out-of-distribution detection. In: Proceeding of ECCV. LNCS, vol. 13684, pp. 691–708. Springer (2022). https://doi.org/10.1007/978-3-031-20053-3_40
43. Sun, Y., Ming, Y., Zhu, X., Li, Y.: Out-of-distribution detection with deep nearest neighbors. In: Proceedings of ICML, pp. 20827–20840. PMLR (2022). https://proceedings.mlr.press/v162/sun22d
44. Tajwar, F., Kumar, A., Xie, S.M., Liang, P.: No true state-of-the-art? OOD detection methods are inconsistent across datasets. CoRR (2021). https://doi.org/10.48550/arXiv.2109.05554

45. Wang, H., Li, Z., Feng, L., Zhang, W.: ViM: Out-of-distribution with virtual-logit matching. In: Proceedings of CVPR, pp. 4921–4930. IEEE/CVF (2022). https://doi.org/10.1109/CVPR52688.2022.00487
46. Xiao, H., Rasul, K., Vollgraf, R.: Fashion-MNIST: a novel image dataset for benchmarking machine learning algorithms
47. Yang, J., et al.: OpenOOD: benchmarking generalized out-of-distribution detection. In: NeurIPS (2022). http://papers.nips.cc/paper_files/paper/2022/hash/d201587e3a84fc4761eadc743e9b3f35-Abstract-Datasets_and_Benchmarks.html
48. Zhang, J., et al.: OpenOOD v1.5: Enhanced benchmark for out-of-distribution detection. CoRR (2023). https://doi.org/10.48550/arXiv.2306.09301
49. Zhang, J., et al.: Out-of-distribution detection based on in-distribution data patterns memorization with modern hopfield energy. In: Proceedings of ICLR (2022). https://openreview.net/forum?id=KkazG4lgKL
50. Zhang, Z., Xiang, X.: Decoupling maxlogit for out-of-distribution detection. In: Proceedings of CVPR, pp. 3388–3397. IEEE/CVF (2023). https://doi.org/10.1109/CVPR52729.2023.00330

Guiding Enumerative Program Synthesis with Large Language Models

Yixuan Li[1(✉)] ⓘ, Julian Parsert[1,2,3] ⓘ, and Elizabeth Polgreen[1(✉)] ⓘ

[1] University of Edinburgh, Edinburgh, UK
{yixuan.li.cs,elizabeth.polgreen}@ed.ac.uk, julian.parsert@gmail.com
[2] University of Oxford, Oxford, UK
[3] University of Innsbruck, Innsbruck, Austria

Abstract. Pre-trained Large Language Models (LLMs) are beginning to dominate the discourse around automatic code generation with natural language specifications. In contrast, the best-performing synthesizers in the domain of formal synthesis with precise logical specifications are still based on enumerative algorithms. In this paper, we evaluate the abilities of LLMs to solve formal synthesis benchmarks by carefully crafting a library of prompts for the domain. When one-shot synthesis fails, we propose a novel enumerative synthesis algorithm, which integrates calls to an LLM into a weighted probabilistic search. This allows the synthesizer to provide the LLM with information about the progress of the enumerator, and the LLM to provide the enumerator with syntactic guidance in an iterative loop. We evaluate our techniques on benchmarks from the Syntax-Guided Synthesis (SyGuS) competition. We find that GPT-3.5 as a stand-alone tool for formal synthesis is easily outperformed by state-of-the-art formal synthesis algorithms, but our approach integrating the LLM into an enumerative synthesis algorithm shows significant performance gains over both the LLM and the enumerative synthesizer alone and the winning SyGuS competition tool.

1 Introduction

Program synthesis is the task of automatically generating programs that satisfy a given specification. It has applications in planning [13], program analysis [16], data-wrangling [17] and more. The dominant techniques for formal program synthesis are based around enumeration [4, 21, 37], and a key challenge is how to guide this enumeration to search a huge space of possible programs efficiently. Syntax-Guided Synthesis(SyGuS) [2] allows the user to restrict the space of possible programs using a context-free grammar, and, in later work, this has been extended using pre-trained probabilistic models such as higher-order grammars [27] and neural networks [31], trained on a dataset of solved synthesis problems. However, obtaining these datasets for pre-training is challenging.

In parallel, the use of pre-trained large language models (LLMs) to generate code is rapidly gaining traction, with impressive results being obtained

ⓒ The Author(s) 2024
A. Gurfinkel and V. Ganesh (Eds.): CAV 2024, LNCS 14682, pp. 280–301, 2024.
https://doi.org/10.1007/978-3-031-65630-9_15

on benchmarks with natural language specifications and input-output examples [14]. These benchmarks are very different in style to the logical specifications that formal program synthesis tackles, as most are procedural code, in Python, and solve classic programming exercise questions that might be asked of students or interview candidates, and that one may find in abundance on sources used in training data such as StackOverflow and GitHub. In contrast, formal program synthesis benchmarks, such as those in the SyGuS competition, require functional code, which must satisfy precise logical specifications derived from problems such as program analysis [16], and are certainly less abundant in sources of publicly available code for training machine learning models.

In this paper, we set out to investigate whether off-the-shelf large language models can solve formal program synthesis problems. We craft a library of prompts, which enables us to solve roughly 50% of the SyGuS competition benchmarks. We hypothesize that, in the cases where the LLM returns only incorrect solutions, the correct solutions are most often in the vicinity of the incorrect solutions, and that, by searching in the neighborhood of the incorrect solutions, we may be able to guide an enumerative synthesizer to find a solution faster. To that end, we construct a probabilistic Context-Free Grammar (pCFG) based on the incorrect solutions proposed by the LLM, and use this to guide an enumerative synthesizer within a CounterExample Guided Inductive Synthesis (CEGIS) loop.

Our final contribution is a full integration of these techniques in a novel CEGIS algorithm with an inline syntactic oracle, in the form of an LLM that is queried by an enumerative synthesis phase. We incorporate information obtained during the synthesis search into the queries, prompting the LLM with partially enumerated functions, incorrect solutions, and counterexamples, and requesting that it provide "helper functions", which we use to update the pCFG guiding the enumerator.

We implement all three techniques described above and evaluate them on benchmarks from the Syntax-Guided Synthesis competition. We compare with two baselines: the first is an enumerative synthesizer where all rules in the grammar are given equal likelihood, and the second is cvc5 [7], the state-of-the-art SyGuS solver. All techniques easily outperform the baseline enumerator, and the final technique outperforms cvc5. Our results demonstrate that, whilst large language models do have the potential to make significant contributions in the domain of formal program synthesis, this can currently only be achieved by combining these techniques with existing algorithms in the literature. Enumerative synthesis is not yet obsolete!

The main contributions of our work are as follows: A set of prompts for prompting a pre-trained Large Language Model to solve formal program synthesis problems (Sect. 4.1); A method for guiding an enumerative synthesizer using LLM-generated probabilistic context-free grammars (Sect. 5.1); A novel approach to integrating an LLM into an enumerative synthesizer (Sect. 6); And, finally, an implementation and evaluation of all of the above on benchmark problems taken from the Syntax-Guided Synthesis competition. The results outperform cvc5, the state-of-the-art synthesizer, as well as our baseline enumerators.

2   Background

Program synthesis focuses on automated program creation that satisfies a high-level specification, which can be comprehensive, such as a basic, unrefined program, or incomplete, like a logical formula or a set of test cases.

Definition 1 (Context-Free Grammar, CFG). *A context-free grammar is a 4-tuple $G = (V, \Sigma, R, S)$. V is a finite set of variables also known as non-terminal symbols. Σ with $\Sigma \cap V = \emptyset$ is called the set of terminal symbols or alphabet. $R \subseteq V \times (V \cup \Sigma)^*$ is a finite relation describing the production rules of the grammar. We define $R_\Sigma = R \cap V \times \Sigma^*$, i.e. the set of rules restricted to those whose right-hand side only consists of terminal symbols. Elements of $(V \cup \Sigma)^*$ are known as words in sentential form. $S \in V$ is the start symbol of the grammar G.*

Given a context-free grammar $G = (V, \Sigma, R, S)$ with $x, y \in (V \cup \Sigma)^*$ and $(\alpha, \beta) \in R$ we say that $x\alpha y$ yields $x\beta y$, written $x\alpha y \to x\beta y$. We say that x derives y written $x \to^* y$ if either $x = y$ or $x \to x_1 \to \ldots x_n \to y$ for $n \geq 0$. Finally, we define the *language* of a grammar $\mathcal{L}^G = \{s \in \Sigma^* \mid S \to^* s\}$. We now introduce two extensions of context-free grammars:

Definition 2 (Weighted Context-Free Grammar, wCFG). *A weighted context-free grammar (wCFG) [29,30] is a 5-tuple $W_G = (V, \Sigma, R, S, W)$ such that (V, Σ, R, S) is a context-free grammar and W is a function assigning a numeric value to each rule $r \in R$.*

Definition 3 (Probabilistic Context-Free Grammar, pCFG). *A probabilistic context-free grammar [29,30] is a 5-tuple $P_G = (V, \Sigma, R, S, \mathbb{P})$ such that (V, Σ, R, S) is a context-free grammar and $\mathbb{P}$ is a probability mass function assigning a probability $\mathbb{P}[r]$ to each rule $r \in R$. $\mathbb{P}_\Sigma$ is the probability mass function that assigns a probability to $\mathbb{P}_\Sigma[r]$ to each rule $r \in R_\Sigma$. A pCFG is a specific instance of a wCFG.*

In general, program synthesis is concerned with the generation (i.e., synthesis) of a program that satisfies a certain specification. Syntax-guided synthesis (SyGuS) describes a standardized function synthesis format that precisely defines a synthesis problem within first-order theories [8]. We will use the notation $\phi[F \mapsto f]$ to denote the replacing of all occurrences of F in ϕ with f while substituting all arguments to f by the arguments of F in the same order.

Definition 4 (Syntax-Guided Synthesis, SyGuS). *A SyGuS problem is a 4-tuple $\langle T, G, \phi, F \rangle$ such that T is a first-order theory, G is a context-free grammar, ϕ is a first-order formula, and F is a function symbol that may occur in ϕ. A solution to a SyGuS problem $\langle T, G, \phi, F \rangle$ is either a function f such that $T \models \phi[F \mapsto f]$ and $f \in \mathcal{L}^G$, or proof that no such function can exist.*

SyGuS closely follows the syntax and semantics of SMT, and hence T usually refers to theories that are also common in SMT. Usually, SMT solvers are queried in the background of SyGuS solvers to verify solution candidates. This connection is made explicit in *Counter-Example Guided Inductive Synthesis* (CEGIS) [39]. CEGIS is a family of algorithms that alternate between a synthesis phase, which searches for a candidate solution that works for a subset of inputs, and a verification phase, where the candidate is checked against all possible inputs. If the verification fails, a counterexample is passed back to the synthesis phase and appended to the subset of inputs used to guide the search. The synthesis phase is often implemented as an enumerative search. An example SyGuS problem is shown in Example 1.

Generative Large Language Models. Generative Large Language Models (LLMs) are advanced Artificial Intelligence (AI) systems based on transformer models and trained on vast datasets to produce human-like text, followed by human-provided instruction prompts [10]. One application of LLMs is generating code from natural language specifications [14].

3   Overview

In this work, we first present a carefully tailored set of prompts that we use to evaluate an LLM's ability to solve formal synthesis problems. We construct an iterative loop where we prompt the LLM, verify the candidate solution, and if the solution fails, we prompt the LLM again.

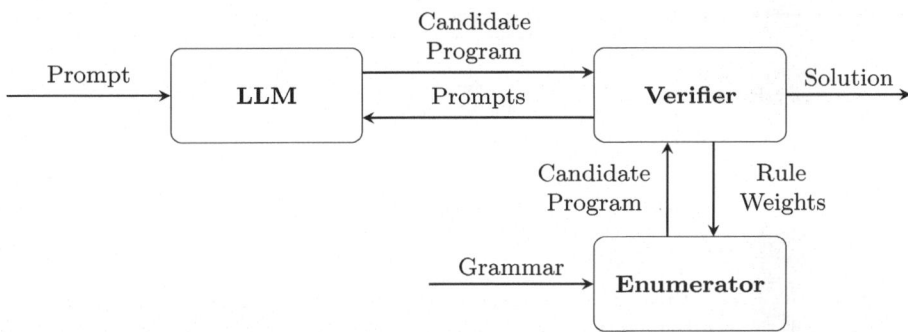

Fig. 1. An overview of pCFG-synth. Both the verifier and the LLM have access to the specification ϕ (which is used to generate the prompt for the LLM, as well as to check whether candidate programs are correct).

We then present two methods for integrating syntactic guidance from pre-trained LLMs into an enumerative CEGIS algorithm. The first method, shown in Fig. 1, prompts an LLM for solutions to the benchmark, and generates a pCFG from these solutions before deploying an enumerative synthesizer, increasing the chance of the LLM solving the synthesis problem outright. We refer to this method as pCFG-synth. The second method, shown in Fig. 2, integrates the prompting within the enumerative synthesizer, allowing the prompts to incorporate additional information obtained during the synthesis process. Here, instead of asking the LLM to provide a full solution, we ask it to provide helper functions to help "a student" complete the partially enumerated program. We use the responses to augment the set of production rules in the grammar and update the weights across the existing production rules. We refer to this approach, which integrates an LLM into an enumerative synthesizer, as iLLM-synth. In this section, we give an overview of these two approaches. The details of the components of both approaches and their relative performances are found in the subsequent sections. We integrate both approaches with a probabilistic top-down enumerator and a weighted search based on the A^* algorithm [19,27].

```
(set-logic LIA)
(synth-fun fn ((vr0 Int) (vr1 Int) (vr2 Int)) Int)
(constraint (>= (fn vr0 vr1 vr2) vr0))
(constraint (>= (fn vr0 vr1 vr2) vr1))
(constraint (>= (fn vr0 vr1 vr2) vr2))
(constraint (or (= vr0 (fn vr0 vr1 vr2)) (or (= vr1 (fn vr0 vr1 vr2))
    (= vr2 (fn vr0 vr1 vr2)))))
(check-synth)
```

Example 1. A SyGuS specification that asks for a program that synthesizes the maximum of 3 inputs. We omit some the grammar and variable declarations for brevity.

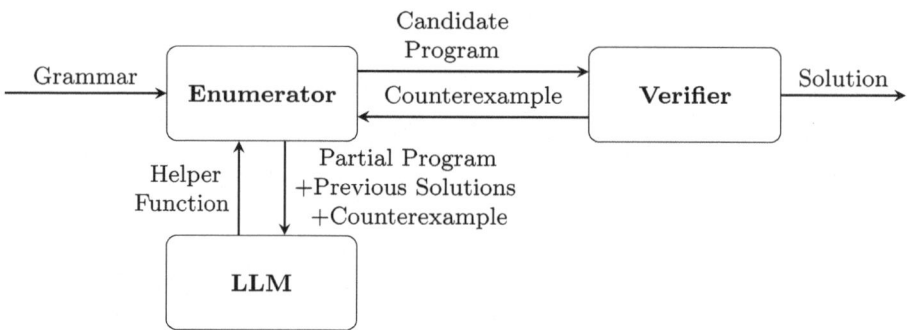

Fig. 2. An overview of iLLM-synth. Both the verifier and the enumerator have access to the specification ϕ (which is used to generate the prompt for the LLM, as well as to check whether candidate programs are correct)

4   Stand-Alone LLM

In this section, we describe how we prompt the LLM as a stand-alone synthesizer. These prompting techniques are then also deployed by pCFG-synth. We use GPT-3.5-turbo as the LLM. Note that the model is not fine-tuned to this problem setting. Furthermore, we rename any functions and variables in the SyGuS benchmarks to generic names to avoid the LLM producing solutions solely based on the function names.

4.1 Prompting the LLM

We design a library of prompts for program synthesis problems with logical specifications and a single target function to synthesize. These prompts are deployed in an iterative loop, until a correct solution is obtained, or the library of prompts is exhausted.

Prompting is an art rather than a science, but we hypothesize that it is better to ask the LLM to give a solution in a language that is more common in the training data, and then request it to translate it into our desired SMT-LIB, and experiment with both Python and Lisp. On a subset of 50 benchmarks, we observed that soliciting responses in Lisp resulted in a 6% enhancement in the resolution of benchmarks compared to utilizing Python (and both were better than asking for SMT-lib directly). It is also reported in the literature that the efficacy of LLMs can be augmented by including emotional stimuli within prompts [28]. Incorporating the emotional prompt leads to an 8% increase in the likelihood of generating accurate solutions compared to standard, non-emotional prompts in our study. Details of our initial prompting experiments are in the extended version of this paper[1].

The following is an example prompt and response sequence for the LIA example shown in Example 1:

```
(set-logic LIA)
(declare-var vr0 Int)
(declare-var vr1 Int)
(declare-var vr2 Int)
(constraint (>= (fn vr0 vr1 vr2) vr0))
(constraint (>= (fn vr0 vr1 vr2) vr1))
(constraint (>= (fn vr0 vr1 vr2) vr2))
(constraint (or (= vr0 (fn vr0 vr1 vr2)) (or (= vr1 (fn vr0 vr1 vr2))
    (= vr2 (fn vr0 vr1 vr2)))))
(check-synth)
You are a good synthesizer. Do you know what "(define-fun fn ((vr0 Int
    ) (vr1 Int) (vr2 Int)) Int" is doing?
Write only one Lisp-like method "defun fn" without any built-in
    methods or arrays.
Requirements:
1. No built-in functions.
2. Never violate the SMT-LIB constraints above.
3. Pay attention to the define functions.
4. Ensure the response contains one and only one function.
5. Do not include any iterations, BitVec, or Int notations in the
    function body.
Write it correctly, or I will lose my job and 100 grandmothers will
    die. Don't disappoint me.
Write only one Lisp-like method "defun fn" that never violates the SMT
    -LIB constraints above.
```

Prompt 1. Prompt for Example 1.

```
(defun fn (vr0 vr1 vr2)
    (ite (>= vr0 vr1) (ite (>= vr0 vr2) vr0 vr2) (ite (>= vr1 vr2) vr1
        vr2)))
```

Response 1. Response from LLM after Prompt 1.

```
You are close to the right answer. Take another guess. You have to try
    something different, think harder. Write a different Lisp method
    that never violates the SMT-LIB constraints above again.
```

Prompt 2. Prompt requesting a revised solution.

Prompts for Invariant Synthesis. Invariant synthesis is a specific instance of program synthesis: given a pre-condition $pre(x)$, transition-relation $trans(x, x')$ and post-condition $post(x)$, the synthesizer is required to provide an invariant inv that satisfies the following constraint: $\forall x, x'.pre(x) \implies inv(x) \wedge (inv(x) \wedge trans(x, x)) \implies inv(x') \wedge inv(x) \implies post(x)$. We find that LLMs struggle to reason about constraints presented in the above format. Inspired by "chain-of-thought" [42] prompting, where the LLM is asked to provide a step-by-step explanation, we augment our prompting strategy for invariants by asking the LLM first to explain the constraints. After requesting this explanation, we follow the same interactive prompt strategy as before.

Lisp to SMT-LIB Converter. The final prompts in our prompt library are to ask the LLM to convert any functions given in Lisp to correct SMT-LIB functions:

```
You are a good programming language converter. Convert the Lisp
    function to SMT-LIB:
Based on the Lisp code provided above, convert the 'defun' Lisp-like
    code to a corresponding SMT-LIB function. Use SMT-LIB syntax
    starting with (define-fun
Follow these guidelines:
1. Only give me the function definition starting with '(define-fun'.
2. Pay attention to types. If there are bit-vector terms, they need to
    be of the same width.
3. Ensure the SMT-LIB function contains one and only one function
    definition starting with '(define-fun'.
4. Do not include any iterations, BitVec, or Int notations in the
    function body.
5. Use the assigned values from the Lisp code during translation.
6. Do not introduce any variables that do not exist in the Lisp
    function.
Rules for SMT-LIB: +, -, *, ite, >, =, <, >=, <=, and, or, not, true,
    false.
```

Prompt 3. Request for converting Lisp to SMT-LIB code for response 1.

Upon receiving a response from the LLM, we extracted the Lisp program and subjected it to format verification. The resulting SMT-LIB code is represented:

```
(define-fun fn ((vr0 Int) (vr1 Int) (vr2 Int)) Int
    (ite (>= vr0 vr1) (ite (>= vr0 vr2) vr0 vr2) (ite (>= vr1 vr2) vr1
        vr2)))
```

Program 1. LLM-Generated program for Example 1.

5   Synthesis with pCFG Guidance: pCFG-synth

We hypothesize that, if the LLM did not propose a correct solution, the correct solution is likely to be roughly in the same "area" as the incorrect solutions it suggested, and so our synthesis algorithm aims to prioritize this area when searching for candidate programs. For simplicity, we use a simple weighted Context-Free Grammar to represent the area of solutions proposed by the LLM. We then present methods for searching the space: the first is a probabilistic top-down search, shown in Algorithm 3; the second is based on an adaptation of the A^* algorithm [19,27], and we integrate both into CEGIS searches as shown in Algorithm 1. The verification phase in Algorithm 1 is implemented via a call to an SMT solver, which checks, for a candidate solution f, whether there exists an input such that the specification is violated, i.e., $\exists x.\neg\phi[F \mapsto f]$.

Algorithm 1. CEGIS with weighted search

1: **procedure** CEGIS(W_G, ϕ)
2:     $cex \leftarrow \emptyset$
3:     **while** *true* **do**
4:         $prog \leftarrow$ ENUMERATE($W_G, \phi, cex,$)
5:         **if** VERIFY($prog, \phi$) **then**
6:             **return** $prog$
7:         **else**
8:             $c \leftarrow$ VERIFY.GET_CEX
9:             $cex \leftarrow cex \cup \{c\}$

5.1   Inferring a Weighted CFG

In this section, we describe how we infer a weighted Context-Free Grammar from the incorrect solutions produced by the large language model.

Definition 5 (Derivations). *Given a context-free grammar G, and a sentence s, the sentence is in the language of the grammar if $S \rightarrow^* s$, where S is the start symbol of the grammar. The derivation of s from S is a sequence of rules such that $S \xrightarrow{r_0} s_1 \xrightarrow{r_1} \ldots s_n \xrightarrow{r_n} s$ and $r_0 \ldots r_n \in R$. We denote the derivation of s by the sequence of rules $r_0, \ldots r_n$ as $D_s = \{r_0, \ldots r_n\}$. The left-most derivation is a derivation such that all rules expand the left-most non-terminal symbol in the sentential form.*

From here on in, all derivations are assumed to be the left-most derivation, and we assume the grammar is unambiguous, i.e., there exists a single left-most derivation for any sentence in the language.

Given a set of possible programs $prog \in \mathcal{L}^G$ generated by the language model, we calculate a weight for each rule $r_i \in R$ as the number of times that rule appears in the left-most derivations of the programs. That is,

$$w[r_i] = \sum_{prog_i \in prog} |r_i| \in D_{prog_i}, \tag{1}$$

where $|r_i|$ is the number of times r_i appears in the derivation. For example, consider Response 1: the weights are calculated as $w[r_1] = 3, w[r_2] = 3, w[r_3] = 3, w[r_4] = 4, w[r_5] = 3$. These correspond to the rules from Example 1:

$$r_1 : \text{Start} \rightarrow (\text{ite StartBool Start Start})$$
$$r_2 : \text{Start} \rightarrow \text{vr0}$$
$$r_3 : \text{Start} \rightarrow \text{vr1}$$
$$r_4 : \text{Start} \rightarrow \text{vr2}$$
$$r_5 : \text{StartBool} \rightarrow (\text{>= Start Start}).$$

Probabilistic Context-Free Grammar. Given a wCFG, we derive a simple pCFG by assuming that the probability associated with a rule $r_i \colon \alpha \rightarrow \beta$ is equal to the weight $w[\alpha \rightarrow \beta]$ of r_i, divided by $|\pi[\alpha]| = |\alpha \times (\Sigma \cup V)^* \in R|$, i.e., the total number of rules that could be applied to α. That is $\mathbb{P}[\alpha \rightarrow \beta] = \frac{w[\alpha \rightarrow \beta]}{|\pi[\alpha]|}$. By extension, $\mathbb{P}_\Sigma[\alpha \rightarrow \beta] = \frac{w[\alpha \rightarrow \beta]}{|\pi[\alpha]|}|$ iff $\beta \in \Sigma$ and 0 otherwise.

5.2   Probabilistic Guided Search

The aim of our algorithm is thus to search the area of programs closest to those with the highest weights in the wCFG, or highest probabilities in the corresponding pCFG. We adapt and implement two search methods for doing this: the first is a probabilistic top-down search. To this end, we first introduce the notion of a grammar tree.

Definition 6 (Grammar tree). *We represent the search space as a grammar tree. Given a context-free grammar $G = (V, \Sigma, R, S)$, the graph of sentential forms, or grammar tree, $T(G)$ defined inductively: S is the root of the tree, and for all $x, y \in (V \cup \Sigma)^*$ with $x \rightarrow y$ and x being a node of the tree, then y is a child node of x.*

To implement our probabilistic guided search, we extend this definition to a probabilistic grammar tree. Given a pCFG, $P_G = (V, \Sigma, R, S, \mathbb{P})$, a probabilistic grammar tree $T(P_G)$ is a directed labelled graph as defined before, but each edge has a corresponding weight ω given by $\mathbb{P}$. We limit the edges to only those needed for the left-most derivations, and so $\mathcal{E}$ and ω are defined as follows:

$$\mathcal{E} = \{x\alpha y \xrightarrow{\alpha \rightarrow \beta} x\beta y \,|\, \alpha \rightarrow \beta \in R, x \in \Sigma^*, \alpha \in V, \beta, y \in (V \cup \Sigma)^*\},$$
$$\omega[\alpha \rightarrow \beta] = \mathbb{P}[\alpha \rightarrow \beta].$$

Note that this guarantees that, for any node, the sum of the weight on the edges leaving that node is equal to 1.

Algorithm 2. Probabilistic top-down enumerator for pCFG-synth

---

1: **procedure** ENUMERATE(W_G, ϕ, cex)
2:     $prog \leftarrow W_G.S$
3:     $d \leftarrow 0$
4:     $previousProgs \leftarrow \emptyset$
5:     $P_G \leftarrow$ BUILDPCFG(W_G)
6:     **while** 1 **do**
7:         **if** $prog \in \Sigma^*$ **then**
8:             $previousProgs \leftarrow previousProgs \cup prog$
9:             **if** $\forall \vec{x} \in cex. \phi(prog, \vec{x})$ **then**
10:                **return** $prog$
11:            **else**
12:                $prog \leftarrow S$
13:                $d \leftarrow 0$
14:        $prog \leftarrow$ REPLACENONTERMINALS($prog, P_G$)
15:        $d \leftarrow d + 1$
16:        **if** $d = maxDepth$ **then**
17:            $prog \leftarrow$ COMPLETEPROGRAM($prog, P_G$)
18:            **if** $prog \in PreviousPrograms$ **then**
19:                $prog \leftarrow S$
20:                $d \leftarrow 0$
21: **procedure** REPLACENONTERMINALS($prog, P_G$)
22:     $NT \leftarrow$ list of nonterminals in $prog$
23:     **for** $\alpha \in NT$ **do**
24:         $(\alpha \times \beta) \sim Cat(|\pi[\alpha]|, \{\mathbb{P}[\pi[\alpha]_1], \mathbb{P}[\pi[\alpha]_2], \ldots\})$ ▷ Sample from distribution
25:         $prog \leftarrow prog.\{\alpha \rightarrow \beta\}$ ▷ apply rule to $prog$
26:     **return** $prog$
27: **procedure** COMPLETEPROGRAM($prog, P_G$)▷ Replaces non-terminal symbols with terminal symbols
28:     $NT \leftarrow$ list of nonterminal symbols in $prog$
29:     **for** $\alpha \in NT$ **do**
30:         $(\alpha \times \beta) \sim Cat(|\pi[\alpha]|, \{\mathbb{P}_\Sigma[\pi[\alpha]_1], \mathbb{P}_\Sigma[\pi[\alpha]_2], \ldots\})$ ▷ Sample
31:         $prog \leftarrow prog.\{nt \rightarrow nt'\}$ ▷ apply rule to $prog$
32:     **return** $prog$

We search this grammar tree using a top-down enumerative synthesizer, shown in Algorithm 2. This enumerates possible programs in the grammar in a top-down manner, expanding non-terminals by randomly sampling from the categorical distribution over the production rules. That is, the search algorithm starts by considering the node corresponding to the start symbol S. It then chooses the next node by sampling from a categorical distribution with event probabilities corresponding to the probabilities on the outgoing edges of the current node. The categorical distribution is a generalization of the Bernoulli distribution and describes the possible results of a random variable that can take one of K possible categories, with the probability of each category separately specified. Formally, to sample a rule $\alpha \times \beta$ to apply to a non-terminal symbol α, we sample from the distribution:

$$(\alpha \times \beta) \sim Cat(|\pi[\alpha]|, \{\mathbb{P}[\pi[\alpha]_1], \mathbb{P}[\pi[\alpha]_2], \ldots\}),$$

where $|\pi[\alpha]|$ is the number of rules that could be applied to α and $\pi[\alpha]_i$ is the ith of those rules, and $\{\mathbb{P}[\pi[\alpha]_1], \mathbb{P}[\pi[\alpha]_2], \ldots\}$ is a vector of probabilities corresponding to those rules.

We then apply the sampled rule, and repeat the process. We use $prog.\{\alpha \to \beta\}$ to indicate the result of substituting the first occurrence of α in a partial program $prog$ with β.

With a naive implementation of this algorithm, the probability of our algorithm generating any sentence s is equal to $\prod_{r_i \in D_s} \mathbb{P}[r_i]$, where D_s is the leftmost derivation of s. However, this will result in the algorithm generating the same programs multiple times, so we modify this algorithm in two ways: First, if we enumerate a complete program that we have seen before, we discard it; Second, we give a maximum depth limit, and if we are approaching the maximum depth limit, we sample only from the outgoing edges that result in complete programs.

Algorithm 3. pCFG-synth

1: **procedure** PCFG-SYNTH($prompts, \phi, G$)
2:      $conv \leftarrow [\,]$
3:      $progs \leftarrow \emptyset$
4:      **while** $prompts \neq \emptyset$ **do**
5:          $response \leftarrow$ LLM($prompts.pop(), conv$)
6:          $conv.append(response)$
7:          $currentProg \leftarrow$ EXTRACTPROGRAM($response$)
8:          **if** $\forall \vec{x} \, \phi(currentProg, \vec{x})$ **then**
9:              **return** $currentProg$
10:         **else**
11:             $progs \leftarrow progs \cup currentProg$
12:     $W \leftarrow$ WEIGHTCOUNTER($prog, G$)
13:     $W_G \leftarrow (G, W)$
14:     $prog \leftarrow$ CEGIS(W_G, ϕ)
15:     **return** $prog$

5.3   Weighted A^* Search

We implement a second variation of pCFG-synth using the A^* weighted search algorithm as the underlying enumerator. A^* is a search algorithm that chooses which paths to extend based on minimizing the cost of the path so far and an estimate of the cost required to extend the path to the goal, i.e., it expands nodes that minimizes $f(x) = c(x) + g(x)$, where $c(x)$ is the cost of the path to

x so far and $g(x)$ is the estimated cost of reaching a goal node from x. This technique was first used for guiding synthesis by Lee et al. [27], and we adapted the algorithm from their work.

To implement our A^* search, we extend the definition of the grammar tree to a weighted grammar tree. Given a pCFG $P_G = (V, \Sigma, R, S, \mathbb{P})$, a weighted grammar tree $T(W_G)$ is a directed labeled graph as defined before, but each edge has a corresponding weight, given as follows:

$$\omega(\alpha \to \beta) = \begin{cases} -\log_2(\mathbb{P}[\alpha \to \beta]) & \text{if } \mathbb{P}[\alpha \to \beta] > 0, \\ \inf & \text{otherwise.} \end{cases}$$

We use the negative log of the probability to ensure that higher weighted edges correspond to those with very low probabilities.

Algorithm 4. A^* search for pCFG-synth

1: **procedure** ENUMERATE(P_G, ϕ, cex)
2:     $Q = \{0, S\}$ ▷ Priority queue of candidates
3:     **while** $Q \neq \emptyset$ **do**
4:         $(f, prog) \leftarrow Q.pop()$ ▷ Remove program with minimal f
5:         **if** $\forall \vec{x} \in cex. \phi(prog, \vec{x})$ **then**
6:             **return** $prog$
7:         **for** $(nt \in prog) \times nt'$ **do**
8:             **if** $(nt \times nt') \in P_G.R$ **then**   ▷ For all applicable rules
9:                 $prog \leftarrow prog.\{nt \to nt'\}$ ▷ apply rule to $prog$
10:                $Q \leftarrow Q \cup (c(prog) + g(prog), prog)$

The A^* algorithm, shown in Algorithm 4, relies on two key functions: first, the function $c(x)$, which computes the cost of the path so far, and second, the function $g(x)$ which estimates the cost to extend the path to a goal node. Assuming x is a sentential form in our language, $c(x)$ and $g(x)$ are given by:

$$c(x) = \sum_{r_i \in D_x} -\log_2(\mathbb{P}[r_i]), \quad g(x) = \begin{cases} 0 & \text{if } x \in \Sigma^*, \\ -\sum_{x_i \in V} \log_2 h(x_i) & \text{otherwise,} \end{cases}$$

where x_i indicates the ith symbol in x, and h is the upper bound of the probabilities of expressions that can be derived from x_i, and is calculated as the fixed point of:

$$\forall \alpha \in V. h(\alpha) = \max_{\alpha \to \beta \in R} \left(\mathbb{P}[\alpha \to \beta] \times \prod_{\beta_i \in V} h(\beta_i) \right),$$

The function $g(x)$ can then be thought of as the product of the probability of each non-terminal symbol in x being converted into a terminal symbol.

Smoothing the Probability Distributions: Since the A^* algorithm will not enumerate any programs whose derivation uses a rule with zero probability, we smooth the weighted grammar as follows, with $\gamma = 0.4$: $w'[\alpha \rightarrow \beta] = 10 \times \left(\frac{w[\alpha \rightarrow \beta]+1}{10} \right)^{\gamma}$.

6 Enumerative Synthesis with an Integrated LLM (iLLM-synth)

The disadvantage of the method described in the preceding section is that the language model cannot benefit from any additional information that the enumerator learns during enumeration, as all prompting happens prior to starting the enumerative synthesis. In this section we describe how we integrate an LLM into an enumerative synthesis algorithm, allowing it to update a probability distribution over the search grammar and to augment the grammar with new production rules, as shown in Algorithm 5.

Algorithm 5. Syntactic feedback generator

1: **procedure** SYNTACTICFEEDBACK($W_G, prog, cex$)
2:      $prompt \leftarrow$ GENERATEPROMPT($prog, cex$)
3:      $response \leftarrow$ LLM($prompt$)
4:      $candidate \leftarrow$ EXTRACTPROGRAM($response$)
5:      $W_G.W \leftarrow W_G.W +$ WEIGHTCOUNTER($response$)
6:      $W_G.R \leftarrow W_G.R \cup (W_G.S \times response$)
7:      **return** W_G

6.1 Integrated Prompting

We construct a prompt that asks the LLM to provide helper functions to assist a student in writing SMT-lib code. We give the LLM the constraints from the target synthesis problem and the partially complete program at the point the enumerator calls the LLM. If the LLM fails to solve the problem with this prompt, we later add the most recently failed candidate solution and the counterexample it failed on. These prompts are shorter than the prompts in those used in Sect. 4 and, therefore, cheaper and faster to run. An example Prompt 4 is as follows:

```
You are teaching a student to write SMT-LIB. The student must write a
    function that satisfies the following constraints:
(constraint (>= (fn vr0 vr1 vr2) vr0))
(constraint (>= (fn vr0 vr1 vr2) vr1))
(constraint (>= (fn vr0 vr1 vr2) vr2))
(constraint (or (= vr0 (fn vr0 vr1 vr2)) (or (= vr1 (fn vr0 vr1 vr2))
    (= vr2 (fn vr0 vr1 vr2)))))
So far, the student has written this code:
(define-fun fn ((vr0 Int) (vr1 Int) (vr2 Int)) Int
    (ite ?? ?? ??))
Can you suggest some helper functions for the student to use to
    complete this code and replace the ??
You must print only the code and nothing else.
```

Prompt 4. Integrated prompt for Example 1.

Algorithm 6. Top-down enumerator for iLLM-synth

```
 1: procedure ENUMERATE(W_G, φ, cex )
 2:     prog ← W_G.S
 3:     d ← 0; i ← 0
 4:     P_G ← BUILDPCFG(W_G)
 5:     while 1 do
 6:         if prog ∈ Σ* then
 7:             if ∀x⃗ ∈ cex. φ(prog, x⃗) then
 8:                 return prog
 9:             else
10:                 prog ← S
11:                 d ← 0
12:         if i%n = 0 then
13:             W_G ← SYNTACTICFEEDBACK(W_G, prog, cex)
14:             P_G ← BUILDPCFG(W_G)
15:         prog ← REPLACENONTERMINALS(prog, P_G)
16:         d ← d + 1
17:         if d = maxDepth then
18:             prog ← COMPLETEPROGRAM(prog, P_G)
19:             if prog ∈ PreviousPrograms then
20:                 prog ← S
21:                 d ← 0
22:         i ← i + 1
```

6.2 Updating the Weighted Grammar

We initialize our algorithm with a weight of 1 for each rule in the grammar. We use the LLM-generated helper functions to augment the grammar in the following way: first, any helper functions will be added directly as new production rules to replace non-terminals of the correct type in the grammar. That is, if the LLM proposes the defined function f, a set of rules of the form $V_i \times f$ are added to the grammar, for all non-terminal symbols V_i such that this rule results in syntactically correct expressions, i.e., V_i must be of the same type as the co-domain of f. This is sufficient to guarantee syntactically correct expressions because any functions proposed by the LLM that are otherwise not well-formed, e.g., they reference variables that are not defined, are discarded. Any new rules are given a weight equal to the average of all the current weights for rules relevant to that non-terminal. The response parser also updates the weights of all existing rules in the grammar, according to Eq. 1, calculated from the set of helper functions the LLM proposed.

6.3 Integrating Syntactic Feedback into Enumerative Search

We integrate the syntactic feedback generator into the probabilistic enumerator, shown in Algorithm 3, and into the A^* weighted search, as shown in Algorithm 7. Both search algorithms call the syntactic feedback generator every n^{th} iteration, where n is a heuristic used to ensure the LLM is not called with the same partial program repeatedly and that the search algorithm has time to exploit the information obtained from the LLM. Note that, when the probabilistic grammar is updated, the h values must be re-calculated in the A^* search.

Algorithm 7. A^* search for iLLM-synth

 1: **procedure** ENUMERATE(P_G, ϕ, cex)
 2:     $Q = \{0, S\}$ ▷ Priority queue of candidates
 3:     $i \leftarrow 0$
 4:     **while** $Q \neq \emptyset$ **do**
 5:         $(f, prog) \leftarrow Q.pop()$ ▷ Remove program with minimal f
 6:         **if** $prog \in \Sigma^*$ **then**
 7:             **if** $\forall \vec{x} \in cex. \phi(prog, \vec{x})$ **then**
 8:                 **return** $prog$
 9:         **if** $i\%n = 0$ **then**
10:             $W_G \leftarrow$ SYNTACTICFEEDBACK($W_G, prog, cex$)
11:             $P_G \leftarrow$ BUILDPCFG(W_G)
12:         **for** $(nt \in prog) \times nt'$ **do**
13:             **if** $(nt \times nt') \in P_G.R$ **then**   ▷ For all applicable rules
14:                 $prog \leftarrow prog.\{nt \rightarrow nt'\}$ ▷ apply rule to $prog$
15:                 $Q \leftarrow Q \cup (c(prog) + g(prog), prog)$
16:         $i \leftarrow i + 1$

---

7 Evaluation

We evaluate our approaches on benchmarks taken from the SyGuS competition [3], each with a grammar that corresponds to the full language of their respective theories. We evaluate across three SyGuS categories: Bit-Vector (BV), Linear Integer Arithmetic (LIA), and Invariants (INV). We evaluate both the LLM as a stand-alone synthesizer, the probabilistic enumerator and A^* implementations with a pre-trained pCFG and the enumerator with a pre-trained syntactic oracle. We utilize OpenAI's GPT-3.5-turbo-16k model to generate the prompts used for the pre-trained pCFG and the standalone LLM evaluation because this model supports longer prompts. We configure this with a temperature of 1.0, conversation-style messaging. We use GPT-3.5-turbo for iLLM-synth, which has shorter prompts. We use the 4.8.12 64-bit version of Z3 for verification and cvc5 version 1.1.0 as a baseline.

Evaluation of the Stand-Alone LLM: We prompt the LLM until it produces up to 6 complete synthesis attempts per benchmark, with the results reported in line 1 of Table 1. Any incomplete solutions are discarded (i.e., functions without a function body), although these are relatively rare, and we discard only 0.85% of programs we generate. In total, the LLM solves 49% of benchmarks, performing better in the invariant and LIA categories than the bit-vector category. On average, for the benchmarks it can solve, it takes 4 attempts to produce a correct solution. The average time for the LLM to generate a program is approximately $5s$ using the OpenAI Python API. However, this is dependent on OpenAI, and we report these times only as estimates in Table 1. We allow the LLM only 6 attempts to solve the problem since, by the 6th iteration, the number of new solutions the LLM finds has dropped to <2% (and it finds 0 new solutions for LIA).

Evaluation of pCFG-synth: We evaluate both variants of pCFG-synth (with the probabilistic enumerator, denoted e-pCFG-synth, and with A^*, denoted A^*-pCFG-synth) using the wCFG obtained from the LLM. As a baseline, we run the same algorithms assigning a weight of 1 to every rule in the grammar (referred to as "enumerator" and A^* respectively in the results). pCFG-synth increases the number of benchmarks the probabilistic enumerator can solve by 30%, but barely increases the number A^* can solve, although the exact sets of benchmarks which A^* and A^*-pCFG-synth solve do differ significantly. We hypothesize that this is because A^*, guided by the pCFG with equal weights for all rules, is very good at generating short solutions, and A^*-pCFG-synth is worse at short solutions but better at generating more complex solutions guided by the pCFG.

We also report the results obtained by the union of the LLM alone and pCFG-synth, i.e., if the LLM solves the benchmark, we do not deploy the enumerator. This is a more realistic representation of how such a technique would be used and demonstrates that the enumerator can overcome shortcomings of the LLM and vice versa. The union of the LLM and A^*-pCFG-synth substantially outperforms cvc5, solving 73 more benchmarks.

Evaluating iLLM-synth: We evaluate both variants of iLLM-synth, denoted e-iLLM-synth and A^*-iLLM-synth. We set the temperature for e-iLLM-synth to 1, but find that A^*-iLLM-synth performs better with a temperature set to 0 which we hypothesize is due to the determinism of the algorithm. We find that iLLM-synth outperforms the enumerator of pCFG-synth, and gets close to the performance of cvc5, suggesting that the ability to prompt the LLM with additional information obtained during enumeration allows the LLM to provide better guidance to the enumerator, as well as to more frequently propose useful helper functions. We do find that iLLM-synth performs less well than methods incorporating the stand-alone LLM on the invariant benchmarks, which is likely because the invariant benchmarks benefit from the custom prompting technique described in Sect. 4.1. Future work would involve identifying further categories of benchmarks that benefit from custom prompts. It is worth noting that neither the probabilistic enumerator nor the A^* implementation includes many of the optimizations that mature solvers such as cvc5 implement, and yet, by integrating these simple algorithms with syntactic feedback from an LLM, they have achieved performance on par with the state-of-the-art enumerative solver.

Failure Modes: We manually examine a sample of the stand-alone LLM errors and give examples of such errors in the extended version of this paper[2]. Broadly, we identify the following common failures: Misunderstandings due to complex constraints (the LLM suggests solutions that are not syntactically close to the correct solution); simple syntactic errors, e.g., applying non-commutative operators to operands in the wrong order, concatenating bit-vectors in the wrong order or hallucinating operations; simple semantic errors, e.g., operators in the wrong order. Errors in the first category are not helpful to our guided enumerators, but the remaining categories of error still allow us to generate a wCFG that is likely to indicate the area of the solution. The benchmarks that cvc5 can solve and our enumerative techniques cannot, tend to have complex constraints and relatively short solutions that use less common operators (e.g., bitwise operators). We hypothesize that the LLM guidance becomes an impediment to the enumerator in these scenarios. In contrast, the average length (in characters) of a solution for benchmarks uniquely solved by the LLM is 4.7x the length of a solution for benchmarks uniquely solved by cvc5. Using the LLM to guide the enumerators increases the length of solutions that the enumerators can find, for instance all solutions found by A^* contain fewer than 3 operators, but A^*-iLLM-synth finds solutions with greater than 20 operators.

Programming-by-Example: We omit benchmarks from the syntax-guided synthesis competition tracks that solely focus on programming-by-example (PBE) (i.e., specifying a program only using input-output examples and a grammar). We omit these benchmarks for two reasons: first, since training data is trivial to generate for PBE, unlike general logical specifications [34], there are many other successful machine-learning driven synthesis techniques that can be trained for PBE techniques [6]. Second; our approaches are effective when the LLM can provide guidance to the enumerator, which comes from prompting the LLM with the logical constraints that form the specification. If we prompt the LLM using the prompting techniques outlined in Sect. 4.1 with a PBE specification, it tends to provide a solution in the form of a large case split over the input examples, which returns specific outputs for each input. This is not useful for guiding the enumerator because the LLM overfits to the examples in the specification and fails to provide any bias towards operators other than "if-then-else". To extend our approach to PBE, we would need to use a prompting approach tailored to input-output examples.

---

[2] https://arxiv.org/html/2403.03997.

Table 1. Summary of results. We run nondeterministic results, marked$^\circ$, 3 times and report the average (standard deviation is less than 1% for all methods except the baseline enumerator for number of benchmarks solved). We highlight the best result in terms of number of benchmarks solved in each category. The timeout is 600 s. Times in *italic* indicate results that may vary depending on load on the OpenAI servers. The times for pCFG-synth do not include the time to call the standalone LLM and generate the wCFGs, but these are included in the times for LLM $\cup$ pCFG-synth.

Methods	BV (384)		LIA (87)		INV (138)		Total (609)	
	#	time(s)	#	time(s)	#	time(s)	#	%
LLM only	137	*13.5*	54	*7.10*	112	*29.2*	303	49.8%
e-pCFG-synth$^\circ$	196.0	48.3	24.0	40.0	25.4	100.5	245.4	40.3%
A^*-pCFG-synth	262	60.1	35	72.7	25	99.7	322	52.9%
LLM $\cup$ e-pCFG-synth	255.0	*37.0*	64.0	*17.20*	117.7	*40.4*	436.7	71.7%
LLM $\cup$ A^*-pCFG-synth	**305.0**	*35.0*	65.0	*18.1*	**118.0**	*33.6*	**488.0**	80.1%
e-iLLM-synth$^\circ$	241.0	*88.2*	63.4	*9.3*	65.3	*25.4*	370.0	60.8%
A^*-iLLM-synth$^\circ$	272.3	*24.6*	**68.3**	*20.8*	67.3	*43.6*	408.0	67.0%
enumerator$^\circ$	142.7	7.2	25.0	1.53	21.0	3.2	188.7	31.0%
A^*	253.0	25.4	34.0	73.19	22.0	31.1	309.0	50.7%
cvc5	292.0	17.1	43.0	19.53	80.0	23.6	415.0	68.1%

8   Threats to Validity

LLM Training Data: The SyGuS problems are publicly available and might be part of the training data for the LLM we use, although we believe the solutions were not publicly available at the time of training.

Reproducibility: These experiments use GPT-3.5, an LLM available via API from OpenAI. We have recorded the responses and parameters generated by the LLM in all experiments, but these may not be reproducible [33] since GPT-3.5 behaves non-deterministically in a way that cannot be seeded. However, we observe very small variations in the number of benchmarks solved in our experiments (although greater variation in the average solving time). It is also possible that OpenAI deprecates this LLM and its associated API or updates it and changes its behavior in the future.

Benchmark Bias: The benchmark set is taken from the SyGuS competition [3], but may not be very diverse and may not be representative of synthesis problems "in the wild". Nevertheless, this is a standard benchmark set used in many formal synthesis papers.

Hyperparameters: We have not invested time in parameter tuning, and better or worse results may be obtained by changing the LLM parameters (temperature), or adjusting the weights, enumeration depth and heuristic functions in the probabilistic enumerator and A^* algorithms.

9   Related Work

Many state-of-the-art of SyGuS solvers are based on enumerative synthesis [4, 21, 27, 37] and use clever heuristics to improve the search speed. Closest to our work is Euphony [27], which uses a pre-trained probabilistic higher-order grammar [9] to guide an A^* search. This requires a library of known solutions for training; an advantage of our approach is it exploits the availability of LLMs pre-trained on large bodies of code in other languages, and disregards the need for a library of known solutions of SyGuS problems for training. Weighted grammars have also been used to guide programming by example [30], and to encode syntactic objectives [20], for instance, for optimizing the length of solutions.

Almost all synthesis algorithms use oracles to give feedback to the synthesis process [24, 25]. The majority of these use *semantic* oracles, which give feedback on the meaning of the program, for example, counterexamples [2]. The LLM in iLLM-synth can be considered a syntactic oracle as it only gives feedback on the syntax of the program. Two approaches [1, 17] can be thought of as using syntactic oracles, which evaluate partial programs (or sentential forms) and tell the synthesizer whether a solution can be derived from the sentential form.

Machine learning techniques have been deployed to improve the efficiency of enumerative synthesis, e.g., reinforcement learning [12, 15, 34] or using neural networks to filter grammars for programming-by-examples problems [31].

LLMs, such as GPT-4 [32] and CoPilot [18], have demonstrated impressive capabilities in generating code and assisting in diverse programming tasks with natural language and input-output specifications [5, 10, 11, 22]. However, their tendency to produce hallucinations, factually incorrect or contextually inappropriate outputs, which poses challenges to users [35, 36, 38]. Closest to our work is Kamath et al., who use LLMs to synthesize loop invariants [26] directly. Our work also demonstrates that LLMs are surprisingly good at synthesizing invariants, but also addresses the question of how to use LLMs in other formal synthesis problems and when they cannot find the solution in one shot. Other work that integrates formal methods with LLMs uses LLMs to generate program annotations for program annotation [41, 43]. Jha et al. [23] and Song et al. [40] integrate an LLM into a CEGIS loop, but, unlike our work, the entire synthesis phase is implemented by an LLM, which does not allow them to benefit from the combined strengths of enumerative solving and LLMs.

10   Conclusions

We have presented a novel integration of LLMs into two enumerative synthesis algorithms, evaluated on benchmarks from the Syntax-Guided Synthesis competition. We found that LLMs and enumerative solvers have distinct strengths and weaknesses when deployed alone. We have demonstrated that, by allowing the enumerative synthesizer to prompt the LLM with information obtained during the enumeration and allowing the LLM to provide syntactic feedback to the enumeration, we can achieve performance that equals and exceeds the state-of-the-art solvers, even with relatively simple enumerative algorithms. We argue that our results show that LLMs have the potential to make significant contributions in the domain of formal program synthesis, but the way to achieve this is by combining these techniques with existing algorithms in the literature. Enumerative synthesis is not dead yet!

Acknowledgements. This work was in part supported by an Amazon Research Award, a Royal Academy of Engineering research fellowship, and the European Research Council (ERC) project FormalWeb3 (Grant ID 101156734).

References

1. Abate, A., David, C., Kesseli, P., Kroening, D., Polgreen, E.: Counterexample guided inductive synthesis modulo theories. In: Chockler, H., Weissenbacher, G. (eds.) CAV 2018. LNCS, vol. 10981, pp. 270–288. Springer, Cham (2018). https://doi.org/10.1007/978-3-319-96145-3_15
2. Alur, R., et al.: Syntax-guided synthesis. IEEE (2013)
3. Alur, R., Fisman, D., Singh, R., Udupa, A.: Syntax guided synthesis competition. https://sygus-org.github.io. Accessed 16 Jan 2024
4. Alur, R., Radhakrishna, A., Udupa, A.: Scaling enumerative program synthesis via divide and conquer. In: Legay, A., Margaria, T. (eds.) TACAS 2017. LNCS, vol. 10205, pp. 319–336. Springer, Heidelberg (2017). https://doi.org/10.1007/978-3-662-54577-5_18
5. Austin, J., et al.: Program synthesis with large language models. arXiv preprint arXiv:2108.07732 (2021)
6. Balog, M., Gaunt, A.L., Brockschmidt, M., Nowozin, S., Tarlow, D.: DeepCoder: learning to write programs. In: ICLR (Poster). OpenReview.net (2017)
7. Barbosa, H., et al.: cvc5: a versatile and industrial-strength SMT solver. In: TACAS 2022. LNCS, vol. 13243, pp. 415–442. Springer, Cham (2022). https://doi.org/10.1007/978-3-030-99524-9_24
8. Barrett, C.W., Sebastiani, R., Seshia, S.A., Tinelli, C.: Satisfiability modulo theories. In: Biere, A., Heule, M., van Maaren, H., Walsh, T. (eds.) Handbook of Satisfiability - Second Edition, Frontiers in Artificial Intelligence and Applications, vol. 336, pp. 1267–1329. IOS Press (2021). https://doi.org/10.3233/FAIA201017
9. Bielik, P., Raychev, V., Vechev, M.T.: PHOG: probabilistic model for code. In: ICML. JMLR Workshop and Conference Proceedings, vol. 48, pp. 2933–2942. JMLR.org (2016)
10. Brown, T., et al.: Language models are few-shot learners. In: Advances in Neural Information Processing Systems, vol. 33, pp. 1877–1901 (2020)
11. Bubeck, S., et al.: Sparks of artificial general intelligence: early experiments with GPT-4. arXiv preprint arXiv:2303.12712 (2023)
12. Bunel, R., Hausknecht, M., Devlin, J., Singh, R., Kohli, P.: Leveraging grammar and reinforcement learning for neural program synthesis. In: International Conference on Learning Representations (2018)
13. Chasins, S.E., Newcomb, J.L.: Using SyGuS to synthesize reactive motion plans. In: SYNT@CAV. EPTCS, vol. 229, pp. 3–20 (2016)
14. Chen, M., et al.: Evaluating large language models trained on code. arXiv preprint arXiv:2107.03374 (2021)

15. Chen, Y., Wang, C., Bastani, O., Dillig, I., Feng, Yu.: Program synthesis using deduction-guided reinforcement learning. In: Lahiri, S.K., Wang, C. (eds.) CAV 2020. LNCS, vol. 12225, pp. 587–610. Springer, Cham (2020). https://doi.org/10.1007/978-3-030-53291-8_30
16. David, C., Kroening, D., Lewis, M.: Using program synthesis for program analysis. In: Davis, M., Fehnker, A., McIver, A., Voronkov, A. (eds.) LPAR 2015. LNCS, vol. 9450, pp. 483–498. Springer, Heidelberg (2015). https://doi.org/10.1007/978-3-662-48899-7_34
17. Feng, Y., Martins, R., Bastani, O., Dillig, I.: Program synthesis using conflict-driven learning. In: PLDI, pp. 420–435. ACM (2018)
18. GitHub, OpenAI: GitHub Copilot (2021)
19. Hart, P.E., Nilsson, N.J., Raphael, B.: A formal basis for the heuristic determination of minimum cost paths. IEEE Trans. Syst. Sci. Cybern. **4**(2), 100–107 (1968)
20. Hu, Q., D'Antoni, L.: Syntax-guided synthesis with quantitative syntactic objectives. In: Chockler, H., Weissenbacher, G. (eds.) CAV 2018. LNCS, vol. 10981, pp. 386–403. Springer, Cham (2018). https://doi.org/10.1007/978-3-319-96145-3_21
21. Huang, K., Qiu, X., Shen, P., Wang, Y.: Reconciling enumerative and deductive program synthesis. In: PLDI, pp. 1159–1174. ACM (2020)
22. Jain, N., et al.: Jigsaw: large language models meet program synthesis. In: ICSE, pp. 1219–1231. ACM (2022)
23. Jha, S.K., et al.: Counterexample guided inductive synthesis using large language models and satisfiability solving. In: MILCOM 2023-2023 IEEE Military Communications Conference (MILCOM), pp. 944–949. IEEE (2023)
24. Jha, S., Gulwani, S., Seshia, S.A., Tiwari, A.: Oracle-guided component-based program synthesis. In: Proceedings of the 32nd ACM/IEEE International Conference on Software Engineering-Volume 1, pp. 215–224 (2010)
25. Jha, S., Seshia, S.A.: A theory of formal synthesis via inductive learning. Acta Informatica **54**, 693–726 (2017)
26. Kamath, A., et al.: Finding inductive loop invariants using large language models (2023)
27. Lee, W., Heo, K., Alur, R., Naik, M.: Accelerating search-based program synthesis using learned probabilistic models. In: PLDI, pp. 436–449. ACM (2018)
28. Li, C., et al.: Large language models understand and can be enhanced by emotional stimuli. arXiv preprint arXiv:2307.11760 (2023)
29. Liang, P., Jordan, M.I., Klein, D.: Learning programs: a hierarchical Bayesian approach. In: ICML, pp. 639–646. Citeseer (2010)
30. Menon, A., Tamuz, O., Gulwani, S., Lampson, B., Kalai, A.: A machine learning framework for programming by example. In: International Conference on Machine Learning, pp. 187–195. PMLR (2013)
31. Morton, K., Hallahan, W.T., Shum, E., Piskac, R., Santolucito, M.: Grammar filtering for syntax-guided synthesis. In: AAAI, pp. 1611–1618. AAAI Press (2020)
32. OpenAI: GPT-4 technical report. arXiv, pp. 2303–08774 (2023)
33. Ouyang, S., Zhang, J.M., Harman, M., Wang, M.: LLM is like a box of chocolates: the non-determinism of ChatGPT in code generation. arXiv preprint arXiv:2308.02828 (2023)
34. Parsert, J., Polgreen, E.: Reinforcement learning and data-generation for syntax-guided synthesis. In: AAAI, pp. 10670–10678. AAAI Press (2024)
35. Pearce, H., Ahmad, B., Tan, B., Dolan-Gavitt, B., Karri, R.: Asleep at the keyboard? Assessing the security of GitHub Copilot's code contributions. In: 2022 IEEE Symposium on Security and Privacy (SP), pp. 754–768. IEEE (2022)

36. Perry, N., Srivastava, M., Kumar, D., Boneh, D.: Do users write more insecure code with AI assistants? In: Proceedings of the 2023 ACM SIGSAC Conference on Computer and Communications Security, pp. 2785–2799 (2023)
37. Reynolds, A., Barbosa, H., Nötzli, A., Barrett, C., Tinelli, C.: CVC4SY: smart and fast term enumeration for syntax-guided synthesis. In: Dillig, I., Tasiran, S. (eds.) CAV 2019. LNCS, vol. 11562, pp. 74–83. Springer, Cham (2019). https://doi.org/10.1007/978-3-030-25543-5_5
38. Sandoval, G., Pearce, H., Nys, T., Karri, R., Garg, S., Dolan-Gavitt, B.: Lost at C: a user study on the security implications of large language model code assistants. In: 32nd USENIX Security Symposium (USENIX Security 2023), pp. 2205–2222. USENIX Association, Anaheim, CA, August 2023
39. Solar-Lezama, A., Tancau, L., Bodik, R., Seshia, S., Saraswat, V.: Combinatorial sketching for finite programs. In: Proceedings of the 12th International Conference on Architectural Support for Programming Languages and Operating Systems, pp. 404–415 (2006)
40. Song, C.H., Wu, J., Washington, C., Sadler, B.M., Chao, W.L., Su, Y.: LLM-planner: few-shot grounded planning for embodied agents with large language models. In: Proceedings of the IEEE/CVF International Conference on Computer Vision, pp. 2998–3009 (2023)
41. Sun, C., Sheng, Y., Padon, O., Barrett, C.: Clover: closed-loop verifiable code generation. arXiv preprint arXiv:2310.17807 (2023)
42. Wei, J., et al.: Chain-of-thought prompting elicits reasoning in large language models. In: NeurIPS (2022)
43. Wu, H., Barrett, C., Narodytska, N.: Lemur: integrating large language models in automated program verification. arXiv preprint arXiv:2310.04870 (2023)

Enchanting Program Specification Synthesis by Large Language Models Using Static Analysis and Program Verification

Cheng Wen[1], Jialun Cao[2,6]([✉]), Jie Su[1], Zhiwu Xu[3], Shengchao Qin[1,5]([✉]),
Mengda He[4], Haokun Li[4], Shing-Chi Cheung[2,6], and Cong Tian[5]

[1] Guangzhou Institute of Technology, Xidian University, Guangzhou, China
[2] The Hong Kong University of Science and Technology, Hong Kong, China
[3] College of Computer Science and Software Engineering, Shenzhen University, Shenzhen, China
[4] Fermat Labs, Huawei, Hong Kong, China
[5] ICTT and ISN Laboratory, Xidian University, Xi'an, China
shengchao.qin@gmail.com
[6] Guangzhou HKUST Fok Ying Tung Research Institute, Guangzhou, China
jcaoap@cse.ust.hk

Abstract. Formal verification provides a rigorous and systematic approach to ensure the correctness and reliability of software systems. Yet, constructing specifications for the full proof relies on domain expertise and non-trivial manpower. In view of such needs, an automated approach for specification synthesis is desired. While existing automated approaches are limited in their versatility, *i.e.*, they either focus only on synthesizing loop invariants for numerical programs, or are tailored for specific types of programs or invariants. Programs involving multiple complicated data types (*e.g.*, arrays, pointers) and code structures (*e.g.*, nested loops, function calls) are often beyond their capabilities. To help bridge this gap, we present AutoSpec, an automated approach to synthesize specifications for automated program verification. It overcomes the shortcomings of existing work in specification versatility, synthesizing satisfiable and adequate specifications for full proof. It is driven by static analysis and program verification, and is empowered by large language models (LLMs). AutoSpec addresses the practical challenges in three ways: (1) driving AutoSpec by static analysis and program verification, LLMs serve as generators to generate candidate specifications, (2) programs are decomposed to direct the attention of LLMs, and (3) candidate specifications are validated in each round to avoid error accumulation during the interaction with LLMs. In this way, AutoSpec can incrementally and iteratively generate satisfiable and adequate specifications. The evaluation shows its effectiveness and usefulness, as it outperforms existing works by successfully verifying 79% of programs through automatic specification synthesis, a significant improvement of 1.592x. It can also be successfully applied to verify the programs in a real-world X509-parser project.

A. Gurfinkel and V. Ganesh (Eds.): CAV 2024, LNCS 14682, pp. 302–328, 2024.
https://doi.org/10.1007/978-3-031-65630-9_16

1   Introduction

Program verification offers a rigorous way to assuring the important properties of a program. Its automation, however, needs to address the challenge of proof construction [1,2]. Domain expertise is required for non-trivial proof construction, where human experts identify important program properties, write the *specifications* (*e.g.*, the pre/post-conditions, invariants, and contracts written in certain *specification languages*), and then use these specifications to prove the properties.

Despite the immense demand for software verification in the industry [3–7], *manual verification by experts remains the primary approach in practice.* To reduce human effort, *automated specification synthesis* is desired. Ideally, given a program and a property to be verified, we expect the specifications that are sufficient for a full proof could be synthesized automatically.

Research gap – Prior works are limited in versatility, *i.e.*, the ability to simultaneously handle *different types of specifications* (*e.g.*, invariants, preconditions, postconditions), *code structures* (*e.g.*, multiple function calls, multiple/nested loops), and *data structures* (*e.g.*, arrays, pointers), leaving room for improvement towards achieving full automation in proof construction. Existing works focus only on loop invariants [8–10], preconditions [11,12], or postconditions [13–15]. Moreover, most works on loop invariant synthesis can only handle numerical programs [2,16–18] or are tailored for specific types of programs or invariants [19–24]. To handle various types of specifications simultaneously and to process programs with various code and data structures, a versatile approach is required.

Challenges – Although the use of large language models (LLMs) such as ChatGPT may provide a straightforward solution to program specification generation, it is not a panacea. The generated specifications are mostly incorrect due to three intrinsic weaknesses of LLMs. First, *LLMs can make mistakes.* Even for the well-trained programming language Python, ChatGPT-4 and ChatGPT-3.5 only achieve 67.0% and 48.1% accuracy in program synthesis [25]. In comparison with programming languages, LLMs are much less trained in specification languages. Therefore, LLMs generally perform worse in synthesizing specifications than programs. Since the generated specifications are error-prone, we need an effective technique to detect incorrect specifications, which are meaningless to verify. Second, *LLMs may not attend to the tokens we want them to.* Self-attention may pay no, less, or wrong attention to the tokens that we want it to. Recent research even pointed out a phenomenon called "lost in the middle" [26], observing that LLMs pay little attention to the middle if the context goes extra long. In our case, the synthesized specifications are desired to capture and describe as many program behaviors as possible. Directly adopting the holistic synthesis (*i.e.*, synthesizing all specifications at once) may yield unsatisfactory outcomes. Third, *errors accumulate in the output of LLMs.* LLMs are auto-regressive. If they make mistakes, these wrong outputs get added to their inputs in the next round, leading to way more wrong outputs. It lays a hidden risk when taking advantage of LLMs' dialogue features, especially in an incremental manner (*i.e.*, incrementally synthesizing specifications based on previously generated ones).

Insight – To address the above challenges, *our key insight is to let static analysis and program verification take the lead, while hiring LLMs to synthesize candidate specifications.* Static analysis parses a given program into pieces, and passes each program piece in turn to LLMs by inserting a placeholder in it. Paying attention to the spotted part, LLMs generate a list of specifications as candidates. Subsequently, a theorem prover validates the generated specifications and keeps the validated ones in the next round of synthesis. The iteration process terminates when the property under verification has been proved, or the iteration reaches a predefined limit.

Solution – Bearing the insight, we present AUTOSPEC, an LLM-empowered framework for generating specifications. It tackles the three above-mentioned limitations of directly adopting LLM in three perspectives. First, *it decomposes the program hierarchically* and employs LLMs to generate specifications incrementally in a bottom-up manner. This allows LLMs to focus on a selected part of the program and generate specifications only for the selected context. Thus, the limitation of context fragmentation could be largely alleviated. Second, *it validates the generated specifications* using theorem provers. Specifications that are inconsistent with programs' behaviors and contradict the properties under verification will be discarded. This post-process ensures that the generated specifications are satisfiable by the source code and the properties under verification. Third, *it iteratively enhances the specifications* by employing LLMs to generate more specifications until they are adequate to verify the properties under verification or the number of iterations reaches the predefined upper bound.

We evaluate the effectiveness of AUTOSPEC by conducting experiments on 251 C programs across four benchmarks, each with specific properties to be verified. We compare AUTOSPEC with three state-of-the-art approaches: Pilat, Code2inv, and CLN2Inv. The result shows AUTOSPEC can successfully handle $79\% (= 199 / 251)$ programs with various structures (*e.g.*, linear/multiple/nested loops, arrays, pointers), while existing approaches can only handle programs with linear loops. As a result, $59.2\% (= (199 - 125) / 125)$ more programs can be successfully handled by AUTOSPEC. The result also shows that AUTOSPEC outperforms these approaches' effectiveness and expressiveness when accurately inferring program specifications. To further indicate its usefulness, we apply AUTOSPEC to a real-world X509-parser project, demonstrating its ability to automatically generate satisfiable and adequate specifications for six functions within a few minutes. Also, the ablation study reveals that the program decomposition and the hierarchical specification generation components contribute most to performance improvement. This paper makes the following contributions:

- **Significance.** We present an automated specification synthesis approach, AUTOSPEC, for program verification. AUTOSPEC is driven by static analysis and program verification, and empowered by LLMs. It can synthesize different types of specifications (*e.g.*, invariants, preconditions, postconditions) for

```
1 #include <limits.h>
2
3 /*@
4 requires \valid(a);
5 requires \valid(b);
6 ensures *a == \old(*b);
7 ensures *b == \old(*a);
8 assigns *a,*b;
9 */
10 void swap(int *a, int *b) {    1. Swap
11   int temp = *a;
12   *a = *b;
13   *b = temp;
14 }
15
16 /*@
17 requires \valid(array+(0..n-1));
18 requires 0 < n < INT_MAX;
19 ensures \forall integer i; 0 < i < n ==> array[i-1] <= array[i];
20 */
21 void bubbleSort(int *array, int n) {    4. bubbleSort
22   if (n <= 0) return;
23   int i, j;
24   /*@
25   loop invariant 0 <= i < n;
26   loop invariant \forall integer k; i <= k < n-1 ==> array[k] <= array[k+1];
27   loop invariant \forall integer k; 0 <= k < i+1 <= n-1 ==> array[k] <= array[i+1];
28   loop assigns i, j, array[0..n-1];
29   */
30   for(i = n - 1; i > 0; i--) {    3. Outer loop
31     /*@
32     loop invariant 0 <= j <= i < n;
33     loop invariant \forall integer k; 0 <= k <= j ==> array[k] <= array[j];
34     loop invariant \forall integer k; 0 <= k < i+1 <= n-1 ==> array[k] <= array[i+1];
35     loop assigns j, array[0..i];
36     */
37     for(j = 0; j < i; j++) {    2. Inner loop
38       if (array[j] > array[j+1]) {
39         swap(&array[j], &array[j+1]);
40       }
41     }
42   }
43 }
44
45 void main() {
46   int array[5000] = {..., 5, 4, 3, 2, 1};
47   bubbleSort(array, 5000);
48   //@ assert \forall int i; 0 < i < 5000 ==> array[i-1] <= array[i];
49 }
```

Fig. 1. ACSL Annotations to Functional Proof of Bubble Sort

programs with various structures (*e.g.*, linear/multiple/nested loops, arrays, pointers).

- **Originality.** AUTOSPEC tackles the practical challenges for applying LLMs to specification synthesis: It decomposes the programs hierarchically to lead LLMs' attention, and validates the specifications at each round to avoid error accumulation. By doing so, AUTOSPEC can incrementally and iteratively generate satisfiable and adequate specifications to verify the desired properties.
- **Usefulness.** We evaluate AUTOSPEC on four benchmarks and a real-world X509-parser. The four benchmarks include 251 programs with linear/multiple/nested loops, array structures, pointers, *etc.*. AUTOSPEC can successfully handle 79% of them, 1.592x outperforming existing works. The experiment result shows the effectiveness, expressiveness, and generalizability of AUTOSPEC.

2   Background and Motivation

Listing 1 illustrates a C program that implements the bubble sort (sorting a 5000-element array of integers in ascending order), where the *property to be verified* (line 48) prescribes that after sorting, any index i between 1 and 4999, the element at array[i-1] is no larger than the element at array[i]. To verify the property, we use a specification language for C programs, ACSL [27] (ANSI/ISO-C Specification Language) to write the proof. It appears in the form of code comments (annotated by //@ ... or /*@ ... */) and does not affect the program execution. The ACSL-annotated program can be directly fed to auto-active verification tool (FRAMA-C [28] in this paper) to prove the properties (Fig. 1).

In the running example, specifications in the program prescribe the *preconditions* (begin with \requires), *postconditions* (begin with \ensures), and *loop invariants* (begin with loop invariant)[1]. To prove the property in line 48, practitioners usually write specifications *in a bottom-up manner*, that is, from line 47 tracing to bubbleSort (line 21), then from line 39, tracing to swap (line 10). Starting from swap, practitioners identify the inputs and outputs of the swap function and write the pre/post-conditions (lines 4–8). In particular, the precondition (lines 4–5) requires the two input pointers to be valid (*i.e.*, they can be safely accessed), which is necessary to ensure the safe execution of the operations involving dereferencing. Additionally, the postcondition ensures that the values of *a and *b are swapped (lines 6–7) and assigned (line 8) during execution.

Then tracing back to where swap is called, *i.e.*, inside bubbleSort, it can be challenging because it contains nested loops. In a bottom-up manner, the ***inner loop*** of bubbleSort (lines 37–41) is first analyzed. In particular, to verify a loop, it is composed of (1) loop invariants (*i.e.*, general conditions that hold before/during/after the loop execution, begin with loop invariant), and possibly (2) the list of assigned variables (begin with assign). In the example, practitioners analyze the inner loop and write specifications in lines 31–36. Specifically, the index j should fall into the range of 0 to n (line 32), the elements from index 0 to j are not larger than the element at j (line 33), and all elements from index 0 to i are smaller than or equal to the element at i+1 (line 34). Also, the variables to be assigned in this inner loop include j and first-i elements in the array (line 35). Similarly, for ***the outer loop*** (lines 30–42), lines 24–29 describe the range of index i (line 25), invariants (lines 26–27) and assigned variables (line 28).

Finally, practitioners analyze bubbleSort (lines 21–43), identifying that the first-n elements of array can be safely accessed (line 17), n must be greater than zero (line 18). After execution, the array is in ascending order (line 19). Once all the specifications are written, they are fed into a prover/verification tool), FRAMA-C [28] which supports ACSL to verify the ***satisfiability*** (*i.e.*, the specifications satisfy the program) and ***adequacy*** (*i.e.*, the specifications are sufficient to verify the desired properties) of all specifications until the desired

---

[1] ACSL has more keywords with rich expressiveness. Refer to the documentation [27].

property verification succeeds. If the verification fails, practitioners debug and refine the specifications.

From this example, we can see that the manual efforts to write specifications are non-trivial. Even for a simple algorithm such as bubble sort. In practice, the program under verification could be on a far larger scale, which brings a huge workload to practitioners, motivating the *automated specification synthesis*.

Motivation – Existing related works can only synthesize loop invariants for programs with a single loop [2,16] or multiple loops [29] on the numerical program. These approaches cannot generate satisfiable and adequate specifications to fully prove the correctness of basic programs such as bubble sort.

Motivated by the research gap, AUTOSPEC is presented. It synthesizes specification in a bottom-up manner, synthesizing versatile specifications (*i.e.*, not only loop invariants, but also precondition, postcondition, and assigned variables, which are necessary for the full proof). It validates the satisfiability of specifications whenever specifications are synthesized, and verifies the adequacy of specifications after all specifications are synthesized.

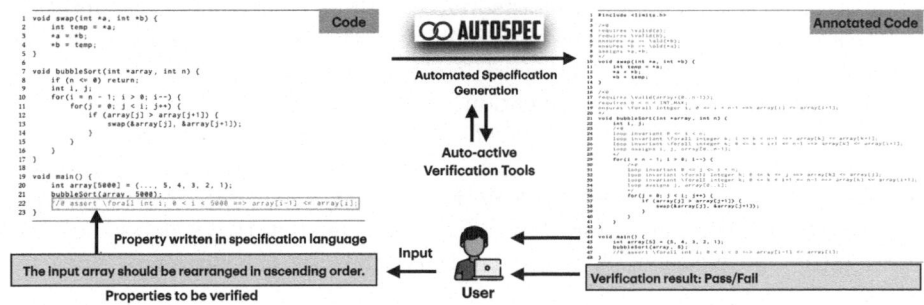

Fig. 2. User Scenario of AUTOSPEC

User Scenario – We envision the user scenario of AUTOSPEC in Fig. 2. Given a program and properties under verification, AUTOSPEC provides a fully automated verification process. It synthesizes the specifications for the program, validates the satisfiability of specifications, verifies the specifications against the desired properties, and outputs the verification result with proof if any.

Note that proof can be provided by AUTOSPEC if the program is correctly implemented (*i.e.*, the properties can be verified). When the given program is syntactically buggy, the program reports the syntactic error at the beginning before launching AUTOSPEC. If the given program is semantically buggy, then AUTOSPEC cannot synthesize adequate specifications for verification, the synthesis terminates when the maximum iteration number is reached.

3   Methodology

Figure 3 shows an **overview** of AUTOSPEC. The workflow comprises three main steps: ❶ **Code Decomposition** (Sect. 3.1). AUTOSPEC statically analyzes a C program by decomposing it into a call graph, where loops are also represented as nodes. The aim of the first step is to generalize the procedure that was previously discussed in Sect. 2 to include the implicit knowledge of simulating interactions between humans and verification tools. By decomposing the program into smaller components, LLMs can iteratively focus on different code components for a more comprehensive specification generation. ❷ **Hierarchical specification generation** (Sect. 3.2). Based on the call graph with loops, AUTOSPEC inserts *placeholders* in each level of the graph in a bottom-up manner. Taking the program in Listing 1 for example, AUTOSPEC inserts the first placeholder (/*@ 1. SPEC PLACEHOLDER */) before swap, and then inserts the second placeholder in the inner loop of Sort. Then, AUTOSPEC iteratively masks the placeholder one at a time with ">>> INFILL <<<" and feeds the masked code into LLMs together with few-shot examples. After querying LLMs, they reply with a set of specifications. AUTOSPEC then fills the generated specifications into the placeholder and proceeds to the next one. Once all the placeholders are filled with LLM-generated specifications, AUTOSPEC proceeds to the next step. ❸ *Specification Validation* (Sect. 3.3). AUTOSPEC feeds the verification conditions of each generated specification into a theorem prover to verify their satisfiability. If the theorem prover confirms the satisfiability of the specifications, they will be annotated as a comment in the source code. Otherwise, if the theorem prover identifies any unsatisfiable specifications (*i.e.*, cannot be satisfied by the program), AUTOSPEC removes those specifications and annotates program with the remaining specifications. Then, AUTOSPEC returns to the second step to insert additional placeholders immediately after the specifications generated in the previous iteration and generate more specifications. This iterative process continues until all the specifications are successfully verified by the prover or until the

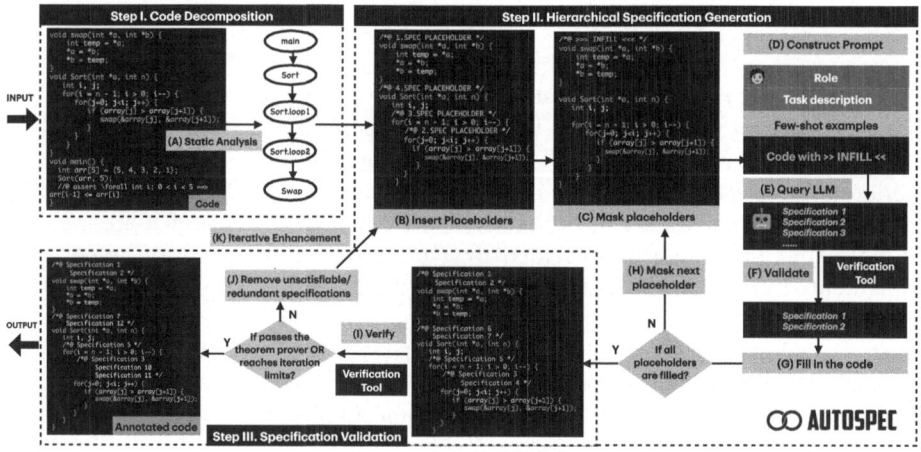

Fig. 3. Overview of AUTOSPEC

Algorithm 1: Construct an Extended Loop/Call Graph

Input: The source code C and the location loc of the assertion to be verify
Output: A call graph G extended with loops

1 $G \leftarrow$ get_function(loc)   // initialize a Graph G
2 $WorkList \leftarrow$ get_function(loc)
3 **while** $WorkList! = \emptyset$ **do**
4     $Fn \leftarrow$ select_and_remove_a_node($WorkList$)   // transitively visit all reachable nodes
5   **for** *each basicBlock bb in Fn* **do**
6   **if** *bb calls a function M* **then**   // If there exist a function call
7   **if** *M is not already a node in G* **then**
8   Add a node M to G
9   Add an edge from Fn to M in G
10          $WorkList \leftarrow WorkList \cup M$ // Add this node (function) to the $WorkList$

11   **if** *bb is a loop entry for loop L* **then**   // If there exist a loop
12   **if** *L is not already a node in G* **then**
13   Add a node L to G
14   Add an edge from Fn to L in G
15          $WorkList \leftarrow WorkList \cup L$ // Add this node (loop) to the $WorkList$

16 **return** G

---

number of iterations reaches the predefined upper limit (in our evaluation, it is set to 5). We will explain the methodology of each step in detail.

3.1 Code Decomposition

Using static analysis, AUTOSPEC constructs a comprehensive call graph for the given program to identify the specific locations where specifications should be added and determine the order in which these specifications should be added. This call graph is an extended version of the traditional one, where loops are also treated as nodes, in addition to functions. This is particularly useful for complex programs where loops can significantly affect the program's behavior.

The algorithm for constructing such a call graph is shown in Algorithm 1. Specifically, the algorithm selects a function that contains the target assertion to be verified as the entry point for the call graph construction. Then, it traverses the abstract syntax tree (AST) of the source code to identify all functions and loops and their calling relationships. For instance, the extended call graph generated for the program in Listing 1 is given in Fig. 3(A).

Then, the specifications are generated step-by-step based on the nodes in the extended call graph. When generating the specification for a node, one only needs to consider the code captured by the node and the specifications of its callees in the extended call graph. Furthermore, modeling loops in addition to functions as separate nodes in the extended call graph allows AUTOSPEC to generate loop invariants, which are essential to program verification. Therefore, code decomposition allows LLMs to focus on small program components to generate specifications, thus reducing the complexity of specification generation and making it more manageable and efficient. And traversing the extended call graph from bottom to top can simulate the programmers' verification process.

3.2   Hierarchical Specification Generation

AUTOSPEC generates specifications for each node in the extended call graph in a hierarchical manner. It starts from the leaf nodes and moves upward to the root node. This bottom-up approach ensures that the specifications for each function or loop are generated within the context of their callers. Algorithm 2 shows the algorithm of hierarchical specification generation. The algorithm takes as input an extended call graph G, an iteration bound t, a large language model, and the assertion to be verified; and outputs an annotated code C with generated specifications. In detail, the algorithm works as follows: First, the algorithm initializes a code template C with the original code without specifications (line 1). The code template, similar to Fig. 3(B), includes placeholders. Each placeholder corresponds to a node in the call graph. These placeholders will be iteratively replaced with the valid specifications generated by the LLMs and validated by the theorem prover, within a maximum of t iterations (line 2).

In each iteration, the algorithm performs the following steps. *First*, AUTOSPEC initializes a stack S with the root node of graph G, which is the target function containing the assertion to be verified (line 3). *Second*, AUTOSPEC pushes the nodes that require specification generation into the stack S and traverses the stack S in a depth-first manner (lines 4–15). For each node f in the stack, the algorithm checks if all the callees of f have their specifications generated in this iteration (lines 7–8). If not, the algorithm pushes the callee nodes into the stack and marks f as not ready for specification generation (lines 9–10). If all of the functions called by f have had their specifications generated, the algorithm will then proceed to generate the specifications for f. (lines 11–15). In particular, AUTOSPEC queries the LLMs to generate a set of candidate specifications $spec_{tmp}$ for f (line 12), and validates $spec_{tmp}$ by examining their syntactic and semantic validity. Any illegal or unsatisfiable specifications are eliminated, and the remaining valid specifications are referred to as $spec_f$ (line 13). The validation process may employ existing provers/verification tools to guarantee soundness. Then, AUTOSPEC inserts the validated specifications into the source code C at the placeholder of f (line 14), and pops up the node f from the stack, indicating that f has its specification generated in this iteration (line 15). *Third*, AUTOSPEC examines whether the whole verification task has been completed, that is, whether the generated specifications are adequate to verify the target assertion (line 16). If it does, AUTOSPEC proceeds to simplify the annotated code C by eliminating redundant or unnecessary specifications (line 17) and then terminates (line 18). Otherwise, it is assumed that the specifications generated so far are satisfiable, though they may be inadequate. And AUTOSPEC will start another iteration to generate additional specifications while retaining those already generated. *Finally*, the algorithm returns the annotated code C with the generated specifications as the output (line 19). After several iterations, if the whole verification task remains incomplete, the programmer can make a decision on whether to involve professionals to continue with the verification process for the annotated code C.

Algorithm 2: Hierarchical Specification Generation

Input: A loop/call Graph G, an iteration bound t, a Large Language Model LLM, and the assertion ass to be verified
Output: Annotated Code C with generated specifications

```
1   C.init()                                              // initialize the code (without specifications)
2   for i in range(0, t) do                               // iteratively enhancing specifications
3   |   Initialize a stack S with the root node of G
4   |   while S is not empty do
5   |   |   f = S.top()                                    // get the element at the top of the stack
6   |   |   allgen = true
7   |   |   for each callee in f.callees() do
8   |   |   |   if spec generation for callee has not been done in i^th iteration then
9   |   |   |   |   S.push(callee)                         // push all callee into the stack
10  |   |   |   |   allgen = false
11  |   |   if allgen == true then
12  |   |   |   spec_tmp = spec_generation(C, f, LLM)      // query LLM to generate specification candidates
13  |   |   |   spec_f = spec_validation(C, spec_tmp)      // specification validation
14  |   |   |   C.insert(spec_f)                           // insert the specifications into the code template
15  |   |   S.pop()                                        // pop up the top element f of the stack
16  |   if spec_validation(C, ass) then   // determine whether the whole verification task has been completed
17  |   |   simplify(C)                                    // eliminating redundant specifications
18  |   |   break
19  return C
```

Consider the extended call graph in Fig. 3(A) for example. AutoSpec first pushes the main function, the sort function, the sort.loop1 loop, the sort.loop2 loop, and the swap function into the stack in order, as all of them, except the swap function have some callee nodes that require specification generation. Then, it generates specifications for each function or loop in the stack in reserve order. This order echoes what is described in Sect. 2. AutoSpec will leverage the power of LLMs to generate candidate specifications for each component/function (*i.e.*, spec_generation function in line 12). In the following, we discuss how AutoSpec utilizes LLMs for generating specifications.

Specification generation by LLMs. To employ LLMs in producing precise and reliable responses in the specified format, AutoSpec automatically generates a prompt for each specification generation task. This prompt is a natural language query that includes the role setting, task description, a few examples showing the desired specifications, and the source code with a highlighted placeholder (*e.g.*, Fig. 3(C)). The prompt template used in AutoSpec is shown in Fig. 3(D). Specifically, a prompt typically consists of the following elements: a system message, code with a placeholder, and an output indicator. The system message provides the specification generation task description and the specification language, which are called *context*. AutoSpec sets the **role** of LLMs as "*As an experienced C/C++ programmer, I employ a behavioral interface specification language that utilizes Hoare style pre/post-conditions, as well as invariants, to annotate my C/C++ source code*". The system message also indicates the task's instructions, such as "*Fill in the >>> INFILL <<<*". As explained in Sect. 3.1, when querying LLMs for the specifications of a component (*i.e.*, a function or loop), the code of this component and the specifications of its callees in the call graph are needed. That is to say, the irrelevant code that is not called by this component can be omitted, allowing LLMs to maintain their focus on the target component and reduces unnecessary token costs. Finally, AUTOSPEC uses the output format /@ ... / to indicate the generated specifications, which is crucial for programmatically processing the responses of LLMs.

To improve the quality of the generated specifications, AUTOSPEC employs the prompt engineering technique of few-shot prompting [30]. To achieve this, the prompts are designed to include a few relevant input-output examples. Feeding LLMs a few examples can guide them in leveraging previous knowledge and experiences to generate the desired outputs. This, in turn, enables LLMs to effectively handle novel situations. In particular, few-shot prompting allows LLMs to facilitate the learning of syntax and semantics of specification language through in-context learning. For example, consider a prompt that includes an input-output example with a loop invariant for an array that initializes all elements to 0, such as \forall integer j; 0 <= j < i ==> ((char*)p)[j] == 0;. With this example, AUTOSPEC is able to generate a valid loop invariant that involves using quantifiers for the inner loop of bubbleSort in a single query.

3.3 Specification Validation

The hierarchical specification generation algorithm also employs specification validation (*i.e.*, spec_validation() in line 13) and specification simplification (*i.e.*, simplify() in line 17) techniques to ensure the quality of the specifications.

Specification Validation. Once candidate specifications have been generated for a component, AUTOSPEC will check their syntactic and semantic validity (*i.e.*, legality and satisfiability), as shown in Fig. 3(F). Specifically, for a function, the legality and satisfiability of the generated specifications are checked immediately. While for a loop, the legality is checked immediately, but the satisfiability check is postponed until the outermost loop. This is because inner loops often use variables defined in some of their outer loops (*e.g.*, variable i in the bubbleSort example), and the satisfiability of all loop invariants needs to be verified simultaneously.

AUTOSPEC leverages the verification tool (*i.e.*, FRAMA-C) to verify the specifications. If the verification tool returns a compilation error, AUTOSPEC identifies the illegal specification where the error occurs and continues verifying without it if there are still some candidates. Otherwise, if the verification tool returns a verification failure, AUTOSPEC identifies the unsatisfiable specification which fails during verification and continues verifying without it if there are still some candidates. Finally, if the verification succeeds, the specifications will be correspondingly inserted into the code as a comment (Fig. 3(G)).

In addition, AUTOSPEC also validates whether the generated specifications are adequate to verify the target assertion (line 16), which is the same as the validation above but with the target assertion. Note that, the validation phase is

Table 1. Statistics of Benchmarks.

Benchmarks/Project	Description	Num of Prog	Types of Specifications	Ave LoC	Num of Spec
Frama-C-problems [31]	Programs with function calls, nested/multiple loops, arrays, pointers	51	pre/post-conditions, loop invariants	17.43	1~3
X509-parser [32]	A real-world software implements a X.509 certificate parser	6	pre/post-conditions, loop invariants	82.33	3~19
SyGuS [33]	Programs with a single loop	133	loop invariants	22.56	1~12
OOPSLA-13 [34]	Programs with a single loop or nested/multiple loops	46	loop invariants	30.28	1~3
SV-COMP [35]	Programs with more complex nested/multiple loops	21	loop invariants	24.33	1~5

crucial to AUTOSPEC as it ensures that the generated specifications are not only legal and satisfiable but also adequate to verify the target assertion (Fig. 3(I)).

Specification Simplification (Optional). The objective of specification simplification is to provide users with a concise and elegant specification that facilitates manual inspection and aids in understanding the implementation. This process could be *optional* if one's goal is simply to complete the verification task without placing importance on the specifications. After successfully verifying the assertion, we proceed to systematically remove specifications that are not needed for their verification, one by one. Our main idea is that a specification is unnecessary if the assertion is still verifiable without it. We repeat this process until we reach the minimal set of specifications for manual reading.

There are two main reasons to eliminate specifications: (1) The specification is considered weak and does not capture relevant properties of the verification task. For example, both the loop invariant i > 0 and i > 1 are satisfiable, but i > 0 can be safely removed. (2) The specification is semantically similar to another specification. For example, both \forall integer i; 0 < i < n ==> array[i-1] <= array[i]; and \forall integer i; 0 <= i < n-1 ==> array[i] <= array[i+1]; accurately describe the post-condition of bubbleSort. Removing either of them has no impact on the verification results.

4 Evaluation

The experiments aim to answer the following research questions:

RQ1. Can AutoSpec generate specifications for various properties effectively? We aim to comprehensively characterize the effectiveness of AUTOSPEC against various types of specifications including pre/post-conditions, loop invariants.

RQ2. Can AutoSpec generate specifications for loop invariant effectively? Loop invariant, as a major specification type, is known for its difficulty and significance. We select three benchmarks with linear and nested loop structures and compare them with state-of-the-art approaches.

RQ3. Is AutoSpec efficient? We compare the AUTOSPEC's overhead incurred by LLM querying and theorem proving with the baselines.

RQ4. Does every step of AutoSpec contribute to the final effectiveness? We conduct an ablation study on each part of the AUTOSPEC's design, showing the distinct contribution made independently.

4.1   Evaluation Setup

Benchmark. We conducted evaluations on four benchmarks and a real-world project. The statistical details of these benchmarks can be found in Table 1. The FRAMA-C-problems [31] benchmark and the X509-parser [32] comprises programs that involve multiple functions or loops, requiring the formulation of pre/post-conditions, loop invariants, *etc.*. The SyGuS [33] benchmark only includes programs with linear loop structures. While the OOPSLA-13 [34] and SV-COMP [35] benchmarks include programs with nested or multiple loops, making them suitable for evaluating the versatility and diversity of generated specifications. Please note that we assume the programs being verified are free of compilation errors, and the properties being verified are consistent with the programs. If there are any inconsistencies between the code and properties, AUTOSPEC is expected to fail the verification after the iterations end.

Baselines. For RQ1, as previous works have primarily relied on manually written specifications for the deductive verification of functional correctness for C/C++ programs [36,37], we then conduct our approach based on this baseline, and use the ablation study to demonstrate the contribution of different parts of the design in AUTOSPEC in RQ4. For RQ2, we compare with Code2Inv [2], a learning-based approach for generating linear loop invariants[2]. Although there are newer approaches built on Code2Inv such as CLN2INV [16], their replicable toolkit is only applicable to the benchmark they used (*i.e.*, SyGuS [33]) and incomplete, failing to apply to other benchmarks. Additionally, for RQ2, we also compared with Pilat [29] using the default settings.

Configuration. For implementation, we use ChatGPT's API *gpt-3.5-turbo-0613*. We configure the parameters in API as follows: max_token: 2048, temperature: 0.7. To show the generalizability of AUTOSPEC, we also utilize *Llama-2-70b* for conducting a comparable experiment (Sect. 5). Lastly, we employ FRAMA-C [28,38] and its WP plugin to verify the specifications.

4.2   RQ1. Effectiveness on General Specification

Table 2 shows the results of AUTOSPEC on the FRAMA-C-problems benchmark. This benchmark consists of 51 C programs, divided into eight categories (as indicated in the entry *Type*). Each type contains several programs. The size of the programs ranges from 9 to 36 lines of code (the entry *LoC*). We also list the number of functions and loop structures defined in the program. Most programs contain a main function, with one or more loop structures. Since we could not

---

[2] We reproduce their implementation using the provided replicable package and run the tool on two additional benchmarks following their instructions. However, in their original setting, the maximal time limit for each program is set to 12 h, which is far from affordable. So we lowered the threshold to 1 h for efficiency.

Table 2. Effectiveness of AUTOSPEC in General Specification Generation

| Benchmark Information | | | | AUTOSPEC | | | | | |
Type	Program	LoC	Component (Func, Loop)	Success	Ratio	Iterations	Generated Spec	Correct Spec	Time(s) mean ± std
general_wp_problems	absolute_value.c	15	1 (1,0)	✔	5/5	1,1,1,1,1	7,7,7,7,7	7/7	14.17 ± 8.74
	add.c	11	1 (1,0)	✔	5/5	1,1,1,1,1	3,3,3,3,3	2/2	14.36 ± 8.20
	ani.c	18	2 (1,1)	✗	0/5	-,-,-,-,-	41,33,26,20,24	3/4	–
	diff.c	10	1 (1,0)	✔	5/5	1,1,1,1,1	2,2,2,2,2	1/1	8.85 ± 5.72
	gcd.c	22	1 (1,0)	✗	0/5	-,-,-,-,-	3,6,8,5,5	2/5	–
	max_of_2.c	15	1 (1,0)	✔	5/5	1,1,1,1,1	4,3,5,3,5	2/2	17.64 ± 11.24
	power.c	18	2 (1,1)	N/A	–	–	–	–	–
	simple_interest.c	14	1 (1,0)	✔	5/5	1,1,1,1,1	5,5,5,5,5	5/5	15.34 ± 8.60
	swap.c	16	1 (1,0)	✔	5/5	1,1,1,1,1	3,3,3,3,3	2/2	15.36 ± 8.66
	triangle_angles.c	14	1 (1,0)	✔	5/5	1,1,1,1,1	7,5,6,4,5	4/4	23.99 ± 13.67
	triangle_sides.c	16	1 (1,0)	✔	5/5	1,1,1,1,1	3,3,3,2,2	2/2	20.11 ± 11.41
	wp1.c	14	1 (1,0)	✗	0/5	-,-,-,-,-	1,4,1,4,2	3/3	–
pointers	add_pointers.c	19	1 (1,0)	✔	5/5	1,1,1,1,1	3,4,4,4,4	2/2	10.00 ± 5.85
	add_pointers_3_vars.c	20	1 (1,0)	✔	5/5	2,5,3,-,3	3,6,10,14,4	3/3	74.45 ± 47.78
	div_rem.c	12	1 (1,0)	✔	5/5	1,1,1,1,1	7,8,7,7,7	4/4	14.66 ± 8.39
	incr_a_by_b.c	13	1 (1,0)	✔	5/5	1,1,1,1,1	6,6,6,4,6	3/3	18.82 ± 13.43
	max_pointers.c	16	1 (1,0)	✔	5/5	1,1,1,1,1	5,4,4,5,5	4/4	41.73 ± 15.74
	order_3.c	36	1 (1,0)	✗	0/5	-,-,-,-,-	16,19,15,6,12	3/4	–
	reset_1st.c	16	1 (1,0)	✔	5/5	1,1,1,1,1	7,5,4,6,5	4/4	15.23 ± 9.42
	swap_pointer.c	13	1 (1,0)	✔	5/5	1,1,1,1,1	5,5,5,5,5	2/2	10.72 ± 6.00
loops	1.c	9	1 (0,1)	✔	5/5	1,1,1,1,1	2,2,2,2,2	1/1	2.35 ± 2.23
	2.c	17	2 (1,1)	✗	0/5	-,-,-,-,-	8,10,11,11,5	2/5	–
	3.c	18	2 (1,1)	✗	0/5	-,-,-,-,-	10,6,7,5,6	3/4	–
	4.c	18	2 (1,1)	N/A	–	–	–	–	–
	fact.c	19	2 (1,1)	✗	0/5	-,-,-,-,-	3,8,7,6,6	3/7	–
	mult.c	16	2 (1,1)	✗	0/5	-,-,-,-,-	6,14,10,9,16	2/3	–
	sum_digits.c	17	2 (1,1)	✗	0/5	-,-,-,-,-	7,13,13,12,11	-	–
	sum_even.c	16	2 (1,1)	✗	0/5	-,-,-,-,-	9,14,16,18,19	2/3	–
immutable_arrays	array_sum.c	16	2 (1,1)	✗	0/5	-,-,-,-,-	5,4,4,3,4	3/5	–
	binary_search.c	24	2 (1,1)	✔	1/5	3,-,-,-,-	16,16,30,36,19	7/7	739.62 ± 239.59
	check_evens_in_array.c	19	2 (1,1)	✗	0/5	-,-,-,-,-	11,18,15,13,16	4/6	–
	max.c	20	2 (1,1)	✔	5/5	1,1,1,1,1	10,9,12,8,7	5/5	40.11 ± 29.49
	occurences_of_x.c	26	2 (1,1)	✔	5/5	2,1,1,1,2	16,12,10,14,12	3/3	121.83 ± 75.04
	sample.c	19	1 (0,1)	✔	5/5	1,1,1,1,1	3,3,4,3,3	1/1	16.89 ± 10.47
	search.c	17	2 (1,1)	✗	0/5	-,-,-,-,-	12,14,16,16,12	5/8	–
	search_2.c	18	2 (1,1)	✔	4/5	1,3,2,-,3	13,18,19,10,16	5/5	155.32 ± 175.44
mutable_arrays	array_double.c	19	2 (1,1)	✔	4/5	-,2,2,2,3	12,17,19,16,17	4/4	81.44± 21.14
	bubble_sort.c	26	3 (1,2)	✔	3/5	-,2,3,3,-	9,12,15,12,15	10/10	448.76 ± 554.81
more_arrays	equal_arrays.c	15	2 (1,1)	✗	0/5	-,-,-,-,-	9,14,15,13,8	5/7	–
	replace_evens.c	17	2 (1,1)	✔	5/5	1,1,1,1,1	13,12,15,20,14	3/3	52.33 ± 17.30
	reverse_array.c	23	2 (1,1)	✗	0/5	-,-,-,-,-	10,7,14,13,18	5/-	–
arrays_and_loops	1.c	10	1 (1,0)	✔	5/5	1,1,1,1,1	3,2,3,2,3	1/1	3.22 ± 2.07
	2.c	18	2 (1,1)	✔	5/5	1,1,1,1,1	10,10,10,10,10	2/2	30.15 ± 27.79
	3.c	19	1 (1,0)	✔	5/5	1,1,1,1,1	9,10,10,4,9	2/2	12.05 ± 7.09
	4.c	18	2 (1,1)	✔	5/5	1,1,1,1,1	12,10,10,8,0	2/2	18.34 ± 13.46
	5.c	18	2 (1,1)	✗	0/5	-,-,-,-,-	12,10,10,4,9	3/4	–
miscellaneous	array_find.c	20	2 (1,1)	✗	0/5	-,-,-,-,-	7,7,7,7,7	4/7	–
	array_max_advanced.c	20	2 (1,1)	✔	5/5	1,1,1,1,1	5,6,5,6,5	2/2	31.99 ± 34.41
	array_swap.c	18	1 (1,0)	✔	5/5	1,1,1,1,1	8,4,7,8,4	3/3	26.05 ± 30.72
	increment_arr.c	17	2 (1,1)	✗	0/5	-,-,-,-,-	2,2,2,2,2	3/6	–
	max_of_2.c	14	1 (1,0)	✔	5/5	1,1,1,1,1	2,3,3,2,3	1/1	9.98 ± 10.31
Overall				31 / 51					89.17 ± 172.75

find other previous work that can automatically generate various types of specifications to complete the verification task on FRAMA-C-problems benchmark, we hereby show the effectiveness of AUTOSPEC in detail.

Overall, 31/51 of these programs can be successfully solved by AUTOSPEC. In particular, due to the randomness of LLMs, we ran the experiment five times for each program and reported the detailed results. The success rate is tabulated in Table 2, column *Ratio*. It shows that the results are stable over five runs. Almost all passed cases can be successfully solved in five runs, with only a few exceptions (*e.g.*, 1/5, 4/5). The stable result shows that the randomness of LLMs has little impact on the effectiveness of AUTOSPEC. Furthermore, AUTOSPEC enables an iterative enhancement on specification generation. We hereby show the number of iterations used for success generation (column *Iterations*). Most cases can be solved in the first iteration. While the iterative enhancement also contributes to certain improvements. For example, add_pointers_3_vars.c in the pointers category needs two more iterations to generate adequate specifications to pass the theorem prover. In addition, we also report the number of generated specifications that are correct by using the ground truth in the benchmark as a reference,

Table 3. Effectiveness on a Real-world X.509 Certificate Parser Project

Function Information				AutoSpec					
Project	Function	Feature	LoC	Success	Ratio	Iterations	Generated Spec	Correct Spec	Time(s) mean ± std
X509-parser	check_ia5_string	loop; buffer pointer	60	✔	5/5	1,1,2,1,1	13,11,14,13,11	6/6	20.89 ± 10.51
	verify_correct_time_use	switch-case	90	✔	5/5	1,1,3,1,2	10,19,23,15,16	3/3	24.16 ± 11.73
	bufs_differ	loop; buffer pointer	55	✔	5/5	1,1,1,1,1	17,17,20,16,15	5/5	12.49 ± 5.11
	parse_null	call the function bufs_differ; buffer pointer	87	✔	2/5	-,-,1,1,-	25,36,44,33,34	13/13	260.96 ± 118.58
	parse_algoid_params_none	call the function parse_null and bufs_differ	136	✔	2/5	-,2,-,-,2	184,92,156,142,96	19/19	957.14 ± 446.56
	time_components	shift operation; multiple data type	63	✔	5/5	1,1,1,1,1	11,17,16,13,17	7/7	11.82 ± 5.34
Overall				**6 / 6**					214.58 ± 389.58

as shown in column *Correct Spec*. We can see that for the failed cases, there is at least one generated specification that is correct. This shows that the generated specifications are not excessive, and still have the potential to improve. Finally, in terms of overhead (column *Time(s)*), AutoSpec processes a case in minutes, from 2.53 s to 12 min, with an average of 89.17 s.

A Real-World X509 Parser Project. The X509-parser project, which aims to ensure the absence of runtime errors, has undergone verification by Frama-C and the ACSL specification language. Note that the specifications for this project were manually added throughout 5 months [3]. It is currently impractical to seamlessly apply AutoSpec to the entire project without human intervention. We manually extracted 6 representative functions without specifications. These functions handle pointer dereference, multiple data types, shift operations, *etc.*. For each function, we set a verification target that accurately describes its functional correctness properties. AutoSpec generates specifications for these functions, as shown in Table 3. Surprisingly, all 6 functions were solved by AutoSpec. Through our comprehensive manual examination of the generated specifications, we found that AutoSpec can generate a variety of specifications not previously written by the developer. These specifications play a crucial role in ensuring functional correctness. Considering that it takes five calendar months to write specifications for the whole X509-parser project [3], AutoSpec can automatically generate the required specifications for the functions in X509-parser in a few minutes. We believe that AutoSpec could be useful for real-world verification tasks.

4.3 RQ2. Effectiveness on Loop Invariants

Table 4 shows the effectiveness of AutoSpec in generating specifications of loop invariants compared with three baselines. In particular, the SyGuS benchmark consists of 133 C programs. Each program contains only one loop structure. We compare AutoSpec with three baselines: Pilat [29], Code2Inv [2] and CLN2INV [16] on this benchmark. The result is shown in Table 4 under *SyGuS* entry. Pailt fails to generate valid specifications for all cases in this benchmark, as all the specifications it generates are either unsatisfiable or irrelevant. On the other hand, Code2Inv and CLN2INV perform better, solving 73 and 124 programs, respectively. AutoSpec can handle a comparable number of cases,

Table 4. Effectiveness on Loop Invariants Synthesis

SyGuS [33] (133 C Programs with One Loop)

Info		AutoSpec		Pailt		Code2Inv		CLN2Inv	
ID	LoC	Success	Time(s)	Success	Time(s)	Success	Time(s)	Success	Time
1	29	✔	6.65	✗	–	✔	4950.78	✔	4.32
2	20	✔	5.97	✗	–	✗	–	✔	4.11
3	18	✗	36.24	✗	–	✗	–	✔	0.22
4	13	✗	32.28	✗	–	✗	–	✔	0.21
5	17	✔	19.22	✗	–	✗	–	✔	2.48
6	21	✗	142.95	✗	–	✗	–	✔	1.7
7	15	✔	57.15	✗	–	✔	128.03	✔	3.47
8	15	✔	92.75	✗	–	✔	72.74	✔	3.13
9	25	✔	39.66	✗	–	✗	–	✔	3.04
10	21	✗	295.83	✗	–	✔	53.39	✔	3.14
11	18	✔	77.48	✗	–	✔	145.02	✔	3.33
12	30	✔	106.137	✗	–	✔	71.97	✔	3.37
13	31	✔	240.24	✗	–	✔	39.82	✔	3.07
14	18	✔	79.59	✗	–	✔	21.9	✔	3.23
15	20	✔	13.66	✗	–	✔	274.79	✔	2.43
16	22	✔	30.31	✗	–	✗	–	✔	6.16
17	15	✔	24.97	✗	–	✗	–	✔	2.31
18	22	✔	23.7	✗	–	✗	–	✔	6.47
19	33	✔	21.41	✗	–	✗	–	✔	2.47
20	22	✔	16.59	✗	–	✔	53.57	✔	9.78
					113 more cases are omitted due to space limitation				
Total		114/133		0/133		73/133	248±982.2	124/133	2.1±2.32

OOPSLA-13 [34] (46 C Programs with Various Loop Types)

Info				AutoSpec		Code2Inv		CLN2INV	
ID	LoC	Type	Loop Num.	Success	Time(s) mean ± std	Success	Time(s)	Success	Time(s)
1	23	Linear	1	✔	6.25 ± 7.22	✔	337.8	✔	–
2	27	Linear	1	✔	7.17 ± 7.38	✔	74.36	●	–
3	22	Linear	1	✔	113.47 ± 88.10	✔	46.22	✗	–
4	28	Linear	1	✔	6.04 ± 7.64	✗	–	✗	–
5	30	Linear	1	✔	8.59 ± 9.80	✗	–	●	–
6	31	Linear	1	✔	41.62 ± 24.06	✗	–	✗	–
7	30	Linear	1	✔	12.66 ± 15.12	✗	–	●	–
8	24	Linear	1	✔	3.40 ± 3.25	✗	–	●	–
9	27	Linear	1	✗	–	✗	–	✗	–
10	26	Linear	1	✔	9.40 ± 7.29	✗	–	✗	–
11	26	Linear	1	✔	16.82 ± 16.90	✗	–	✗	–
12	25	Linear	1	✔	51.27 ± 34.43	✗	–	✗	–
13	25	Linear	1	✔	12.57 ± 10.57	✗	–	●	–
14	29	Linear	1	✔	19.42 ± 11.52	✗	–	✗	–
15	37	Linear	1	✔	58.85 ± 13.83	✗	–	●	–
16	37	Linear	1	✗	–	✗	–	✗	–
17	27	Linear	1	✔	4.80 ± 3.62	✔	66.4	✗	–
18	24	Linear	1	✔	19.86 ± 12.17	✗	–	●	–
19	23	Linear	1	✔	10.34 ± 7.59	✗	–	✗	–
20	25	Linear	1	✗	–	✗	–	●	–
21	24	Linear	1	✔	12.09 ± 7.97	✗	–	✗	–
22	22	Linear	1	✔	11.79 ± 11.14	✔	29.96	✗	–
23	28	Linear	1	✔	32.71 ± 24.14	✗	–	✗	–
24	23	Linear	1	✔	12.84 ± 7.20	✗	–	✗	–
25	62	Linear	1	✔	6.64 ± 4.62	✗	–	✗	–
26	32	Linear	1	✔	44.89 ± 49.35	✗	–	✗	–
27	34	Linear	1	✗	–	✗	–	✗	–
28	26	Linear	1	✔	11.92 ± 9.78	✗	–	✗	–
29	35	Linear	1	✔	16.21 ± 14.83	✗	–	✗	–
30	29	Linear	1	✔	140.51 ± 67.06	✗	–	●	–
31	51	Multiple	4	✗	–	✗	–	✗	–
32	36	Multiple	2	✔	71.74 ± 60.13	✗	–	✗	–
33	27	Multiple	2	✔	94.02 ± 58.68	✔	26.97	✗	–
34	33	Multiple	2	✔	57.32 ± 39.28	✗	–	●	–
35	27	Nested	3	✔	58.26 ± 54.18	✗	–	✗	–
36	30	Nested	2	✔	84.23 ± 57.52	✔	17.42	✗	–
37	23	Nested	2	✗	–	✔	0.26	✗	–
38	22	Nested	2	✔	105.28 ± 60.01	✗	–	●	–
39	35	Nested	2	✔	96.50 ± 68.99	✗	–	✗	–
40	26	Nested	3	✔	139.88 ± 92.53	✔	147.89	✗	–
41	30	Nested	3	✗	–	✗	–	✗	–
42	29	Nested	3	✔	228.71 ± 218.43	✗	–	✗	–
43	39	Nested	3	✗	–	✗	–	●	–
44	61	Nested	4	✗	–	✗	–	✗	–
45	46	Nested	3	✔	202.78 ± 185.39	✗	–	●	–
46	24	Nested	3	✔	86.61 ± 50.22	✗	–	✗	–
Total				38/46	68.92 ± 171.13	9/46	83.0 ± 104.8	0/46	

SV-COMP (21 C programs with multiple/nested loops)

Benchmark Information				AutoSpec	
Type	Program	LoC	Loop	Success	Time(s)
quantifier-free	afnp2014_true-unreach-call.c	17	1	✔	40.69 ± 34.37
	bhmr2007_true-unreach-call.c	31	1	✔	4.50 ± 2.61
	cggmp2005_true-unreach-call.c	18	1	✔	128.04 ± 53.74
	count_up_down_true-unreach-call...	22	1	✔	18.44 ± 15.77
	css2003_true-unreach-call.c	19	1	✔	88.07 ± 74.35
	ddlm2013_true-unreach-call.c	33	1	✗	–
	down_true-unreach-call.c	21	2	✔	269.98 ± 224.05
	half_2_true-unreach-call.c	25	2	✗	–
	hhk2008_true-unreach-call.c	26	1	✔	8.49 ± 5.87
	jm2006_variant_true-unreach-call.c	30	1	✔	22.52 ± 14.55
	jm2006_true-unreach-call.c	25	1	✔	123.61 ± 100.31
	large_const_true-unreach-call.c	37	2	✗	–
	nest-if3_true-unreach-call.c	19	2	✔	107.05 ± 73.11
	nested6_true-unreach-call.c	31	3	✗	–
	nested9_true-unreach-call.c	23	3	✔	274.87 ± 156.77
	seq_true-unreach-call.c	33	3	✗	–
	sum01_true-unreach-call...	20	1	✔	8.12 ± 6.41
	terminator_03_true-unreach-call...	20	1	✔	26.09 ± 22.98
	up_true-unreach-call.c	30	2	✔	374.38 ± 291.44
quantifier	array_true-unreach-call1.c	13	1	✔	5.88 ± 3.78
	array_true-unreach-call2.c	18	1	✔	32.53 ± 27.11
Total				16/21	217.9 ± 451.7

namely, 114 programs in this benchmark. Although CLN2INV can solve 10 more cases in this benchmark, it cannot handle any cases in the OOPSLA-13 benchmark. Although CLN2INV can successfully parse 19 out of 46 cases (denoted as ●), CLN2INV fails to construct satisfiable invariants that are adequate to verify the programs, resulting in a score of 0/46. This could be due to the overfitting of machine learning methods to specific datasets. Code2Inv, on the other hand, can handle 9 out of 46 cases. In comparison, AUTOSPEC can solve 38/46 (82.60%), which significantly outperforms existing approaches.

Furthermore, we consider a more difficult benchmark, SV-COMP. Due to the unsatisfactory results of the existing approaches, we have opted to exclusively present the results obtained using AUTOSPEC. As shown in Table 4 under *SV-COMP* entry, AUTOSPEC can solve 16 out of 21 programs with an average time of 3 min. Note that there are three programs with 3-fold nested loop structures in this benchmark. AUTOSPEC can solve one of them, while for the other two programs, AUTOSPEC can generate several satisfiable specifications, but there are still one or two specifications that cannot be generated after five iterations.

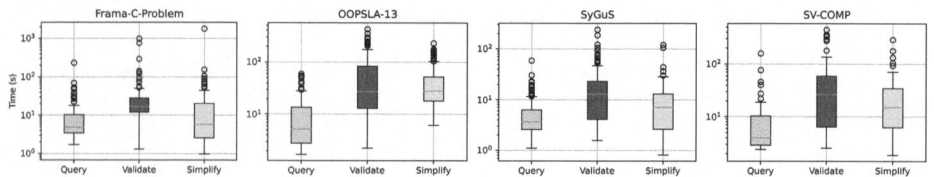

Fig. 4. Overhead of AutoSpec on Four Benchmarks.

4.4 RQ3. Efficiency of AutoSpec

In the first RQs, we can observe that AutoSpec can generate satisfiable and adequate specifications for the proof ranging from 2.35 to 739.62 s (*i.e.*, 0.04 to 12.33 min). In this RQ, we illustrate the composition of the overhead in AutoSpec across sub-tasks, *i.e.*, the time required for querying the LLM for specifications, validating and verifying the specifications against the theorem prover, and simplifying the specifications (optional). The results for these four benchmarks are presented in Fig. 4.

We can see that for the four benchmarks, validating and verifying the specifications (*Validate*) takes the most time, ranging from 1.3 to 994.9 s. Querying the LLMs (*Query*) takes the least time, averaging less than 10 s. It is noteworthy that, unlike existing works that tend to generate a lot of candidate specifications and check their validity for one hour [16] to 12 h [2], AutoSpec takes far less time in validating (*e.g.*, 1.2 s to 3.88 min). This is because AutoSpec generates fewer but higher-quality specifications. The efficiency of AutoSpec makes it both practical and cost-effective for various applications.

In addition, the time required for simplifying the specifications (*Simplify*) may vary depending on the number of generated specifications. A larger number of specifications leads to a longer simplification process. Nonetheless, given the fact that the simplification step is optional in AutoSpec, and considering the benefit of faster solving brought about by the concise and elegant specifications, the cost of simplification is justified.

4.5 RQ4. Ablation Study

Finally, we evaluate the contribution made by each part of AutoSpec's design. The results are shown in Table 5. We conduct the evaluation on FRAMA-C-problems benchmark [31] under seven settings: (1) - (4) settings under *Base ChatGPT* entry directly feed the C program together with the desired properties to be verified into ChatGPT, with zero-/one-/two-/three-shot. These settings are designed to compare with the decomposed manner adopted by AutoSpec. Setting (5) under entry *Decomposed* adopts the code decomposition (*i.e.*, Step 1 of AutoSpec) with three-shot, because it shows the best result according to the results of the previous settings. Settings (6) and (7) are respectively configured with only one pass (*i.e.*, without enhancement) and five iterations (*i.e.*, with enhancement), showing the improvement brought by the iterative enhancement

Table 5. Experiment Result of Ablation Study

Type	Base ChatGPT				Decomposition	Iterative Enhancement	
	(1) 0-shot	(2) 1-shot	(3) 2-shot	(4) 3-shot	(5) 3-shot	(6) Pass@1	(7) Iter@5
Loops	1	1	1	1	1	1	1
Immutable_arrays	0	0	0	0	3	4	5
Mutable_arrays	0	0	0	0	0	0	2
Arrays_and_loops	1	0	1	1	4	4	4
More_arrays	0	0	0	0	1	1	1
General_wp_problems	2	4	3	5	8	8	8
Pointers	0	2	0	1	6	6	7
Miscellaneous	1	1	1	1	3	3	3
Total	5	8	6	9	26	27	**31**

(Step (K) in Fig. 3). The last row shows the total number of programs that can be successfully solved under the corresponding settings.

Table 5 shows an ascending trend in the number of solved programs, from 5 to 31 over 51. On the one hand, it is hardly possible to directly ask ChatGPT to generate specifications for the entire program. The input-output examples bring only a limited improvement (from 5 to 9) in the performance. On the other hand, code decomposition and hierarchical specification generation bring a significant improvement (from 9 to 26). This shows the contribution made by the first two steps of AUTOSPEC. Furthermore, the contribution of iterative enhancement can be observed in the last two columns, from 27 to 31. Overall, the ablation study shows that every step in AUTOSPEC has a positive impact on the final result and that the idea of code decomposition and hierarchical specification generation brings the biggest improvement.

4.6 Case Studies

We discuss 3 representative cases to show how iterative enhancement contributes (Fig. 5), and situations where AUTOSPEC fails to handle (Fig. 6 and Fig. 7).

Case 1. A Success Case Made by Validation and Iterative Enhancement. We show how specification validation and iterative enhancement help AUTOSPEC to generate satisfiable and adequate specifications. The program presented below computes the sum of three values stored in pointers. In the first iteration, only two specifications (lines @newinlinkFig5listing:case32 and @newinlinkFig5listing:case33) are generated, which respectively require three pointers should be valid (line @newinlinkFig5listing:case32), and the result of add is the sum (line @newinlinkFig5listing:case33). However, these two specifications alone are inadequate to verify the property due to the lack of a specification describing whether the values of the pointers have been modified within the add function. AUTOSPEC then inserts placeholders immediately after the two generated specifications and continues to the second iteration of enhancement. The subsequently generated specification (line @newinlinkFig5listing:case34) states the add function has no assignment behavior, making the verification succeed.

Case 2. A Failing Case Due to Missing Context. We present an example where AUTOSPEC fails to generate adequate specifications due to *the lack of necessary context*. The code for the pow in <math.h> is not directly accessible. Currently, AUTOSPEC does not automatically trace all the dependencies and include their code in the prompt. LLMs can hardly figure out what pow is expected to do. As a result, the specification for this function cannot be generated despite all attempts made by AUTOSPEC. This case shows a possible improvement by adding more dependencies in the prompt.

```
1 /*@
2 requires \valid(a) && \valid(b) && \valid(r);
3 ensures \result == *a + *b + *r;
4 assigns \nothing;
5 */
6 int add(int *a, int *b, int *r)
7 {
8    return *a + *b + *r;
9
10 }
```

Fig. 5. Case 1

```
1 #include <math.h>
2 /*@
3 requires n >= 0;
4 ensures \result == (\pow(2, n+1)) - 1;
5 assigns \nothing;
6 */
7 int fun(int n) {
8    double y = 0;
9    double i = 0;
10   /*@
11   loop invariant y == (\pow(2, i)) - 1;
12   loop invariant i <= n;
13   loop assigns i, y;
14   */
15   while(i <= n) {
16       y = y + pow(2.0, i);
17       i = i + 1;
18   }
19   return y;
20 }
```

Fig. 6. Case 2

Case 3. A Failing Case Due to the Need for User-Defined Axioms.
We illustrate an example where AUTOSPEC fails to produce sufficient specifications, necessitating *user-defined axioms*. The factorial function encompasses
a nonlinear loop, typically necessitating the formulation of axioms or lemmas
by domain experts to aid in the proof process. Presently, AUTOSPEC does not
include axioms in the prompt or provided examples, posing a challenge for LLM
to generate these supportive axioms. This example underscores the importance
of addressing the axiom generation issue for AUTOSPEC for future work, in order
to handle intricate examples effectively.

5   Threats to Validity

There are three major validity threats. The first concerns **the data leakage
problem**. We addressed this threat in two folds. First, we directly apply LLMs
to generate the specifications (Sect. 4.5). The unsatisfactory result (success rate:
5/51) shows that the chance of overfitting to the benchmark is low. Second, we
followed a recent practice [39] for the data leakage threat. We randomly sampled
100 programs from three benchmarks in RQ2 (*i.e.*, SyGuS, OOPSLA-13, and SV-
COMP) in a ratio of 50:25:25 and mutated these programs by variable renaming
(*e.g.*, renaming x to m) and statement/branch switching (*e.g.*, negotiating the
if-condition, and switching the statements in if and else branches) without
changing the semantics of the program manually. Then we applied AUTOSPEC

```
1  /*@
2  axiomatic Factorial {
3       logic integer fact(integer n);
4       axiom case_n:
5         \forall integer n;
6           n >= 1 ==> fact(n) == n*fact(n-1);
7
8       axiom case_0:
9         fact(0) == 1;
10 }
11 */
12
13 /*@
14 requires n >= 0;
15 ensures \result == fact(n);
16 assigns \nothing ;
17 */
18 int factorial(int n) {
19      int i = 1;
20      int f = 1;
21      /*@
22      loop invariant f == fact(i-1);
23      loop invariant 0 < i;
24      loop invariant i <= n+1;
25      loop assigns i, f;
26      */
27      while (i <= n) {
28          f = f * i;
29          i = i + 1;
30      }
31      return f;
32 }
33
34 void main() {
35      int t = factorial(5);
36      //@ assert t == 120;
37 }
```

Fig. 7. Case 3

over the 100 mutated programs. The experiment shows that *98% results hold after the programs are mutated.* It further confirmed that the validity threat of data leakage is low. The second concerns **the generalizability to different LLMs.** To address this concern, we implemented AUTOSPEC to a popular and open-source LLM called *Llama-2-70b* and ran it on the same benchmark used in RQ1. Similar results were observed, with AUTOSPEC (Llama2) achieving a score of 25/51 compared to the score of 31/51 achieved by AUTOSPEC (Chat-GPT). The third concerns **the scalability of AutoSpec.** We have evaluated a real-world X509-parser project and achieved unexpectedly good performance. However, completing the whole verification task on the entire project remains challenging. The evidence suggests that AUTOSPEC has the potential to assist participants in writing specifications for real-world programs.

6 Related Work

Specification Synthesis. While there exist various approaches and techniques for generating program specifications from natural language [40–42], this paper primarily focuses on specification generation based on the programming language. There has been work using data mining to infer specifications [43–46]. Several of these techniques use dynamic traces to infer possible invariants and preconditions from test cases, and static analysis to check the validity and completeness of the inferred specifications [47–49]. While others apply domain knowledge and statically infer specifications from the source code [43,50,51]. Several works have been conducted to address the challenging sub-problem of loop invariant inference, including CLN2INV [16], Code2Inv [2], G-CLN [17] and Fib [52]. Additionally, there are also studies dedicated to termination specification inference [23]. A recent study, SpecFuzzer [53], combines grammar-based fuzzing, dynamic invariant detection, and mutation analysis to generate class specifications for Java methods in an automated manner. Our approach differs from these techniques as it statically generates comprehensive contracts for each loop and function, yielding reliable outcomes necessary for verification.

Assisting Program Analysis and Verification with LLMs. In recent years, there has been a growing interest in applying LLMs to assist program analysis tasks [54], such as fuzz testing [55,56], static analysis [57–59], program verification [60–62], bug reproduction [63] and bug repair [64–66]. For example, Baldur [60] is a proof-synthesis tool that uses transformer-based pre-trained large language models fine-tuned on proofs to generate and repair whole proofs. In contrast, AUTOSPEC focuses on generating various types of program specifications and leveraging the auto-active verification tool to complete the verification task, while Baldur focuses on automatically generating proofs for the theorems. Li *et al.* [59] investigated the potential of LLMs in enhancing static analysis by posing relevant queries. They specifically focused on UBITest [67], a bug-finding tool for detecting use-before-initialization bugs. The study revealed that those false positives can be significantly reduced by asking precisely crafted questions related to function-level behaviors or summaries. Ma *et al.* [68] and Sun *et al.* [58] explore the capabilities of LLMs when performing various program analysis tasks such as control flow graph construction, call graph analysis, and code summarization. Pei *et al.* [69] use LLMs to reason about program invariants with decent performance. These diverse applications underline the vast potential of LLMs in program analysis. AUTOSPEC complements these efforts by showcasing the effectiveness of LLMs in generating practical and elegant program specifications, thereby enabling complete automation of deductive verification.

7   Conclusion

In this paper, we presented AUTOSPEC, a novel approach for generating program specifications from source code. Our approach leverages the power of Large Language Models (LLMs) to infer the candidate program specifications in a bottom-up manner, and then validates them using provers/verification tools and iteratively enhances them. The evaluation results demonstrate that our approach to specification generation achieves full automation and cost-effectiveness, which is a major bottleneck for formal verification.

Acknowledgements. This work was supported in part by the National Natural Science Foundation of China (Nos. 62372304, 62302375, 62192734), the China Postdoctoral Science Foundation funded project (No. 2023M723736), the Fundamental Research Funds for the Central Universities, and the Hong Kong SAR RGC/GRF No. 16207120.

References

1. Hähnle, R., Huisman, M.: Deductive software verification: from pen-and-paper proofs to industrial tools. In: Steffen, B., Woeginger, G. (eds.) Computing and Software Science. LNCS, vol. 10000, pp. 345–373. Springer, Cham (2019). https://doi.org/10.1007/978-3-319-91908-9_18
2. Si, X., Dai, H., Raghothaman, M., Naik, M., Song, L.: Learning loop invariants for program verification. Adv. Neural Inf. Process. Syst. **31**, 1–12 (2018)
3. Ebalard, A., Mouy, P., Benadjila, R.: Journey to a rte-free x. 509 parser. In: Symposium sur la sécurité des technologies de l'information et des communications (SSTIC 2019) (2019)
4. Efremov, D., Mandrykin, M., Khoroshilov, A.: Deductive verification of unmodified linux kernel library functions. In: Margaria, T., Steffen, B. (eds.) ISoLA 2018. LNCS, vol. 11245, pp. 216–234. Springer, Cham (2018). https://doi.org/10.1007/978-3-030-03421-4_15
5. Dordowsky, F.: An experimental study using acsl and frama-c to formulate and verify low-level requirements from a do-178c compliant avionics project. arXiv preprint arXiv:1508.03894 (2015)
6. Blanchard, A., Kosmatov, N., Lemerre, M., Loulergue, F.: A case study on formal verification of the anaxagoros hypervisor paging system with frama-C. In: Núñez, M., Güdemann, M. (eds.) FMICS 2015. LNCS, vol. 9128, pp. 15–30. Springer, Cham (2015). https://doi.org/10.1007/978-3-319-19458-5_2

7. Kosmatov, N., Lemerre, M., Alec, C.: A case study on verification of a cloud hypervisor by proof and structural testing. In: Seidl, M., Tillmann, N. (eds.) TAP 2014. LNCS, vol. 8570, pp. 158–164. Springer, Cham (2014). https://doi.org/10. 1007/978-3-319-09099-3_12

8. Dillig, I., Dillig, T., Li, B., McMillan, K.: Inductive invariant generation via abductive inference. Acm Sigplan Not. **48**(10), 443–456 (2013)

9. Lin, Y., et al.: Inferring loop invariants for multi-path loops. In: 2021 International Symposium on Theoretical Aspects of Software Engineering (TASE), pp. 63–70. IEEE (2021)

10. Yu, S., Wang, T., Wang, J.: Loop invariant inference through smt solving enhanced reinforcement learning. In: Proceedings of the 32nd ACM SIGSOFT International Symposium on Software Testing and Analysis, pp. 175–187 (2023)

11. Cousot, P., Cousot, R., Fähndrich, M., Logozzo, F.: Automatic inference of necessary preconditions. In: Giacobazzi, R., Berdine, J., Mastroeni, I. (eds.) VMCAI 2013. LNCS, vol. 7737, pp. 128–148. Springer, Heidelberg (2013). https://doi.org/ 10.1007/978-3-642-35873-9_10

12. Padhi, S., Sharma, R., Millstein, T.: Data-driven precondition inference with learned features. ACM SIGPLAN Not. **51**(6), 42–56 (2016)

13. Popeea, C., Chin, W.-N.: Inferring disjunctive postconditions. In: Okada, M., Satoh, I. (eds.) ASIAN 2006. LNCS, vol. 4435, pp. 331–345. Springer, Heidelberg (2007). https://doi.org/10.1007/978-3-540-77505-8_26

14. Su, J., Arafat, M., Dyer, R.: Using consensus to automatically infer post-conditions. In: Proceedings of the 40th International Conference on Software Engineering: Companion Proceedings, pp. 202–203 (2018)

15. Singleton, J.L., Leavens, G.T., Rajan, H., Cok, D.: An algorithm and tool to infer practical postconditions. In: Proceedings of the 40th International Conference on Software Engineering: Companion Proceedings, pp. 313–314 (2018)

16. Ryan, G., Wong, J., Yao, J., Gu, R., Jana, S.: Cln2inv: learning loop invariants with continuous logic network. In: International Conference on Learning Representations (2020)

17. Yao, J., Ryan, G., Wong, J., Jana, S., Gu, R.: Learning nonlinear loop invariants with gated continuous logic networks. In: Proceedings of the 41st ACM SIGPLAN Conference on Programming Language Design and Implementation, pp. 106–120 (2020)

18. Gupta, A., Rybalchenko, A.: InvGen: an efficient invariant generator. In: Bouajjani, A., Maler, O. (eds.) CAV 2009. LNCS, vol. 5643, pp. 634–640. Springer, Heidelberg (2009). https://doi.org/10.1007/978-3-642-02658-4_48

19. Le, Q.L., Gherghina, C., Qin, S., Chin, W.-N.: Shape analysis via second-order biabduction. In: Biere, A., Bloem, R. (eds.) CAV 2014. LNCS, vol. 8559, pp. 52–68. Springer, Cham (2014). https://doi.org/10.1007/978-3-319-08867-9_4

20. Wang, Q., Chen, M., Xue, B., Zhan, N., Katoen, J.-P.: Synthesizing invariant barrier certificates via difference-of-convex programming. In: Silva, A., Leino, K.R.M. (eds.) CAV 2021. LNCS, vol. 12759, pp. 443–466. Springer, Cham (2021). https:// doi.org/10.1007/978-3-030-81685-8_21

21. Feng, Y., Zhang, L., Jansen, D.N., Zhan, N., Xia, B.: Finding polynomial loop invariants for probabilistic programs. In: D'Souza, D., Narayan Kumar, K. (eds.) ATVA 2017. LNCS, vol. 10482, pp. 400–416. Springer, Cham (2017). https://doi. org/10.1007/978-3-319-68167-2_26

22. Gan, T., Xia, B., Xue, B., Zhan, N., Dai, L.: Nonlinear craig interpolant generation. In: Lahiri, S.K., Wang, C. (eds.) CAV 2020. LNCS, vol. 12224, pp. 415–438. Springer, Cham (2020). https://doi.org/10.1007/978-3-030-53288-8_20

23. Le, T.C., Qin, S., Chin, W.N.: Termination and non-termination specification infer-
    ence. In: The 36th ACM SIGPLAN Conference on Programming Language Design
    and Implementation, pp. 489–498 (2015)
24. Vazquez-Chanlatte, M., Seshia, S.A.: Maximum causal entropy specification infer-
    ence from demonstrations. In: Lahiri, S.K., Wang, C. (eds.) CAV 2020. LNCS, vol.
    12225, pp. 255–278. Springer, Cham (2020). https://doi.org/10.1007/978-3-030-
    53291-8_15
25. OpenAI. GPT-4 technical report. CoRR arxiv:2303.08774 (2023)
26. Liu, N.F., et al.: Lost in the middle: how language models use long contexts. arXiv
    preprint arXiv:2307.03172 (2023)
27. Baudin, P., Filliâtre, J.-C., Marché, C., Monate, B., Moy, Y., Prevosto, V.: Acsl:
    Ansi/iso c specification (2021)
28. FRAMA-C. Frama-c, software analyzer. Accessed 15 Jan 2024
29. de Oliveira, S., Bensalem, S., Prevosto, V.: Polynomial invariants by linear algebra.
    In: Artho, C., Legay, A., Peled, D. (eds.) ATVA 2016. LNCS, vol. 9938, pp. 479–494.
    Springer, Cham (2016). https://doi.org/10.1007/978-3-319-46520-3_30
30. Brown, T.B., et al.: Language models are few-shot learners. In: Larochelle, H., Ran-
    zato, M., Hadsell, R., Balcan, M.F., Lin, H.T. (eds.) Advances in Neural Informa-
    tion Processing Systems 33: Annual Conference on Neural Information Processing
    Systems 2020, NeurIPS 2020, 6–12 December 2020, virtual (2020)
31. FRAMA-C. A repository dedicated for problems related to verification of programs
    using the tool frama-c. Accessed 15 Jan 2024
32. A rte-free x.509 parser. Accessed 15 Jan 2024
33. Alur, R., Fisman, D., Padhi, S., Singh, R., Udupa, A.: Sygus-comp 2018: results
    and analysis. CoRR arxiv:1904.07146 (2019)
34. Dillig, I., Dillig, T., Li, B., McMillan, K.: Inductive invariant generation via abduc-
    tive inference. In: Proceedings of the 2013 ACM SIGPLAN International Confer-
    ence on Object Oriented Programming Systems Languages & Applications, OOP-
    SLA 2013, pp. 443–456. Association for Computing Machinery, New York (2013)
35. Beyer, D.: Progress on software verification: SV-COMP 2022. In: TACAS 2022.
    LNCS, vol. 13244, pp. 375–402. Springer, Cham (2022). https://doi.org/10.1007/
    978-3-030-99527-0_20
36. Baudin, P., Bobot, F., Correnson, L., Dargaye, Z., Blanchard, A.: Wp plug-in
    manual. Frama-c. com (2020)
37. Blanchard, A., Loulergue, F., Kosmatov, N.: Towards full proof automation in
    frama-C using auto-active verification. In: Badger, J.M., Rozier, K.Y. (eds.) NFM
    2019. LNCS, vol. 11460, pp. 88–105. Springer, Cham (2019). https://doi.org/10.
    1007/978-3-030-20652-9_6
38. Kirchner, F., Kosmatov, N., Prevosto, V., Signoles, J., Yakobowski, B.: Frama-c:
    a software analysis perspective. Formal Aspects Comput. 27, 573–609 (2015)
39. Wu, Y., et al.: How effective are neural networks for fixing security vulnerabilities.
    In: Just, R., Fraser, G. (eds.) Proceedings of the 32nd ACM SIGSOFT Interna-
    tional Symposium on Software Testing and Analysis, ISSTA 2023, Seattle, WA,
    USA, 17–21 July 2023, pp. 1282–1294. ACM (2023)
40. Cosler, M., Hahn, C., Mendoza, D., Schmitt, F., Trippel, C.: nl2spec: interactively
    translating unstructured natural language to temporal logics with large language
    models. In: Enea, C., Lal, A. (eds.) Computer Aided Verification, pp. 383–396.
    Springer, Cham (2023). https://doi.org/10.1007/978-3-031-37703-7_18

41. Zhai, J., et al.: C2s: translating natural language comments to formal program specifications. In: Proceedings of the 28th ACM Joint Meeting on European Software Engineering Conference and Symposium on the Foundations of Software Engineering, pp. 25–37 (2020)

42. Giannakopoulou, D., Pressburger, T., Mavridou, A., Schumann, J.: Generation of formal requirements from structured natural language. In: Madhavji, N., Pasquale, L., Ferrari, A., Gnesi, S. (eds.) REFSQ 2020. LNCS, vol. 12045, pp. 19–35. Springer, Cham (2020). https://doi.org/10.1007/978-3-030-44429-7_2

43. Beckman, N.E., Nori, A.V.: Probabilistic, modular and scalable inference of typestate specifications. In: Proceedings of the 32nd ACM SIGPLAN Conference on Programming Language Design and Implementation, pp. 211–221 (2011)

44. Lo, D., Khoo, S.C., Liu, C.: Efficient mining of iterative patterns for software specification discovery. In: The 13th ACM SIGKDD International Conference on Knowledge Discovery and Data Mining, pp. 460–469 (2007)

45. Le, T.B.D., Lo, D.: Deep specification mining. In: Proceedings of the 27th ACM SIGSOFT International Symposium on Software Testing and Analysis, pp. 106–117 (2018)

46. Kang, H.J., Lo, D.: Adversarial specification mining. ACM Trans. Softw. Eng. Methodol. (TOSEM) **30**(2), 1–40 (2021)

47. Ammons, G., Bodik, R., Larus, J.R.: Mining specifications. ACM Sigplan Notices **37**(1), 4–16 (2002)

48. Yang, J., Evans, D., Bhardwaj, D., Bhat, T., Das, M.: Perracotta: mining temporal api rules from imperfect traces. In: Proceedings of the 28th International Conference on Software Engineering, pp. 282–291 (2006)

49. Nimmer, J.W.: Automatic generation and checking of program specifications. PhD thesis, Massachusetts Institute of Technology (2002)

50. Ramanathan, M.K., Grama, A., Jagannathan, S.: Static specification inference using predicate mining. ACM SIGPLAN Not. **42**(6), 123–134 (2007)

51. Shoham, S., Yahav, E., Fink, S., Pistoia, M.: Static specification mining using automata-based abstractions. In: Proceedings of the 2007 International Symposium on Software Testing and Analysis, pp. 174–184 (2007)

52. Lin, S.W., Sun, J., Xiao, H., Liu, Y., Sanán, D., Hansen, H.: Fib: squeezing loop invariants by interpolation between forward/backward predicate transformers. In: 2017 32nd IEEE/ACM International Conference on Automated Software Engineering (ASE), pp. 793–803 (2017)

53. Molina, F., d'Amorim, M., Aguirre, N.: Fuzzing class specifications. In: Proceedings of the 44th International Conference on Software Engineering, pp. 1008–1020 (2022)

54. Hou, X., et al.: Large language models for software engineering: a systematic literature review. CoRR arxiv:2308.10620 (2023)

55. Deng, Y., Xia, C.S., Peng, H., Yang, C., Zhang, L.: Large language models are zero-shot fuzzers: Fuzzing deep-learning libraries via large language models. In: Just, R., Fraser, G. (eds.) Proceedings of the 32nd ACM SIGSOFT International Symposium on Software Testing and Analysis, ISSTA 2023, Seattle, WA, USA, 2023, pp. 423–435. ACM (2023)

56. Lemieux, C., Inala, J.P., Lahiri, S.K., Sen, S.: Codamosa: escaping coverage plateaus in test generation with pre-trained large language models. In: 45th IEEE/ACM International Conference on Software Engineering, ICSE 2023, Melbourne, Australia, 2023, pp. 919–931. IEEE (2023)

57. Wen, C., et al.: Automatically inspecting thousands of static bug warnings with large language model: how far are we? ACM Trans. Knowl. Disc. Data **18**(7), 1–34 (2024)

58. Sun, W., et al.: Automatic code summarization via chatgpt: how far are we? CoRR arxiv:2305.12865 (2023)

59. Li, H., Hao, Y., Zhai, Y., Qian, Z.: Poster: assisting static analysis with large language models: a chatgpt experiment. In: 44th IEEE Symposium on Security and Privacy, SP 2023, San Francisco, CA, USA, 2023. IEEE (2023)

60. First, E., Rabe, M.N., Ringer, T., Brun, Y.: Baldur: whole-proof generation and repair with large language models. In: ESEC/FSE '23: 31th ACM Joint European Software Engineering Conference and Symposium on the Foundations of Software Engineering. ACM (2023)

61. Wu, H., Barrett, C., Narodytska, N.: Lemur: integrating large language models in automated program verification. arXiv preprint arXiv:2310.04870 (2023)

62. Yang, K., et al.: Leandojo: theorem proving with retrieval-augmented language models. arXiv preprint arXiv:2306.15626 (2023)

63. Kang, S., Yoon, J., Yoo, S.: Large language models are few-shot testers: exploring llm-based general bug reproduction. In: 45th IEEE/ACM International Conference on Software Engineering, ICSE 2023, Melbourne, Australia, 14–20 May 2023, pp. 2312–2323. IEEE (2023)

64. Pearce, H., Tan, B., Ahmad, B., Karri, R., Dolan-Gavitt, B.: Examining zero-shot vulnerability repair with large language models. In: 44th IEEE Symposium on Security and Privacy, SP 2023, San Francisco, CA, USA, 21–25 May 2023, pp. 2339–2356. IEEE (2023)

65. Xia, C.S., Wei, Y., Zhang, L.: Automated program repair in the era of large pre-trained language models. In: 45th IEEE/ACM International Conference on Software Engineering, ICSE 2023, Melbourne, Australia, 14–20 May 2023, pp. 1482–1494. IEEE (2023)

66. Fan, Z., Gao, X., Mirchev, M., Roychoudhury, A., Tan, S.H.: Automated repair of programs from large language models. In: 45th IEEE/ACM International Conference on Software Engineering, ICSE 2023, Melbourne, Australia, 14–20 May 2023, pp. 1469–1481. IEEE (2023)

67. Zhai, Y., et al.: Ubitect: a precise and scalable method to detect use-before-initialization bugs in linux kernel. In: Devanbu, P., Cohen, M.B., Zimmermann, T. (eds.) ESEC/FSE '20: 28th ACM Joint European Software Engineering Conference and Symposium on the Foundations of Software Engineering, Virtual Event, USA, 8–13 November 2020, pp. 221–232. ACM (2020)

68. Ma, W., et al.: The scope of chatgpt in software engineering: a thorough investigation. CoRR arxiv:2305.12138 (2023)

69. Pei, K., Bieber, D., Shi, K., Sutton, C., Yin, P.: Can large language models reason about program invariants? (2023)

Verifying Global Two-Safety Properties in Neural Networks with Confidence

Anagha Athavale[1,2]($\boxtimes$), Ezio Bartocci[1], Maria Christakis[1], Matteo Maffei[1], Dejan Nickovic[2], and Georg Weissenbacher[1]

[1] TU Wien, Vienna, Austria
anagha.athavale@tuwien.ac.at
[2] AIT Austrian Institute of Technology, Vienna, Austria

Abstract. We present the first automated verification technique for confidence-based 2-safety properties, such as global robustness and global fairness, in deep neural networks (DNNs). Our approach combines self-composition to leverage existing reachability analysis techniques and a novel abstraction of the softmax function, which is amenable to automated verification. We characterize and prove the soundness of our static analysis technique. Furthermore, we implement it on top of Marabou, a safety analysis tool for neural networks, conducting a performance evaluation on several publicly available benchmarks for DNN verification.

1 Introduction

Deep neural networks (DNNs) [1, 2] encountered tremendous success in the recent past due to their ability to infer highly nonlinear relations from data, learn accurate predictive models, and make smart decisions with little or no human intervention. Despite their success, the correctness of neural networks remains a major concern due to their complexity and lack of transparency. This is especially the case for safety- and security-critical applications where errors and biases can have serious undesired consequences, such as in medical diagnosis [3], self-driving cars [4], or financial systems [5]. New techniques that can prove mathematical guarantees concerning the behavior of neural networks are the need of the hour [6]. An effective approach to address this issue is the use of automatic verification techniques, which can either formally prove that the network adheres to a specified property or return a concrete input (witness) demonstrating a violation of the property [7].

Robustness and *fairness* are two important properties of neural networks. Robustness refers to the neural network's ability to make accurate predictions even in the presence of input perturbations. In particular, a robust neural network is able to produce accurate results without being overly sensitive to small changes in the input. Fairness, on the other hand, refers to a neural network's ability to make unbiased and equitable predictions, particularly in cases where the input data may contain sensitive attributes such as gender, race, or age. A neural network that is not fair may produce biased results that discriminate against certain groups, which can have serious ethical and social implications.

A. Gurfinkel and V. Ganesh (Eds.): CAV 2024, LNCS 14682, pp. 329–351, 2024.
https://doi.org/10.1007/978-3-031-65630-9_17

Local Robustness and Fairness provide the dominant perspective in verification and adversarial testing of DNNs. Local robustness [8–11] intuitively requires the DNN to have the following property with respect to a given input x – it has to make the same prediction for the input x as for all the points in the vicinity of x. Local fairness [8,12,13] is defined in a similar way, with the distance metric used for the inputs being the main difference. Both properties can be formalized as safety properties. This has led to the design of a variety of SMT-based techniques [10,14,15], which encode the neural networks and the property to be verified as an SMT solving problem in order to enable automated verification. Other works approach the verification problem using static analysis [16–19] which over-approximates DNN executions, thereby compromising precision for higher scalability. Alternative verification techniques include mixed-integer programming [20–22] and modified simplex algorithms [9,23].

Figure 1 (a) illustrates the properties of local robustness. It shows the classification of an input $\vec{x}$ that includes two (continuous) features x_1 and x_2. The pair of purple points is not a counterexample to robustness, as both inputs lie within the same class. The green and blue points, however, represent counterexamples to local robustness, as they fall on different sides of the decision boundaries.

The above example shows two major limitations of local properties. First, there are always inputs arbitrarily close to the decision boundary, which then constitute counterexamples to local robustness. Second, local robustness is defined only for a specific input. Consequently, it does not provide any guarantees for any other input. It follows that the robustness of the entire neural network cannot be assessed with local robustness only.

Global Robustness and Fairness. The limitation of the local definition for robustness and fairness indicates the need for a global property that evaluates the expected input/output relation over *all pairs of inputs*.

We first observe that global robustness and fairness of DNNs are *hyperproperties*, i.e. properties that relate multiple executions of the model. Khedr et al. [24] and Biswas et al. [25] recently introduced the first verification techniques for hyperproperties in DNNs. These works assume that the inputs contain categorical variables. Based on this strong assumption, these two approaches partition the input space based on categorical features to avoid comparing inputs close to decision boundaries, which would lead to a non-satisfiable property. This is illustrated in Fig. 1 (b). Here, we assume that $\vec{x}$ includes a categorical feature x_3 in addition to the continuous features x_1 and x_2. The left (right) part of Fig. 1 (b) depicts classes and inputs in the partition based on the categorical feature x_3 with value v (v'). Consequently, only pairs of inputs belonging to the *same* partition are compared. Inputs belonging to two different partitions (e.g. green points in Fig. 1 (b)) deviate in at least one categorical feature and can hence be assumed to violate the premise that these inputs are "close". According to this approach, a classification in a secure network can only change with different categorical values. Any two points that lie in the same partition but belong to different classes (e.g. the pair of blue points in Fig. 1 (b)) are considered counterexamples to the global property. This leads to a strong limitation

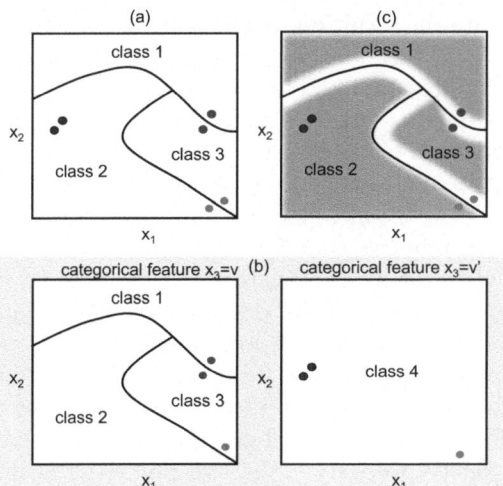

Fig. 1. (a) Local, (b) partitioned-global and (c) our confidence-based robustness. x_1 and x_2 denote continuous input points, while x_3 denotes a categorical input in the partitioned-global approach (b). The shades of gray in (c) depict the level of confidence of the neural network with respect to the given inputs – dark gray denotes high while white denotes low confidence level. The neural network is robust to the pair of purple points in all three cases (a), (b) and (c). The neural network is not robust for the pair of blue points in the case of local and partitioned-global (b) robustness, but is robust according to our definition (c). Finally, the neural network is not robust for the pair of green points according to both the local and our confidence-based global robustness (a) and (c), but is robust with respect to the partitioned-global robustness (b). The global partitioning method does not catch the counterexample, because the two green points are in separate partitions. (Color figure online)

that does not admit two classes to result from continuous inputs only, as typically required for robustness. As a result, the two approaches [24,25] address only verification of global fairness.

Our Contributions. Inspired by the work of Chen et al. [26] on properties of rule-based security classifiers, we adopt a *confidence-based* view on global robustness and fairness for DNN. The idea is to compare all input pairs which are (1) sufficiently close and (2) for which at least one of them yields a high confidence classification. This intuitive definition expects robust and fair DNNs to generate outputs with low confidence near the decision boundary.

We therefore propose *confidence-based 2-safety property*, the first definition that unifies global robustness and fairness for DNNs. Our definition highlights the hyperproperty nature of global properties and uses the confidence in the DNN as a first class citizen.

We briefly illustrate the intuition behind our confidence-based 2-safety property definition with focus on robustness in Fig. 1 (c), in which the input space is colored into shades of gray and where every gray value corresponds to a confidence of the network. Darker shades of gray represent higher levels of confidence for the given classification. Our definition captures two reasonable assumptions: (1) continuous inputs can also trigger changes in classification, and (2) the confidence of the neural network at a decision boundary must be relatively low. In essence, our definition requires that for any input with high-confidence, all its ϵ-neighbour inputs yield the same class (e.g. the two purple points in Fig. 1 (c)). This notion discards inputs near the decision boundaries as counterexamples, as long as they result in outputs with low confidence (e.g. the two blue points in Fig. 1 (c)). Systems satisfying the 2-safety properties hence guarantee that input points classified with a high confidence are immune to adversarial perturbation attacks. In Fig. 1 (c), the pair of green inputs witness the violation of the confidence-based 2-safety property – the two points lie in different classes and one of them has an output with high confidence.

This confidence-based view makes a conceptual change to the definition of global properties, as it requires relating not only inputs, but also confidence values to the outputs. This conceptual change poses a significant challenge to the verification problem because checking a confidence-based property on a DNN requires reasoning about its *softmax* layer, which is not supported by the state-of-the-art DNN verification tools [23, 27–31]. To solve this problem, we develop the first verification method that supports DNNs with softmax, in which we use a linearized over-approximation of the softmax function. We then combine it with self-composition [32] in order to verify confidence-based 2-safety properties. We formally prove the soundness of our analysis technique, characterizing, in particular, the error bounds of our softmax over-approximation.

We demonstrate our approach[1]in Marabou [23], a state-of-the-art analysis tool for local robustness based on a modified simplex algorithm, which we extend to support global robustness and global fairness. We show that by combining our method with binary search, we can go beyond verification and synthesize the minimum confidence for which the DNN is globally robust or fair. We finally conduct a performance evaluation on four neural networks trained with publicly available datasets to demonstrate the effectiveness of our approach in identifying counterexamples and proving global robustness and fairness properties.

2   Background

2.1   Feed-Forward Neural Networks

In feed-forward neural networks data flows uni-directionally, which means there are no back edges. An input layer receives the inputs that move via one or multiple hidden layers to the output layer [33]. A layer has multiple neurons, each connected to the neurons in the next layer using a set of weights. Each layer also

---

[1] https://github.com/anaghaathavale/Global_2Safety_with_Confidence.git.

has an associated bias. Weight and bias selection is crucial to the performance of a neural network and is performed during the training phase. Outputs are calculated by processing the inputs using weights and biases, followed by applying the activation functions and then propagating the processed inputs through the network [34].

Formally, a feed-forward neural network $f : \mathbb{R}^m \to \mathbb{R}^n$ is modeled as a directed acyclic graph $G = (V, E)$ that consists of a set (finite) of nodes V and a set of edges $E \subseteq V \times V$.[2] The nodes V are partitioned into l layers V^i with $1 \leq i \leq l$, where V^1 and V^l represent the input and output layers, and $V^2, \ldots, V^{l-1}$ represent the hidden layers, respectively. We use $v_{i,j}$ to denote node j in layer i. The edges E connect nodes in V^{i-1} with their successor nodes in V^i (for $1 < i \leq l$).

Each node $v_{i,j}$ has an input and an output, where the latter is derived from the former by means of an activation function. We use $\mathrm{in}(v_{i,j})$ and $\mathrm{out}(v_{i,j})$ to denote the input and output value of node $v_{i,j}$, respectively. The output is determined by

$$\mathrm{out}(v_{i,j}) = a_{i,j}(\mathrm{in}(v_{i,j})),\tag{1}$$

where $a_{i,j}$ is the activation function. The input to node $v_{i,j}$ in layer V^i is determined by the outputs of its predecessors $v_{i-1,1}, \ldots, v_{i-1,k}$ in V^{i-1} and weights associated with the edges $(v_{i-1,k}, v_{i,j}) \in E$ for $1 \leq k \leq |V^{i-1}|$:

$$\mathrm{in}(v_{i,j}) = \sum_{k=1}^{|V^{i-1}|} \mathrm{weight}((v_{i-1,k}, v_{i,j})) \cdot \mathrm{out}(v_{i-1,k})$$

The values of the nodes in the input layer V^1 are determined by the input $\vec{x}$ to $f(\vec{x})$, i.e.,

$$(\mathrm{in}(v_{1,1}), \ldots, \mathrm{in}(v_{1,m})) = \vec{x}.$$

The output of the final layer V^l is then computed by propagating the inputs according to the activation functions (see Eq. 1 above). Consequently, a graph G with $|V^1| = m$ input and $|V^l| = n$ output nodes induces a function $f : \mathbb{R}^m \to \mathbb{R}^n$ whose semantics is determined by the activation functions.

In this paper, we concentrate on the Rectified Linear Unit (ReLU) activation function, which is frequently applied to the hidden layers of deep neural networks. For a (scalar) input value x, ReLU returns the maximum of 0 and x, i.e.

$$\mathrm{ReLU}(x) = \max(0, x).$$

In neural networks that are used as classifiers and map an input $\vec{x}$ to one of m labels in a set of classes C, the final layer typically employs a softmax function to ensure that the output represents normalized probabilities corresponding to each of the n classes. Mathematically,

$$\mathrm{softmax}(\vec{z})_i = \frac{e^{z_i}}{\sum_{j=1}^{n} e^{z_j}}\tag{2}$$

---

[2] We follow the formalization of [35] and omit the biases for simplicity.

where $\vec{z}$ represents the values $\text{out}(v_{l-1,i})$ for $1 \leq i \leq n$ and $n = |V^{l-1}|$, and z_i is the ith element in $\vec{z}$. This induces a function $y : \mathbb{R}^n \rightarrow [0,1]^n$ mapping every output of V^{l-1} to a confidence score in the range $[0,1]$. Consequently, $f(\vec{x})$ outputs a probability distribution over the possible labels in C, where each component of the output vector represents the probability of input $\vec{x}$ belonging to the corresponding class. We use $\text{conf}(f(\vec{x}))$ to refer to the highest probability value in the softmax layer of $f(\vec{x})$ and call it the *confidence*, i.e.,

$$\text{conf}(f(\vec{x})) = \max(\text{out}(v_{l,1}), \ldots, \text{out}(v_{l,n})) \tag{3}$$

Finally, a function class : $\mathbb{R}^m \rightarrow C$ then maps the output of f to the class C corresponding to the highest probability in $f(\vec{x})$:

$$\text{class}(f(\vec{x})) = \underset{1 \leq i \leq n}{\arg\max}(\text{out}(v_{l,i})) \tag{4}$$

2.2   Hyperproperties

Hyperproperties [36] are a class of properties that capture relationships between multiple execution traces. This is in contrast to traditional properties, which are evaluated over individual traces.

To define traces in the context of feed-forward neural networks, we extend our notation out to layers as follows:

$$\text{out}(V^i) = (\text{out}(v_{i,1}), \ldots, \text{out}(v_{i,k}))$$

where $k = |V^i|$. Let $\text{in}(V^i)$ be defined similarly. The corresponding trace π for $f(\vec{x})$ is then formally defined as

$$\pi = \text{in}(V^1), \text{out}(V^1), \ldots, \text{in}(V^l), \text{out}(V^l)$$

where $\text{in}(V^1) = \vec{x}$.

Note that each execution is entirely determined by the input value $\vec{x}$ (assuming that the function f implemented by the network is deterministic). Quantifying over traces π of $f(\vec{x})$ hence corresponds to quantifying over the corresponding inputs $\vec{x}$. A traditional safety property would then quantify over the inputs $\vec{x}$, e.g.

$$\forall \vec{x} \, . \, \text{conf}(f(\vec{x})) \geq \kappa,$$

stating that the confidence of each classification of the network should be larger than a threshold κ. Another example of a traditional safety property is local robustness, given in Definition 1 in Subsect. 2.4.

A hyperproperty, on the other hand, refers to, and quantifies over, more than one trace. An example would be

$$\forall \vec{x}, \vec{x}' \, . \, \frac{|f(\vec{x})_i - f(\vec{x}')_i|}{||\vec{x} - \vec{x}'||} \leq K_i, 1 \leq i \leq n \tag{5}$$

where $f(\vec{x})_i$ denotes $\text{out}(v_{l,i})$. Equation 5 states that K_i sets the maximum limit of the Lipschitz constant for $f(\vec{x})_i$. A hyperproperty central to this paper is global robustness, defined in Definition 2 Subsect. 2.4.

Hyperproperties are used to capture important properties that involve multiple inputs, such as robustness and fairness. By verifying hyperproperties of neural networks, we can ensure that they behave correctly across all possible input traces.

2.3   Relational Verification and Self-composition

Hyperproperties are verified by means of so-called relational verification techniques: the idea is to verify if k program executions satisfy a given property [37], expressing invariants on inputs and outputs of such executions. Several security properties (e.g., information flow) can be expressed by relating two executions of the same program differing in the inputs: such properties are called 2-safety properties. Global robustness in neural networks can also be seen as a 2-safety property [8].

2-safety properties can be verified in a generic way by self-composition [37]: the idea is to compose the program with itself and to relate the two executions. In the context of neural networks, the self-composition of a network f is readily defined as a function over

$$f(\vec{x}) \times f(\vec{x}') = \lambda(\vec{x}, \vec{x}') \cdot (f(\vec{x}), f(\vec{x}')) \tag{6}$$

where $(\vec{x}, \vec{x}')$ denotes the concatenation of the vectors $\vec{x}$ and $\vec{x}'$ and $\lambda\vec{x} \cdot f(\vec{x})$ denotes the lambda term that binds $\vec{x}$ in $f(\vec{x})$. The underlying graph $G = (V, E)$ is simply duplicated, i.e., we obtain a graph $G \times G' = (V \cup V', E \cup E')$ where V' and E' are primed copies of V and E.

A counterexample to a universal 2-safety property over the self-composition of f comprises of a pair of traces of f witnessing the property violation.

2.4   Robustness and Fairness

Robustness in neural networks refers to the ability of a model to perform consistently in the presence of small perturbations of the input data. The common approach to address robustness in neural networks is to define it as a *local robustness* [38] property. For an input $\vec{x}$, a neural network is locally robust if it yields the same classification for $\vec{x}$ and all inputs $\vec{x}'$ within distance ϵ from $\vec{x}$ [39]:

Definition 1 (Local Robustness). *A model f is locally ϵ-robust at point $\vec{x}$ if*

$$\forall \vec{x}' \cdot ||\vec{x} - \vec{x}'|| \le \epsilon \rightarrow \text{class}(f(\vec{x})) = \text{class}(f(\vec{x}'))$$

Local robustness, therefore, is defined only for inputs within a distance ϵ of a specific $\vec{x}$ and, thus, does not provide global guarantees. Here $||\cdot||$ represents the distance metric used over the input space. Intuitively, global robustness tackles this problem by requiring that the local robustness property must hold for *every* input within the input space [8]. Definition 2 gives the general definition of global robustness used in [26,40]. It essentially states that all input points in a small neighborhood ϵ, are mapped to the same class.

Definition 2 (Global robustness). *A model f is globally ϵ-robust if*

$$\forall \vec{x}, \vec{x}' \, . \, ||\vec{x} - \vec{x}'|| \leq \epsilon \rightarrow \text{class}(f(\vec{x})) = \text{class}(f(\vec{x}'))$$

Clearly, global robustness as formalized in Definition 2 makes sense only for selected distance metrics, which in particular avoid comparing inputs close to the decision borders. For instance, [40] addresses this by introducing an additional class $\perp$ to which class($f(\vec{x})$) evaluates whenever the difference between the highest and second-highest probability falls below a certain threshold (determined by the Lipschitz constants of f). The global robustness requirement is then relaxed at these points.

Definition 3 (Global fairness) *A model is said to be globally fair if:*

$$\forall \vec{x} = (x_s, \vec{x_n}), \vec{x}' = (x'_s, \vec{x_n}').$$
$$||\vec{x_n} - \vec{x_n}'|| \leq \epsilon \wedge (x_s \neq x'_s) \rightarrow \text{class}(f(\vec{x})) = \text{class}(f(\vec{x}'))$$

where x_s and x_n are the sensitive and non-sensitive attributes of $\vec{x}$, respectively.

[24,25] address a similar problem, which arises in the context of fairness, by partitioning the input space based on categorical features. In general, if the input to a decision-making neural network comprises of certain sensitive attributes, say age or gender, the network is said to be fair if the sensitive attributes do not influence its decisions [8]. Definition 3 gives the general definition of global fairness used in [24,25].

Ensuring fairness in neural networks is important because these models are increasingly being used in decision-making processes that can have significant impacts on peoples' lives. For example, a hiring algorithm that discriminates against certain groups of job applicants based on their race or gender could perpetuate existing biases and inequalities in the workplace [41].

3   Confidence Based Global Verification of Feed-Forward Neural Networks

We now formalize confidence-based 2-safety property, the first definition that unifies global robustness and fairness for DNNs in Definition 4. It is a hyperproperty that takes the confidence of the decision into account when checking for the safety of the network. Before we give the actual definition, we introduce additional notation. Given an input $\vec{x} = (x_1, \ldots, x_n)$, we assume that its every component x_i is either a *categorical* or *real* value. We then define the distance $d(x_i, x'_i)$ as $|x_i - x'_i|$ when x_i is real-valued. We use instead the following distance:

$$d(x_i, x'_i) = \begin{cases} 0, & \text{if } x_i = x'_i \\ 1, & \text{otherwise} \end{cases}$$

when x_i is a categorical value. We define $cond(\vec{x}, \vec{x}', \vec{\epsilon})$ as a (generic) Boolean *condition* that relates inputs $\vec{x}$ and $\vec{x}'$ to a tolerance vector $\vec{\epsilon}$.

Definition 4 (Confidence-based global 2-safety). *A model f is said to be globally 2-safe for confidence $\kappa > 0$ and tolerance $\vec{\epsilon}$ iff*

$$\forall \vec{x}, \vec{x}' \, . \, \mathrm{cond}(\vec{x}, \vec{x}', \vec{\epsilon}) \wedge \mathrm{conf}(f(\vec{x})) > \kappa \implies \mathrm{class}(f(\vec{x})) = \mathrm{class}(f(\vec{x}'))$$

Next, we instantiate the above 2-safety property for confidence-based global robustness and fairness.

For *confidence-based global robustness*, cond is defined as:

$$\mathrm{cond}(\vec{x}, \vec{x}', \vec{\epsilon}) = \bigwedge_{i \in [1,n]} d(x_i, x_i') \leq \epsilon_i$$

For *confidence-based global fairness*, $\vec{x}$ can be split into sensitive $\vec{x}_s$ and non-sensitive $\vec{x_n}$ attributes. For confidence-based global fairness,

$$\mathrm{cond}(\vec{x}, \vec{x}', \vec{\epsilon}) = \bigwedge_{x_i \in \vec{x}_s} d(x_i, x_i') > 0 \wedge \bigwedge_{x_i \in \vec{x_n}} d(x_i, x_i') \leq \epsilon_i$$

where for any categorical $x_i \in \vec{x_n}$, its associated tolerance threshold $\epsilon_i = 0.5$.

Intuitively, confidence-based global fairness ensures that for any data instance, x classified with high confidence κ, no other data instance, x', that only differs with x in the value of the sensitive attribute (e.g. age, gender, ethnicity) shall be classified to a different class.

As defined in Sect. 2, $f(x)$ represents the feed-forward neural network, which maps inputs to classes with corresponding confidence scores. By introducing the threshold κ, our definition effectively ignores classification mismatches that arise from decisions with low confidence. The rationale is as follows:

- Different classifications close to decision boundaries need to be allowed, as safety can otherwise only be satisfied by degenerate neural networks that map all inputs to a single label.
- On the other hand, input points classified with a high confidence should be immune to adversarial perturbations and also uphold fairness.

3.1   Encoding 2-Safety Properties as Product Neural Network

In this section, we reduce checking of the 2-safety hyperproperty in Definition 4 to a safety property over a single trace. Given a neural network f (as defined earlier in Sect. 2), the product neural network is formed by composing a copy of the original neural network with itself. Checking 2-safety then reduces to checking an ordinary safety property for the self-composed neural network that consists of two copies of the original neural network, each with its own copy of the variables.

Table 1. Marabou's piecewise linear constraints

Equation	::=	Sum $\Diamond$ Constant with $\Diamond \in \{\leq, \geq, =\}$
		and Sum ::= Sum + Constant · Variable | Constant · Variable
MaxConstraint	::=	Variable = max(VariableList)
		and VariableList ::= VariableList, Variable | Variable
AbsConstraint	::=	Variable = |Variable|
ReLUConstraint	::=	Variable = ReLU(Variable)
Disjunction	::=	(Disjunction $\vee$ Equation) | Equation

The product neural network is now treated as the model to be verified. A product network allows the reduction of a hyperproperty to a trace property, thereby reducing the problem of hyperproperty verification to a standard verification problem, which can be solved using an existing standard verification technique.

Product Neural Network. We encode $f(\vec{x})$ using piecewise linear constraints (see Table 1). Each node $v_{i,j}$ is represented by two variables $\mathsf{in}_{i,j}$ and $\mathsf{out}_{i,j}$ representing its input and output, respectively. Inputs and outputs are related by the following constraints:

$$\mathsf{in}_{i,j} = \sum_{k=1}^{|V^{i-1}|} w_{i,j}^{i-1,k} \cdot \mathsf{out}_{(i-1,)k} \quad \wedge \quad \mathsf{out}_{i,j} = a_{i,j}(\mathsf{in}_{i,j})$$

where $w_{i,j}^{i-1,k}$ is the weight associated with the edge $(v_{i-1,k}, v_{i,j})$ and $a_{i,j}$ is the activation function of node $v_{i,j}$. To encode the self-composition, we duplicate all variables and constraints by introducing primed counterparts $\mathsf{in}'_{i,j}$ and $\mathsf{out}'_{i,j}$ for $\mathsf{in}_{i,j}$ and $\mathsf{out}_{i,j}$.

Transfer Functions and Operators. ReLUs can be readily encoded using $\mathsf{out}_{i,j} = \mathrm{ReLU}(\mathsf{in}_{i,j})$. There is, however, no direct way to encode softmax using the constraints in Table 1, hence we defer the discussion to Subsect. 3.2.

The conf operator can be implemented using the max constraint (cf. Eq. 3). The operator class as well as the implication, on the other hand, are not necessarily supported by state-of-the-art static analysis tools for DNNs. For instance, they are not supported by Marabou [23], on which we base our implementation. For reference, Table 1 illustrates the linear constraints supported by Marabou. We thus introduce an encoding, which we detail below.

First, checking the validity of the implication in Definition 4 can be reduced to checking the unsatisfiability of

$$\mathrm{cond}(\vec{x}, \vec{x'}, \vec{\epsilon}) \wedge \mathrm{conf}(f(\vec{x})) > \kappa \wedge \mathrm{class}(f(\vec{x})) \neq \mathrm{class}(f(\vec{x'})) \tag{7}$$

However, the grammar in Table 1 provides no means to encode disequality or class (which returns the *index* of the largest element of a vector). To implement disequality, we perform a case split over all $n = |V^l|$ labels by instantiating the encoding of the entire network over $\text{out}_{l,i}$ and $\text{out}'_{l,i}$ for $1 \leq i \leq n$. To implement this in Marabou, we execute a separate query for every case.

To handle the operator class, we can encode the disequality $\text{class}(f(\vec{x})) \neq \text{class}(f(\vec{x}'))$ as:

$$\ldots \wedge \overbrace{\max(\text{out}_{l,1}, \ldots, \text{out}_{l,n})}^{\text{conf}(f(\vec{x}))} > \kappa \wedge (\max(\text{out}_{l,1}, \ldots, \text{out}_{l,n}) - \text{out}_{l,i} = 0) \wedge$$
$$(\max(\text{out}'_{l,1}, \ldots, \text{out}'_{l,n}) - \text{out}'_{l,i} \neq 0) \quad (8)$$

The constraint $(\max(\text{out}_{l,1}, \ldots, \text{out}_{l,n}) - \text{out}_{l,i} = 0)$ ensures that $\text{out}_{l,i}$ corresponds to the largest element in $f(\vec{x})$ (and hence that $\text{class}(f(\vec{x}) = i)$. Consequently, if $(\max(\text{out}'_{l,1}, \ldots, \text{out}'_{l,n}) - \text{out}'_{l,i} \neq 0)$, then we can conclude that $\text{class}(f(\vec{x}')) \neq i$ and hence the safety constraint is violated.

Since, Marabou does not support the disequality operator, we check whether $(\max(\text{out}'_{l,1}, \ldots, \text{out}'_{l,n}) - \text{out}'_{l,i} < 0)$ and $(\max(\text{out}'_{l,1}, \ldots, \text{out}'_{l,n}) - \text{out}'_{l,i} > 0)$, and if both constraints are not satisfied, we know that $(\max(\text{out}'_{l,1}, \ldots, \text{out}'_{l,n}) - \text{out}'_{l,i} \neq 0)$.

While the above transformation is equivalence preserving, the encoding of softmax requires an approximation, described in the following subsection.

3.2   Softmax Approximation

Softmax in Terms of Max and Sig. We can approximate softmax using a max operator and a sigmoid function as follows. Consider $\text{softmax}(\vec{z})_i$ (cf. Eq. 2), for $i = 1$,

$$\text{softmax}(\vec{z})_1 = \frac{1}{1 + (e^{z_2} + \cdots + e^{z_n})e^{-z_1}} \quad (9)$$

$$= \frac{1}{1 + e^{\log(e^{z_2} + \cdots + e^{z_n})}e^{-z_1}} = \frac{1}{1 + e^{(-z_1 + \log(e^{z_2} + \cdots + e^{z_n}))}} \quad (10)$$

We can now generalize the result from (9) for i

$$\text{softmax}(\vec{z})_i = \frac{1}{1 + e^{(-z_i + \log(\sum_{j \neq i}^n e^{z_j}))}} = \text{Sig}(z_i - \underset{\substack{1 \\ j \neq i}}{\overset{n}{\text{LSE}}}(z_j)) \quad (11)$$

where LSE (the *log-sum-exp*) is:

$$\underset{\substack{1 \\ j \neq i}}{\overset{n}{\text{LSE}}}(z_j) = \log(\sum_{j=1, j \neq i}^n e_j^z) \text{ and } \text{Sig}(x) = \frac{1}{1 + e^{-x}}$$

We know from [42] that LSE is bounded:

$$\max_1^n(z_i) \leq \underset{1}{\overset{n}{\text{LSE}}}(z_i) \leq \max_1^n(z_i) + \log(n) \quad (12)$$

with $max_1^n(z_i) = max(z_1, \cdots, z_n)$, in particlular, when $z_1 = \cdots = z_n$, we have:

$$\text{LSE}_1^n(z_i) = max_1^n(z_i) + log(n) \tag{13}$$

Then softmax has as lower bound:

$$\text{softmax}(\vec{z})_i \geq \text{Sig}(z_i - max_1^n_{j \neq i}(z_j) + log(n-1)) \tag{14}$$

and as upper bound:

$$\text{softmax}(\vec{z})_i \leq \text{Sig}(z_i - max_1^n_{j \neq i}(z_j)) \tag{15}$$

When $n = 2$, the softmax is equivalent to the sigmoid:

$$\text{softmax}(\vec{z})_1 = \text{Sig}(z_1 - z_2) \text{ and } \text{softmax}(\vec{z})_2 = \text{Sig}(z_2 - z_1) \tag{16}$$

Now that we know how to approximate a softmax using a sigmoid and max, we need to find a piece-wise linear approximation of sigmoid since sigmoid is also a non-linear exponential function.

Piece-Wise Approximation of Sigmoid. We approximate sigmoid as a piece-wise linear function using the Remez exchange algorithm [43]. The Remez algorithm is an iterative algorithm that finds simpler approximations to functions. It aims to minimize the maximum absolute difference between the approximated polynomial and the actual function. The algorithm takes a maximum acceptable error δ and generates l linear segments to approximate the sigmoid function such that the error is less than δ. We use the Remez algorithm to approximate the sigmoid in the interval $[\text{Sig}^{-1}(\delta), \text{Sig}^{-1}(1-\delta)]$, where Sig^{-1} is the inverse function of the sigmoid. The inverse of sigmoid is the logit function i.e., $\text{Sig}^{-1}(y) = logit(y) = log(y)/(1-y)$. For example, if the user sets δ to 0.0006, then the input domain for the algorithm lies in $[-7.423034723582278, 7.423034723582278]$. Thus, the approximated sigmoid is:

$$|\widehat{\text{Sig}}(x) - \text{Sig}(x)| \leq \delta$$

We approximate softmax with its lower bound:

$$\widehat{\text{softmax}}(\vec{z})_i = \widehat{\text{Sig}}(z_i - max_1^n_{j \neq i}(z_j) + log(n-1)) - \delta \tag{17}$$

and the upper bound for the softmax is:

$$\widehat{\text{softmax}}(\vec{z})_i \leq \text{softmax}(\vec{z})_i \leq \widehat{\text{Sig}}(z_i - max_1^n_{j \neq i}(z_j)) + \delta \tag{18}$$

Theorem 1. *Let* softmax *and* $\widehat{\text{softmax}}$ *compute the real and linearly approximated softmax (with precision δ), respectively for the last layer of $n \geq 2$ neurons $\vec{z}$ of a neural network and $z_i = max(z_1, \cdots, z_n)$. Then, we have the following result:*

$$\forall \vec{z}. \ \text{softmax}(\vec{z})_i - \widehat{\text{softmax}}(\vec{z})_i \leq \frac{n-2}{(\sqrt{n-1}+1)^2} + 2\delta$$

Proof. We refer to [44]. □

Theorem 2. *(Class consistency) Let f and $\hat{f}$ denote the real and the approximated (with precision δ) neural networks with $n \geq 2$ outputs, respectively. Then:*

$$\text{conf}(\hat{f}(\vec{x})) > \frac{1}{2} \implies \text{class}(\hat{f}(\vec{x})) = \text{class}(f(\vec{x}))$$

Proof. We refer to [44]. □

Soundness. For the confidence-based 2-safety property discussed before, our analysis provides a soundness guarantee. This means that whenever the analysis reports that the property specified in Definition 4 holds, then the property also holds true in the concrete execution.

Theorem 3. *(Soundness) Let f and $\hat{f}$ be the original neural network and over-approximated neural network, respectively. Let $b_{n,\delta}$ be the error bound of the approximated softmax ($b_{n,\delta} = \frac{n-2}{(\sqrt{n-1}+1)^2} + 2\delta$ (see Theorem 1)). Then we have the following soundness guarantee: Whenever the approximated neural network is 2-safe for $\text{conf}(\hat{f}(\vec{x})) > (\kappa - b_{n,\delta})$, the real neural network is 2-safe for $\text{conf}(f(\vec{x})) > \kappa$, given $\text{conf}(\hat{f}(\vec{x})) > \frac{1}{2}$. Formally:*

$$\begin{pmatrix} \forall \vec{x}, \vec{x'}. \ \text{cond}(\vec{x}, \vec{x'}, \vec{\epsilon}) \wedge \text{conf}(\hat{f}(\vec{x})) > (\kappa - b_{n,\delta}) \\ \implies \text{class}(\hat{f}(\vec{x})) = \text{class}(\hat{f}(\vec{x'})) \end{pmatrix} \implies$$

$$\begin{pmatrix} \forall \vec{x}, \vec{x'}. \ \text{cond}(\vec{x}, \vec{x'}, \vec{\epsilon}) \wedge \text{conf}(f(\vec{x})) > \kappa \\ \implies \text{class}(f(\vec{x})) = \text{class}(f(\vec{x'})) \end{pmatrix}, \ \text{with} \ \text{conf}(\hat{f}(\vec{x})) > \frac{1}{2}$$

Proof. We refer to [44]. □

4   Implementation

For the implementation of our technique, we use the state-of-the-art neural network verification tool Marabou [23] as our solver. In this section, we describe how we encode the confidence-based 2-safety property in Marabou. Note that such an encoding can be expressed in a similar way for virtually any off-the-shelf neural network verifier.

Marabou [23]. Marabou is a simplex-based linear programming neural network verification and analysis tool. Marabou is capable to address queries about network's properties, such as local robustness, by encoding them into constraint satisfaction problems. It supports fully-connected feed-forward neural networks. A network can be encoded as a set of linear constraints representing the weighted sum of the neurons' outputs feeding the next neuron's input, and a set of non-linear constraints defining the activation functions. A verification query to Marabou comprises a neural network along with a property that needs to be verified. This property is defined as "linear and nonlinear constraints on the network's inputs and outputs" [23]. In Marabou, network's neurons are treated as variables. As a result, the verification problem involves identifying a variable assignment that satisfies all the constraints at the same time, or establishing that such an assignment does not exist. The tool uses a variant of the *Simplex* algorithm at its core to make the variable assignment satisfy the linear constraints. During the execution, the tool adjusts the variable assignment to either fix a linear or a non-linear constraint violation. Although the technique implemented in Marabou is sound and complete, the tool can work only with piece-wise linear activation functions (including ReLU function and the max function) to guarantee termination. Additionally, an essential aspect of Marabou's verification approach is deduction – specifically, deriving more precise lower and upper bounds for each variable. The tool leverages these bounds to relax piece-wise linear constraints into linear ones by considering one of its segments.

The original network g is a function of the following: input parameters, neurons, neuron connection weights, layer biases, ReLU activation functions and output classes. To make Marabou amenable for verification of 2-safety properties, we need a product neural network. This means that the execution is tracked over two copies of the original network, g and g' (cf. Subsect. 2.3). Let X_i denote the set of input variables to g and let X_i' be a set of primed copies of the variables in X_i. As a result, we obtain a self-composition $g(X_i) \times g'(X_i')$ of g over the input variables $X_i \cup X_i'$.

Next, we extend the output layer with softmax function in order to extract the confidence scores with which output classes are predicted.

Linearized Sigmoid. We explain our linearized sigmoid function in this subsection. This function is used to implement an approximated piece-wise linear sigmoid function. Let the outputs of the last inner layer $l-1$ be represented by z_i for $1 \leq i \leq n$, where n is the number of output classes. In Marabou, we first encode the linear piece-wise sigmoid function which we obtain by setting the maximum acceptable error to 0.005. This provides us with a piece-wise linear approximated sigmoid with 35 segments of the form $q_j = \{m_j \cdot z_i + c_j, \mid LB \leq z_i \leq UB\}$, where z_i is the variable representing the output node whose confidence we want to find. We encode each segment as an equation in and represent it using a variable q_j. Next, we need to select the applicable segment corresponding to the value of z_i. Unfortunately, Marabou does not provide a conditional construct. So, we deploy the min and max functions to emulate if-then-else.

First, we split the sigmoid into two convex pieces S_1 and S_2. Figure 2 illustrates this step using a simplified approximation of sigmoid with 4 linear segments q_1, q_2, q_3, and q_4. The resulting value of S_1 can now be expressed as $S_1 = \min(\max(0, q_1, q_2), 0.5)$. Similarly, $S_1 = \max(\min(0.5, q_3, q_4), 1)$. The values 0 and

1 are the minimum and maximum values of the sigmoid function and 0.5 is the value of sigmoid at the splitting point. Second, we combine the convex segments by adding them:

$$S = \min(\max(0, q_1, q_2), 0.5) + \max(\min(0.5, q_3, q_4), 1) - 0.5$$

Note that we have 35 segments instead of four used in our simplified explanation.

Linearized Softmax. The next step consists in implementing the softmax function using the output of the sigmoid function and the max function (see Eq. 17). To this end, we find the maximum of all output nodes excluding the current one, and subtract that maximum from the current output value. Finally, we apply the linearized sigmoid (cf. Sect. 4), to obtain the result of softmax.

We repeat the above steps for all output nodes to obtain the softmax values corresponding to all output classes. Finally, we find the maximum value of these softmax outputs, which represents the confidence.

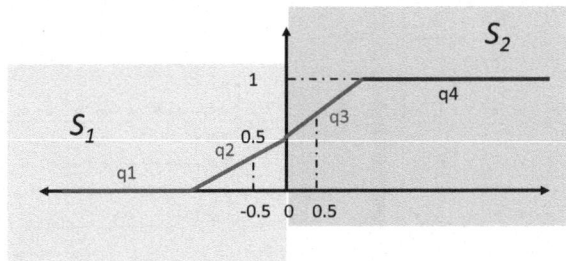

Fig. 2. (Simplified) Approximation of sigmoid with 4 linear segments

5   Experimental Evaluation

For our evaluation, we used four publicly available benchmark datasets to evaluate our technique. We pre-process the datasets to remove null entries, select relevant categorical attributes, and hot-encode them. For each dataset, we train a fully connected feed-forward neural network with up to 50 neurons and ReLU activation functions.

German Credit: The German Credit Risk dataset [45] describes individuals requesting credit from a bank and classified, based on their characteristics, in two categories ("good" or "bad") of credit risk. The dataset comprises 1000 entries.

Adult: The Adult dataset, also referred to as the "Census Income" dataset, is used to estimate whether a person's income surpasses $50,000 per year based on census information [46].

COMPAS: COMPAS ("Correctional Offender Management Profiling for Alternative Sanctions") is a widely-used commercial algorithm that is utilized by judges and parole officers to assess the probability of criminal defendants committing future crimes, also known as recidivism [47].

Law School: The Law School Admissions Council (LSAC) provides a dataset called Law School Admissions, which includes information on approximately 27,000 law students from 1991 to 1997. The dataset tracks the students' progress through law school, graduation, and bar exams. It uses two types of academic scores (LSAT and GPA) to predict their likelihood of passing the bar exam [48].

We use TensorFlow for training neural networks and the NN verifier Marabou [23] whose implementation is publicly available. The accuracies for the deployed models are as follows: German Credit: 0.71; COMPAS: 0.74; Law: 0.94; Adult: 0.77. In our experiments, adding more layers or nodes per layer did not result in an increased accuracy. We run all our experiments using a single AMD EPYC 7713 64-Core Processor, Ubuntu 22.04 LTS Operating System with 32 GB RAM.

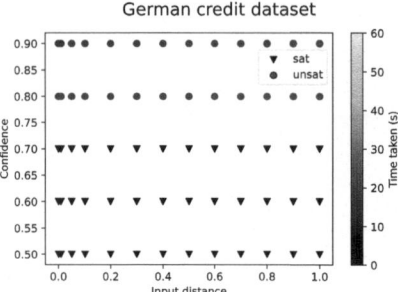

Fig. 3. Input distance vs. confidence for German credit dataset

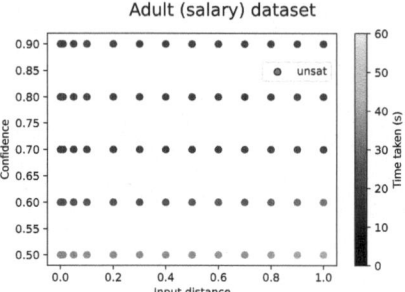

Fig. 4. Input distance vs. confidence for adult dataset

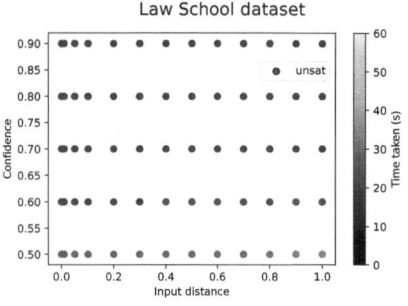

Fig. 5. Input distance vs. confidence for law school dataset

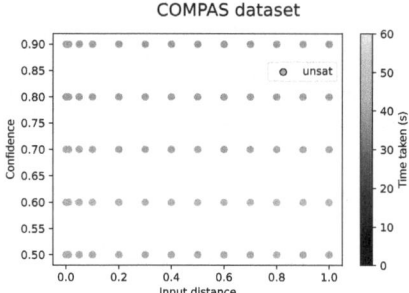

Fig. 6. Input distance vs. confidence for COMPAS dataset

First, we present our confidence-based global robustness results. We evaluate our implementation on the neural networks trained with the benchmark datasets for various combinations of input distance and confidence values. We aim to find proofs for globally robust neural networks. The plots in Figs. 3, 4, 5 and 6 show our experimental results as scatter plots. Markers denoting 'sat' correspond to the query resulting in a counter-example. A counter-example here means that for the input distance and confidence values in that query, the inputs are classified into different output classes. The 'unsat' markers stand for the query being proved (i.e. the model is robust), which means that for the corresponding input distance and confidence threshold, the inputs are classified to the same output class and the model is globally robust. The color bar on the right side denotes the time taken in seconds to run each query; the time scale goes from deep purple to blue, green and yellow as the time taken increases from 0 to 60 sec. The plot in Fig. 3 depicts the effect of varying input distance and confidence on the German credit benchmark. We ran our query with the confidence-based global robustness property for input distance, ϵ and confidence κ values ranging from 0.001 to 1.0 and 0.5 to 0.9, respectively. Observe that for κ values below 0.7, the model is sat i.e. we find counter-examples. However, for confidence values above 0.75, even for larger input distances, the queries result in unsat and a proof that the model is robust above a confidence threshold of 0.75.

The plots in Figs. 4, 5 and 6 show the results for neural networks trained with Adult, Law School, and COMPAS datasets. As can be observed from the scatter plots, these models are robust. For confidence values above 0.5, they are 2-safe and we are successfully able to prove this rather fast in 50 s or less.

Table 2. Global fairness on German credit/COMPAS datasets for various criteria

Dataset	Sensitive attribute	Confidence threshold	Result	Time taken
German credit	Gender	0.5	unsat	10.232 s
German credit	Age	0.5	unsat	11.478 s
COMPAS	Gender	0.5	sat	7.423 s
COMPAS	Ethnicity	0.5	sat	18.293 s
COMPAS	Ethnicity	0.99	sat	25.846 s
COMPAS	Ethnicity	0.999	unsat	171 min 15 s

Next, we present the results for confidence-based global fairness verification, which are shown in Table 2. Each row in the table depicts the verification result for a NN along with the sensitive attribute and confidence threshold considered. If the result is 'unsat', it means that the query is proved (i.e. the model is fair). In other words, for the corresponding sensitive attribute and confidence value constraints, the inputs are classified to the same output class and the model is globally fair. On the other hand, 'sat' corresponds to the query resulting in a counter-example. A counter-example here means that for the corresponding sensitive attribute and confidence threshold in the query, the inputs are classified into different output classes.

The German credit model is proved to be globally fair for confidence values above 0.5 for sensitive attributes Gender and Age. Running our query with the confidence-based global fairness property for the COMPAS model, with Gender as the sensitive attribute gives counter-examples for all confidence values. Additionally, when Ethnicity is considered as the sensitive attribute while verifying the COMPAS model, we find counter-examples for lower confidence values. However, the model is proved to be globally fair for confidence values above 0.999.

We combined our method with binary search, to synthesize the minimum confidence for which the DNN is globally robust or fair. We perform the binary search, starting with confidence 0.5. If the model is unsat, we are done. Else, we check for confidence $mid = (0.5 + 1)/2$, and continue in this way till we find the minimum confidence accurate to the nearest 0.05. For instance, binary search combined with our method, on German credit gave us 0.75 (in 45 s) to be the minimum confidence for which the DNN is globally robust.

Our experimental results on 2-safety properties (with regard to both, global robustness and global fairness), clearly point out that taking confidence along with input distance into account is crucial when verifying neural networks.

5.1   Discussion

Soundness. Our proof of soundness guarantees that if our approach yields that a model is robust or fair for a given confidence and input distance, the model is indeed safe. In case of the German Credit model, for instance, the model is indeed globally robust for all input distances when the confidence is at least 0.75. Moreover, we can use binary search to find the minimal confidence value above which a model is robust. Our approach guarantees soundness and when a model is found to be safe, it is indeed safe. However, if a counterexample is found, it may be a false positive. False positives (or spurious counterexamples) may in general stem either from overapproximations of the underlying reachability analysis tool or from our own softmax approximation. In our implementation, the former are not present since Marabou is complete (i.e., it does not have false positives), whereas our softmax approximation yields a confidence error that depends on the number of DNN-outputs, as formalized in Theorem 1 and quantified in its proof. For DNNs with two outputs, such as German Credit, Adult, and Law School, there is no error, whereas for three outputs (COMPAS) the error is $\sim$ 0.171. Hence, if we want to certify a three-output DNN for confidence x, we run our analysis for confidence $x - 0.171$: if no attack is found, we can certify the network for confidence x (soundness), otherwise we know the counterexample violates the 2-safety property (completeness of Marabou) for confidence in between x and $x - 0.171$ (the possible imprecision is due to our softmax overapproximation). We report counterexamples in this paper on German Credit and on COMPAS: the former are true positives (2-output DNN), whereas the latter are counterexamples for confidence in between 0.999 (the confidence we can certify the network for) and 0.828. We ran the network on the counterexample reported by Marabou and found the real confidence to be 0.969. Hence, the network is for sure fair for a confidence higher than 0.999, unfair for confidence levels lower than 0.969, while we cannot decide it for the confidence levels in the interval between 0.969 and 0.999. This means that on our datasets, our analysis is very accurate.

Threats to Validity. Presuming a high level of confidence as a precondition can make low-confidence networks vacuously safe. However, an accurate but low-confidence network is not desirable in the first place. This concept is known in the literature as miscalibration. The Expected Calibration Error is defined as weighted average over the absolute difference between confidence and accuracy. In scenarios where accurate confidence measures are crucial, the goal is to reduce the Maximum Calibration Error [49] that is the maximum discrepancy between confidence and accuracy.

This is orthogonal to our work and there is an entire field of research [50,51] aiming at minimizing such calibration errors.

6   Conclusion

We introduce the first automated method to verify 2-safety properties such as global robustness and global fairness in DNNs based on the confidence level. To handle the nonlinear softmax function computing the confidence, we approximate it with a piece-wise linear function for which we can bound the approximation error. We then compute the self-composition of the DNN with the approximated softmax and we show how to leverage existing tools such as Marabou to verify 2-safety properties. We prove that our analysis on the approximated network is sound with respect to the original one when the value of confidence is greater than 0.5 in the approximated one. We successfully evaluate our approach on four different DNNs, proving global robustness and global fairness in some cases while finding counterexamples in others.

While we improve over recent verifiers for global properties that are limited to binary classifiers [25], a limitation of our current approach is that we can only handle DNNs with few (two to five) outputs, since the approximation error increases with the number of outputs. We plan to overcome this limitation in future work by devising more accurate abstractions of softmax.

To improve scalability, we will investigate how to refine our approach by integrating pruning strategies, such as those developed in [25], which we intend to refine to fit our static analysis framework.

We also plan to explore more sophisticated and effective verification techniques for 2-safety properties, possibly tailored to specific DNN structures.

Finally, we plan to complement our verification approach with testing techniques to further explore the generated counterexamples.

Acknowledgements. The work published in this paper is a part of the AI4CSM project that has received funding within the ECSEL JU in collaboration with the European Union's H2020 Framework Programme (H2020/2014-2020) and National Authorities, under grant agreement No. 101007326. This work was also partially supported by the WWTF project ICT22-023, by the WWTF project 10.47379/ICT19018, by the European Research Council (ERC) under the European Union's Horizon 2020 research (grant agreement 771527-BROWSEC), by the Austrian Science Fund (FWF) 10.55776/F85 (project F8510-N); the Vienna Science and Technology Fund (WWTF) through [ForSmart Grant ID: 10.47379/ICT22007]; the Austrian Research Promotion Agency (FFG) through the COMET K1 SBA.

References

1. Gurney, K.: An Introduction to Neural Networks. CRC Press, Boca Raton (1997)
2. Goodfellow, I.J., Bengio, Y., Courville, A.C.: Deep Learning. Adaptive Computation and Machine Learning. MIT Press, Cambridge (2016)
3. Amato, F., López, A., Peña-Méndez, E.M., Vaňhara, P., Hampl, A., Havel, J.: Artificial neural networks in medical diagnosis (2013)
4. Rao, Q., Frtunikj, J.: Deep learning for self-driving cars: chances and challenges. In: Proceedings of the 1st International Workshop on Software Engineering for AI in Autonomous Systems, pp. 35–38 (2018)
5. Duan, J.: Financial system modeling using deep neural networks (DNNs) for effective risk assessment and prediction. J. Franklin Inst. **356**(8), 4716–4731 (2019)
6. Tran, H., Xiang, W., Johnson, T.T.: Verification approaches for learning-enabled autonomous cyber-physical systems. IEEE Des. Test **39**(1), 24–34 (2022)
7. Bjesse, P.: What is formal verification?. ACM SIGDA Newsl. **35**(24), 1–es (2005)
8. Seshia, S.A., Desai, A., Dreossi, T., Fremont, D.J., Ghosh, S., Kim, E., Shivakumar, S., Vazquez-Chanlatte, M., Yue, X.: Formal specification for deep neural networks. In: Lahiri, S.K., Wang, C. (eds.) ATVA 2018. LNCS, vol. 11138, pp. 20–34. Springer, Cham (2018). https://doi.org/10.1007/978-3-030-01090-4_2
9. Katz, G., Barrett, C., Dill, D.L., Julian, K., Kochenderfer, M.J.: Reluplex: an efficient SMT solver for verifying deep neural networks. In: Majumdar, R., Kunčak, V. (eds.) CAV 2017. LNCS, vol. 10426, pp. 97–117. Springer, Cham (2017). https://doi.org/10.1007/978-3-319-63387-9_5
10. Huang, X., Kwiatkowska, M., Wang, S., Wu, M.: Safety verification of deep neural networks. In: Majumdar, R., Kunčak, V. (eds.) CAV 2017. LNCS, vol. 10426, pp. 3–29. Springer, Cham (2017). https://doi.org/10.1007/978-3-319-63387-9_1
11. Gopinath, D., Katz, G., Păsăreanu, C.S., Barrett, C.: DeepSafe: a data-driven approach for assessing robustness of neural networks. In: Lahiri, S.K., Wang, C. (eds.) ATVA 2018. LNCS, vol. 11138, pp. 3–19. Springer, Cham (2018). https://doi.org/10.1007/978-3-030-01090-4_1
12. Urban, C., Christakis, M., Wüstholz, V., Zhang, F.: Perfectly parallel fairness certification of neural networks. Proc. ACM Program. Lang. **4**(OOPSLA), 1–30 (2020)
13. Xie, X., Zhang, F., Hu, X., Ma, L.: Deepgemini: verifying dependency fairness for deep neural network. Proceedings of the AAAI Conference on Artificial Intelligence, vol. 37, pp. 15251–15259 (2023)
14. Pulina, L., Tacchella, A.: Challenging SMT solvers to verify neural networks. AI Commun. **25**(2), 117–135 (2012)

15. Li, J., Liu, J., Yang, P., Chen, L., Huang, X., Zhang, L.: Analyzing deep neural networks with symbolic propagation: towards higher precision and faster verification. In: Chang, B.-Y.E. (ed.) SAS 2019. LNCS, vol. 11822, pp. 296–319. Springer, Cham (2019). https://doi.org/10.1007/978-3-030-32304-2_15
16. Pulina, L., Tacchella, A.: An abstraction-refinement approach to verification of artificial neural networks. In: Touili, T., Cook, B., Jackson, P. (eds.) CAV 2010. LNCS, vol. 6174, pp. 243–257. Springer, Heidelberg (2010). https://doi.org/10.1007/978-3-642-14295-6_24
17. Singh, G., Gehr, T., Püschel, M., Vechev, M.: An abstract domain for certifying neural networks. Proc. ACM Program. Lang. **3**(POPL), 1–30 (2019)
18. Gehr, T., Mirman, M., Drachsler-Cohen, D., Tsankov, P., Chaudhuri, S., Vechev, M.: AI2: safety and robustness certification of neural networks with abstract interpretation. In: 2018 IEEE Symposium on Security and Privacy (SP), pp. 3–18. IEEE (2018)
19. Baninajjar, A., Hosseini, K., Rezine, A., Aminifar, A.: Safedeep: a scalable robustness verification framework for deep neural networks. In: ICASSP 2023 - 2023 IEEE International Conference on Acoustics, Speech and Signal Processing (ICASSP), pp. 1–5 (2023)
20. Cheng, C.-H., Nührenberg, G., Ruess, H.: Maximum resilience of artificial neural networks. In: D'Souza, D., Narayan Kumar, K. (eds.) ATVA 2017. LNCS, vol. 10482, pp. 251–268. Springer, Cham (2017). https://doi.org/10.1007/978-3-319-68167-2_18
21. Tjeng, V., Xiao, K., Tedrake, R.: Evaluating robustness of neural networks with mixed integer programming. arXiv preprint arXiv:1711.07356 (2017)
22. Dutta, S., Jha, S., Sankaranarayanan, S., Tiwari, A.: Output range analysis for deep feedforward neural networks. In: Dutle, A., Muñoz, C., Narkawicz, A. (eds.) NFM 2018. LNCS, vol. 10811, pp. 121–138. Springer, Cham (2018). https://doi.org/10.1007/978-3-319-77935-5_9
23. Katz, G., et al.: The Marabou framework for verification and analysis of deep neural networks. In: Dillig, I., Tasiran, S. (eds.) CAV 2019. LNCS, vol. 11561, pp. 443–452. Springer, Cham (2019). https://doi.org/10.1007/978-3-030-25540-4_26
24. Khedr, H., Shoukry, Y.: Certifair: a framework for certified global fairness of neural networks. arXiv preprint arXiv:2205.09927 (2022)
25. Biswas, S., Rajan, H.: Fairify: fairness verification of neural networks. In: 45th IEEE/ACM International Conference on Software Engineering. ICSE 2023, Melbourne, Australia, 14–20 May 2023, pp. 1546–1558. IEEE (2023)
26. Chen, Y., Wang, S., Qin, Y., Liao, X., Jana, S., Wagner, D.: Learning security classifiers with verified global robustness properties. In: Proceedings of the 2021 ACM SIGSAC Conference on Computer and Communications Security, pp. 477–494 (2021)
27. Wang, S., et al.: Beta-crown: efficient bound propagation with per-neuron split constraints for neural network robustness verification. In: Advances in Neural Information Processing Systems, vol. 34, pp. 29909–29921 (2021)
28. Xu, K., et al.: Fast and complete: enabling complete neural network verification with rapid and massively parallel incomplete verifiers. arXiv preprint arXiv:2011.13824 (2020)
29. Zhang, H., Weng, T.-W., Chen, P.-Y., Hsieh, C.-J., Daniel, L.: Efficient neural network robustness certification with general activation functions. In: Advances in Neural Information Processing Systems, vol. 31 (2018)

30. Ferrari, C., Muller, M.N., Jovanovic, N., Vechev, M.: Complete verification via multi-neuron relaxation guided branch-and-bound. arXiv preprint arXiv:2205.00263 (2022)
31. Bak, S., Tran, H.-D., Hobbs, K., Johnson, T.T.: Improved geometric path enumeration for verifying ReLU neural networks. In: Lahiri, S.K., Wang, C. (eds.) CAV 2020. LNCS, vol. 12224, pp. 66–96. Springer, Cham (2020). https://doi.org/10. 1007/978-3-030-53288-8_4
32. Barthe, G., D'Argenio, P.R., Rezk, T.: Secure information flow by self-composition. Math. Struct. Comput. Sci. **21**(6), 1207–1252 (2011)
33. Huang, G.-B.: Learning capability and storage capacity of two-hidden-layer feedforward networks. IEEE Trans. Neural Netw. **14**(2), 274–281 (2003)
34. Sharma, S., Sharma, S., Athaiya, A.: Activation functions in neural networks. Towards Data Sci. **6**(12), 310–316 (2017)
35. Albarghouthi, A., et al.: Introduction to neural network verification. Found. Trends® Program. Lang. **7**(1–2), 1–157 (2021)
36. Clarkson, M.R., Schneider, F.B.: Hyperproperties. J. Comput. Secur. **18**(6), 1157–1210 (2010)
37. Barthe, Gilles, Crespo, Juan Manuel, Kunz, César.: Relational verification using product programs. In: Butler, Michael, Schulte, Wolfram (eds.) FM 2011. LNCS, vol. 6664, pp. 200–214. Springer, Heidelberg (2011). https://doi.org/10.1007/978-3-642-21437-0_17
38. Bastani, O., Ioannou, Y., Lampropoulos, L., Vytiniotis, D., Nori, A., Criminisi, A.: Measuring neural net robustness with constraints. In: Advances in Neural Information Processing Systems, vol. 29 (2016)
39. Mangal, R., Nori, A.V., Orso, A.: Robustness of neural networks: a probabilistic and practical approach. In: 2019 IEEE/ACM 41st International Conference on Software Engineering: New Ideas and Emerging Results (ICSE-NIER), pp. 93–96. IEEE (2019)
40. Leino, K., Wang, Z., Fredrikson, M.: Globally-robust neural networks. In: International Conference on Machine Learning, pp. 6212–6222. PMLR (2021)
41. Binns, R.: Fairness in machine learning: lessons from political philosophy. In: Conference on Fairness, Accountability and Transparency, pp. 149–159. PMLR (2018)
42. Pant, Y.V., Abbas, H., Mangharam, R.: Smooth operator: control using the smooth robustness of temporal logic. In: 2017 IEEE Conference on Control Technology and Applications (CCTA), pp. 1235–1240. IEEE (2017)
43. Remez, E.Y.: Sur la détermination des polynômes d'approximation de degré donnée (1934)
44. Athavale, A., Bartocci, E., Christakis, M., Maffei, M., Nickovic, D., Weissenbacher, G.: Verifying global two-safety properties in neural networks with confidence. arXiv preprint arXiv:2405.14400 (2024)
45. Hofmann, H., German credit dataset. UCI Machine 2023 Repository. University of California, School of Information and Computer Science, Irvine (1994). http://archive.ics.uci.edu/ml
46. Dua, D., Graff, C.: UCI machine 2023 repository (2017)
47. Larson, J. (2017). https://github.com/propublica/compas-analysis
48. Wightman, L.F.: LSAC national longitudinal bar passage study. LSAC research report series (1998)
49. Naeini, M.P., Cooper, G., Hauskrecht, M.: Obtaining well calibrated probabilities using Bayesian binning. In: Proceedings of the AAAI Conference on Artificial Intelligence, vol. 29 (2015)

50. Guo, C., Pleiss, G., Sun, Y., Weinberger, K.Q.: On calibration of modern neural networks. In: International Conference on Machine Learning, pp. 1321–1330. PMLR (2017)
51. Ao, S., Rueger, S., Siddharthan, A.: Two sides of miscalibration: identifying over and under-confidence prediction for network calibration. In: Uncertainty in Artificial Intelligence, pp. 77–87. PMLR (2023)

Certified Robust Accuracy of Neural Networks Are Bounded Due to Bayes Errors

Ruihan Zhang[✉] and Jun Sun

Singapore Management University, Singapore, Singapore
{rhzhang,junsun}@smu.edu.sg

Abstract. Adversarial examples pose a security threat to many critical systems built on neural networks. While certified training improves robustness, it also decreases accuracy noticeably. Despite various proposals for addressing this issue, the significant accuracy drop remains. More importantly, it is not clear whether there is a certain fundamental limit on achieving robustness whilst maintaining accuracy. In this work, we offer a novel perspective based on Bayes errors. By adopting Bayes error to robustness analysis, we investigate the limit of certified robust accuracy, taking into account data distribution uncertainties. We first show that the accuracy inevitably decreases in the pursuit of robustness due to changed Bayes error in the altered data distribution. Subsequently, we establish an upper bound for certified robust accuracy, considering the distribution of individual classes and their boundaries. Our theoretical results are empirically evaluated on real-world datasets and are shown to be consistent with the limited success of existing certified training results, *e.g.*, for CIFAR10, our analysis results in an upper bound (of certified robust accuracy) of 67.49%, meanwhile existing approaches are only able to increase it from 53.89% in 2017 to 62.84% in 2023.

1 Introduction

Neural networks have achieved remarkable success in various applications, including many security-critical systems such as self-driving cars [24], and face-recognition-based authentication systems [44]. Unfortunately, several security issues of neural networks have been discovered as well. Arguably the most notable one is the presence of adversarial examples. Adversarial examples are inputs that are carefully crafted by adding human imperceptible perturbation to normal inputs to trigger wrong predictions [25]. Their existence poses a significant threat when the neural networks are deployed in security-critical scenarios. For example, adversarial examples can mislead road sign recognition systems of self-driving cars and cause accidents [24]. The increasing adoption of machine learning in security-sensitive domains raises concerns about the robustness of these models against adversarial examples [38].

To defend against adversarial examples, various methods for improving a model's robustness have been proposed. Two main categories are adversarial training [3,58] and certified training [35,45], both of which aim to improve a model's accuracy in the presence of adversarial examples. Adversarial training works by training the network with a mix of normal and adversarial examples, either pre-generated or generated during

A. Gurfinkel and V. Ganesh (Eds.): CAV 2024, LNCS 14682, pp. 352–376, 2024.
https://doi.org/10.1007/978-3-031-65630-9_18

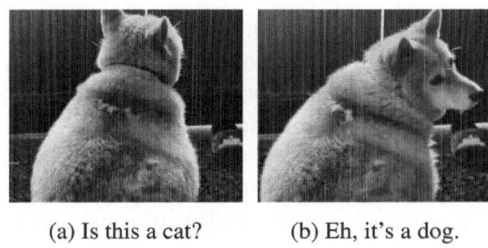

(a) Is this a cat?   (b) Eh, it's a dog.

Fig. 1. The picture at left may look like a cat. In fact, it can be the back of a dog.

training. Methods in this category do not provide a formal robustness guarantee [63], leaving the system potentially vulnerable to new types of adversarial attacks [31,49].

In contrast, certified training aims to provide a formal guarantee of robustness. A method in this category typically incorporates robustness verification techniques [60] during training, *i.e.*, they aim to find a valuation of network parameters such that the model is provably robust with respect to the training samples. However, they are found to reduce the model's accuracy significantly [9]. Recent studies have shown that state-of-the-art certified training can result in up to 60% accuracy drop on CIFAR-10 [32] (at vicinity size 8/255). This is unacceptable for many real-world applications. Although numerous researchers attempt to enhance certified training methods, there seems to be an invisible hurdle preventing them from achieving a level of accuracy similar to that of vanilla models. Despite attempts to explore it using the limit of certain abstraction domains [33], in general, whether there is such a theoretical upper bound on certified robust accuracy or not remains an open problem.

In this work, we offer a novel perspective and argue that Bayes errors may be one of the reasons why there is such an invisible hurdle. The Bayes error, in the context of statistics and machine learning, is a fundamental concept related to the inherent uncertainty in any classification system [20]. It represents the minimum error rate for any classifier on a given problem and is determined by the overlap in the probability distributions of the classes to be predicted [13]. Thus, we study whether the Bayes errors put a limit on certified robust accuracy.

To understand how Bayes Error is relevant, we can consider it from the uncertainty in neural network learning. Most existing classifiers learn using a data set which gives a unique and certain label for each input [26]. Yet, this may not be the case in reality. That is, not every input may have a 100% certain label (due to reasons such as information loss during the picture-capturing process). Intuitively, we show a real-world example in Fig. 1. This image looks like a cat, while it is, in fact, also possible to be a dog. The point is that unless we know how this photo was taken, and there is no information loss during the photo taking, there may always be a certain level of uncertainty when we label the data. These uncertainties call for Bayes errors and actually bounds both vanilla and certified robust accuracy.

This work has two objectives. First, we aim to analyse whether the quest for robustness inevitably decreases model accuracy, from the perspective of Bayes errors. This requires examining how the inherent, irreducible error in class probability distributions influences the robustness of classifiers (with respect to perturbations). We show that given the definition of robustness, the data distribution undergoes a convolution within the vicinity (*i.e.*, the region around an input which is defined by the perturbation budget). Second, we intend to quantify this potential decrease, *i.e.*, what are the upper bounds on the optimal certified robust accuracy? We show that such an upper bound can be derived independently from the classification algorithm. Through a detailed exploration of how each input may contribute to the Bayes errors, our study aims to enhance the understanding of their contribution to classification robustness.

We apply our analysis to multiple benchmark data sets and the corresponding models. From every data set, we observe that the convolved distribution has an increased Bayes error compared with the original distribution. This implies that pursuing robustness would in turn increase uncertainty, and decrease accuracy as we show in our analysis. Second, we contrast the state-of-the-art (SOTA) certified robust accuracy against the upper bound derived using our approach. This is to verify if the bound is empirically effective. We find that the bound is indeed higher than the state-of-the-art certified robust accuracy. We further investigate the relationship between the robustness upper bound and the perturbation vicinity size. When vicinity size grows, we expectedly obtain a decreased upper bound, on every data set used in our study.

2   Preliminary and Problem Definition

In this section, we review the relevant background of this study, including the fundamentals of robustness in machine learning, *e.g.*, its definition and verification. We also recall statistical decision theory, highlighting its relevance to classification. After that, we define our research problem.

In machine learning, the learner, denoted as a function $h : \mathbb{X} \to \mathbb{Y}$, is used to predict outputs $h(x) \in \mathbb{Y}$ based on a (possibly high dimensional) input point $x \in \mathbb{X}$. The quality of h can be measured by a problem-dependent loss function $\ell(h, \mathbf{x}, \mathbf{y})$ [66]. The choice of the loss function depends on the specific problem and data. Common options include the cross-entropy loss for classification and the mean squared error loss for regression. We focus on the classification problem in this work. Classification is the problem of assigning a class to each input [34], *i.e.*, the learner's task is to map an input to a discrete class and the learner is often called a classifier.

Definition 1 (Classifier). *In machine learning, a classifier maps an input x from an input space $\mathbb{X}$ to a discrete class y in the output space $\mathbb{Y}$. The output space $\mathbb{Y}$ is a (typically finite) set of discrete categories. Formally,*

$$h : x \mapsto \hat{y}, \quad x \in \mathbb{X}, \hat{y} \in \mathbb{Y}, \quad \mathbb{Y} = \{ \text{class}_i \mid i \in \mathbb{Z}^+, i \le N_y \} \tag{1}$$

where N_y is the total number of categories the classifier can assign such that $|\mathbb{Y}| = N_y$.

For example, a spam classifier maps an email to { spam, non-spam }. The input vector for an email may embody the length of the message, the frequency of certain keywords in the body of the message, or the vectorised email body [34]. A learning example contains an input and a label. A classifier can learn from labelled email examples and predict labels for other email examples. The classifier's predictions are then compared with the labels of the email under test to measure the performance of the classifier, *e.g.*, a zero-one misclassification loss may be defined over $\{\text{spam}, \text{non-spam}\} \times \{\text{spam}, \text{non-spam}\}$ by $l(\hat{y}, y) = \mathbf{1}_{\hat{y} \neq y}$. A lower loss on the test sample set indicates a more accurate classifier.

2.1 Robustness in Classification

A classifier may not be robust as small changes in input data might lead to significant changes in the predictions made by a classifier [47]. Consider the spam classifier example. Surprisingly, the removal of a single seemingly unimportant word from an email may switch the classifier's decision from spam to non-spam [55]. This phenomenon highlights the existence of adversarial examples, which are defined as follows.

Definition 2 (Adversarial example [17,25]). *Given a classifier $h : \mathbb{X} \to \mathbb{Y}$ and an input-label pair $(\boldsymbol{x}, y) \in \mathbb{X} \times \mathbb{Y}$, an adversarial example $\boldsymbol{x}' \in \mathbb{X}$ is an input that is similar to $\boldsymbol{x}$ but is classified wrongly, e.g., $h(\boldsymbol{x}') \neq y$. The difference between $\boldsymbol{x}$ and $\boldsymbol{x}'$ can be measured by a distance function d, and we often require the distance between $\boldsymbol{x}'$ and $\boldsymbol{x}$ to be smaller than some threshold ϵ. We assume $\boldsymbol{x}$ is correctly classified, i.e., $h(\boldsymbol{x}) = y$.*

Consider the case of the spam email. If a single word is removed, the Levenshtein distance (a measure of the number of edits needed to change one text into another) is 1. An adversarial example based on such a small change could be used with malicious intent. Even though removing a common word like 'just' does not alter the nature of a spam email, it might be enough to prevent it from being detected by the spam classifier. Therefore, robustness against such attacks is needed such that spam would not evade detection by just changing a few words. Formally, robustness is defined as follows [30].

Definition 3 (Classifier robustness against perturbations). *Given classifier h and example $(\boldsymbol{x}, y) \in \mathbb{X} \times \mathbb{Y}$, we say that h is robust with respect to vicinity $\{\boldsymbol{x}' \mid d(\boldsymbol{x}, \boldsymbol{x}') \leq \epsilon\}$, i.e., $\text{Rob}\left(h, \boldsymbol{x}, y; (d, \epsilon)\right)$, only if the following condition is satisfied.*

$$\neg \exists \, \boldsymbol{x}' \in \mathbb{X}. \, d(\boldsymbol{x}, \boldsymbol{x}') \leq \epsilon \wedge h(\boldsymbol{x}') \neq y \tag{2}$$

Definition 3 involves the concept of vicinity, which is a subset of the input space, *i.e.* $\subset \mathbb{X}$. It is usually determined by an input and a budget for perturbation. For instance, give an input $\boldsymbol{x}$, we can define its vicinity as $\mathbb{V}_{\boldsymbol{x}} = \{\boldsymbol{x}' \mid d(\boldsymbol{x}, \boldsymbol{x}') \leq \epsilon\}$. However, this set representation may be inconvenient sometimes. Thus, we give an equivalent function form as follows.

$$v_{\boldsymbol{x}}(\boldsymbol{x}') = \begin{cases} \left(\int_{\mathbb{V}_{\boldsymbol{x}}} d\boldsymbol{x}''\right)^{-1}, & \text{if } \boldsymbol{x}' \in \mathbb{V}_{\boldsymbol{x}} \\ 0, & \text{otherwise} \end{cases} \tag{3}$$

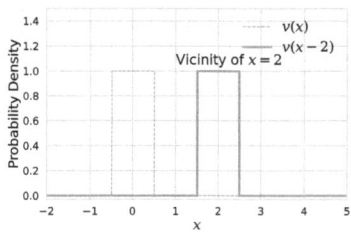
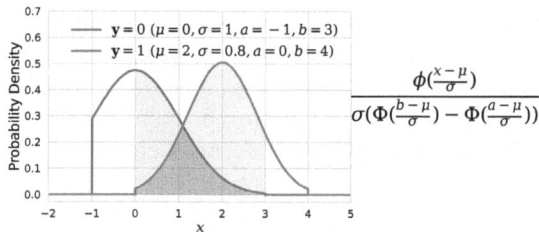

(a) Vicinity function $v(x)$ is shown in blue ($\epsilon = 0.5$). To get the vicinity at a specific input $x = 2$, we simply shift $v(x)$ along the positive direction of the x-axis by 2.

(b) The grey-shaded area represents the Bayes error, characterising the overlap between the two distributions (truncated normal as expressed). The union of the light colour-shaded area and the grey-shaded area represents the proportion of inputs that *have* uncertainty, *i.e.*, $p(\mathbf{x} \in \mathbb{K}_D)$.

Fig. 2. 1D visualizations of vicinity function and Bayes error. A vicinity function is a rectangular function that returns a constant value if an input is in the vicinity. We use two PDFs of the truncated normal distribution to visualise the Bayes error.

Essentially, Equation (3) can be viewed as a probability density function uniformly defined over the vicinity around an input x. Now we shift the x-coordinate by x, we get

$$v_0(x' - x) = \begin{cases} \left(\int_{\mathbb{V}_0} dx''\right)^{-1}, & \text{if } x' - x \in \mathbb{V}_0 \\ 0, & \text{otherwise} \end{cases} \tag{4}$$

Assuming that the vicinity function is translation invariant, we can drop the subscript 0, and use a positive constant ϵ_v to represent $\int_{\mathbb{V}_0} dx''$. Thus, the vicinity function $v : \mathbb{X} \to \{0, \epsilon_v^{-1}\}$ can be expressed as

$$v(x) = \begin{cases} \epsilon_v^{-1} & \text{if } x \in \mathbb{V}_0 \\ 0, & \text{otherwise} \end{cases} \tag{5}$$

Since these representations are equivalent, we choose either representation based on the contexts. An example of a one-dimensional input's vicinity is shown in Fig. 2a.

Achieving robustness is challenging. Verifying whether $\mathrm{Rob}\left(h, x, y; \mathbb{V}_x\right)$ holds for a given classifier h is complicated since examining every example within a vicinity is impractical. Consequently, accurately estimating a classifier's robustness on specific inputs, as well as its robustness on a given data distribution, presents significant challenges. Existing methods for evaluating robustness include empirical evaluation (*i.e.*, adversarial attacks) [14], robustness verification [17,28], and others [57].

Adversarial attacks take one or more steps to search for adversarial examples within a vicinity. Let $\mathrm{AttS}\left(h, x, y; \mathbb{V}x\right)$ denote the success of an **att**ack in finding adversarial examples in $\mathbb{V}_x$. The failure rate of this attack on classifier h can serve as an estimation for the classifier's expected robustness, as outlined below.

$$\mathrm{AttS}\left(h, x, y; \mathbb{V}x\right) \to \neg\,\mathrm{Rob}\left(h, x, y; \mathbb{V}_x\right) \tag{6}$$

Another perspective contends that any non-zero rate of false negatives in the detection of adversarial examples is problematic. To this end, a condition Vrob is to be established, such that given a classifier h, it satisfies

$$\forall\, (\boldsymbol{x}, y) \in \mathbb{X} \times \mathbb{Y}.\ \mathrm{Vrob}\left(h, \boldsymbol{x}, y; \mathbb{V}_{\boldsymbol{x}}\right) \to \text{Formula 2} \tag{7}$$

This method refers to robustness verification and the condition Vrob is the verification result of **rob**ustness. There are two categories of robustness verification methods, *i.e.*, incomplete deterministic verification [28] and complete deterministic verification [28]. Any deterministic verification method that fulfils Formula 7 qualifies as an incomplete verification. If a method further fulfils Formula 8, it qualifies as a complete verification. In both cases, if the verification result $\mathrm{Vrob}\left(h, \boldsymbol{x}, y; \mathbb{V}_{\boldsymbol{x}}\right)$ is True, *i.e.*, verified, the classifier is considered to have deterministic robustness certification [28] for input $\boldsymbol{x}$ within the vicinity $\mathbb{V}_{\boldsymbol{x}}$, and the average certification likelihood is often called certified robust accuracy [45]. Certified robust accuracy can serve as a lower bound for the classifier's expected robustness.

$$\forall\, (\boldsymbol{x}, y) \in \mathbb{X} \times \mathbb{Y}.\ \mathrm{Vrob}\left(h, \boldsymbol{x}, y; \mathbb{V}_{\boldsymbol{x}}\right) \leftarrow \mathrm{Rob}\left(h, \boldsymbol{x}, y; \mathbb{V}_{\boldsymbol{x}}\right) \tag{8}$$

These verification methods can be used to optimise classifiers during training, and such a practice refers to certified training [28,53], which is defined as follows.

$$\min_{h}\ \mathrm{E}_{(\mathbf{x},\mathbf{y}) \sim D}\left[\sup_{\boldsymbol{x}' \in \mathbb{V}(\mathbf{x}),\ k \neq \mathbf{y}} \left(\ell(h, \boldsymbol{x}', \mathbf{y}) - \ell(h, \boldsymbol{x}', k)\right)\right] \tag{9}$$

Here, the neural network verification methods are used to soundly approximate the worst loss that can be induced by any perturbation within the vicinity of each training sample. However, after years of research [6,46,64], certified training still faces challenges. Existing certified training methods often result in a significant drop in the model's accuracy [10,40]. For instance, the best accuracy achieved by certified training is typically half of that of the standard training on the CIFAR-10 data set [45,51]. Such a significantly reduced accuracy often means that the model is unacceptable in practice.

In summary, to evaluate whether h attains robustness at example $(\boldsymbol{x}, y)$ within the vicinity $\mathbb{V}_{\boldsymbol{x}}$, existing methods include checking $\mathrm{AttS}\left(h, \boldsymbol{x}, y; \mathbb{V}\boldsymbol{x}\right)$ through adversarial attacks or $\mathrm{V}\left(h, \boldsymbol{x}, y; \mathbb{V}_{\boldsymbol{x}}\right)$ through robustness verification. The expected robustness over a given distribution D, denoted by

$$\mathrm{E}_{(\mathbf{x},\mathbf{y}) \sim D}\left[\mathbf{1}_{\mathrm{Rob}\left(h, \mathbf{x}, \mathbf{y}; \mathbb{V}_{\mathbf{x}}\right)}\right] \tag{10}$$

which can be overestimated by attack success rate $(\mathrm{E}_{(\mathbf{x},\mathbf{y}) \sim D}\left[\mathbf{1}_{\mathrm{AttS}}\right])$ or underestimated by certified robust accuracy $(\mathrm{E}_{(\mathbf{x},\mathbf{y}) \sim D}\left[\mathbf{1}_{\mathrm{Vrob}}\right])$. $\mathbf{1}_{\mathrm{condition}}$ is the indicator function that returns 1 if the condition is True, and 0 otherwise.

2.2 Bayes Rules for Distributions

In the following, we introduce the notion of Bayes Error and how it reflects a classification distribution. We consider a scenario where an input $\mathbf{x}$ is to be classified into one class in $\mathbb{Y}$, in particular, $y = k$ with prior class probability $P(y = k)$ where $k \in \mathbb{Y}$. Let $p(x|y = k)$ denote the class likelihood, that is, the conditional probability density of x given that it belongs to class k. The probability that the input x belongs to a specific class k, namely the posterior probability $p(y = k|x)$, is given by Bayes' theorem.

$$p(y = k|x) = \frac{p(x|y = k)P(y = k)}{p(x)} \tag{11}$$

where $p(x)$ is the probability density function of x, i.e., $p(x) = \sum_{k \in \mathbb{Y}} p(x|y = k)P(y = k)$. This classifier assigns an input x to the class with the highest posterior and is called the Bayes classifier, which is the optimal classifier. The classification error associated with the Bayes classifier is outlined as follows.

Definition 4 (Bayes error). *Given a distribution D over $\mathbb{X} \times \mathbb{Y}$, the error associated with the Bayes classifier is called the Bayes error (rate), denoted as β_D. The Bayes error can be expressed [13, 15] as:*

$$\beta_D = E_{(x,y) \sim D} \left[1 - \max_k p(y = k|x) \right]$$
$$= \int \left(1 - \max_k p(y = k|x = x) \right) p(x) dx \tag{12}$$

Besides, since the Bayes classifier is optimal [42], this optimality gives rise to the following definition of the Bayes error [34].

$$\beta_D = \min_{\text{measurable } h} E_{(x,y) \sim D} \left[1_{h(x) \neq y} \right] \tag{13}$$

where the Bayes error is defined as the minimum of the errors achieved by measurable functions $h : \mathbb{X} \rightarrow \mathbb{Y}$. Hereby, (any) classifier h with an error rate equal to β_D can be called a Bayes classifier.

An example illustrating the Bayes error is given in Fig. 2b. The Bayes error fundamentally reflects the inherent uncertainty in classification tasks. It is the (irreducible) minimal error rate achievable by any classifier for a specific problem, influenced by the overlap amount among the class probability distributions. An input having a certain (deterministic) label can be formally expressed as $\max_k p(y = k|x = x) = 1$. We can also represent this using the ceiling $\lceil \cdot \rceil$ or floor $\lfloor \cdot \rfloor$ function within the interval $[0, 1]$. Specifically, the ceiling function returns the smallest integer greater than or equal to the input. Consequently, it returns 1 for any number from 0 (exclusive) up to 1 and returns 0 if the input is 0. This shows that the input's label has uncertainty if $1 - \max_k p(y = k|x = x) > 0$ and does not have uncertainty otherwise. We write $\mathbb{K}_D = \{ x \mid 1 - \max_k p(y = k|x = x) > 0 \}$ to denote the set of every input whose label has uncertainty. The Bayes error provides a yardstick for other classifiers [18,42], e.g., a classifier may be deemed effective if its error rate approximates the Bayes error.

As highlighted in Eqs. (11) and (12), the calculation of Bayes error is contingent upon knowing the prior distribution. In practical situations, since this distribution is not analytically known, the strategy is to estimate Bayes error using the observable portion of the distribution, e.g., training data characteristics, through approximations [11,19,52,61] or by computing its upper [5,13,21] and lower [1,65,67] bounds.

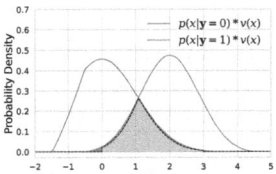 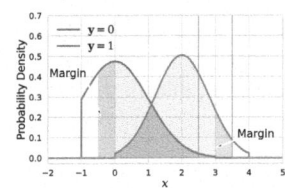 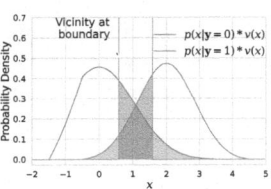

(a) Convolution of distributions from Fig. 2b with the vicinity function from Fig. 2a, resulting in flatter and smoother distributions with increased shaded areas.

(b) Demonstration of the margin contributing to $\zeta_D^\sharp$. In a 1D problem, the width of $\mathbb{K}_D^*$ is essentially the vicinity width.

(c) Union of shaded areas indicating the lower bound of irreducible robustness error and upper bound of certified robust accuracy.

Fig. 3. Visualizing the convolution of distributions, the marginal contribution to Bayes error, and the bounds of robustness error and certified robust accuracy.

Problem Definition. Next, we define the problem that we study. Despite the many proposals on certified training, noticeable suboptimality in robustness persists, especially compared with vanilla accuracy. Our objective is to ascertain whether this limitation comes from insufficient optimisation, or if there exists a fundamental upper bound that inherently limits the certified robust accuracy. Furthermore, if such an upper bound does exist, we aim to investigate how we can compute it, and how we can validate our result.

3   An Upper Bound of Robustness from Bayes Error

In this section, we present a method that attempts to address our research problem defined above, from a Bayes error perspective. Particularly, we hypothesise that the Bayes error plays a vital role in estimating the robustness that can be achieved by any classifier. First, we prove that certified training increases the Bayes error, which poses an upper bound on the robustness that can be achieved by any classifier. Second, we present how the upper bounds of certified robust accuracy can be calculated from a given distribution.

3.1   Certified Training Increases Bayes Error

Certified robustness can be viewed as a way of optimizing the classifier with an altered data distribution instead of the original distribution [37]. This is because due to the requirement of robustness, an input may be forced with a label of some of its neighbors in the vicinity, instead of its original label. In the following, we investigate how the robustness requirement influences the data distribution, further affecting the Bayes error. We hypothesise that the altered distribution worsens Bayes error. We begin by defining a "label-assignment" action that alters a distribution, from a local perspective.

Suppose there is a distribution D over the space $\mathbb{X} \times \mathbb{Y}$. From a local (example) perspective, an example $(\boldsymbol{x}, y) \in \mathbb{X} \times \mathbb{Y}$ assigns its label to a specific domain $\mathbb{S} \subset \mathbb{X}$ ($\mathbb{S}$ can be a vicinity) by directly altering the joint probability in $\mathbb{S}$. Specifically, this alteration is a process that adds $\Delta p(y = y, \mathbf{x} = \boldsymbol{x})$ to the original $p(y = y, \mathbf{x} = \boldsymbol{x})$, and adds $\Delta p(y = y, \mathbf{x} = \boldsymbol{x}')$ to the original $p(y = y, \mathbf{x} = \boldsymbol{x}')$ for any example $\boldsymbol{x}' \in \mathbb{S}$, where Δp denotes a change in the joint distribution function (of $\mathbf{x}, \mathbf{y}$) such that

$$
\Delta p'(y = k, \mathbf{x} = \boldsymbol{x}) = \begin{cases} 0, & \text{if } k \neq y \\ p_{\text{ori}}(y = k, \mathbf{x} = \boldsymbol{x}) \left(\frac{1}{\int_s d\boldsymbol{x}'} - 1 \right), & \text{otherwise} \end{cases}
$$

$$
\Delta p(y = k, \mathbf{x} = \boldsymbol{x}') = \begin{cases} 0, & \text{if } k \neq y \\ \frac{1}{\int_s d\boldsymbol{x}'} p_{\text{ori}}(y = k, \mathbf{x} = \boldsymbol{x}), & \text{otherwise} \end{cases}
\tag{14}
$$

We then explain why this label assignment aligns with the robustness criteria. In the context of robustness, for every input in the training set, every neighbour point in the vicinity around the input gets the label of this input. Meanwhile, an input may fall within more than one vicinity. Thus, an input gets labels assigned from multiple neighbours, and each label's influence depends on its source's joint probability. Intuitively, examples with higher joint probability have a stronger influence on its vicinity.

Equation (14) captures the effect of an input's label on its neighbours, from an individual input perspective. We next set out from a distributional perspective which is supposed to match our individual input perspective. When all examples in the original distribution concurrently assign labels to their respective vicinity, the effect is equivalent to convolving this given distribution with the vicinity (function). This convolved distribution represents the target of certified robustness optimization, as captured by Throrem 1.

Theorem 1. *Given a distribution D for classification, optimising for higher certified robustness does not optimise the classifiers to fit D. Rather, it optimises classifiers towards $D * v$, i.e., convolved distribution between D and vicinity $v(\boldsymbol{x})$.*

Proof. Optimising for certified robustness tunes classifiers to have a higher probability of satisfying Formula 2. Therefore, the objective is to maximise

$$
\mathbb{E}_{(\mathbf{x},\mathbf{y}) \sim D} \left[\lfloor \int_{\mathbb{X}} v(\mathbf{x} - \boldsymbol{x}') \cdot \mathbf{1}_{y=h(\boldsymbol{x}')} d\boldsymbol{x}' \rfloor \right]
$$

$$
= \sum_k \int_{\mathbb{X}} \lfloor \int_{\mathbb{X}} v(\boldsymbol{x} - \boldsymbol{x}') \cdot \mathbf{1}_{k=h(\boldsymbol{x}')} d\boldsymbol{x}' \rfloor p(\boldsymbol{x}, k) d\boldsymbol{x}
\tag{15}
$$

Denote $\mu_k(\boldsymbol{x}) = \int_{\mathbb{X}} v(\boldsymbol{x} - \boldsymbol{x}') \cdot \mathbf{1}_{k=h(\boldsymbol{x}')} d\boldsymbol{x}'$, then the objective can be expressed as $\sum_k \int_{\mathbb{X}} \lfloor \mu_{k^*}(\boldsymbol{x}) \rfloor p(\boldsymbol{x}, k) d\boldsymbol{x}$. Suppose μ_k for each $\boldsymbol{x}$ is the variational function we tune to maximise the objective. As the floor function is monotonically increasing, maximising the original objective is equivalent to maximising $\sum_k \int_{\mathbb{X}} \mu_k(\boldsymbol{x}) p(\boldsymbol{x}, k) d\boldsymbol{x}$, which equals

$$
\sum_k \int_{\mathbb{X}} \int_{\mathbb{X}} v(\boldsymbol{x} - \boldsymbol{x}') \cdot \mathbf{1}_{k=h(\boldsymbol{x}')} d\boldsymbol{x}' p(\boldsymbol{x}, k) d\boldsymbol{x}
$$

$$
= \sum_k \int_{\mathbb{X}} \int_{\mathbb{X}} v(\boldsymbol{x}' - \boldsymbol{x}) p(\boldsymbol{x}, k) d\boldsymbol{x} \cdot \mathbf{1}_{k=h(\boldsymbol{x}')} d\boldsymbol{x}'
\tag{16}
$$

Observe the convolution form $(p_k * v)(x') = \int_{\mathbb{X}} v(x' - x)p(x, k)dx$, and the objective becomes $\sum_k \int_{\mathbb{X}} (p_k * v)(x') \cdot \mathbf{1}_{k=h(x')} dx'$. Thus, the target distribution of optimising for certified robustness is indeed the convolved distribution of the given one.   □

Note that Throrem 1 is not particularly for existing certified training approaches but rather any approach to achieving certified robustness. Hereafter, we use D to denote the original distribution, p to denote the conditional distributions (of each class) from D, D' to denote the convolved distribution, and q to denote the conditional distributions (of each class) from D'. Thus, the Bayes error of D' can be expressed as

$$\beta_{D'} = \mathrm{E}_{(\mathbf{x},\mathbf{y}) \sim D'} \left[1 - \max_k q(\mathbf{y} = k | \mathbf{x}) \right] \tag{17}$$

The subsequent question is to study the Bayes error with respect to the convolved distribution D'. Throrem 2 suggests that Bayes error grows when D is transformed into D', as illustrated in Fig. 3a.

Theorem 2. *Given a distribution D for classification, its convolved distribution D' has an equal or larger Bayes error, i.e., $\beta_D \leq \beta_{D'}$.*

Proof. Consider D is a distribution of random variables $\mathbf{x}$ and $\mathbf{y}$. Let $p_k(x)$ be the conditional distribution of $\mathbf{x}$ given $\mathbf{y} = k$. We need to prove that the Bayes error between p_k is less than or equal to the Bayes error between $p_k * v$, where v is a probability density function (PDF). First, let us prove that $((\max_k(p_k)) * v)(x) \geq \max_k((p_k * v)(x))$. Expanding both sides, we get $\int \max_k(p_k(x - x')v(x'))dx'$ at left. We get $\max_k(\int p_k(x - x')v(x')dx')$ at right. We can see that left $\geq \int p_k(x - x')v(x')dx'$ for any k. Therefore, the maximum can be brought out from the integral and thus the left side is proved to be greater than or equal to the right side. Then, we use the equality that the integral of $((\max_k p_k) * v)(x)$ is actually the same as the integral of $(\max_k p_k)(x)$. This is because v itself is a PDF. Therefore, we get

$$\int \left(1 - (\max_k p_k)(x) \right) dx \leq \int \left(1 - \max_k((p_k * v)(x)) \right) dx \tag{18}$$

□

Intuitively, when robustness is required, new labels are assigned to data in the vicinity of the training inputs. But, these new labels sometimes contradict the original labels or contradict themselves. As a result, the convolved distribution invariably exhibits larger uncertainty, represented by an increased Bayes error. For instance, let us consider a separable distribution with a unique boundary. The condition $d(x, x') \leq \epsilon$ implies that x and x', near the boundary, should be assigned the same label even if their ground-truth labels are different, leading to a non-zero Bayes error.

3.2   Irreducible Robustness Error and Robustness Upper Bound

We have proved that the optimal robustness is equal to or lower than the optimal accuracy. We now would like to find a quantitative upper bound for robustness. We first define the irreducible expected error rate across all classifiers regarding robustness, as expressed in Equation (19) where $\zeta_D^\sharp$ represents the irreducible robustness error on distribution D.

$$\zeta_D^\sharp = \inf_{\text{measurable } h} E_{(\mathbf{x},\mathbf{y}) \sim D} \left[1 - \mathbf{1}_{\text{Rob}\left(h,\mathbf{x},\mathbf{y};\mathbb{V}_\mathbf{x}\right)} \right] \tag{19}$$

This concept is analogous to Equation (13), where the Bayes error is described as the irreducible vanilla error rate achievable by any classifier. Then, the upper bound of expected robustness is 1 minus the lower bound of $\zeta_D^\sharp$.

Recall Definition 3, the condition $\text{Rob}(h, \boldsymbol{x}, y; (d, \epsilon))$ holds only if Formula 2 is met, where $(\boldsymbol{x}, y) \in \mathbb{X} \times \mathbb{Y}$. Nevertheless, Formula 2 alone is not a sufficient condition for $\text{Rob}\left(h, \boldsymbol{x}, y; (d, \epsilon)\right)$. According to Definition 2, $\text{Rob}\left(h, \boldsymbol{x}, y; (d, \epsilon)\right)$ also requires that no input in the vicinity of $\boldsymbol{x}$ should be classified incorrectly, as expressed in Formula 20. Formally, $\text{Rob}\left(h, \boldsymbol{x}, y; (d, \epsilon)\right) \iff$ Formula 2 $\wedge$ Formula 20.

$$\neg \exists \, (\boldsymbol{x}', y') \in \mathbb{X} \times \mathbb{Y}. \, p(\boldsymbol{x}', y') > 0 \, \wedge \, d(\boldsymbol{x}, \boldsymbol{x}') \leq \epsilon \, \wedge \, h(\boldsymbol{x}') \neq y' \tag{20}$$

Equation (20) suggests that if the ground-truth labels of inputs in the vicinity of $\boldsymbol{x}$ are different from the labels of $\boldsymbol{x}$, then a prerequisite of robustness is missing such that robustness cannot be attained. The conjunction of Formula 2 and 20 clarifies that robustness asks for general correctness across the (local) input domain, rather than just local consistency. From this conjunction, we can derive that for a classifier to attain robustness at an input, it is necessary that the posterior probability associated with this input is entirely certain, which is formally captured in Throrem 3. Further, given a distribution, the proportion of examples with uncertain labels can serve as a lower bound for the proportion of examples without robustness.

Theorem 3. *Given a distribution D over $\mathbb{X} \times \mathbb{Y}$, the irreducible robustness error is greater than or equal to the probability that an input is in $\mathbb{K}_D$.*

$$\zeta_D^\sharp \geq \int \lceil 1 - \max_k p(\mathbf{y} = k|\mathbf{x} = \boldsymbol{x}) \rceil \, p(\boldsymbol{x}) d\boldsymbol{x} \geq \beta_D \tag{21}$$

When $\lceil 1 - \max_k p(\mathbf{y} = k|\mathbf{x} = \boldsymbol{x}) \rceil = 0$, there is one and only one class has a posterior probability of 1 at input $\boldsymbol{x}$, resulting in a non-zero contribution to the Bayes error.

Proof. Assume some classifier h attains robustness at input $\boldsymbol{x}$, and the posterior probability is not certain, *i.e.*, $1 - \max_k p(\mathbf{y} = k \mid \mathbf{x} = \boldsymbol{x}) > 0$. The latter infers that there exists some (non-zero probability) examples of $(\boldsymbol{x}, y_1)$ pair and some $(\boldsymbol{x}, y_2)$ pair, and $y_1 \neq y_2$. The prediction for $\boldsymbol{x}$ differs from at least one of either y_1 and y_2. Formally, the latter condition in our assumption entails $(h(\boldsymbol{x}) \neq y_1 \vee h(\boldsymbol{x}) \neq y_2)$, which then entails

$$\exists \boldsymbol{x}' \in \mathbb{V}_\boldsymbol{x}. \, h(\boldsymbol{x}') \neq y_1 \vee h(\boldsymbol{x}') \neq y_2 \qquad \text{(because } \boldsymbol{x} \in \mathbb{V}_\boldsymbol{x})$$
$$\exists \boldsymbol{x}' \in \mathbb{V}_\boldsymbol{x} \, \exists y' \in \mathbb{Y}. \, p(\boldsymbol{x}', y') > 0 \, \wedge \, h(\boldsymbol{x}') \neq y' \quad \text{(Disjunction Elimination)} \tag{22}$$

Condition (22) contradicts the former condition in our assumption, *i.e.*, Condition 20. Thus, robustness may only be attained if there is no label uncertainty at an input. $\qquad\square$

Uncertainty contributes to an irreducible error in both vanilla accuracy and robustness. The irreducible robustness error is at least the Bayes error. We are further interested in refining this boundary in scenarios where we know the value of the Bayes error but lack information about the posterior probabilities. To this end, we develop Corollary 1.

Corollary 1. *Given a distribution D over $\mathbb{X} \times \mathbb{Y}$, its irreducible robustness error is at least as large as the Bayes error multiplied by the number of classes divided by one less than the number of classes, i.e.,*

$$\zeta_D^{\sharp} \geq \frac{|\mathbb{Y}|}{|\mathbb{Y}| - 1}\beta_D \tag{23}$$

where $|\mathbb{Y}|$ denotes the number of classes.

Proof. we have that $\zeta_D^{\sharp} \geq \int_{\mathbb{K}_D} p(\boldsymbol{x})d\boldsymbol{x} = \int_{\mathbb{K}_D}(1 - \max_k p(y = k|\mathbf{x} = \boldsymbol{x}) + \max_k p(y = k|\mathbf{x} = \boldsymbol{x}))p(\boldsymbol{x})d\boldsymbol{x} = \beta_D + \int_{\mathbb{K}_D}(\max_k p(y = k|\mathbf{x} = \boldsymbol{x}))p(\boldsymbol{x})d\boldsymbol{x} \geq \int_{\mathbb{K}_D} p(\boldsymbol{x})/|\mathbb{Y}| \, d\boldsymbol{x} + \beta_D$. Thus, we can prove that $\int_{\mathbb{K}_D} p(\boldsymbol{x})d\boldsymbol{x} \geq \beta_D |\mathbb{Y}| /(|\mathbb{Y}| - 1)$ $\square$

In Threorem 3 and Corollary 1, the lower bounds for the $\zeta_D^{\sharp}$ are established based on that a single input needs to have a deterministic label. Still, there are additional conditions that, if unmet, will prevent a classifier from attaining robustness for a given input. For instance, we can expand the certainty requirement from a single input to encompass any input within its vicinity. The input neighbours in the vicinity with uncertain labels can also contribute to the irreducible robustness error. Given an input $\boldsymbol{x}$ such that $\boldsymbol{x} \notin \mathbb{K}_D$, if there exists an $\boldsymbol{x}'$ within this vicinity of $\boldsymbol{x}$ such that $\boldsymbol{x}' \in \mathbb{K}_D$, robustness at $\boldsymbol{x}$ cannot be attained. All such $\boldsymbol{x}$ forms a domain $\mathbb{K}^*{}_D$. $\mathbb{K}^*{}_D$ can be considered as a thin margin around $\mathbb{K}_D$, as shown in Fig. 3b. This expansion results in a more stringent condition. Consequently, we will likely identify a tightened lower bound for $\zeta_D^{\sharp}$.

Corollary 2. *Given a distribution D over $\mathbb{X} \times \mathbb{Y}$, then*

$$\zeta_D^{\sharp} \geq 2 \cdot \epsilon_{\text{eff}} \cdot p_{\min} \cdot \left(\int_{\mathbb{K}_D} d\boldsymbol{x} \right)^{\frac{\dim \mathbb{X} - 1}{\dim \mathbb{X}}} + \int_{\mathbb{K}_D} p(\boldsymbol{x})d\boldsymbol{x} \tag{24}$$

where ϵ_{eff} denotes the radius of the vicinity according to the definition of robustness, e.g., for L^2-perturbation, ϵ_{eff} equals to the radius ϵ. For general perturbations,

$$\frac{\pi^{\dim \mathbb{X}/2}}{\Gamma\left(\frac{\dim \mathbb{X}}{2} + 1\right)}\epsilon_{\text{eff}}^{\dim \mathbb{X}} = \int_{\mathbb{X}} \lceil v(\boldsymbol{x}) \rceil d\boldsymbol{x} \tag{25}$$

Proof. $\mathbb{K}_D^*$ emerges when a perturbation vicinity sweeps along the boundary of $\mathbb{K}_D$ and the isoperimetric inequality suggests that the volume of this marginal domain is minimized when both vicinity and $\mathbb{K}_D$ are dim $\mathbb{X}$-spheres.

Thus, a lower bound of the volume of $\mathbb{K}_D^*$ can be expressed as the volume difference between two concentric spheres which is again greater than the product of their radius difference and the surface area of the inner sphere. Thus, the volume of $\mathbb{K}_D^*$ is lower bounded by

$$\epsilon_{\text{eff}} \cdot \text{vol}(\mathbb{K}_D)^{\frac{\dim \mathbb{X}-1}{\dim \mathbb{X}}} \cdot \frac{2\pi^{\dim \mathbb{X}/2}}{\Gamma\left(\frac{\dim \mathbb{X}}{2}\right)} \left(\pi^{-\dim \mathbb{X}/2} \Gamma\left(\frac{\dim \mathbb{X}}{2}+1\right)\right)^{\frac{\dim \mathbb{X}-1}{\dim \mathbb{X}}} \tag{26}$$

where Γ represents the gamma function, and for all positive real numbers $\Gamma(z) = \int_0^\infty t^{z-1} e^{-t} \, dt$. We further simplify Equation (26) to $\epsilon_{\text{eff}} \cdot \text{vol}(\mathbb{K}_D)^{(\dim \mathbb{X}-1)/(\dim \mathbb{X})} \cdot \gamma$, where $\gamma \geq 2$ for $\dim \mathbb{X} > 1$ and a lower bound of $\text{vol}(\mathbb{K}_D^*)$ is thus $2 \cdot \epsilon_{\text{eff}} \cdot (\int_{\mathbb{K}_D} d\boldsymbol{x})^{(\dim \mathbb{X}-1)/(\dim \mathbb{X})}$. In very high dimensions, the (minimum) volume of $\mathbb{K}_D^*$ is almost linearly related to the volume of $\mathbb{K}_D$. The irreducible error contributed by the marginal domain to robustness can be expressed as $\int_{\mathbb{K}_D^*} p(\boldsymbol{x}) d\boldsymbol{x}$. It is greater than or equal to $\int_{\mathbb{K}_D^*} p_{\min} d\boldsymbol{x}$, where $p_{\min} = \min_{\boldsymbol{x}} p(\boldsymbol{x})$. Thus, this irreducible error $\geq p_{\min} \cdot \text{vol}(\mathbb{K}_D^*)$, contributes to the irreducible robustness error as the first term in Equation (24). This corollary is particularly useful if we know the non-zero $p_{\min}$ of the distribution. □

In short, Throrem 3, Corollary 1, and Corollary 2 suggest how we can get lower bounds of irreducible robustness error $\zeta_D^\sharp$ from the original distribution D, with lower bound from Corollary 2 being the tightest among three. Given a distribution, $\zeta_D^\sharp$ has two sources. One is the examples that have uncertain labels (which contribute to the error directly), and the other is the examples that have neighbours whose labels are uncertain (which contribute to the error indirectly). Additionally, when the Bayes error β_D of a distribution is non-zero, the irreducible error of robustness $\zeta_D^\sharp$ is also non-zero and is greater than the Bayes error.

Theoretically, there is another way to tighten the bound provided by Throrem 3. If we know the convolved distribution D' obtained in Sect. 3.1, the $\zeta_D^\sharp$ can be calculated as $p(\mathbf{x} \in \mathbb{K}_{D'})$, i.e., the probability (in convolved distribution) that input has a deterministic label. Thus,

$$\zeta_D^\sharp = \mathbb{E}_{(\mathbf{x},\mathbf{y}) \sim D'} \left[1 - \lfloor \max_k q(\mathbf{y} = k|\mathbf{x}) \rfloor \right] \tag{27}$$

Since $D' = D * v$, as vicinity size grows, the Bayes error of D' also grows, and thus the irreducible robustness error $\zeta_D^\sharp$ grows.

The least upper bound of robustness on a given data distribution D can then be written as $1 - \zeta_D^\sharp$, and 1 minus any lower bound of $\zeta_D^\sharp$ presented above serves as an upper bound of robustness on a given data distribution D. These upper bounds are directly derived from the data distribution D and the vicinity function v, independent of any specific classifier.

Although we have been using both Formulae 2 and (20) throughout this subsection, the existing studies only rely on Formula 2 [28] for practical evaluation of certified robust accuracy. Intuitively, we sometimes do not know the true label of a neighbour $\boldsymbol{x}'$ in an input $\boldsymbol{x}$'s vicinity, and thus use the $\boldsymbol{x}$'s label instead. Consequently, the correctness of $\boldsymbol{x}'$ prediction is neglected. Instead, only the consistency between predictions on $\boldsymbol{x}'$ and $\boldsymbol{x}$, as well as the correctness of prediction on $\boldsymbol{x}$, are considered. This simplification could result in a different certified robust accuracy for classifiers and exceed our upper bounds of robustness on a given data distribution (Throrem 3). To this end, we also present the irreducible robustness error ζ_D in Equation (28) and the corresponding upper bound for such robustness on a given data distribution $1 - \zeta_D$. We use Fig. 3c to illustrate its effect.

$$\zeta_D = \int_{\mathbb{K}_{D^\dagger}} q(\boldsymbol{x})d\boldsymbol{x} + \int_{\mathbb{X}\backslash\mathbb{K}_{D^\dagger}} \left(1 - \max_k q(\mathrm{y} = k|\mathrm{x} = \boldsymbol{x})\right) q(\boldsymbol{x})d\boldsymbol{x} \qquad (28)$$

where $D^\dagger$ is a distribution obtained from convolving the vicinity function v and the "hardened" distribution of D', i.e., each $p_{\mathrm{hard}}(\mathrm{y} = k_{\mathrm{max}}|\mathrm{x} = \boldsymbol{x}) = q(\boldsymbol{x})$ and for other $k \neq k_{\mathrm{max}}$, $p_{\mathrm{hard}}(\mathrm{y} = k|\mathrm{x} = \boldsymbol{x}) = 0$. Then, $p_{D^\dagger} = p_{\mathrm{hard}} * v$. Recall that q is the conditional distribution of D'. In Equation (28), its first term suggests no input close to the boundary can attain robustness. For inputs not close to the boundary, as indicated by the second term, their optimal robustness on a given data distribution depends on the correctness of the prediction. In terms of Fig. 3c, the first term corresponds to the shaded area bounded by the vicinity, and the second term corresponds to all shaded areas outside the curve. Although Equation (28) has tackled the label-missing challenges in practice, this theoretical evaluation of the irreducible error (in certified robust accuracy) could still rely on the knowledge of distribution. Thus, distribution estimating techniques are also needed when facing sampled data from an unknown distribution.

4   Experiment and Results

In this section, we empirically test our results discussed above by designing and answering three research questions: 1) does certified training always result in a classifier on a distribution with a higher Bayes error; 2) is our computed upper bound of robustness indeed higher than the robustness achieved by all the existing certified training classifiers; and 3) does the upper bound of robustness change when the vicinity increases, and if so how does it change?

The experiments are conducted with four data sets: two synthetic ones (i.e., Moons and Chan [8]) and two standard benchmarks (i.e., FashionMNIST [59] and CIFAR-10 [23]). Moons is used for binary classification with two-dimensional features, where each class's distribution is described analytically with specific likelihood equations, and uses a three-layer Multi-Layer Perceptron (MLP) neural network for classification. The Chan data set, also for binary classification with two-dimensional features, differs in that it does not follow a standard PDF pattern, requiring kernel density estimation (KDE) for non-parametric PDF estimation, and also uses the three-layer MLP. FashionMNIST, a collection of fashion item images, involves a 10-class classification task with 784-dimensional inputs (28×28 pixel grayscale images). Each class has an equal prior probability, and their conditional distributions are estimated non-parametrically using KDE. CIFAR-10 uses images with a resolution of 32×32 pixels. Similar to FashionMNIST, it has a balanced class distribution and is estimated using KDE. We use a seven-layer convolutional neural network (CNN-7) [45] as the classifier of both FashionMNIST and CIFAR-10. We adopt a direct approach [20] to compute the original Bayes error of both FashionMNIST and CIFAR-10 [20].

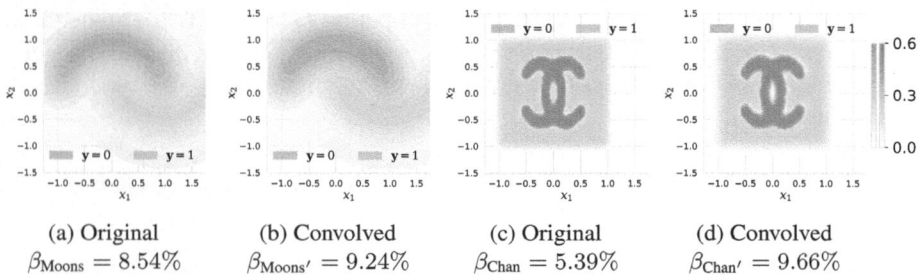

| (a) Original | (b) Convolved | (c) Original | (d) Convolved |
| $\beta_{\text{Moons}} = 8.54\%$ | $\beta_{\text{Moons}'} = 9.24\%$ | $\beta_{\text{Chan}} = 5.39\%$ | $\beta_{\text{Chan}'} = 9.66\%$ |

Fig. 4. The conditional distribution before and after convolution for (a, b) Moons and (c, d) Chan. For both Moons and Chan, L^∞ size is set at $\epsilon = 0.15$. We also report the Bayes error to show the change of inherent uncertainty in each distribution.

To train the classifiers, two approaches are adopted, *i.e.*, empirical error minimization (ERM [54]) for standard training, and the state-of-the-art (SOTA) small-box method for certified training [35]. The performance of these classifiers is evaluated using two metrics: vanilla accuracy and certified robust accuracy [35]. Note that, certified robust accuracy measures the proportion of predictions that can be certified as robust in terms of satisfying Formula 2.

RQ1: Does the Bayes error indeed grow when certified training is applied? We would like to check if the Bayes error indeed sees a growth when certified training is used. To do that, we first need to obtain the altered distribution used in the context of certified training. As explained in Sect. 3.1, certified training extends the label of an input to its vicinity, and thus results in a convolutional effect across the entire given distribution. Therefore, we can obtain a convolved distribution of each given distribution with each vicinity. Then, we compare the original distribution and the convolved distribution of a given data set, and the Bayes error of the distribution before and after convolution.

We use the Moons and Chan data sets, setting a L^∞ vicinity at $\epsilon = 0.15$. Then, we get the convolved distribution of each data set (using FFT-based convolution, implemented through `scipy.signal.fftconvolve`) and the results are demonstrated in Fig. 4. Observing the comparison shown in Fig. 4(a, b) and (c, d), we can see that the original distribution has gone through a "melting" process, *i.e.*, the peaks of each distribution becomes lower, and the spread increases. For example, in Fig. 4b, the upper moon's centre region (around $x_1 = 0, x_2 = 0.6$) has a higher concentration of inputs from the lower moon than that in (a). This is because convolution with a rectangular function, *e.g.*, vicinity function in our case, is essentially smoothing the original conditional distribution.

To quantify the increased overlap between the density function of each distribution after convolution, we compute their Bayes error. For Moons, the original Bayes error (Fig. 4a) is 8.54%, while the Bayes error after convolution is 9.24%. Similarly, for Chan, Bayes error increases from 5.39% (c) to 9.66% (d). As expected, the Bayes errors do grow, with the growth ranging from 8% to nearly 80%.

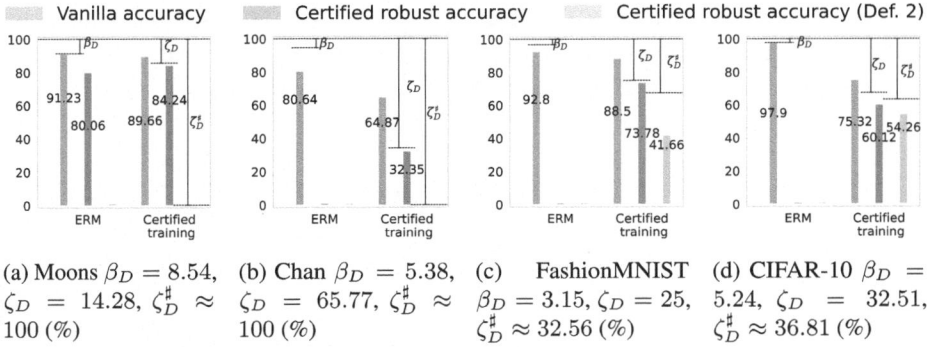

(a) Moons $\beta_D = 8.54$, $\zeta_D = 14.28$, $\zeta_D^\sharp \approx 100\,(\%)$, (b) Chan $\beta_D = 5.38$, $\zeta_D = 65.77$, $\zeta_D^\sharp \approx 100\,(\%)$, (c) FashionMNIST $\beta_D = 3.15$, $\zeta_D = 25$, $\zeta_D^\sharp \approx 32.56\,(\%)$, (d) CIFAR-10 $\beta_D = 5.24$, $\zeta_D = 32.51$, $\zeta_D^\sharp \approx 36.81\,(\%)$

Fig. 5. Upper bounds of robustness/accuracy and the state-of-the-art classifier's performance. The L^∞ vicinity size for certified training /certified robust accuracy for each data set is $\epsilon = 0.15, 0.15, 0.1, 2/255$ for Moons, Chan, FashionMNIST, and CIFAR-10.

We find that convolving with the same vicinity function results in very different growth in the Bayes error. This is likely due to the shape of the original density function. For instance, each moon in the Moons distribution can be approximately seen as a single-modal distribution, and the density function does not have sharp changes. In contrast, the density function of each class's conditional distribution in Chan has sharper value changes at the central region (around $x_1 = 0, x_2 = 0.5$). This may suggest that the Chan distribution exhibits a larger shape change to its original distribution after convolution than Moons. Particularly, in Chan, we observe that the class with the highest probability at the central region changes. Originally, class-0 examples have a higher density in this region. However, after convolution, we can see from Fig. 4d that this region is filled more with class-1 examples than class-0 examples. Essentially, this change shows a significant prediction change in the Bayes classifier. This is likely because convolution has a larger influence on the distributions with features with high (2D) frequencies.

In summary, by comparing the Bayes error before and after distribution alteration, we conclude that the Bayes error does increase when certified training is used, which aligns with Throrem 2. Moreover, the distribution alteration has a larger impact on distributions with high-frequency features than on originally smooth distributions.

RQ2: Is our upper bound of robustness empirically effective? Next, we check whether the computed upper bound of robustness is indeed higher than the existing robustness evaluation in practice. To do that, we apply the closed-form Equation (28) numerically to compute the irreducible robustness error ζ_D for each data set/distribution D. The upper bound of certified robust accuracy is $1 - \zeta_D$. Then, we use ERM and certified training to optimise the corresponding classifier of each data set. As such, we get two trained classifiers for each data set. For each classifier, we compute its performance metrics and compare the classifiers' performance against our upper bounds. We remark that the accuracy and certified robust accuracy may fluctuate when the sample size is not sufficiently large, as seen in Fig. 6. For example, if we are only given five samples, there is a high chance we get a very high or very low accuracy. For this reason, we gradually increase the sample size of test sets and observe its converged value.

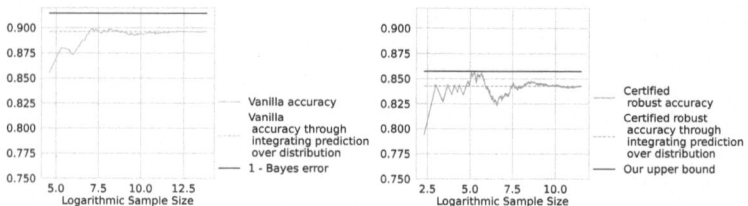

Fig. 6. As sample size grows, the accuracy converges to a value below *1 - Bayes-error*. Similarly, the certified robust accuracy converges to a value below our upper bound of robustness. The figures are computed based on the Moons data set.

The results are shown in Fig. 5. For each data set, the computed value ζ_D is detailed in the caption. The certified robust accuracy is represented by bars in the graph. For example, the MLP for the Moons dataset (seen in Fig. 5a) is trained twice. Initially, it is trained with ERM, achieving a vanilla accuracy of 91.23%, which is nearly the optimal vanilla accuracy of 91.46% (calculated as $1 - 8.54\%$). Here, the certified robust accuracy is about 80% with an L^∞ vicinity of $\epsilon = 0.15$. When trained a second time with certified training, the MLP's vanilla accuracy slightly decreases to 89.66%, but its certified robust accuracy improves by 5.1%, at 84.24%. The improved certified robust accuracy is below the theoretical upper bound (marked by a dashed line in Fig. 5a, below the annotation ζ_D), which is calculated to be 85.72% ($1-14.28\%$). Furthermore, the gap between the certified robust accuracy of this classifier and its upper limit is relatively small, approximately 1.5% in absolute percentage points.

Based on the result, we have multiple observations. First, we find that $1 - \zeta_D$ consistently exceeds the certified robust accuracy achieved by state-of-the-art method [35] across various datasets in Fig. 5. This gap, ranging from 1.5% to 7.1%, indicates the potential for further improving classifier robustness within these theoretical limits. For example, the Moons dataset has a small gap, suggesting limited room for improvement, while larger gaps in datasets like the Chan, FashionMNIST, and CIFAR-10 indicate more significant opportunities for increasing the robustness.

Second, we note that ζ_D consistently surpasses the Bayes error β_D by a significant margin for all D. For example, in the Moons dataset, ζ_D is 14.2%, which is 66% higher than its β_D of 8.54%. This implies that robustness against perturbations is challenging, even when the inherent uncertainty of the data is considered. In datasets like Fashion-MNIST and CIFAR-10, despite their low Bayes error of 3.1%-5.2%, their ζ_D are at least six times higher (25.0%-32.7%). This indicates that factors other than inherent data uncertainty are affecting robustness. These factors are likely the newly generated uncertainty from certified training. Moreover, some gaps between ζ_D and β_D are particularly large (*e.g.*, Fig. 5b). Such instances highlight the robustness challenges presented by each dataset can vary. Recall Fig. 4d, the distribution of Chan can be particularly sensitive to convolution with vicinity.

Third, recall that the upper bound ζ_D and certified robust accuracy are based on Formula 2 and Equation (28), and they do not consider the correctness of the label (Definition 2). If we take into consideration the correctness of the examples in the vicinity, we can compute a tighter bound $\zeta_D^{\sharp}$ based on Equation (20), and certified robust accuracy (from Def. 2) is calculated by sampling a large finite number of neighbours of the input and evaluating their correctness. As the test sample size grows, more examples appear in the vicinity of some training samples, and the likelihood of correctly predicting all of them decreases. This result is also illustrated in the right-most columns in Fig. 5. As observed, certified robust accuracy (from Def. 2) is always lower than $1 - \zeta_D^{\sharp}$. For instance, the certified robust accuracy of Moons (and Chan) decreases from 84.24% (and 32.35%) respectively to less than 10^{-7}, and that of FashionMNIST (and CIFAR-10) decreases from 73.78% (and 60.12%) to 41.66% (and 54.26%) respectively. Such large reductions indicate a potential need for rethinking the robustness requirement, which may lead to different ways of defining and achieving robustness.

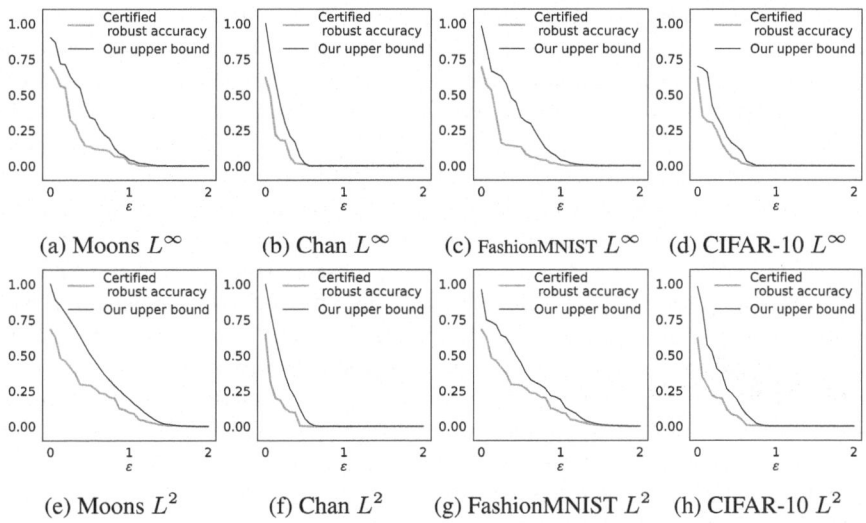

(a) Moons L^∞ (b) Chan L^∞ (c) FashionMNIST L^∞ (d) CIFAR-10 L^∞

(e) Moons L^2 (f) Chan L^2 (g) FashionMNIST L^2 (h) CIFAR-10 L^2

Fig. 7. As epsilon increases, we plot the robustness upper bound change as well as classifiers' certified robust accuracy change in the Moons and Chan dataset.

RQ3: How does the upper bound of robustness vary when the vicinity size grows? In the following, we investigate what can influence the value of irreducible robustness error/upper bound of certified robust accuracy. We already know that when the vicinity grows, it empirically becomes more difficult for a classifier to be robust [35]. The question is then: how about the irreducible robustness error? Is it dependent on the size of the vicinity? If so, how are they correlated? To answer this question, we extend our experiment to cover various vicinity shapes (L^∞ and L^2), and different vicinity sizes (from 0 to 2).

The results are shown in Fig. 7. Each sub-figure in Fig. 7 illustrates the impact of increasing the vicinity size (ϵ) on the upper bound $(1 - \zeta_D)$. For instance, in Fig. 7a, we present the change of $1 - \zeta_D$ as well as the classifier's certified robust accuracy after certified training. We observe that for all datasets (Moons, Chan, FashionMNIST, CIFAR-10) and norms (L^∞ and L^2), as the vicinity size grows, both the robustness upper bound and certified robust accuracy decrease monotonically. This indicates an inverse relationship between the upper bound and vicinity size. This finding aligns with our intuition that when vicinity size grows it becomes more difficult for a classifier to be robust. Notably, the CIFAR-10/Chan dataset shows a sharper decline in the upper bound than Moons/FashionMNIST, suggesting that some data distributions may inherently withstand perturbation better, which is consistent with our previous findings. Implementation of our experiment is available on our GitHub page[1].

5   Related Works

This work is closely related to research on Bayes errors and certified training. Computing the Bayes error of a given data distribution has been studied for over half a century [12]. Several works have derived upper and lower bounds of the Bayes error and proposed ways to estimate those bounds. Various f-divergences, such as the Bhattacharyya distance [13] or the Henze-Penrose divergence [7,43], have been studied. Other approaches include directly estimating the Bayes error with f-divergence representation instead of using a bound [36], and computing the Bayes error of generative models learned using normalizing flows [22,48]. More recently, a method has been proposed to evaluate Bayes error estimators on real-world datasets [41], for which we usually do not know the true Bayes error. While these existing studies concentrate on vanilla accuracy, our approach extends the study into the realm of robustness. Besides, some studies may argue that the real-world datasets are well-separated so therefore the Bayes error predicted by the theorems may not be as severe [62]. However, due to the information loss (photo-taking or compression), Bayes errors inevitably exist. For instance, Over 1/3 of CIFAR-10 inputs have been re-annotated by human annotators to have non-fixed labels (CIFAR-10H) [39], indicating non-zero uncertainty. Hence, calculating irreducible error, regardless of severity, holds significance in understanding the inherent limit of certified robustness.

Many certified training techniques have been developed to increase certified robust accuracy, including branch-and-bound [4,16,56], linear relaxation [2,32,46], Lipschitz or curvature verification [29,50], and others [27]. In addition, a number of training techniques have been proposed specifically for improving certified robustness [28], which include warm-up training [45], small boxes [35], and so on. Certified robust accuracy has seen only limited growth over the past decade, prompting research efforts to understand why. Besides the Bayes error perspective, there exists an explanation for this problem from the standpoint of the abstraction domain [33]. However, note that these studies often only focus on the concept of interval arithmetic. Additionally, factors such as the trade-off between certified robustness and vanilla accuracy have also been explored [37,51].

---

[1] https://github.com/cat-claws/irreducible-robustness-error.

6 Conclusion

In this work, we study the limit of classification robustness against perturbations. We are motivated by the observation that the robustness of existing certified classifiers tends to be suboptimal, and hypothesise that there is an irreducible robustness error linked to the classification distribution itself. We formally prove that this irreducible robustness error does exist and is greater than the Bayes error. Further, we present how to calculate the upper bound of robustness based on the data distribution and the vicinity within which we demand robustness. Besides, this work also provides empirical experiments that compute our upper bound on common machine learning data sets. Results show that our robustness upper bound is empirically effective. We conclude that the limit of classification robustness can be well elaborated from the Bayes error perspective and we hope that the upper bound we derive can enlighten future developments on certified training and other robust-classifier training.

Acknowledgements. We thank anonymous reviewers for their constructive feedback. This research is supported by the Ministry of Education, Singapore under its Academic Research Fund Tier 3 (Award ID: MOET32020-0004). Any opinions, findings and conclusions or recommendations expressed in this material are those of the author(s) and do not reflect the views of the Ministry of Education, Singapore.

Disclosure of Interests. The authors have no competing interests to declare that are relevant to the content of this article.

References

1. Antos, A., Devroye, L., Gyorfi, L.: Lower bounds for Bayes error estimation. IEEE Trans. Pattern Anal. Mach. Intell. **21**(7), 643–645 (1999). https://doi.org/10.1109/34.777375
2. Baader, M., Mueller, M.N., Mao, Y., Vechev, M.: Expressivity of reLU-networks under convex relaxations. In: The Twelfth International Conference on Learning Representations (2024). https://openreview.net/forum?id=awHTL3Hpto
3. Bai, T., Luo, J., Zhao, J., Wen, B., Wang, Q.: Recent advances in adversarial training for adversarial robustness. In: Zhou, Z.H. (ed.) Proceedings of the Thirtieth International Joint Conference on Artificial Intelligence, IJCAI-21. pp. 4312–4321. International Joint Conferences on Artificial Intelligence Organization (8 2021). https://doi.org/10.24963/ijcai.2021/591, https://doi.org/10.24963/ijcai.2021/591, survey Track
4. Bak, S., Tran, H.D., Hobbs, K., Johnson, T.T.: Improved geometric path enumeration for verifying Relu neural networks. In: Lahiri, S.K., Wang, C. (eds.) Computer Aided Verification, pp. 66–96. Springer International Publishing, Cham (2020)
5. Balagani, K.S., Phoha, V.V.: On the relationship between dependence tree classification error and Bayes error rate. IEEE Trans. Pattern Anal. Mach. Intell. **29**(10), 1866–1868 (2007). https://doi.org/10.1109/TPAMI.2007.1184
6. Balunovic, M., Vechev, M.T.: Adversarial training and provable defenses: bridging the gap. In: 8th International Conference on Learning Representations, ICLR 2020, Addis Ababa, Ethiopia, April 26-30, 2020. OpenReview.net (2020). https://openreview.net/forum?id=SJxSDxrKDr

7. Berisha, V., Wisler, A., Hero, A.O., Spanias, A.: Empirically estimable classification bounds based on a nonparametric divergence measure. IEEE Trans. Signal Process. **64**(3), 580–591 (2016). https://doi.org/10.1109/TSP.2015.2477805

8. Chen, Q., Cao, F., Xing, Y., Liang, J.: Evaluating classification model against Bayes error rate. IEEE Trans. Pattern Anal. Mach. Intell. **45**(8), 9639–9653 (2023). https://doi.org/10.1109/TPAMI.2023.3240194

9. Chiang, P., Ni, R., Abdelkader, A., Zhu, C., Studer, C., Goldstein, T.: Certified defenses for adversarial patches. In: 8th International Conference on Learning Representations, ICLR 2020, Addis Ababa, Ethiopia, April 26-30, 2020. OpenReview.net (2020). https://openreview.net/forum?id=HyeaSkrYPH

10. Cohen, J., Rosenfeld, E., Kolter, Z.: Certified adversarial robustness via randomized smoothing. In: Chaudhuri, K., Salakhutdinov, R. (eds.) Proceedings of the 36th International Conference on Machine Learning. Proceedings of Machine Learning Research, vol. 97, pp. 1310–1320. PMLR, PMLR (09–15 Jun 2019). https://proceedings.mlr.press/v97/cohen19c.html

11. Dučinskas, K., Zikarienundefined, E.: Actual error rates in classification of the t-distributed random field observation based on plug-in linear discriminant function. Informatica **26**(4), 557–568 (Jan 2015)

12. Fukunaga, K., Hostetler, L.: k-nearest-neighbor Bayes-risk estimation. IEEE Trans. Inf. Theory **21**(3), 285–293 (1975). https://doi.org/10.1109/TIT.1975.1055373

13. Fukunaga, K.: Introduction to Statistical Pattern Recognition, 2nd edn. Academic Press Professional Inc, USA (1990)

14. Ganin, Y., et al.: Domain-adversarial training of neural networks. J. Mach. Learn. Res. **17**(59), 1–35 (2016). http://jmlr.org/papers/v17/15-239.html

15. Garber, F., Djouadi, A.: Bounds on the Bayes classification error based on pairwise risk functions. IEEE Trans. Pattern Anal. Mach. Intell. **10**(2), 281–288 (1988). https://doi.org/10.1109/34.3891

16. Gehr, T., Mirman, M., Drachsler-Cohen, D., Tsankov, P., Chaudhuri, S., Vechev, M.: Ai2: Safety and robustness certification of neural networks with abstract interpretation. In: 2018 IEEE Symposium on Security and Privacy (SP), pp. 3–18 (2018). https://doi.org/10.1109/SP.2018.00058

17. Goodfellow, I.J., Shlens, J., Szegedy, C.: Explaining and harnessing adversarial examples. In: Bengio, Y., LeCun, Y. (eds.) 3rd International Conference on Learning Representations, ICLR 2015, San Diego, CA, USA, May 7–9, 2015, Conference Track Proceedings (2015). http://arxiv.org/abs/1412.6572

18. Hastie, T., Tibshirani, R., Friedman, J.: The Elements of Statistical Learning. Springer, 2 edn. (2009). https://hastie.su.domains/Papers/ESLII.pdf

19. Hummels, D.M.: Nonparametric estimation of the Bayes error. Ph.D. thesis, Purdue University (1987). https://docs.lib.purdue.edu/dissertations/AAI8814491/

20. Ishida, T., Yamane, I., Charoenphakdee, N., Niu, G., Sugiyama, M.: Is the performance of my deep network too good to be true? a direct approach to estimating the Bayes error in binary classification. In: The Eleventh International Conference on Learning Representations (2023). https://openreview.net/forum?id=FZdJQgy05rz

21. Kang, H.J., Doermann, D.: Product approximation by minimizing the upper bound of Bayes error rate for Bayesian combination of classifiers. In: Proceedings of the 17th International Conference on Pattern Recognition, 2004. ICPR 2004, vol. 1, pp. 252–255 Vol.1 (2004). https://doi.org/10.1109/ICPR.2004.1334071

22. Kingma, D.P., Dhariwal, P.: Glow: Generative flow with invertible 1x1 convolutions. In: Bengio, S., Wallach, H., Larochelle, H., Grauman, K., Cesa-Bianchi, N., Garnett, R. (eds.) Advances in Neural Information Processing Systems. vol. 31. Curran Associates, Inc. (2018). https://proceedings.neurips.cc/paper_files/paper/2018/file/d139db6a236200b21cc7f752979132d0-Paper.pdf

23. Krizhevsky, A., Hinton, G., et al.: Learning multiple layers of features from tiny images (2009)
24. Kurakin, A., Goodfellow, I.J., Bengio, S.: Adversarial examples in the physical world. In: 5th International Conference on Learning Representations, ICLR 2017, Toulon, France, April 24–26, 2017, Workshop Track Proceedings. OpenReview.net (2017). https://openreview.net/forum?id=HJGU3Rodl
25. Kurakin, A., Goodfellow, I.J., Bengio, S.: Adversarial machine learning at scale. In: 5th International Conference on Learning Representations, ICLR 2017, Toulon, France, April 24–26, 2017, Conference Track Proceedings. OpenReview.net (2017). https://openreview.net/forum?id=BJm4T4Kgx
26. LeCun, Y., Cortes, C., Burges, C.: http://yann.lecun.com/exdb/mnist/
27. Lecuyer, M., Atlidakis, V., Geambasu, R., Hsu, D., Jana, S.: Certified robustness to adversarial examples with differential privacy. In: 2019 IEEE Symposium on Security and Privacy (SP), pp. 656–672. IEEE (2019)
28. Li, L., Xie, T., Li, B.: Sok: Certified robustness for deep neural networks. In: 44th IEEE Symposium on Security and Privacy, SP 2023, San Francisco, CA, USA, 22-26 May 2023. IEEE (2023). https://arxiv.org/abs/2009.04131
29. Li, Q., Haque, S., Anil, C., Lucas, J., Grosse, R.B., Jacobsen, J.H.: Preventing gradient attenuation in lipschitz constrained convolutional networks. In: Wallach, H., Larochelle, H., Beygelzimer, A., d'Alché-Buc, F., Fox, E., Garnett, R. (eds.) Advances in Neural Information Processing Systems. vol. 32. Curran Associates, Inc. (2019). https://proceedings.neurips.cc/paper_files/paper/2019/file/1ce3e6e3f452828e23a0c94572bef9d9-Paper.pdf
30. Lin, W., et al.: Robustness verification of classification deep neural networks via linear programming. In: Proceedings of the IEEE/CVF Conference on Computer Vision and Pattern Recognition (CVPR), pp. 11418–11427 (June 2019)
31. Liu, H., Zhu, X., Lei, Z., Li, S.Z.: Adaptiveface: adaptive margin and sampling for face recognition. In: Proceedings of the IEEE/CVF Conference on Computer Vision and Pattern Recognition (CVPR) (June 2019)
32. Lyu, Z., Guo, M., Wu, T., Xu, G., Zhang, K., Lin, D.: Towards evaluating and training verifiably robust neural networks. In: Proceedings of the IEEE/CVF Conference on Computer Vision and Pattern Recognition (CVPR), pp. 4308–4317 (June 2021)
33. Mirman, M., Baader, M., Vechev, M.T.: The fundamental limits of interval arithmetic for neural networks. CoRR **abs/2112.05235** (2021). https://arxiv.org/abs/2112.05235
34. Mohri, M., Rostamizadeh, A., Talwalkar, A.: Foundations of Machine Learning. The MIT Press (2012)
35. Müller, M.N., Eckert, F., Fischer, M., Vechev, M.T.: Certified training: small boxes are all you need. CoRR **abs/2210.04871** (2022). https://doi.org/10.48550/arXiv.2210.04871, https://doi.org/10.48550/arXiv.2210.04871
36. Noshad, M., Xu, L., Hero, A.: Learning to benchmark: Determining best achievable misclassification error from training data. arXiv preprint arXiv:1909.07192 (2019)
37. Pang, T., Lin, M., Yang, X., Zhu, J., Yan, S.: Robustness and accuracy could be reconcilable by (proper) definition. In: Chaudhuri, K., Jegelka, S., Song, L., Szepesvári, C., Niu, G., Sabato, S. (eds.) International Conference on Machine Learning, ICML 2022, 17–23 July 2022, Baltimore, Maryland, USA. Proceedings of Machine Learning Research, vol. 162, pp. 17258–17277. PMLR (2022). https://proceedings.mlr.press/v162/pang22a.html
38. Papernot, N., McDaniel, P.D., Goodfellow, I.J.: Transferability in machine learning: from phenomena to black-box attacks using adversarial samples. CoRR **abs/1605.07277** (2016). http://arxiv.org/abs/1605.07277
39. Peterson, J.C., Battleday, R.M., Griffiths, T.L., Russakovsky, O.: Human uncertainty makes classification more robust. In: Proceedings of the IEEE/CVF International Conference on Computer Vision (ICCV) (October 2019)

40. Raghunathan, A., Steinhardt, J., Liang, P.: Certified defenses against adversarial examples. In: 6th International Conference on Learning Representations, ICLR 2018, Vancouver, BC, Canada, April 30 - May 3, 2018, Conference Track Proceedings. OpenReview.net (2018). https://openreview.net/forum?id=Bys4ob-Rb
41. Renggli, C., Rimanic, L., Hollenstein, N., Zhang, C.: Evaluating bayes error estimators on real-world datasets with feebee. In: Vanschoren, J., Yeung, S. (eds.) Proceedings of the Neural Information Processing Systems Track on Datasets and Benchmarks 1, NeurIPS Datasets and Benchmarks 2021, December 2021, virtual (2021). https://datasets-benchmarks-proceedings.neurips.cc/paper/2021/hash/045117b0e0a11a242b9765e79cbf113f-Abstract-round2.html
42. Ripley, B.D.: Pattern recognition and neural networks. Cambridge Univ. Press (1996). https://doi.org/10.1017/CBO9780511812651
43. Sekeh, S.Y., Oselio, B., Hero, A.O.: Learning to bound the multi-class Bayes error. IEEE Trans. Signal Process. **68**, 3793–3807 (2020). https://doi.org/10.1109/TSP.2020.2994807
44. Sharif, M., Bhagavatula, S., Bauer, L., Reiter, M.K.: Accessorize to a crime: Real and stealthy attacks on state-of-the-art face recognition. In: Proceedings of the 2016 ACM SIGSAC Conference on Computer and Communications Security, pp. 1528–1540. CCS '16, Association for Computing Machinery, New York, NY, USA (2016). https://doi.org/10.1145/2976749.2978392
45. Shi, Z., Wang, Y., Zhang, H., Yi, J., Hsieh, C.J.: Fast certified robust training with short warmup. In: Ranzato, M., Beygelzimer, A., Dauphin, Y., Liang, P., Vaughan, J.W. (eds.) Advances in Neural Information Processing Systems. vol. 34, pp. 18335–18349. Curran Associates, Inc. (2021). https://proceedings.neurips.cc/paper/2021/file/988f9153ac4fd966ea302dd9ab9bae15-Paper.pdf
46. Singh, G., Gehr, T., Püschel, M., Vechev, M.: An abstract domain for certifying neural networks. Proc. ACM Program. Lang. **3**(POPL) (Jan 2019). https://doi.org/10.1145/3290354
47. Szegedy, C., et al.: Intriguing properties of neural networks. In: Bengio, Y., LeCun, Y. (eds.) 2nd International Conference on Learning Representations, ICLR 2014, Banff, AB, Canada, April 14–16, 2014, Conference Track Proceedings (2014). http://arxiv.org/abs/1312.6199
48. Theisen, R., Wang, H., Varshney, L.R., Xiong, C., Socher, R.: Evaluating state-of-the-art classification models against bayes optimality. In: Ranzato, M., Beygelzimer, A., Dauphin, Y., Liang, P., Vaughan, J.W. (eds.) Advances in Neural Information Processing Systems. vol. 34, pp. 9367–9377. Curran Associates, Inc. (2021). https://proceedings.neurips.cc/paper_files/paper/2021/file/4e0ccd2b894f717df5ebc12f4282ee70-Paper.pdf
49. Tramer, F., Carlini, N., Brendel, W., Madry, A.: On adaptive attacks to adversarial example defenses. In: Larochelle, H., Ranzato, M., Hadsell, R., Balcan, M., Lin, H. (eds.) Advances in Neural Information Processing Systems. vol. 33, pp. 1633–1645. Curran Associates, Inc. (2020). https://proceedings.neurips.cc/paper_files/paper/2020/file/11f38f8ecd71867b42433548d1078e38-Paper.pdf
50. Trockman, A., Kolter, J.Z.: Orthogonalizing convolutional layers with the cayley transform. In: International Conference on Learning Representations (2021). https://openreview.net/forum?id=Pbj8H_jEHYv
51. Tsipras, D., Santurkar, S., Engstrom, L., Turner, A., Madry, A.: Robustness may be at odds with accuracy. In: 7th International Conference on Learning Representations, ICLR 2019, New Orleans, LA, USA, May 6–9, 2019. OpenReview.net (2019). https://openreview.net/forum?id=SyxAb30cY7
52. Tumer, K., Ghosh, J.: Estimating the Bayes error rate through classifier combining. In: Proceedings of 13th International Conference on Pattern Recognition, vol. 2, pp. 695–699 (1996). https://doi.org/10.1109/ICPR.1996.546912
53. Vaishnavi, P., Eykholt, K., Rahmati, A.: Accelerating certified robustness training via knowledge transfer. CoRR **abs/2210.14283** (2022). https://doi.org/10.48550/arXiv.2210.14283

54. Vapnik, V.N.: The Nature of Statistical Learning Theory. Springer New York, New York, NY (2000). https://doi.org/10.1007/978-1-4757-3264-1
55. Wang, C., Zhang, D., Huang, S., Li, X., Ding, L.: Crafting adversarial email content against machine learning based spam email detection. In: Proceedings of the 2021 International Symposium on Advanced Security on Software and Systems, pp. 23–28. ASSS '21, Association for Computing Machinery, New York, NY, USA (2021). https://doi.org/10.1145/3457340.3458302
56. Wang, S., Pei, K., Whitehouse, J., Yang, J., Jana, S.: Formal security analysis of neural networks using symbolic intervals. In: 27th USENIX Security Symposium (USENIX Security 18), pp. 1599–1614. USENIX Association, Baltimore, MD (Aug 2018). https://www.usenix.org/conference/usenixsecurity18/presentation/wang-shiqi
57. Weng, T., et al.: Evaluating the robustness of neural networks: an extreme value theory approach. In: 6th International Conference on Learning Representations, ICLR 2018, Vancouver, BC, Canada, April 30 - May 3, 2018, Conference Track Proceedings. OpenReview.net (2018). https://openreview.net/forum?id=BkUHlMZ0b
58. Wong, E., Rice, L., Kolter, J.Z.: Fast is better than free: revisiting adversarial training. In: 8th International Conference on Learning Representations, ICLR 2020, Addis Ababa, Ethiopia, April 26–30, 2020. OpenReview.net (2020). https://openreview.net/forum?id=BJx040EFvH
59. Xiao, H., Rasul, K., Vollgraf, R.: Fashion-mnist: a novel image dataset for benchmarking machine learning algorithms. CoRR **abs/1708.07747** (2017). http://arxiv.org/abs/1708.07747
60. Xu, K., et al.: Automatic perturbation analysis for scalable certified robustness and beyond. In: Larochelle, H., Ranzato, M., Hadsell, R., Balcan, M., Lin, H. (eds.) Advances in Neural Information Processing Systems. vol. 33, pp. 1129–1141. Curran Associates, Inc. (2020). https://proceedings.neurips.cc/paper/2020/file/0cbc5671ae26f67871cb914d81ef8fc1-Paper.pdf
61. Yang, S.H., Hu, B.-G.: Discriminative feature selection by nonparametric Bayes error minimization. IEEE Trans. Knowl. Data Eng. **24**(8), 1422–1434 (2012). https://doi.org/10.1109/TKDE.2011.92
62. Yang, Y.Y., Rashtchian, C., Zhang, H., Salakhutdinov, R.R., Chaudhuri, K.: A closer look at accuracy vs. robustness. Adv. Neural Inform. Process. Syst. **33**, 8588–8601 (2020)
63. Zhang, H., Chen, H., Song, Z., Boning, D.S., Dhillon, I.S., Hsieh, C.: The limitations of adversarial training and the blind-spot attack. In: 7th International Conference on Learning Representations, ICLR 2019, New Orleans, LA, USA, May 6–9, 2019. OpenReview.net (2019). https://openreview.net/forum?id=HylTBhA5tQ
64. Zhang, H., Weng, T.W., Chen, P.Y., Hsieh, C.J., Daniel, L.: Efficient neural network robustness certification with general activation functions. In: Proceedings of the 32nd International Conference on Neural Information Processing Systems. NIPS'18, vol. 31, p. 4944-4953. Curran Associates Inc., Red Hook, NY, USA (2018)
65. Zhang, J.G., Deng, H.W.: Gene selection for classification of microarray data based on the bayes error. BMC Bioinform. **8**(1), 370 (Oct 2007). https://doi.org/10.1186/1471-2105-8-370
66. Zhang, T.: Statistical behavior and consistency of classification methods based on convex risk minimization. Ann. Stat. **32**(1), 56–85 (2004). https://doi.org/10.1214/aos/1079120130
67. Zhao, M.J., Edakunni, N., Pocock, A., Brown, G.: Beyond Fano's inequality: bounds on the optimal f-score, ber, and cost-sensitive risk and their implications. J. Mach. Learn. Res. **14**(32), 1033–1090 (2013). http://jmlr.org/papers/v14/zhao13a.html

Boosting Few-Pixel Robustness Verification via Covering Verification Designs

Yuval Shapira$^{(\boxtimes)}$, Naor Wiesel, Shahar Shabelman, and Dana Drachsler-Cohen

Technion, Haifa, Israel
{shapirayuval,wieselnaor,shabelman}@campus.technion.ac.il,
ddana@ee.technion.ac.il

Abstract. Proving local robustness is crucial to increase the reliability of neural networks. While many verifiers prove robustness in L_∞ ϵ-balls, very little work deals with robustness verification in L_0 ϵ-balls, capturing robustness to few pixel attacks. This verification introduces a combinatorial challenge, because the space of pixels to perturb is discrete and of exponential size. A previous work relies on covering designs to identify sets for defining L_∞ neighborhoods, which if proven robust imply that the L_0 ϵ-ball is robust. However, the number of neighborhoods to verify remains very high, leading to a high analysis time. We propose *covering verification designs*, a combinatorial design that tailors effective but analysis-incompatible coverings to L_0 robustness verification. The challenge is that computing a covering verification design introduces a high time and memory overhead, which is intensified in our setting, where multiple candidate coverings are required to identify how to reduce the overall analysis time. We introduce CoVerD, an L_0 robustness verifier that selects between different candidate coverings *without constructing them*, but by predicting their block size distribution. This prediction relies on a theorem providing closed-form expressions for the mean and variance of this distribution. CoVerD constructs the chosen covering verification design *on-the-fly*, while keeping the memory consumption minimal and enabling to parallelize the analysis. The experimental results show that CoVerD reduces the verification time on average by up to 5.1x compared to prior work and that it scales to larger L_0 ϵ-balls.

1 Introduction

Neural networks are very successful in various applications, most notably in image recognition tasks [14]. However, neural networks are also vulnerable to adversarial example attacks [17,33]. In an adversarial example attack, an attacker slightly perturbs the input to mislead the network. Many attack models and different kinds of perturbations have been considered for neural networks implementing image classifiers [15,26,33]. The most commonly studied perturbations are L_p perturbations, where p is 0 [9,40], 1 [10], 2 [4,33] or ∞ [4,15]. For L_p perturbations, the attacker is given a small budget ϵ and the goal is to find a perturbed input in the L_p ϵ-ball that causes misclassification.

© The Author(s) 2024
A. Gurfinkel and V. Ganesh (Eds.): CAV 2024, LNCS 14682, pp. 377–400, 2024.
https://doi.org/10.1007/978-3-031-65630-9_19

In response to adversarial attacks, many verifiers have been proposed to reason about the robustness of neural networks in a given neighborhood of inputs. Most deterministic robustness verifiers analyze robustness in L_∞ ϵ-balls [2,13, 21,25,32,34], while some deterministic verifiers analyze L_2 ϵ-balls [19,22] or L_1 ϵ-balls [38,41]. Probabilistic verifiers, often leveraging randomized smoothing [6], have been proposed for analyzing L_p ϵ-balls for $p \in \{0,1,2,\infty\}$ [11,23,28,39]. Other verifiers analyze neighborhoods defined by semantic or geometric features (e.g., brightness or rotation) [3,20,24]. An existing gap is deterministically verifying robustness in L_0 ϵ-balls, for a small ϵ, also known as robustness to few pixel attacks. In L_0 ϵ-balls, ϵ is the number of pixels that can be perturbed. Since ϵ is an integer (as opposed to a real number), we denote it as t. L_0 t-balls consist of *discrete perturbations*, unlike many other attack models whose perturbations are continuous. Thus, their analysis is a challenging combinatorial problem. Theoretically, robustness verification of an L_0 t-ball can be reduced into a set of robustness verification tasks over L_∞ neighborhoods, each allows a specific set of t pixels to be perturbed. However, this approach is infeasible in practice for $t > 2$, since the number of the L_∞ neighborhoods that need to be proven robust is $\binom{v}{t}$, where v is the number of pixels. To illustrate, for MNIST images, where $v = 784$, the number of neighborhoods is $1.6 \cdot 10^{10}$ for $t = 4$, $2.4 \cdot 10^{12}$ for $t = 5$, and $3.2 \cdot 10^{14}$ for $t = 6$. That is, every *minimal* increase of t (by one) increases the neighborhood size by *two orders of magnitude*.

A recent work proposes a deterministic L_0 robustness verifier for few pixel attacks, called Calzone [30]. Calzone builds on two main observations. First, if a network is robust to perturbations of a *specific* set of k pixels, then it is also robust to perturbations of any subsumed set of these pixels. Second, often L_∞ robustness verifiers can analyze robustness to arbitrary perturbations of k *specific* pixels, for values of k that are significantly larger than t. They thus reduce the problem of verifying robustness in an L_0 t-ball to proving robustness in a set of L_∞ neighborhoods defined by a set of k-sized pixel sets, subsuming all possible sets of t pixels. To compute the k-sized pixel sets, they rely on *covering designs* [16,35]. Given parameters (v, k, t), a covering is a set of k-sized sets that cover all subsets of size t of a set $[v] = \{1, \ldots, v\}$ (e.g., the pixel set). Covering designs is a field in combinatorics providing construction techniques to compute coverings. The challenge is to compute a covering of minimal size. While many covering constructions have been proposed, computing an optimal covering is an open combinatorial problem for most values of v, k and t. Further, most best-known coverings for $t > 3$ are far from the best general lower bound, known as the Schönheim bound [29]. This severely impacts the analysis time of Calzone. In practice, Calzone often does not complete within the five hour timeout when analyzing L_0 5-balls. To scale, it is crucial to lower the number of analyzed sets. While there are effective covering constructions renowned for the small coverings they compute, they are limited to specific values of v and k, which are incompatible for the analysis of L_0 robustness. Since Calzone treats covering constructions as black-box, it is limited to rely on analysis-compatible coverings and cannot benefit from these effective constructions.

To boost the robustness verification of few pixel attacks, we propose a new covering type, called a *covering verification design* (CVD), tailoring covering designs for L_0 robustness verification. CVD relies on a highly effective construction to obtain an analysis-incompatible covering and *partially induces* it to an analysis-compatible covering, where sets can have different sizes. Although the exact sets and their sizes depend on a random choice, we prove that the mean and variance of the set sizes are independent of this choice and have closed-form expressions. Partially inducing this effective construction has been proposed before [27], however it has been proposed for another combinatorial design, requiring a bound on the maximal set size in the covering, unlike CVD. We demonstrate that the sizes of CVDs are *lower* by 8% for $t = 4$ and by 15% for $t = 5$ than the respective Schönheim lower bound. This improvement, enabled by considering a new type of coverings, is remarkable for scaling L_0 robustness analysis. To date, for analysis-compatible values of v and k and for $t \geq 3$, it is impossible to obtain an optimal covering design, and even if we obtained it, its size is *at least* the Schönheim bound. In particular, Calzone's considered coverings are larger by 4x than the Schönheim lower bound for $t = 4$ and by 8.4x for $t = 5$. While promising, CVDs raise a practical challenge: their construction as well as their final size introduce a high memory overhead. Further, to minimize the analysis time, the verifier chooses between *multiple* coverings. However, the total memory overhead makes it infeasible to store these coverings in a covering database without limiting their size (like Calzone does).

We introduce CoVerD, an L_0 robustness verifier, boosting Calzone's performance by leveraging CVDs. CoVerD has two main components, *planning* and *analysis*. The planning component predicts the CVD that will allow it to minimize the overall analysis time. To reduce the memory overhead, it predicts the best CVD out of many candidates, *without constructing the candidates*. This prediction relies on estimating the set size distribution of a candidate covering, using our expressions for the mean and variance. The analysis component constructs the chosen CVD. The challenge is that the original covering that is being induced may be too large to fit the memory. To cope, CoVerD induces the covering while constructing the original covering. Further, it constructs *on-the-fly* a partitioning of the CVD so that the analysis can be parallelized over multiple GPUs. Another advantage of the on-the-fly construction is that CoVerD does not need to prepare coverings for every image dimension in advance. This both saves memory consumption and makes CoVerD suitable for *any* image classifier, without requiring to precompute coverings for new image dimensions, as Calzone requires.

We evaluate CoVerD on convolutional and fully-connected networks, trained for MNIST, Fashion-MNIST, and CIFAR-10. CoVerD is faster than Calzone in verifying robust t-balls on average by 2.8x for $t = 4$ and by 5.1x for $t = 5$. Further, CoVerD scales to more challenging t-balls than Calzone. In particular, it verifies some 6-balls, which Calzone does not consider at all, within 42 minutes.

2 Background

In this section, we define the problem of verifying robustness of an image classifier in an L_0 t-ball and provide background on Calzone [30].

L_0 Robustness Verification. We address the problem of determining the local robustness of an image classifier in an L_0 t-ball of an image x. An image classifier N takes as input an image x consisting of v pixels, each ranges over $[0, 1]$ (all definitions extend to colored images, but omitted for simplicity's sake). It returns a vector consisting of a score for every possible class. The classification the classifier N assigns to an input image x is the class with the maximal score: $c_x = \texttt{argmax}(N(x))$. We focus on classifiers implemented by neural networks. Specifically, our focus is on fully-connected and convolutional networks, since many L_∞ robustness verifiers can analyze them [2,13,21,25,32,34]. However, like Calzone, CoVerD is not coupled to the underlying implementation of the classifier and can reason about any classifier for which there are L_∞ robustness verifiers that it can rely on. The problem we study is determining whether a classifier N is locally robust in the L_0 t-ball of an input x, for $t \geq 2$. That is, whether every input whose L_0 distance from x is at most t is classified by N as x is classified. Formally, the t-ball of x is $B_t(x) = \{x' \mid ||x' - x||_0 \leq t\}$ and N is locally robust in $B_t(x)$ if $\forall x' \in B_t(x).\ \texttt{argmax}(N(x')) = \texttt{argmax}(N(x))$. We note that the L_0 distance of two images is the number of pixels that the images differ, that is $||x' - x||_0 = |\{i \in [v] \mid x_i \neq x_i'\}|$ (where $[v] = \{1, \ldots, v\}$). In other words, an L_0 perturbation to an image x can arbitrarily perturb up to t pixels in x.

Calzone. Calzone, depicted in Fig. 1, is an L_0 robustness verifier. It verifies by determining the robustness of a classifier N in all neighborhoods in which a specific set of pixels S is arbitrarily perturbed, for every $S \subseteq [v]$ of size t. Namely, to prove robustness, it has to determine for every such S whether N classifies the same all inputs in the neighborhood consisting of all images that are identical to x in all pixels, but the pixels in S. We denote this neighborhood by $I_S(x) = \{x' \in [0,1]^v \mid \forall i \notin S.\ x_i' = x_i\}$. Such neighborhoods can be specified as a sequence of intervals, one for every pixel, where the ith interval is $[0, 1]$ if $i \in S$ (i.e., it can be perturbed) or $[x_i, x_i]$ if $i \notin S$ (i.e., it cannot be perturbed). Most existing L_∞ robustness verifiers can determine the robustness of such interval neighborhoods. However, verifying $\binom{v}{t}$ interval neighborhoods, one for every selection of t pixels to perturb, is practically infeasible for $t > 2$. Instead, Calzone builds on the following observation: if N is locally robust in a neighborhood $I_{S'}(x)$ for $S' \subseteq [v]$ of size $k > t$, then N is also robust in every $I_S(x)$, for $S \subseteq S'$ of size t. This observation allows Calzone to leverage *covering designs* to reduce the number of neighborhoods analyzed by an L_∞ verifier. Given three numbers (v, k, t), for $t \leq k \leq v$, a covering $C(v, k, t)$ is a set of *blocks*, where (1) each block is subset of size k of $[v]$ and (2) the blocks cover all subsets of $[v]$ of size t: for every $S \subseteq [v]$ of size t, there is a block $B \in C(v, k, t)$ such that $S \subseteq B$. Coverings are evaluated by their size, $|C(v, k, t)|$, where the smaller the better. We next describe the components of Calzone: analysis, planning and covering database.

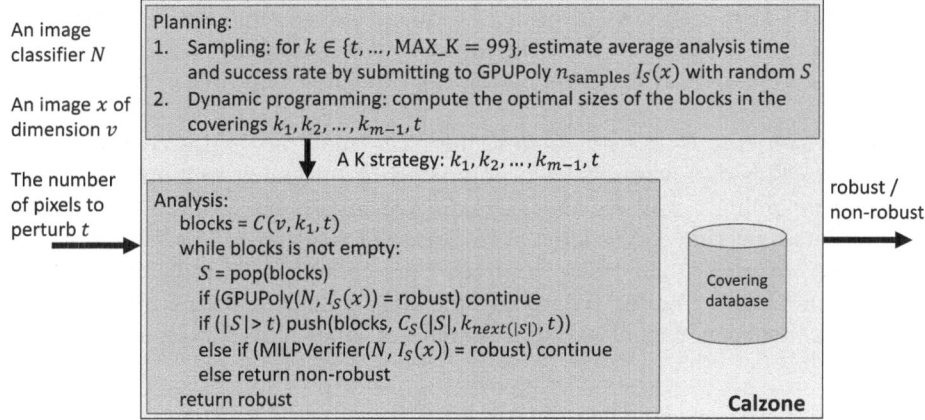

Fig. 1. The Calzone L_0 robustness verifier.

Calzone's Analysis. Calzone begins the analysis by obtaining a covering $C(v, k_1, t)$ from its covering database, where k_1 is determined by the planning component (described shortly). It pushes all blocks in the covering into a stack. It then iteratively pops a block S from the stack and verifies the robustness of N in $I_S(x)$ by running GPUPoly [25]. GPUPoly is a sound L_∞ robustness verifier which is highly scalable because it performs the analysis on a GPU. However, it relies on a linear relaxation and thus may fail proving robustness due to over-approximation errors. If it determines that $I_S(x)$ is robust, Calzone continues to the next block. Otherwise, Calzone performs an exact analysis or refines the block. If $|S| = t$, Calzone invokes a sound and complete mixed-integer linear programming (MILP) verifier [34]. If it determines that $I_S(x)$ is not robust, Calzone returns *non-robust*, otherwise Calzone continues to the next block. If $|S|$ is greater than t, Calzone refines S by pushing to the stack all blocks in a covering for S and t. The blocks' size is k_{i+1}, which is the block size following the current block size $k_i = |S|$, as determined by the planning component. The covering is obtained by retrieving from the covering database the covering $C(|S|, k_{i+1}, t)$ and renaming the numbers in the blocks to range over the numbers in S (instead of $[|S|]$), denoted as $C_S(|S|, k_{i+1}, t)$. If Calzone observes an empty stack, it returns *robust*. This analysis is proven sound and complete. To scale, Calzone parallelizes the analysis over multiple GPUs (for GPUPoly) and CPUs (for the MILP verifier). Technically, the first covering is split between the GPUs, each independently analyzes its assigned blocks and refines if needed.

Calzone's Planning. The planning determines the block sizes of the first covering and of the refinements' coverings. These are given as a K *strategy*, a decreasing series $k_1 > \ldots > k_m$, where $k_1 \leq \text{MAX\_K} = 99$ and $k_m = t$. Calzone predicts the K strategy that minimizes the overall analysis time using dynamic programming, defined over the analysis time of the first covering, the average fraction of blocks that will be refined, and the analysis time of the refined blocks. This computation requires GPUPoly's success rate and average analysis time for neighborhoods $I_S(x)$, for all $|S| \leq$ MAX_K. These are estimated by sampling $n_{\text{samples}} = 400$ sets S for every $k \leq$ MAX_K and submitting their neighborhood $I_S(x)$ to GPUPoly.

Calzone's Covering Database. As described, the analysis obtains coverings from a database. This database has been populated by obtaining well-optimized coverings from online resources and extending them for large values of v and k using general covering constructions. Because of these general constructions, the database's coverings tend to be far from the Schönheim bound [29], the best-known general lower bound, especially for large values of v (the image dimension). This inefficiency results in longer analysis, since more blocks are analyzed.

3   Our Approach: Covering Verification Designs

To scale Calzone's analysis, it is crucial to reduce the number of blocks that are analyzed by GPUPoly or the MILP verifier. A dominant contributor to this number is the size of the first covering, for two reasons. First, the first covering is over a large v (the image dimension), thus its size is significantly larger than the sizes of coverings added upon refinement, which are over significantly smaller v (typically $v \leq 80$ and at most $v \leq$ MAX_K). Second, the first covering has an accumulative effect on the number of refinements, and consequently it dominates the analysis time. Reducing this size is theoretically possible by relying on *finite geometry covering constructions* [1,16,27], which are renowned for computing very small coverings. However, finite geometry coverings are limited to (v, k, t) triples in which v and k are defined by related mathematical expressions over t. In Calzone's analysis, the first covering has to be defined over a given v (the image dimension) and t (the number of perturbed pixels). Thus, for some values of v and t, there is no finite geometry covering. For the other values, there are very few values for k, leading to long analysis either because they are large and have a low success rate, triggering many refinements, or small and have very large coverings. We propose to tailor *induced coverings* for L_0 robustness analysis in order to leverage finite geometry coverings. To this end, we introduce a new type of a covering design, called a *covering verification design* (CVD). We next provide background on finite geometry coverings and induced coverings. We then define *partially-induced coverings* and our new covering type. We discuss its properties, its effectiveness, and the practical challenges in integrating it to L_0 verification.

Finite Geometry Coverings. Finite geometry covering constructions are widely known for obtaining small (sometimes optimal) coverings [1,16,27]. Popular finite geometry constructions rely on projective geometry (PG) or affine geometry (AG). We focus on PG, but our approach extends to AG. A PG construction views the problem of constructing a covering for a given (v, k, t) from a finite geometry point of view, where v is the

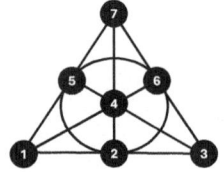

Fig. 2. The Fano Plane.

number of points in the geometry. It constructs coverings by computing flats (linear subspaces) of dimension $t - 1$, each containing k points. Since every t points from $[v]$ are contained in at least one flat [27], the flats provide a covering. Figure 2 shows *the Fano plane*, a well-known example. In this example, there are $v = 7$ points, the flats are of dimension $t - 1 = 1$ (the lines and the circle), each containing $k = 3$ points. The set of flats forms a covering, where each flat is a block: $C(7, 3, 2) = \{\{1, 2, 3\}, \{1, 4, 6\}, \{1, 5, 7\}, \{2, 4, 7\}, \{2, 5, 6\}, \{3, 4, 5\}, \{3, 6, 7\}\}$. PG coverings exist for triples where $v = \frac{q^{m+1}-1}{q-1}$ and $k = \frac{q^t-1}{q-1}$, for a prime power q and $m \geq t \geq 2$ (it also exists for $m = t - 1$, but then $v = k$, which is unhelpful to our analysis). Because PG is restricted to such triples, Calzone cannot effectively leverage it for the first covering, whose v and t are given. This is because for common image dimensions (e.g., $v = 784$ for MNIST and $v = 1024$ for CIFAR-10), there are no suitable q and m. Even if there are suitable q and m, there are very few possible k values, which are unlikely to include or be close to an optimal value of k. Thus, either they are smaller than an optimal k, leading to larger coverings and a longer analysis time, or that they are larger than an optimal k and have a lower success rate, leading to many refinements, resulting, again, in a longer analysis time. For example, for $v = 364$ and $t = 5$, the only suitable values are $q = 3$ and $m = 5$ (i.e., $364 = (3^{5+1} - 1)/(3 - 1)$), namely there is only one triple for these values of v and t. In this triple, $k = (3^5 - 1)/(3 - 1) = 121$. Since $k \approx \frac{v}{3}$, neighborhoods $I_S(x)$ for which $|S| = 121$ are not likely to be robust, thus such k is likely to have a low success rate. *Induced coverings* [16] enable to leverage finite geometry coverings for other (v, k, t) triples, as next explained.

Induced Coverings. Given $v \leq v'$ and $k \leq k'$, a covering $C(v', k', t)$ can be *induced* to form a covering $C(v, k, t)$ [16]. The induced covering is obtained in three steps. First, we select a subset of numbers of size v, denoted $L \subseteq [v']$, and remove every $l \in [v'] \setminus L$ from every block in $C(v', k', t')$. This results in a set of blocks of different sizes that covers all subsets of L of size t [27, Lemma 1]. This follows since every subset $S \subseteq L$ of size t is a subset of $[v']$ and thus there is $B \in C(v', k', t)$ such that $S \subseteq B$. The first step removes from B only numbers from $[v'] \setminus L$ and thus S is contained in the respective block to B after this step. The next two steps fix blocks whose size is not k. The second step extends every block whose size is smaller than k with numbers from L. The third step refines every block whose size is larger than k to multiple blocks of size k that cover all of its subsets of size t. This step significantly increases the number of blocks, unless the number of blocks larger than k is negligible. We note that these steps provide a covering over the numbers in L (i.e., $C_L(|L|, k, t)$). A covering for $(|L|, k, t)$ can be obtained by renaming the numbers to range over $[|L|]$.

Partially-induced Covering. Our new covering design is an instance of a *partially-induced covering*. A partially-induced covering is the set of blocks obtained by the first step, where the blocks cover all subsets of L of size t and are of different sizes. For example, for the Fano plane and $L_1 = \{4, 5, 6, 7\}$, the partially-induced covering is: $C_1 = \{\{\}, \{4, 6\}, \{5, 7\}, \{4, 7\}, \{5, 6\}, \{4, 5\}, \{6, 7\}\}$, while for $L_2 = \{1, 2, 3, 4\}$, it is: $C_2 = \{\{1, 2, 3\}, \{1, 4\}, \{1\}, \{2, 4\}, \{2\}, \{3, 4\}, \{3\}\}$. Partially-induced coverings have two benefits in our setting: (1) by not extending blocks whose size is smaller than k, we increase the likelihood that GPUPoly will prove their robustness, and (2) by not refining blocks whose size is larger than k, we (a) preserve the number of blocks as in the original covering, (b) provide GPUPoly an opportunity to verify these blocks, and (c) rely on the optimal refinement sizes (computed by the dynamic programming) for blocks that GPUPoly fails proving robustness. Our covering design partially induces PG coverings, to obtain additional benefits for L_0 robustness verification.

Covering Verification Designs. Given the number of pixels v and the number of pixels to perturb t, a covering verification design (CVD) is the set of blocks obtained by partially inducing a PG covering $C(v', k', t)$, where $v \leq v'$, using a random set of numbers $L \subseteq [v']$ of size v. The numbers in the blocks can later be renamed to range over $[v]$. For example, since the Fano plane is a PG covering, the partially-induced coverings C_1 and C_2 are CVDs. A CVD has two important properties. First, it is a partially-induced covering and thus has all the aforementioned advantages in our setting. In particular, its size is equal to the size of the original covering, which is highly beneficial since CVD induces from PG coverings, known for their small size. Second, although different sets L lead to different block size distributions, we prove that the mean block size and its variance are *the same* regardless of the choice of L. Further, we identify closed-form expressions for them and show that the variance is bounded by the mean. For example, although the block size distributions of C_1 and C_2 are different, they have the same average block size ($\frac{12}{7}$) and the same variance ($\frac{24}{49}$). This property has practical advantages: (1) it allows us to estimate the block size distribution (Sect. 4.2), and (2) since the variance is bounded by the mean, the smaller the mean block size, the less likely that there are very large blocks, which are less likely to be proven robust by GPUPoly. To prove this property, we rely on the fact that PG coverings (and AG coverings) are also a combinatorial design called a *balanced incomplete block design* (BIBD) [7, Part VII, Proposition 2.36]. We next describe BIBD and then state our theorem on its mean and variance.

BIBD. Given positive integers (v, b, r, k, λ), a BIBD is a set of b blocks, each is a subset of $[v]$ of size k, such that every $i \in [v]$ appears in r blocks and every $i \neq j \in [v]$ appear together in λ blocks. For example, the Fano plane is a BIBD with $v = 7, b = 7, r = 3, k = 3, \lambda = 1$. This is because it has $b = 7$ blocks, each block is a subset of $[v] = \{1, \ldots, 7\}$ of size $k = 3$, every number in $\{1, \ldots, 7\}$ appears in $r = 3$ blocks and every two different numbers appear together in $\lambda = 1$ block. Given a BIBD with parameters (v', b, r, k', λ), we define a partially-induced BIBD for $v \leq v'$ by selecting a subset of numbers $L \subseteq [v']$ of size v and removing every $l \in [v'] \setminus L$ from every block in the BIBD (empty blocks or repetitive blocks are kept). While the distribution of the induced blocks' sizes depends on L, the mean block size and its variance depend only on v, v', k'.

Theorem 1. *Given a* (v', b, r, k', λ)*-BIBD, for* $v' > 1$*, and* $1 \leq v \leq v'$*, for every* $L \subseteq [v']$ *of size* v*, the mean* $\mu_{v',k',v}$ *and variance* $\sigma^2_{v',k',v}$ *of the block sizes in the partially-induced BIBD satisfy:*

1. $\mu_{v',k',v} = \frac{vk'}{v'}$
2. $\sigma^2_{v',k',v} = \mu_{v',k',v}\left(1 + \frac{(v-1)(k'-1)}{v'-1} - \mu_{v',k',v}\right) = \frac{vk'}{v'}\left(1 + \frac{(v-1)(k'-1)}{v'-1} - \frac{vk'}{v'}\right)$
3. $\sigma^2_{v',k',v} \leq \mu_{v',k',v}$

Proof. 1. We prove $\mu_{v',k',v} = \frac{vk'}{v'}$.

Since $|L| = v$ and r is the number of occurrences of every number in all blocks, the sum of the sizes of the induced blocks is vr. By counting arguments, for a BIBD it holds that $rv' = bk'$ [7, Part II, Proposition 1.2], and so $r = \frac{bk'}{v'}$. That is, the sum of the induced blocks' sizes is $\frac{vbk'}{v'}$. The mean is obtained by dividing by the number of blocks b: $\mu_{v',k',v} = \frac{vk'}{v'}$.

2. We prove $\sigma^2_{v',k',v} = \mu_{v',k',v}\left(1 + \frac{(v-1)(k'-1)}{v'-1} - \mu_{v',k',v}\right)$.

Let $Z \in \mathbb{N}_0^b$ be a vector such that, for every $n \in [b]$, Z_n is the size of block n in the partially-induced BIBD. It can be written as $Z = A^T x_L$, where A represents the BIBD and x_L the set L, used for partially inducing the BIBD. The matrix A is a $v' \times b$ incidence matrix, where $A[m,n] = 1$ if m is in block n and $A[m,n] = 0$ otherwise. The vector x_L is a v'-dimensional vector, where $x_L[m] = 1$ if $m \in L$ and $x_L[m] = 0$ otherwise. Thus, the average of the squares of the block sizes, denoted $\mathbb{E}[Z^2]$, is $\mathbb{E}[Z^2] = \frac{1}{b}\left(\sum_{n=1}^b (A^T x_L)_n^2\right) = \frac{1}{b}\|A^T x_L\|_2^2$ (1).

By the variance definition, $\sigma^2_{v',k',v} = \mathbb{E}[Z^2] - \mu^2_{v',k',v}$. Thus, we need to show: $\mathbb{E}[Z^2] = \mu_{v',k',v}(1 + \frac{(v-1)(k'-1)}{v'-1}) = \frac{vk'}{v'}(1 + \frac{(v-1)(k'-1)}{v'-1}) = \frac{k'}{v'}v + \frac{k'(k'-1)}{v'(v'-1)}v(v-1)$. By counting arguments [7], we have $\frac{k'}{v'} = \frac{r}{b}$ and $\frac{k'(k'-1)}{v'(v'-1)} = \frac{\lambda}{b}$. Namely, it suffices to show: $\mathbb{E}[Z^2] = \frac{1}{b}(rv + \lambda v(v-1))$. By (1), we can show $\|A^T x_L\|_2^2 = rv + \lambda v(v-1)$. We prove by induction on $v = |L|$ that $\|A^T x_L\|_2^2 = rv + \lambda v(v-1)$:

Base For $v = 1$, we show $\|A^T x_L\|_2^2 = r \cdot 1 + \lambda \cdot 1 \cdot 0$: Since $v = |L| = 1$, by definition of a BIBD, the vector of the induced blocks' sizes Z has r ones and the rest are zeros. Thus, $\|Z\|_2^2 = r$. Since $Z = A^T x_L$, the claim follows.

Induction hypothesis. Assume that the claim holds for every $1, \ldots, v$.

Step Let $L \subseteq [v']$ such that $|L| = v+1$. Pick some $i \in L$ and define $L' = L \setminus \{i\}$ of size v. We get $x_L = x_{L'} + e_i$, where e_i is the ith standard unit vector. Thus:

$$\|A^T x_L\|_2^2 = \|A^T(x_{L'} + e_i)\|_2^2 = \|A^T x_{L'}\|_2^2 + \|A^T e_i\|_2^2 + 2\langle A^T x_{L'}, A^T e_i \rangle$$

- By the induction hypothesis, $\|A^T x_{L'}\|_2^2 = rv + \lambda v(v-1)$.
- Since e_i can be viewed as $x_{L''}$ for some L'' of size 1, we get $\|A^T e_i\|_2^2 = r$.
- We show $\langle A^T x_{L'}, A^T e_i \rangle = x_{L'}^T (AA^T) e_i = \lambda v$: Since A is an incidence matrix of a BIBD, AA^T is the matrix with r on the diagonal and λ elsewhere [7, Part II, Theorem 1.8]. Therefore, $(AA^T) e_i$ is a vector whose entries are λ except for the ith entry which is r. The vector $x_{L'}$ has v ones and 0 on the ith entry (since $i \notin L'$). Thus, their dot product is $x_{L'}^T (AA^T) e_i = \lambda v$.

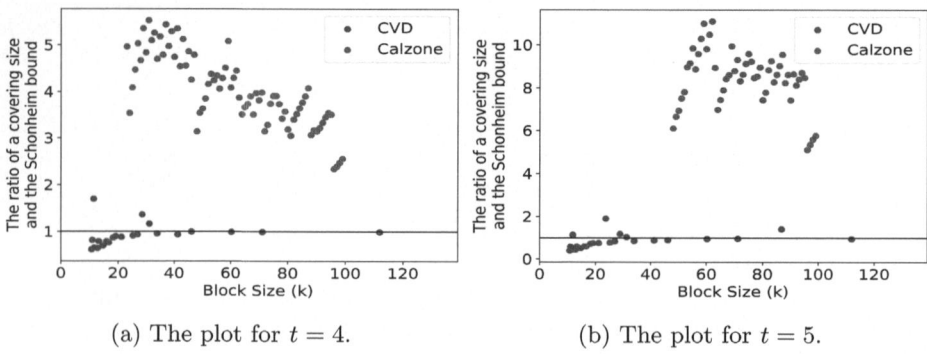

(a) The plot for $t = 4$.   (b) The plot for $t = 5$.

Fig. 3. The ratio of CVD sizes and their respective Schönheim bound vs. the ratio of Calzone's covering sizes and their Schönheim bound. The black line is ratio 1, i.e., coverings whose sizes are equal to the respective Schönheim bound. (Color figure online)

Putting it all together: $\|A^T x_L\|_2^2 = rv + \lambda v(v-1) + r + 2\lambda v = r(v+1) + \lambda(v+1)v$.

3. We show $\sigma_{v',k',v}^2 \leq \mu_{v',k',v}$ by showing that $1 + \frac{(v-1)(k'-1)}{v'-1} - \mu_{v',k',v} \leq 1$. Since $\mu_{v',k',v} = \frac{vk'}{v'}$, we show $\frac{(v-1)(k'-1)}{v'-1} \leq \frac{vk'}{v'}$. We have $1 \leq v \leq v'$ and $1 < v'$, thus we get $\frac{v-1}{v'-1} \leq \frac{v}{v'}$. Since $k'-1 \geq 0$, we get $\frac{(v-1)(k'-1)}{v'-1} \leq \frac{v(k'-1)}{v'} \leq \frac{vk'}{v'}$.

□

Size of Covering Verification Designs. CVDs enable us to obtain coverings whose sizes are small, often close or better than their respective Schönheim bound. Given a CVD whose mean block size is a real number k, we define its respective Schönheim bound as the bound for the covering design of $(v, \lceil k \rceil, t)$. Note that this bound is not a lower bound on the size of the CVD, since the CVD can have blocks larger than $\lceil k \rceil$ and thereby be smaller than covering designs for $(v, \lceil k \rceil, t)$. Still, comparing to this bound enables understanding how much smaller our coverings are compared to the coverings considered by Calzone, whose sizes are lower bounded by the Schönheim bound. Figure 3 shows the ratio of the sizes of our CVDs and their respective Schönheim bound and the ratio of the sizes of Calzone's covering designs and their Schönheim bound. The comparison is for $v = 784$ and $t = 4$ (Fig. 3a) and $t = 5$ (Fig. 3b). We compute CVDs from different PG coverings and the figure shows CVDs whose mean block size k is at least 10. For Calzone, we show all coverings in its database. The plots demonstrate that typically the size of a CVD is smaller or equal to the Schönheim bound, and on average, the ratio is 0.92 for $t = 4$ and 0.85 for $t = 5$. In contrast, Calzone's coverings are significantly larger than the Schönheim bound, on average the ratio is 4.04 for $t = 4$ and 8.44 for $t = 5$. The plots also show that Calzone has many more coverings than the number of CVDs. This is because Calzone relies on general techniques to compute coverings and thus it can generate a covering

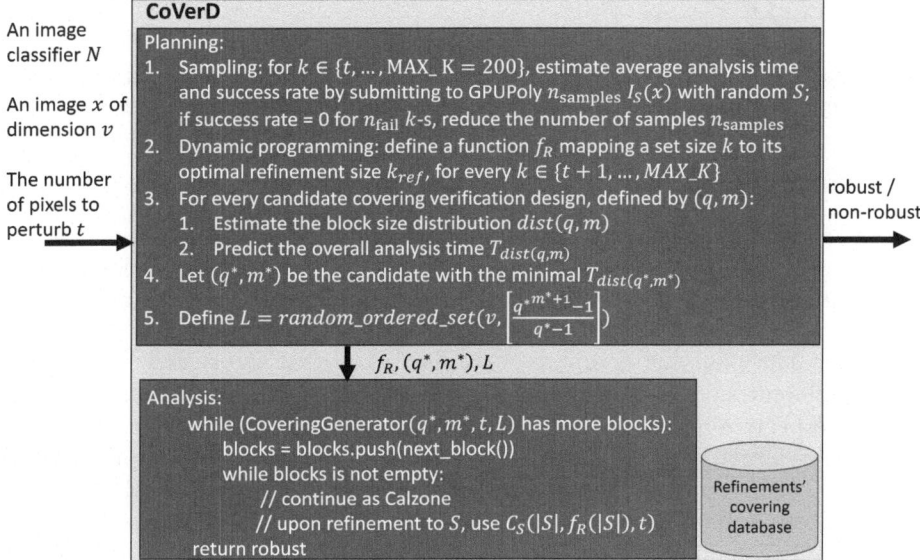

Fig. 4. CoVerD: An L_0 robustness verifier.

for every $k \leq \mathrm{MAX\_K} = 99$ (except that it is limited to coverings with at most 10^7 blocks). In contrast, our CVDs induce PG coverings and are thus limited to coverings whose mean block size is given by the expression given in Theorem 1, over v' and k' such that there is a PG covering for (v', k', t).

Challenge: Memory Consumption. The main challenge in computing CVDs is that it requires to compute a PG covering for large values of v' and k', which poses a high memory overhead. To illustrate, in our experiments, CoVerD uses a CVD induced from a PG covering for $(v' = 1508598, k' = 88741, t = 5)$. If CoVerD stored this covering in the memory, it would require 124GB of memory, assuming each number in a block takes a byte. To cope, CoVerD computes the partially-induced covering during the PG covering construction. However, even the partially-induced coverings can consume a lot of memory, since the number of blocks can be large. Calzone faced a similar challenge and coped by restricting the size of the covering designs to at most 10^7, which allowed it to keep all coverings in the covering database. While CoVerD could take a similar approach, this would prevent it from picking CVDs of larger size which overall may lead to a lower analysis time (since they will require fewer refinements). Instead, CoVerD generates a CVD *on-the-fly* and uses the covering database only for the refinements, which tend to require coverings of significantly smaller size than the first covering. Another advantage of building the CVD on-the-fly is that it enables CoVerD to analyze any classifier over any image dimension, without any special adaptation. This is in contrast to Calzone, which requires to extend its covering database upon every new image dimension v.

4   CoVerD

In this section, we present CoVerD, our L_0 robustness verifier. We first describe our system and its components and then provide a running example.

4.1   Our System

Figure 4 shows CoVerD that, given an image classifier N, an image x with v pixels, and the maximal number of perturbed pixels t, returns whether N is robust in the t-ball of x. We next describe its planning and analysis components.

Planning. The planning component consists of several steps. First, it samples sets of different sizes k to estimate the success rate and average analysis time of their respective neighborhoods, like Calzone. Since CoVerD considers CVDs, it can observe larger block sizes than Calzone, thus the maximal sampled set size is MAX_K = 200, unlike 99 in Calzone. Because of the larger bound, CoVerD is likely to observe many more k values whose success rate is zero. To save execution time while still enabling to determine the success rate and average analysis time of large k values, CoVerD reduces the number of samples after observing n_{fail} times k values whose success rate is zero. Second, the planning component relies on Calzone's dynamic programming for computing a K strategy, but uses it differently. Since CoVerD begins the analysis from a CVD consisting of different sized blocks, there is no single K strategy. Instead, it runs Calzone's dynamic programming for every $k \in \{t+1, \ldots, \text{MAX\_K}\}$ to define a function f_R mapping every set size k to the best set size to use upon a refinement of a set of size k. Then, the planning component iterates over every candidate CVD and picks the best CVD for the analysis. It picks between the candidates *without* constructing them, as the construction is time and memory intensive and we wish to execute it only for the chosen candidate. To pick the best candidate, it leverages two observations. First, a CVD candidate is uniquely defined by the parameters of the PG covering, (q, m) (formally, its parameters are (q, m, t) but t is identical in all our PG coverings), so it suffices to pick a pair (q, m) which can later be used to construct the CVD. Second, to predict the CVD with the minimal analysis time, only the *block sizes* are needed. In Sect. 4.2, we describe how to estimate a CVD's block size distribution $dist(q, m)$ and estimate its analysis time $T_{dist(q,m)}$, in order to predict the best CVD. Given the best candidate (q^*, m^*), it randomly samples an ordered set L of v indices from v', which is a function of (q^*, m^*).

Analysis. After determining the best (q^*, m^*), L, and the refinement mapping f_R, CoVerD continues to analyze the robustness of the classifier N in the t-ball of the given image x. The analysis constructs the CVD on-the-fly block-by-block. Technically, there is a covering generator that constructs the blocks one-by-one. Every block is pushed to the stack of blocks to verify, and then the analysis proceeds as Calzone. That is, the block is popped, submitted to GPUPoly, and if needed, refinement is executed. After the block is verified (directly or by refinement), the next block in the CVD is obtained from the covering generator. We note that although CoVerD could use CVDs for refinements, the coverings for refinements are smaller than the first covering since these coverings are for triples $(\tilde{v}, \tilde{k}, t)$ where $\tilde{v}$ is typically few dozens and at most MAX_K = 200, whereas the first covering is for a triple $(\tilde{v}, \tilde{k}, t)$ where $\tilde{v}$ is the image dimension. Like Calzone, CoVerD parallelizes the analysis on GPUs. Thus, our covering generator generates disjoint parts of the covering, described in Sect. 4.3.

4.2 Choosing a Covering Verification Design

In this section, we describe how CoVerD predicts the CVD that enables CoVerD to minimize the overall analysis time. We begin with describing the CVD candidates, then describe how CoVerD estimates their block size distributions, and finally explain how CoVerD predicts the CVD leading to the minimal analysis time.

Candidates. A CVD candidate is defined by the PG covering from which it is partially-induced. Recall that a PG covering is defined for triples (v', k', t), where $v' = \frac{q^{m+1}-1}{q-1}$ and $k' = \frac{q^t-1}{q-1}$ for a prime power q and $m \geq t \geq 2$. By Theorem 1, given a PG covering, the mean block size of the CVD has a closed-form expression $\mu_{v',k',v} = \frac{vk'}{v'} = \frac{v(q^t-1)}{q^{m+1}-1}$. By this expression, given q, as m increases $\mu_{v',k',v}$ decreases, and given m, as q increases $\mu_{v',k',v}$ decreases. Further, this expression approaches 0 for high values of q or m. Thus, to obtain a *finite* set of candidates, we provide a positive lower bound on $\mu_{v',k',v}$, denoted MIN_K (our implementation sets it to t). That is, the finite set of candidates CoVerD considers is:

$$\{(q,m) \in \mathbb{N}^2 \mid q \text{ is a prime power, } m \geq t, \ v' \geq v, \ \mu_{v',k',v} \geq \text{MIN\_K}\}$$

Estimating the Block Size Distribution. For every CVD candidate, defined by (q, m), CoVerD estimates the distribution of its block sizes. While Theorem 1 provides expressions for the mean block size and the variance, it does not define the block size distribution. We empirically observe that our CVDs have the property that the distribution of their block sizes resembles a discrete approximation of a Gaussian distribution with mean $\mu_{v',k',v}$ and variance $\sigma^2_{v',k',v}$. The higher the mean and the number of blocks, the higher the resemblance. Figure 5a visualizes this resemblance for a CVD, with $v = 784$, induced from a PG with parameters $q = 17$, $m = 5$, and $t = 5$. We believe this resemblance exists because a CVD is partially-induced from a PG covering given *a random set of numbers* L. This resemblance may not hold for other choices of L, for example for the choice of L proposed by [27], which compute a partially-induced covering whose maximal block size is bounded (unlike our CVD). Because of this resemblance, we model the block size as drawn from the Gaussian distribution with the true mean and variance $\mathcal{G}\left(\mu_{v',k',v}, \sigma^2_{v',k',v}\right)$. Even if this modeling is imprecise, in practice, it is sufficient to allow CoVerD identify the candidate CVD leading to the minimal analysis time. Formally, given a CVD candidate defined by (q, m), the distribution of the block sizes is $dist(q,m) = \{N_k^{q,m} \mid k \leq \text{MAX\_K}\}$, where $N_k^{q,m}$ is our estimation of the number of blocks of size

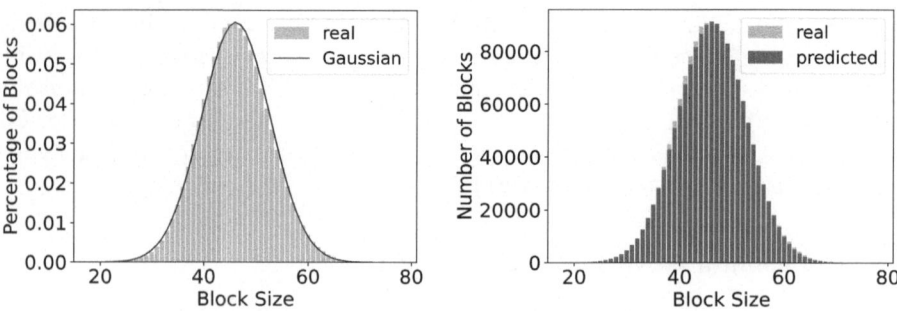

(a) The block size distribution of a CVD and (b) Our estimated block size distribution the respective Gaussian distribution.   vs. the distribution of a respective CVD.

Fig. 5. Block size distributions.

k in this CVD. We define the probability that a block size in this CVD is of size k as: $\mathbb{P}(k - 0.5 < Z \leq k + 0.5) = \Phi\left(\frac{(k+0.5)-\mu_{v',k',v}}{\sigma_{v',k',v}}\right) - \Phi\left(\frac{(k-0.5)-\mu_{v',k',v}}{\sigma_{v',k',v}}\right),$ where $Z \sim \mathcal{G}\left(\mu_{v',k',v}, \sigma^2_{v',k',v}\right)$ and Φ is the cumulative distribution function (CDF) of a Gaussian distribution with mean 0 and variance 1. The number of blocks $b^{q,m}$ is identical to the number of blocks in the PG covering, which has a closed-form expression [16]. Thus, the estimated number of blocks of size k is: $\tilde{N}^{q,m}_k = b^{q,m} \cdot \mathbb{P}(k-0.5 < Z \leq k+0.5)$. To make the estimated number an integer, we define $N^{q,m}_k$ as the floor of $\tilde{N}^{q,m}_k$ and add 1 with probability of the remainder: $N^{q,m}_k = \left\lfloor \tilde{N}^{q,m}_k \right\rfloor + X$ where $X \sim \text{Bern}\left(\tilde{N}^{q,m}_k - \left\lfloor \tilde{N}^{q,m}_k \right\rfloor\right)$. Figure 5b visualizes how close our estimation of the block size distribution is to the distribution of the CVD shown in Fig. 5a. We note that CoVerD considers a candidate and estimates its block size distribution only if its estimated number of overly large blocks (larger than MAX_K) is close to zero. Formally, it considers candidates that satisfy $b^{q,m} \cdot \left(1 - \Phi\left(\frac{\text{MAX\_K}-\mu_{v',k',v}}{\sigma_{v',k',v}}\right)\right) \leq \epsilon$, where ϵ is a small number. This is the reason that $dist(q,m) = \{N^{q,m}_k \mid k \leq \text{MAX\_K}\}$ consists of estimations only for blocks whose size is at most MAX_K.

Predicting the Best CVD. Given the candidates and their estimated block size distributions, CoVerD chooses the CVD which will enable CoVerD to minimize the overall analysis time. To this end, it predicts for every candidate CVD its overall analysis time. The prediction relies on: (1) the estimated number of blocks $N^{q,m}_k$ of size k, (2) the average analysis time of a block of size k, denoted $k\_array[k][time]$ (given by the initial sampling), (3) the fraction of the non-robust blocks of size k, which is one minus the success rate of k, denoted $k\_array[k][success]$ (given by the initial sampling) and (4) the analysis time of refining a non-robust block of size k, denoted $T(k)$ (given by the dynamic programming, as defined in [30]). Similarly to Calzone's dynamic programming,

---

Algorithm 1: CoveringGenerator(q, m, t, L, i_{GPU})

Input: PG parameters (q, m, t), an ordered set of v indices $L = [s_1, \ldots, s_v]$
      which is a subset of $[\frac{q^{m+1}-1}{q-1}]$, and an index of a GPU i_{GPU}.

Output: A stream of the covering verification design's blocks.

1   $\forall i \in [v]$. $P[:,i] =$ a unique vector in $\mathbb{F}_q^{m+1}$ computed for s_i $// \ P \in \mathbb{F}_q^{(m+1) \times v}$

2   $\mathcal{M} = [M \in \mathbb{F}_q^{(m-t+1) \times (m+1)} \mid M$ is full rank and in reduced row echelon form$]$

3   **for** $j = 0; j < |\mathcal{M}|; j + +$ **do**

4   **if** j *modulo GPUs* $\neq i_{GPU}$ **then** continue

5      $R = \mathcal{M}[j] \times P$

6   block $= \{i \in [v] \mid R[:,i] = \mathbf{0}\}$ $//$ generate induced block

7   output block

---

the analysis time is the sum of the analysis time of verifying all blocks in the CVD and the analysis time of the refinements of the non-robust blocks:

$$T_{dist(q,m)} = \sum_{k=t}^{\text{MAX\_K}} N_k^{q,m} \cdot (k\_array[k][time] + (1 - k\_array[k][success]) \cdot T(k))$$

This computation ignores blocks of size less than t since they do not cover any subset of size t and need not be analyzed to prove L_0 robustness. After predicting the analysis time of every candidate, CoVerD picks the candidate with the minimal time.

4.3 Constructing a Covering Verification Design

In this section, we present our covering generator that computes a CVD. The covering generator operates as an independent process, one for every GPU, that outputs blocks a-synchronically. At every iteration, every GPU worker obtains a block from its covering generator, analyzes it with GPUPoly, and refines if needed. If the block is robust or its refinement does not detect an adversarial example, the GPU worker obtains the next block from the covering generator. The covering generator relies on the chosen CVD's parameters q and m and the ordered set L from the planning component. It computes the PG covering for (q, m, t) block-by-block and induces it to obtain a CVD. Generally, its construction follows the meta-algorithm of generating PG coverings described in [16]. The novel parts are our implementation of inducing blocks immediately upon generating them and partitioning them to enable their analysis to proceed in parallel over the available GPUs. We next describe the covering generator.

    Algorithm 1 shows the algorithm of our covering generator. It takes as input the PG parameters (q, m, t), an ordered set L of v indices from $[v']$ (where $v' = \frac{q^{m+1}-1}{q-1}$), and the GPU index i_{GPU}. As described in Sect. 3, a PG construction for (v', k', t) views v' as the number of points in the geometry. Formally, given the finite field $\mathbb{F}_q$ of order q, we identify the points of the geometry as a subset

$W \subset \mathbb{F}_q^{m+1}$ of size v' (technically, these points are representatives of equivalence classes over $\mathbb{F}_q^{m+1}$, as explained in [16]). To later partially-induce the covering using L, Algorithm 1 maps every index in L to a unique point in W and stores all points (column vectors) in a matrix P (Line 1). Then, Algorithm 1 begins to construct the PG covering by computing flats (linear subspaces) of dimension $t - 1$, each containing $k' = \frac{q^t - 1}{q - 1}$ points. As described in [16], every block in the PG covering is a solution (a set of points in W) to $m - t + 1$ independent linear equations over $m + 1$ variables. Such a linear system can be represented as a full rank matrix, where its solutions are vectors in the matrix's null space. Thus, to compute the blocks in the PG covering, Algorithm 1 defines a set of matrices $\mathcal{M}$, each is over $\mathbb{F}_q$, of dimension $(m - t + 1) \times (m + 1)$, and full rank (equal to $m - t + 1$). Each matrix has exactly k' points in W in its null space. These points form a PG block (a flat of dimension $t - 1$). To avoid block duplication, the matrices in $\mathcal{M}$ need to have different null spaces. Thus, Algorithm 1 considers matrices in reduced row echelon form, i.e., $\mathcal{M}$ is all full rank $(m - t + 1) \times (m + 1)$ matrices over $\mathbb{F}_q$ in reduced row echelon form (Line 2). The covering generator then iterates these matrices. To avoid a high memory overhead, the matrix $\mathcal{M}[j]$ is generated only upon reaching its index j. If j belongs to the disjoint part of the given GPU, its induced block is generated (Line 4). To construct a PG block, one needs to compute all the points in the null space of $\mathcal{M}[j]$. However, the generator requires only the partially-induced blocks. Thus, it *immediately induces* the block by obtaining all points s_i, for $i \in [v]$, whose respective point $P[:, i]$ belongs to the null space of $\mathcal{M}[j]$. To this end, it defines R as the multiplication of $\mathcal{M}[j]$ and P (Line 5), forms the induced block by identifying the points that are in the null space of $\mathcal{M}[j]$ (i.e., every s_i satisfying $R[:, i] = \mathbf{0}$), and makes the induced block a subset of $[v]$ by mapping every s_i in the induced block to i (Line 6).

4.4   A Running Example

In this section, we describe a real execution of CoVerD, for an MNIST image, a fully-connected network ($6\times200\_PGD$ in Sect. 5), and $t = 4$. CoVerD begins with the planning component. It first estimates the success rate and average analysis time of blocks. For every $k \in \{4, 5, \ldots, 200\}$, it samples blocks S (subsets of $[784]$) of size k and submits their neighborhood $I_S(x) = \{x' \in [0, 1]^v \mid \forall i \notin S. \; x'_i = x_i\}$ to GPUPoly. Based on all samples for k, it estimates the success rate and the average analysis time. For instance, for $k = 34$ the success rate is 94.05% and the average analysis time is 16.19ms, while for $k = 41$ they are 65.85% and 16.96ms. Then, CoVerD runs Calzone's dynamic programming to map every $k \in \{5, 6, \ldots, 200\}$ to the refinement size. For example, $k = 34$ is mapped to 28 and $k = 41$ to 33. Next, CoVerD determines the CVD for the first covering, out of 50 candidates. For each candidate, it predicts the block size distribution and the respective overall analysis time of this candidate. To this end, it computes the mean, variance, and number of blocks using the closed-form expressions. For example, the CVD of the candidate ($q = 23, m = 4$) has mean block size 34.087, variance 32.518 and $292, 561$ blocks. The CVD of ($q = 19, m = 4$) has mean block size 41.263, variance 38.867, and 137, 561 blocks. Although the second candidate has less than half the number of blocks of the first candidate, CoVerD predicts that using the first candidate will enable a faster analysis. This is because its success rate is significantly higher and thus it will require fewer refinements (e.g., the success rate of its mean block size is 94.05%, whereas the second candidate's success rate of the mean block size is 65.85%). The estimated analysis times (in minutes) are $T_{dist(23,4)} = 21.20$ and $T_{dist(19,4)} = 27.92$. The last step of the planning component samples an ordered set L of size 784 (the number of pixels in the MNIST image) from $[\frac{23^5-1}{23-1}] = [292561]$. In total, the planning component takes 63.5 s.

Then, CoVerD continues to the analysis component. It starts by creating eight instances of the covering generator (Algorithm 1), one for each GPU. A covering generator creates blocks for its GPU one-by-one, given $q^* = 23$, $m^* = 4$, $t = 4$ and L. For every CVD block S, the GPU worker defines its neighborhood $I_S(x)$ and submits to GPUPoly. If GPUPoly verifies successfully, the next CVD block is obtained. If GPUPoly fails proving robustness, S is refined. As example, if a block S of size 34 is refined, the analysis pushes to the stack all blocks in the covering $C_S(34, 28, 4)$, which is the covering for $(34, 28, 4)$ that is in the covering database, where the numbers are renamed to range over the numbers in S. In this example, GPUPoly is invoked 659, 326 times, where 44% of these calls are for blocks in the CVD. The maximal size of block submitted to GPUPoly is 62 and the minimal size is 8. In particular, CoVerD did not submit any block of size $t = 4$ (i.e., there are no calls to the MILP verifier). The analysis takes 23.49 min, which is only 10.8% higher than the estimated time.

5 Evaluation

In this section, we describe the experimental evaluation of CoVerD on multiple datasets and networks and compare it to Calzone.

Implementation and Setup. We implemented CoVerD[1] as an extension of Calzone[2]. Experiments ran on a dual AMD EPYC 7713 server, 2TB RAM, eight NVIDIA A100 GPUs and Ubuntu 20.04.1. We evaluate CoVerD on the networks evaluated by Calzone, whose architectures are described in ERAN[3]. We consider networks trained for popular image datasets: MNIST and Fashion-MNIST, consisting of 28×28 greyscale images, and CIFAR-10, consisting of 32×32 colored images. CoVerD's hyper-parameters are: the maximal block size is MAX_K = 200, the number of samples is initially $n_{\text{samples}} = 400$ and after $n_{\text{fail}} = 10$ failures, it is reduced to $n_{\text{samples}} = 24$, and the bound on the estimated number of overly large blocks is $\epsilon = 0.01$. Our covering database, used for the refinement steps, contains coverings for $v, k \leq 200$, $t \leq 6$. The covering sizes are restricted to at most 500, 000 blocks. This limitation is stricter than Calzone, which limited to

---

[1] https://github.com/YuvShap/CoVerD.
[2] https://github.com/YuvShap/calzone.
[3] https://github.com/eth-sri/eran.

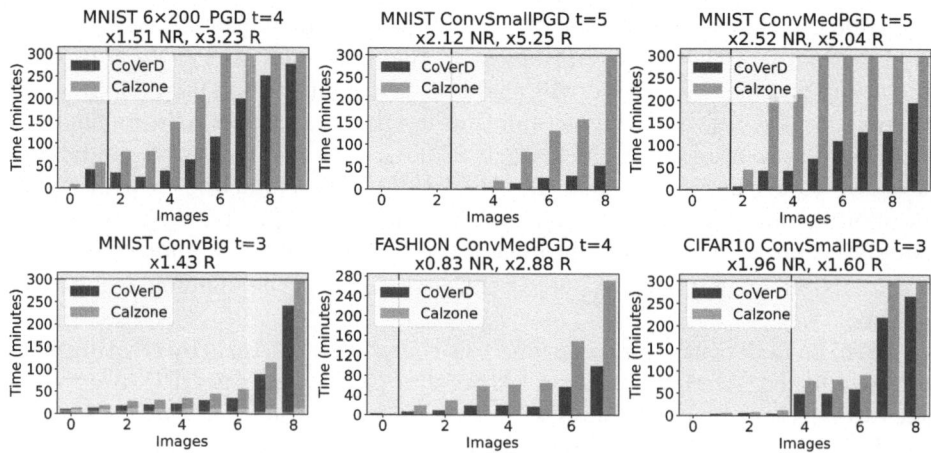

Fig. 6. CoVerD vs. Calzone on Calzone's most challenging benchmarks.

10^7, but in practice this is unnoticeable since CoVerD only uses the coverings for refinements, and even Calzone typically refines to coverings whose size is at most $500,000$. Like Calzone, the database consists of coverings computed by extending coverings from the La Jolla Covering Repository Tables[4] using construction techniques from [16, Section 6.1]. Additionally, our database includes finite geometry coverings (for $v, k \leq 200$, $t \leq 6$) and extends coverings using the dynamic programming of [16, Section 5]. Like Calzone, We ran CoVerD with eight GPUPoly instances and five MILP instances, except for the CIFAR-10 network where it ran 50 MILP instances. For the matrix multiplication over finite fields (Algorithm 1), CoVerD relies on an effective library [18] and considers only prime numbers for q (since matrix multiplication is too slow for prime powers).

Comparison to Calzone. We begin by evaluating CoVerD on Calzone's benchmarks (i.e., the same networks, images and timeouts) for $t \geq 3$. Figure 6 shows the comparison for the most challenging benchmarks of Calzone, and Fig. 7 shows comparisons for $t = 4$ (the plots for $t = 3$ are shown in [31, Appendix A]). For a given network and t, the plot shows the execution time in minutes of CoVerD and Calzone for every t-ball. The x-axis orders the t-balls by CoVerD's output: non-robust (in light red background), robust (in light green background), and timeout (in light blue background, e.g., Fig. 7, top). Within each section, the t-balls are sorted by their execution time for clearer visuality. Timeouts, of CoVerD or Calzone, are shown by bars reaching the red horizontal line. The lower part of each bar shows in a lighter color the execution time of the initial sampling (unless it is too short to be visible in the plot). The sampling time is highlighted since Calzone and CoVerD sample slightly differently: Calzone samples 400 sets of size k, for every $k \leq 99$, while CoVerD samples up to $k \leq 200$ and reduces

---

[4] https://ljcr.dmgordon.org/cover/table.html.

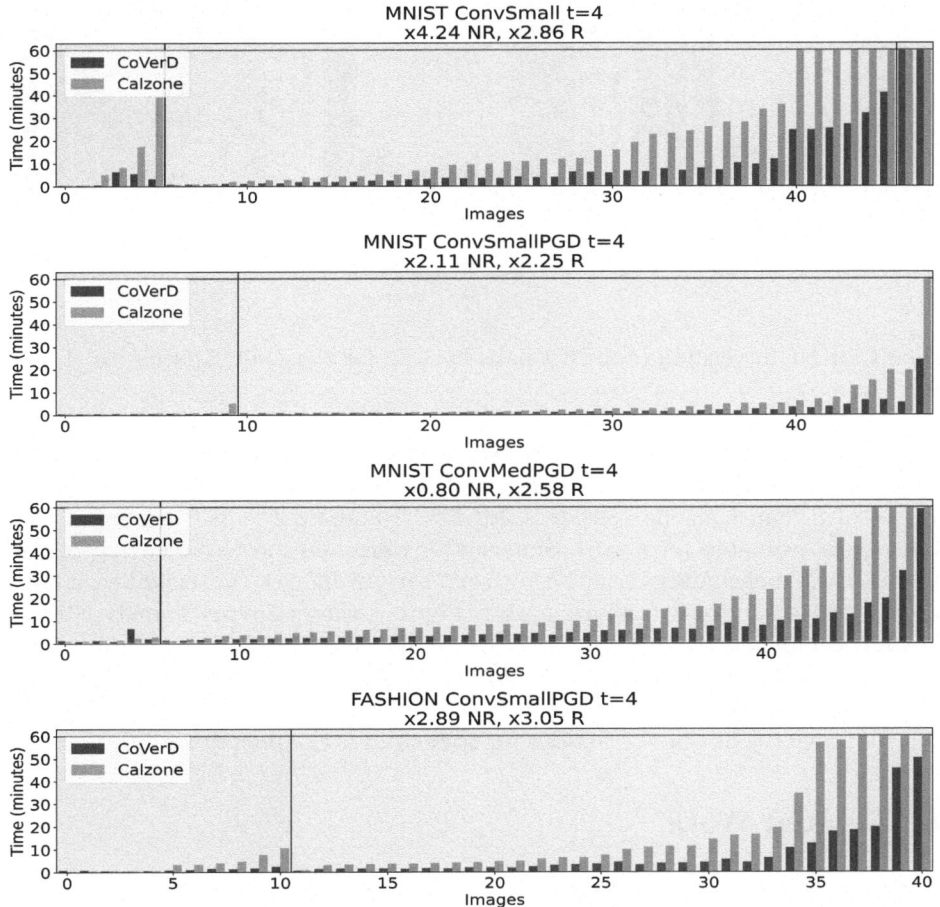

Fig. 7. CoVerD vs. Calzone for $t = 4$.

the number of samples after observing ten k values whose average success rate is zero. We note that the other computations of the planning component take a few seconds. The plots' titles include the speedup in the average analysis time of CoVerD over Calzone for non-robust t-balls (NR) and for robust t-balls (R).

The plots show that, on the most challenging benchmarks (Fig. 6), CoVerD is always faster than Calzone, except for two non-robust t-balls which CoVerD completes their analysis within 140 s. In the plots of Fig. 7, CoVerD is always faster than Calzone except for thirteen 4-balls whose analysis terminates within seven minutes by both verifiers. In the other plots (Fig. 9 in [31, Appendix A]), where $t = 3$, Calzone is sometimes faster, but in these cases the analysis time is typically short. In other words, the significance of CoVerD is in shortening the analysis time of t-balls with long analysis time. On average, CoVerD is faster

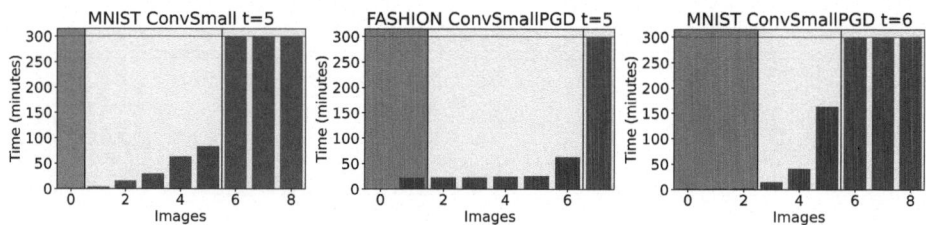

Fig. 8. CoVerD's new benchmarks.

than Calzone in verifying robust t-balls by 1.3x for $t = 3$, by 2.8x for $t = 4$, and by 5.1x for $t = 5$.

Challenging Benchmarks. Next, we show more challenging benchmarks than Calzone. We evaluate the robustness of three networks for t-balls with larger values of t than Calzone considers, for $t = 5$ and for $t = 6$ (we remind that Calzone is evaluated for $t \leq 5$). Similarly to Calzone's most challenging benchmarks, these benchmarks evaluate CoVerD for ten images (misclassified images are discarded) and a five hour timeout. Figure 8 shows CoVerD's analysis time. CoVerD completes the analysis for 73% t-balls. Further, it verifies robustness in some 6-balls within 42 minutes. As before, CoVerD is significantly faster for non-robust t-balls.

We provide additional statistics on CoVerD in [31, Appendix A].

6   Related Work

In this section, we discuss the closest related work.

Robustness Verification of Neural Networks. Many works propose robustness verifiers for neural networks. Most works focus on local robustness in L_∞ neighborhoods, defined by a series of intervals [2,12,13,21,25,32,34,36,37]. Some verifiers provide a complete analysis, i.e., they determine whether a network is robust in the given neighborhood [12,21,34]. These approaches typically rely on constraint solving (SAT/SMT solvers or MILP solvers) and thus they often do not scale to large networks. Incomplete verifiers scale the analysis by over-approximating the non-linear computations of the network (e.g., the activation functions) by linear approximations or abstract domains [13,25,32,36]. Several local robustness verifiers address L_2-balls, e.g., by computing a bound on the network's global or local Lipschitz constant [19,22], or L_1-balls [38,41]. Other approaches analyze robustness in L_p-balls for $p \in \{0, 1, 2, \infty\}$ using randomized smoothing [6,11,23,28,39], providing probabilistic guarantees. To the best of our knowledge, Calzone [30] is the first work to deterministically verify local robustness in L_0-balls. Other works prove robustness in neighborhoods defined by high-level features [3,20,24].

Covering and Combinatorial Designs. CVD is related to several combinatorial designs: the combinatorial design defined by [27], covering designs [16] and balanced incomplete block designs [7]. Covering designs, in particular finite geometry coverings, have been leveraged in various domains, including file information retrieval [27], file organization [1] and coding theory [5]. General combinatorial designs have also been leveraged in various domains in computer science [8].

7   Conclusion

We present CoVerD, an L_0 robustness verifier for neural networks. CoVerD boosts the performance of a previous L_0 robustness verifier by employing several ideas. First, it relies on a covering verification design (CVD), a new combinatorial design partially inducing a projective geometry covering. Second, it chooses between candidate CVDs without constructing them but only predicting their block size distribution. Third, it constructs the chosen CVD on-the-fly to keep the memory overhead minimal. We evaluate CoVerD on fully-connected and convolutional networks. We show that it boosts the performance of proving a network's robustness to at most t perturbed pixels on average by 2.8x, for $t = 4$, and by 5.1x, for $t = 5$. For $t = 6$, CoVerD sometimes proves robustness within 42 minutes.

References

1. Abraham, C., Ghosh, S., Ray-Chaudhuri, D.: File organization schemes based on finite geometries. Inf. Control **12**(2), 143–163 (1968)
2. Anderson, G., Pailoor, S., Dillig, I., Chaudhuri, S.: Optimization and abstraction: a synergistic approach for analyzing neural network robustness. In: Proceedings of the 40th ACM SIGPLAN Conference on Programming Language Design and Implementation, PLDI (2019)
3. Balunovic, M., Baader, M., Singh, G., Gehr, T., Vechev, M.T.: Certifying geometric robustness of neural networks. In: Advances in Neural Information Processing Systems 32: Annual Conference on Neural Information Processing Systems, NeurIPS (2019)
4. Carlini, N., Wagner, D.A.: Towards evaluating the robustness of neural networks. In: IEEE Symposium on Security and Privacy, SP (2017)
5. Chan, A., Games, R.: (n,k,t))-covering systems and error-trapping decoding (corresp.). IEEE Trans. Inform. Theory **27**(5), 643–646 (1981)
6. Cohen, J., Rosenfeld, E., Kolter, J.Z.: Certified adversarial robustness via randomized smoothing. In: Proceedings of the 36th International Conference on Machine Learning, ICML. vol. 97. PMLR (2019)
7. Colbourn, C.J., Dinitz, J.H. (eds.): Handbook of Combinatorial Designs. Chapman and Hall/CRC, 2nd edn. (2006). https://doi.org/10.1201/9781420010541
8. Colbourn, C.J., van Oorschot, P.C.: Applications of combinatorial designs in computer science. ACM Comput. Surv. **21**(2), 223–250 (Jun 1989)

9. Croce, F., Andriushchenko, M., Singh, N.D., Flammarion, N., Hein, M.: Sparsers: A versatile framework for query-efficient sparse black-box adversarial attacks. In: Thirty-Sixth AAAI Conference on Artificial Intelligence, AAAI Thirty-Fourth Conference on Innovative Applications of Artificial Intelligence, IAAI , The Twelveth Symposium on Educational Advances in Artificial Intelligence, EAAI. AAAI Press (2022)

10. Croce, F., Hein, M.: Mind the box: l_1-apgd for sparse adversarial attacks on image classifiers. In: Proceedings of the 38th International Conference on Machine Learning, ICML. PMLR (2021)

11. Dvijotham, K.D., et al.: A framework for robustness certification of smoothed classifiers using f-divergences. In: 8th International Conference on Learning Representations, ICLR. OpenReview.net (2020)

12. Ehlers, R.: Formal Verification of Piece-Wise Linear Feed-Forward Neural Networks. In: D'Souza, D., Narayan Kumar, K. (eds.) Automated Technology for Verification and Analysis, pp. 269–286. Springer International Publishing, Cham (2017). https://doi.org/10.1007/978-3-319-68167-2_19

13. Gehr, T., Mirman, M., Drachsler-Cohen, D., Tsankov, P., Chaudhuri, S., Vechev, M.T.: AI2: safety and robustness certification of neural networks with abstract interpretation. In: IEEE Symposium on Security and Privacy, SP (2018)

14. Goodfellow, I., Bengio, Y., Courville, A.: Deep Learning. MIT Press (2016). http://www.deeplearningbook.org

15. Goodfellow, I.J., Shlens, J., Szegedy, C.: Explaining and harnessing adversarial examples. In: 3rd International Conference on Learning Representations, ICLR (2015)

16. Gordon, D.M., Kuperberg, G., Patashnik, O.: New constructions for covering designs. J. COMBIN. DESIGNS **3**, 269–284 (1995)

17. Grosse, K., Papernot, N., Manoharan, P., Backes, M., McDaniel, P.D.: Adversarial perturbations against deep neural networks for malware classification. CoRR **abs/1606.04435** (2016)

18. Hostetter, M.: Galois: A performant NumPy extension for Galois fields (11 2020). https://github.com/mhostetter/galois

19. Huang, Y., Zhang, H., Shi, Y., Kolter, J.Z., Anandkumar, A.: Training certifiably robust neural networks with efficient local lipschitz bounds. In: Advances in Neural Information Processing Systems 34: Annual Conference on Neural Information Processing Systems NeurIPS (2021)

20. Kabaha, A., Drachsler-Cohen, D.: Boosting robustness verification of semantic feature neighborhoods. In: Singh, G., Urban, C. (eds.) Static Analysis: 29th International Symposium, SAS 2022, Auckland, New Zealand, December 5–7, 2022, Proceedings, pp. 299–324. Springer Nature Switzerland, Cham (2022). https://doi.org/10.1007/978-3-031-22308-2_14

21. Katz, G., Barrett, C.W., Dill, D.L., Julian, K., Kochenderfer, M.J.: Reluplex: an efficient SMT solver for verifying deep neural networks. In: Computer Aided Verification - 29th International Conference, CAV (2017)

22. Leino, K., Wang, Z., Fredrikson, M.: Globally-robust neural networks. In: Proceedings of the 38th International Conference on Machine Learning, ICML. Proceedings of Machine Learning Research, vol. 139. PMLR (2021)

23. Li, B., Chen, C., Wang, W., Carin, L.: Certified adversarial robustness with additive noise. In: Advances in Neural Information Processing Systems 32: Annual Conference on Neural Information Processing Systems, NeurIPS (2019)

24. Mohapatra, J., Weng, T., Chen, P., Liu, S., Daniel, L.: Towards verifying robustness of neural networks against A family of semantic perturbations. In: IEEE/CVF Conference on Computer Vision and Pattern Recognition, CVPR (2020)
25. Müller, C., Serre, F., Singh, G., Püschel, M., Vechev, M.T.: Scaling polyhedral neural network verification on gpus. In: Proceedings of Machine Learning and Systems MLSys (2021)
26. Papernot, N., McDaniel, P.D., Jha, S., Fredrikson, M., Celik, Z.B., Swami, A.: The limitations of deep learning in adversarial settings. In: IEEE European Symposium on Security and Privacy, EuroS&P (2016)
27. Ray-Chaudhuri, D.K.: Combinatorial information retrieval systems for files. SIAM J. Appl. Math. **16**(5), 973-992 (sep 1968)
28. Salman, H., et al.: Provably robust deep learning via adversarially trained smoothed classifiers. In: Wallach, H.M., Larochelle, H., Beygelzimer, A., d'Alché-Buc, F., Fox, E.B., Garnett, R. (eds.) Advances in Neural Information Processing Systems 32: Annual Conference on Neural Information Processing Systems, NeurIPS. pp. 11289–11300 (2019)
29. Schönheim, J.: On coverings. Pac. J. Math. **14**(4), 1405–1411 (1964)
30. Shapira, Y., Avneri, E., Drachsler-Cohen, D.: Deep learning robustness verification for few-pixel attacks. Proc. ACM Program. Lang. **7**(OOPSLA1) (2023)
31. Shapira, Y., Wiesel, N., Shabelman, S., Drachsler-Cohen, D.: Boosting few-pixel robustness verification via covering verification designs. CoRR **abs/2405.10924** (2024)
32. Singh, G., Gehr, T., Püschel, M., Vechev, M.T.: An abstract domain for certifying neural networks. PACMPL **3**(POPL) (2019)
33. Szegedy, C., Zaremba, W., Sutskever, I., Bruna, J., Erhan, D., Goodfellow, I.J., Fergus, R.: Intriguing properties of neural networks. In: 2nd International Conference on Learning Representations, ICLR (2014)
34. Tjeng, V., Xiao, K.Y., Tedrake, R.: Evaluating robustness of neural networks with mixed integer programming. In: 7th International Conference on Learning Representations, ICLR (2019)
35. Todorov, D.: Combinatorial coverings. Ph.D. thesis, PhD thesis, University of Sofia, 1985 (1985)
36. Wang, S., et al.: Beta-crown: Efficient bound propagation with per-neuron split constraints for neural network robustness verification. In: Advances in Neural Information Processing Systems 34: Annual Conference on Neural Information Processing Systems (2021)
37. Wu, H., et al.: Parallelization techniques for verifying neural networks. In: Formal Methods in Computer Aided Design, FMCAD. IEEE (2020)
38. Wu, Y., Zhang, M.: Tightening robustness verification of convolutional neural networks with fine-grained linear approximation. In: Thirty-Fifth AAAI Conference on Artificial Intelligence, AAAI, pp. 11674–11681. AAAI Press (2021)
39. Yang, G., Duan, T., Hu, J.E., Salman, H., Razenshteyn, I.P., Li, J.: Randomized smoothing of all shapes and sizes. In: Proceedings of the 37th International Conference on Machine Learning, ICML. Proceedings of Machine Learning Research, vol. 119. PMLR (2020)
40. Yuviler, T., Drachsler-Cohen, D.: One pixel adversarial attacks via sketched programs. Proc. ACM Program. Lang. **7**(PLDI) (2023)
41. Zhang, H., Weng, T., Chen, P., Hsieh, C., Daniel, L.: Efficient neural network robustness certification with general activation functions. In: Advances in Neural Information Processing Systems 31: Annual Conference on Neural Information Processing Systems, NeurIPS (2018)

Unifying Qualitative and Quantitative Safety Verification of DNN-Controlled Systems

Dapeng Zhi[1], Peixin Wang[2(✉)] , Si Liu[3] , C.-H. Luke Ong[2] , and Min Zhang[1]

[1] Shanghai Key Laboratory of Trustworthy Computing,
East China Normal University, Shanghai, China
[2] Nanyang Technological University, Singapore, Singapore
peixin.wang@ntu.edu.sg
[3] ETH Zurich, Zurich, Switzerland

Abstract. The rapid advance of deep reinforcement learning techniques enables the oversight of safety-critical systems through the utilization of Deep Neural Networks (DNNs). This underscores the pressing need to promptly establish certified safety guarantees for such DNN-controlled systems. Most of the existing verification approaches rely on qualitative approaches, predominantly employing reachability analysis. However, qualitative verification proves inadequate for DNN-controlled systems as their behaviors exhibit stochastic tendencies when operating in open and adversarial environments. In this paper, we propose a novel framework for unifying both qualitative and quantitative safety verification problems of DNN-controlled systems. This is achieved by formulating the verification tasks as the synthesis of valid neural barrier certificates (NBCs). Initially, the framework seeks to establish almost-sure safety guarantees through qualitative verification. In cases where qualitative verification fails, our quantitative verification method is invoked, yielding precise lower and upper bounds on probabilistic safety across both infinite and finite time horizons. To facilitate the synthesis of NBCs, we introduce their k-inductive variants. We also devise a simulation-guided approach for training NBCs, aiming to achieve tightness in computing precise certified lower and upper bounds. We prototype our approach into a tool called and showcase its efficacy on four classic DNN-controlled systems.

Keywords: Safety verification · DNN-controlled systems · Neural barrier certificates

1 Introduction

The widespread adoption of deep reinforcement learning techniques has propelled advancements in autonomous systems, endowing them with adaptive decision-making capabilities by Deep Neural Networks (DNNs) [36]. Ensuring the safety of these DNN-controlled systems emerges as a critical concern, necessitating the

© The Author(s) 2024
A. Gurfinkel and V. Ganesh (Eds.): CAV 2024, LNCS 14682, pp. 401–426, 2024.
https://doi.org/10.1007/978-3-031-65630-9_20

provision of certified safety guarantees. Formal methods, renowned for their rigorousness and automaticity in delivering verified safety assurances, stand as a promising means to address this concern. However, most of the existing formal verification approaches rely on qualitative approaches, predominantly employing reachability analysis [47]. Despite their significance, qualitative results fall short for DNN-controlled systems due to the constant influence of various uncertainties from different sources, such as environment noises [68], unreliable sensors [55], and even malicious attacks [67]. When qualitative verification fails, it becomes both desirable and practical to obtain quantitative guarantees, including quantified lower and upper bounds on the safety probabilities of the systems. This necessitates the use of quantitative verification engines [47].

Quantitative verification has proven its efficacy in enhancing the design and deployment across a variety of applications, including autonomous systems [33], self-adaptive systems [13], distributed communication protocols [26], and probabilistic programs [57]. These applications are commonly modeled using automata-based quantitative formalisms [25], such as Markov chains, timed automata, and hybrid automata, and undergo verification using tools such as Prism [32] and STORM [27]. Nonetheless, the quantitative verification of DNN-controlled systems is challenging due to the incorporation of intricate and almost inexplicable decision-making models by DNNs [46]. Compounding the issue, the difficulty is amplified by the continuous and infinite state space, as well as the non-linear dynamics inherent in DNN-controlled systems. First, building a faithful automata-based probabilistic model for a DNN-controlled system is challenging. This difficulty arises as one cannot predict the action a DNN might take until a specific state is provided, and exhaustively enumerating all continuous states is impractical. Second, even if such a model is constructed under certain constraints, such as bounded steps [9] and state abstractions [31], verification is susceptible to state exploration issues—a well-known problem in model checking [52]. For instance, the verification process can take up to 50 minutes for just 7 steps [9].

Leveraging barrier certificates (BCs) for verification emerges as a promising technique for formally establishing the safety of non-linear and stochastic systems [34,43]. A BC partitions the state space of the system into two parts, ensuring that all trajectories starting from a given initial set, located within one side of the BC, cannot reach a given set of states (deemed to be unsafe), located on the other side, almost surely (i.e., with probability 1) or with probability at least $p \in [0, 1)$. Once a BC is computed, it can be used to certify systems' safety properties either qualitatively or quantitatively. Recently, studies have shown that BCs can be implemented and trained in neural forms called Neural Barrier Certificates (NBCs). NBCs facilitate the synthesis of BCs and improve their expressiveness [1,37,38,58,70]. A relevant survey is delegated to [18].

In this paper, we propose a unified framework for both qualitatively and quantitatively verifying the safety of DNN-controlled systems by leveraging NBCs. The key idea is to reduce both qualitative and quantitative verification problems into a cohesive synthesis task of their respective NBCs. Specifically, we first seek to establish almost-sure safety guarantees through qualitative verification. In cases where qualitative verification fails, our quantitative verification method is invoked, yielding precise lower and upper bounds on probabilistic safety across both infinite and finite time horizons.

We also establish relevant theoretical results. In qualitative verification, we prove that an NBC satisfying corresponding conditions serves as a qualitative safety certificate. In the quantitative counterpart, we establish that valid NBCs can be utilized to calculate certified upper and lower bounds on the probabilistic safety of systems, encompassing both infinite and finite time horizons. For infinite time horizons, as the lower bounds on probabilistic safety approach zero, indicating a decreasing trend in safety probabilities along the time horizon, we provide both linearly and exponentially decreasing lower and upper bounds on the safety probabilities over finite time horizons.

To facilitate the synthesis of valid NBCs, we further relax their constraints by defining their k-inductive variants [6]. This necessitates the conditions to be inductive for k-compositions of the transition relation within a specified bound k [11]. Consequently, synthesizing a qualified NBC becomes more manageable under these k-inductive conditions, while ensuring safety guarantees. As valid NBCs are not unique and yield different certified bounds, we devise a simulation-guided approach to train potential NBCs. This approach aims to enhance their capability to produce more precise certified bounds. Specifically, we estimate safety probabilities through simulation. The differences between the simulation results and the bounds provided by potential NBCs are incorporated into the loss function. This integration can yield more precise certified bounds after potential NBCs are successfully validated.

We prototype our approach into a tool, called UniQQ, and apply it to four classic DNN-controlled problems. The experimental results showcase the effectiveness of our unified verification approach in delivering both qualitative and quantitative safety guarantees across diverse noise scenarios. Additionally, the results underscore the efficacy of k-inductive variants in reducing verification overhead, by 25% on average, and that of our simulation-based training method in yielding tighter safety bounds, with an up to 47.5% improvement over ordinary training approaches.

Contributions. Overall, we make the following contributions.

1. We present a novel framework that unifies both qualitative and quantitative safety verification of DNN-controlled systems by reducing these verification problems into the cohesive task of synthesizing NBCs.
2. We establish relevant theoretical results, including new constraints of NBCs for both qualitative and quantitative safety verification and the associated lower and upper bounds for safety probabilities in both linear and exponential forms.
3. To accelerate training, we relax the constraints of NBCs by introducing their k-inductive variants. We also present a simulation-guided approach designed to train potential NBCs to compute safety bounds as tightly as possible.

4. We develop a prototype of our approach, showcasing its efficacy across four classic DNN-controlled systems.

All omitted proofs and supplementary experimental results can be found in the full version [71].

2 Preliminaries

Let $\mathbb{N}$, $\mathbb{Z}$, and $\mathbb{R}$ be the sets of natural numbers, integers, and real numbers, respectively.

2.1 DNN-Controlled Systems

We consider DNN-controlled systems where the control policies are implemented by deep neural networks and suppose the networks are trained for specific tasks. Formally, a DNN-controlled system is a tuple $M = (S, S_0, A, \pi, f, R)$, where $S \subseteq \mathbb{R}^n$ is the set of (possibly continuous and infinite) system states, $S_0 \subseteq S$ is the set of initial states, A is the set of actions, $\pi : S \to A$ is the trained policy implemented by a neural network, $f : S \times A \to S$ is the system dynamics, and $R : S \times A \times S \to \mathbb{R}$ is the reward function.

Trajectories. A trained DNN-controlled system $M = (S, S_0, A, \pi, f, R)$ is a decision-making system that continuously interacts with the environment. At each time step $t \in \mathbb{N}_0$, it observes a state s_t and feeds s_t into its planted NN to compute the optimal action $a_t = \pi(s_t)$ that shall be taken. Action a_t is then performed, which transits s_t into the next state $s_{t+1} = f(s_t, a_t)$ via the system dynamics f and earns a reward $r_{t+1} = R(s_t, a_t, s_{t+1})$. Given an initial state $s_0 \in S_0$, a sequence of states generated during interaction is called a *trajectory*, denoted as $\omega = \{s_t\}_{t \in \mathbb{N}_0}$. To ease the notation, we denote by ω_t the t-th element of ω, i.e., $\omega_t = s_t$, and by Ω the set of all trajectories.

State Perturbations. As DNN-controlled systems collect state information via sensors, uncertainties inevitably originate from sensor errors, equipment inaccuracy, or even adversarial attacks [66,68]. Therefore, the observed states of the systems can be perturbed and actions are computed based on the perturbed states. Formally, an observed state at time step t is $\hat{s}_t := s_t + \delta_t$ where $\delta_t \sim \mu$ is a random noise and μ is a probability distribution over $\mathbb{R}^n$. We denote by $W := \text{supp}(\mu)$ the support of μ. Due to perturbation, the actual successor state is $s_{t+1} := f(s_t, \hat{a}_t)$ with $\hat{a}_t := \pi(\hat{s}_t)$ and the reward is $r_{t+1} := R(s_t, \hat{a}_t, s_{t+1})$. Note that the successor state and the reward are calculated according to the actual state and the action on the perturbed state, and this update is common [68]. We then denote a DNN-controlled system M perturbed by a noise distribution μ as $M_\mu = (S, S_0, A, \pi, f, R, \mu)$.

Assumptions. Given a DNN-controlled system $M = (S, S_0, A, \pi, f, R)$, we assume that the state space S is compact in the Euclidean topology of $\mathbb{R}^n$, its system dynamics f and trained policy π are Lipschitz continuous. We further assume that the system has forward invariance [62], i.e., all the states fall into the state space. These assumptions are common in control theory [4,72]. For perturbation, we require that the noise distribution μ either has bounded support or is a product of independent univariate distributions.

Probability Space. Given a DNN-controlled system $M_\mu = (S, S_0, A, \pi, f, R, \mu)$, for each initial state $s_0 \in S_0$, there exists a *probability space* $(\Omega_{s_0}, \mathcal{F}_{s_0}, \mathbb{P}_{s_0})$ such that Ω_{s_0} is the set of all trajectories starting from s_0 by the environmental interaction, $\mathcal{F}_{s_0}$ is a σ-algebra over Ω_{s_0} (i.e., a collection of subsets of Ω_{s_0} that contains the empty set $\emptyset$ and is closed under complementation and countable union), and $\mathbb{P}_{s_0} : \mathcal{F}_{s_0} \to [0, 1]$ is a probability measure on $\mathcal{F}_{s_0}$. We denote the expectation operator in this probability space by $\mathbb{E}_{s_0}$.

2.2   Barrier Certificate and Its Neural Implementation

Barrier certificates (BCs) are powerful tools to certify the safety of continuous-time dynamical systems. In the following we describe the discrete-time BCs which this work is based upon. We refer readers to [42,44] for details about continuous-time BCs.

Definition 1 (Discrete-time Barrier Certificates). *Given a DNN-controlled system* $M = (S, S_0, A, f, \pi, R)$ *with an unsafe set* $S_u \subseteq S$ *such that* $S_u \cap S_0 = \emptyset$. *A discrete-time barrier certificate is a real-valued function* $B : S \to \mathbb{R}$ *such that for some constant* $\lambda \in (0, 1]$, *it holds that:*

$$B(s) \leq 0 \qquad \qquad \text{for all } s \in S_0, \qquad (1)$$

$$B(s) > 0 \qquad \qquad \text{for all } s \in S_u, \qquad (2)$$

$$B(f(s, \pi(s))) - B(s) + \lambda \cdot B(s) \leq 0 \qquad \qquad \text{for all } s \in S. \qquad (3)$$

If there exists such a BC for the system M, then M is safe, i.e., the system cannot reach a state in the unsafe set S_u from the initial set S_0. The intuition is that: Condition (3) implies that for any $s \in S$ such that $B(s) \leq 0$, $B(f(s, \pi(s))) \leq 0$. Since Condition (1) asserts that the initial value of B is not greater than zero, any trajectory $\omega \in \Omega_{s_0}$ starting from an initial state $s_0 \in S_0$ cannot enter the unsafe set S_u, where $B(s) > 0$ (see Condition (2)), thereby ensuring the safety of the system.

Finding a BC is restricted to the expressiveness of templates. For example, even if there exists a function satisfying Condition (1) to (3), it may be not found under polynomial forms. Recent work [41,69,70] proposes a neural implementation of BCs as deep neural networks, leveraging the expressiveness of neural networks. The neural implementation of a BC is called a neural barrier certificate (NBC), which consists of training and validation. First, a learner trains a neural network (NN) to fit over a finite set of samples the conditions for a BC. After training, an NBC is then checked whether it meets the conditions. This is achieved by a verifier using SMT solvers [41,70] or other methods like

Sum-of-Squares programming [69]. If the validation result is false, a set of counterexamples can be generated for future training. This iteration is repeated until a trained candidate is validated or a given timeout is reached. This training and validation iteration is called CounterExample-Guided Inductive Synthesis (CEGIS) [2].

3   Verification Problem and Our Framework

3.1   Problem Statement

We consider the safety of DNN-controlled systems from both qualitative and quantitative perspectives. Below we fix a DNN-controlled system $M_\mu = (S, S_0, A, \pi, f, R, \mu)$ and an unsafe set $S_u \subseteq S$ such that $S_0 \cap S_u = \emptyset$ throughout the paper.

Definition 2 (Almost-Sure Safety). *The system M_μ is almost-surely (a.s.) safe, if a.s. no trajectories starting from any initial state $s_0 \in S_0$ enter S_u, i.e.,*

$$\forall s_0 \in S_0.\omega \in \Omega_{s_0} \implies \omega_t \notin S_u \ \forall t \in \mathbb{N}.$$

This almost-sure safety is a qualitative property and we call it "almost-sure" due to the stochasticity from state perturbations. Since the almost-sure safety does not always exist with the increase of state perturbations, we propose the notion of probabilistic safety over infinite time horizons.

Definition 3 (Probabilistic Safety over Infinite Time Horizons). *The system M_μ is probabilistically safe over infinite time horizons with $[l_{\inf}, u_{\inf}]$, where $0 \leq l_{\inf} \leq u_{\inf} \leq 1$, if the probability of not entering S_u falls into $[l_{\inf}, u_{\inf}]$ for all the trajectories from any initial state $s_0 \in S_0$, i.e.,*

$$\forall s_0 \in S_0.\mathbb{P}_{s_0} \left[\{ \omega \in \Omega_{s_0} \mid \omega_t \notin S_u \text{ for all } t \in \mathbb{N} \} \right] \in [l_{\inf}, u_{\inf}].$$

The probabilistic safety is a quantitative property and $l_{\inf}, u_{\inf}$ are called *lower* and *upper* bounds on the safety probabilities over infinite time horizons, respectively. Once both bounds equal one, it implies the almost-sure safety. When the lower bound $l_{\inf} = 0$, indicating that the system reaches the unsafe region at some time step $T < \infty$, it is significant to figure out how the safety probability decreases over the finite time horizon. Therefore, we present the probabilistic safety over finite time horizons as follows.

Definition 4 (Probabilistic Safety over Finite Time Horizons). *The system M_μ is probabilistically safe over a finite time horizon $T \in [0, \infty)$ with $[l_{\text{fin}}, u_{\text{fin}}]$, where $0 \leq l_{\text{fin}} \leq u_{\text{fin}} \leq 1$, if the probability of not entering S_u within T falls into $[l_{\text{fin}}, u_{\text{fin}}]$ for all the trajectories starting from any initial state $s_0 \in S_0$,*

$$\forall s_0 \in S_0.\mathbb{P}_{s_0} \left[\{ \omega \in \Omega_{s_0} \mid \omega_t \notin S_u \text{ for all } t \leq T \} \right] \in [l_{\text{fin}}, u_{\text{fin}}].$$

Safety Verification Problems of DNN-Controlled Systems. Consider a DNN-controlled system $M_\mu = (S, S_0, A, \pi, f, R, \mu)$ with an unsafe set $S_u \in S$ such that $S_0 \cap S_u = \emptyset$. We formulate the qualitative and quantitative safety verification problems of M_μ as follows:

1. **Qualitative Verification (QV):** To answer whether M_μ is almost-surely safe.
2. **Quantitative Verification over Infinite Time Horizons (QVITH):** To compute certified lower and upper bounds $l_{\inf}, u_{\inf}$ on the safety probability of M_μ over infinite time horizons.
3. **Quantitative Verification over Finite Time Horizons (QVFTH):** To compute certified lower and upper bounds $l_{\text{fin}}, u_{\text{fin}}$ on the safety probability of M_μ over a finite time horizon T.

3.2 Overview of Our Framework

We first provide an overview of our unified framework designed to address the three safety verification problems. Our framework builds on two fundamental results: (i) all the problems can be reduced to the task of defining BCs under specific conditions, and the defined BCs can be used to certify almost-sure safety for **QV** or safety bounds for **QVITH** and **QVFTH**, respectively, and (ii) these BCs can be implemented and trained in neural forms. The fundamental results are presented in Sects. 4 to 6, respectively.

The synthesis of NBCs has a preset timeout threshold, i.e., it will fail if NBCs cannot be successfully synthesized within the time threshold. The procedure of our framework is sketched in Fig. 1, which consists of the following three steps:

Step 1: QV. We try to synthesize an NBC satisfying conditions in Theorem 1. If such an NBC is successfully synthesized, we can conclude that the system M_μ is almost-surely safe by Theorem 1 and finish the verification. Alternatively, we can resort to synthesizing a k-inductive NBC in Theorem 8 whose conditions are weaker than those in Theorem 1. If the synthesis fails, we proceed to quantitative verification.

Step 2: QVITH. We try to synthesize two NBCs under the conditions in Theorems 2 and 3, respectively. If the synthesis fails, a timeout will be reported and the process will be terminated. Otherwise, we can obtain the lower bound $l_{\inf}$ and the upper bound $u_{\inf}$ on probabilistic safety over infinite time horizons. Alternatively, we can choose to synthesize the k-inductive variants of NBCs in Theorems 9 and 10. If the lower bound $l_{\inf}$ is no less than some preset safety threshold $\delta \in (0, 1)$, we terminate the verification. The purpose of setting δ is to prevent the verification from returning a meaningless lower bound such as 0. If $l_{\inf}$ is less than δ, we resort to computing safety bounds over finite time horizons.

Step 3: QVFTH. We try to synthesize two NBCs satisfying conditions in Theorems 4 and 6, respectively. If the synthesis fails, a timeout will be reported and the verification will terminate. Otherwise, we can compute the linear lower and upper bounds on probabilistic safety over finite time horizons according

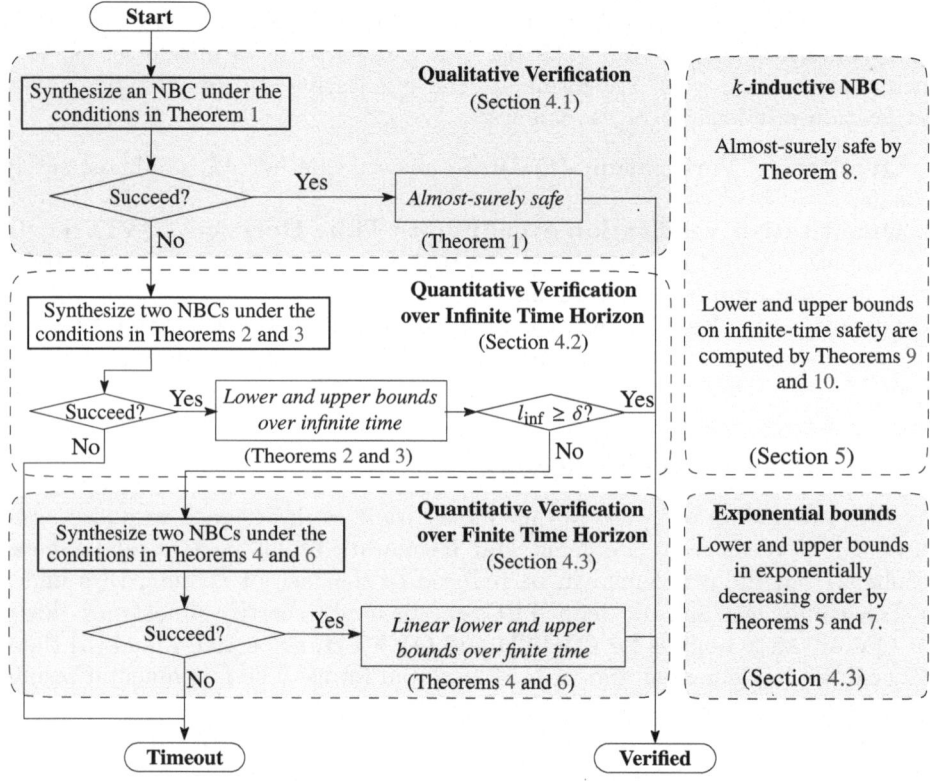

Fig. 1. UniQQ: The unified verification framework.

to the synthesized NBCs. Alternatively, we can choose to synthesize two NBCs satisfying conditions in Theorems 5 and 7 to achieve exponential bounds, which might be tighter than linear ones.

4   Qualitative and Quantitative Safety Verification

In this section, we reduce all three safety verification problems of DNN-controlled systems into a cohesive problem of defining corresponding BCs. We establish specific conditions for candidate BCs and provide formulas for computing lower and upper bounds for quantitative verification based on the defined BCs.

4.1   Qualitative Safety Verification

Theorem 1 (Almost-Sure Safety). *Given an M_μ with an initial set S_0 and an unsafe set S_u, if there exists a barrier certificate $B : S \to \mathbb{R}$ such that for some constant $\lambda \in (0, 1]$, the following conditions hold:*

$$B(s) \leq 0 \qquad \qquad \text{for all } s \in S_0, \quad (4)$$

$$B(s) > 0 \qquad \qquad \text{for all } s \in S_u, \quad (5)$$

$$B(f(s, \pi(s + \delta))) - B(s) + \lambda \cdot B(s) \leq 0 \qquad \text{for all } (s, \delta) \in S \times W, \quad (6)$$

then M_μ is almost-surely safe, i.e., $\forall s_0 \in S_0.\ \omega \in \Omega_{s_0} \implies \omega_t \notin S_u \ \forall t \in \mathbb{N}$.

Intuition. The BC in Theorem 1 is similar to that in Definition 1 except Condition (6), in which we consider all stochastic behaviors of the system from state perturbations. The proof of Theorem 1 resembles that in [43, Proposition 2].

Proof. We prove Theorem 1 by contradiction. Assume that there exists a barrier certificate B satisfying conditions (4)-(6), but the system is unsafe, i.e., there is a time step $T > 0$ and an initial state $s_0 \in S_0$ such that $s_T \in S_u$. Condition (6) implies that for any state $s \in S$ such that $B(s) \leq 0$ and a noise $\delta \in W$, the value of B at the next step is no more than zero, i.e., $B(f(s, \pi(s + \delta))) \leq 0$. As a result, $B(s_T)$ must be no more than zero, which is contradictory to Condition (5). Therefore, the system with a BC in Theorem 1 is almost-surely safe. $\square$

4.2   Quantitative Safety Verification over Infinite Time Horizon

Below we present the state-dependent lower and upper bounds on probabilistic safety over infinite time horizons.

Theorem 2 (Lower Bounds on Infinite-time Safety). *Given an M_μ with an initial set S_0 and an unsafe set S_u, if there exists a barrier certificate B : $S \to \mathbb{R}$ such that for some constant $\epsilon \in [0, 1]$, the following conditions hold:*

$$B(s) \geq 0 \qquad \qquad \text{for all } s \in S, \quad (7)$$

$$B(s) \leq \epsilon \qquad \qquad \text{for all } s \in S_0, \quad (8)$$

$$B(s) \geq 1 \qquad \qquad \text{for all } s \in S_u, \quad (9)$$

$$\mathbb{E}_{\delta \sim \mu}[B(f(s, \pi(s + \delta))) \mid s] - B(s) \leq 0 \qquad \text{for all } s \in S \setminus S_u, \quad (10)$$

then the safety probability over infinite time horizons is bounded from below by

$$\forall s_0 \in S_0.\ \mathbb{P}_{s_0}\left[\{\omega \in \Omega_{s_0} \mid \omega_t \notin S_u \text{ for all } t \in \mathbb{N}\}\right] \geq 1 - B(s_0). \quad (11)$$

Intuition. A BC under conditions in Theorem 2 is a non-negative real-valued function satisfying the supermartingale property, i.e., the expected value of the function remains non-increasing at every time step for all states not in S_u (see Condition (10)). The proof of Theorem 2 resembles that in [43, Theorem 15].

Proof (Sketch). To obtain the lower bound in Eq. (11), we first construct a stochastic process $\{X_t\}_{t \geq 0}$ where $X_t = B(s_t)$ with the safe initial state $s_0 \in S_0$ (see Condition (8)). Let κ be the first time that the system enters the unsafe set S_u. Then we prove that the stopped process of $\{X_t\}_{t \geq 0}$ w.r.t. κ is a non-negative supermartingale by Condition (7) and Condition (10). By Condition (9) and Ville's inequality [54], we have that $\mathbb{P}_{s_0}[s_t \in S_u \text{ for some } t \in \mathbb{N}] \leq X_0 = B(s_0)$. Finally, we obtain the lower bound in Eq. (11) by the complementation of the above upper bound.

Theorem 3 (Upper Bounds on Infinite-time Safety). *Given an M_μ with an initial set S_0 and an unsafe set S_u, if there exists a barrier certificate B : $S \to \mathbb{R}$ such that for some constants $\gamma \in (0,1)$, $0 \le \epsilon' < \epsilon \le 1$, the following conditions hold:*

$$0 \le B(s) \le 1 \qquad\qquad\qquad\qquad\qquad\qquad \text{for all } s \in S, \qquad (12)$$
$$B(s) \ge \epsilon \qquad\qquad\qquad\qquad\qquad\qquad\qquad \text{for all } s \in S_0, \qquad (13)$$
$$B(s) \le \epsilon' \qquad\qquad\qquad\qquad\qquad\qquad\qquad \text{for all } s \in S_u, \qquad (14)$$
$$B(s) - \gamma \cdot \mathbb{E}_{\delta \sim \mu}[B(f(s, \pi(s + \delta))) \mid s] \le 0 \qquad \text{for all } s \in S \setminus S_u, \qquad (15)$$

then the safety probability over infinite time horizons is bounded from above by

$$\forall s_0 \in S_0. \ \mathbb{P}_{s_0}\left[\{\omega \in \Omega_{s_0} \mid \omega_t \notin S_u \text{ for all } t \in \mathbb{N}\}\right] \le 1 - B(s_0). \qquad (16)$$

Intuition. A BC under conditions in Theorem 3 is a bounded non-negative function satisfying the γ-scaled submartingale property [53], i.e., the expected value of B is increasing at each time step for states not in S_u (Condition (15)). We prove the theorem by Optional Stopping Theorem [56], while the former work [50] is based on fixed-point theory [17].

Proof (Sketch). The proof is similar to that in Theorem 2. To obtain the upper bound in Eq. (16), we first construct a stochastic process $\{Y_t\}_{t \ge 0}$ such that $Y_t = \gamma^t B(s_t)$ with the safe initial state $s_0 \in S_0$ (see Condition (13) and Condition (14)). Let κ be the first time that the system enters the unsafe set S_u. Then we prove that the stopped process of $\{Y_t\}_{t \ge 0}$ w.r.t. κ is a submartingale by Condition (12) and Condition (15). By applying the Optional Stopping Theorem [56], we derive that $\mathbb{P}_{s_0}[s_t \in S_u \text{ for some } t \in \mathbb{N}] \ge B(s_0)$. Finally, we obtain the upper bound in Eq. (16) by the complementation of the derived lower bound.

4.3 Quantitative Safety Verification over Finite Time Horizon

When the safety probability over infinite time horizons exhibits a decline, it becomes advantageous to analyze the decreasing changes over finite time horizons. In the following, we present our theoretical results on finite-time safety verification, starting with two results related to lower bounds.

Theorem 4 (Linear Lower Bounds on Finite-time Safety). *Given an M_μ with an initial set S_0 and an unsafe set S_u, if there exists a barrier certificate B : $S \to \mathbb{R}$ such that for some constants $\lambda > \epsilon \ge 0$ and $c \ge 0$, the following conditions hold:*

$$B(s) \ge 0 \qquad\qquad\qquad\qquad\qquad\qquad\qquad \text{for all } s \in S, \qquad (17)$$
$$B(s) \le \epsilon \qquad\qquad\qquad\qquad\qquad\qquad\qquad \text{for all } s \in S_0, \qquad (18)$$
$$B(s) \ge \lambda \qquad\qquad\qquad\qquad\qquad\qquad\qquad \text{for all } s \in S_u, \qquad (19)$$
$$\mathbb{E}_{\delta \sim \mu}[B(f(s, \pi(s + \delta))) \mid s] - B(s) \le c \qquad\quad \text{for all } s \in S, \qquad (20)$$

then the safety probability over a finite time horizon T is bounded from below by

$$\forall s_0 \in S_0. \, \mathbb{P}_{s_0} \left[\{ \omega \in \Omega_{s_0} \mid \omega_t \notin S_u \text{ for all } t \leq T \} \right] \geq 1 - (B(s_0) + cT)/\lambda.$$

Intuition. A BC in Theorem 4 satisfies the c-martingale property [49], i.e., the expected value of B can increase at every time step as long as it is bounded by a constant c (Condition (20)), which is less conservative than the supermartingle property (Condition (10)), at the cost providing safety guarantees over finite time horizons. We prove the theorem by Ville's Inequality [54] and the proof resembles that in [6, Theorem 9].

Theorem 5 (Exponential Lower Bounds on Finite-time Safety). *Given an M_μ if there exists a function $B : S \to \mathbb{R}$ such that for some constants $\alpha > 0, \beta \in \mathbb{R}$, and $\gamma \in [0, 1)$, the following conditions hold:*

$$B(s) \geq 0 \qquad\qquad\qquad\qquad\qquad \text{for all } s \in S, \qquad (21)$$
$$B(s) \leq \gamma \qquad\qquad\qquad\qquad\qquad \text{for all } s \in S_0, \qquad (22)$$
$$B(s) \geq 1 \qquad\qquad\qquad\qquad\qquad \text{for all } s \in S_u, \qquad (23)$$
$$\alpha \mathbb{E}_{\delta \sim \mu}[B(f(s, \pi(s + \delta))) \mid s] - B(s) \leq \alpha\beta \qquad \text{for all } s \in S \setminus S_u. \qquad (24)$$

then the safety probability over a finite time horizon T is bounded from below by

$$\forall s_0 \in S_0. \, \mathbb{P}_{s_0} \left[\{ \omega \in \Omega_{s_0} \mid \omega_t \notin S_u \text{ for all } t \leq T \} \right] \geq 1 - \frac{\alpha\beta}{\alpha - 1} + \left(\frac{\alpha\beta}{\alpha - 1} - B(s_0) \right) \cdot \alpha^{-T}.$$

Intuition. A BC in Theorem 5 satisfies that its α-scaled expectation can increase at most $\alpha\beta$ at every time step (Condition (24)). We establish a new result in discrete-time DNN-controlled systems and prove it by the discrete version of Gronwall's Inequality [24], which is inspired by former work [60] in continuous-time dynamical systems.

Then we propose our two results of upper bounds on safety probabilities.

Theorem 6 (Linear Upper Bounds on Finite-time Safety). *Given an M_μ with an initial set S_0 and an unsafe set S_u, if there exists a barrier function $B : S \to \mathbb{R}$ such that for some constants $\beta \in (0, 1), \beta < \alpha < 1 + \beta, c \geq 0$, the following conditions hold:*

$$B(s) \geq 0 \qquad\qquad\qquad\qquad\qquad \text{for all } s \in S, \qquad (25)$$
$$B(s) \leq \beta \qquad\qquad\qquad\qquad\qquad \text{for all } s \in S \setminus S_u, \qquad (26)$$
$$\alpha \leq B(s) \leq 1 + \beta \qquad\qquad\qquad\qquad \text{for all } s \in S_u, \qquad (27)$$
$$\mathbb{E}_{\delta \sim \mu}[B(f(s, \pi(s + \delta))) \mid s] - B(s) \geq c \qquad \text{for all } s \in S \setminus S_u. \qquad (28)$$

then the safety probability over a finite time horizon T is bounded from above by

$$\forall s_0 \in S_0. \, \mathbb{P}_{s_0} \left[\{ \omega \in \Omega_{s_0} \mid \omega_t \notin S_u \text{ for all } t \leq T \} \right] \leq 1 - B(s_0) - \frac{1}{2} c \cdot T + \beta.$$

Intuition. A BC in Theorem 6 is non-negative and its value is bounded when states are in S_u (Condition (27)). Moreover, Condition (28) is the inverse of the c-martingale property in Theorem 4, i.e., the expected value of B should increase at least c at every time step.

Theorem 7 (Exponential Upper Bounds on Finite-Time Safety). *Given an M_μ with an initial set S_0 and an unsafe set S_u, if there exists a barrier function $B : S \to \mathbb{R}$ such that for some constants $K' \leq K < 0$, $\epsilon > 0$ and a non-empty interval $[a, b]$, the following conditions hold:*

$$B(s) \geq 0 \qquad\qquad\qquad\qquad\qquad\qquad \text{for all } s \in S \setminus S_u, \quad (29)$$
$$K' \leq B(s) \leq K \qquad\qquad\qquad\qquad\qquad \text{for all } s \in S_u, \quad (30)$$
$$\mathbb{E}_{\delta \sim \mu}[B(f(s, \pi(s + \delta))) \mid s] - B(s) \leq -\epsilon \qquad \text{for all } s \in S \setminus S_u, \quad (31)$$
$$a \leq B(f(s, \pi(s + \delta))) - B(s) \leq b \qquad \text{for all } s \in S \setminus S_u \text{ and } \delta \in W, \quad (32)$$

then the safety probability over a finite time horizon T is bounded from above by

$$\forall s_0 \in S_0. \; \mathbb{P}_{s_0}\left[\{\omega \in \Omega_{s_0} \mid \omega_t \notin S_u \text{ for all } t \leq T\}\right] \leq exp(-\frac{2(\epsilon \cdot T - B(s_0))^2}{T \cdot (b - a)^2}).$$

Intuition. A BC under Conditions (29) to (32) is a difference-bounded ranking supermartingale [16]. Condition (31) is the supermartingale difference condition, i.e., the expectation of B should decrease at least ϵ at each time step, while Condition (32) implies that the update of B should be bounded. We prove this theorem by Hoeffding's Inequality on Supermartingales [28] and the proof resembles that in the work [16].

Remark 1. In this section, we establish relevant theoretical results from the perspectives of qualitative and quantitative verification. In qualitative verification, we prove that an NBC satisfying corresponding conditions serves as a qualitative safety certificate. In the quantitative counterpart, we establish that valid NBCs can be utilized to calculate certified upper and lower bounds on the probabilistic safety of systems. It is worth noting that, for unifying safety verification in Fig. 1, new theoretical results (Theorem 5 and Theorem 6) are established, which mitigates the gaps of existing results [42,43].

Common conditions of different BCs. To clarify the construction of different BCs, we give three common categories of their conditions. The first two categories define the bounds of BCs for initial states and unsafe states, ensuring they are disjoint. The third category specifies the monotonicity of the (expected) BC values for successor states, yielding the possibility of the system reaching the unsafe set.

5   Relaxed k-Inductive Barrier Certificates

We now introduce k-inductive barrier certificates, capable of offering both qualitative and quantitative safety guarantees, while relaxing the strict conditions for safety through the utilization of the k-induction principle [11,20]. Prior to presenting our theoretical results, we first define the notion of k-inductive update functions as follows.

Definition 5 (k-inductive Update Functions). *Given an $M_\mu = (S, S_0, A, \pi, f, R, \mu)$, a k-inductive update function $g_{\pi,f}^k$ with respect to π, f is defined recursively, i.e.,*

$$g_{\pi,f}^k(s_t, \Delta_t^k) = \begin{cases} g_{\pi,f}(g_{\pi,f}^{k-1}(s_t, \Delta_t^{k-1}), \delta_{t+k-1}) & \text{if } k > 1 \\ f(s_t, \pi(s_t + \delta_t)) & \text{if } k = 1 \\ s_t & \text{if } k = 0 \end{cases}$$

where $\Delta_t^k = [\delta_t, \delta_{t+1}, \ldots, \delta_{t+k-1}]$ is a noise vector of length k with each $\delta_t \sim \mu$, and $g_{\pi,f}(s_t, \delta_t) := f(s_t, \pi(s_t + \delta_t))$.

Intuitively, $g_{\pi,f}^k$ computes the value of a state after k steps given a k-dimensional noise vector $\Delta^k \in W^k \subseteq \mathbb{R}^{n \times k}$, where $W = \text{supp}(\mu)$ is the support of μ. To calculate the expectation w.r.t. k-dimensional noises, we denote by μ^k the product measure on W^k.

5.1 k-Inductive Barrier Certificates for Qualitative Safety

Theorem 8 (k-inductive Variant of Almost-Sure Safety). *Given an M_μ with an initial set S_0 and an unsafe set S_u, if there exists a k-inductive barrier certificate $B : S \to \mathbb{R}$ such that the following conditions hold:*

$$\bigwedge_{0 \leq i < k} B(g_{\pi,f}^i(s, \Delta^i)) \leq 0 \qquad\qquad \forall (s, \Delta^i) \in S_0 \times W^i, \tag{33}$$

$$B(s) > 0 \qquad\qquad \forall s \in S_u, \tag{34}$$

$$\bigwedge_{0 \leq i < k}(B(g_{\pi,f}^i(s, \Delta^i)) \leq 0) \implies B(g_{\pi,f}^k(s, \Delta^k)) \leq 0 \quad \forall (s, \Delta^i) \in S \times W^i, \tag{35}$$

then the system M_μ is almost-surely safe, i.e., $\forall s_0 \in S_0.\ \omega \in \Omega_{s_0} \implies \omega_t \notin S_u\ \forall t \in \mathbb{N}$.

Intuition. Condition (33) implies that the state sequences starting from the safe set will remain in the safe set for the next $k - 1$ consecutive time steps, while Condition (35) means that for any k consecutive time steps, if the system is safe, then the system will still be safe at the $(k + 1)$-th time step. We prove the theorem by contradiction.

Note that Condition (35) contains an implication, in order to compute the k-inductive BC, we replace it with its sufficient condition:

$$- B(g_{\pi,f}^k(s, \Delta^k)) - \sum_{0 \leq i < k} \tau_i \cdot (-B(g_{\pi,f}^i(s, \Delta^i))) \geq 0,\ \forall (s, \Delta^i) \in S \times W^i. \tag{36}$$

If there exist $\tau_0, \ldots, \tau_{k-1} \geq 0$ satisfying Eq. (36), Condition (35) is satisfied.

5.2 k-Inductive Barrier Certificates for Quantitative Safety

Theorem 9 (k-inductive Lower Bounds on Infinite-time Safety). *Given an M_μ, if there exists a k-inductive barrier certificate $B : S \to \mathbb{R}$ such that for some constants $k \in \mathbb{N}_{\geq 1}$, $\epsilon \in [0, 1]$ and $c \geq 0$, the following conditions hold:*

$$
\begin{aligned}
&B(s) \geq 0 &&\text{for all } s \in S &&(37)\\
&B(s) \leq \epsilon &&\text{for all } s \in S_0, &&(38)\\
&B(s) \geq 1 &&\text{for all } s \in S_u, &&(39)\\
&\mathbb{E}_{\delta \sim \mu}[B(f(s, \pi(s + \delta))) \mid s] - B(s) \leq c &&\text{for all } s \in S, &&(40)\\
&\mathbb{E}_{\Delta^k \sim \mu^k}[B(f_{\pi,f}^k(s, \Delta^k)) \mid s] - B(s) \leq 0 &&\text{for all } s \in S, &&(41)
\end{aligned}
$$

then the safety probability over infinite time horizons is bounded from below by

$$
\forall s_0 \in S_0. \; \mathbb{P}_{s_0}\left[\{\omega_0 \in \Omega_{s_0} \mid \omega_t \notin S_u \text{ for all } t \in \mathbb{N}\}\right] \geq 1 - kB(s_0) - \frac{k(k-1)c}{2}.
$$

Intuition. Condition (40) requires the barrier certificate to be a c-martingale at every time step and Condition (41) requires the barrier certificate sampled after every k-th step to be a supermartingale. We prove the theorem by Ville's Inequality [54].

Theorem 10 (k-inductive Upper Bounds on Infinite-time Safety). *Given an M_μ, if there exists a barrier certificate $B : S \to \mathbb{R}$ such that for some constant $\gamma \in (0, 1)$, $0 \leq \epsilon' < \epsilon \leq 1$, $c \leq 0$ the following conditions hold:*

$$
\begin{aligned}
&0 \leq B(s) \leq 1 &&\text{for all } s \in S &&(42)\\
&B(s) \geq \epsilon &&\text{for all } s \in S_0, &&(43)\\
&B(s) \leq \epsilon' &&\text{for all } s \in S_u, &&(44)\\
&\mathbb{E}_{\delta \sim \mu}[B(f(s, \pi(s + \delta))) \mid s] - B(s) \geq c &&\text{for all } s \in S, &&(45)\\
&B(s) - \gamma^k \cdot \mathbb{E}_{\Delta^k \sim \mu^k}[B(g_{\pi,f}^k(s, \Delta^k)) \mid s] \leq 0 &&\text{for all } s \in S \setminus S_u, &&(46)
\end{aligned}
$$

then the safety probability over infinite time horizons is bounded from above by

$$
\forall s_0 \in S_0. \; \mathbb{P}_{s_0}\left[\{\omega \in \Omega_{s_0} \mid \omega_t \notin X_u \text{ for all } t \in \mathbb{N}\}\right] \leq 1 - kB(s_0) - \frac{k(k-1)c}{2}.
$$

Intuition. This BC is non-negative and bounded (Condition 42). Condition (45) is the inverse of the c-martingale property, while Condition (46) requires the barrier certificate sampled after every k-th step to be a γ^k-scaled submartingale. We prove the theorem by the Optional Stopping Theorem [56].

Remark 2. To make the probabilistic bounds in Theorem 9 and Theorem 10 non-trivial, the value of k should be bounded by

$$
1 \leq k \leq \frac{(c - 2B(s_0)) + \sqrt{4B(s_0)^2 + c^2 - 4c(B(s_0) - 2)}}{2c}.
$$

Remark 3. In this section, we relax constraints to facilitate the synthesis of valid NBCs by defining their k-inductive variants [6]. Thus, synthesizing a valid NBC becomes more manageable under these k-inductive conditions, while ensuring safety guarantees. Besides, to our best knowledge, Theorem 10 is the first relaxation conclusion for upper bounds on infinite-time safety.

6 Synthesis of Neural Barrier Certificates

In this section, we show that the BCs defined in the previous sections for DNN-controlled systems can be implemented and synthesized in the form of DNNs, akin to those for linear or nonlinear stochastic systems [69].

We adopt the CEGIS-based method [2] to train and validate target NBCs. Figure 2 sketches the workflow. In each loop iteration, we train a candidate BC in the form of a neural network which is then passed to the validation. If the validation result is false, we compute a set of counterexamples for future training. This iteration is repeated until a trained candidate is validated or a given timeout is reached. Moreover, we propose a simulation-guided training method by adding additional terms to the loss functions to improve the tightness of upper and lower bounds calculated by the trained NBCs.

We present the synthesis of NBCs in Theorem 2 for probabilistic safety over infinite time horizons, as an example. We defer to the full version [71] the synthesis of other NBCs.

6.1 Training Candidate NBCs

Two pivotal factors in the training phase are the generation of training data and the construction of the loss function.

Training Data Discretization. As the state space S is possibly continuous and infinite, we choose a finite set of states for training candidate NBCs. This can be achieved by discretizing the state space S and constructing a *discretization* $\tilde{S} \subseteq S$ such that for each $s \in S$, there is a $\tilde{s} \in \tilde{S}$ with $||s - \tilde{s}||_1 < \tau$, where $\tau > 0$ is called the granularity of $\tilde{S}$. As S is compact and thus bounded, this discretization can be computed by simply picking the vertices of a grid with sufficiently small cells. For the re-training after validation failure, $\tilde{S}$ will be reconstructed with counterexamples and a smaller granularity τ. Once the discretization $\tilde{S}$ is obtained, we construct two finite sets $\tilde{S}_0 := \tilde{S} \cap S_0$ and $\tilde{S}_u := \tilde{S} \cap S_u$ used for the training process.

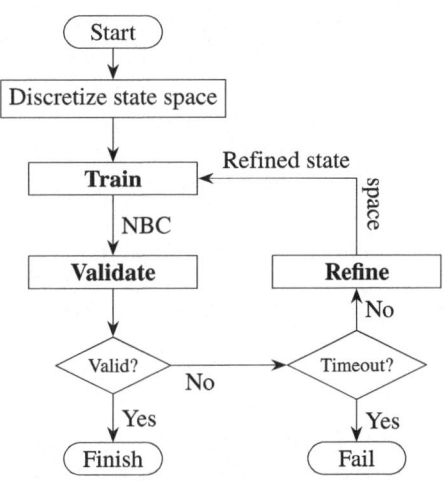

Fig. 2. CEGIS-based NBC synthesis [2].

Loss Function Construction. A candidate NBC is initialized as a neural network h_θ w.r.t. the network parameter θ. h_θ is trained by minimizing the following loss function:

$$\mathcal{L}(\theta) := k_1 \cdot \mathcal{L}_1(\theta) + k_2 \cdot \mathcal{L}_2(\theta) + k_3 \cdot \mathcal{L}_3(\theta) + k_4 \cdot \mathcal{L}_4(\theta) + k_5 \cdot \mathcal{L}_5(\theta)$$

where $k_i \in \mathbb{R}$, $i = 1, \cdots, 5$ are the algorithmic parameters balancing the loss terms.

The first loss term is defined via the condition in Condition (7) as:

$$\mathcal{L}_1(\theta) = \frac{1}{|\tilde{S}|} \sum_{s \in \tilde{S}} (\max\{0 - h_\theta(s), 0\})$$

Intuitively, a loss will incur if either $h_\theta(s)$ is less than zero for any $s \in \tilde{S}$.

Correspondingly, the second and third loss terms are defined via Condition (8) and (9) as:

$$\mathcal{L}_2(\theta) = \frac{1}{|\tilde{S}_0|} \sum_{s \in \tilde{S}_0} (\max\{h_\theta(s) - \epsilon, 0\}), \text{ and } \mathcal{L}_3(\theta) = \frac{1}{|\tilde{S}_u|} \sum_{s \in \tilde{S}_u} (\max\{1 - h_\theta(s), 0\}).$$

The fourth loss term is defined via the condition in Condition (10) as:

$$\mathcal{L}_4(\theta) = \frac{1}{|\tilde{S} \setminus \tilde{S}_u|} \sum_{s \in \tilde{S} \setminus \tilde{S}_u} \left(\max\{ \sum_{s' \in \mathcal{D}_s} \frac{h_\theta(s')}{N} - h_\theta(s) + \zeta, 0\} \right)$$

where for each $s \in \tilde{S} \setminus \tilde{S}_u$, $\mathcal{D}_s$ is the set of its successor states such that $\mathcal{D}_s := \{s' \mid s' = f(s, \pi(s + \delta_i)), \delta_i \sim \mu, i \in [1, N]\}$, $N > 0$ is the sample number of successor states. We use the mean of $h_\theta(\cdot)$ at the N successor states to approximate the expected value $\mathbb{E}_{\delta \sim \mu}[B(f(s, \pi(s + \delta)))]$ for each $s \in \tilde{S} \setminus \tilde{S}_u$, and $\zeta > 0$ to tighten the condition.

Simulation-Guided Loss Term. A trained BC that satisfies the above four conditions can provide lower bounds on probabilistic safety over infinite time horizons for the system. However, these conditions have nothing to do with the tightness of lower bounds and we may obtain a trivial zero-valued lower bound by the trained BC.

To assure the tightness of lower bounds from trained NBCs, we propose a simulation-guided method based on Eq. (11). For each $s_0 \in \tilde{S}_0$, we execute the control system $N' > 0$ episodes, and calculate the safety frequency $\mathbb{f}_s$ of all the N' trajectories over infinite time horizons. Based on the statistical results, the last loss term is defined as:

$$\mathcal{L}_5(\theta) = \frac{1}{|\tilde{S}_0|} \sum_{s \in \tilde{S}_0} (\max\{\mathbb{f}_s + h_\theta(s) - 1, 0\})$$

Intuitively, this term is to enforce the value of the derived lower bound to approach the statistical result as closely as possible, ensuring its tightness.

We emphasize that our simulation-guided method plus the NBC validation (see next section) is sound, as we will validate the trained BC to ensure it satisfies all the BC conditions (see also Theorem 12).

6.2   NBC Validation

A candidate NBC h_θ is valid if it meets the Conditions (7) to (10). The first three conditions condition can be checked by the following constraint

$$\inf_{s \in S} h_\theta(s) \geq 0 \ \wedge \ \sup_{s \in S_0} h_\theta(s) \leq \epsilon \ \wedge \ \inf_{s \in S_u} h_\theta(s) \geq 1$$

using the interval bound propagation approach [23,59]. When any state violates the above equation, it is treated as a counterexample and added to $\tilde{S}$ for future training.

For Condition (10), Theorem 11 reduces the validation from infinite states to finite ones, which are easier to check.

Theorem 11. *Given an M_μ and a function $B : S \rightarrow \mathbb{R}$, we have $\mathbb{E}_{\delta \sim \mu}[B(f(s, \pi(s + \delta))) \mid s] - B(s) \leq 0$ for any state $s \in S \setminus S_u$ if the formula below*

$$\mathbb{E}_{\delta \sim \mu}[B(f(\tilde{s}, \pi(\tilde{s} + \delta))) \mid \tilde{s}] \leq B(\tilde{s}) - \zeta \tag{47}$$

holds for any state $\tilde{s} \in \tilde{S} \setminus \tilde{S}_u$, where $\zeta = \tau \cdot L_B \cdot (1 + L_f \cdot (1 + L_\pi))$ with L_f, L_π, L_B being the Lipschitz constants of f, π and B, respectively.

To check the satisfiablility of Eq. (47) in h_θ and a state $\tilde{s}$, we need to compute the expected value $\mathbb{E}_{\delta \sim \mu}[h_\theta(f(\tilde{s}, \pi(\tilde{s} + \delta))) \mid \tilde{s}]$. However, it is difficult to compute its closed form because h_θ is provided in the form of neural networks. Hence, We bound the expected value $\mathbb{E}_{\delta \sim \mu}[h_\theta(f(\tilde{s}, \pi(\tilde{s} + \delta))) \mid \tilde{s}]$ via interval arithmetic [23, 59] instead of computing it, which is inspired by the work [35,72]. In particular, given the noise distribution μ and its support $W = \{\delta \in \mathbb{R}^n \mid \mu(\delta) > 0\}$, we first partition W into finitely $m \geq 1$ cells, i.e., $\text{cell}(W) = \{W_1, \cdots, W_m\}$, and use $\text{maxvol} = \max_{W_i \in \text{cell}(W)} \text{vol}(W_i)$ to denote the maximal volume with respect to the Lebesgue measure of any cell in the partition, respectively. For the expected value in Eq. (47), we bound it from above:

$$\mathbb{E}_{\delta \sim \mu}[h_\theta(f(\tilde{s}, \pi(\tilde{s} + \delta))) \mid \tilde{s}] \leq \sum_{W_i \in \text{cell}(W)} \text{maxvol} \cdot \sup_\delta F(\delta)$$

where, $F(\delta) = h_\theta(f(\tilde{s}, \pi(\tilde{s} + \delta)))$. The supremum can be calculated via interval arithmetic. We refer interested readers to [35,72] for more details.

Theorem 12 (Soundness). *If a trained NBC is valid, it can certify the almost-sure safety for the qualitative verification, or the derived bound by the NBC is a certified lower/upper bound on the safety probability for the quantitative case.*

The proof of soundness is straightforward by the NBC validation.

7   Evaluation

Our experimental goals encompass evaluating the effectiveness of (i) the qualitative and quantitative verification methods within our framework, (ii) the k-inductive BCs, and (iii) the simulation-guided training method, respectively.

7.1   Benchmarks and Experimental Setup

We assess the effectiveness of our approach on four classic DNN-controlled tasks from public benchmarks: Pendulum and Cartpole from the DRL training platform OpenAI's Gym [12], while B1 and Tora commonly used by the state-of-the-art safety verification tools [30]. All experiments are executed on a workstation running Ubuntu 18.04, with a 32-core AMD Ryzen Threadripper CPU, 128 GB RAM, and a single 24564MiB GPU.

The NBCs in this work are small fully-connected feedforward networks (FNNs) i.e., four-layer ReLU FNNs with $4\times64\times64\times1$. For the safety verification of DNN-controlled systems, we consider

Table 1. Qualitative verification results.

Task	Perturbation	Verification	k	#Fail.
CP	0	✓	1	0
	$r = 0.01$	**Unknown**	1	0
	$r = 0.01$	✓	2	0
	$r = 0.03$	**Unknown**	1	207
PD	$r = 0$	✓	1	0
	$r = 0.01$	**Unknown**	1	675
	$r = 0.03$	**Unknown**	1	720
Tora	$r = 0$	✓	1	0
	$r = 0.02$	**Unknown**	1	0
	$r = 0.02$	✓	2	0
	$r = 0.04$	**Unknown**	1	1113
B1	$r = 0$	✓	1	0
	$r = 0.1$	✓	1	0
	$r = 0.2$	**Unknown**	1	43

state perturbations of uniform noises with zero means and different radii. Specifically, for each state $s = (s_1, \ldots, s_n)$, we add noises $X_1, \ldots, X_n$ to each dimension of s and obtain the perturbed state $(s_1 + X_1, \ldots, s_n + X_n)$, where $X_i \sim \mathbf{U}(-r, r)$ ($1 \le i \le n$, $r \ge 0$). We adopt the CEGIS-based method in Fig. 2 to train and validate target NBCs. For qualitative and various quantitative safety verification of these four systems, each synthesis of an NBC requires 3 iterations on average and each iteration produces an average of 1827 counterexamples.

For qualitative evaluations, the existence of an NBC in Theorem 1 can ensure the almost-sure safety of the whole system. Due to the data sparsity of an initial state, we randomly choose 10,000 initial states (instead of a single one) from the initial set S_0. For quantitative evaluations, to measure the quantitative safety probabilities from the system level, we calculate the mean values of lower/upper bounds by NBCs on these 10,000 states under different perturbations. The correctness of such system-level safety bounds is witnessed by Theorem 12 as each lower/upper bound on a single state s_0 is a certified bound for the exact safety probability from s_0, and thus the same holds on the system level. We also simulate 10,000 episodes starting from each of these 10,000 initial states under different perturbations and use the statistical results as the baseline.

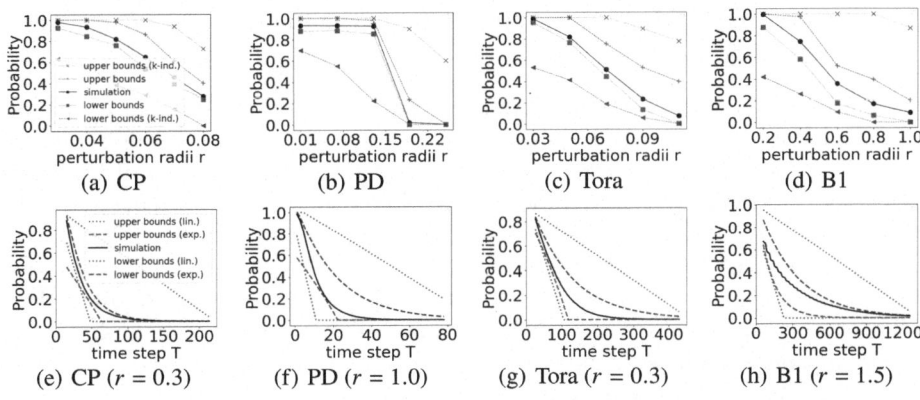

Fig. 3. The certified upper and lower bounds over infinite (a-d) and finite (e-h) time horizons, respectively, and their comparison with the simulation results. (Color figure online)

7.2   Effectiveness of Qualitative Safety Verification

Table 1 shows the qualitative verification results under different perturbation radii r's and induction bounds k's. Given a perturbed DNN-controlled system, we verify its qualitative safety by training an NBC under the conditions in Theorem 1. Once such an NBC is trained and validated, the system is verified to be almost-surely safe, marked as ✓. If no valid barrier certificates are trained within a given timeout, the result is marked as **Unknown**.

As for simulation, we record the number of those episodes where the system enters the unsafe region, marked as the column **#Fail.** in the table. We can observe that for the systems that are successfully verified by NBCs, no failed episodes are detected by simulation. For systems with failed episodes by simulation, no corresponding NBCs can be trained and validated. The consistency experimentally reflects the effectiveness of our approach.

Furthermore, we note that for CP with $r = 0.01$ and Tora with $r = 0.02$, there are no failed episodes, but no NBCs in Theorem 1 can be synthesized for these systems. By applying Theorem 8, we find the 2-inductive NBCs, which ensures the safety of the systems. It demonstrates that k-inductive variants can relax the conditions of NBCs and thus ease the synthesis of valid NBCs for qualitative safety verification.

As the perturbation radius increases, ensuring almost-sure safety becomes challenging, and qualitative verification only results in the conclusion of **Unknown**. Consequently, we proceed to conduct quantitative verification over infinite time horizons.

7.3 Effectiveness of Quantitative Safety Verification over Infinite Time Horizon

Figure 3 (a-d) show the certified upper and lower bounds and simulation results (i.e., black lines marked with '•') over infinite time horizons. The red lines marked with '■' and blue lines marked with '+' represent the mean values of the lower bounds in Theorem 2 and the upper bounds in Theorem 3 on the chosen 10,000 initial states calculated by the corresponding NBCs, respectively. The purple lines marked with '▲' and green lines marked with '×' represent the mean values of the 2-inductive upper and lower bounds calculated by the corresponding NBCs in Theorems 10 and 9, respectively. We can find that the certified bounds enclose the simulation outcomes, demonstrating the effectiveness of our trained NBCs.

Table 2 shows a comparison of average synthesis time (in seconds) for different NBCs. The synthesis time includes both training time and validation time. On average, the training time is 846 s and the validation time is 498 s. We observe that the synthesis time of 2-inductive NBCs is 25% faster than that of normal NBCs, at

Table 2. Synthesis time for different NBCs.

Task	Lower	2-Lower	Upper	2-Upper
CP	2318.5	1876.0	2891.9	2275.3
PD	1941.6	1524.0	2282.7	1491.5
Tora	280.3	218.5	895.1	650.7
B1	587.4	313.6	1127.3	840.1

the sacrifice of tightness. Note that the tightness of certified bounds depends on specific systems and perturbations. Investigating what factors influence the tightness to yield tighter bounds is an interesting future work to explore.

Approaching zero for infinite time horizons, the lower bounds indicate a declining trend in safety probabilities over time. Therefore, we proceed to conduct quantitative verification over finite time horizons, providing both linear and exponential lower and upper bounds.

7.4 Effectiveness of Quantitative Safety Verification over Finite Time Horizon

Figure 3 (e-h) depict the certified upper and lower bounds and simulation results (i.e., black lines) over finite time horizons from the system level. Fix a sufficiently large noise level for each system, the x-axis represents the time horizon, while the y-axis corresponds to the safety probabilities. The purple lines and blue lines represent the mean values of the exponential lower and upper bounds calculated by the corresponding NBCs in Theorem 5 and Theorem 7, respectively. The red lines and green lines represent the mean values of the linear lower and upper bounds calculated by the corresponding NBCs in Theorem 4 and Theorem 6, respectively. The results indicate that our computed certified bounds encapsulate the statistical outcomes. Moreover, the exponential upper bounds are always tighter than the linear upper bounds, and the exponential lower bounds become tighter than the linear ones with the increase of time. It is worth exploring the factors to generate tighter results in future work.

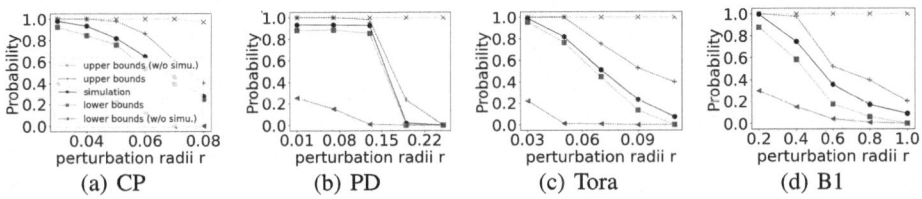

Fig. 4. The certified bounds w/ and w/o simulation-guided loss terms over infinite time horizons. (Color figure online)

7.5   Effectiveness of Simulation-Guided Loss Term

The simulation-guided loss term is proposed in Sect. 6.1 to tighten the certified bounds calculated by NBCs. To evaluate its effectiveness, we choose NBCs in Theorems 2 and 3, and train them with and without the simulation-guided loss terms. The comparison between them is shown in Fig. 4. The red lines marked with '■' and blue lines marked with '+' represent the mean values of the bounds in Theorems 2 and 3 on initial states calculated by the corresponding NBCs trained with the simulation-guided loss terms, respectively. The purple lines with '▲' and green lines with '×' represent the mean values of the bounds calculated by the NBCs trained without the simulation-guided loss terms. Apparently, the upper and lower bounds derived by NBCs trained without the simulation-guided loss terms are looser than the bounds trained with these terms. Specifically, the results computed by NBCs with simulation-guided loss terms can achieve an average improvement of 47.5% for lower bounds and 31.7% for upper bounds, respectively. Hence, it is fair to conclude that accounting for simulation-guided loss terms is essential when conducting quantitative safety verification.

8   Related Work

Barrier Certificates for Stochastic Systems. Our unified safety verification framework draws inspiration from research on the formal verification of stochastic systems employing barrier certificates. Prajna *et al.* [42–44] propose the use of barrier certificates in the safety verification of stochastic systems. This idea has been further expanded through data-driven approaches [45] and k-inductive variants [6]. As the dual problem of computing safety probabilities, computing reachability probabilities in stochastic dynamical systems has been studied for both infinite [22,62,63] and finite time horizons [60,61]. Alireza *et al.* [3] represent non-negative repulsing supermartingales as neural networks and use them to derive upper bounds on the finite-time reachability probability. Probabilistic programs, viewed as stochastic models, have their reachability and termination probabilities investigated using proof rules [21] and martingale-based approaches [7,15,16], where the latter are subsequently unified through order-theoretic fixed-point approaches [50,51,53].

Formal Verification of DNN-Controlled Systems. Modeling DNN-controlled systems as Markov Decision Processes (MDPs) and verifying these models using probabilistic model checkers, such as PRISM [32] and STORM [27], constitutes a quantitative verification approach. Bacci and Parker [9,10] employ abstract interpretation to construct interval MDPs and yield safety probabilities within bounded time. Carr *et al.* [14] propose probabilistic verification of DNN-controlled systems by constraining the analysis to partially observable finite-state models. Amir *et al.* propose a scalable approach based on DNN verification techniques to first support complex properties such as liveness [5].

Reachability analysis is a pivotal qualitative approach in the safety verification of DNN-controlled systems. Bacci *et al.* [8] introduce a linear over-approximation-based method for calculating reachable set invariants over an infinite time horizon for DNN-controlled systems. Other reachability analysis approaches, such as Verisig [30] and Polar [29], focus solely on bounded time. These approaches do not consider perturbations as they assume actions on states to be deterministic.

Barrier Certificates for Training and Verifying DNN Controllers. BC-based methods [1,41] have recently been investigated for training and verifying DNN controllers. The key idea is to train a safe DNN controller through inter-active computations of corresponding barrier certificates to ensure qualitative safety [19,64]. Vishnu *et al.* [40] present a data-driven algorithm for training a neural network to represent the closure certificates in [39]. Existing BC-based approaches for the verification of DNN-controlled systems focus solely on qualitative aspects but neglect the consideration of perturbations [40,48,65]. Our approach complements them by accommodating the inherent uncertainty in DNN-controlled systems.

9 Conclusion and Future Work

We have systematically studied the BC-based qualitative and quantitative safety verification of DNN-controlled systems. This involves unifying and transforming the verification problems into a general task of training corresponding neural certificate barriers. We have also defined the conditions that a trained certificate should satisfy, along with the corresponding lower and upper bounds presented in both linear and exponential forms and k-inductive variants. Through the unification of these verification problems, we have established a comprehensive framework for delivering various safety guarantees, whether qualitatively or quantitatively, in a unified manner.

Our framework sheds light on the quest for scalable and multipurpose safety verification of DNN-controlled systems. It accommodates both qualitative and quantitative aspects in verified results, spans both finite and infinite time horizons, and encompasses certified bounds presented in both linear and exponential forms. Our work also showcases the potential to circumvent verification challenges posed by DNN controllers. From our experiments, we acknowledge that both qualitative and quantitative verification results are significantly dependent on the quality of the trained NBCs. Our next step is to explore more sophisticated deep learning methods and hyperparameter settings (e.g., the architecture of NBCs and the k-inductive horizon) to train valid NBCs for achieving more precise verification results.

Acknowledgments. We thank the anonymous reviewers for their valuable comments. The work has been supported by the NSFC Programs (62161146001, 62372176), Huawei Technologies Co., Ltd., the Shanghai International Joint Lab (22510750100), the Shanghai Trusted Industry Internet Software Collaborative Innovation Center, and the National Research Foundation, Singapore, under its RSS Scheme (NRF-RSS2022-009).

References

1. Abate, A., Ahmed, D., Edwards, A., Giacobbe, M., Peruffo, A.: FOSSIL: a software tool for the formal synthesis of lyapunov functions and barrier certificates using neural networks. In: HSCC, pp. 24:1–24:11 (2021)
2. Abate, A., David, C., Kesseli, P., Kroening, D., Polgreen, E.: Counterexample guided inductive synthesis modulo theories. In: CAV, pp. 270–288 (2018)
3. Abate, A., Edwards, A., Giacobbe, M., Punchihewa, H., Roy, D.: Quantitative verification with neural networks. In: CONCUR. LIPIcs, vol. 279, pp. 22:1–22:18 (2023)
4. Ames, A.D., Coogan, S., Egerstedt, M., Notomista, G., Sreenath, K., Tabuada, P.: Control barrier functions: Theory and applications. In: ECC, pp. 3420–3431 (2019)
5. Amir, G., Schapira, M., Katz, G.: Towards scalable verification of deep reinforcement learning. In: FMCAD, pp. 193–203 (2021)
6. Anand, M., Murali, V., Trivedi, A., Zamani, M.: k-inductive barrier certificates for stochastic systems. In: HSCC, pp. 12:1–12:11 (2022)
7. Asadi, A., Chatterjee, K., Fu, H., Goharshady, A.K., Mahdavi, M.: Polynomial reachability witnesses via stellensätze. In: PLDI, pp. 772–787 (2021)
8. Bacci, E., Giacobbe, M., Parker, D.: Verifying reinforcement learning up to infinity. In: IJCAI, pp. 2154–2160 (2021)
9. Bacci, E., Parker, D.: Probabilistic guarantees for safe deep reinforcement learning. In: FORMATS, pp. 231–248 (2020)
10. Bacci, E., Parker, D.: Verified probabilistic policies for deep reinforcement learning. In: NFM, pp. 193–212 (2022)
11. Brain, M., Joshi, S., Kroening, D., Schrammel, P.: Safety verification and refutation by k-invariants and k-induction. In: SAS, pp. 145–161 (2015)
12. Brockman, G., et al.: OpenAI Gym (2016). arXiv:1606.01540
13. Calinescu, R., Ghezzi, C., Kwiatkowska, M., Mirandola, R.: Self-adaptive software needs quantitative verification at runtime. Commun. ACM **55**(9), 69–77 (2012)
14. Carr, S., Jansen, N., Topcu, U.: Task-aware verifiable RNN-based policies for partially observable markov decision processes. Artif. Intell. Res. **72**, 819–847 (2021)
15. Chakarov, A., Sankaranarayanan, S.: Probabilistic program analysis with martingales. In: Sharygina, N., Veith, H. (eds.) CAV 2013. LNCS, vol. 8044, pp. 511–526. Springer, Heidelberg (2013). https://doi.org/10.1007/978-3-642-39799-8_34
16. Chatterjee, K., Fu, H., Novotný, P., Hasheminezhad, R.: Algorithmic analysis of qualitative and quantitative termination problems for affine probabilistic programs. In: POPL, pp. 327–342 (2016)

17. Cousot, P., Cousot, R.: Constructive versions of tarski's fixed point theorems. Pac. J. Math. **82**(1), 43–57 (1979)
18. Dawson, C., Gao, S., Fan, C.: Safe control with learned certificates: a survey of neural lyapunov, barrier, and contraction methods for robotics and control. IEEE Trans. Robot. **39**, 1749–1767 (2023)
19. Deshmukh, J., Kapinski, J., Yamaguchi, T., Prokhorov, D.: Learning deep neural network controllers for dynamical systems with safety guarantees. In: ICCAD, pp. 1–7 (2019)
20. Donaldson, A.F., Haller, L., Kroening, D., Rümmer, P.: Software verification using k-induction. In: SAS, pp. 351–368 (2011)
21. Feng, S., Chen, M., Su, H., Kaminski, B.L., Katoen, J., Zhan, N.: Lower bounds for possibly divergent probabilistic programs. Proc. ACM Program. Lang. **7**(OOPSLA1), 696–726 (2023)
22. Feng, S., Chen, M., Xue, B., Sankaranarayanan, S., Zhan, N.: Unbounded-time safety verification of stochastic differential dynamics. In: CAV, pp. 327–348 (2020)
23. Gowal, S., et al.: On the effectiveness of interval bound propagation for training verifiably robust models. CoRR arXiv: 1810.12715 (2018)
24. Gronwall, T.H.: Note on the derivatives with respect to a parameter of the solutions of a system of differential equations. Annals Math. 292–296 (1919)
25. Hahn, E.M., et al.: The 2019 comparison of tools for the analysis of quantitative formal models: (QComp 2019 competition report). In: TACAS, pp. 69–92 (2019)
26. Hamers, R., Jongmans, S.: Discourje: Runtime verification of communication protocols in clojure. In: TACAS, pp. 266–284 (2020)
27. Hensel, C., Junges, S., Katoen, J.P., Quatmann, T., Volk, M.: The probabilistic model checker storm. Inter. J. Softw. Tools Technol. Trans. 1–22 (2021)
28. Hoeffding, W.: Probability inequalities for sums of bounded random variables. The collected works of Wassily Hoeffding, pp. 409–426 (1994)
29. Huang, C., Fan, J., Chen, X., Li, W., Zhu, Q.: Polar: a polynomial arithmetic framework for verifying neural-network controlled systems. In: ATVA, pp. 414–430 (2022)
30. Ivanov, R., Carpenter, T., Weimer, J., Alur, R., Pappas, G., Lee, I.: Verisig 2.0: Verification of neural network controllers using taylor model preconditioning. In: CAV, pp. 249–262 (2021)
31. Jin, P., Tian, J., Zhi, D., et al.: Trainify: a CEGAR-driven training and verification framework for safe deep reinforcement learning. In: CAV, pp. 193–218 (2022)
32. Kwiatkowska, M., Norman, G., Parker, D.: Prism 4.0: verification of probabilistic real-time systems. In: CAV, pp. 585–591 (2011)
33. Kwiatkowska, M., Norman, G., Parker, D.: Probabilistic model checking and autonomy. Annu. Rev. Control Robot. Auton. Syst. **5**, 385–410 (2022)
34. Lavaei, A., Soudjani, S., Frazzoli, E.: Safety barrier certificates for stochastic hybrid systems. In: ACC, pp. 880–885 (2022)
35. Lechner, M., Zikelic, D., Chatterjee, K., Henzinger, T.A.: Stability verification in stochastic control systems via neural network supermartingales. In: AAAI, pp. 7326–7336 (2022)
36. Lillicrap, T., et al.: Continuous control with deep reinforcement learning. CoRR abs/ arXiv: 1509.02971 (2015)
37. Mathiesen, F.B., Calvert, S.C., Laurenti, L.: Safety certification for stochastic systems via neural barrier functions. IEEE Control Syst. Lett. **7**, 973–978 (2022)
38. Meng, Y., Qin, Z., Fan, C.: Reactive and safe road user simulations using neural barrier certificates. In: IROS, pp. 6299–6306 (2021)

39. Murali, V., Trivedi, A., Zamani, M.: Closure certificates. In: HSCC, pp. 10:1–10:11 (2024)
40. Nadali, A., Murali, V., Trivedi, A., Zamani, M.: Neural closure certificates. In: AAAI, pp. 21446–21453 (2024)
41. Peruffo, A., Ahmed, D., Abate, A.: Automated and formal synthesis of neural barrier certificates for dynamical models. In: TACAS, pp. 370–388 (2021)
42. Prajna, S., Jadbabaie, A.: Safety verification of hybrid systems using barrier certificates. In: Alur, R., Pappas, G.J. (eds.) HSCC, pp. 477–492 (2004)
43. Prajna, S., Jadbabaie, A., Pappas, G.J.: A framework for worst-case and stochastic safety verification using barrier certificates. IEEE Trans. Automat. Contr. **52**(8), 1415–1428 (2007)
44. Prajna, S., Rantzer, A.: On the necessity of barrier certificates. IFAC Proc. Vol. **38**(1), 526–531 (2005)
45. Salamati, A., Lavaei, A., Soudjani, S., Zamani, M.: Data-driven safety verification of stochastic systems via barrier certificates. In: ADHS, pp. 7–12 (2021)
46. Samek, W., Montavon, G., Lapuschkin, S., et al.: Explaining deep neural networks and beyond: a review of methods and applications. Proc. IEEE **109**(3), 247–278 (2021)
47. Seshia, S.A., Sadigh, D., Sastry, S.S.: Toward verified artificial intelligence. Commun. ACM **65**(7), 46–55 (2022)
48. Sha, M., et al.: Synthesizing barrier certificates of neural network controlled continuous systems via approximations. In: DAC, pp. 631–636 (2021)
49. Steinhardt, J., Tedrake, R.: Finite-time regional verification of stochastic non-linear systems. Int. J. Robotics Res. **31**(7), 901–923 (2012)
50. Takisaka, T., Oyabu, Y., Urabe, N., Hasuo, I.: Ranking and repulsing supermartingales for reachability in probabilistic programs. In: ATVA, pp. 476–493 (2018)
51. Takisaka, T., Oyabu, Y., Urabe, N., Hasuo, I.: Ranking and repulsing supermartingales for reachability in randomized programs. ACM Trans. Prog. Lang. Syst. **43**(2), 5:1–5:46 (2021)
52. Tschaikowski, M., Tribastone, M.: Tackling continuous state-space explosion in a markovian process algebra. Theoret. Comput. Sci. **517**, 1–33 (2014)
53. Urabe, N., Hara, M., Hasuo, I.: Categorical liveness checking by corecursive algebras. In: LICS, pp. 1–12 (2017)
54. Ville, J.: Etude critique de la notion de collectif (1939)
55. Wan, X., Zeng, L., Sun, M.: Exploring the vulnerability of deep reinforcement learning-based emergency control for low carbon power systems. In: IJCAI, pp. 3954–3961 (2022)
56. Williams, D.: Probability with martingales. Cambridge university press (1991)
57. Winkler, T., Gehnen, C., Katoen, J.: Model checking temporal properties of recursive probabilistic programs. In: FOSSACS, pp. 449–469 (2022)
58. Xia, J., Hu, M., Chen, X., Chen, M.: Accelerated synthesis of neural network-based barrier certificates using collaborative learning. In: Proceedings of the 59th ACM/IEEE Design Automation Conference, pp. 1201–1206 (2022)
59. Xu, K., et al.: Automatic perturbation analysis for scalable certified robustness and beyond. In: NeurIPS (2020)
60. Xue, B.: A new framework for bounding reachability probabilities of continuous-time stochastic systems. CoRR abs/ arxiv: 2312.15843 (2023)
61. Xue, B., Fränzle, M., Zhan, N.: Inner-approximating reachable sets for polynomial systems with time-varying uncertainties. IEEE Trans. Autom. Control **65**(4), 1468–1483 (2020)

62. Xue, B., Li, R., Zhan, N., Fränzle, M.: Reach-avoid analysis for stochastic discrete-time systems. In: ACC, pp. 4879–4885 (2021)
63. Xue, B., Zhan, N., Fränzle, M.: Reach-avoid analysis for polynomial stochastic differential equations. IEEE Trans. Autom. Control (2023)
64. Yang, Z., et al.: An iterative scheme of safe reinforcement learning for nonlinear systems via barrier certificate generation. In: CAV, pp. 467–490 (2021)
65. Zeng, X., Yang, Z., Zhang, L., Tang, X., Zeng, Z., Liu, Z.: Safety verification of nonlinear systems with bayesian neural network controllers. In: AAAI, pp. 15278–15286 (2023)
66. Zhang, H., Gu, J., Zhang, Z., Du, L., et al.: Backdoor attacks against deep reinforcement learning based traffic signal control systems. Peer Peer Netw. Appl. **16**(1), 466–474 (2023)
67. Zhang, H., Chen, H., Boning, D.S., Hsieh, C.: Robust reinforcement learning on state observations with learned optimal adversary. In: ICLR (2021)
68. Zhang, H., et al.: Robust deep reinforcement learning against adversarial perturbations on state observations. In: NeurIPS, pp. 21024–21037 (2020)
69. Zhao, H., Qi, N., Dehbi, L., Zeng, X., Yang, Z.: Formal synthesis of neural barrier certificates for continuous systems via counterexample guided learning. ACM Trans. Embed. Comput. Syst. **22**(5s), 146:1–146:21 (2023)
70. Zhao, H., Zeng, X., Chen, T., Liu, Z.: Synthesizing barrier certificates using neural networks. In: HSCC, pp. 1–11 (2020)
71. Zhi, D., Wang, P., Liu, S., Ong, L., Zhang, M.: Unifying qualitative and quantitative safety verification of dnn-controlled systems. CoRR abs/ arXiv: 2404.01769 (2024)
72. Zikelic, D., Lechner, M., Henzinger, T.A., Chatterjee, K.: Learning control policies for stochastic systems with reach-avoid guarantees. In: AAAI, pp. 11926–11935 (2023)

Author Index

A

Abate, Alessandro III-161, III-395
Abdulla, Parosh Aziz II-19
Alt, Leonardo I-466
Althoff, Matthias III-259
Amir, Guy II-249
An, Jie III-282
Ang, Zhendong II-182
Antonopoulos, Timos II-233
Armborst, Lukas II-3
Athavale, Anagha II-329
Atig, Mohamed Faouzi II-19
Azeem, Muqsit II-265

B

Barrett, Clark I-3, II-249
Bartocci, Ezio II-329
Basin, David II-156
Bassa, Alp I-3
Bassan, Shahaf II-249
Baumeister, Jan II-207
Becchi, Anna II-219
Berger, Martin III-209
Bertram, Noah II-109
Besson, Frédéric I-325
Beutner, Raven III-3
Biere, Armin I-133
Bjørner, Nikolaj I-26
Bonakdarpour, Borzoo III-3
Bonsangue, Marcello III-555
Bos, Pieter II-3
Bosamiya, Jay I-348
Brauße, Franz I-219
Britikov, Konstantin I-466
Brockman, Mikael I-453
Bryant, Randal E. I-110
Bu, Lei III-329

C

Cai, Shaowei I-68
Cano, Filip II-233
Cao, Jialun II-302

Chajed, Tej II-86
Chaudhuri, Swarat III-41
Cheung, Shing-Chi II-302
Chiari, Michele I-387
Cho, Chanhee I-348
Christakis, Maria II-329
Cimatti, Alessandro I-234, II-219
Cohen, Albert I-279

D

D'Antoni, Loris III-27
Daggitt, Matthew II-249
Dai, Aochu III-520
Das, Sarbojit II-19
Dillig, Işıl I-3, III-41
Dimitrova, Rayna III-135
Ding, Jianqiang III-307
Dohmen, Taylor III-184
Drachsler-Cohen, Dana II-377
Dureja, Rohit I-203
Dxo, I-453

E

Eilers, Marco I-362
Elacqua, Matthew II-233

F

Faller, Tobias I-133
Fazekas, Katalin I-133
Fedyukovich, Grigory I-466
Feldman, Yotam M. Y. II-71
Feng, Yuan III-533
Ferles, Kostas I-3
Fijalkow, Nathanaël III-209
Finkbeiner, Bernd II-207, III-3, III-64, III-87
Fleury, Mathias I-133
Frenkel, Eden II-86
Frenkel, Hadar III-87
Froleyks, Nils I-133

G

Geatti, Luca   I-387
Giacobbe, Mirco   III-161, III-395
Gigante, Nicola   I-387
Griggio, Alberto   I-234
Grobelna, Marta   II-265
Grosser, Tobias   I-279
Guan, Ji   III-533

H

Habermehl, Peter   I-42
Hasuo, Ichiro   III-282, III-467
Havlena, Vojtěch   I-42
He, Mengda   II-302
Hečko, Michal   I-42
Heim, Philippe   III-135
Heule, Marijn J. H.   I-110
Hipler, Raik   II-133
Holík, Lukáš   I-42
Hsu, Justin   II-109
Hsu, Tzu-Han   III-3
Huang, Pei   II-249
Hublet, François   II-156
Huisman, Marieke   II-3

I

Irfan, Ahmed   I-203
Isac, Omri   II-249

J

Jiang, Hanru   III-495
Johannsen, Chris   I-203
Johnson, Keith J. C.   III-27
Jonsson, Bengt   II-19
Judson, Samuel   II-233
Julian, Kyle   II-249
Junges, Sebastian   III-467

K

Kallwies, Hannes   II-133
Kanav, Sudeep   II-265
Katz, Guy   II-249
Khasidashvili, Zurab   I-219
Kincaid, Zachary   I-89, I-431
Kohn, Florian   II-207
Kokke, Wen   II-249
Komendantskaya, Ekaterina   II-249
Könighofer, Bettina   II-233
Konsta, Alyzia-Maria   III-373

Korovin, Konstantin   I-219
Křetínský, Jan   II-265
Krstić, Srđan   II-156

N

Laarman, Alfons   III-555
Lahav, Ori   II-249
Lai, Tean   II-109
Lengál, Ondřej   I-42
Lercher, Florian   III-259
Leucker, Martin   II-133
Li, Haokun   II-302
Li, Jianwen   I-234
Li, Xuandong   III-329
Li, Yixuan   II-280
Liang, Zhen   III-307
Lima, Leonardo   II-156
Lin, Fangzhen   I-409
Lin, Yi   III-112
Liu, Jiamou   III-420
Liu, Si   II-401
Liu, Wenxia   III-329
Lluch Lafuente, Alberto   III-373
Löhr, Florian   II-207
Lundfall, Martin   I-453
Luo, Ziqing   II-44

M

Maffei, Matteo   II-329
Manfredi, Guido   II-207
Martinelli Tabajara, Lucas   III-112
Matheja, Christoph   III-373
Mathur, Umang   II-182
McMillan, Kenneth L.   I-255
Meel, Kuldeep S.   I-153
Meggendorfer, Tobias   III-359
Mei, Jingyi   III-555
Metzger, Niklas   III-64, III-87
Miltner, Anders   III-41
Mohr, Stefanie   II-265
Moses, Yoram   III-64
Muduli, Sujit Kumar   I-480
Müller, Peter   I-362
Murphy, Charlie   I-89
Myreen, Magnus O.   I-153

N

Nachmanson, Lev   I-26
Nayak, Satya Prakash   III-135

Nickovic, Dejan II-329
Niemetz, Aina I-178
Nukala, Karthik I-203

O
Ong, C.-H. Luke II-401
Ozdemir, Alex I-3

P
Padon, Oded II-71, II-86
Padulkar, Rohan Ravikumar I-480
Pailoor, Shankara I-3
Paraskevopoulou, Zoe I-453
Parno, Bryan I-348
Parsert, Julian II-280
Perez, Mateo III-184
Piskac, Ruzica II-233
Pitchanathan, Arjun I-279
Polgreen, Elizabeth II-280
Pollitt, Florian I-133
Pradella, Matteo I-387
Preiner, Mathias I-178

Q
Qian, Yuhang I-68
Qin, Shengchao II-302

R
Reeves, Joseph E. I-110
Refaeli, Idan II-249
Ren, Dejin III-307
Reps, Thomas III-27
Reynolds, Andrew III-27
Rieder, Sabine II-265
Roy, Diptarko III-395
Roy, Subhajit I-480
Rozier, Kristin Yvonne I-203
Rubbens, Robert II-3

S
Sagonas, Konstantinos II-19
Şakar, Ömer II-3
Sánchez, César II-133
Sato, Sota III-282
Scaglione, Giuseppe II-219
Schirmer, Sebastian II-207
Schmuck, Anne-Kathrin III-135
Schnitzer, Yannik III-161
Schwerhoff, Malte I-362

Seidl, Helmut I-303
Shabelman, Shahar II-377
Shankar, Natarajan I-203
Shapira, Yuval II-377
Shapiro, Scott J. II-233
Sharygina, Natasha I-466
Shi, Yuhui III-329
Shoham, Sharon II-71, II-86
Siber, Julian III-87
Siegel, Stephen F. II-44
Somenzi, Fabio III-184
Soos, Mate I-153, I-453
Stade, Yannick I-303
Su, Jie II-302
Sun, Jun II-352

T
Tagomori, Teruhiro II-249
Takisaka, Toru III-420
Talpin, Jean-Pierre I-325
Tan, Yong Kiam I-153
Tasche, Philip II-3
Tian, Cong II-302
Tilscher, Sarah I-303
Tinelli, Cesare I-203
Torens, Christoph II-207
Traytel, Dmitriy II-156
Trivedi, Ashutosh III-184
Turrini, Andrea III-533

V
Valizadeh, Mojtaba III-209
van den Haak, Lars B. II-3
Vardi, Moshe Y. I-203, III-112
Vegt, Marck van der III-467

W
Wang, Changjiang III-420
Wang, Chenglin I-409
Wang, Jiawan III-329
Wang, Peixin II-401
Wang, Yuning III-232
Wang, Ziteng III-41
Watanabe, Kazuki III-467
Wei, Jiaqi III-329
Weininger, Maximilian III-359
Weissenbacher, Georg II-329

Wen, Cheng   II-302
Wiesel, Naor   II-377
Wilcox, James R.   II-71
Wu, Chenyu   III-307
Wu, Haoze   II-249
Wu, Min   II-249
Wu, Taoran   III-307

X

Xia, Yechuan   I-234
Xu, Zhiwu   II-302
Xue, Bai   III-307

Y

Yan, Peng   III-495
Yang, Jiong   I-153
Ying, Mingsheng   III-520, III-533

Yu, Nengkun   III-495
Yuan, Shenghao   I-325

Z

Zeljić, Aleksandar   II-249
Zhang, Libo   III-420
Zhang, Min   II-249, II-401
Zhang, Muzimiao   III-329
Zhang, Ruihan   II-352
Zhang, Yunbo   III-443
Zhang, Zhenya   III-282
Zhao, Mengyu   I-68
Zhi, Dapeng   II-401
Zhou, Yi   I-348
Zhu, He   III-232
Zhu, Shaowei   I-431, III-443
Zinenko, Oleksandr   I-279
Zlatkin, Ilia   I-466
Zohar, Yoni   I-178